RESCUE AT SEA

RESCUE AT SEA

**An International History of Lifesaving,
Coastal Rescue Craft and Organisations**

Clayton Evans

Conway Maritime Press

This book is dedicated to all the brave souls who, throughout history,
have risked their lives to assist those in peril on the sea.

First published in 2003 by
Conway Maritime Press, a division of
Chrysalis Books plc
The Chrysalis Building
Bramley Road
London W10 6SP
www.conwaymaritime.com

A member of **Chrysalis** Books plc

ISBN 0-85177-934-4

Editorial & Design by Pagenine,
34 Woodlane, Falmouth, Cornwall, England
www.pagenine.co.uk

Printed in Singapore

Contents

Part I

Coastal Lifesaving; A History

Part II

The Evolution of Coastal Rescue Craft; Origins to the Present Day

Part III

The Oceanic Safety Net

Part IV

Today's Maritime Rescue Services

Acknowledgements

Countless organisations and individuals provided invaluable information for the production of this book. To name them all would require another chapter unto itself although I hope I have succeeded in naming as many individuals as possible who made a significant contribution of material and/or advice.

On the home front, I would like to thank my dear wife Gail for the many hours she spent editing the text, attempting to translate and providing thoughtful insight and recommendations. I would also like to express my appreciation to my friends and colleagues at the Canadian Coast Guard who provided me with the support and latitude at work to complete the task.

On the research front there are a few names who deserve specific mention for their extraordinary efforts on my behalf. These include Edward Wake-Walker, Public Relations Director of the RNLI who supported me throughout the project and enabled me to obtain many copies of individual lifeboat conference papers. Also at the RNLI, I would like to thank Barry Cox, Honorary Librarian of the Institution, for his invaluable work categorizing both the ILC papers and all the articles of the RNLI's journal, *The Lifeboat*.

In the United States I would like to make special mention of the assistance rendered by two people. William D. Wilkinson, Director Emeritus of the Mariners' Museum and a leading expert on lifeboat design and development, was instrumental in providing me with a plethora of information on both the early American lifesaving services and American rescue craft. To him I owe a great debt of gratitude. I would also like to thank Colin Mackenzie, Librarian at the Nautical Research Centre in Petaluma, California, for the wealth of material he has collected on lifeboats and lifesaving services around the world, many copies of which he forwarded to me.

Finally, and most importantly, I would like to thank my publisher, John Lee of Conway Maritime Press, for recognizing the importance of this topic and having the vision and zeal to make it a reality.

The following are but a few of the many individuals who assisted in the creation of this book.

Åland Islands
Dag Lindholm, Svante G. Svensson (ASRS); Henrik Karlsson (Åland Islands Maritime Museum); Kenneth Gustavsson (Ålands Museum)

Australia
John O'Callaghan (Port Albert Maritime Museum); Karen Jackson (Western Australia Maritime Museum); Penny Cuthbert (Australian National Maritime Museum); Andrew Magnusson (South Australian Maritime Museum); Malcolm Wilson (AVCGF); Gabrielle Vaughan (Portland Maritime Discovery Centre); Peter Agnew (SLSA); Yvonne Whittington (Queensland Emergency Services)

Belgium
Rita Bertens (Belgisch Loodswezen Zeereddingsdienst); Peter De Becker (VBZR); Urbain Ureel

Bermuda
Scott Simmons (RCC Bermuda)

British Virgin Islands
Alexandra Greenspon (VISAR)

Canada
Max Birch, Alan Bilodeau, John Palliser, Pablo Sobrino, Jon Churchill, Joanne McNish, Daryl Mintenko, Micheline Brodeur, Anthony Toxopeus, Fred Moxey, Eric Tolonen, Crew of CCG Station Bamfield (CCG); Derek Bechthold (Marine Museum of the Great Lakes); Lucy the Librarian (Greater Victoria Public Library); Dan Conlin (Maritime Museum of the Atlantic); Staff of Hydrographic Services Office (HSO) of Royal Canadian Navy, Esquimalt, BC; Ken Lewis (CLI); Adrian Lee (CCGA); Mabel Walter

Chile
Camilo Cabrera Parada (CVBS)

China
Li Jianping (Maritime Rescue and Salvage Bureau)

Denmark
Morten Sylvester (Strandingsmuseum St. George); Helle Bæk Nielsen (Kystfiskermuseum Løkken); Ole Skovgaard Jensen (Farvandsvaesnet)

Faroe Islands
Eli Lyngvej-Larsen (Royal Danish

—— ACKNOWLEDGEMENTS ——

Navy)

Finland
Tina Liira (Finnish Lifeboat Society);
Capt. Paul Lammi (Finnish Lifeboat
Society); Maija Fast (Maritime
Museum of Finland); Marita Penttilä
(Finnish Lifeboat Society)

France
Amiral Michel Merveilleux du
Vignaux (SNSM); B. Denis (SNSM);
Contre-Amiral (2s) Francois Besson

Germany
Hermann C. Helms, Uwe Klein,
Dr. Bernd Anders, Andreas
Lubkowitz (DGzRS); Peter Baltes
(Wrackmuseum Cuxhaven);
Christiane Hennet (Deutsches
Museum); Lutz Zetzsche
(http//:www.sea-rescue.de)

Greece
Captain G. Siamos (HCG)

Guatemala
Capitán Erick Alejandro Sanchez
Muñiz (Guatemalan Navy); Rosa
Isabel Valladares Sanchez

Iceland
Sigurour Vioarsson (ICESAR)

India
Jog Raj (ICG)

Ireland
Capt. W.A. Kirwen (ICG); Tom MacGinty
(Irish National Maritime Museum)

Italy
Giulia Boetto (Museo delle Navi)

Japan
Ryuichi Takei (JLI); Masaki
Furukawa (JCG)

Malta
Major E. Mallia (Armed Forces of Malta)

Morocco

Abdelilah El Mezouar (La Marine
Marchande)
Namibia
Grant Hull (SRIN)

Netherlands
S.E. Wiebenga, Kees Brinkman
(KNRM); Ms. A. Jonker (Redding
Museum Dorus Rijkers); Ab Hoving
(Rijksmuseum, Amsterdam); C.P.P.
van Romburgh (Nederlands
Scheepvaartmuseum); Anton Kos
(Zuiderzeemuseum).

Netherlands Antilles
Yolanda Croes (SARFA); Joseph (Joe)
W. Peterson (SSRF)

New Zealand
Rosemary Deane (NZNMM), Max
Dowell, Walter Baguley (SLI); Kerry
Stenhouse, Kevin Rangi (RNZCGF)

Norway
Dagfinn Bakka (Horten
Redningsselskapets Museum); Elsie Marie
Thorstvedt (Norsk Sjofartsmuseum);
Magnus A. Stene, Dag Hennum, Svein
Jarle Hambre, Jan Øyvind Larsen, Uni
Knudsen (NSSR)

Poland
Robert Orlowski (PRO); Krzysztof
Selke (MSPiR)

Portugal
José Manuel Baptista Coelho Rita (ISN)

South Africa
Ian Wienburg, Krista French (NSRI)

Spain
Enric Garcia Domingo (Museu
Maritim); Drassanes Reials de
Barcelona); Miguel San Claudio
Santa Cruz (Museo Nacional de
Arqueología Marítima); Jesús M.
Uribe Echaburu (SASEMAR)

Sweden
Rolf Westerström (SSRS); Carl
Gunnar-Olsson (Sjohistorika Museet

Stockholm); Mikael Ekeblad
(Goteborg Maritime Museum)

Tunisia
Rear Admiral Brahim Barrak (Service
National de Surveillance Cotiere)

Turkey
Varol Atalay (DDD), Mustafa Böke
(Kiyi Emniyeti)

United Kingdom
Edward Wake-Walker, Derek King,
Ray Kipling, Barry Cox, Ian
Ventham, Michael Woodroffe,
Shelley Woodroffe, Janet Smith,
Clem Watson, Gerry Keeling,
Lorraine Peterson, Neil Chaplin,
Brian Miles (RNLI); Nicholas Leach,
Denis J. Horgan (Lifeboat
Enthusiasts Society); Michael Porter
(Maritime Museum of Scotland); Eric
Teare (Isle of Man); Christine Bell &
B. Calderwood (Grace Darling
Museum); P. Parker (Lowestoft &
East Suffolk Maritime Society); Karen
Howard (Merseyside Maritime
Museum); Simon Stephens, Lucy
Waite, Joanna Buddle (National
Maritime Museum); Olive Graham
(Newcastle Libraries and Information
Service); Jenny Bennett, Krista
Taylor (Pagenine); Clive Lawford,
David and Sharon Fisher, Eric Fry.

United States of America
William D. Wilkinson (AFRAS); Mike
Monteith, Mike McCormack, Robert
M. Browning (USCG); Chris Havern
(USCG Historians Office); Dennis
Noble (USCG Ret'd); Colin
Mackenzie (Nautical Research
Centre); George Schwartz, Carolle
Morini (Peabody Essex); Susan
Russell (Maine Maritime Museum);
Carie Foley (Massachusetts Historical
Society); Margherita M. Desy (USS
Constitution Museum); Prof. Lionel
Casson (NYU); Nicholas Wardle
(SEARCH)

Uruguay
Guillermo Pérez Lavagnini (ADES)

Preface

When I began researching for this book in 1995 my intention was to provide an update to E.W. Middleton's, *Lifeboats of the World*, published in 1978. Essentially, this work was to be an overview of contemporary maritime rescue organisations and their craft. As time went on, however, I began to realise that there was far more to the story of lifesaving than just the modern day. The stories of each individual nation and its particular lifesaving organisation began to reveal international connections, some going back as far as the late 18th Century. These humanitarian bonds between nations continue today in the form of the International Lifeboat Federation (ILF). In order to understand today's rescue organisations, I felt it imperative that the reader also understand how and why they originated. As a result, much of my work has taken on a historical focus as described in the first two parts of the book. In order to keep pace with my original intent and provide an up-to-date reference text, in the final two parts I have attempted to balance the historical with the contemporary. Where historical information pertaining to a particular nation or organisation has not been provided in the first two sections of the book, I have endeavoured to provide it within the national chapters of Part IV.

It should be noted that much of my research was limited to material available in the English language as the cost of translation was prohibitive. To some extent, the book's focus on the coastal lifesaving history of both Great Britain and the United States is a product of that availability. These countries did, however, play key roles in the history of lifesaving at sea and provide divergent examples of the development of both private and public rescue services. It is my hope that, in future, more information can be obtained or translated so that additional material can be included in any subsequent edition.

The choice of profiled countries and organisations was based solely on the February 1997 List of International Lifeboat Federation Members. All the organisations that responded to my requests for information have been included. Again, I hope that any future edition will update the maritime rescue services section to include all ILF members. It should be noted that there are hundreds of other maritime rescue organisations around the world not covered in this book; many are small independent societies. Their work is just as important as that of the organisations profiled but time and space has allowed me to select only the principal few. A great deal of information regarding these organisations is available at some of the excellent lifesaving sites on the World Wide Web.

Rescue at Sea focuses on one primary element of lifesaving at sea through the ages: lifeboats and other relatively small coastal rescue craft. This is not unintentional – I am a lifeboat coxswain by profession and must claim a bias. In recent decades there has been a distinct lack of international reference work dealing with small-boat rescue and the lifesaving organisations that use such craft either as their principal rescue tool or as part of their overall lifesaving arsenal. It is this void I am attempting to fill.

There are, of course, many other vital elements to both the history of lifesaving at sea and the modern maritime search and rescue (SAR) network around the world. There are thousands of air personnel manning helicopters and fixed-wing aircraft, many of which are specifically designated for lifesaving. Countless men and women crew the offshore and oceanic patrols aboard large coast guard cutters, buoy tenders, ice breakers and scientific research vessels as well as naval and other patrol craft designated to help those in peril on the world's oceans. Thousands of dedicated professionals and volunteers operate the SAR communications network enveloping the world, standing by 24 hours a day for any sign of distress. There are also thousands of support personnel who administer, raise funds, maintain and provide training for these organisations. Although I have made brief mention of these, I have done them a disservice through this brevity and I only hope that another author will take on the task of writing their fascinating story in far greater detail at some future date.

This volume owes much to the hundreds of individuals who wrote books, articles and conference papers over the last 200 or so years. I have merely collected their thoughts and ideas and, hopefully, provided the connections between them. I have endeavoured to provide footnotes and references to these men and women; without their efforts my work would not have been possible. I only hope that all of you who write the books, essays and workshop papers regarding lifeboats and lifesaving today, continue to do so. Although such work may seem to be of only contemporary relevance, it is not. Down the historical road it is your documents that will provide a portal to the past from which works such as this may be derived.

Clayton Evans

Foreword

From time immemorial, the sea has provided man with a bountiful source of food, a means of transportation, and a source of seemingly boundless pleasure. We have learned to enjoy and yet still to curse, we love and fear the sea in its many forms and moods. It provides for us yet strikes back with mortal fury when we transgress the bounds.

Whether driven by primitive preservation instincts or by a more evolved sense of humanity, the tradition of man helping his fellow man at sea has prevailed for as long as history itself and today this ethic serves as the cornerstone of the modern response to distress at sea. Under the terms of international conventions all vessels must respond to calls for aid from fellow mariners regardless of nationality, creed or cause.

In the early 19th Century enlightened philanthropists became aware that this traditional ethic alone was insufficient to ensure that seafarers' calls for help would be answered, and dedicated maritime rescue associations were thus born. In coastal towns and villages a great and proud new order came into being – volunteers who would raise funds to establish rescue associations served alongside seafarers prepared to put their own lives at risk to assist the stranger at sea.

Before long these locally formed societies consolidated into national institutions, many of which provided the roots of the modern world's great maritime search and rescue organisations. Today there are hundreds of thousands of people around the globe involved with the provision of dedicated maritime rescue services, either as volunteers or as full-time professionals.

The national institutions gathered together for the first time in 1924 at the International Lifeboat Conference to share information and generate new ideas toward the furtherance of their common goal – saving lives. This union of rescue organisations latterly formed itself into the International Lifeboat Federation (ILF), the only global body of its kind, which now comprises 87 member organisations from 62 countries from the largest to the smallest. Recognising the important contribution that ILF members make to safety at sea, the International Maritime Organisation granted the Federation consultative status in 1985 and awarded it the "International Maritime Prize" in 1998.

The International Lifeboat Conference has been held almost every four years since 1924 and, as this book goes to press, preparations are being finalised for the first conference of the third millennium, to be held in Cape Town in March 2003.

Unfortunately not all regions of the world enjoy the same level of rescue service nor is it the case that a seafarer in peril will be guaranteed the same degree of response no matter what the circumstances. Much has been achieved – but much is yet to be done. This book by Clayton Evans is timely in its publication. As we turn the pages of history into the new millennium it records the development of dedicated maritime search and rescue services around the world – we heartily endorse it.

As you enjoy this book, please remember the men and women who have toiled selflessly, some at the cost of their own lives, to help their fellow seafarers in need. Spare a thought also for the hundreds of rescuers, from many organisations around the globe, who will put to sea on such missions even as you read. Please support this wonderful cause in any way you can.

Gerry Keeling
International Development Manager
International Lifeboat Federation

PART I

COASTAL LIFESAVING;
A HISTORY

INTRODUCTION

The Unknown Saviour

While much of the story that is about to unfold is about lifeboats and wreck, rescue and tragedy, it is also about humanity and, in particular, the character of the individual. It is about those unique souls who have maintained selfless fortitude to risk their own lives for the sake of others in peril at sea. Such a person is a saviour of life. This book deals primarily with the development of organised sea rescue services around the world and the tools used to conduct those rescues. Although institutional organisation and safe and efficient rescue craft are the key to every successful coast guard and lifeboat service in the world today, it is still through the effort, determination, and selflessness of the individual that hundreds of thousands of lives have been saved.

'A Fishing Boat Saving the Crew of a Ship in Distress off Sheringham'. Before the existence of dedicated lifeboats and lifesaving agencies, it was up to the spirit of the individual and collaborative human endeavour to assist those in peril at sea. *National Maritime Museum, London*

The rescuer is, and always has been, a different breed. There are those who are born to it and there are those who find themselves members of the club by chance and circumstance. Regardless of background, they all share the common bond of sacrifice in the name of humanity. It took a certain kind of person in 1800 to leave the warmth of hearth and family to face the full onslaught of a North Sea gale, tearing through the freezing surf in a primitive oar-powered wooden lifeboat, wearing only oilskins for protection. The same holds true in the year 2003 for the person who is willing to strap themselves to a spider-thread wire beneath 5 tons (5.1 tonnes) of gyrating machinery, in the same type of weather, possibly even in the same place, all in the hope of saving someone's life. It is only the technology that has changed.

The unknown saviour was one of these unique souls, probably a seafarer or fisherman who made his or her living from the sea. These original rescuers helped to establish the rules of humanitarian conduct along the coasts of the civilised world, as well as on the high seas. For, unlike man's chaotic endeavours on terra firma, universal rules of assistance are still followed at sea. For this reason, too, the nationality of the unknown saviour is of no vital importance. Organised sea rescue started with this individual and the recognition that unless someone, somewhere, started lending a helping hand to the shipwrecked and drowning, not only would the carnage continue unabated, but one day it could be them or their loved ones who stared at a sea of blank faces as they slipped beneath the sea. As history progressed and the annals of human conflict continued to grow, there remained only one common enemy with which the entire race could consider itself at war, and that was the brute force and wrath of the sea and its elements. A bond would develop amongst seafarers and water travellers the world over: when it came to survival at sea they were their brother's keeper.

The Ancient World

There is no available evidence to suggest that any efforts were made to establish dedicated lifesaving facilities in the Ancient World. From the contemporary perspective it seems difficult to accept that such incredibly complex mercantile societies as the Phoenicians, Greeks, Mesopotamians and Romans would not have had some means of aiding distressed mariners somewhere in their respective empires but in classical times human life was both short and expendable. Any resources that may have been allocated for assisting in shipwreck would most probably have been aimed at benefiting the shipowner through the salvage of cargo. The salvage of life would have been merely an adjunct to this more profitable pursuit. Losses of ships and cargo would, no doubt, have been staggering at times: every time a vessel sailed on a trading adventure into the Mediterranean or beyond the odds would certainly have been weighed against it ever returning.

With mercantile interests in mind, the earliest known efforts at safety were initiated by the Ancient Greeks with the establishment of the world's first known lighthouse in the 7th Century BC The light was at Cape Sigeum in Asia Minor and marked a strategic passage to the harbour of Troy, as well as to the Hellespont and the entrance to the Bosphoros.[1] The Ancient Greeks would continue to construct great lighthouses, including the famed Colossus of Rhodes in 285 BC, a human-shaped tower said to have been 108ft (33m) in height and which later became the Fifth Wonder of the World. At the entrance to the great port of Alexandria in Egypt another massive beacon was established in 261 BC. The Pharos Lighthouse, which would become known as the Seventh Wonder of the World, was named after the island on which it was placed and was thought to have stood some 450ft (140m) in height, an incredible feat of engineering by the standards of the period. Both the Greeks and later the Romans would eventually construct a string of lighthouses throughout their empires.

One of the most important lighthouses in the Roman Empire was constructed in 50 AD during the reign of Emperor Claudius.[2] The light marked the treacherous entrance to the River Tiber and the port of Ostia, the primary overseas trading centre for the heart of the Roman Empire, the city of Rome itself. Ostia and its light may hold some significance in the story of coastal lifesaving, as it is possible that some of the first waterborne measures for assisting shipwrecked mariners may have been established here. In the year 62 AD it was recorded that some 200 vessels were lost while moored in the harbour, primarily due to the lack of protection from strong southwest winds.[3] These figures did not even include vessels lost in the approaches to the harbour or in adjacent waters. Losses were so great that a Guild of Divers was established at the port, assigned the constant task of salvaging both ships and cargo. Another safety measure commonly undertaken at the port was that of towage by small pulling boats. It would seem likely that the interests of both the salvage and towage organisations at the Port of Ostia, although obviously commercial in nature, may at times have resulted in the rescue of ships and seafarers. Thus, it is quite possible that Ostia may have seen the earliest implementation of dedicated resources to assist ships and seafarers at sea, albeit due to commercial, not humanitarian, motivations.

This sculpture, from a 3rd Century sarcophagus, depicts a scene at the ancient Roman port of Ostia. A man in the water is about to be recovered by a small boat; while it is possible that this is a depiction of early lifesaving, it is more probable that the man was a member of one of the local diving guilds that salvaged cargo from wrecks. Such commercial endeavours did, however, spur on the development of the first maritime safety measures, such as lighthouses and organised salvage teams.

The tower at extreme left may have been a watchtower established to monitor the port's entrance for security and safety. *Ny Carlsberg Glyptotek, Copenhagen.*

CHAPTER 2

Before the Lifeboat

In terms of western civilisation, throughout the Middle Ages and well into the 18th Century, the role of the lifesaver remained rather undefined. Life was generally harsh and short and helping a fellow man was not always a top priority when one's own survival was tested on a daily basis. Indeed, on many a shore the news of shipwreck was generally received with keen interest by the coastal population, not as a signal for all to reach out to assist others in difficulty, but as a sign of opportunity to plunder the tragic remains. There were many tales where victims were left to die on the beach, as would-be saviours focused their attentions on the pillaging of wreck. Indeed, it was common practice on many hostile shores for 'wreckers' to set false fires to confuse hapless mariners into running aground. Those seafarers who survived the wreck were, in many cases, unceremoniously put to death. In order to deter such activity, the crime of 'Putting out false lights in order to bring any ship into danger' was added to the early Sea Laws of Oleron, aspects of which evolved into the basic tenets of the maritime law of both France and Britain. Punishment for such crimes was severe and no one was excluded, not even pilots. The Sea Laws of Oleron for example, provided a description of the punishment that could be exacted upon a pilot who was suspected of having ill intentions:

> If any pilot designedly misguide a ship that it may be cast away, he shall be put to a rigorous death and hang in chains; and if the lord of the place where a ship be thus lost abet such villains in order to have a share of the wreck, his person shall be fastened to a stake in the midst of his own mansion, which, being fired at the four corners, shall be burnt to the ground and he with it.[4]

As if this punishment alone were not enough to dissuade any pilots of wrong doing, if the master and crew of a vessel even 'suspected' the pilot of having evil intentions regarding their vessel, they were at liberty to decapitate him on the spot!

In the Baltic the tribes of the Norsemen had a savage reputation for seizing all wrecks and deciding whether any survivors should live or die. Certain codes of the original German common law (known as the Laws of the Visigoths) were enacted to deal with this problem. In the 13th Century, Earl Birger, one of the Regents of Sweden, issued a proclamation against the ill treatment and pillage of the shipwrecked.[5] In the Mediterranean, the Neapolitan Constitution also established measures that severely punished any, and all, who failed to assist persons in distress, or who plundered any wreck. Although one would hope that these very early laws were instituted and adopted for the sake of humanity, it is quite probable that the commercial interests of the national aristocracies were also concerned with claiming the prizes for themselves as the natural bounty of their domain.[6] In Britain laws to assist the shipwrecked were legislated in 1752. An Act of Parliament was passed which declared it a capital crime for anyone caught 'plundering any vessel either in distress or shipwrecked or preventing the escape of any person that endeavours to save life'.[7]

It would seem that it was not only evil intentions of coastal folk that could cause grief to mariners in the days before lifesaving services, but also superstition. In Scotland in the early 17th Century it was believed that a curse would be struck upon any would-be rescuer who saved the shipwrecked from their inevitable doom. In Noel Methley's, *The Lifeboat and Its Story*, written in 1912, a common sentiment of these earlier times is passed on. Methley quotes a narrative by Sir Walter Scott in which he refers to an incident in the Scottish Hebrides:

It is remarkable that, in an archipelago where so many persons must be necessarily endangered by the waves, so strange and inhuman a maxim should have engraffed itself upon the minds of a people otherwise kind, moral, and hospitable. But all with whom I have spoken agree that it was almost general in the beginning of the eighteenth century, and was with difficulty weeded out by the sedulous instructions of the clergy and the rigorous injunctions of the proprietors. There is little doubt it had been originally introduced as an excuse for suffering those who attempted to escape from the wreck to perish unassisted, so that, there being no survivor, she might be considered as lawful plunder. A story was told me, I hope an untrue one, that a vessel having got ashore among the breakers on one of the remote Zetland Islands, five or six men, the whole or greater part of the unfortunate crew, endeavoured to land by assistance of a hawser, which they had secured to a rock. The inhabitants were assembled, and looked on with some uncertainty, till an old man said: 'Sirs, if these men come ashore, the additional mouths will eat all the meal we have in store for winter; and how are we to get more?' A young fellow, moved with this argument, struck the rope asunder with his axe, and all the poor wretches were immersed in the breakers and perished.[8]

It is undoubtedly true that in terms of shore-side response to shipwreck, examples of man's nature, both good and bad, did occur. What was probably a more common scenario, in this period of abject poverty and depravation, was that the incentive of salvage might have been the drawing card by which many rescuers came to the site of a shipwreck. Once arriving on the scene however, the salvation of human life came before the latter, more material, duties.

It is difficult for a modern reader to even contemplate the sheer magnitude of the loss of ships and human life during the great age of sail. The fates of passengers and crew were generally in the grip of the elements and all factors continually conspired against a vessel's safe arrival. A severe winter storm could leave literally hundreds of ships wrecked all over a nation's coast. For example, in three separate gales in 1821, 1824 and 1829, no fewer than 169 vessels were lost on the east coast of England between the Humber and the Tees, a distance of only about 80 nautical miles. In a single gale, on 13 January 1843, 103 British vessels were lost in one day. During March 1850 – the year in which more accurate annual wreck accounts began – no less then 134 vessels were lost around the coasts of Great Britain, an average of four a day.[9] The *Abstract of Wrecks for 1850* paints a chilling picture of the resultant loss of life. It was estimated that in addition to the 681 vessels wrecked, more than 784 lives were lost. The perils of ocean travel

'Clearing A Wreck'. This work by John Templeton depicts the aftermath of a shipwreck on the English coast, circa 1840. At one time, entire coastal communities, particularly those adjacent to hazardous locations, would depend on the salvage of wreck for much of their sustenance and livelihood. Acts of treachery were not uncommon, with false lights being lit to lure ships to their destruction and entire crews being murdered. Over time, however, the profession of the 'wrecker' evolved into a somewhat more legitimate trade as aristocracies and governments sought to control the plunder and ensure that they received their fair share. Various 'sea laws' were developed to control the activity and in many coastal states local 'wreckmasters' were assigned the duties of organising salvage crews and recovering wrecks. Eventually these same men would form the core of the first lifesaving crews.
National Maritime Museum, London

are highly evident in the accounts of that year, which were provided by Lloyd's as follows: '30th March, 206 lost on the *Royal Adelaide* steamer on the Tongue Sand at the entrance to the Thames; 18th June, 41 lost in the *Orion* steamer off Port Patrick; 20th November, 99 lost in the bark *Edmond*, wrecked in Killkee Bay, County Clare, on the west coast of Ireland'.

The latter was undoubtedly full of emigrants just setting out on their journey to the New World.

Horrific tales of shipwreck abounded the world over. There is perhaps no better description of the tragedy and utter horror of shipwreck than that provided in a letter by a witness to the carnage that followed the loss of the American bark *Mexico* wrecked off the coast of Long Island on 2 January 1837 with her entire crew and all the 112 emigrant passengers. There were no lifesaving facilities in place to assist them.[10] The letter was sent to the editor of the *Boston Mercantile Journal* and serves as a reminder to the modern reader of the inherent dangers of sea travel during the days of sail:

On reaching Hempstead, I concluded to go somewhat off the road, to look at the place where the ship Mexico *was cast away. In half an hour we came to Lott's Tavern, some four or five miles this side of the beach where the ship lay – and here, in his barn had been deposited the bodies of the ill-fated passengers which had been thrown upon the shore. I went out to the barn. The doors were open, and such a scene as presented itself to my view, I certainly could never have contemplated. It was dreadful – a frightful scene of horror.*

Forty or fifty bodies, of all ages and sexes, were lying before me, over the floor, all frozen and as solid as marble – and all except a few, in the very dresses in which they perished. Some with their hands clenched, as if for warmth, and almost everyone with an arm crooked, and bent as it would in clinging to the rigging.

There were scattered about among the number, four or five beautiful little girls, from six to sixteen years of age, their cheeks and lips as red as roses, with their calm blue eyes open, looking you in the face as if they would speak. I could hardly realize that they were dead. I could perceive a resemblance to each other, and supposed them to be the daughters of a passenger named Pepper, who perished, together with his wife and all his family.

...I saw one poor negro sailor, a tall man, with his head thrown back, his lips parted, and his now sightless eye-balls turned upwards, and his arms crossed over his breast, as if imploring heaven for aid. The poor fellow had evidently frozen while in the act of fervent prayer.... Such scenes show us indeed how powerful and feeble are all human efforts, when contending against the storms and tempest which sweep with resistless violence over the face of the deep. And yet the vessel was so near the shore, that the shreaks and moans of the poor creatures were heard through that bitter, dreadful

'Wreck Chart for Britain and Ireland for 1889'. In the 19th Century the onset of the industrial revolution resulted in a tremendous increase in the amount of maritime traffic all over the world. During the age of sail ocean travel was fraught with dangers as ships struggled with the vagaries of wind and weather. The development of the first steamships also resulted in many a calamity as the engines were often poorly maintained and unreliable. The amount of shipwreck and maritime casualty could only be considered massive by today's standards. This chart shows the losses around only one small, albeit very busy, part of the globe, that of the coast of the British Isles. In a one-year period ending 30 June 1890 no fewer than 4,366 shipwrecks (represented by the dots) were recorded with 406 lives being lost. The number of lives lost was half that recorded in 1851, the year in which a major expansion of lifeboat stations around Great Britain and Ireland began.
RNLI

night, till towards morning, the last groan died away, and all was hushed in death, and the murmer of the raging billows was all the sound that then met the ear.

After the storm the wreck was approached, and here and there were seen columns, pillars of ice, which had formed on the frozen bodies, as the sea broke over.[11]

'The Great Storm of November 26th, 1703, Wherein Rear Admiral Beaumont was lost on the Goodwin Sands…'. With no lifesaving mechanisms in existence, ships and sailors were most often left to the perils of the seas; hundreds often succumbed within sight of horrified onlookers ashore. In this case, however, a local mayor could not stand to witness the scores of stranded seamen awaiting their fate on the offshore sandbanks. He took matters into his own hands and rescued many with the help of some loyal followers. *National Maritime Museum, London*

But before the advent of organised lifesaving, humanity was not always the callous ignorer of calamity; not all those who found themselves subject to the perils of the sea would meet the same fate as the unfortunate souls on the *Mexico*. There were individuals who would seek to assist the shipwrecked and provide the beginnings of lifesaving. In 1639 for example, historical record states that a Dutch whaler was wrecked off the inhospitable coast of Spitzbergen in Norway. The local inhabitants quickly launched three boats and rescued 19 of those on board. It was reported that the feet of the shipwrecked men were placed in brine and that they were provided with food and shelter.[12] Accounts also tell of an event in November 1703 when a fleet of British ships was driven ashore by a hurricane off the coast of Kent. Although

countless lives were lost, several hundred seamen made it to the sandbars of the Goodwin Sands, where they were in danger from the rising tides. In spite of the appeals of the Mayor of Deal to local boatmen 'and revenue men', all refused to render assistance. Eventually, the Mayor himself, with several other brave souls, put out to the sands and rescued scores of sailors.

Governments also began to expand laws to encompass aid to the shipwrecked, rather than merely protection of the wreck itself. Some of the earliest recorded measures for the promotion of coastal lifesaving originated in Nordic kingdoms such as Sweden, Finland, and the Åland Islands, in the 13th Century (see Part IV). In The

Netherlands, King Charles V passed laws aimed at curbing the traditional habit of plundering ships and thereby defined the role of the *jutter*, or salvor, as a legitimate profession along The Netherlands' outer coasts. These men, in spite of past indiscretions, now saved life before cargo. It should be noted, however, that removing the people from the wreck also meant that the ship was rendered derelict and subject to salvage. The early Dutch Sea Laws also established the role of the 'wreck master', a local coastal officer who was responsible to the crown and who ensured that his employer received a fair share of the now legitimised plunder. Although these first legal measures were principally related to the control of revenue, they did initiate a new ethic among seagoing men. There was now honour in the coasting profession and it was from these roots that the lifesaving crews of the future would be drawn.

Similar royal edicts began to appear in other European countries. In 1691 Don Pedro II of Portugal passed a law stating that all coastal forts in his domain must, when necessary, send out vessels to aid the shipwrecked. In 1692 Sweden's King Charles XI required the Swedish Diving Guild to assist those in peril as part of their salvage duties.[13] [14]

Further measures to assist the shipwrecked were also established by members of the upper class and aristocracy at specific locations. One of these was Bamburgh, on the coast of Northumberland, northeast England, at a castle built in 547 AD for King Ida, the ruler of the ancient Anglian Kingdom of Bernicia. In the year 1721 Nathaniel, Third Baron Crewe of Stene and Bishop of Durham, passed away and donated his entire estate, castle and all, for the provision of charitable deeds. For decades thereafter trustees managed the estate and, in respect of the wishes of Baron Crewe, several charitable services were provided to the local populace. During the latter half of the 18th Century one of the Trustees was a member of the local clergy, Archdeacon John Sharpe (1723-92), who had a keen interest in the plight of the shipwrecked and who recognised the strategic location of the castle. Beginning in the 1750s Archdeacon Sharpe encouraged lifesaving efforts through the reconstruction of the castle to ensure its continued usage as a visual beacon for those at sea, and, through the auspices of Trinity House, pushed for lighthouses to be set up on the adjacent islands. In a document written on Christmas Eve 1771, he further extended the services on behalf of those shipwrecked in the vicinity of the castle. Such measures included the establishment of coastal patrols on horseback during the storm season; signals for mariners to be flown from the castle; the sounding of bells and cannon at regular intervals in the event of fog; accommodation and refuge in the castle for survivors of

Bamburgh Castle was located on a notoriously dangerous headland on the coast of Northumberland. A charitable trust, originally established by the Bishop of Durham in 1722, began in the 1750s to provide aid to mariners in distress, probably, in part, because of the castle's particular vantage point above the scene of many a nautical disaster. In later years this charitable trust would become involved in the development of the 'life-boat'. Although it is open to debate as to whether Bamburgh was the location of the world's first lifeboat station, as has been claimed, this famous castle undoubtedly played a vital role in the early development of organised coastal lifesaving in Great Britain.
National Maritime Museum, London.

Wreck of the East Indiaman *Halsewell*

Before the introduction of dedicated lifeboats and other facilities, survivors of shipwreck could only count on the goodwill of the local populace to assist in matters of lifesaving. Yet, there are countless tales of mariners helping other mariners. Pilot boats and cutters were commonly used as rescue craft. Coastal pilots were generally out at sea, regardless of the weather, in search of vessels requiring their services. By the very nature of their work, these men possessed the best seamanship skills to assist in sea rescues: superior boat-handling abilities and in-depth local knowledge. It would be these brave and hearty souls and others of their ilk, who would form the core crews of the newly emerging lifeboat societies.

It was not only seamen who lent assistance to the shipwrecked in these early times; in many cases help was also provided by landsmen. On 6 January 1786 the British East Indiaman, *Halsewell*, was blown ashore by hurricane-force winds on the Isle of Purbeck, Dorset. With over 240 persons onboard the ship came to rest within what was described as a 'fearful chasm' at the bottom of a 100ft (30.5m) cliff. Given the resounding din of the tempest and the vessel's obscured position below the cliffs, not one of its signal guns was heard. As time went on, scores of people perished attempting to seek refuge in the cave. Eventually,

> *…with the utmost difficulty and risk, one or two contrived to scale the cliff, and news of the wreck was conveyed by them to the nearest dwellings…then at length the countryside was roused, and efforts were made to rescue the survivors from their perilous position. The method adopted was as follows: two men stood at the cliff's edge and were securely fastened by ropes to bars driven into the ground. Behind them were two more men similarly lashed, and then two more, and so on. Between the successive couples a rope was passed and lowered down the cliff, and by its means the wretched men and women were at last brought to safety.*[15]

In the end, only 74 of the *Halsewell*'s 240 were saved, but those who did survive most certainly owed their lives to the humanitarian spirit of these early lifesavers.

wreck; the use of a large speaking trumpet. It is interesting to note that the use of the gun as a signal not only attracted would-be rescuers to the scene, but also alerted the local customs officers to come at once to control any attempt at plunder. Provision was also made to ensure that local boatmen were notified to launch in the event of shipwreck. Furthermore, towards the end of his tenure as Trustee of the Bishop Crewe Estate, Archdeacon Sharpe would play an instrumental role in the development of a safer design of rescue boat.

These early efforts to establish dedicated services to assist the shipwrecked proved that an awareness of the problem was developing. As trade and emigration to the colonies of European nations rapidly expanded, so too did the number of shipwrecks. Eventually it would take the concerted efforts of a few generous and progressive minds to pave the way for dedicated lifesaving services around the world.

CHAPTER 3

The Chinese Lifesaving Associations

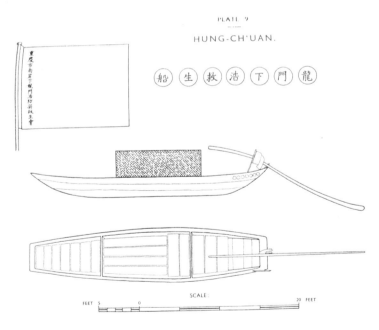

PLATE 9

HUNG-CH'UAN.

船 生 救 浩 下 門 龍

SCALE:
FEET 5   0   20 FEET

A drawing of the *Lungmenhao Lower Section Lifeboat* as displayed by the engraved characters on her stern. Painted a distinctive red colour, the *Hung Ch'uan*, or lifeboat, belonged to the society at Chinkiang. This particular society became known as the 'Dare to Die' Service and was instrumental in saving thousands of lives in and around the treacherous gorges of the upper Yangtze River. *Worcester, G.R.G.*

Throughout China's 5,000-year history, death by drowning and the natural calamity of flooding have held special meaning for her people. Indeed, the Huanghe (Yellow River) has been dubbed by writers as 'China's Sorrow'. To this day, thousands of Chinese people succumb to the annual raging torrents of floodwater, just as they have for generations. Ancient Chinese history recalls a well known tale about a man named Qu Yuan, who committed ritual suicide by drowning himself in the Miluo River close to where it drains into Dongting Lake in south central Hunan Province.[16] A contemporary of both Kongzi (Confucius) and *Art of War* author Sonzi, Qu lived at the very end of the Zhou Dynasty (1122 to 221 BC) during the 'Warring States' period. This was an era of massive civil strife and great political treachery. Qu Yuan was the scholarly advisor to the King of Chu state and chose a time-honoured, watery death to protest the rampant corruption of his time. Upon hearing of his plight local fishermen took to their long and slender paddled boats and dashed out on to the lake to try to locate and rescue him, but to no avail. The attempt to save him, one of the first maritime lifesaving operations ever recorded, has been re-enacted ever since in an annual public waterside remembrance ceremony held around the Summer Solstice and known as Duan Wu. In the west, this has been adopted in annual Dragon Boat Racing Festivals, along the lines of a regatta.[17]

14

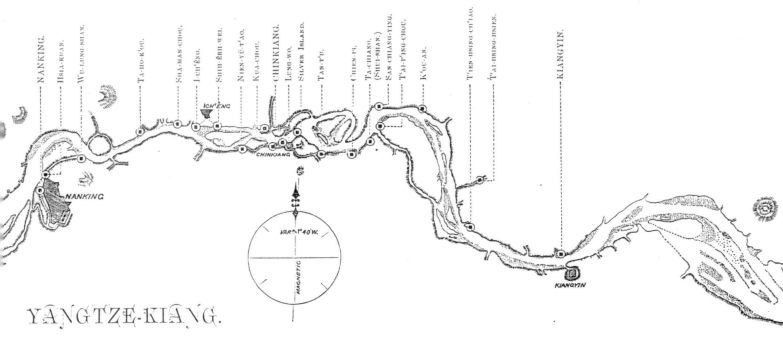

YANGTZE-KIANG.

LANGSHAN TO NANKING.

The saving of life from drowning and the creation of the tools and organisations to conduct such measures required a civilised approach to humanity. In China a measure of civilisation existed long before anything comparable could even be envisaged in the western world; it should therefore come as no surprise that, as well as the many inventions attributed to the Chinese, there can be added the development of the organised rescue service. Trade and transport into the Chinese interior followed her great rivers and canals, which were rife with perils, both natural and man-made. Traders and travellers had to brave massive rapids and gorges and silted-up shoals. Coastal mariners faced typhoons known as da feng or 'striking winds', tropical cyclones of Force 10 and more, as well as pirates and other scoundrels. To assist those traversing the trade routes, benevolent societies were established throughout China to provide boats that escorted junks through the most treacherous areas, as well as refuge to the shipwrecked, and the recovery of bodies. (This latter, somewhat melancholy, duty was of high importance in Chinese culture as it was paramount for a man to know where his ancestors were buried. The inability to recover a relative's corpse was a personal tragedy, second only to the actual death of the person.) It is thought that some of these organisations have origins as far back as the 13th Century when the earliest resuscitation methods were being promoted in China.[18]

A map showing lifeboat stations in the vicinity of Chinkiang around 1893. The Chinkiang Association for Saving Life, established as early as 1708, was revitalised in the 1860s with the creation of the stations seen above. Records indicate that the first estuarine lifesaving stations with dedicated rescue vessels in China were established in Chungking around 1737, although this may have occurred much earlier. Although the rescue sampans were not coastal boats, carrying out most of their work on the Yangtze River, they represent the first recorded use of boats specifically dedicated for lifesaving in the world.
China, Imperial Maritime Customs

Few, if any, translated records exist of the earliest benevolent societies in China, but it is quite probable that they were in existence long before the first known record, which appears in 1708. In that year, the Chinkiang Association for Saving Life was established by a committee of benefactors on the lower reaches of the Yangtze River, in the vicinity of Nanking, Jiangsu Province.[19] A ceremonial tablet was placed at Tantu by the District Magistrate in remembrance of the original committee which established the association. It seems, however, that the organisation's original focus was on dealing with drowning victims and teaching methods for reviving the apparently drowned, as there is no mention of the association acquiring lifeboats until 1796.[20]

15

There are, however, records of actual river lifeboats from elsewhere in China dating back to 1737. This precedes the introduction of dedicated lifeboats in Europe by approximately 40 years. In the Szechwan region of the Upper Yangtze River it is stated that, in 1737, five lifeboats were supplied by 'Imperial command' to be placed on the main river and a tributary, although there is no mention of exactly who was operating them. It would seem that over time they might have become neglected and disappeared from historical record.[21]

Fortunately there is a much more accurate record of lifeboats in China in the 19th Century. The concept of river lifeboats in the Upper Yangtze saw a resurgence in 1854, when a prosperous merchant named Li Yung-kuei, who lived near one of the dreaded gorges of the Yangtze known as the Hsint'an, initiated the idea of collecting subscriptions from passing junks in order to pay for lifeboats to escort them through the narrows. His idea was widely received and soon three lifeboats were built along the lines of the traditional sampans ('three strake' boats) of the area. Li decided that the lifeboats should be highly visible and easy to recognise, so he had them painted bright red. Red is a most auspicious colour in Chinese culture symbolising 'life energy', so its selection was not purely based on visual impact. The name Red Boats, or Hung-ch'uan, became synonymous with lifeboats in China's inland waterways. Li's new association quickly gained the admiration and respect of travellers and, as a testament to the dangers the lifeboat men faced, it became known as the kan-ssu-tang or 'Dare to Die' service.[22] By 1875 there were 13 river lifeboats placed at various locations adjacent to the gorges and, in 1883, it is said that a High Official from Hunan was rescued by a Red Boat, after which he petitioned that the service should be expanded and supported by the government. This was done and a special department was subsequently established by the Emperor, known as the Chiu-sheng Chu or Life-Saving Bureau.[23] In 1899 records state that 1,473 lives were saved by the Red Boats and, in 1900, 285 Chinese civilians and 33 foreigners were saved by these vessels when the German steamer *Suihsing* was lost on a rock in the K'ungling Rapid (see Sidebar).

Although the Dare to Die service was not the only lifeboat association in China in the 1800s (there were others at Shanghai, Wuhu, Kiukiang and on Donting Lake), it was certainly one of the most organised, with a stringent set of rules for the men in its employ. The boats were to patrol the gorges at all times by cruising up and down the eddies and rapids, and would be strategically placed according to the level of the river, the severity of the rapids and the flow of traffic. Up-bound junks were considered to be in more danger than those heading downstream and they would be escorted through a rapid by a Red Boat. If a wreck occurred and the cry of chiu-ming! (save life!) was heard, then a cannon was to be fired summoning all boats. Remuneration for the crew included 1,200 units of the currency of the day for survivors and 400 for the drowned. In addition, the lifeboatmen were strictly forbidden to undertake any salvage and would ensure that all was returned to its rightful owner. By 1901 there were 44 Red Boats on the Upper Yangtze, although this appears to have been the heyday of the Chinese river lifeboats. With the demise of Imperial China, the Red Boats' days were numbered, although G.R.G. Worcester, chronicler of the river craft of China, notes that in 1940 there was still one of these vessels manned by a couple of elderly lifeboatmen at Chungking near a treacherous set of rapids known as Long Kou, the 'Dragon's Mouth'. However, these two benevolent old souls were probably the last of their kind.

Loss of the German Steamship *Suihsing*

Although there are a number of historical books on the subject of early lifesaving in China, most have yet to be translated from the original language.[24] This more contemporary account of a rescue by lifesaving sampan provides an insight into the vessel's effectiveness in the turbulent waters and the skill and daring of their crews. It is taken from G.R.G. Worcester's, *The Junks and Sampans of the Upper Yangtze*.

That year [1900] was also remarkable for the first total wreck of a foreign steamer, the German S.S. Suihsing, on her maiden voyage up from Ichang. Unskillfully handled against the advice of the pilot, she ran on to a rock in the K'ungling Rapid and drifted down in a sinking condition. The crew had commandeered the ship's two boats and lowered them, and one was sunk by the ship's wash, but the red boats played their part and made trip after trip to the shore with rescued Chinese passengers. In this way considerable loss of life was avoided, though many, including the captain, who had generously parted with his lifebelt, were drowned. Thirty-three foreign passengers and 285 Chinese were rescued in all, and a collection of $300 was made by the British Consul at Ichang for the crews of the red boats in recognition of their services.[25]

CHAPTER 4

Humane Societies in the West

The Chinese idea of a benevolent 'lifesaving' or 'humane' society first appeared in Europe around 1757 when records indicate that the ancient methods of resuscitating the apparently drowned were being demonstrated in France and The Netherlands. In 1767 the 'Institution for the Recovery of Drowned Persons' was established in The Netherlands. Whether the fact that the Dutch had strong trading links with the Far East had any connection with the adaptation of the idea in a European context is difficult to say, but the chronological connection appears to be more then coincidental. Regardless, the idea of an organisation whose principal objective was to assist the survivor of wreck and near drowning, and to teach the newly developed principles of resuscitation, would quickly catch on in other countries. In 1774 the British 'Humane Society for the Recovery of Persons Apparently Drowned' (known later as the Royal Humane Society) would be established, espousing the same principles as its Dutch counterpart. In 1785 the idea would also spread to the New World in the form of the 'Humane Society of the Commonwealth of Massachusetts', the original lifesaving society in America. The international connections are best exemplified by a quote from the founding 'Rules' of that Society which stated:

> Upon these considerations, societies have been formed in various parts of Europe for promoting attempts to recover persons from apparent death, especially in cases of suffocation and drowning. The Humane Society established in Great Britain, in 1774, has been very successful. Within ten years from its institution, out of 1300 persons apparently dead from drowning, 790 have been restored to their friends and country. Many of them, no doubt, useful and valuable men.
>
> For an institution of this nature a considerable fund is necessary. And many occasional expenses will unavoidably occur. The cause of humanity,

THE INSTITUTION OF THE Humane Society OF THE Commonwealth of MASSACHUSETTS: WITH THE RULES For regulating said SOCIETY, AND

The Methods of Treatment to be used with Persons apparently dead ; with a Number of recent Cases proving the happy Effects thereof.

BOSTON: Printed in the Year 1788.

however, deserves every encouragement. And to promote that cause, it is to be hoped the benevolent will liberally subscribe.

A Society is now formed for these salutary purposes in this Commonwealth. And the following plan and arrangements are submitted to the inspection of the publick.[26]

These new societies focused on dealing with the aftermath of wreck and did not, for the most part, take an intervening or preventive approach to lifesaving. The primary goal of the early humane societies, aside from the education of the public as to the methods of resuscitating the survivors of wreck, was also to promote the development of safety measures and acts of heroism through the provision of awards.

From a coastal lifesaving perspective the humane societies were not a solution to the problem but did provide a partial remedy for the plight of the shipwrecked. Their establishment, in a European context, represented a truly significant change in the prevailing attitudes of the day. For the first time it was proven to an increasingly enlightened populace that private citizens could collectively form associations separate, to a great extent, from church and state, for the benefit of the common good and the pursuit of humanitarian goals. Another very significant and ground-breaking approach taken by these fledgling European societies, and one that would be of great importance in the future development of coastal lifesaving services around the world, was that many were national in scope and, as such, proved that lifesaving measures could be extended beyond the confines of purely local interest to the needs of a nation as a whole.

It should be stated that the humane societies were not entirely hands-off when it came to the provision of resources to coastal lifesaving. Houses of Refuge, dwellings which provided shelter, warmth and food for those survivors of shipwreck fortunate enough to reach them, were established by the Massachusetts Humane Society (MHS) along the remote New England coast in its formative years (see Chapter I-6). In Britain the Royal Humane Society continually provided awards to inventors of better boats and lifesaving appliances, including such historically important apparatus as Captain Manby's line-throwing mortar, one of the original devices for transferring a line from shore to a vessel in distress.

However, the reality remained that, in spite of the aforementioned measures, little or no effort was expended to prevent loss of life on the water through direct intervention at the wreck site. This could only be done with the use of boats and other apparatus. None of the humane societies seemed ready to grasp this concept (although the MHS would eventually establish the first lifeboat station in the United States in 1807) and it would be the people most directly affected by the carnage of shipwreck, the shipowners and inhabitants of coastal communities large and small, who would initiate the development of such services on a local level.

The Rescue of Persons Apparently Drowned

One of the main objectives of the early humane societies was to teach the practice of resuscitating the apparently drowned, a technique which had originated in China in the Middle Ages. The methodology had been brought to Europe by traders and merchants to the Far East. Part of the Chinese technique, described below, is as sound today as it was 500 years ago, particularly in the context of modern theories on hypothermia and near drowning.

On rescuing a drowning man, the crew are to lose no time changing the patient's clothes for the dry ones of the Society, after which a tisane of ginger is to be administered. The boatmen are on no account to give up the patient for dead because he may be perfectly insensible, and they are to be careful not to place the patient near a fire, as such a measure would force the cold inwards and lessen the chances of recovery.[27]

By the mid 18th Century these theories and practices were being taught at the internationally renowned medical university at Leidon, in The Netherlands. Additional methods were slowly incorporated, including the introduction of mouth-to-mouth resuscitation, as well as several more dubious remedies such as filling the person's lungs with tobacco smoke, or rolling them over a log. In 1767 a Dutch 'Institution for the Recovery of Drowned Persons' was established, followed closely by the creation of similar societies in other progressive nations. Strange remedies aside, within four years of the humane society's creation in Holland some 160 people had been saved from near drowning through the promulgation of these new techniques. Most of the western societies eventually evolved into public safety organisations associated more with swimming than coastal lifesaving. In their early years, however, they would provide key support for the development of the first lifesaving craft and facilities. They also rewarded individual acts of heroism through the provision of the first lifesaving medals.

An 18th-Century Dutch oil painting showing an early method of resuscitating the apparently drowned – survivors were placed over barrels to help drain their lungs of seawater.
KNRM

CHAPTER 5

The Local Lifeboat Societies

It is difficult to say just exactly when or where the world's first dedicated rescue vessel was established, although evidence suggests that the Dutch would be the first to undertake such provision. This is not surprising as The Netherlands has one of the most treacherous stretches of coastline in the world. The lowlands of this nation extend far offshore in great sandbanks, which, when combined with the full fury of a North Sea gale in the days of sail, brought doom to countless ships. Scores of East Indiamen were lost on their return from trading voyages to the Far East and seamen accused the local citizens of making little or no effort to aid the shipwrecked. There were also serious reports of plundering and a committee of investigation was established through the influence of parties who were being financially affected.[28] Thus, commercial interests were one of the primary instigating factors for the establishment of the early lifesaving facilities. Of particular importance was the ability to protect wreck from plunder and to salvage and store the remaining cargo and valuables so that they could be returned to their rightful owner. For obvious reasons this objective was of primary concern to ship- and cargo-owners and to the relatively new, burgeoning underwriting industry in The Netherlands.[29]

The Committee published its recommendations on 13 October 1768. They included such new ideas as 'partitioning of beaches, installation of official beachcombers to patrol the beach, and the provision of equipment for saving people and goods, which included a boat'.[30] The recommendations were national in scope, but called for each of the Dutch provinces to construct a boat and carriage of the stated design and to place them at local villages. The vessels were to be manned by the local citizenry and were to be stationed at such locations as Scheveningen, Zaandvort, Texel, Vlieland, Egmond van Zee and Oostvoorne. Unfortunately, this earliest attempt at providing dedicated rescue vessels was destined for failure. It would seem that with no organised

structure in place to man and maintain the craft, there was little will on the part of the local populace to utilise the boats on their own. This, and the rather unseaworthy appearance of the boats themselves, which looked more like small canal barges than vessels designed for use in breaking surf, probably combined to bring about their eventual demise. In fact, there is no real record of whether these vessels were ever put to use at all.

This would be the first of many misguided attempts to establish dedicated rescue vessels by well-intentioned governments, aristocrats and humane societies in many nations well into the next century. Without fail all such symbolic efforts would result in the same fate as did the lifeboats of West Friesland. With no strong supporting organisation the shore-based rescue boat was doomed to fail.

An early depiction of the 'life-boat' rescuing the crew of a stricken sailing ship at the mouth of the River Tyne in Northumberland. One of the earliest and most successful local lifesaving societies in the world was established to protect mariners in these same waters beginning in 1789.
Author's Collection

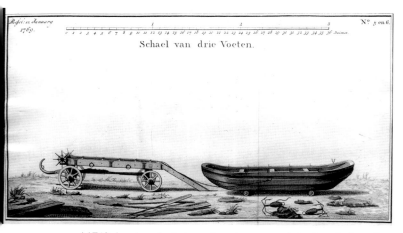

A 1769 drawing of what may have been one of the first dedicated coastal lifesaving vessels in the world. Sponsored by shipping and insurance interests directly affected by the mounting losses of both property and life on Dutch shores, these vessels were intended for use in the Frisian Islands to be operated by local crews. It is not certain, however, whether they were actually used, or even constructed. The drawing shows the rescue boat, its carriage, complete with launching rollers and hand-winches for recovery, as well as the rowing and steering oars and grapples used for anchoring and veering down on wrecks. Given the rather barge-like appearance of these craft, the fact that they may never have been used might be considered a blessing in disguise for their intended crews.
KNRM, Redding Museum Dorus Rijkers

Great Britain has been referred to by many historians as the 'Cradle of the Lifeboat', and rightfully so. Although the concept of humane societies and the use of dedicated rescue craft may have had international origins, as seen on the rivers of China, it would be the British and the Irish who would be the first to successfully operate dedicated rescue vessels in a coastal environment, first on a local and later on a national basis. The British would also go on to invent a new, specialised type of rescue vessel, the 'life-boat', which would have far superior sea-keeping characteristics than the earlier conventional small boats in use. Britain proved that dedicated rescue vessels could be operated successfully over time and was the first nation to combine an effective organisational structure with the new tool of the lifeboat.

The concept of a localised organisation promoting assistance to the shipwrecked was not new to Great Britain – as has been seen with the implementation of charitable measures at Bamburgh Castle in Northumberland as early as the 1750s.[31] In 1776, however, came the creation of a successful localised rescue service with its own dedicated rescue vessels. The world's first

such coastal lifesaving station was established at Formby Point, on the banks of the River Mersey and was administered by the Liverpool Docks Trust. As had been the case eight years earlier in The Netherlands, the Formby lifesaving station was established primarily at the behest of commercial interests with a humanitarian tinge. The port of Liverpool was then a major centre for global trade and was the location of the world's first commercial or 'wet' dock, constructed back in 1715. Since its inception substantial port dues had been continually paid to the docks trust and had been used, in addition to funding the dock expansion, to institute such safety measures as a pilotage service and the building of lighthouses. In 1764 a catastrophe occurred in which 18 vessels were stranded at the entrance to the port and more than 75 lives were lost. It was estimated that lost revenue through port duties was in the order of £18,000. As a result of this and earlier calamities, it was recommended that the port's safety measures be extended to provide a dedicated and permanently manned rescue boat at Formby Point, a strategic location at the entrance to the Mersey. As time went on, the financial backing for this boat would extend beyond the primary source of allotments from port duties to direct contributions from shipowners and underwriters such as the Liverpool Underwriters and the West Indies Association who, interestingly enough, would only provide remuneration if one of their own vessels was salved!

The main proponent of these improvements was the Head Dock Master and Principal Water Bailiff for Liverpool, Captain William Hutchinson, an experienced mariner and an ingenious man who had a keen awareness of the plight of seafarers. Hutchinson eagerly promoted the relatively new concepts of maritime safety and rescue techniques and also solicited the creation of a local Humane Society along the lines of the recently established Royal Humane Society. In 1777 he published a book, one of the first of its kind, entitled *A Treatise on Practical Seamanship*, in which he espoused that to 'save the lives of distressed people on board wrecks…the best methods that experiments may produce, should be represented and described in prints, for the purpose of being distributed among our ships, and amongst the inhabitants along our sea coasts, to be made as public as possible, and rewards of a guinea certain should be allowed to the poor people on shore for every human life saved by them from wrecks, and vessels forced on shore, and Liverpool leads the way for this noble purpose'.[32]

The first mention of a 'boat' being placed at Formby appears in a 1776 map of the approaches to the Port of Liverpool and the entrances to the River Mersey, on which it states:

On the Strand, about a Mile below Formby Lower Land Mark there is a boat House, and a Boat kept ready to save lives from Vessels forced on Shore on that Coast, and a Guinea, or more, Reward is paid by the Corporation for every human Life that is Saved by means of this Boat, &c.[33]

Eventually there would be three lifeboats operated by the Liverpool Docks Trust, including one of the new Shields type lifeboats constructed by Henry Greathead, at Formby (see Chapter II-5); the other two were located at Hoylake and Liverpool proper. It is interesting to note that William Hutchinson would also be instrumental in helping to establish a similar docks trust, or harbour authority, for the port of Dublin, Ireland. As in Liverpool, the Dublin Docks Trust would establish the first dedicated lifesaving vessels in Ireland beginning in 1800 (see Part IV).[34]

The boats of Formby and Dublin were a relative success because of the strong organisational structures surrounding them. The boats of the Liverpool Docks Trust were not manned by volunteers and eventually had a fully paid keeper to tend each vessel with the crews being paid for exercises and call-outs. Maintenance and training were closely supervised with monthly practices. Although the Liverpool boats appear to have had their ups and downs in terms of operation and management throughout the political tumult of the next three decades, the vessels would remain in operation until 1894, at which time they would be amalgamated into the Royal National Lifeboat Institution (RNLI), having been in operation for some 118 years.

The Dutch having proposed the concept of dedicated coastal rescue vessels, and William Hutchinson having developed the support structure to effectively operate them, 1789 would see further advancements in coastal lifesaving, both in terms of technology and organisation. This was the year that a small ship and its crew would add their names to the litany of destruction and loss of life on the treacherous Northumberland coast. The events surrounding the loss of this one vessel would forever change the way coastal lifesaving was conducted around the world.

On 15 March 1789 the collier *Adventure* ran aground on the notorious Herd Sand at the mouth of the River Tyne. The perils of Tynemouth had to be traversed by all vessels trying to reach Newcastle and North and South Shields, all of which were becoming increasingly popular ports of call in the burgeoning coal trade. These hazards were aptly described by Captain Hutchinson himself in his treatises: '...the entrance into the harbour is very narrow, with dangerous rocks on one side, and a steep sand bank on the other, with a hard shoal bar a-cros [sic], where the waves of the sea frequently run very high...'.[35]

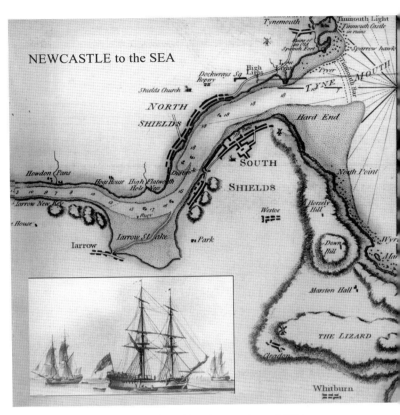

The treacherous mouth of the River Tyne from a chart of 1794. The image shows the Herd Sand (referred to as the Hard End) and the Tynemouth Bar. The picture inset is of a two-masted snow, similar to the *Adventure*, lost at this exact location in March 1789 with her entire crew. This tragedy was the catalyst for the development of the first design of true 'life-boat'.
Tyne and Wear Museums Service

A tragic scene unfolded. Gradually, as the *Adventure* succumbed to the constant onslaught of the breakers, the crew were seen to vanish from ship and rigging one by one, some vainly attempting to reach the shore. In the end all were lost and not one effort had been made from land to assist the hapless crew. Hundreds had witnessed the carnage, including a rather prominent group of local businessmen with keen interests in local shipping and marine insurance. These men watched the entire calamity during the course of a meeting at their reading room and coffeehouse, located high on a bluff known locally as the Lawe. So shocked was one member of the group, Cuthbert Heron, that he 'offered a Reward for any Seaman to go off to save the Men's Lives; which was refused; the greatest Part of the Crew of the *Adventure* perished within 300 yards of the Shore, and in sight of a multitude of Spectators'.[36] A decision was made by the 'Gentlemen of the Lawe House', as they became known, to run a contest in a local newspaper; the winner would receive two guineas for the best design of a boat 'which would not be liable to be overset by sea, and which moreover, would retain its buoyancy when manned and when nearly full of water'.[37] A committee was then established, led by a Mr Nicholas Fairles, to review the results and decide upon a winner.

A REWARD OF TWO GUINEAS
will be given to any Perfon producing a PLAN (which fhall be approved of by the Committee appointed for that Purpofe, as the beft) of a BOAT, capable of containing 24 Perfons, and calculated to go through a very fhoal, heavy, broken Sea : The Intention of it being to preferve the Lives of Seamen, from Ships coming afhore, in hard Gales of Wind.
Plans will be received on any Day, at the Law-Houfe, South-Shields : and the Committee will meet at THREE o'Clock on the 10th of June, 1789, to determine who fhall be entitled to the Reward.
The Committee will be obliged to any Gentleman favouring them with his Hints, or fending a Plan prior to that Day.

The advertisement for the best design for a boat to go out in heavy surf and recover persons from shipwrecks, and return safely with all onboard, as submitted to the *Newcastle Advertiser* on 2 May 1789 by the Lawe House Committee.
Newcastle Central Library

The competition would result in the invention and construction of the world's first boat built specifically to save life at sea. In other words, although the term would not come into common use until the beginning of the 19th Century, this was the world's first true 'life-boat' (now commonly spelt as lifeboat). Constructed by a South Shields boatbuilder by the name of Henry Greathead this new vessel, which later became known as the *Original*, was launched in the autumn of 1789, and first saw service on 30 January 1790 at which time it was advertised as having exceeded all expectations (see Chapter II-5).

The Gentlemen of the Lawe House not only initiated the competition for a safer boat they also formed a local humanitarian organisation to operate the new vessel, known as the Tyneside Humane Society. This would become the first local voluntary lifeboat society in the world, for, although the crews would at times be 'rewarded' for their rescue efforts, they remained primarily volunteers. Thus, the Gentlemen of the Lawe House had promoted and directly assisted in the development of the tool – the lifeboat – and combined that tool with an effective mechanism to run it, a local volunteer society.

In April 1789 they recommended to Trinity House – the governing body for lighthouses and pilots in England, Wales and Ireland – that the boat under construction be stationed at South Shields and that beacons be placed at advantageous points at the mouth of the Tyne. The Trinity Brethren approved the recommendations, as did the 'Committee of Trade at Newcastle' who provided financial support to construct and maintain the new rescue boat. Monies would also be solicited from a voluntary levy on local shipping that transited in and out of the Tyne. Once again, vested commercial interests played a major role in the establishment of dedicated rescue craft, including the personal interests of members of the Lawe House Committee themselves, who had obvious financial concerns regarding losses off the Tynemouth. (Some years earlier these same individuals had been instrumental in establishing one of the first mutual insurance associations in Great Britain as a means to address their significant financial losses through shipwreck as well as the relative monopoly of the London underwriters.[38])

It should be mentioned that the Gentlemen of the Lawe House were not alone in pursuing the concept of a purpose-built rescue boat and developing a voluntary humane society at this time. Similar efforts were being investigated by the Bamburgh Trust during the late 1780s. Many historians have described Bamburgh Castle as the world's first lifeboat station but this probably was not the case, although Archdeacon Sharpe's interests in developing a specialised type of lifesaving vessel did precede those of the Lawe House. In 1788 the Archdeacon began corresponding with a coachbuilder named Lionel Lukin, who claimed to have designed a new 'unimmergible' boat (see Chapter II-3). In the spring of 1789 a local craft – a coble – was sent to Mr Lukin's workshop in London to be altered into one of his unimmergibles through the addition of such features as cork flotation and air cases. However, according to Adrian Osler's well researched book, *Mr Greathead's Lifeboats*, there is little evidence to prove that the altered coble made it back to Bamburgh prior to the establishment of the boat at South Shields, as is stated in most historical accounts. Although in later correspondence Mr Lukin claimed that the vessel met with great success, contemporary accounts of wreck in the Bamburgh area reveal a distinct lack of historical record of the vessel actually being used for lifesaving.[39] In 1802 the Bamburgh Trust would in fact purchase one of Mr Greathead's lifeboats for use in the local vicinity.[40] Lack of historical documentation aside, the Bamburgh Trust and its efforts at establishing the earliest of dedicated lifesaving facilities remains important in the history of rescue at sea.

The career of the world's first coastal 'life-boat' and the Tynemouth Humane Society which operated it, would not be uneventful. The appropriation of adequate funding – an inherent problem that dogs all lifesaving organisations, past and present – would create ongoing problems for the fledgling society. Even though scores of lives, and cargoes and ships were saved by the new vessel, public and commercial interest quickly waned and by 1795 external problems, such as the war with France, had only further distracted public interest and sympathy. That same year the Tynemouth Society had to appeal to Trinity House for basic operating funds as the annual subscriptions had dried up. Problems were again evident in 1797 when Nicholas Fairles published another public appeal for financial support and met with minimal success.

Fortunately, other events that year would significantly change things for the better. Once again, a prominent individual would witness a shipwreck at the mouth of the Tyne and be moved to action. The man was Hugh Earl Percy, Second Duke of Northumberland – a name that would be synonymous with the charitable cause of lifeboats in years to come. What the Duke witnessed, however, was not the horror of drowning seafarers, but the rescue of an entire crew and the salvage of a cargo by none other than the South Shields lifeboat. Moved by the event and by Mr Fairles's petition, the Duke placed an order with Henry Greathead for a second boat, the first in almost a decade, that would be stationed on his property at North Shields; he also established an annuity to ensure the vessel's ongoing operation. Within its first two years, this new lifeboat saved the crews of three vessels and, as a measure of the newly expanded Society's success, in the year 1802 more than 200 lives were saved in the mouth of the Tyne by the North and South Shields lifeboats alone.[41]

The new lifesaving vessels promoted by the Lawe Committee and built by Henry Greathead, attracted further national and international interest as the lifeboat concept began to catch on, riding the philanthropic wave and the enlightened sense of humanity arising in many European nations during the latter part of the 18th Century. The idea of the lifeboat as an entity, a type of vessel specifically designed to face the elements, save lives, and around which fledgling lifesaving organisations could rally, had now been established. In 1800, the year following the construction of the North Shields boat, the Duke purchased the third of Greathead's lifeboats, which he then donated to the port of Oporto, Portugal. Unfortunately there is no record of what became of this early lifeboat, although it is quite probable that, once again, the strong British commercial interests at the port, combined with the treacherous bar at its entrance, probably influenced the decision to place it there (see

Like any relatively new organisation, the local lifeboat societies faced many birthing pains, both at sea and ashore. In this case the Committee of the North Shields Lifeboat Society expresses, through a public petition, its frustration with local crews taking the lifeboat out without authorisation, leaving the boat and boathouse in utter disarray and absconding with any remuneration donated to the lifeboat charity by those saved.
South Tyneside Library

Part IV). Also in 1800 a Mr Cathcart Dempster purchased one of the lifeboats to be stationed at St Andrews, Scotland, with the financial assistance of the insurance underwriter Lloyd's. On 10 January 1800 the *Meanwell*, out of Scarborough, was wrecked off St Andrews in a horrific storm. Due to the violence of the tempest, Mr Dempster was unable to convince any of the local fishermen to take up oars. Instead, Dempster, a Major Horsburgh who was one of the local magistrates, and a ship's master by the name of Stewart volunteered their own services and others soon followed. The spirit of the cause was kindled and all 12 sailors were saved.

The new appreciation for the lifeboat was a result of two factors. First was the relative success of the Shields boats themselves – although as we shall see in the following chapters, there would eventually be many detractors of the design. Second was the promotion of this success. In 1802 Henry Greathead and certain members of the Lawe House Committee set out to create the first concerted public relations campaign to promote the lifeboat and the need to assist the shipwrecked – educating the public and the powers that be was just as important to organisational survival as the boats themselves.

Through the assistance of such notable contemporaries as the Second Duke of Northumberland, Sir John Swinburne, a relation of the Duke and a local philanthropist, and Rowland Burdon, a Member of Parliament for the County of Durham, Greathead was able to petition Parliament to establish a committee to review the merits of his new boat and, at the same time, attract considerable interest from the press of the day. His petition was successful and considerable financial remuneration was awarded by both Parliament and the Royal Society for the Arts. More importantly, however, the publicity surrounding the petition and the personal contacts made by Mr Greathead himself while residing in London resulted in Lloyd's of London becoming interested in the cause. This was not the first time that Lloyd's had provided funds for lifeboats, limited funds had been previously provided to St Andrews and other locations in the British Isles. But in 1802, thanks to recent reforms, the Committee of Lloyd's had become flush with spare capital and a prominent member, John Julius Angerstein, felt inclined to direct some of the funds towards the high-profile cause of the day. In May of that year a fund of £2,000 was set aside to promote such a cause, with the condition that no more then £50 per community would be provided once the boat had been constructed and put in place.[42]

By 1810 Greathead would have constructed 44 lifeboats for local organisations in the United Kingdom and Ireland, and around the world. The publicity surrounding the success of the new boat caught the attention of benevolent societies, individuals, governments and aristocracies throughout Europe. In addition to the Oporto lifeboat, several of Greathead's boats were built in The Netherlands where the first was stationed at the village of Terheyden around 1808; still others were purchased for use in Sweden, Russia, Lithuania, Denmark, Poland, India, Germany and, curiously enough, one was even purchased by the Government of the United States.[43]

Local organisations would be established throughout Britain. In 1800 the Suffolk Humane Society, using one of Greathead's boats, was formed from local subscriptions, followed in 1804 by the Norfolk Shipwreck Association.

In 1807 the Suffolk Society would approach none other than Lionel Lukin to help them design a new type of lifeboat based on local craft; they had had little success with the original Shields boat provided in 1801 with the assistance of Lloyd's (see Chapter II-7). Eventually, and inevitably, lifeboat societies would emerge in Lincolnshire, Anglesey, North Devon, Tees Bay, Newcastle and Dover, and individual lifeboats financed by local subscription or by individuals began to appear in ever greater numbers. There were also examples of lifeboats operated and manned by the Coastguard, the Royal Navy, various Harbour Trustees and Boards, and even Trinity House.[44] Although the organisational focus in Britain and many other countries would slowly move towards a national approach, several local societies would carry on for many decades, some well into the 20th Century. In fact, in 1913, there were still 15 separate local lifeboat organisations in the United Kingdom operating independently of the RNLI.

The Wreck of the Brig, *Mary and Margaret*

Local lifeboat societies were the pioneers of organised lifesaving. Examples of early rescues abound in contemporary newspaper accounts. Of all the local societies, the Tyne Lifeboat Institution, founded in 1789, is probably the most prominent. The principal role of this society was 'For the Preservation of Life From Shipwreck' and its creation led to the development of the first true coastal lifeboat. The following is an account of a rescue conducted by the first lifeboat (the *Original*), at the mouth of the River Tyne on 20 March 1792.

Thursday, in an amazingly high tide, two Brigs were swept by the rapidity of the tide to the southward of the Tyne bar, when they attempted to take the harbour. One of them after bearing much on the Herdsand got itself in a place called The Wheel, and from thence into the harbour, but the other the Mary and Margaret of Sunderland, being loaden with rails etc, and after being particularly hard struck upon a wreck (it is supposed) which lay in The Wheel, when she soon filled with water, and is entirely gone to pieces. About an hour before she began to break up, the boat, which was constructed about two years ago, for the purpose of saving the lives of seamen when in imminent danger, near the mouth of this port, was launched, and in a few minutes, reached the poor wretches in the wreck, and brought them all safe onshore. It created astonishment and admiration in the numerous spectators, when they saw the boat go through the breakers, that would have filled and sunk, any other machine, but one of its construction.[45]

CHAPTER 6

The Spread to the New World

The origins of organised coastal lifesaving in the United States go back to the years immediately after the American Revolution and the relatively parallel creation of two separate maritime entities, one private and one public, during the 1780s. As the amount of commerce and maritime traffic increased in and around the New World so, too, did the frequency of maritime calamity. Many wrecks involved overcrowded emigrant ships, crammed full of unfortunate souls whose only hope in life was to start afresh, in a new land. In May 1784 Dr May, a British physician and proponent of the Royal Humane Society, came to Boston, Massachusetts, and suggested the establishment of a similar humanitarian organisation in America. His suggestions did not fall upon deaf ears: humane societies were appearing all over the world at this time and many of the notable names in Boston society would support the views that evoked 'a new realization of the necessity to become your brother's keeper'.[46]

In 1785 the Humane Society of the Commonwealth of Massachusetts was founded; one of its primary objectives was to render assistance to the apparently drowned and the survivors of shipwreck. Prominent founding members and supporters included the then Governor of Massachusetts, James Bowdoin, as well as two founders of the Harvard Medical School, and such notable contemporaries as Paul Revere, John Hancock and Dr Samuel Adams. Starting in 1787 the Massachusetts Humane Society would begin construction of 'houses of refuge', otherwise described as humane or charity houses, which would be strategically placed along the New England coast:

The Society...[has] created for the benefit of Shipwrecked Mariners a number of huts, or small buildings, furnished with necessaries for their Relief, viz. one on Lovell's Island, in the harbour of Boston, situated on the north east side, on a rising ground, about fifty rods from the shore; one on the outer beach of Nantucket, about forty rods from Strawberry-Hill, so called; and one on Scituate beach, a mile to the southward of the fourth cliff, so called, and nearly opposite to White's ferry.
Massachusetts Humane Society, Boston; 1788.[47]

The Society's then-meagre resources, extracted solely from voluntary contributions, did not provide for the construction of lifeboats; this would come at a later date. The houses of refuge provided relief for those fortunate enough to survive shipwreck on the desolate shores and contained 'food, candles, [a] tinderbox for making fire, kindling and fuel'.[48] The Massachusetts Humane Society and a similar contemporary body known as the Merrimac Humane Society, thus initiated the development of the first dedicated lifesaving facilities in New England.

The twilight of the 18th Century saw not only private philanthropic efforts to establish coastal lifesaving services in the new United States, but also the birth of another maritime service, this time a public organisation that would become one of the fundamental cornerstones of the latterday United States Coast Guard (USCG). On 4 August 1790 President George Washington was authorised by an act of Congress to have constructed 'so many boats or cutters, not exceeding ten, as may be necessary' for use in the United States Revenue-Cutter Service, sometimes referred to as the Revenue-Marine. This service preceded the creation of the United States Navy and the vessels of the Revenue-Marine, whose primary duty was the enforcement of customs, came under the direct control of the Treasury Department.[49] The role of the Revenue-Marine would become less specific throughout the 19th Century, with military, anti-slavery and quarantine duties being included in the roster. From the inception of the service the revenue cutter crews always adhered to the common principle of assisting fellow mariners in distress and, on many occasions, acted on that convention. By 1832 the

The United States Revenue Cutter *Eagle* chases and, ultimately, captures the French privateer *Bon Pere* during the Quasi War, 1798-1801. Initially used for customs enforcement, the cutters were recruited to assist the US Navy in times of armed conflict, a tradition that continues to this day with the USCG. In 1832 they were assigned the duty of aiding ships in distress off the Atlantic seaboard during the winter season; they thus performed the world's first lifesaving patrols.
USCG

Treasury Department had officially recognised that one of the evolving roles of the Revenue-Marine was the saving of life. In December of that year Congress authorised the President, 'to cause any suitable number of public vessels, adapted to the purpose, to cruise upon the coast, in the severe portion of the season, when the public service will allow of it, and to afford such aid to distressed navigators as their circumstances and necessities may require, and such public vessels shall go to sea prepared fully to render such assistance'.[50] The small and seaworthy revenue cutters were then the only government vessels capable of carrying out these perilous duties and so the offshore patrols became the United States' first step towards an organised public rescue service (see Chapter II-16).

Back on the coast, in 1791 the Massachusetts Humane Society was officially incorporated and in 1807 established the first lifeboat station in the United States at Cohasset, Massachusetts. A 30ft (9m) whaleboat was constructed by a Mr William Raymond of Nantucket, along the lines of similar contemporary boats.[51] No evidence suggests that this boat was altered in any way for lifesaving, merely that it was chosen because of its inherent sea-keeping abilities and its popularity with local boatmen. Records do indicate, however, that one of Henry Greathead's lifeboats was purchased by the US Government in 1805. Although it is not known whether this particular boat was provided to the MHS or not.

The Massachusetts Humane Society saved thousands of lives over the course of its existence and by 1845 its resources consisted of 18 stations, equipped with Francis-type metallic lifeboats, Captain Manby's line-throwing mortars and, in some cases, rocket apparatus (see Chapters I-12 and II-9). The Society also continued to maintain houses of refuge at every station.[52] The crews consisted entirely of volunteers, although almost to a man the individuals in question were somehow connected to the rather prominent salvage and wrecking industry that thrived on the coasts of New England at this time.

Just as in Europe, the formation of early lifesaving organisations in America, such as the MHS and the later New York Shipwreck Society, was not entirely for humanitarian reasons but was spurred on by individuals involved in commercial shipping and insurance. The marine underwriters of such cities as Boston, Philadelphia, and New York had a vested interest in seeing that some form of service was established, not only to save passengers and crew, but also to save ships and cargo.

Before the establishment of the humane societies an intricate private salvage and rescue network already existed along the shores of New England, administered by the Boards of Underwriters of these cities who, in turn, had agents representing their interests, strategically located along the coast, at points where shipwrecks were most likely to occur.[53] Many of these agents became the voluntary 'keepers' of the first humane stations (see Chapter I-16). In some jurisdictions these 'wreckmasters', as they were called, would evolve into agents of the government, for the state had always had a vested financial interest in the preservation of wreck. In February 1787 the State of New York legitimised the profession and appointed 'Coast Masters' or Officers, 'to protect the interest of the (ship)owner of the wrecked vessel and thus the insurers, as well as the interest of the State'.[54] The agents chose the crews of the first lifeboats from the best of the local surfmen and, for the most part, local boats were used. Such men would use their well-honed skills to save lives but once that valiant deed had been achieved they became salvagers. The early humane stations were by no means perfect, but they were certainly a step in the right direction.

In Canada, then known as British North America, similar, less organised efforts were being made to establish basic lifesaving services by the Crown Colony of Nova Scotia. Canada's story of lifesaving at sea begins out in the Atlantic, at Sable Island, a treacherous body of shifting sand some 200 miles east of Halifax. The island, with its dangerous currents and outlying sandbanks, was a natural trap for passing ships also hindered by the fact that the island's existence was not even commonly known prior to 1800. In 1797 the then Governor of Nova Scotia, Sir John Wentworth, attempted to establish a government presence on the island after the wreck of the *Princess Amelia*. He commissioned two brothers, Andrew and William Miller, as 'Keepers of Sable Island' and proclaimed that their duties should include, 'The preservation of the Lives of all such Unfortunate persons as may from time to time be cast on shore on the (said island) or the Banks and Shoals adjacent thereto...'.[55] Unfortunately, the two brothers only

survived one season on the remote island, during which time they ran out of food and were harassed by 'marauders'. (The island had long been a haven for pirates and vagabonds and horrendous stories of wreck and calamity had reached the ears of the Halifax elite, particularly after the wreck of the *Frances* in 1799, which resulted in rather exaggerated stories involving ghosts and murder.)

The year before the wreck of the *Frances* Sir John had dispatched the schooner *Black Snake* of Liverpool, Nova Scotia, 'to pick up known castaways, and to leave a small party to remain over the winter and render assistance towards the future of life and property'.[56] Through this action, Canada's first lifesaving station was permanently established on 10 October 1801. The first 'Superintendent' or Keeper of the lifesaving station was John Morris, a retired Royal Navy man of good reputation. Wentworth wanted to provide some permanency to the settlement and he ensured that the new Superintendent was a 'gentleman', who would be accompanied by his family. The hired men who went with Morris were also encouraged to take their families. The original establishment provided houses for the keepers and the shipwrecked, storage for any salvaged goods, guns and ammunition to ward off unwanted 'wreckers and marauders', as well as for 'boats and carriages'.[57] The Humane Establishment at Sable Island was the first station in North America to have a dedicated rescue boat and it was one of the most enduring, remaining in operation until 1947 when it was made redundant by the efficiencies of modern navigational tools such as radar.

An early surfboat and line-throwing gun of the Massachusetts Humane Society, the first lifesaving organisation in the United States. *USCG*

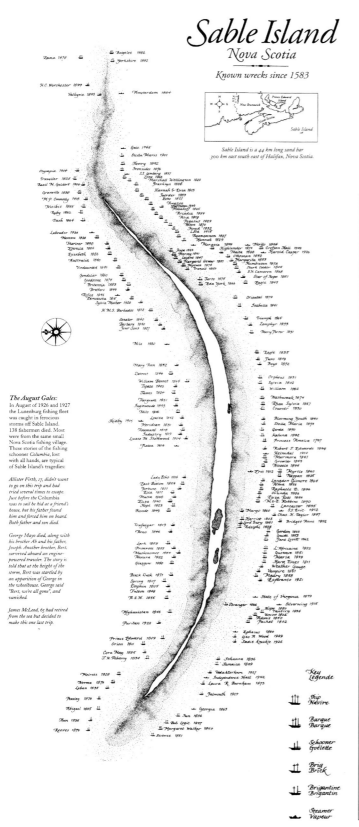

Sable Island
Nova Scotia

Known wrecks since 1583

Sable Island is a 44 km long sand bar 300 km east south east of Halifax, Nova Scotia.

A contemporary wreck chart of Sable Island off the coast of Nova Scotia helps illustrate the staggering toll of ships and mariners which this tendril of drifting sand has taken during recorded history. It is no wonder that the island became the site of the first permanently-manned lifesaving station in the New World.
Maritime Museum of the Atlantic, Halifax

The August Gales:
In August of 1926 and 1927 the Lunenburg fishing fleet was caught in ferocious storms off Sable Island. 138 fishermen died. Most were from the same small Nova Scotia fishing village. These stories of the fishing schooner *Columbia*, lost with all hands, are typical of Sable Island's tragedies:

Allister Firth, 17, didn't want to go on this trip and had tried several times to escape. Just before the Columbia was to sail he hid at a friend's house, but his father found him and forced him on board. Both father and son died.

George Mayo died, along with his brother Ab and his father, Joseph. Another brother, Bert, survived aboard an engine-powered trawler. The story is told that at the height of the storm, Bert was startled by an apparition of George in the wheelhouse. George said "Bert, we're all gone", and vanished.

James McLeod, 65, had retired from the sea but decided to make this one last trip.

The Rescue of the Crew of a New England Fishing Schooner

Some of the earliest measures of providing assistance to the shipwrecked along the vast expanses of remote, exposed and uninhabited coastline in the Americas involved the establishment of Houses of Refuge at sites where wrecks were frequent. Although this was only beneficial to those who actually survived a wreck and made it safely to shore, such structures saved countless lives and must have brought welcome salvation for those who chanced upon them. The following letter, written to the Massachusetts Humane Society in February 1788 by the owner of a fishing schooner lost outside Boston, gives an excellent early example of the great public service provided by the houses and the humane society.

This may certify, that in the night of the 14th of December last, a small schooner sailed from this place bound to Cape-Ann, having on board, besides the captain Mr John Bishop, four persons, viz. Capt. Philip Haskel, Mr Joseph Plumber, Mr Ephraim Ellery, and Mr Smith. The wind being very high, before day, the schooner was driven upon the rocks, called Ram-head near Lovell's Island, in the lower harbour. With great difficulty the people got upon the island, and to their inexpressible joy, reached the house lately erected by the Humane Society, for the preservation of shipwrecked seamen, in which they found every necessary for warming, drying and making themselves comfortable.

The people all wish to express their gratitude to the Founders of that benevolent institution, and acknowledge that, under God, they owe the preservation of their lives to the shelter, and the means of comfort which they found in it, as the night was extremely cold, and they were entirely wet before it was possible to get upon the shore.

On behalf of the people belonging to the schooner, and the passengers on board.
Robert Williams, Owner of the Schooner.[58]

Key
Legende

⚓ *Ship*
Navire

⚓ *Barque*
Barque

⚓ *Schooner*
Goélette

⚓ *Brig*
Brick

⚓ *Brigantine*
Brigantin

⚓ *Steamer*
Vapeur

CHAPTER 7

Great Britain; The 'Shipwreck' Institution

In 1802 a new local lifeboat society, similar to those being formed in England and Scotland was established at Douglas on the Isle of Man. The island had known many tragedies, including a storm that hit Douglas Bay on the evening of 21 September 1787 when the Manx fishing fleet was caught at sea: 50 boats were dashed to pieces and more than 160 lives were lost with no attempts made to rescue the hapless mariners.[59]

In 1808 a man by the name of Sir William Hillary would move to Douglas and become part of the lifesaving society. Sir William was a soldier by experience who had spent many years in the Mediterranean where, at one point, he had been equerry to Prince Frederick, son of King George III. He had also gained a keen love of the sea during his travels and become an avid and experienced sailor and boatman. In spite of personal and financial troubles which would plague him his entire life, Sir William would put his heart and soul into the concept of revitalising the already waning lifesaving society on the Isle of Man. Eventually, and more significantly, he would promote the concept of a 'National' lifesaving organisation for the United Kingdom, which would provide direct aid to the shipwrecked through the provision of lifeboats, line-throwing apparatus and awards for bravery.

However, the idea of a 'national' British lifesaving organisation was not entirely Hillary's. Others had promoted the concept before him. In 1801 Prime Minister William Pitt and the Marquis of Hertford recognised the success of the Duke of Northumberland and the Tyneside Humane Society, and the need to establish similar vessels, 'from the Northern Ports to London' and considered raising the idea in the House of Lords'.[60] But they were thwarted by a change of government.

By the 1820s most of Britain's locally-run lifesaving societies were in shambles. In a few rare cases, where strong organisational guidelines and reliable funds had been established, the societies continued: in Tynemouth, Liverpool, Norfolk and Suffolk. But by 1821 so deplorable was the nationwide state of coastal lifesaving that the Government commissioned Captain George Manby to travel the country and submit a report on the status of such facilities. A member of the Royal Artillery, Manby would later co-invent a line-throwing mortar for shooting ropes to stricken vessels from shore (see Chapter I-12). He was very active in the workings of the Suffolk Humane Society and in the cause of aiding the shipwrecked in general. He, too, had promoted the concept of a national society for aiding the shipwrecked. His report reflects his bias towards line-throwing apparatus to assist those wrecked on a lee shore; at the same time his comments give us some insight into the contemporary plight of the great many boats that had been placed around the country, particularly after 1802.

Sir William Hillary, founder of the 'Institution for the Preservation of Life from Shipwreck' in 1824. Known more simply as the 'Shipwreck Institution', this was the world's first 'national' movement in aid of the shipwrecked. *RNLI*

The boat, generally called the life-boat, though admirably calculated for particular services, is so large and cumbrous, that it is at times very difficult to convey it to the point of danger; and its unwieldy size exposes it so much to the force of the winds and waves, that to get it off from a flat beach in a storm is utterly impracticable. It differs also much in its construction from that particular form of boat which obtains in different maritime districts, to which, it is well known, those who use it are stubbornly attached, and in which alone they possess skill and feel confidence. These and other causes have not only thrown the life-boat into disuse, but have produced such neglect of it, that in some places I found it decaying, and, in others, actually gone to decay and falling to pieces.[61]

Sir William Hillary also recognised that lifeboats and societies around the country were on the decline. He realised that for the lifesaving cause to survive and even spread to those parts of the country where no such services existed, a truly nationwide perspective must be put forward. Similar to the concept of the Royal Humane Society, in terms of national context, the new lifesaving society would promote the cause throughout the country and would pool its resources to ensure success. Sir William developed his soulful and emotional views through personal involvement in several rescues in and around Douglas. In 1822 he assisted in the rescue of persons from the Royal Navy Cutter *Vigilant*, which had gone aground on St Mary's Isle in Douglas Bay. Apparently the Douglas lifeboat had been wrecked in 1814 and had not been replaced. Having witnessed the peril of the *Vigilant* Sir William proceeded to the harbour and commandeered a small rowing boat, which he crewed with naval officers. Together they rescued the *Vigilant* and towed her to safety. Less than 10 weeks later a second Royal Navy vessel, the 18-gun brig *Racehorse*, was wrecked on Langness Point. Five boats were summoned by Sir William and dispatched to the scene. Tragically, on the final run to rescue survivors, the last boat was swamped and nine men drowned. These incidents provided the catalyst for Sir William's 'Appeal to the British Nation', a document that he would publish in February 1823 and promulgate to promote the cause of a national lifesaving service.

For many years, and in many countries, the melancholy and fateful shipwrecks which I have witnessed, have excited a powerful interest in my mind for the situation of those who are exposed to this awful calamity; but the idea of the advantages which would result from the establishment of a

national institution for the preservation of human life from the perils of the sea, first suggested itself to me during my residence on a part of the coast often exposed to the most distressing scenes of misery, and where the dreadful storms of the last Autumn prevailed with unusual violence.[62]

His eloquent appeal called for the British nation, a nation of seafarers, to rise up and face the challenge and his prose exemplified the best of humanitarian intentions. He proposed to hold a series of public meetings. The primary objectives of the new institution would be:

1) The preservation of life from shipwreck.

2) Assistance for vessels in distress.

3) The Preservation of ships and property, even when the saving of life was not involved, or after the crew and passengers were already rescued.

4) The prevention of plunder and robbery from stranded vessels.

5) The succour and support of rescued persons, by providing medical aid, food, clothing, shelter and, finally, the means of reaching their homes and friends again.

6) The bestowing of suitable rewards on those who saved life and assisted vessels in distress, and the provision of help for the families of men who lost their lives in such heroic service.[63]

As one can gather from these grand intentions, Sir William's aim was to go beyond the local lifeboat and create an all-encompassing national coastal lifesaving entity. At first he made little progress, but eventually his appeal reached London where it was received with interest by many in the upper echelons of power, including Mr Thomas Wilson, Member of Parliament for the City, who was taken by Sir William's zeal and the cause itself. Wilson believed that it was the duty of those engaged in foreign commerce and shipping, which included many of his constituents, to assist in such a plan. Wilson would continue to be a driving force behind the cause for decades to come.

On 4 March 1824 a powerful and influential group of men congregated at the London Tavern; among their number were the famed abolitionist William Wilberforce and Captain Manby himself. The meeting was presided over by Dr Manners Sutton, Archbishop of Canterbury, and its result was the creation of the 'Royal National Institution for the Preservation of Life from Shipwreck' an organisation that, in later years, would be revamped and renamed as the present day Royal National Lifeboat Institution (RNLI).

Interestingly enough, on 25 February 1824, Sir William received a letter from an elderly man who offered his support stating: 'Having seen in the *Morning Herald* a notice of the commencement of a most laudable institution for the purpose of saving lives from shipwreck, I shall be most happy to contribute anything in my power to the success of the proposed Institution'. The man was the 82-year-old Lionel Lukin, designer of the 'Unimmergible' Boat.

A new chapter had now opened in the history of lifesaving at sea and, thanks primarily to the organisational efforts and skill of Thomas Wilson, Sir William returned victorious to the Isle of Man. In 1826 he formed a local chapter of the organisation and, by 1829, had established four lifeboats of Plenty's design (see Chapter II-8) to be stationed around the island. For the Isle of Man his efforts could not come too soon: between 1821 and 1842 there would be no fewer than 144 wrecks

AN APPEAL

TO THE

BRITISH NATION,

ON THE

HUMANITY AND POLICY

OF FORMING

A National Institution,

FOR THE PRESERVATION OF

LIVES AND PROPERTY FROM SHIPWRECK.

BY SIR WILLIAM HILLARY, BART.

LONDON:
PRINTED FOR G. AND W. B. WHITTAKER,
AVE-MARIA-LANE.

1823.

The cover of William Hillary's 1823 'Appeal to the British Nation' for the establishment of a national shipwreck institution. In this document Hillary set out his ideals for the new institution, which included providing assistance to the 'people and vessels of every nation, whether in peace or war'.
RNLI

on the island with the resultant loss of 172 lives. Sir William himself was seldom far from the action: in 1825 he assisted at the wreck of the steamer *City of Glasgow*, where 62 lives were saved and, later in that same year, helped to rescue 20 men from the brig *Leopard* and the sloop *Fancy*. There were many other occasions when Sir William set out but perhaps the most famous was on 20 November 1830 when his lifeboat rescued the entire crew of the mail steamer *St George*. The steamer's anchor cable had parted in a howling storm and she had been driven ashore. Sir William, aided by two other 'gentlemen' and a crew of 14, proceeded in a new Palmer-designed lifeboat – so new that one of the air cases had yet to be installed (see Chapter II-8) – and successfully took off all 22 persons onboard. In the process of the daring rescue, Sir William and three others were washed off the lifeboat but were later recovered. He continued to lead the party safely ashore in spite of the fact that 'he had his chest crushed and a rib broken'.[64] He was then 59 years old (see Sidebar).

The new institution burgeoned. Given the high status it had achieved in its formative years, including the patronage of His Majesty King George IV, revenues through donation quietly soared to more than £10,000, a phenomenal sum for the day. The first annual report stated that the committee had established lifeboats at 14 stations including two in Scotland and two in Ireland, adding to the 39 lifeboats already in existence and run by local societies and benevolent institutions. But the new group, which would soon become known as the 'Shipwreck Institution' did not seek to amalgamate or consolidate with the local lifesaving organisations. Instead, it developed as a national body that not only had its own lifeboats at strategic locations, but also sought to assist the 'independent' organisations, including providing them with lifeboats and awards. In addition, in the first year, the Institution would provide 16 of Manby's mortar apparatus to various locations.

Sir William Hillary died in Douglas, Isle of Man, on 5 January 1847. In his life he had been awarded two gold medals for bravery by his own Institution. His cause had been noble and the success of his endeavours great. Although the Shipwreck Institution would, in future, have its trials and tribulations, he had left a lasting legacy. His was the concept of a national lifesaving organisation for the world and he formalised the soon-to-be-accepted international ethic that any lifesaving measures taken 'should extend to all without distinction of country, in war and in peace' and that 'every stranger, whom the disasters of the sea may cast on her shores, should never look for refuge in vain'. The universal nature of lifesaving at sea was now established.

The Wreck of the Paddle-Steamer *St George*

In the early hours of Saturday 20 November 1830 the RMS *St George*, at anchor off the Port of Douglas, Isle of Man, was driven on to the treacherous Conister Reef by a tremendous onshore gale. Fortunately, all the passengers had been transferred ashore the previous day. But the crew of 22 had remained aboard and now huddled inside what remained of the shattered hulk. Time was of the essence as massive seas were gradually grinding the ship to pieces beneath their very feet.

Sir William Hillary mustered a crew of 13 to man the Douglas lifeboat. At first light they began the treacherous pull to Conister Reef. The seas were described as mountainous but somehow the lifeboat beat her way to the wreck site, in full view of a throng of onlookers on shore. The plan was to take the lifeboat to windward of the disaster, drop an anchor, and then veer down within reach of the wreck and take off the crew. The first attempt failed a few yards short of the ship, the breaking surf around the *St George* almost swamping the lifeboat. Lieutenant John Tudor, the commanding officer of the steamer, begged the lifeboat crew to save themselves and leave his crew to survive as best they could, but Hillary and his men carried on. On the second attempt they veered down into what they thought were calmer seas between the wreck and the reef. The move proved almost fatal for all concerned. In the confused seas and chaotic surge, the lifeboat was tossed about like a cork,

the boat being at one point 'vertical to the sea'. Her rudder was smashed and Sir William and three of his crew were thrown into the watery cauldron to be bashed between the rock and the heaving ship. Miraculously, all of them somehow made it back into the lifeboat. Sir William suffered several broken ribs and a crushed chest after being slammed against the hull of the *St George* and was eventually rescued by Lieutenant Tudor and another man who managed to lift him clear. For two hours he remained onboard, and eventually directed what remained of the shattered lifeboat into a safer location where he and the

Sir William Hillary and his Manx crew approach the wreck of the RMS *St George* impaled on Conister Reef during the fierce storm of 20 November 1830. Miraculously, all 22 onboard the steamer were saved and the rescue earned Hillary a Gold Medal.
Manx Museum

crew of the paddle steamer were slung onboard with ropes.

Still the adventure was not over. Thirty-six men now clung together in a lifeboat just 30ft (9m) in length and already damaged by reef and ship, with both air cases crushed. To add to their misery, there remained only two oars on board. Realising their predicament and sensing that they might not make it from the stern of the wreck to the more protected waters in the lee of the reef, Sir William kept a rope attached from the *St George* to the stern of the lifeboat. In the event of a further upset, this would be their lifeline back to the partial safety of the wreck. In the end, however, it proved a hindrance to their escape. Inevitably, with very little freeboard and not much reserve buoyancy, the lifeboat capsized once again. All 36 men hung on to the lifeboat which, now tethered to the wreck, was dashed like a pendulum against the reef. In the end, one brave soul swam under the up-turned lifeboat and cut the rope. Then a miracle occurred: a huge wave picked up the Douglas lifeboat and all the men and washed them piece-meal right over Conister Reef. Sir William himself described it as 'intervention of merciful providence'. All survived and in the much calmer seas were recovered by harbour boats manned by more volunteers.

For his valiant actions that day Sir William Hillary would receive the Gold Medal. Those who had survived the incident would always remember that fate, as much as brute force and seamanship, had played a large part in their rescue.

CHAPTER 8

Early European Lifeboat Services

The problems of shipwreck and loss of life that prompted the creation of Sir William's Shipwreck Institution were, of course, not exclusive to Great Britain. Other nations recognised the need and saw the merits of creating organised lifeboat services. In The Netherlands both the North and South Holland Lifeboat Institution (NZHRM), and the South Holland Institution for Saving the Shipwrecked (ZHRM) were founded in November of 1824, just eight months after the formation of Britain's Shipwreck Institution. Their mutual creation was largely due to public concern over the increasing number of shipwrecks and the enormous loss of life on the treacherous Dutch coast. In October 1824 the Dutch frigate *De Vreede* went aground off the village of Den Helder, near the Frisian Gap, with heavy losses among both the shipwrecked and the fishermen attempting to rescue them. The catastrophe solidified the calls for a more organised and reliable lifeboat institution, earlier attempts by the Dutch government and commercial interests having failed in 1769. The Dutch Monarchy had also placed six Greathead lifeboats at strategic coastal locations during the early 1800s but, yet again, lack of organisation and continuity allowed both stations and craft to fall into disrepair. Also, the rather heavy and cumbersome boats were probably not best suited to the Dutch coast with its shallow beaches and offshore sandbanks.

The reason for two separate institutions, one based in Amsterdam, the other in Rotterdam, was related to the influence of The Netherlands Pilotage Authority whose administration was split on the same geographic lines and

who took 'an active interest in the formation of the rescue organizations'.[65] For the next 167 years these Societies would work closely together on thousands of rescues.

During 1824 and 1825 at approximately the same time that other facilities were being established in The Netherlands and the UK, local humane societies began to appear on France's Atlantic coast, the earliest being the Société Humaine de Boulogne. The French stations operated both lifeboats and line-throwing apparatus. Other locally supported lifeboats were established at Dunkerque, Calais, Le Havre, Marseille, Grau du Roi and Honfleur.[66] As was seen elsewhere in Europe at the time, most of these local lifeboats eventually fell into disrepair. Political turmoil and a lack of continuity ruled the day. Those that survived did so primarily through the support of local benefactors and merchants (see Sidebar).

In 1828 His Majesty King Miguel of Portugal recognised the merits of the Oporto lifeboat and ordered the construction of a station on the beach at St John. A new lifeboat was purchased, as well as a line-throwing mortar (possibly a Manby type), and a house of refuge was constructed, complete with an infirmary and a stock of dry clothing.[67] Like so many others, the Asilo dos Naufragos eventually ran into disrepair through sheer neglect.

The coast of Belgium is only about 40 miles (65km) long but has been the scene of many horrendous wrecks over the centuries. The Belgian Sea Rescue Service was established by Royal Decree in October 1838. This publicly-funded lifesaving organisation remains in operation to this day and is one of the earliest known state-run rescue services in the western world. In spite of the failures of publicly-funded lifeboats and services elsewhere in Europe, the Belgian service flourished. Its first stations were located at Ostend, Nieuwpoort, Blankenberghe and

A model of one of the early Greathead-type lifeboats constructed by the Dutch Monarchy for use on the outer coasts of The Netherlands. The carriage is rather unique in that it suspended the boat, rather than carrying it. The large wheels were designed not to get bogged down in the sand and to allow the boat to be launched in a sufficient depth of water. *KNRM, Redding Museum Dorus Rijkers*

An early scene of lifesaving off the Dutch coast, 1833. The lifeboat from Noordwijk heads to sea in aid of the stranded ship *Gräfin Pläter*. KNRM

able to hold down another job, many in the local fishery. Eventually many lifeboat crews were drawn from the pilotage service and, in 1840, the Rescue Service became a branch of that authority. The only exception to this was at Ostend, where enough qualified volunteers were available to man the station. All the original stations housed line-throwing guns and breeches buoy gear, in the same fashion as the early French rescue services. Due to the sandy nature of the Belgian coast most of the early rescue craft were relatively lightweight surfboats (around 2 tons [2.04 tonnes]) of about 30ft (9m) in length, with air cases at either end (which rendered them 'insubmersible' but not self-righting), and were considered to be self-bailing. They were launched off iron carriages and, in most cases, were drawn by hand, although horses could be used if greater distances had to be crossed.

Knokke and, by the turn of the century, four more were established at Adinkerke, Coq, Zeebrugge and Heyst. Eventually a ninth station was set up at the new port of Zeebrugge when it was completed.[68]

The Belgian station crews were paid a stipend to train and remain available for the lifeboat service, although most were

The Loss of the *Amphitrite*

Not all stories of rescue and survival at sea have happy endings, despite the valiant and concerted efforts of the rescuers. On 30 August 1833, the British ship *Amphitrite*, on route from Woolwich with a human cargo of 120 women and children condemned for transport to the penal colony at Botany Bay in Australia, was blown across the Strait of Dover by a strong nor'wester. The events of this day provide an excellent example of the valour of the crew of one of the earliest European human societies and of an incident, which in the end would spur on the development of a larger, national lifesaving network in France, the Société Centrale de Sauvetage des Naufragés.

At around 5pm, the old and dilapidated vessel was in an extremely precarious position less than a mile off Boulogne. She anchored, but the tide would soon be changing and then the seas would get up even more. Almost immediately a crew of local volunteers was mustered to man the Boulogne Humane Society's lifeboat and, without even the protection of life preservers, they rowed out into the tempest. It took them four attempts to make it over the bar and when they finally came alongside the vessel they were shocked to find that the captain refused all offers of assistance. In his opinion all was fine and the *Amphitrite* would ride out the storm at anchor. It was obvious to the would-be lifesavers that the passengers and crew did not share his opinion and that panic was rising on deck. The lifeboat crew screamed through the howling gale, attempting to apprise the master of the forthcoming change in tide, but his mind was set. Finally they convinced him that, at least, a line should be made fast to shore. Reluctantly, they departed with the line but,

when almost back on shore, the rope became taught and almost capsized the lifeboat. In a frantic attempt to save their own lives, the rescuers cut the line. By now the tide had turned and from their position the lifesavers could see that the inevitable destruction of the *Amphitrite* was beginning. The seas were now of such magnitude that the lifeboat itself barely made it to shore.

Incredibly, one of her crew, a young man by the name of Pierre-Antoine Henin, plunged into the surf in a desperate attempt to get another line from the vessel. For over an hour he swam through the surf to the stricken ship and, even when he made it alongside, his yells were barely heard above the din. Bedlam had broken out on the heaving deck of the *Amphitrite*, yet the captain maintained his state of denial. It is thought that his refusal of help was based on his fear of losing the £50 bounty that he would receive for the delivery of the women and children; as far as he was concerned the passengers, most of whom were prostitutes and petty criminals, would simply escape if they made it ashore. By now, however, the poor people were desperate and ignored the captain's dictatorial powers; they passed a line to Pierre-Antoine who, with almost super-human strength, started back for the shore. Exhausted he was eventually hauled out of the sea at the breakwater by the large crowd that had gathered to witness the calamity – he no longer had the rope.

Now, all anyone could do was watch in horror as, one by one, the ship's boats were launched, only to crash against the hull and spill the ill-fated occupants into the sea. Within hours the *Amphitrite* had been smashed to pieces and 130 of her passengers and crew, including the arrogant master, had gone to a watery grave.[69]

CHAPTER 9

Great Britain; The 'Lifeboat' Institution

The initial successes and momentum of Sir William Hillary's Shipwreck Institution would quickly fade, despite the substantial funds and the immense expansion in the provision of lifeboats, rocket apparatus and awards for bravery. After 1824 political and economic turmoil would beset the United Kingdom and most of Europe and in 1826 an economic panic swept the nation and riots ensued. The times were not conducive to the formative years of a voluntary lifesaving organisation. By the mid 1840s the overall state of lifeboats had, once again, diminished to the point 'that among all the Lifeboats in the United Kingdom there were perhaps not a dozen really efficient boats';[70] this out of an original total of 96 lifeboats in Britain and Ireland, 30 of which belonged to the Shipwreck Institution. Public interest had waned and many of the lifeboats were abandoned and left to rot. From 1841 to 1850 no public appeals were even made on behalf of the Institution.

Nevertheless, heroic deeds did occur during this downturn. In 1830 Sir William Hillary took part in the incredible rescue of the Royal Mail Steamer *St George*, and in 1838 William and Grace Darling carried out their famous rescue of the survivors of the steamer *Forfarshire* (see Chapter I-14). Although the fortunes of the Institution were waning, the fact remained that since its inception in 1824 an estimated 6,716 lives had been saved, and 74 gold and 429 silver medals had been awarded to 'officers, boatmen, and other persons' for service in the salvation of human life. In addition, the monumental sum of £5,500 had been spent on the provision of lifeboats and rocket apparatus around the coasts of Britain and Ireland.[71]

Thus, the infrastructure of the world's first national lifesaving institution having been sorely neglected for over two decades faced the question, would it ever recover? The catalyst for change came on 4 December 1849 when the South Shields lifeboat set out in a heavy sea to rescue the crew from the brig *Betsy*, which had been wrecked on the Herd Sand, that same natural hazard that had claimed the entire crew of the *Adventure* in 1789. The strong ebb current raised the seas and, while alongside the wreck, the lifeboat was upended and capsized throwing all 24 crew into the sea – 20 perished. To add to the loss, all the men were drawn from the best local Tynemouth pilots. The lifeboat was one of Greathead's original design and, although this had been the first tragedy to strike the Tynemouth lifeboats in over 60 years, the accident served to fuel two fires. First and foremost, it rekindled public sentiment and support for the lifeboat cause. Second, recognition was now given to the idea that perhaps a better and safer design of lifeboat could be developed, possibly one that could incorporate some of the safety principles such as self-righting put forward by men like William Wouldhave (see Chapter II-4).

Britain was now coming out of the economic and political doldrums of the previous two decades and some very notable personalities of the period set about revitalising the lifeboat service. Recognising that the nation's lifeboats were in general disrepair, that great stretches of the coast had no lifesaving facilities at all, and that a new lifeboat design was entirely warranted, such notables as Britain's Prince Albert, the Belgian King, and Queen Victoria lent their considerable support to the revitalised cause. The original President of the Shipwreck Institution, the Earl of Liverpool, had passed away in 1828 and since then no one had taken up the post. At last, in 1851, Algernon, the Fourth Duke of Northumberland, assumed the role. Algernon, also known as the 'Sailor

Duke', was a Royal Navy man of compassionate nature who had risen through the ranks to become First Lord of the Admiralty. His seafaring background combined with a strong and intellectually disposed nature to provide the perfect mix for the regeneration of the lifeboat ideal in Great Britain. There would be no looking back.

With the help of a new Committee of Management that included some of the founding members such as Mr Thomas Wilson and Mr George Palmer, then both in their 80s, the Duke of Northumberland began to initiate far-reaching changes. The new committee took over all the existing stations, formed numerous local branches both on the coast and inland (therefore initiating a broader base of support for the cause), and created the position of Inspector of Lifeboats to ensure that no lifeboat belonging to the Institution would ever again fall into disrepair through apathy or neglect and that regular training exercises would be carried out. It was also the decision of the Committee that it would become the central authority to which all the local branches would report on a 'service or quarterly basis', and 'a fixed scale of payments to the coxswains and crews of the Life-boats on all occasions of their going afloat in them, whether on service or quarterly exercise...in addition to an annual salary to the coxswains' would be established.[72]

Another significant and far-sighted decision was to publish a journal on a regular basis, which was to be known as *The Lifeboat*. The journal would outline the workings and heroic rescues of the Institution and would become a tool for disseminating information throughout the British Isles. Public relations was now as integral a part of a successful volunteer lifesaving organisation as was the lifeboat itself. A spirited young barrister named Richard Lewis was hired as Secretary of the Institution. In the 30 years that he would hold the post, the annual income of the Institution would rise from a mere few hundred, to more than £58,000 per annum, and the number of lifeboats belonging to the Institution and placed in service from 30 in 1850 (in various states of repair), to close to 300 by the turn of the century. Just as organisational strength and integrity had ensured the survival of a few of the earliest local lifesaving organisations in Britain, the same would now hold true, for the first time, on a national level.

In 1854 the structure and mandate of the Institution would also be changed. Two of the original objectives of the Shipwreck Institution would be transferred to other organisations. Line-throwing apparatus was passed to the Board of Trade. The Merchant Shipping Act of that year stipulated that the Board of Trade, through the auspices of HM Coastguard, should 'assist in lifesaving proportional to private and local exertions' and it was agreed that the maintenance and provision of all coastal lifesaving apparatus such as rockets and breeches buoy should become the domain of this public body, as is the case today. The second change was the transfer of the responsibility for the care of shipwreck survivors to the Shipwrecked Fishermen and Mariners Royal Benevolent Society who, in turn, would hand over the control of their nine lifeboats, at various locations around the country, to the Institution.

Next it was decided that the name of the organisation should be altered to represent its new, more focused role, and the name 'Royal National Life-boat Institution (founded in 1824 for the Preservation of Life from Shipwreck)' was taken up; by many the organisation would now be referred to as, simply, the 'Lifeboat Institution' or the RNLI.

Another result of the Act was the implementation of a subsidy for the revitalised Institution of £2,000 per annum to be granted from the Mercantile Marine Fund. It is undoubtedly true that this sum greatly contributed to the revitalisation of the service but it came with a caveat: acceptance of these funds meant that a senior Coastguard officer or an official of the Board of Trade must sit on each local lifeboat committee and be in attendance to countersign any expenditures. This was to be the situation until successful voluntary fund-raising mechanisms could be established. If ever there was an incentive to raise funds, surely this was one. By 1860 the subsidy and the shackles of state bureaucracy had been cast off and the RNLI has survived entirely on voluntary support ever since.

Thus, the loss of the South Shields lifeboat initiated great change within the organisation and was also the precursor for the development of an improved lifeboat. The Duke of Northumberland held a second competition, similar to that run by the Gentlemen of the Lawe House in 1789, for the design of a lifeboat that would best meet a set of published standards. This time, the prize would be 100 guineas. More than 280 entries were submitted from the UK, France, Germany, The Netherlands, the United States and beyond. The eventual result was the creation of the standard self-righting, self-bailing (SR-SB) lifeboat. This would be the precursor of future generations of lifeboats in Britain and abroad and, through its highly visible success, would become the perfect champion for the cause (see Chapter II-8).

The competition report presented by Captain John Washington, an expert on lifeboats and a member of the Committee of the RNLI, analysed the previous state of lifeboats throughout the country and provided a prognosis for the future. The Institution would excel and grow through the remainder of the 19th Century and, through the words of Captain Washington, we recognise that lessons learnt, would not soon be forgotten.

It affords both a warning as to the past and an encouragement as to the future: a warning to those who have allowed the boats at certain stations to fall into decay, while it teaches us that humane intentions, in order to be serviceable to our fellow-creatures, must be fully and efficiently carried into action. On the other hand, it offers a cheering encouragement to the future, inasmuch as the number of lives saved from shipwreck through the instrumentality of lifeboats, mortars, and rockets (even in their present imperfect, and, on many parts of the coast, ill-organized state), affords undoubted proof of the value of such means for preserving life. Wherever the boats have been looked after, and the crews well trained, as at Liverpool, Shields, and on the coasts of Norfolk and Suffolk, the most signal success has rewarded their exertions. This fact is most encouraging, and cannot be too strongly insisted upon. It is the most gratifying reward to the several local committees and individuals who have perseveringly done their

The original RNLI Headquarters, depicted here, was in London, where it remained until 1972. Property was then purchased for the existing head office and maintenance depot at Poole, Dorset.
RNLI

duty, and gives firm ground of encouragement for the future.... The success that has attended exertions in one place may fairly be reckoned in another. There seems no reason why a very few years should not see a life-boat stationed at each of the exposed points on the most frequented parts of the coasts of the United Kingdom; by means of which – with the blessing of Devine Providence upon the endeavours of those who undertake the work – the best results to the cause of humanity may confidently be anticipated.[73]

And so it was.

The *Forest Hall* and the Lynmouth Lifeboat

The solidification of Sir William Hillary's ideal of a truly national lifeboat service for Britain and Ireland after 1851, in the form of the RNLI, would result in the most efficient voluntary coastal lifesaving organisation the world had ever seen. Hundreds of rescues would be carried out every year and thousands of lives would be saved. The Institution would eventually become a national icon and the culture of the lifeboat would become firmly established within the British psyche. It is practically impossible to pick out one particular rescue as the most historic as there have been entire volumes written about the hundreds of heroic deeds conducted by the lifeboats and crews of the RNLI. Nevertheless, there is one famous rescue that occurred off the southern shores of the Bristol Channel and exemplifies the power of humanitarian deeds when community spirit combines with sheer grit and determination to resolve a crisis at sea.

On the evening of 12 January 1899 a terrific storm was raging in the Bristol Channel, pounding the shores of North Devon and wreaking havoc throughout England and Wales. During the day, the 1,900-ton, fully-rigged ship *Forest Hall* had departed Bristol under tow and, with a skeleton crew of 15 men, was attempting to make St David's Head off the southwest tip of Wales, whence the ship would make her own way under sail to Liverpool, where a cargo and fresh crew were waiting. As the weather deteriorated the captains of both the tug and the tow realised that making their destination was no longer an option. The seas had become so large and the effects of the wind so strong, that less and less progress was being made. They attempted to alter course for the relative protection of Carmarthen Bay but in the process the tow-line rose taut out of the seas and almost immediately parted. On the *Forest Hall* Captain James Uliss immediately had his crew set enough sail to gain control of the vessel, while the tug, after several attempts to re-secure the tow-line, was forced to abandon the situation and head for safety.

Soon after the tug's departure a series of huge breaking seas washed over the ship, knocking the quartermaster off the helm. With the ship's wheel spinning freely, her rudder was smashed and disabled. Her fate was now sealed – she would drift helplessly towards the southeast and the 800ft (245m) high cliffs of the North Devon coast. Both anchors were dropped and all cable was paid out, but even this last-ditch effort to save the ship had little effect; merely slowing the rate of drift as she dragged towards the shore. At about 6 o'clock in the evening Captain Uliss decided the time had come to declare a distress, and several rockets were fired.

Huddled in their storm-bound houses ashore, several residents of the tiny community of Porlock Weir sighted the signals as well as the dim outline of a large sailing vessel through the blinding spray. Almost immediately, a message was sent by telegraph to the village of Lynmouth, some 13 miles to the east,

and windward of the distressed vessel, where a lifeboat was stationed. The honorary secretary of the Lynmouth lifeboat, who also happened to be the local vicar, summoned the coxswain and crew to the station, where the Standard Self-Righting lifeboat, *Louisa*, was kept. Both the vicar and the coxswain, John Crocombe, agreed that conditions were too severe to launch the boat in the local harbour where immense seas were sweeping across the breakwater. The only hope for the ship rested in somehow transporting the 5-ton *Louisa* overland to the more protected harbour of Porlock. Although the small ports were only 13 miles apart as the crow flies, the road between them went up and down the steep Countisbury and Porlock Hills, between high banks and village walls, and across a rough expanse of Exmoor. Such a feat had never before been attempted.

Undaunted by lack of precedent, the lifeboat crew and the community of Lynmouth set to work. Dozens of horses were mustered from local farms, workers with pickaxes and shovels set out to clear the road ahead of the lifeboat and her carriage – all in the black of night, during one of the most horrendous storms of the year. A wheel fell off the lifeboat carriage at the top of Countisbury Hill. It was repaired. On the vast wilds of Exmoor the road was too rough and narrow in parts. The lifeboat was placed on skids and dragged towards its destination while volunteers tore down stone gates to allow the carriage through. On the final, treacherous descent down the narrow road to Porlock – more a footpath than a carriage route – the rescuers were blocked by a protruding stone wall, which they immediately began to disassemble. Woken by the commotion outside her residence, an elderly woman expressed her consternation regarding the racket at such an ungodly hour. When advised of the situation, she put on her coat, and joined the rest in tearing down the obstruction.

Miraculously the *Louisa* was launched just 10 hours and 30 minutes after leaving Lynmouth. Without food or rest, Coxswain Crocombe and his 13 crew set out to the storm-ravaged *Forest Hall*, now perilously close to shore in Porlock Bay. Thankfully for those onboard the ship, the two anchors were now somehow holding in the shallower water and, although the seas were breaking right over her, the ship's mighty iron hull was fit for the trial.

As day dawned Captain Uliss was able to make out what seemed like an apparition: the Lynmouth lifeboat was approaching through the driving rain and spray. At the same time, the tug returned to aid in the rescue attempt. Several of the lifeboat crew were able to board the ship and assist her beleaguered crew, most of whom were almost unconscious from exposure and seasickness. A tow-line was secured, the anchors lifted and, in spite of the severe weather, the *Forest Hall*, under escort and partially manned by the lifeboat crew, made her way to safe haven in Barry, South Wales. There, almost 24 hours after they had left their homes, the valiant crew of the *Louisa* were at last able to eat and rest. They returned across the Bristol Channel the next day. [74]

CHAPTER 10

The United States Life-Saving Service

As a result of numerous wrecks, including the tragic loss of the *Mexico* in 1837 (see Chapter I-2), a movement was begun to improve and consolidate lifesaving services along the New England coast, the only stations then in existence being those established by the Massachusetts Humane Society from 1787. Most of the earliest government initiatives at maritime safety in the United States involved the building of lighthouses. In June 1845 the United States Government sent two naval lieutenants to Europe to investigate various lighthouse systems, particularly those in Great Britain, France and Belgium. In their report published the following year, these men made special mention of their visit to Liverpool and of the merits of the system in effect there since 1776 – with the lifeboats being connected to the harbour and lighthouse authority, and crews being paid, rather then strictly volunteers.[75]

In August 1848 a physician and New Jersey Congressman, Dr William A. Newell, made a plea for government assistance in the setting up of more extensive coastal rescue services. His 'vigorous and victorious' appeal resulted in Congress sanctioning the provision of $10,000 for the establishment of 'surfboats, rockets, carronades, and other necessary apparatus for the better preservation of life and property from shipwrecks on the coast of New Jersey...'.[76] Like most of the earliest proponents of dedicated lifesaving facilities around the world, Newell had been moved to pursue such endeavours after witnessing a terrible shipwreck. He witnessed first-hand the loss of the Austrian brig *Terasto*, and 13 of her crew off the remote shores of Barnegat Inlet, New Jersey, with no resources being available to render assistance. In addition, Newell had also amassed some chilling statistics that served to strengthen his argument. In the period between 12 April 1839 and 31 July 1848, there had been no fewer then 338 'recorded' shipwrecks along the coasts of Long Island and New Jersey, of which some 158 had been in his New Jersey constituency alone.[77] Indeed, Newell had appealed for funds in 1847 when he requested $5,000 to provide existing lighthouses and their keepers with lifeboats and rescue apparatus. In the end this sum was approved by Congress but was given to the MHS to upgrade their facilities, which were in dire need of a financial injection. Aside from the assignment of certain Revenue Cutters to patrol the outer banks, and the odd financial grant to organisations such as the MHS, this was the US Government's first direct involvement in coastal lifesaving and was followed the next year by the $10,000 for New Jersey.

This new system of government-funded lifesaving stations was to be administered by the Treasury Department through the Revenue Marine. Captain Douglas Ottinger was assigned the duty of liaising with the New York Board of Underwriters to decide upon the best locations for the new stations, all of which, albeit in New Jersey, were on the approaches to their rapidly expanding seaport. In addition, the Board and Captain Ottinger sought the advise of R.B. Forbes of the MHS for recommendations regarding types of lifeboats, line-throwing devices and other tools of the trade. It was soon recognised that the system of stations needed to be expanded to other areas of the northeast and, in 1849, further funds were allocated by Congress under the instigation of the Philadelphia Board of Underwriters to establish stations on the southern half of the New Jersey Coast, from Little Egg Harbour to Cape May.[78] In addition, Captain Ottinger let it be known that, in his opinion, the northern approaches to New York were shockingly devoid of lifesaving facilities. In a letter to Dr Newell in January 1849 he wrote: 'I have omitted to mention that the seacoast of Long Island is sadly in need of surfboats and houses to save and shelter the shipwrecked, and hope that important part of our shore will be cared for'.[79]

Partially following Captain Ottinger's initiative in March 1849 Congress approved a further $20,000 for the maintenance and expansion of lifesaving facilities and with some of this 'The Life-Saving Benevolent Association of New York' was formed to help oversee the establishment of facilities on Long Island. The new Society's stated purpose was to 'encourage meritorious conduct, to grant rewards, donations, and premiums in money and medals, to procure and use life-boats, boat and stationhouses, with articles and materials to afford facilities in saving life, in cases of shipwreck or otherwise, and, by themselves or others, to perform any similar services of benevolence and charity'.[80]

In 1850 another $20,000 was allocated, half of which provided for the establishment of more stations in Long Island and one at Watch Hill, Rhode Island, with the other half providing 26 extra Francis-type metallic surfboats (see Chapter II-9) to be used at other locations around the United States at the discretion of the local Customs Agents.[81] These included boats for Maine, the MHS, New Hampshire, North and South Carolina, Georgia, Florida, and Texas.[82] By 1854 there were some 55 Government lifesaving stations along the coasts of New York and New Jersey, essentially one every five miles. There were also some 82 other stations and lifeboats around the country, including 23 boats provided for use on Lake Michigan.[83]

The new public system was not without its flaws, however. The New Jersey and Long Island stations suffered from serious neglect over the years. Many lives were lost due to various deficiencies such as lack of maintenance, gaps in coastal coverage and, most notably, lack of experience of many of the keepers, who, in various cases, were chosen because of their political connections rather than their seafaring skills (see Chapter II-16). Equipment was not maintained because it was used so infrequently and no one, other than the voluntary keepers, was assigned such duties. The early wooden-bottomed metal surfboats suffered immensely from such neglect. Most were unseaworthy within a few years, with their air-tanks rusting through and their bottoms cracking.

A high degree of social mobility combined with low population density in general, and almost non-existent financial incentives for the men (other then salvage rights), ensured an almost complete lack of continuity amongst lifesaving crews. The coastline of the United States, like Canada to the north, was vast and sparsely populated which created problems of coverage and manpower. The question was not whether to man boats with paid crew or volunteers, but whether there was anyone to man the stations at all. Such problems were relatively exclusive to North America and it was this reality that would lead the United States and, eventually, Canada, to the development of non-volunteer services.

In 1854 a series of tragic wrecks, including that of the *Powhatten* off the coast of New Jersey with the loss of 300 lives, highlighted the poor condition of the government stations and spurred on reforms that included the assignment of two paid Superintendents – one for Long Island, the other for New Jersey – at a cost of $750 per man, as well as the establishment of keepers at each of the station, to be paid $200 per annum. According to one chronicler of the early government stations: 'Partial improvement in the service resulted; but the absence of drilled and disciplined crews, of regulations of any kind for the government of those concerned, and above all of energetic central administration of its affairs, were radical defects, and the record continued to be one of meager benefits checkered by the saddest failures'.[84]

The fact remained, however, that despite the inefficiencies of this early service and the rather negative views espoused during and after its tenure, many successful rescues were carried out and thousands of lives were saved. In fact, contemporary records indicate that from 1850 to 1870 in which the first state-funded service existed, there were some 272 wrecks recorded on the coasts of New York and New Jersey, and from these 4,168 lives were saved, and only 512 lost. No one could argue in 1870 that the situation, however imperfect, was not a vast improvement on the dark days before 1850, when disasters such as that which befell the *Mexico*, were commonplace. Notable successes of the early American service included:

...the saving of 204 emigrants and crew of the English ship Henry *by the surf-boat at Bridgehampton Station on Long Island in June 1851. Of 270 emigrants and crew from the English ship* Catherine *by the life-boat and apparatus at the Amaganset Station on Long Island. Of 100 persons from the ship* Chauncey Jerome Jun., *by the life-boat and life-car of the Long Branch Station, New Jersey, in January 1854. Of 201 passengers and the crew of the ship* Ayrshire, *through a terrific surf and during a severe snow-storm, by the apparatus and life-car of the Squan Beach Station, New Jersey, on the 12th January 1850. Of 290 persons from the ship* Georgia, *by the apparatus and life-car of the Long Beach Station, Long Island, in December 1852. Of 234 persons from the ship* Cornelius Grinnell *by the apparatus and life-car of the Squan Beach Station, New Jersey, on the night of the 13th January 1853. Of 200 passengers and the crew of the ship* Seaduck *by the apparatus and life-car of the Long Beach Station, New Jersey, in April 1853.*[85]

One of the more notable rescues by the early service was that of the emigrant ship *Ayrshire*, which, on the night of 12 January 1850, ran aground at Squan Beach, New Jersey, during a horrific snow storm. There were more than 200 souls onboard and despite the surf running so high that a boat could not be launched, the local crew was able to save all but one by shooting out a line and transferring everyone to shore using one of the patented lifecars co-invented by Captain Ottinger and constructed by Joseph Francis and his Novelty Ironworks Company of New York (see Sidebar p.55).[86]

The chaos and destruction of the American Civil War marked the death knell of the early government stations, as all but one of the Francis metallic lifeboats were commandeered for use in the Hatteras Campaign, and the system never fully recovered. During the winter of 1870 and 1871, a series of horrendous storms wreaked havoc on the eastern seaboard causing numerous deaths as well as calls for the reform of existing government-sponsored services to 'check the terrible fatalities off our coasts'.[87]

In 1871 the US Government recognised that the system of 'straggling apologies of lifesaving stations' was not working; it was inefficient and was costing lives.[88] In April the Secretary of the Treasury, George S. Boutwell, appealed to Congress for funds with which to thoroughly revitalise the service; a vast sum of $200,000 was authorised. The new Chief of the Revenue Marine, a young lawyer from Maine by the name of Sumner Kimball, immediately tasked Revenue Marine Captain John Faunce with the job of touring the country to inspect what remained of the state-funded lifesaving facilities and to submit a report as to what remedial action was required. On 9 August Captain Faunce delivered his rather damning report – in one location he had discovered the sole remaining Francis metallic surfboat being used as a pig trough! As a result, a mission was started to totally overhaul the coastal rescue network of the United States. A mission that, for Sumner Kimball, would last the next 44 years.

One of Kimball's first reforms was to rid the service of incompetent keepers and political appointees. He and his staff also set about establishing rules of conduct for the keepers and crews, as well as nightly beach patrols connecting the stations. This duty was carried out by full-time, paid *surfmen*, who worked for the individual keepers and who were chosen by him for their experience and fitness for the job. The decision to pay these men was made in light of the previous difficulties in manning stations and would set the trend for the eventual establishment of paid crews around the country. A comprehensive set of examinations was also devised for both keepers and surfmen, who would have to sit before a carefully picked review board prior to being

hired. Dozens of new stations were built around the country, including ones to fill in the gaps between existing facilities, making the distance between the now fully-manned seasonal stations no more then five miles on the more active coasts, such as those of New England. Keepers were to keep accurate logbooks regarding such items as the particulars of crew on duty, drills conducted, and weather conditions. These documents, as well as any wreck reports, were to be forwarded weekly to Mr Kimball's office in Washington, DC. Officers of the Revenue Marine were maintained as Local or District Superintendents. These men were given the responsibility for budgetary control over their area, as well as overseeing the constant inspection of individual stations, the running of drills and that all aspects of every operation were being carried out to the highest standards of the service. The basic rules of conduct evolved into a comprehensive code of regulations that undoubtedly added greatly to the efficiency of the developing organisation.

The increased professionalism paid off almost immediately. In the winter of 1871-72 there was not one life lost to shipwreck on the shores of New Jersey or Long Island.[89] In the following year there was one. The complete revitalisation and strengthening of the system did not take place overnight however, and mishaps did occur. Due to limited funds the stations were seasonal. The keepers were employed year-round, but the surfmen

Sumner Kimball was the Superintendent of the USLSS for its entire existence, from 1871 to 1915. He retired when the service became part of the new USCG in 1915. *USCG*

were employed only during the months of heavy weather. Generally, on the east coast, this was from September to May. There were instances of wrecks occurring during the so-called 'quiet' months when the keepers were unable to track down the requisite volunteers. There were also the inevitable cases of wrecks whose situation was either so severe as to make any attempt at rescue fatal for the lifesavers as well, or there was no station close enough to be of assistance.

A USLSS crew proudly shows off their surfboat and carriage at the USLSS Station, Salisbury Beach, Massachusetts.
USCG

In June 1878 two opposing Bills were placed before Congress regarding the state of the lifesaving service. One called for its annexation into the US Navy, the other for its further expansion as an independent branch of the Treasury, with even more Government support and funding. Due to the concerted efforts and letter-writing campaign of many benevolent and free-thinking souls, particularly those prominent individuals who had been involved in the earliest lifesaving societies along the eastern seaboard, the naval bill was squashed in favour of a stronger civilian service. The new Act of Congress allowed for the '...organization of the service into a separate and definite establishment, detached from the Revenue Marine, in conjunction with which it had hitherto existed, and placed under the charge of a General Superintendent...'.[90]

The United States Life-Saving Service (USLSS) was thereby officially formed, with Sumner Kimball as its General Superintendent. In 1878 the service boasted 148 stations of various shapes and descriptions, including 16 on the Great Lakes and Rivers, five houses of refuge on the coast of Florida and, for the first time, two new stations on the Pacific coast.[91] By 1879, only eight years after the inception of the revitalised service, there had been 5,981 lives saved within the jurisdiction of the USLSS, with only 306 being lost, 197 of whom were from wrecks beyond station coverage.[92]

A typical USLSS facility was a picturesque structure, not at all similar to the drab, utilitarian warehouses that the government might construct today. The types of stations were broken into three categories: lifesaving station,

lifeboat station, and house of refuge. From an architectural perspective all the service's buildings were simultaneously beautiful and practical.[93] Lifesaving stations employed full-time paid crews of six or seven men and a keeper, and used either surfboats or a combination of a surfboat and a lifeboat – this being the preference on the Atlantic seaboard of New Jersey and Long Island. Rather confusingly 'Lifeboat stations' had nothing to do with the type of boat stationed there. These were volunteer-type stations modelled after those operated by the RNLI, but with paid keepers. In the end, the lifeboat station concept, originally used at the more remote locations on the Atlantic coast and at the Great Lakes and Pacific stations, would be replaced by the fully-manned system as volunteer crews continued to be difficult to maintain.

The houses of refuge were originally stand-alone structures similar to those devised by the MHS back in the 1780s, but eventually had paid keepers, with signs being posted along the beach pointing in the direction of the house. This method of lifesaving was exclusive to the eastern coast of Florida.[94]

The USLSS would become well known for pioneering innovative rescue techniques including the development of motorised lifeboats (MLBs) and the use of telephones for connecting a network of stations with one another and with the district and national headquarters, thus providing the ability to combine and coordinate rescues and gear for large-scale operations. In 1890 Sumner Kimball noted that the communications link had been instrumental in the success of a massive rescue the previous year:

A notable illustration of the benefit of such a combination of crews was the work achieved near Cape Henlopen in the great storm of September 10, 11 and 12 last, one of the most destructive that has ever visited our coast, when the crews of three stations, under the leadership of Captain Clampitt, of the Lewes Station, rescued the crews of 22 stranded vessels – 194 persons – by the use of every form of rescuing appliance; 23 being landed with the surf-boats, 16 with the self-righting life-boat, 135 with the breeches buoy, and 20 with the life-car – not a life being lost. [95]

Stories of valour and heroism within the USLSS would fill volumes and many a gallant crew perished while attempting to save those in peril (see Chapter I-13). A great deal of public support for the service was promoted through the publication of details of these very rescues with the release of the various Annual Reports of the USLSS. Sumner Kimball wasted no time in ensuring that his assistant, William D. O'Connor, a noted journalist and humanitarian who wrote details of the various rescues in an eloquent and captivating fashion distributed these reports to prominent members of society, as well as to significant members of the press. In essence, Sumner Kimball realised, as do all successful maritime rescue organisations of today, that a positive public image was the key to survival, whether public or private.

At its peak, just prior to the outbreak of the First World War, the USLSS was comprised of a grand total of 281 stations – 201 on the Atlantic and Gulf coasts, 61 on the Great Lakes, and 19 on the Pacific Coast (there was even a station in Nome, Alaska). From 1871 to 1914 the crews and vessels of the USLSS were responsible for saving the life of, or otherwise assisting, an incredible 178,741 people within the scope of their operations. Only 1,455 unfortunate souls were lost – less then 1% of the total in peril during this period of almost 50 years; an admirable feat by any measure.[96]

In 1915 the USLSS was amalgamated with the Revenue Cutter Service to form the United States Coast Guard. Thus ended a rather uniquely independent and focused public lifesaving organisation whose almost legendary leader, Sumner Kimball, retired along with it. After 50 years of public service he would be remembered as one of the greatest advocates of maritime safety of all time.

The Station at Salisbury Beach with surfboats at the ready (c. 1880). USCG

Rescue of Salvage Men

The very nature of coastal lifesaving, in extreme sea and weather conditions, meant that lifesaving crews had to improvise and adapt their equipment and techniques to whatever disaster confronted them. An excellent example of the innovative thinking of one USLSS Keeper was provided by Sumner Kimball, Superintendent of the Service, at an International Life-Saving Conference in 1889.

In the great storm of September last the keeper of the Hunniwell's Beach Station, on the coast of Maine, was notified that a wrecking crew of fifteen persons who were at work upon a vessel which had some time before struck upon Glover's Rock, some 5 miles distant from the station and out of sight, had hoisted a signal of distress. He put a heaving-stick, the Lyle gun, a shot-line, a whip-line, a breeches-buoy, and a spare line into the surf boat, and with his crew set out for the rock. Arriving, he found the wreckers in danger of being engulfed by the growing sea, and that the boat could not approach near enough to enable him to reach the rock with the heaving-stick. He therefore anchored his boat, set the shot-line box on the stern, lashed the gun upon the after thwart, loaded it with a 1-ounce cartridge of powder, and fired, casting the line almost into the hands of the imperiled men. It was found impossible, however, to take them off with the breeches-buoy without great risk of their being dashed upon the projecting points of the rock. Fortunately there was a small dory upon the rock, by means of which, with the use of the line, the whole number was drawn in six trips safely to the surf-boat, which took them ashore through a sea which the keeper describes as heavy as he ever saw.

For sake of interest Mr Kimball went on to add that 'in the same storm the crew of the Lewes Station, Delaware, fired the gun from the upper window of a fish-house and landed the crew of a vessel into the loft with the breeches-buoy'.[97]

CHAPTER 11

An International Movement

The Danish Lifesaving Service was established in 1851. This image shows the high-ended traditional Danish-style pulling surfboat from the village of Løkken being launched. Note the use of rollers under the keel to transport the boat to the surfzone.

Løkken Kystfiskerimuseum, Denmark

Like Britain, both The Netherlands and Belgium had established enduring coastal lifeboat organisations, in 1824 and 1838 respectively. Many of the early attempts in other countries, however, had been unsuccessful prior to 1851. These failures were a direct result of social apathy and political tumult; the same factors that had almost resulted in the demise of Hillary's Shipwreck Institution in Britain. The creation of the RNLI in 1851 coincided with a period of relative political and economic stability in Europe that would allow governments and individuals alike to re-align their focus towards humanitarian measures. The rapid success of the RNLI in consolidating and championing coastal lifesaving was recognised in other countries and within a short time the Institution's Committee of Management found itself fielding correspondence from other nations interested in establishing similar 'voluntary' organisations, or enquiring about matters of recognised expertise, such as the designs of lifeboats. Thus, the second half of the 19th Century would see a rapid expansion of lifeboat and lifesaving organisations around the world, all inspired by the success of the RNLI.

In 1851 the Danish Government, through the progressive efforts of C.B. Claudi, 'Commissioner for the Supervision of the Dunes', established a national lifeboat service to help eliminate the ongoing carnage, particularly off the west coast of Jutland where, like Germany and The Netherlands to the south, extensive beaches faced the full onslaught of the North Sea. In the same year the Prussian Government set up similar, albeit limited, measures for its Baltic coast. In May 1865 a national lifesaving organisation similar to the RNLI, known as the Deutsche Gessellschaft zer Rettung Schiffbruchiger (DGzRS), was formed through the concerted efforts of enlightened individuals such as Mr George Breusing of Bremen.

In Scandinavia the governments of both Norway and Sweden established state-financed lifeboat services in 1854. Although these organisations saved a great many lives, their stations were few and far between and, once again, eventually succumbed to the whims of a treasurer's pen. In Norway, July 1891, the Norsk Selskab til Skibbrudnes (NSSR), a private national lifesaving organisation based around the provision of lifeboats and lifesaving apparatus, was formed through the direct efforts of Dr Oscar Tybring. In Sweden the state-funded

A team of horses pulls an early German surfboat closer to the scene of a shipwreck.
DGzRS

organisation would last somewhat longer, being replaced in June of 1907 by the Svenska Sallskapet for Raddning of Skeppsbrutne (SSRS), a national, voluntary organisation.

In Canada the original Humane Establishment at Sable Island was expanded by the Government of Nova Scotia to include additional lifeboat stations and houses of refuge on some of the other outlying and remote problem areas, such as Seal and St Paul Islands. In 1867, the year Canada entered into Confederation, these stations would be taken over by the new Dominion Government and expanded throughout the country as a national service.

After 1851 other locations in the British Empire began to establish lifeboat and lifesaving services, albeit primarily on a localised basis. These included the construction of several lifeboats of Peake's (see Chapter II-8) design for use in Australian ports around 1858. New Zealand would introduce localised lifesaving services as early as 1861. Entries in the RNLI's Journal, *The Lifeboat*, in 1866 make mention of British-designed lifeboats being ordered for India and South Africa as well.[98]

In Spain, early government attempts to establish lifeboat stations failed but in 1880 a national voluntary organisation along the lines of the RNLI was created, subsidised by the state. The Sociedad Espanola de Salvamento de Naufragos (SESN) would be highly successful – it is credited with having saved more than 1,134 lives by 1907. A similar national voluntary organisation, the Instituto de Socorros a Naufragos (ISN), would be established in Portugal in 1892.

In 1854 Monsieur Th. Gudin of France who, in his youth, had lost a brother to shipwreck, began

campaigning for a national organisation and, in 1865, the Société Centrale de Sauvetage des Naufragés (SCSN) was formed. In 1873 another lifeboat service was established in France, which would become national in scope. La Société des Hospitaliers Sauveteurs Bretons (HSB) was originally created to assist the families of lifeboatmen who were lost or injured while trying to assist others. The HSB would eventually expand its role to the provision of lifeboats and lifesaving gear throughout the country and, eventually, in the French Colonies of Algeria and Morocco as well. The society would become one of the more innovative organisations in the early days of coastal lifesaving with public education campaigns and promotion of international conferences on lifesaving.

In 1869 international interests established a lifeboat for the Bosphorous in Turkey, using British personnel for training and supervision. In Imperial Russia measures for establishing coastal lifesaving facilities began in 1874 when certain British residents of St Petersburg bought two RNLI Standard Self-Righting (SR) lifeboats as a gift for the Russian Grand Duke and Duchess. This followed the creation of the Russian Society for the Preservation of Life from Shipwreck in 1872. In March 1897 the Suomen Meripelastusseura was founded in Helsinki, Finland, then under the control of Tsarist Russia.

In 1896 the Imperial Japanese Lifeboat Society was formed along the lines of the Russian and Spanish Institutions, with the Chief Patron of the Society being the Imperial Prince himself. There is also evidence to suggest that many of the original Chinese Benevolent Societies were revitalised during the latter half of the 18th Century when European Colonial influence was at its peak.

This chronology is by no means exhaustive; there were

CADIZ.—BOTE «SALVAVIDAS» CON APARATO «LANZA-CABOS BOXER», PREPARADO PARA BOTARLO AL AGUA.
(Regálala à la Sociedad Española de Salvamento de Náufragos por la testamentaria de D. Diego F. Montañés.)

The rescue cause spread throughout Europe. This drawing depicts a new lifeboat of the RNLI's Standard Self-Righting type which was purchased by the SESN for use at Cadiz in the 1880s.
Enric Garcia-Domingo, Museu Marítim, Barcelona

many more organisations, particularly on a local level, that sprang up all over the world. But what all these new coastal lifesaving organisations symbolised, whether national or local in stature, was an almost universal acceptance of a common ideal that surpassed national boundaries to encompass the concept of helping mankind, of whatever race or creed, from the common perils of the sea. A unique spirit of internationalism had evolved, along with an equally unique relationship in world affairs: the RNLI, a private humanitarian body belonging to one nation, became the role model and advisor to lifesaving organisations and foreign governments the world over.

The idea of creating an international umbrella organisation to promote assistance to the shipwrecked was not invented by the RNLI and, indeed, had been promoted for some time. In 1812 Captain Manby had written *An Essay on the Preservation of Shipwrecked Persons...* in which he called for the spread of lifesaving societies beyond England, stating that, 'For this purpose, I would propose, that Societies be formed in the different maritime countries for such objects'.[99] In 1835 the Société Centrale des Naufragés et de l'Union des Nations was established in Paris under the direct patronage of the King of France. Its principal objective was 'to establish in every country, and in as many localities as possible, life saving methods that would prevent, or reduce, disasters at sea'.[100] Several chapters of this organisation were, indeed, established in other nations, in particular Britain, Portugal and the United States. In the United States the chapter was established in 1843 by none other then Joseph Francis, the inventor of the metallic lifeboat, and was called the American Shipwreck and Humane Society.[101] In 1884 a well-known French philanthropist named Emile Robin (1818-1915) became Vice-President of the Société Centrale de Sauvetage des Naufragés and immediately, through his own means and influence, began to promote the spread of lifesaving facilities around the world. Robin established a strong relationship with the DGzRS in Germany, providing them with a trust fund of 216,000 gold marks, and having their craftsmen build lifeboats and rocket apparatus, which were then donated to existing and emerging societies in France, The Netherlands, Spain, Portugal, and Russia. Rocket apparatus and carriages went to Finland, Sweden, and Norway. Both Hungary and Romania also received rettungsraketen, and some of the gear found its way to more exotic locations such as San Sebastián, Mexico, Madeira and Tunisia. The trust fund was also used in Germany to provide relief for the survivors of shipwreck and to assist the widows and families of mariners lost at sea. In 1897 Robin became an honorary life member of the DGzRS and, in 1901, a new lifeboat, to be stationed at Amrum was named after him. Robin continued to be involved with the promotion of lifesaving facilities around the world until he was well into his 90s.[102]

The development of coastal lifesaving organisations transcending all borders fostered the promotion of maritime safety measures for deep-sea shipping as well. Throughout the latter half of the 19th Century several international conferences and expositions were held to promote the cause of lifesaving and the development of lifesaving and safety equipment for seafarers and ships' passengers, as well as coastal lifesavers. In 1876, for example, a large exhibition was held in Brussels to promote the lifesaving cause and to provide inventors and companies with a venue at which to display their new safety products.[103] The international conferences on lifesaving at sea continued and by the turn of the century had helped nurture other conferences, which resulted in such international safety measures as the Regulations for the Prevention of Collisions at Sea and the Regulations for the Safety of Life at Sea (SOLAS). The latter convention pertained to the provision of safety apparatus on board commercial shipping. In August 1908 an International Congress of Maritime Life-Saving was held in St Nazaire, France. Many of the European coastal lifesaving organisations attended. The conference allowed lifeboat and lifesaving experts from the various nations to collaborate and share information specific to coastal lifesaving. The idea caught on and, although the political turmoil surrounding the Great War intervened, the RNLI held a conference on lifeboats and lifesaving in London in 1924 to coincide with their 100th-Anniversary celebrations. Seven nations were welcomed by the host country: Denmark, France, Japan, The Netherlands, Norway, Spain, and Sweden. The 1st International Lifeboat Conference, as it was called, was proclaimed a resounding success.

The Japanese delegate, Count Yoshii, passed a unanimous motion proclaiming, 'That an International Lifeboat Organisation be formed on the lines of the Red Cross Society with all the National Lifeboat Societies as its members, and that copies of this resolution be sent to all maritime countries, the Headquarters of the League of Nations in Geneva and the League of Nations of all Countries'.[104] The Committee of the RNLI and the delegates at the meeting decided that the conference should be staged every four years in a different host country; the idea being to share and disseminate knowledge related specifically to coastal lifesaving. The primary focus of the meetings would be technical – that is designs and modifications of rescue craft and gear – but additional emphasis would eventually be placed on administration and organisation, as well as fund-raising and public relations.

The first International Lifeboat Conference (ILC) was held in London in 1924 to coincide with the 100th Anniversary of the founding of the RNLI.

In this photo from that conference, several lifeboats are seen cruising the Thames on parade. In addition to the UK, seven lifesaving nations attended the inaugural conference, including Denmark, France, Japan, The Netherlands, Norway, Spain and Sweden. Aside from an interruption caused by the Second World War, the ILCs have been held at intervals of four years ever since and have proven to be an excellent venue to share information on technology and other lifesaving matters.
RNLI

Although Count Yoshii's vision of an international lifeboat body along the lines of the Red Cross may not have come to fruition, an 'International Lifeboat Federation', or ILF, was formed, with the RNLI maintaining the central secretariat. The ILF has ensured that the conferences have, indeed, occurred every four years and, apart from an 11-year interruption caused by the Second World War, have continued until the most recent gathering, the 19th International Lifeboat Conference, in Cape Town, South Africa, 2003. Topics of discussion at the conference have expanded to include such subjects as crew training and public education, but the core subject remains the same: rescue-craft technology. The ILF has also promoted the cause of lifesaving at sea in the international forum, including the issue of neutrality of rescue vessels in times of armed conflict. To this end in 1987 the ILF was granted consultative status by the International Maritime Organisation (IMO), the maritime arm of the United Nations, thus allowing the more than 40 countries and 70 lifesaving organisations who are now members of the Federation to express their views on maritime search-and-rescue in a unified capacity.

The Wreck of the *Arcadia*

Spurred on by early proponents of international measures for assisting the shipwrecked, such as Captain George Manby and Sir William Hillary, other international humanitarians pursued such ideals in the latter half of the 19th Century. They included such notable philanthropists as Emile Robin in France and Dorothea Dix in the United States. Miss Dix, one of the first reformers of hospitals, military infirmaries and asylums for the mentally ill around the world, also had a profound influence on the provision of lifesaving facilities in both the United States, with the MHS, and Canada, with the early humane stations established by the Crown Colony of Nova Scotia. Dix visited several countries during her travels, always keeping a keen eye open for new and improved lifesaving gear. Through her correspondence and connections, she initiated some of the first cohesive links between the emerging lifesaving societies in both the old and new worlds (see Chapters I-14, II-9, and Part IV). The following rescue story describes the direct results of the extraordinary efforts of this prominent Bostonian, who raised funds for the provision of lifeboats on the shores of remote Sable Island, in another country, far away.

On 11 February 1854 *Reliance*, the first of the new Francis Metallic lifeboats – financed through the concerted efforts of Miss Dix among others – arrived at Sable Island along with a line-throwing gun and a patented life-car. It had taken over a year for the lifeboat and equipment to make its way to the island from New York – ironically the original shipment had not made it to Nova Scotia, having been shipwrecked along the way.

A little more than two weeks later, very early on the morning of 27 February, one of the junior keepers of the Sable Island Humane Establishment, James Farquhar, was riding his trusty steed on a beach patrol on the eastern shores of Sable Island, a treacherous barrier of drifting sand some 200 miles east of Halifax. There had been a severe blow the previous evening and James soon noticed a steady stream of flotsam appearing along the beach. It quickly became apparent that something horrific had occurred during the night's tempest. Through the gloom of the early dawn he noticed a distinct change in the line of breakers about 200 yards offshore. The waves were peaking in one spot and spray was shooting high in the air, as if a new reef had been created. The object upon which the waves were breaking was the large American three-masted ship *Arcadia*, on route from Antwerp to New York with 1,000 tons (1,020 tonnes) of cargo onboard; she had run aground on the south side of the bar. As the sun rose, Farquhar could see that the stern of the ship was completely awash and, much to his shock and dismay, he could also just make out, huddled on the ship's bows, a great mass of humanity. In addition to the vessel's crew of 21, she also carried 147 German immigrants. By 9 o'clock that morning Farquhar had relayed a message to the Main Station on the island and to the Superintendent of the Sable Island Humane Establishment, Matthew McKenna.

McKenna and his crew immediately set off down the beach, towing behind them the newly acquired lifeboat on its carriage. By the time they arrived the situation had become extremely dire. The *Arcadia* was now almost entirely awash, having heeled to seaward, and both her mizzen and main masts had crashed to the sea. Somehow, four of her crew – the first mate and three seamen – had made it to the bar with one of the ship's boats and were soon rescued by the Sable Island crew in *Reliance*. The mate advised McKenna that the ship had been aground on the bar since 6pm the previous day, that the captain had been injured in the resulting mayhem and was thus incapacitated. With the *Arcadia*'s mate onboard, the *Reliance* set out for the wreck in horrendous conditions: the wind and tide were combining to create tumultuous seas, which at first drove McKenna and his crew right past the wreck. It would not be until 3pm that they would finally reach the *Arcadia* and, with only two hours of daylight remaining, the lifesaving crew wasted no time in loading the surfboat with passengers. Six trips were made and 80 souls – men, women and children – were carried to the beach. The seas were rising even more, and two further attempts were made to reach the wreck, but 'the oars and thole pins were broken by the violence of the sea'. The men tried to secure a line to the *Arcadia*, but the longshore current running parallel to the beach was so strong as to break the line. Nothing more could be done until day break, and then only if the storm abated. Throughout the long and horrible night, those who had made it ashore listened to the distant wailing of their loved ones still stranded aboard. The scene onshore was, according to McKenna, one that 'could be imagined but not described', as families were separated, possibly forever.

At first light, the *Reliance* set out once again, the storm having calmed considerably. Ten more trips were made before midday and by the end not one of the passengers or crew of the *Arcadia* was lost – a fitting tribute to both the skill of the Sable Island lifesavers, and the seaworthiness of the first purpose-built lifeboat to be stationed there.

When news of the rescue reached Dorothea Dix, she immediately wrote a letter to the Shipwrecked Fishermen and Mariners Royal Benevolent Society in Great Britain to have the exploits of McKenna and his crew recognised. As a result, McKenna was awarded the gold lifesaving medal of the society and every member of the crew won the silver. Dorothea stated in her letter that such medals are 'evidence that your services in a lonely and desolate island are honorably estimated, and gratefully recorded'. The strong esteem in which the Sable Island crew held Miss Dix and her international efforts were summed up by the words of Superintendent McKenna who wrote, 'I shall think of her with feelings of gratitude while memory lasts'.[105]

WRECK OF THE "ARCADIA," ON SABLE ISLAND.

The metallic surfboat *Reliance* was put to work only two weeks after her arrival on Sable Island, Nova Scotia, saving all on board the stranded American ship *Arcadia* on 27 February 1854.

Although the island was part of British North America, the surfboat and other lifesaving apparatus were provided through the concerted efforts of Dorothea Dix, a Bostonian. *Maritime Museum of the Atlantic*

CHAPTER 12

Wreck Guns and Rockets

While the lifeboat is prepared for launching, members of a German lifesaving crew fire flares to illuminate the stricken ship. Another fires a line-throwing rocket to the wreck in order to establish a connection for the breeches-buoy apparatus.
Wrackmuseum, Cuxhaven

It would be unjust to conclude any history of coastal lifesaving without mentioning the efforts of those individuals who invented and operated rescue apparatus designed to 'communicate', or transfer, lines and rescue apparatus to vessels in distress, from shore. These included line-throwing mortars and guns, as well as rockets and associated gear. As is still the case, not all coastal rescues could be carried out safely by lifeboat. In many cases of shipwreck, primarily where vessels had been caught on a lee shore and ended up in large breaking surf, or up against steep cliffs, any efforts at rescue by lifeboat might have also spelt disaster for the rescuers. In many cases, lifeboat crews did attempt to pluck survivors from such precarious circumstances. Through incredible displays of seamanship and raw daring countless lives were saved but the reality was that many lifeboat crews were lost attempting such rescues.

From the earliest days of organised lifesaving there were those who promoted the idea that it was better to rescue the shipwrecked *from* shore, using equipment designed to transfer lines and gear to a vessel in distress, rather than risk other lives in launching boats. Such ideas were sound but not all wrecks were close enough to allow lines to be 'shot' out to them, and just as circumstances of a particular wreck may not have been suitable for a rescue by lifeboat, the same reasoning held true for rescue by wreck gun, or rocket. The reality was that both methods of saving lives had their particular advantages and disadvantages and, when used in conjunction with one another or directly for the purpose for which they were best suited, the end result was a coastal lifesaving force that could handle and adapt to almost all shipwreck scenarios.

The earliest attempts to develop methods to transfer lifelines to a wreck from shore involved ballistics. Muskets, mortars and cannons were used to fire a ball, or some other form of projectile, over the stricken vessel; a line attached to the missile, could be used to haul out stronger ropes, as well as blocks, and various types of slings for transferring persons back to shore. The first recorded experimentation with such an apparatus took place in England, at the Royal Arsenal at Woolwich on 29 August 1791: a Sergeant Bell of the Royal Artillery tested his mortar and projectile before a Committee of the Society for the Encouragement of Arts, Manufacturing and Commerce. (With few exceptions in the years to come, almost all the inventors of shore-launched lifesaving apparatus would be artillerymen with an obvious affinity for such affairs.) Bell's demonstration was reported to have been a resounding success, with the projectile carrying a deep-sea line a distance of 400 yards (365m). It is interesting to note, in a quote from Bell, that he states the apparent usefulness of his invention for places such as the Shields Bar (Tynemouth). One wonders, therefore, whether his efforts had any connection whatsoever to the affairs surrounding the invention of the lifeboat and the creation of the Tynemouth Humane Society during the same period?

There is every reason to conclude that this contrivance would be very useful at all ports of difficult access both at home and abroad where ships reliable [are liable] to strike ground before they enter the harbour [such] as Shields Bar, and other similar situations, when a line might be thrown over the ship, which might probably be the means of saving both lives and property; and, moreover, if a ship was driven ashore near such a place, the apparatus might easily be removed to afford assistance, and the whole performance is so exceedingly simple that any person seeing it done would not want any further instruction.[106]

Some earlier authorities have unfortunately dismissed Bell's efforts as being designed to transfer lines in the opposite direction – ie from ship to shore – and therefore as not directly related to the development of beach-launched devices. His comments above serve to correct the record. Although Bell's device was successful and he was awarded 50 guineas by the adjudicating society and promoted to the rank of Lieutenant, the device never seems to have been put to practical use. In fact this may have been due to his death not long after the tests were completed.[107]

The man who expanded on Bell's ideas and who perfected the line-throwing mortar, was Captain George William Manby, the same individual who, along with Sir William Hillary, had become one of the founders of the National Shipwreck Institution in Great Britain. George Manby had shown an interest in shooting lines from mortars at a young age. Born in Norfolk in 1765, Manby had apparently begun experimenting at the age of 15, when he is reported to have drawn attention to himself by shooting a line over the local church, unfortunately breaking a window in the process. His keen interest in such matters led him to join the Royal Artillery where, by 1807, he was the Barracks Master at Yarmouth, on the coast of Norfolk. During that year Manby witnessed the tragic loss of the gun-brig *Snipe*, the chilling effects of which rekindled his inventive curiosity regarding the line-throwing mortar.

The dreadful events of the 18th of February, 1807, when His Majesty's gun-brig Snipe *was driven on shore near Haven's Mouth at Yarmouth, first made an impression upon my mind, which has never been effaced. At the close of that melancholy scene, after several hours of fruitless attempt to save the crew, upwards of sixty persons were lost, though not more than fifty yards from shore, and this wholly owing to the impossibility of conveying a rope to their assistance. At that crisis a ray of hope*

beamed upon me, and I resolved immediately to devote my mind to the discovery of some means for affording relief in cases of similar distress and difficulty.[108]

Manby set about doing just that. He devised a relatively reliable line-throwing mortar that was light enough to be portable, and a shot, or projectile, that was not as prone as previous inventions to snap the line upon firing. His means to ensure that the line would not disconnect due to the shock and instantaneous acceleration caused by the explosion of the charge was to utilise a leather 'shock absorber' connecting the line to the projectile. His first mortar was put to the test with the Suffolk Humane Society in 1808, when seven lives were saved from a wrecked schooner. The apparatus was then adopted by the Society, making Yarmouth the first lifesaving station in the world with a dedicated 'Wreck Gun'. Manby also came up with some other innovations for his lifesaving apparatus, including a rather ominous looking cannon ball that belched flame. The idea was to alleviate the difficulties of night rescues where, without some form of luminous trail behind the projectile, it was practically impossible to discern whether or not the shot was successful in reaching its target. He also proposed the use of a life cot – essentially a rectangular canvas box – to convey survivors back to the beach. Like Bell, Manby tested his mortar at the Royal Arsenal, this time before a Committee of fellow Artillery officers on 18 and 20 May 1811, and achieved several successful shots in the range of 250 yards (230m). The Committee recommended procurement of the devices, which led to an address being moved in the British Parliament to the Prince Regent by William Wilberforce 'praying that he would be graciously pleased to order that Captain Manby's invention should be stationed on different parts of the coast, &c., and assuring him that the House would make good the expense'.[109]

Several of the guns were subsequently purchased under the auspices of the Navy Board and provided to 'various stations, where they were watched by the coastguard assisted by volunteers'.[110] These would be the first volunteer lifesaving brigades for shore-side rescue. Although administration of the 'beach apparatus', as the mortars became known, changed hands many times, the system of manning the equipment remains in effect in Britain to this day.

By the year 1814 some 45 of the mortars were in use around the country and, in the following decade, were credited with having saved more than 200 lives. In 1823 Manby was awarded the monumental sum of £2,000 and made an Honorary Member of the Royal Humane Society. The proven success of Captain Manby's Mortar would result in the devices being purchased by other countries, including Portugal and Spain, and the MHS in the United States.

A drawing of Captain Manby's Line-Throwing Mortar taken from his 1812 treatise on the subject.
Author's Collection

Manby's Mortar would be the mainstay for communicating lines to shipwreck for many years. Eventually, the device would be overshadowed to some degree by the introduction of rockets, and other guns would be developed, particularly in the United States and France. In the former Manby's invention would eventually give way to the mortar devised by Mr Robert P. Parrott and Captain Douglas Ottinger of the Revenue Marine in New York. This device used a cylindrical shot and had an average range of around 400 yards (365m). It appears to have been developed in the late 1840s for use with the early lifesaving stations in New Jersey, as it was a Parrott Mortar that was used along with one of Francis's Life-Cars in the *Ayrshire* rescue of 1850, resulting in over 200 lives saved (see Sidebar p.55). Although 25 of these guns were later ordered by Superintendent Sumner Kimball for the USLSS in 1877, they appear not to have been favoured by the lifesaving crews because of the dangers associated with the violent recoil of the mortar.[111]

The next apparatus of note in the United States was the gun devised by Edward S. Hunt of Weymouth, Massachusetts, for the MHS. *Hunt's Gun and Projectile for Effecting Communication with Shipwrecked Vessels*, boasted that it had, 'a longer range, a truer aim, especially in a high wind; and comparative cheapness'.[112] The innovative feature of this device was the projectile itself, a semi-hollow, tin cylinder that, unlike previous projectiles, had a considerable amount of the messenger-line flaked 'within' it. According to Hunt, his method minimised line-drag on the projectile, thereby increasing the range – in previous guns the line was generally 'faked', or flaked, outside the device, either on the

ground, or in a flaking box. One of Hunt's guns was donated by the MHS to the RNLI in 1879 and was sent to the Royal Arsenal at Woolwich for testing – it received negative reviews. Indeed, the relatively light weight of the projectile, which allowed it to drift in a high wind, made it unpopular with rescue crews in the US as well.

In 1877 Sumner Kimball recruited a young army officer, Lieutenant D.A. Lyle from the Army Ordnance Department, to work with Captain Merryman, Chief Inspector of the USLSS, experimenting with the different devices, both guns and rockets, then available for line-throwing. Lyle was a graduate of the Massachusetts Institute of Technology (MIT) and West Point where, in fact, he would spend his later years as a Professor of Philosophy. Lyle's and Merryman's objective was to produce a report and recommend, or design, a new means of shooting lines to a shipwreck that was safe, efficient in terms of range and ease of operation, and would be accepted by lifesaving crews. They decided that the ballistic method was the most safe and reliable means and the result was the invention of the Lyle Gun in 1878. Essentially a beach canon, it weighed 185lb (84kg) and shot a 17lb (7.7kg), 14$\frac{1}{2}$in (400mm) bullet-shaped projectile to an amazing 700 yards (640m). Lyle set the gun, projectiles, lines and all ancillary gear, on to an easily moved cart, which he called the 'beach apparatus'. The Lyle Gun was highly successful and, like Manby's earlier invention, became the mainstay in other countries as well. It was so successful in fact, that Lyle Guns remained in service at some United States Coast Guard Stations right up until 1962, at which time such means of rescue appear to have been superseded by the helicopter.[113]

A USLSS Lyle Gun and all the connecting gear was referred to as the 'beach apparatus'. In this photograph we find, moving in a clockwise direction from the gun itself, the faking gear, a faking box and projectile, faking gear with line on it, the breeches-buoy on top of the A-frame used to support the line, blocks and tackle, the tail-hold, or sand anchor (the crossed boards) and the shovels and picks used to set that anchor.
In the background one can see the carriage used to transport the beach apparatus to the scene of a wreck, along with gas-lamps, heaving sticks and Coston flares.
USCG

As mentioned, efforts were being made to develop line-throwing ordnance in France as well. In 1872 the Société Centrale de Sauvetage des Naufragés, developed three guns of various sizes and ranges. The first was known as the *mousketon* (carbine), with a range of 80-100 yards (73-91m). This device, like similar line-throwing guns today, was designed to be shoulder fired. Interestingly, the mousketon's messenger-line apparently carried cork floats to assist in recovering persons from the surf. The second gun was known as the *espingole* (blunderbuss), which was designed to shoot wooden or iron arrows approximately 250 yards (230m). This rather ominous instrument was approximately 3ft (0.9m) long, weighed 40lb (18kg), had a calibre of 1lb (450g) and, if the line disconnected from the shot for whatever reason, was known to reach 1,000 yards (914m)! The last French line-throwing gun of note was the *Perrier* (swivel gun), with a calibre of 4lb (1.8kg), which appears to have been a naval canon adapted for the purpose of lifesaving.[114] In addition to these French endeavours, a Monsieur Delvigne is credited with conducting extensive research into adaptable *flechés* (lifesaving arrows) for use in guns not specifically designed for lifesaving. His method allowed the charge and the projectile to be fired from only part of a cannon barrel; thus limiting the amount of recoil and range, and allowing vessels to use their own guns to save themselves.[115]

The other primary means of transferring lines developed in the 19th Century was, of course, by rocket. Ever since the Chinese invention had been introduced to Europe, engineers had been experimenting with its use. In 1807 a Cornishman by the name of Henry Trengrouse began testing with rockets as a means to transfer lines after witnessing the loss of more than 100 people off the frigate *Anson* in Mount's Bay. The relative cheapness and

portability of rockets as compared to mortars was sufficiently significant to catch the attention of the Admiralty and the Board of Trade and, by 1821, some locations had been equipped with rocket apparatus. Aside from the lower cost, the other distinct advantage of the rocket was that the acceleration of the projectile was far more gradual, thus greatly reducing the chance of line breakage. Rockets also left a fiery trail, which allowed both rescued and rescuer to follow the track of the line. However, Trengrouse's rocket does not seem to have met with wide acceptance, primarily owing to the lack of reliability of the rockets themselves. Rockets were unstable when stored over time, were very temperamental when subjected to the vagaries of weather.

It would not be until 1832 that John Dennet, from the Isle of Wight, would further expand on the principle and develop a rocket apparatus that would shoot 250 yards (230m). Four of his devices were purchased by the Board of Customs and put to use on the island. Lieutenant Colonel Boxer of the Royal Artillery, also stationed on the Isle of Wight, would further develop Dennet's invention by doubling the rockets, making them a two-stage apparatus, much like the lunar rockets of the 1960s and 1970s. The range of the Boxer Rocket was thus extended to over 400 yards (366m) and, by the late 1860s, these

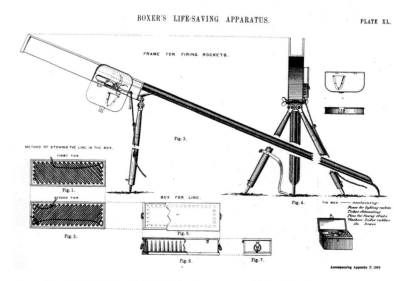

A profile of Lt Col Boxer's Life-Saving Apparatus, which utilised a two-stage rocket to convey a line to the shipwreck.
Author's Collection

devices began to find widespread acceptance amongst 'coastguards' throughout the United Kingdom. Indeed, in Britain the use of the improved rockets for transferring lines was so successful that, from 1870 to 1911, roughly 10,000 lives were saved from shipwreck through the use of rockets and the breeches-buoy.[116]

A similar rocket was developed in the 1840s for use in the United States by Robert Cunningham of Massachusetts; and is said to have reached distances in the range of 1,000 yards (914m). But eventually, as rescue organisations amalgamated in America, the Lyle Gun became the mechanism of choice.

Brief mention should also be made of the means by which survivors were transferred to shore along the lines sent out by the line-throwing apparatus. The earliest methods appear to have merely involved the lines themselves, then primitive boards, or 'bosun's chairs' were introduced. Manby recommended the rope-lashing method, as well as his 'life-cot' which, unto itself, does not appear to have had any inherent flotation. Boxer's experiments with rocket apparatus on the Isle of Wight would eventually involve another officer, Kisbee, who felt that a more secure form of transferring personnel was required. Kisbee invented the 'breeches-buoy', essentially a circular cork float or life-ring (also known as a kisbee ring), with canvas breeches attached beneath. The breeches-buoy was easily suspended from a line, the survivor could not fall out or be dashed against the side of the wreck and, even better, it floated, for in many cases, although a person might have been suspended by the life-line, they were not necessarily clear of the sea. The breeches-buoy became the most popular device, on both sides of the Atlantic, because it was cost-effective, and extremely light and portable.

Another means of conveyance from shipwreck, used in both the United States and Canada, was the 'Life-Car', built by Joseph Francis of New York in 1847.[117] Francis was already well known for his patented metallic lifeboats constructed by his firm, the Novelty Iron Works Company in Brooklyn (see Chapter II-9). The life-car resembled something akin to a small submarine and was constructed of corrugated metal, pressed into shape by means of hydraulic pressure. The idea was that, unlike a breeches-buoy, multiple survivors (six or seven) could be brought back to shore at each haul of the line, thus speeding up the evacuation. The life-car had a small hatch on top through which survivors could enter. They would then lie down inside the device and, in a semi-watertight state, the life-car would be hauled back to shore through the surf and weather. The main drawbacks of the device were that it was heavy and required considerably more manpower to operate as well as time to set up. The life-car did, however, have uses,

particularly over longer distances, where low elevations made the lifelines prone to dip into the surf before coming onshore. Francis's life-car was instrumental in the success of several rescues including the *Ayrshire* off the Coast of New Jersey, and the schooner *Hartzel* on Lake Michigan in 1880. The Instituto de Socorros a Naufragos of Portugal purchased one of Francis's life-cars in 1852.[118] They were regularly used for lifesaving by the USLSS right up until 1899, and exercised at some stations until 1940.[119] It was estimated that between 1850 and 1853, 2,150 lives were saved through the use of this apparatus along the approaches to New York Harbor alone.[120]

Regardless of the type of equipment used, most line-throwing apparatus became part of the rescue kit of the same organisations that were operating the lifeboats. In the United States and Canada the government-operated lifesaving services used both boats and beach apparatus. In most of continental European, either the state-run, or privately-run voluntary societies did the same. In fact, as the concept of dedicated coastal lifesaving resources spread around the world after 1851, so, too, did the technology. Eventually line-throwing brigades would appear in New Zealand, South Australia, and other distant corners of the globe. In Britain, the process of administering and operating the line-throwing apparatus developed somewhat differently.

The earliest mortar apparatus, which dated back to 1811, was provided by the state, to be operated primarily by the private lifesaving societies, such as those at Suffolk and Tyneside, and to be watched over by government agents, then known as the 'Preventive Waterguard'. The Preventive Waterguard had been formed in 1809 as a law enforcement entity designed to assist the Board of Customs in stamping out the rampant smuggling that was plaguing Britain and its treasury. So widespread was this problem around the end of the 18th Century, that Napoleon Bonaparte confided from his exile on St Helena, that his massive military campaigns had been primarily funded through profits received from the illicit smuggling of French goods to Great Britain, all of which had been financed by the merchants of London![121] The Preventive Waterguard men operated small boats, in specific areas of the coast, and worked closely with the offshore revenue cutters and the 'Riding Officers' on land, to form what was then called the Coast Blockade. In 1822 all of the three entities of the Coast Blockade were combined to form the Coastguard, which was charged, by regulation, to ensure that all line-throwing apparatus was tested by the societies, or whatever body managed them, on a regular basis, with an officer of the Coastguard overseeing such activities.

The early Coastguard boat crews were, for obvious reasons, fine seamen and boat operators, with keen local knowledge; they were an extremely handy resource in the early days of the Shipwreck Institution. From 1824 until 1852 over one third of all medals for bravery issued were awarded to Coastguard officers and crew utilising either their own boats or crewing on lifeboats owned by the local societies.[122] In 1851 Captain Washington stated in his report on the state of lifesaving apparatus in the British nation that 91 Coastguard stations had rockets, or mortars, or both and that, although the state of such equipment was somewhat in decline…

> …at 22 stations where a record has been kept, not less then 243 lives have been saved by them, besides several crews at Caistor, near Yarmouth, and many lives at eight other stations, where no account has been kept of the number. The veteran Captain Manby may reflect with just gratification in his declining years that the mortar he was instrumental in bringing into use as a means of saving life, has proved very serviceable.[123]

Strangely, in 1852, an edict was passed that Coastguards in the United Kingdom were no longer to crew the lifeboats belonging to the RNLI, or any of the local societies. It was felt by the authorities that their other duties, regarding customs and surveillance, were too important. This did not end the lifesaving duties of the Coastguard however, and, in 1855, the organisation was given the responsibility for the supervision of all mortar and rocket stations in Britain and Ireland. These included stations and equipment provided by the government (Board of Trade), as well as those previously operated by the RNLI, the Shipwrecked Fishermen and Mariners Royal Benevolent Society, and the local humane societies. The Coastguard (HMCG) would eventually evolve into a national maritime safety agency, the revenue aspects remaining with the Customs Service, with the provision and supervision of local volunteer beach line-throwing crews as one of its main responsibilities; this relationship continues to this day, the Coastguard being part of the UK Maritime and Coastguard Agency (MCA).

The Loss of the Immigrant Ship *Ayrshire*

The rescue of 201 men, women and children on a cold and stormy night on 12 January 1850 by the keeper and crew of one of the earliest government lifesaving stations in the United States was one of the first successful, large-scale rescues using line-throwing apparatus and the new life-car and proved to many that large-scale saving of life was possible and that not all shipwrecks had to result in the tragic scenes reminiscent of those following the loss of the *Mexico*, on similar shores (see Chapter I-2).

While attempting to ride out a strong northeaster under shortened sail the British immigrant ship *Ayrshire*, bound for New York, struck a sandbar a few hundred yards from the Squan Beach Life-Saving Station on the coast of New Jersey. Before long, all her masts and rigging had come down, while almost all the terrified passengers and crew tried to keep cover in the small deckhouses. Whoever could not fit inside was lashed to the vessel to avoid being washed away. The scene onboard was later described by one of the survivors, Mrs A.E. Bell: the 'ship lay over so that one side was almost under water and men were compelled to come and pass strips of blanket and ropes around the women for fear they would slip overboard. The waves beat against the side of the ship with fearful force, keeping a continual shower of water flying over everybody who was on deck.'[126]

The captain had no means by which to send out a distress signal. Their saving grace would rest in the fact that they had been wrecked so close to a lifesaving station and that, somehow, through all the tumult of roaring wind and crashing seas, someone ashore either heard their cries for help or noticed the dim light of the few small

storm lanterns that remained in operation. Their guardian angel would come in the form of Captain John B. Maxon, Keeper of the Squan Beach Station and, soon, bright flashes from shore, followed by the thump of an appliance landing on the heaving deck, would signify that measures were being mounted for their rescue.

Keeper Maxon described the scene to Walter Jones, President of the New York Board of Underwriters and key proponent of the establishment of the early government lifesaving service in the United States:

> Sir, I was present, and superintended and sent the line by mortar on board the ship Ayrshire, on the 12th of January, 1850, and by means of the Metallic Life-car, we landed in safety her passengers, in all, two hundred and one, which, in my opinion, at that time, could not have otherwise been saved, as the sea was so bad that no open boat could have lived. We attached the line to the shot and fired it from the mortar. It fell directly across the wreck, and was caught by the crew on board, and the hawser hauled off, to which we attached the Metallic Life-car, and pulled her to and from the wreck through a terrific foaming surf. Every soul…men, women, children and infants…came through the surf during that cold snow-storm, dry and comfortable.[127]

Lamentably, one life was lost. A man by the name of Bell, unrelated to Mrs A.E. Bell, refused to wait while his sister and her three daughters went ashore in the life-car. Ignoring the orders of the *Ayrshire*'s crew, he jumped on to the outside of the car and was soon swept away by the pounding surf as the device dipped from sea to sea on its way to shore.

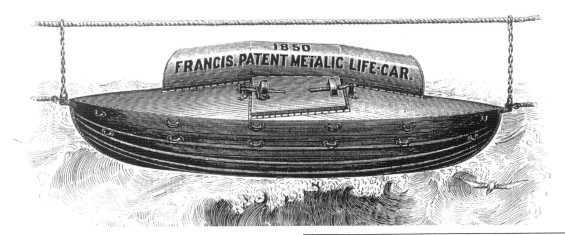

Rescue by life-car. Unlike the breeches-buoy, this lifesaving device was designed to go through high surf in a submarine-like fashion. Although setting up the life-car took far more time and manpower than the breeches-buoy, the car was able to transport up to seven persons at a time and function in much more severe weather and sea conditions than the far more exposed breeches-buoy.
Author's collection

Captain Manby's Gun and the Wreck of the Brig *Elizabeth*

This rescue involves the first recorded use of a line-throwing mortar, or gun, to save lives. On 12 February 1808 the brig *Elizabeth* was driven aground off Yarmouth beach in a strong northeasterly gale. This area of the Norfolk coast has always been a notorious lee shore, and once again appeared ready to claim further victims. The *Elizabeth* was soon awash in the breakers, and her captain and crew took to the rigging in a last ditch attempt to survive the elements. Fortunately however, Captain George Manby of the Royal Artillery and Barrack Master at Yarmouth had been experimenting with mortars and guns to convey a line to shipwrecks. The rest of the story is borrowed from an account of the incident in Robert Malster's, *Saved From the Sea*.

Time after time the beachmen tried to get a boat off the beach, and time after time the waves flung it back. Benumbed with cold and with the exhaustion of despair creeping through them, the crew of the Elizabeth resigned themselves to almost imminent death. As soon as he heard of what was happening Manby bustled down the beach with his mortar and all his equipment. It took a little more time to set it up, but soon all was ready; he fired, and the shot swung in a great arc towards the vessel, the line curving out behind. His aim was true, and the line dropped across the wreck. On this occasion the mortar line was used to drag a boat off the beach and out to the Elizabeth; all seven members of the crew were saved in this fashion.[124]

The Wreck of the British Ship *Veronese*

The *Veronese* rescue is historically significant for being one of the largest ever conducted with line-throwing rockets, life-lines and a breeches-buoy. Over the course of two days Portuguese lifesaving crews saved hundreds of passengers and crew, dragging them all, one by one, through immense surf.

The Veronese, a British cargo boat, carrying two hundred people on board, passengers and crew included, ran aground in the middle of the night of 16th, January 1913, on the rocks of the Nossa Senhora da Boa Nova beach to the north of Leixies. The sea flooded the cabins and holds, forcing dozens of frightened passengers to flee to the quarterdeck where they again found that the sea was sweeping across the decks, taking some of them with it [nineteen were lost]. Sharp rocks extended for some three hundred and fifty metres into the sea and surrounded the ship, which could not move or use its own lifeboats. On land the sirens and bells of the Veronese could be heard, but nothing could be done because of the storm. The nearest firemen, the police, some soldiers and the populace rushed down to the shore at the sound of the alarm bell. A rocket line was launched nineteen times from the beach without once reaching the Veronese…the wind, fog, rain, the ten metre high waves, all combined to divert the six millimeter cable when it wasn't actually being slashed on the rocks. At last, the line reached the ship, and by means of it the hauling cable for the breeches-buoy was sent over, the means by which ninety-eight survivors would be saved in an uninterrupted operation which lasted for fifty-two hours. The first to be carried thus ashore was a fifteen year old girl, Dorothy Alcoy, and it was said that on the crowded decks of the Veronese, a passageway was opened to allow youth and beauty to be rescued before all else.[125]

The account then goes on to say that as the seas abated somewhat two lifeboats were launched and, still using the breeches-buoy, all the remaining passengers and crew were slung on board these craft, eventually bringing them ashore by the boatload.

CHAPTER 13

The Toll on the Rescuers

Those who brave the perils of the surf and seas to assist others do so knowing that they may never return. On many occasions, especially in the early days of coastal lifesaving by oar and sail, they did not. The broad scope of this book allows only for the citation of a few examples regarding losses of lifeboats and crews and deals with some of the more significant and tragic stories. Almost all maritime rescue organisations in the world have lost members to the ravages of the cause and it would not be fair to write a book such as this without giving the reader some idea of the losses incurred, nor would it be fair to the memory of the thousands of individuals who have sacrificed their own lives while attempting to save others in peril at sea.

As lifeboat and lifesaving technology improved so, too, did the chances of survival for the rescuers themselves. Losses of lifesaving crews, like the losses of the ships and people they were trying to save, were much higher in the days before mechanised propulsion, radio communications and radar. For example, between the creation of Sir William Hillary's National Shipwreck Institution in 1824 and the present day, the RNLI has lost 437 crew in the line of duty; 312 before the First World War and the introduction of mechanised propulsion.

We begin, then, with a few examples of lifeboat disasters from the days of sail and oar, and follow with some tragic tales from the mechanised era, proving that, in spite of technical advances, the business of coastal lifesaving remains a dangerous one. For the sake of brevity, and clarity, in some cases quotations have been taken directly from historical accounts, as well as from Boards of Inquiry, in order to provide a brief chronological overview.

Great Britain
Hartley, Northumberland, 1810.
At Hartley, on the coast of Northumberland, five miles north of Tynemouth, in the year 1810, one of Greathead's life-boats, carried overland from Blyth, rescued the crews of several fishing cobles that were prevented landing by a high sea tumbling suddenly upon the coast, unaccompanied by wind. On returning towards the shore, the boat got too near the South Bush Rock, when a heavy sea broke on board and split her in halves; the result was, that the whole crew, 34 in number, were drowned.[128]

Appledore, Devon, 1833.
At Appledore, Devon, in December, 1833, the life-boat, in going off to the brig Mary Anne, *of Exeter, stranded on the Northam Burrows, was struck by a heavy sea, and turned end over end it is believed; two of the crew who had lashed themselves to the thwarts were drowned, a third got his lashings loose enough to keep his head above water in the bottom of the boat, and was taken out alive when the boat drove on shore, bottom up, about an hour after. On this occasion three men were drowned; the remainder of the crew were taken off the life-boat by another boat.* [In his report to the Duke of Northumberland Captain Washington added that] *had this boat had the power of self-righting, there seems no reason why the men should not have been saved.*[129]

Robin Hood's Bay, Yorkshire, 1843.
At Robin Hood's Bay, on the coast of Yorkshire, seven miles south of Whitby, in February of 1843, the life-boat went off to the assistance of a stranded vessel, the Ann *of London, during a fresh northerly gale. The life-boat had got alongside the wreck, and was taking in the crew, and it is supposed, four or five men jumped into her at once on one side, and a heavy sea striking her at the same time, she capsized. Many of the crew got on her bottom, while three remained under, and in this state she was drifted towards the shore on the opposite side*

of the bay. On seeing the accident from the shore, five gallant fellows launched a coble (fitted with air-cases as a life-boat), and tried to pull off to the rescue; but she had hardly encountered two seas, when she was turned end over end; two of her crew were drowned, and she drifted ashore bottom up. On this occasion Lieut. Lingard, RN, of the Coast Guard service, and 11 men, lost their lives. Three men came on shore safely under the life-boat, and some on her bottom, the others were washed off. Had the life-boat possessed the power of self-righting; there seems no reason why most, if not all her crew, should not have been saved. [130]

Tynemouth, Northumberland, 1849.

On 4 December 1849 one of Greathead's lifeboats departed in a heavy sea to rescue the crew of the brig *Betsy*, wrecked on Herd Sand. With the combination of the large sea opposed by a strong ebb tide working against them, the boat made the wreck and tied fast off the quarter. Just when the crew of the *Betsy* were about to descend 'a heavy knot of sea recoiling from the bow of the vessel caught the bow of the [life-]boat and turned her up on end, throwing the whole of the crew and the water into the stern sheets'. The lifeboat drifted back to the beach through the boiling surf with most of her crew of 24 'Pilots of the Tyne' beneath her capsized hull. In the end, 20 of the crew were lost, while the remainder, plus the crew of the *Betsy*, were rescued by two other lifeboats of the Tynemouth Humane Society, which had come to their aid. The public outcry following this tragic loss

The lifeboat being launched by a crew of 'Pilots of the Tyne'. In 1849 a crew such as this attempted to save those on the brig *Betsy* being dashed upon the Herd Sand. Tragically, the Greathead lifeboat capsized in the process and 20 of her crew were lost. This event would, however, induce the Duke of Northumberland to hold a competition for a safer design of lifeboat.
South Tyneside Library

resulted in the Duke of Northumberland's Competition for a better design of lifeboat, and the consequential restructuring of the Royal National Institution for the Preservation of Life from Shipwreck into the RNLI.

United States
Barnegat Life Saving Station, 1886.

On the morning of 11 February 1886 the Austrian barque *Kraljevika* ran aground on Barnegat Shoals off New Jersey in thick fog and a strong northeast wind. After seeing the signals of distress, the keeper of the Barnegat Life Saving Station, Joel Ridgeway, advised an adjacent station and summoned his crew to launch the surfboat. The seas were the largest seen in many years, so severe that the crew became seriously fatigued before even reaching the wreck. Ridgeway decided they would have to return to regain strength and that they would have to 'turn the boat around in the storm and run for the beach'. The breaking seas were immense and, in the 'wild turmoil of waters…a towering wave reared its frowning crest close astern [but] the boat could not rise to it. An instant later there came a thundering roar as tons upon tons of water broke with savage [force] upon the boat, twirled it around broadside and rolling it over and over like a chip, the men being thrown in all directions.' Three surfmen lost their lives, one being either struck by an oar or crushed by the boat, while the other two drowned in the surf. Strangely enough and unbeknownst to the lifesaving crew, there were no survivors left on the *Kraljevika*. The situation had become so dire as the ship broke apart around them that her crew had braved the surf and departed into the hail, snow, and dark of night in one of the ship's boats – only six survivors made it to shore.[131]

Great Britain
Loss of the Southport & St Anne's Lifeboats, Lancashire, 1886.

This tragic loss deserves more than a brief mention, not only because of the scale of the disaster, but also because of the longterm effects that it would have on both lifeboat design and the workings of the RNLI. On 9 December 1886 the German barque *Mexico*, fully laden, and with a crew of 13 men, attempted to beat her way out of Liverpool, into the teeth of a full southwest gale. During the day many saw the ship trying to make headway offshore against the full force of the rising tempest. She was gradually driven to leeward and, at about 9pm, in the howling dark, found herself aground in the treacherous shallows at the mouth of the Ribble, off Southport, Lancashire. Owing to her deep draught and the fact that the beaches and sandbanks in the area extended far offshore, the *Mexico* was by no means close to land, but was being subjected to massive breakers and hell-bent destruction.

A contemporary depiction of the capsizing of the British lifeboat *Eliza Fernley* while attempting to rescue the crew of the German barque *Mexico* during the hurricane of 9 and 10 December 1886, off Southport, Lancashire. By the time the dawn rose, two lifeboats and 27 of their crew would be lost, making this one of the worst lifeboat disasters in the history of the RNLI. *RNLI*

'We had just got alongside [the ship] and were just getting ready to cast anchor when a wave came and capsized us in a jiffy. Why, mate, believe me but the weight of the water alone was enough to have killed us…'.[133] The *Eliza Fernley* was a standard self-righting lifeboat of recent design, but from all accounts it seems that the weight of the unset anchor, hanging off the bow, would not allow her to re-right and she rolled several times. Eventually, she would drift into shallow water some three miles west of Southport, where the two survivors would come ashore dazed and in shock.

The lifeboat from St Anne's, the *Laura Janet*, faired no better. She had been successfully launched at 10:25pm from her location on the north side of the river mouth from whence 'she proceeded for about 500 yards under oars, and then made sail, crossing the Salt House Bank'.[134] What happened after this will never be known for the crew of the *Laura Janet* never returned. Thirteen men were lost and only three bodies were recovered, still hanging in the thwarts of the capsized boat found on the beach the next morning. It is thought that the conditions were so severe that the *Laura Janet*, also a standard self-righter, was overwhelmed by breaking seas in shallow water and, once on her beam ends, and striking bottom continuously, she would have been impossible to steer, or keep her in an upright position.

The barque's distress signals were seen by three of the local lifeboat stations – at Southport, St Anne's and Lytham – all of which immediately began efforts to come to her assistance. Winds were estimated as Force 7, and the 'tide setting against the wind caused the sea to break heavily, rendering it extremely dangerous to boats'.[132] The Southport lifeboat, the *Eliza Fernley*, led by Coxswain Charles Hodge, was transported four miles down the beach by horse and carriage so as to launch to windward of the wreck. The gale had risen even more and was now accompanied by driving sleet and hail, so severe that one of the horses pulling the lifeboat became spooked and had to be replaced, further delaying the launch. It was as if the horse knew something the men did not. Coxswain Hodge had assembled his entire crew, plus three extra men, for he knew it would be rough-going to the scene of the disaster and that fatigue would be a factor. They launched through the breaking surf, and the cheers of the onlookers and launch party could be heard above the roar. The boat was beaten back several times but eventually reached the *Mexico* at about 1am when a light was spotted on what remained of the ship's mizzenmast, the main and foremast having already been blown away. From here on, everything went from bad to worse. While trying to manhandle the lifeboat in appalling conditions, at night, with a massive and confused sea breaking all around them, Hodge made the fateful decision to drop an anchor and veer down on the wreck. The attempt would cost the lives of all but two of the crew of 16, including Coxswain Hodge. According to one of the two survivors,

The loss of the other boats and fellow lifesavers was unknown to the crew from Lytham, who set out in the lifeboat *Charles Biggs* against obviously monumental odds and succeeded where the others had failed. According to the Coxswain J. Clarkson:

The Lytham boat was launched successfully at five minutes past ten, signals of distress having been seen at 9:30pm, December 9th, bearing about SW from the boat-house; she proceeded down river under oars for a mile and a half, and then set sail, steering about SSW, the wind being WNW, wind and sea about abeam. The boat was filled four or five times, and when a quarter of a mile from the ship, the sails were taken in and the masts down. After getting the oars out, a heavy breaking sea struck her, throwing the boat over with her gunwale under water, the sudden lurch breaking three of the oars. The boat subsequently got safely alongside the ship and was successful in rescuing the crew. [135]

Coxswain Clarkson added that, 'We had great difficulty getting at the men on the boat [the *Mexico*], for the sea was breaking over her in great mountain waves.... The men jumped safely into our boat, except one who missed the boat, but was fortunately caught by one of our crew, and had a most miraculous escape.'[136]

Twenty-seven lifeboatmen lost their lives that night. The weather remained so severe that the next day the coxswain of the Blackpool lifeboat was washed overboard by the seas and was almost lost while searching for survivors. The tragedy sent shock waves through the RNLI and the nation. All three boats had been Standard Self-Righters, and both the Southport and St Anne's boats had already carried out many successful rescues in adverse conditions, saving dozens of lives. However, the Lytham boat was a newer version, somewhat longer and narrower, with larger air cases and a swing, or drop, keel to assist when sailing.

As a result of the inquiry that followed the disaster, it was determined that previous self-righters did not have sufficient inherent re-righting qualities and that all future lifeboats should have the new features incorporated in their construction. Self-righting tests at the builders' trials were also updated as previous tests had always been conducted 'lightship', and did not take into consideration the weight of crew and equipment, whether ballast tanks were full or sails set. All future trials were conducted with these considerations in mind, and the self-righting features of lifeboats were adjusted accordingly.

The tragedy also revised the debate about the seaworthiness of self-righters for all coastal-rescue applications. A consulting naval architect was hired by the Institution to study the problem and make recommendations. G.L. Watson would become an instrumental force in the development of future lifeboats, including the world's earliest steam and motor lifeboats. He would promote the idea of larger, more stable, non-self-righting lifeboats for rescue work offshore, while leaving the less sea-kindly, but inherently self-righting boats for the near shore and surf work (see Chapter II-11).

The *Mexico* disaster not only spurred on developments in lifeboat design, it also induced a fundamental restructuring of the RNLI's inner workings, in particular its methods of raising funds and its treatment of dependants of lifeboatmen lost at sea. The result was the establishment of a new public charitable fund-raising campaign that became known as the Lifeboat Saturday Fund, as well as the introduction of more substantial pensions for widow's and dependants (see Chapter I-16).

Norway
Loss of the *Risør*, 1913.
The loss of a lifeboat was not always caused by events directly surrounding a rescue attempt. Lifeboats were expected to go out in all conditions and sometimes the sea itself would claim its toll. Such was the case of the Norwegian sailing lifeboat *Risør*, based at the small port of the same name. In the fall of 1913 the Colin Archer-designed lifeboat was newly arrived at *Risør*, with Johannes Martinson as master, and a crew of three. They had a busy time looking after the local boats of the offshore fishery, and they towed in 88 vessels in that one season alone.

On 3 December *Risør* sailed from Kragenø and arrived at her home port that evening. The weather had been calm and fine but the temperature was higher than normal. However, the barometer fell sharply, and by the night of 4 December an incredible storm wreaked havoc upon the Norwegian coast. During the night doors were blown open and windows smashed in. A storm surge washed through the village of Risør, rushing over the wharf and washing many of the boats out to sea. All along the coast, vessels that could find shelter did, while others tried to ride out the ravages of wind and weather at sea. There were countless reports of shipwreck.

Captain Martinson somehow kept his lifeboat unharmed in the confines of the harbour, but he now realised that the *Risør* had to head out to sea to search for any vessels that may not have been so fortunate in the storm. By 7:30am the winds had abated somewhat and the storm surge had fallen about 18in (0.5m). Many of the locals advised him to wait, saying that it was too risky, but Martinson replied, 'It is right after a night like that, that we have something to do on the sea'. The people of Risør watched the lifeboat leave until she was out of sight at about 9:30am. At noon, the steamship *Capella*, spotted the *Risør* about four miles offshore in extremely rough conditions, running under a reefed mainsail. It was the last time Captain Martinson and his crew were ever seen. No trace of the vessel or crew were ever found – this was the only time in the 107-year history of the Norwegian Society for Sea Rescue, that a lifeboat and her entire crew were lost.[137]

The Netherlands
Hoek van Holland and Terschelling, loss of the *President van Heel* and the *Brandaris*, 1921
The weekend of 21-22 October 1921 was tragic for the two lifeboat societies in Holland. Both the NZHRM and the ZHRM would lose vessels and crew while trying to assist vessels in distress, in hurricane-force winds. On the Saturday, the steam lifeboat *President van Heel* of the ZHRM, left her base at the Hook of Holland. She had been tasked to assist a French vessel reported to be in distress, but before she could clear the entrance to the shipping canal, she was capsized by the breaking seas and six of her crew of seven were lost. (This was the same lifeboat that had conducted a valiant rescue in 1907 when, in extremely perilous circumstances, she plucked

survivors from the British passenger steamer *Berlin*, wrecked on the pier at the entrance to the River Maas [See Chapter II-10; Steam Powered Lifeboats].) In spite of this loss the *President van Heel* was salved, and continued in service until 1930.[138]

Meanwhile, further to the north, the German schooner *Liesbeth*, fully laden and with a crew of six, had struck the treacherous Stanley Reef in the Engelsmans Gat, while trying to make a run for safer water. The crew of the NZHRM pulling boat from Cocksdorp saw her signals of distress and launched soon after. Against incredible odds, the lifeboat, with nothing more than manpower, made it to the *Liesbeth*, only to be swamped by a huge breaker and washed to leeward. Undaunted, the crew recovered and, with enormous effort, regained the wreck. They were successful in rescuing the entire crew, who slid down ropes into the lifeboat and, with the strong winds behind them, safely returned to shore. But their happiness was short-lived. Another NZHRM lifeboat had also been sent to the *Liesbeth*'s aid. The *Brandaris*, a large and powerful motor lifeboat from Terschelling, was en route to the stricken vessel in order to assist should the smaller pulling boat run into difficulty. The *Brandaris* was one of the largest and most powerful lifeboats in the world. She had departed her base and successfully made it through the breakers out to sea. She was also reported underway in heavy weather some two hours later by the people of Vlieland, making her way towards the *Liesbeth*. This would be the last time anyone would see either the *Brandaris* or her crew of four. What caused the sudden disappearance will never be known and, in the words of the board of inquiry that followed, 'The council is unable to establish the cause of the loss of the *Brandaris* through lack of evidence. In any rescue operation in stormy weather at sea there is always an element of danger. However, the *Brandaris* was adequately equipped to carry out such missions, she was well maintained and she had a skilled crew especially trained for rescue service.'[139]

Great Britain
Welsh Coast, 1947.

In April 1947 the 7,000-ton steamship *Santampa*, running light up the Bristol Channel was caught in a strong onshore blow and was unable to maintain enough steerage to avoid being driven ashore. Eventually, she was able to drop an anchor in the vicinity of Sker Point but, as her position remained precarious, the 45ft (13.75m) Watson lifeboat from Mumbles was called out to assist. Coxswain William Gannon and his crew of seven were last seen receiving signals regarding the position of the *Santampa*, before pounding their way across the bay to Sker Point. According to all accounts, as the lifeboat headed towards the *Santampa*, one of the ship's anchor

cables parted and she was blown onto the rock ledge below the point. There she immediately began to break up in the heavy seas, with the crew of 41 men huddling in the midships section. A Coastguard rocket crew attempted to transfer a line, but to no avail. The midships section rolled off the ledge into deep water taking the entire complement with it. Ironically, the bow and stern sections, the latter of which held the crew's quarters, remained intact and the next day were found to have stayed relatively dry. But the dawn's light also revealed another tragedy – as the tide receded, the capsized hull of the Mumbles lifeboat was found amongst the wreckage, along with the lifeless bodies of all her crew. At the board of inquiry it was determined that the lifeboat had been overwhelmed by an immense breaking wave when Coxswain Gammon and his crew, in the finest tradition of the service, had bravely gone into the frenzied waters off Sker Point in a last-ditched attempt to save those on board the *Santampa*.

United States
Oregon, Columbia River Bar, 1961.

On 12 January 1961 the conditions at the mouth of the Columbia River were described as winds SSE at 55kt, with a heavy breaking sea on the bar. The area has earned its reputation as one of the more notorious locations in the 'Graveyard of the Pacific' – a region of treacherous rocks, reefs and bars extending north from Oregon to the west coast of Vancouver Island in Canada, that has claimed hundreds of ships and lives since earliest times. The fishing vessel *Mermaid* radioed the USCG to advise them she had lost her rudder while attempting to cross the bar and was in danger of drifting into the breakers.

A 40ft (12m) utility boat (UTB) and a 36ft (11m) motor lifeboat (MLB) from the Cape Disappointment Lifeboat Station on the Washington side of the river were already on scene but, due to the immense sea conditions, were unable to provide assistance. A 52ft (16m) Type F MLB, the *Triumph*, from the Point Adams Lifeboat Station, Oregon, was tasked to assist and by the time she arrived on scene the *Mermaid* was drifting into the shallows off Peacock Spit, on the north side of the bar. Through skill and daring, the six men on the *Triumph* succeeded in transferring a towline to the *Mermaid* and began to drag her to safer water. In the great breaking seas the surge of the towline caused it to snap and, in turning around to pass another line, the *Triumph* was struck by an immense wave, which capsized her, throwing most of the crew into the water. One crewman managed to swim to the *Mermaid*, and somehow made it onboard, while one of the engineers, Gordon E. Huggins, remained with the *Triumph* until she hit the beach – only he would survive.

The plight of the *Mermaid* and the other two lifeboats,

had become even worse. At about the same time that the crew of the *Triumph* had been swept away, the 40ft UTB, attempting to stand-by the stricken vessel, was also hit by a large breaking wave and capsized (not being self-righting it is assumed it sank). The 36ft MLB, struck by the same series of breakers and with her stern compartment flooded under the impact, was somehow able to retrieve the three crewmen from the UTB. The coxswain of the 36 Footer then made a fateful decision. Realising that two lifeboats had already been lost and that his own vessel had been seriously damaged, he made for the nearest safe haven, the Columbia River Lightship, and transferred his survivors and crew, before his own lifeboat sank. It was a decision that saved all their lives. Another 36ft MLB had been sent to assist the *Mermaid*, and she, too, had succeeded in setting up a tow. Unfortunately, this line would also part. The *Mermaid* and her hapless crew, along with the crewmen from the *Triumph*, would be last seen disappearing into the breakers of Peacock Spit, into the black of night and driving spume, all onboard being lost.[140]

Germany
Heligoland, 1967.
On 23 February 1967 the large DGzRS rescue cruiser, the *Adolph Bermpohl*, was tasked to assist the fishing vessel, *J.C. Wriede*, reported in distress in hurricane-force winds. The fishing vessel's position was about 45 nautical miles northwest of the rescue cruiser's homeport of Cuxhaven, on the Island of Heligoland. Sea conditions were said to be in excess of 20ft (6.0m). Approximately one hour after departing, the *Adolph Bermpohl* was diverted to assist another vessel, the Dutch fishing boat, *Burgermeester van Kampen*, reported to be taking on water to the north of Heligoland and in need of immediate assistance.

At 5.13pm the rescue cruiser arrived on scene and, in what must have been an incredible feat of seamanship given the state of wind and sea, launched the small daughter boat, *Vegesack*. The *Vegesack* had a crew of three and their mission was to come alongside the stricken fishing vessel and recover the crew. At 6.19pm the coxswain radioed that the *Vegesack* had been successful in rescuing the crew and that the *Adolph Bermpohl* would escort the small rescue craft back to harbour – the sea conditions were deemed to be too severe to attempt a recovery of the *Vegesack*. This would be the last communication ever received from the rescue cruiser or her crew. The *Adolph Bermpohl* was located the following morning by a passing freighter, her masts and rigging had been crushed and there was damage to its superstructure. There was no sign of her crew. The *Vegesack* was also located the next day, capsized, and also without crew or passengers. She, too, had suffered damage to the superstructure.

In the official enquiry that followed the only clue came from the lightkeeper on Heligoland. He advised that at around 6.45pm on the night of the loss, the running lights of a small vessel were seen in the treacherous north entrance to Cuxhaven. The vessel also appeared to have her searchlights aimed down over the side. One possible scenario was that the coxswain of the *Adolph Bermpohl*, being keenly aware of the nightmare that his crew and the survivors must have been going through on the *Vegesack*, had decided to attempt either to transfer the personnel, or recover the boat, in order to get everyone to the comparative safety of the larger rescue cruiser. It was probably at this point, the moment of transfer, when all were on deck and at their most vulnerable, that an immense breaking sea knocked over the two vessels throwing all into the turmoil of sea and spray. The truth of what actually happened will, however, never be known.[141]

The Netherlands
Loss of the Lifeboat *Christiaen Huygens*, 1975.
On 26 March 1975 distress flares were spotted by the Dutch Coast Guard in the treacherous Haaksgronden, near the town of Den Helder. The flares were coming from the sailing yacht *Hasco III*, disabled and adrift in the treacherous sandbars and breaking seas. The large, 53-ton lifeboat *Suzanna* of the NZHRM was dispatched from Den Helder. Coxswain J.J. Bijl, decided to tow the smaller, 26ft (8m) Vlet class lifeboat *Christiaen Huygens* behind: if the vessel in distress was in shallow water, or too close to the beach, the *Suzanna* would not be able to render assistance, and the smaller boat would have to be sent in.

The wind was reported as Force 4 to 5, with waves in the order of 7ft (2m). The previous two days, however, had seen consistent winds of Force 6 to 7, and the seas were probably much larger, as a strong ebb tide was working against them. When within visual range of the stricken yacht, Coxswain Bijl could see her lights in the dark of night, but could not raise anyone on the radio. From her position however, it was clear that the smaller lifeboat would have to be sent in.

Three of the crew from the *Suzanna*, Second Coxswain J. Post, Engineer C. van der Oord and crewman A. van Duivenbooden, boarded the *Christiaen Huygens* and headed for the yacht at about 11.30pm. Coxswain Bijl soon lost radio communication with the *Christiaen Huygens* but this was not out of the ordinary. Eventually, through his binoculars, he spotted what looked like some of his crew on the deck of the *Hasco III*. His relief was shortlived. Soon after, more red flares shot towards the sky. Unbeknownst to those on the *Suzanna*, the *Christiaen Huygens* had been broached by a huge breaking sea and two of her crew were clinging helplessly to the overturned hull. One, van Duivenbooden, was washed away from the lifeboat, but somehow, 'after what he thought was about an hour', was able to make it to the stricken yacht, and was hauled onboard. He was the only one of the *Christiaen Huygen's* crew to survive, being washed ashore with the yacht and her crew. The bodies of the other two crewmen were found the next day along the shores of the sandbanks not far from the overturned hull of the *Christiaen Huygens*. [142]

Great Britain
Cornwall, 1981.

On the evening of 19 December 1981 hurricane-force winds were blowing off the southwest coast of England. The MV *Union Star* radioed that she was disabled and adrift in the vicinity of Tater Du lighthouse on the south coast of Cornwall. The *Union Star* was a small coaster, with six people onboard including the captain and his family. A large rescue helicopter was dispatched from RNAS Culdrose as was the RNLI lifeboat *Solomon Browne* from nearby Penlee Point. The helicopter was the first on scene, but the frenzy of wind and sea spray made it impossible to lower a recovery line. By this time the *Union Star's* anchor cables had parted and she was drifting into the breakers under sheer, vertical cliffs. It is estimated that the seas were in the range of 30 to 40ft (9.3 to 12.2m) and at one point the mast of the stricken vessel came within 6ft (1.8m) of the helicopter's main rotor. The only chance of survival for the people onboard rested with Coxswain Trevelyan Richards and his handpicked crew of seven on the *Solomon Browne*. In his book *Strong to Save*, Ray Kipling provides an apt description of what followed.

> *At 12 minutes past eight, the Penlee lifeboat hit the water. Reaching the* Union Star, *Trevelyan Richards drove his lifeboat in again and again, hitting the ship, and trying to get the people to come out on deck and be rescued. Even when the ship was right in the broken surf, just yards from the base of the cliffs, the lifeboat kept going in. At 21 minutes past nine, the Penlee lifeboat radios the coastguard: 'We got four off at the moment, male and female. There's two left onboard...'. Then there was a bang, the message was cut short and nothing further was ever heard from the* Solomon Browne. [143]

What exactly transpired in those fateful moments will never be known. It is thought that Coxswain Richards was making another attempt to close on the *Union Star* to rescue the last two survivors when the lifeboat was either struck by a massive sea that washed her over the ship, or the ship herself rolled over on top of the boat. The *Solomon Browne* was smashed to pieces by the forces of sea and stone and all the brave souls on both the lifeboat and the stricken vessel, 14 in all, perished. Coxswain Trevelyan Richards was posthumously awarded the RNLI's Gold Medal.

Canada
Middle Cove, Newfoundland, 1989.

On 15 October 1989, at approximately 5.15pm, the Royal Newfoundland Constabulary advised the MRSC in St John's, Newfoundland, that 'windsurfers' were in trouble at Middle Cove Beach, approximately 9½ miles (15km) north of that city. The SAR system was put in motion and, at about 5.45pm, a rigid-hull inflatable from the Canadian Coast Guard (CCGS) ship *Sir Wilfred Grenfell* departed St John's ahead of the mother ship, which had also been tasked. It turned out that the individuals in distress were in fact wet-suited swimmers who had decided to do some body surfing in the exposed cove. One had become fatigued in the extreme conditions and had been unable to reach shore. In the cove itself the conditions were described as breaking seas in the 20 to 25ft range.

A second rigid-hull inflatable, FRC *244*, was launched from *Sir Wilfred Grenfell*. By now a considerable crowd of onlookers had gathered on the bluffs overlooking Middle Cove. At approximately 7.45pm, after a transfer of personnel between the two rescue craft, an attempt was made by the three-man crew of FRC *244* to recover the individual from the confines of the cove. To the horror of all on shore, as the FRC began her approach to the victim, an extremely large sea broke astern, sending her careening, out of control and crashing into an exposed reef. All three coastguards were thrown into the water and, with a combination of massive breakers, powerful undertow and a steep, rocky beach working against them, their fates were sealed. Three members of the Canadian Coast Guard and the swimmer they were trying to rescue lost their lives.

United States
Quillayute River, Washington, 1997.

Tucked away in the northwest corner of the continental United States is the small community of La Push, Washington, located at the entrance to the Quillayute River. Like almost all the main ports on the outer coasts of Oregon and Washington, the river at La Push flows directly into the open Pacific, creating a natural coastal bar and, on occasion, impassable surf conditions. Such was the case on the evening of 12 February 1997 when a faint distress call was heard from a sailing vessel reporting that she was on the bar, and taking on water. The radio watch crew at the USCG Station Quillayute River received the call and immediately paged out the crew for the duty 44ft (13.4m) self-righting motor lifeboat, the MLB *44-363*. The man at the helm was Boatswain's Mate Second class David Bosley, he was accompanied by Engineer Matthew Schlimme, Seaman Clinton Miniken and Seaman Apprentice Benjamin Wingo, just six months in the Coast Guard. The lifeboat was underway in short order, and quickly reached the river mouth, pounding through 20ft (6.0m) breaking surf. At this point the Officer-in-Charge of the station, Master Chief George A. LaForge, arrived to supervise, and a call was received from the Coast Guard Group HQ in Seattle advising to delay launching as they believed the distress call might have been a hoax. The station attempted to raise *44-363* to advise them of this information but received a brief reply of 'we're busy,' which probably signified that they were then crossing the bar and would be able to communicate more in a few moments.

Master Chief LaForge then had his Second-in-Command, Boatswain's Mate First class Jonathan Placido prepare a second 44 Footer, while he proceeded to the lookout to check the conditions on the bar. Soon after, on the *44-363* Bosley advised that they had safely transited the bar, and La Forge assumed they would now be beyond the treacherous bluffs of James Island and heading out into deeper water. It was at this point that a weak radio message of 'we rolled the boat', and 'disoriented', was heard from the lifeboat and LaForge could just make out an intermittent searchlight at the base of James Island. He realised that *44-363* had not made it out of the surf zone and was now caught in the treacherous breakers at the base of the island's cliffs. There were no further communications from Bosley or the lifeboat. LaForge immediately requested helicopter assistance from the USCG Air Stations at Pt Angeles and Astoria. Seattle still believed the original distress call was a hoax, but a Coast Guard lifeboat was now in peril and resources were tasked.

Onboard what remained of *44-363* clung the only surviving crewmember, Seaman Apprentice Benjamin Wingo. Immediately upon crossing the bar in the mountainous surf, *44-363* had strayed out of deep water and struck bottom; she was almost simultaneously hit by a large breaking sea, which rolled her 180 degrees. The vessel was severely damaged, but all the crew had remained, and the terse radio message about the roll over had been sent out. Almost immediately another huge sea completely rolled the boat over, tossing her on top of some adjacent rocks and tearing off the wheelhouse top, along with Bosley and Miniken, both of whom were lost. Only Schlimme and Wingo were still in the boat. The older, more experienced engineer, quickly advised the junior man to re-attach his safety harness to the lifeboat. A third massive breaker struck the *44-363* and, when the vessel came back, Schlimme was also washed away. Just 16 days later he was to have retired from the United States Coast Guard.

Wingo tried in vain to get below, through the hatch to the forward compartment, where he would at least find

The crumpled hull of the USCG MLB 44-363 resting on the stone beach of James Island off La Push, Washington, in February 1997, a solemn reminder of the power of breaking seas. *USCG*

some protection within the corten-steel hull. But the impact of the MLB crashing against the rocks had warped the hull and the hatch was seized. He quickly fired off three flares from his pyro vest, which were seen at the station. The MLB's engines were still running and the navigation lights were still on, but there was no means of controlling her as she drifted astern into an exposed cove on the south side of James Island. Miraculously *44-363* drifted through the breakers in the cove and came ashore upright, where Wingo, banged up but still alive, was able to clamber off on to the beach. Matthew Schlimme's last words to the young apprentice seaman had saved his life. Wingo was able to crawl to the top of a bluff on James Island and activate his strobe light to await rescue later that evening; he was the only survivor of MLB *44-363*.

But the incident was by no means over: the original distress call had not, after all, been a hoax. A small yacht with two people onboard was now drifting helplessly close to the same breaking seas that had claimed the lifeboat. A second 44 footer from the station, under the command of Petty Officer Placido, had headed out into the storm in response to Wingo's flares. At one point the station lost communication with Placido's boat. Finally, however, they received word: they, too, had suffered wave damage and their antennae had been knocked out; they were now communicating by hand-held radio. The helicopters arrived on scene in weather conditions beyond borderline for their machines. One of the helicopter crew later stated that, 'Someone was watching out for us'. A brief radio communication was heard between the USCG HH-65 helicopter from Pt. Angeles and the sailboat, 'You have thirty seconds before you hit the rocks. Prepare yourselves.' Somehow, Commander Paul A. Langlois, on the HH-65 hoisted the two crew off the sailboat just in time.[144]

CHAPTER 14
Coastal Heroines

The making of a Victorian heroine. One of the many depictions of Grace Darling and her father William, keeper of the Longstone Light, rowing to aid the survivors on the steamship *Forfarshire* in 1839. *Grace Darling Museum, Bamburgh*

Great Britain.
Grace Darling and the Wreck of the *Forfarshire*, 1838.

Together they put forth, Father and Child!
Each grasps an oar, and struggling on they go –
Rivals in effort; alike intent
Here to elude and there surmount, they watch
The billows lengthening, mutually crossed
And shattered, and re-gathering their might;
As if the tumult, by the Almighty's will
Were, in the conscious sea, roused and prolonged
That woman's fortitude – so tried, so proved –
May brighten more and more!

The poet, William Wordsworth, penned these words in remembrance of the passing of 26-year-old Grace Darling, the lighthouse keeper's daughter, and one of the most famous heroines in the history of maritime rescue. Grace was born in 1815 with the sea in her blood. Her grandfather was the groundskeeper for the Crewe Trustees at Bamburgh Castle; her father, William Darling, was the keeper at Longstone Light, where Grace and her mother, Thomasin, were residing that fateful morning of 7 September 1838.

The weather had been foul for days, the North Sea winds blasting the Northumberland coast from all directions, finally settling into a strong northeaster providing a nasty leeshore for any ships in the area. One such was the 366-ton, side-wheel steamer *Forfarshire*, trying desperately to make it from Hull to Dundee. Rigged as an auxiliary topsail schooner, the *Forfarshire* had been experiencing boiler troubles, a plight not uncommon in early steamships. Despite the problems and the uncertain weather, the captain, a man by the name of Humble, decided to set sail and venture forth. It would be a fatal decision. As the wind swung around in the night the *Forfarshire* was driven on to Big Harcar Rock. For most onboard the suffering would be brief: the ship quickly broke in two just aft of the paddle wheels, the stern section disappearing into the dark tumult, taking with it almost all the passengers and most of the crew, including Captain Humble and his wife. The wreck was within a mile of the Longstone Lighthouse. On board the remains of the *Forfarshire* clung 11 souls including a woman and her two young children. Some of the crew were able to escape on one of the ship's boats, but they left the rest helpless.

Grace and her father had spent the previous evening securing things around the lighthouse, and had spent a sleepless night listening to the howling storm. Grace rose early and through the dawn could see the grim outline of what remained of the *Forfarshire*, but it was after seven o'clock that the Darlings made out any signs of life on the wreck.

Accounts vary on what happened next; some contemporaries say that Grace pleaded with her father to make efforts to render assistance, while others state that she pleaded with him to let her join him in the rescue. Regardless of the version, history states that this small woman, slight of build and just over 5ft (1.5m) in height, joined her father in the station's coble – a vessel probably not unlike that used as a basis for Lionel Lukin's modified lifeboat design – to cross the hazardous passage to the wreck. Mrs Darling helped launch her husband and daughter into the storm and, although it was only about 1,000 yards in direct distance to the wreck, they had to row a circuitous route of over a mile in the most appalling of conditions to avoid the surging rocks and reefs. Upon reaching the wreck it became apparent that more than one trip would be needed if all were to be rescued, and William Darling scrambled off the coble on to the rock, leaving young Grace to fend off and keep the frail craft from being dashed to pieces. In the first boatload came the four men as well as the mother – both the children had already perished. William clambered back on board and, with two of the men, grabbed the oars while Grace attended to the despairing mother, wrapping her with blankets.

Upon making Longstone, Grace took the woman and two of the survivors to the lighthouse where she and her mother tended to them. William Darling returned to the wreck with the assistance of the other two survivors. It is testament to their grit and fortitude that these two brave men were so capable and so ready to return to the place from which they had just so narrowly escaped. In the end, through sheer luck and seamanship, William Darling was able to recover the remaining five persons and transport them back to safety. Undoubtedly, one of the primary factors in everyone's survival that storm-tossed morning was William Darling's consummate skill and local knowledge, yet it was his daughter, Grace, who stole the show.

When news of the rescue trickled out the entire country became enthralled by the story. *The Times* of London summed up the national mood by stating 'Is there, in the whole field of history or of fiction, even one instance of female heroism to compare for one moment with this?' Grace and her father received gold medals from the Royal Humane Society, silver medals from the Shipwreck Institution (forerunner of the RNLI), as well as a

Women from local communities, many of them close relatives of the lifeboat's crew, have helped to launch and recover lifeboats in Great Britain and Ireland since the early days of the RNLI. In this photograph from the 1950s, local women help recover the Dungeness Lifeboat.
RNLI

substantial stipend from the Duke of Northumberland, the eternal benefactor of the lifeboat. Sadly, Grace Darling died of consumption in 1842 and will always be remembered as the youthful queen of maritime rescue.

Women play an integral role in the history of coastal lifesaving. In most cases, however, their participation has either been ignored by history or overshadowed by the deeds of men. While Grace Darling has always been the most famous of sea-rescue heroines, her courage was not without precedent. Women had been directly involved in lifesaving from the earliest days: it was women who took in shipwreck survivors and clothed and fed them; it was parties of women that would follow their husbands and men-folk to the surf-line, and help them launch the lifeboat into the darkness, not knowing whether they would ever return; it was also women who, on many occasions, just like Grace Darling, put their own lives at risk to rescue those in peril. The following are a few brief examples of other heroines from around the world.

Ireland
The Pidgeon Sisters, 1760s.

One of Ireland's earliest recorded rescues by boat was conducted by a pair of sisters in the Port of Dublin in the 1760s.

...John Pidgeon, watchman of the South Wall works, who supplemented his work by rowing sight-seers round the piles and out to the Poolbeg anchorage. His son Ned helped him, but was fatally injured by burglars. John Pidgeon died soon after, his wife died of shock at the news of Ned's demise, and two orphan daughters, Rachel and Mary, were all that remained of the Pidgeon family. They bravely took up the boating business. One October night in the 1760s a severe gale swept Dublin Bay and two ships were wrecked at Ringsend. The two girls with great courage rowed over to Ringsend and saved a man, who turned out to be a widower from the flourishing colonial city of Philadelphia, and his child. The grateful widower married Mary Pidgeon, and Rachel went with them to live in Philadelphia.[145]

Canada
Mary Hichens of Seal Island, 1823.

Mary was the wife of Captain Richard Hichens, a shipmaster residing in the Colony of Nova Scotia. For many years she had listened to the melancholy tales of ships being lost on the nearby islands, the most notorious of which was Seal Island, located off the southern tip of the colony, on the primary trade and fishing route in and out of the Bay of Fundy. There were such tales as that of a man who was found frozen on the shores of Seal Island, with his body fixed in the motion of striking a spark. Captain Hichens himself had been wrecked some years previously on Cape Sable Island and had been fortunate enough to find a homestead there, complete with food and a hearth. Mary convinced Richard that they should move to Seal Island to offer similar services. They left for the island in 1823 along with their extended family, and from then on almost no one perished on those desolate shores. Eventually, the first dedicated coastal lifeboat in the Colony would be constructed and built for Seal Island, to be used in conjunction with the lighthouse and houses of refuge instituted by the efforts of Mary Hichens.[146]

Great Britain
From *The Lifeboat*, January, 1865.

Voted the Silver Medal of the Institution, and a copy of its vote of thanks on parchment, to Miss Alice R. Le Geyt, in admiration of her prompt and courageous conduct in rowing a small boat into the surf at the risk of her life, and rescuing two little boys who had fallen into the sea from the outer pier at Lyme Regis, Dorset, on the 4th of August. Again, in October, 1879, the Committee of the National Lifeboat Institution voted the Silver Medal of the Institution, and a copy of the vote inscribed on vellum, to Miss Ellen Francis

Women rescuing lifesavers. On 26 January 1883 the RNLI lifeboat from Mumbles, South Wales, capsized while attempting to rescue the crew of the barque *Amiral Prinz Adalbert*, which had blown ashore beneath Mumbles lighthouse. Two of the lighthouse keeper's daughters, a Miss Jessie Ace and a Mrs Wright, risked life and limb, and braved the breaking seas and slippery rocks below the light to save two of the lifeboat's crew.
Author's Collection

Prideaux Brune, Miss Gertrude Rose Prideaux Brune, Miss Mary Katherine Prideaux Brune, Miss Beatrix May Prideaux Brune, and Miss Nora O'Shaughnessy, in acknowledgement of their intrepid and prompt service in proceeding through heavy surf in their rowing boat, and saving, at considerable risk of life, a sailor from a boat which had been capsized by a squall of wind off Bray Hill, Padstow Harbour, Cornwall, on the 9th August. When the accident occurred, the ladies' boat was being towed astern of a fishing-boat, and Miss Ellen Prideaux Brune, with great gallantry and determination, asked to be cast off, and, with her companions, she proceeded with all possible dispatch to the rescue of the drowning sailor. All the ladies showed great courage, presence of mind, and marked ability in the management of their small boat. They ran great risk in getting the man into it, on account of the strong tide and sea on at the time.[147]

Germany
A Prussian Grace Darling,
from *The Lifeboat*, 1 July 1867.

At Pilau, in Prussia, now lives a woman who has for some years consecrated her life to the noble and dangerous task of rescuing persons from drowning. Whenever a tempest comes on, day or night, Catherine Kleinfeldt, who is the widow of a sailor, is ready with a boat, in which she puts out to sea, and frequently goes farther than any other, in order to give help to those who may be shipwrecked. More than 300 individuals have been saved by her efforts; and, accustomed for 20 years to make voyages with her husband, she possesses a skill and hardihood that render these efforts unusually successful. When she is seen, the greatest respect is paid to her, and the sailors regard her as their guardian angel; the very children of the fishermen go on their knees to her, and kiss the skirt of her dress. The Prussian and other Governments have decreed her medals, and the Principality of Pilau has made her an honorary citizen for life. She is about sixty years of age, with an athletic figure of great strength; she has a masculine countenance, which, however, is softened by the benevolent expression that it constantly wears.

United States
Edith Morgan, 1878 and '79
The daughter of Keeper Sanford W. Morgan of the Grande Pointe au Sable Life-Saving Station in Michigan, Edith Morgan had lifesaving in her blood. In the winter of 1878, like almost all the USLSS stations on the Great Lakes, Grande Pointe had been shut down for the season and the only residents remaining were Keeper Morgan, Edith and her younger brothers. Thus, when a sudden storm sprang up and two men were seen off the station in a capsized boat, it was up to the Morgans to make an attempt in their small boat, with the youngest son, only a child, manning the steering oar. The boat was nearly swamped, and Keeper Morgan decided to head for shore and see what crew he could muster from their winter residences to man the surfboat. Edith and her father set about clearing the beach of logs and debris, so that the surfboat could have clear passage. Eventually, a crew arrived and the two men were saved.

Within a year, in December 1879, Edith would be instrumental in the rescue of 18 people from the steamer *City of Toledo*, which ran aground in a blinding snowstorm just south of the station. Early attempts to rescue the passengers and crew by surfboat had been thwarted by the extreme icing conditions, which made the oars as heavy as

lead within minutes and rendered them useless. The beach apparatus was sent for. A line was successfully shot out to the steamer but 'the ice upon the vessel prevented [the breeches-buoy lines] from being fixed at a sufficient height above the deck to keep them from immersion in water, where the ice formed on them so quickly as to make them hard to manage, and [the lines] were at the same time subjected to the heavy drag of a strong current'.[148]

There were very few men at hand to help pull on the ice-choked lines and Edith did not hesitate in joining the men, standing in knee high snow, where she 'tugged away with them upon the whip line for five to six hours, until every one of the eighteen persons on board were safely landed. It is testified that if not for her assistance some of the persons on board must have certainly perished.'[149] Edith Morgan's exemplary efforts on these two occasions did not go unnoticed and in 1880 she was awarded the Congressional Silver Life-Saving Medal.

Dorothea Dix, 1802-1887
and Martha Coston 1828-1902
Most early lifeboats were transported by horse and carriage. The horses were generally disconnected from the carriage before the lifeboat entered the water, as they could become spooked by the surging seas. To launch a heavy lifeboat took many spare hands and, in many of the smaller communities throughout Europe and North America, where extra help was at a premium, it was women who stepped in to help. One such was Margaret Armstrong of the small village of Cresswell, Northumberland. As a child in 1873, Margaret had witnessed the loss of her father and three brothers, when their fishing coble capsized. Afterwards a lifeboat was stationed at Cresswell and, for fifty years, Margaret Armstrong attended every launching.[150]

There were also the all-too important women fund-raisers. After the tragic loss of the Southport and St Anne's lifeboats in 1887, Marion Macara, the wife of an influential member of the RNLI's Committee of Management, was instrumental in establishing the first 'Ladies Auxiliary Committee' to help raise money for the highly successful Lifeboat Saturday Fund which resulted in the establishment of several similar women's fund-raising committees throughout the country. In 1921 a Ladies Lifeboat Guild was formed in Great Britain, the women raising money by providing lectures, selling souvenirs and educating the public on the cause of the lifeboat. A similar organisation was formed in the United States in 1880. The Women's National Relief Association, later renamed the Blue Anchor Society, assisted the humanitarian efforts of the USLSS by raising funds to provide food and clothing for survivors of shipwreck.[151]

The United States also produced two other truly remarkable women whose efforts in the cause of coastal lifesaving would not soon be forgotten: Dorothea Lynde Dix and Martha J. Coston.

Dorothea Dix (1802-87) was born and raised in Boston, Massachusetts. Brought up in a strict, orthodox fashion by her grandmother, Dorothea became a teacher and, eventually, started a school of her own. With a strong independent streak and a will of iron, by the time she was 33, she had become one of the primary instigating forces for social reform in New England, particularly with regards to the improvement of hospitals, prisons and asylums for the mentally handicapped. Dorothea spent her summer months in the Canadian Colonies, where she found the bracing climate much to her liking. While in St John's, Newfoundland, in 1853, she witnessed a vicious storm, which caused the loss of many vessels and lives. Returning to Halifax, Nova Scotia, where she was campaigning for the creation of the Nova Scotia Hospital Foundation, Dorothea became acquainted with Hugh Bell, the Chairman of the Board of Works, a man who was also responsible for the Sable Island Humane Establishment far out in the Atlantic. It was from Mr Bell that Dorothea learned of the lunatics said to have been banished to the island, as there was no insane asylum in the colony at the time. Drawn by her concern for both the shipwrecked and the infirm, and undaunted by the prospects of another ocean crossing, she immediately set sail on a government schooner bound for the island. When she arrived she was appalled by the living conditions and lack of equipment at the humane establishment. Then, while she was there, a schooner called the *Guide* ran aground on a sandbar on the south side of the island. With great difficulty most of the crew was rescued by the superintendent of the asylum, M.D. McKenna, and his men in the station surfboat. Unfortunately the captain of the schooner remained aboard – his crew saying that he had gone mad in the chaos of the stranding. It was their opinion that he was 'a raving lunatic' and that there was no point in trying to rescue him. It was at this juncture that,

> *Dorothea Dix turned up on the beach, having come there on horse-back, and harangued the men to make one more effort to get the reluctant captain, advising them to secure him if necessary for his safety. This they managed to do and, in a short while, the stricken man was ashore, bound hand and foot. No one was disposed to release a man who had been violent, and it was Miss Dix herself who cut the bonds. Taking his arm and talking quietly, for she was a very gentle woman in dealing with illness, whatever she was to stubborn officials, Miss Dix was able to calm the master of the schooner; at her persuasion he finally thanked those who had risked their lives to get him ashore....*[152]

Miss Dix returned to Boston where she immediately set about raising funds for the provision of lifeboats and line-throwing apparatus for the Humane Establishment. Through her connections in the upper echelons of society in New York and Philadelphia, and with Captain Robert B Forbes of the MHS, she was able to purchase four Francis metallic lifeboats, as well as a patented life-car and a wreck gun (see Chapters I-12, II-9 and Part IV, 'Canada'). This incredible woman who, during the American Civil War would become the Chief of Nursing for the Union Army, had thus been instrumental in providing some of the first lifeboats and lifesaving gear for the Canadian colonies, and helped lay the foundation for the eventual creation of an organised lifeboat service in the country.

Martha J. Coston was another unusual and exceptional lady. Described as a 'tall woman with blonde hair and blue eyes who was considered a great beauty in her time', she would promote the cause of assisting the shipwrecked around the world through the Coston Night Signal. At the age of 21, when she had three children to care for, Martha's husband, Benjamin Franklin Coston, a research scientist with the US Navy, died from complications related to inhaling chemical fumes. He was just 26. Faced with the prospect of abject poverty and destitution, Martha remembered that her husband had unsuccessfully experimented with a form of night signal, or flare, that would allow vessels to communicate with one another at night, there being no other means available in the 1840s. In her opinion, the box that held the remnants of his experiments and his notes held the key to her family's survival.

Martha took the gamble and funnelled all her remaining resources into perfecting the signals, which she quickly realised also had a very significant contribution to make to coastal lifesaving. Through a combination of strong intellect, business sense, courage and charm, Martha was able to come up with a safer, and more reliable, chemical combination for the signals envisaged by her husband. Much to the disdain of many prominent detractors in the US Navy, her signals were proven to be of great strategic value in 1861 with the outbreak of the American Civil War. Travelling the world, she marketed the Coston Night Signals to European naval authorities. She became well known in the contemporary circles of nobility, visiting Napoleon III of France and Queen Victoria. More importantly, however, from a lifesaving perspective, the Coston Signal became standard equipment in the United States Life-Saving Service, where it was used for beach illumination to draw attention to a shipwreck, light up the shoreline for a beach launching or, on many occasions, to warn ships offshore that they were running into danger. Thousands of lives were saved by this invention; the ingredients of which would eventually evolve into the modern emergency flare.[153]

CHAPTER 15

Lifeboats at War

Armed conflict in the 20th Century, the two World Wars in particular, had a profound effect on the operations of coastal lifesaving organisations in Europe and overseas. With war came the inevitable increase in casualties at sea. For many of the coastal nations of the Atlantic and the Mediterranean the years 1914 to 1918, and 1939 to 1945, were the busiest in lifeboat history. The perils of the sea were combined with the perils of war and the job of lifeboat crews was even more hazardous. In addition to the dangers of enemy fire from aircraft and patrol boats, lifeboatmen had to deal with mines, uncharted wrecks, and coming alongside vessels on fire, many of them with cargoes of ammunition or fuel. Maritime safety measures such as lighthouses, beacons and buoys, taken for granted in peacetime, were extinguished, or removed, further complicating navigation in poor visibility. All marine traffic, including lifeboats, were prohibited from displaying their own navigation lights during night operations. Collisions were common and groundings frequent. In some countries the use of flares to assist in lifesaving was limited and in Britain the use of maroons (a loud, explosive, aerial signal used to summon the lifeboat crew to the station), was also prohibited, thus making call-outs very difficult. Apparently lifeboat maroons did find another wartime use in the City of London however, where they were used to warn citizens of impending air raids during the First World War.[154]

Another consequence of war that had a profound effect on lifeboat services was the call to arms, and the withdrawal of many qualified and younger men to military duty. In some countries with state-funded coastal lifesaving organisations, the lifeboat services essentially ceased to exist either due to occupation by other nations, or the lack of personnel to man the boats. In Canada, for example, there were only three lifesaving stations left operating in the entire country at the end of the Second World War, many of the stations having been replaced by military air-sea rescue crews. In countries with private, voluntary services, as in most of Europe, old lifeboatmen were summoned out of retirement and people previously unconnected with the lifeboat, or even the sea, volunteered to fill the void – many saw the need to replace the lifeboatmen as a call to service, similar to joining the military. Only, in this case, the cause was the salvation of humanity, not the waging of war. Towards the end of the First World War for example, the RNLI lifeboat from Lowestoft, England, struck out for a rescue, with a coxswain named Swan at the helm. '...with a scratch crew of eighteen men, of whom two were over seventy, twelve over sixty, and four over fifty, rescued nine out of twelve men from the sloop *Pomona*, which was wrecked five miles from Southwold in Suffolk, the captain and the two remaining men having been swept away almost at once'.[155]

Two of the most famous heroes of the RNLI, both winners of the Gold Medal of the Institution, Henry Blogg of Cromer, and Robert Cross of Spurn Head, would see lifeboat service in both wars and conduct their award-winning rescues during the Second World War, when they were both well into their 60s.

The First World War was the first great conflict to have a lasting effect on lifeboat services around the world. In Germany, the DGzRS came out of the conflict relatively unscathed. In 1915 the Germans had 133 lifesaving stations, including 52 lifeboat stations, 17 rocket apparatus stations, and 64 combination stations. The Treaty of Versailles resulted in the annexation of parts of Germany into Poland and Denmark, and several stations went with the territory, but their numbers were only reduced to 122 by 1919. During the course of the war, the society was responsible for saving 432 lives in the Baltic and North Seas.

The strong bonds that had developed between the lifeboat societies of Europe prior to 1914 would not be broken by the ravages of armed conflict. All promoted the neutrality of lifesaving vessels in times of war. In June 1920 the DGzRS sent a letter of appreciation to the RNLI, thanking them for their efforts during the war which, through their relationship with the British Admiralty, had ensured that the large German motor lifeboat at Heligoland was not destroyed.[156]

In Britain and Ireland, the First World War had a more severe impact on the men and resources of the RNLI. The new menace of the U-Boat had arrived and was taking its toll around the British Isles. During the four-year conflict the lifeboats and crews of the RNLI would save an astonishing 5,332 lives, many of them foreign seamen, including 98 French, 91 Italians and 98 Americans. For the first time in history, there would be rescues from downed aircraft – 22 in total, 18 in the last year of the war alone.[157] The general order of doing business had changed drastically. The crews of His Majesty's Coastguard were immediately amalgamated into the navy, as had always been the case in times of armed conflict. Their duties, which included the observation of the coast, and thus the reporting of shipwrecks as well as the operation of the line-throwing apparatus, were taken over by a valiant force of 1,400 boy scouts! According to all accounts, these young men became quite proficient at their duties and carried them out very effectively throughout the war. The Royal Navy took responsibility for the launching of lifeboats, which, for obvious reasons, gave rise to a relationship that was not always without conflict. In some instances, the Port Captains were openly obstructionist and lives were lost through a delay in response and a general lack of understanding of the ways of coastal lifesaving. Such problems would recur in the Second World War. In many cases the lifeboat crews would just launch, without waiting for permission. But this was not the case at all the stations; in many locations the relationship worked out exceedingly well, especially given the strict rationing of goods essential to lifeboat operations such as fuel and chandlery items – the Royal Navy had priority access to such materials and were able to pass them on to units of the RNLI.

In the United States, 1915 had seen the creation of the United States Coast Guard and the amalgamation of the United States Life-saving Service and the Revenue Cutter Service into one organisation. The new USCG was now considered to be one of the branches of the nation's military and, as is the case to this day, during times of armed conflict, vessels and personnel could be called to service. The First World War had little or no effect on the coastal lifesaving units of the continental United States, due to their late entry into the conflict and the fact that the limited range of the early U-boats meant that the German Navy concentrated its efforts in European waters. Even so, the USCG did not come out of the conflict unscathed. In 1918 the USCG Cutter *Tampa*, while on convoy duty off the Bay of Biscay, was sunk by a torpedo from U-53, with the loss of her entire crew of 111.[158]

As with most large-scale armed conflicts, the First World War resulted in an acceleration in the development and use of new technologies. The most significant change for coastal lifesaving was the phenomenal increase in the use of the internal-combustion engine in motorised lifeboats, or MLBs. In 1914 the United States led the way in mechanised propulsion, with over half their fleet, more then 100 boats, having internal-combustion motors. The Germans had four MLBs, France and The Netherlands

each had three, and Spain had one.[159] The RNLI ended the war with 19 MLBs, but the increased volume of launchings during the war, coupled with the obviously superior capabilities of the MLB, as proven in such prominent rescues as that of the Hospital Ship *Rohilla* off Tynemouth in 1914 (see Chapter II-12) paved the way for the general acceptance of mechanised propulsion throughout the RNLI. The MLB fleet would be expanded throughout the next 20 years so that, by the start of the Second World War, the RNLI had 145 MLBs and only 15 pulling-and-sailing lifeboats. By 1945 there would be only three remaining pulling-and-sailing boats.[160]

Following the First War, the neutrality of lifeboats in times of armed conflict was discussed at the 1st International Lifeboat Conference, held in London in 1924. Captain Ottar Vogt, the Secretary of the Norwegian Lifeboat Society, called for the establishment of a 'common distinguishing mark for all lifeboats', and recommended displaying the Red Cross, thus identifying the neutrality and humanitarian intent of designated rescue craft to all combatants.[161] The Hague Convention of 1907 had already allowed for the designation of hospital ships in times of war as non-combatants, with the use of the same symbol. The issue was raised again after the Second World War by lifeboat authorities in The Netherlands, where it was felt that, in times of war, all rescue craft should be similarly identified as hospital ships – all white, with a red horizontal stripe on the hull, with the red cross permanently marked to be seen from sea and air. Strangely, citing reasons of bureaucratic complexity, the Red Cross of The Netherlands had refused to permit lifeboats of the Dutch Societies to display the symbol before the outbreak of hostilities in 1939 and, somewhat ironically, it was the occupying forces of the German Navy that registered the lifeboats as non-combatants, and allowed them to display the red cross.[162] The German naval commander for The Netherlands considered lifeboats to be 'small craft', which were encompassed under the provisions of the original 1907 Convention. The designation of coastal lifeboats as non-combatants, subject to specific rules and circumstances, was specifically included in the amended Geneva Convention on the Rules of War in 1949.[163]

The events of the Second World War and the German occupation of most of the European coastal nations provided additional problems for the lifesaving organisations in those countries. In The Netherlands the symbol of the red cross on the lifeboats of the ZHRM and the NZHRM was put to good use. Although the new visual designation for lifeboats was not fully accepted by allied forces during the early part of the war – there were two instances of lifeboats being strafed by aircraft – the Dutch rescue craft were still able to carry out some 600 rescues between 1940 and 1945, with 1,100 seamen and airmen of all nationalities being saved.[164] Relations with German military forces were surprisingly civil when dealing with higher authorities, but there were many problems with local commanders, particularly towards the end of the war. For example, when a German officer commanding troops in the Frisian Islands demanded that the usual armed guard onboard the lifeboat be raised from two to twenty, a complaint was forwarded to the German Admiral in charge of the The Netherlands, and the officer was subsequently replaced.[165] However, the end of the war brought about a change in attitude, and several lifeboat stations were demolished to make way for beach fortifications. As could be expected, the Dutch lifeboat crews were not entirely impartial when it came to dealings with the occupying forces.

In one instance, when the Canadians overran Friesland, the coxswain of a motor lifeboat was ordered by a German officer to transport him and some soldiers to one of the islands. Protests were in vain, and so he tried to win a few hours delay by telling the German officer...that he had to wait for high water. When the officer returned, the lifeboat crew had disappeared with their wives and children and the engines of the boat were disabled....[166]

Three of the Dutch lifeboats fled across the channel during the course of the war, all of them eventually returned. One, the MLB *Zeemanshoop* from Scheveningen, fled on 14 May 1940, just hours after Holland capitulated, carrying her crew and 40 Jewish refugees to England and sanctuary.[167]

When Norway was occupied in April 1940, the lifeboats of the Norsk Selskab til Skibbrudnes (NSSR) were already laid up after their winter patrolling season. Authorities in the German Navy demanded that they be immediately brought back into service and were refused by the NSSR. The German authorities then seized all 28 of the patrolling boats, which were to be painted and armed as coastal patrol boats. Curiously the NSSR was rescued by the German Luftwaffe who recognised the need for a coastal rescue service and intervened on their behalf. In the end, it was decided that the Norwegian lifeboats would remain under their own authority, that they would not carry armed guards on board, but that they would extend their patrolling season throughout the year. In 1944 the German naval authorities changed their mind and seized 18 of the NSSR's vessels, but the strong commercial interests of the offshore fishing industry (vital to both sides as a major food source throughout the war) were able to lobby the Luftwaffe and have the decision reversed. Between 1940 and 1944 Norwegian lifeboats

would assist some 4,409 vessels in difficulty and save 266 lives, 42 of them German. Two Norwegian lifeboats fled for the Shetland Islands during the latter part of the War, apparently after some of the crew 'had come into difficulties with the Germans'.[168]

The effects of the Second World War on the RNLI were much the same as in the earlier conflict, only greater. The first RNLI rescue of the war occurred on 20 September 1939, when the SS *Magdapur* struck a mine off the coast of Suffolk and her crew of 74 was rescued by the Aldeburgh Lifeboat. By war's end lifeboats of the RNLI had saved an astounding 6,376 men, women and children from the perils of war and sea. Thirteen lifeboat crew were lost during the war but only three to enemy action. [169] The busiest time was during the early part of the war. While troops on each side of the Maginot line stared at each other and played cards, casually whiling away the Phoney War, a real war was being fought on the seas around the British Isles. The U-boat blockade had begun and this, combined with the intensive mining of ports and seaways by German forces, meant that in the first seven months 38 naval, 135 British merchant, and 143 foreign merchant vessels were lost around Great Britain. From November 1939 to February 1940 alone, the RNLI would launch 520 times and save 1,552 lives.

By May 1940 France and the lowland countries were being overrun by the Germans and the Phoney War was over. Remnants of the British Expeditionary Force and French forces amassed at Dunkerque in France awaiting rescue. At 1:15pm on 30 May, the RNLI headquarters in London received an urgent telegram from the Ministry of Shipping requesting that they task all motor lifeboats between north Suffolk and West Sussex to proceed to Dover and make ready to assist in the evacuation effort. The remaining forces of the allied army lay along a 9-mile (15-km) stretch of sandy coast where, even at the highest tide, the average ship could come no closer than half a mile. There was an urgent need for craft to ferry military personnel from shallow water to the ships, and small craft of all descriptions were being commandeered from all over the east and southeast coasts of England. The Ramsgate lifeboat was the first of the RNLI's vessels to reach France and behold the scene of utter chaos and devastation: tens of thousands of men were trapped on the beaches, the city was ablaze from a massive aerial bombardment and the enemy was already pinning down the troops and vessels with artillery and machine-gun fire. The water was so shallow that not even the lifeboat could come in close enough and the eight wherries she had towed across the channel were rowed ashore by soldiers and lifeboatmen to ferry personnel to the lifeboat. When no fewer than 160 men were on board, they were taken to deeper water to be transferred to a larger vessel. The

The evacuation of troops of the BEF from Dunkerque, France, 29 May to 3 June 1940 involved hundreds of ships and small boats. The RNLI provided 19 lifeboats for the task, most of which were damaged beyond repair in the action.
Illustrated London News

Ramsgate crew worked non-stop, without sleep, for three days. Almost continuously under fire, she transported 2,800 men from the beaches.[170]

The lifeboat from Margate was the second RNLI vessel on scene, arriving further down the beach, at Nieuport, on the evening of 30 May. In the 24 hours that she worked the beaches she hauled 600 men to the safety of a waiting destroyer, the two coxswains receiving the Distinguished Service Medal.[171] These were the only two lifeboats to be continually operated by RNLI crew through the evacuation. All the others were commandeered by the Navy upon their arrival and their crews sent home after a dispute arose with one of the coxswains about beaching the large lifeboats.[172] It is not known just how many soldiers may have been evacuated by the lifeboats after they were manned by military personnel, although it would have been in the thousands. Of the 19 boats that were commandeered, one was damaged beyond repair and abandoned on the beach. Many returned, but were also damaged beyond repair, including the Eastbourne lifeboat, riddled with 500 bullets.

Almost immediately following the evacuation came the next challenge, the Battle of Britain. In the summer of 1940 the aerial bombardment began and dogfights between the Royal Air Force and the German Luftwaffe became commonplace over the English Channel, the key areas for downed aircraft being the Thames Estuary and the coasts of Kent, Essex and Sussex. The slow speed of the displacement-hulled lifeboats of the RNLI was not always the

best for the 'dash and grab' needs of rescuing airmen, even if they rose to the purpose in heavy weather. Nevertheless, the RNLI during the course of the war, did rescue 142 air crew of all nationalities, including German. Allied naval and air force authorities would eventually develop their own 'Air Sea Rescue Service' utilising high-speed launches known as 'crash' boats, as well as flying boats and other aircraft that could drop survival gear to ditched airmen (see Chapter III-1). The demand for rapid rescue in times of war necessitated such developments, but the advantages of speed in coastal lifesaving would not be forgotten.

In addition to the loss of the 13 lifeboat crew during the war, and the loss of the boats abandoned and damaged in France, the RNLI also lost a lifeboat and station that took a direct hit from a German bomb at Tynemouth, and three new lifeboats under construction in Cowes, Isle of Wight, were also destroyed by bombing. The lifeboats of Jersey and Guernsey, occupied by the Germans, were also destroyed beyond repair. The fleet was, however, augmented by two foreign lifeboats, one Belgian and one French, which fled the invasion in 1940 and were used in the reserve fleet.[173]

In France, the central lifeboat organisation, the SCSN, although subject to the occupation, continued to operate, and were responsible for saving the lives of shipwreck victims and military personnel from several nations. With France being one of the principal theatres of armed conflict, her boats did suffer. Of the 44 motor lifeboats in service in 1939, almost all were destroyed, as were 22 of the 61 pulling lifeboats.[174]

When the United States entered the war in 1941 most of the coastal lifeboat stations believed it would probably be like the previous war, with little extra activity. But this time the U-boats quickly took advantage of the lack of naval protection off the eastern seaboard in the first few months after America's entry. During the entire conflict, 1,500 lives would be saved by coastal and offshore units of the USCG from merchant vessels being torpedoed close to shore. Coastal lifeboat units were also used extensively for beach patrol, keeping an eye out for potential infiltrators as well as for survivors from the carnage offshore. As a branch of the United States Military, the USCG became deeply involved in the war effort, operating a variety of vessels from landing craft at Guadalcanal and Normandy, to frigates hunting U-boats in the North Atlantic. One US Coast Guardsman, Signalman First class Douglas Munro, received the Congressional Medal of Honour for his bravery at Guadalcanal. Over 231,000 men and 10,000 women served in the USCG during the Second World War; 1,918 were lost, one third in enemy action. Personnel of the USCG would also see action in later wars, such as Korea and Vietnam, where their expertise in port security, as well as inshore coastal patrol and defence was put to use.

CHAPTER 16

Methods and Means

Directly we attempt to compare the life-boat services of the world we are faced with difficulties, and before we have gone far we begin to realize that the difficulties are insurmountable. At a first glance we are struck with an apparently world-wide resemblance; we remember that the various systems are organized in the main on English lines, and we reason accordingly. But with the lines and the system the resemblance ends. The conditions in every country, in every district even, are so different that we can follow up no connected argument.[175]

So said Noel T. Methley in his survey of lifeboats and coastal lifesaving organisations around the globe in 1912, and no truer words on the issue were ever written. The means of administering, funding and crewing lifesaving organisations are as varied and diverse as its constituent nations. Every maritime rescue organisation in existence today has evolved as a result of the history, geography and demography of the coastal state in question. Economic priorities and realities have also had a profound effect on organisational structure, as has the extent of a nation's historical and physical connections to the sea. The primary differences among lifesaving organisations throughout history, and which have been carried forward to today, have centred around three inter-related and often very contentious factors: methods of crewing, methods of funding, and methods of management, be they public or private. In terms of crewing, many different structures have existed, from the purely voluntary model to the use of the full-time paid employee. As far as funding is concerned, opinions on the subject vary just as widely, ranging from the exclusive use of entirely private contributions with no inclusion of state or levied funds, to organisations that are entirely supported by state-funds. The differing management styles have generally been established as a direct result of the funding equation. The state-run organisations obviously have an almost total reliance on public funds, while the independent non-government institutions prefer the unshackled revenues of private contributions.

Crew Structures

Volunteerism has always been the core philosophy behind those who risk their lives to save others in peril on the sea. Whether or not some form of remuneration has been offered for the exertions being made has no bearing – in the end, the individual member of a lifesaving crew makes the decision whether or not to take the greatest of personal risks. No one is forced to go out there, they make the choice to sign up for the lifesaving service, and they volunteer for the common benefit of mankind. Variations in crewing have developed with this collective goal in mind, the end result being a high degree of professionalism amongst lifesaving crews, regardless of whether they make their living at the task, or whether they volunteer their efforts for free.

The Volunteer, Then & Now

The earliest dedicated lifesaving crews, those of the local societies in Europe, were volunteers who were generally compensated for going out on a rescue. Due to the strong connection of the earliest lifeboats with commercial shipping and insurance interests many would receive part of the salvage award for ships and cargo saved, after they had completed their humanitarian endeavours. The volunteers were allowed to use the lifeboats for salvage work, which also served as an incentive to try out these new craft. Eventually they would also be paid to show up for lifeboat drills and exercises. In Britain and Ireland such men were drawn from different groups with expertise in handling small boats in rough seas and local waters. They were coastal fishermen and pilots, as well as crofters, small subsistence farmers who also fished in season. In many cases they belonged to the old beach companies, small groups of boatmen who generally resided on one specific part of the coast helping out in rescue, salvage and beach-combing for profit – a line of work also known as hovelling.[176] Many of these beach

'The Old Company of Lowestoft Beachmen'. Many of the early lifesaving crews, particularly in England along the coast of Norfolk and Suffolk, were drawn from local salvagemen, well trained in handling small boats in the worst of local conditions. Here, a group of retired Lowestoft lifeboatmen, all former beachmen, settle in for a game of cards at the old company house in 1890. *W. Broughton & Sons RNLI*

companies saw the first lifeboats as potential competition but when they discovered they could crew these boats for the prestigious duty of lifesaving as *well* as for salvage, they began to sign on. It should be noted that the right of a lifeboat crew to claim salvage of property, other than life, remains in effect with RNLI crews to this day.

The situation in New England was very similar, with the advent of the early stations of the MHS and early government lifesaving service, where volunteers were drawn from the local surfmen, who 'had been saving lives long before the establishment of the federal boathouses'. As was the case in the UK, these men would receive a stipend for going out, and a portion of the salvage award if ship and/or cargo were saved.

A description of a typical RNLI volunteer lifeboat crew and their rates of compensation in 1871 went as follows:

Each boat has its appointed coxswain at a salary of £8, and an assistant at £2 a year. The crew consists, in addition, of a bowman, and as many boatmen as the boat pulls oars. The members of the volunteer crews are enrolled, and, wherever practicable, at least double the number of men required should be so. Such men are mostly resident boatmen, fishermen, or Coastguardmen.
On every occasion of going afloat to save life, the coxswain and each man of the crew receive alike from the funds of the Institution (whether successful or not) 10s., if by day, and £1, if by

night; and 4s. each for every time of going afloat for exercise (at least once a quarter). The rewards for saving life are increased on special occasions when unusual risk or exposure has been incurred.[177]

In many cases they were persons of opportunity, generally with some nautical experience, including men of the Royal Navy, the Coastguard and Trinity House. Circumstances were not always ideal:

...it happens occasionally that the usual skill-full men are not to be procured at the moment when the boat's services are required, some perhaps being ill, others at sea, or engaged in avocations at a distance – in such cases the first well-known oarsman who arrives at the scene of the action and secures a Life-belt, has at once his claim acknowledged to a seat in the boat.[178]

As local and national lifeboat services began to develop in Britain and Europe they were able to draw from these groups as and when necessary. Coasts were well inhabited in many of the nations bordering the Baltic, the North Sea, the English Channel, the Bay of Biscay and the Iberian Peninsula, and lifeboats could be stationed reasonably close together and manned by crews from the local village or hamlet. In many cases, entire families were involved with the local lifeboat from generation to generation, from the crew and the launching party, to the local fundraising guild. It was a source of pride and prestige to be associated with the local lifeboat. There was no need for full-time paid crews; almost all these individuals were suitably employed and secure in their trades, the remuneration was mainly compensation for lost wages, rather then a financial incentive.

Today's volunteer lifesaver differs little in terms of spirit. In some organisations, such as the RNLI, stipends and retainers are still provided for certain members of the crew, such as coxswains and engineers of the large motor lifeboats, many of whom now receive an annual salary. In others, the volunteers receive no compensation at all, other then personal insurance coverage. In certain situations where volunteer lifesavers are requested to use their own vessels, such as with the Canadian and United States Coast Guard Auxiliaries, they may also receive hull insurance, and compensation for fuel and time.

If anything has changed regarding the state of the volunteer lifesaver from the days of old, it would be the type of individuals that are now drawn to the service. Gone are the days of the beach companies; inshore fisheries the world over have succumbed to the onslaught of over-fishing and marine pollution. The merchant marine, both coastal and deep sea, of many of the traditional lifesaving nations is now but a fraction of its former self. All these groups were principal sources of recruitment for volunteer lifeboat crews. Although there are still many volunteers in lifesaving organisations that could refer to themselves as 'professional mariners' by trade or experience, the bulk now come from all walks of life and professions, all of them sharing a common bond with the cause.

In Britain the evolution from the traditional crews started during and after the Second World War when many experienced men had to join the armed services and people of all persuasions stepped in to their roles. By the 1950s and 1960s the traditional sources of lifeboat crews were beginning to diminish while, at the same time, numbers of rescue calls were rising rapidly. This increase occurred partly as a result of the explosion in pleasure boating activity, a phenomenon that was occurring in industrial countries around the globe. One of the solutions to the greater number of call-outs was the advent of the inflatable inshore rescue boat, which, in some respects, did not demand the same level of background and experience as did the more complex offshore motor lifeboats. However, the very physical nature of operating these small boats required a certain level of fitness – in many cases just hanging on was a physical feat of epic proportions – and boat-specific training was provided.

Today's volunteer lifeboat crewmembers, men and women, may come from every walk of life, but their spirit is the same as those of past lifesavers. E.W. Middleton, one-time Chief Inspector of Lifeboats for the RNLI, and chronicler of lifesaving organisations around the world, connected the historical with the contemporary when he penned the following statement, presented in a paper on volunteer crews at the 11th International Lifeboat Conference, at New York, in 1971.

It is possible that as various lifeboat stations came into being…discussions were held on the subject of manning the boats. It seems more likely that there was a unanimous tacit agreement that of course there would be volunteers. The men themselves would decide who should be in charge of the boat as their lives would be in his hands. In fact, the system was no doubt exactly the same as it is today and for exactly the same reason. If the best men, possessed of special skills, are required to carry out dangerous work, then these will be the men who come forward and offer themselves. There may be an occasional exhibitionist among them, who may or may not be accepted by the rest of the crew. If he is accepted they will see that he lives up to his suggested reputation.[179]

The Paid Crewman, Then & Now

For the most part, as nations around the world including the United States and Canada began to emulate the relatively efficient organisational model created by the RNLI, the use of volunteer crew was also copied. While not paid on a constant basis, in almost all cases the volunteers were compensated for lost wages, or were rewarded for their individual efforts on rescues and for conducting exercises.

Such was not the case throughout Europe. At an early stage, Belgium and Denmark introduced salaried crews. The Belgian lifesaving Service, one of the oldest in Europe, was established in 1838 as a state-funded entity, which, in 1840, became a branch of the country's pilotage administration. Due to the relatively short coastline within its jurisdiction – just 40 miles (65km) – the number of lifesaving stations required was substantially lower than in other countries; hence the overall costs were relatively low. It was decided therefore, that most of the crews would receive an annual salary to maintain the vessels and equipment, and to be available at all times. Generally the wage was not sufficient to live on and most still maintained other occupations.

When the state-funded Danish lifesaving service was officially established in 1852, it followed the Belgian model, with paid superintendents at each locale 'who must be thoroughly acquainted with the conditions of the coast at the Station which he is supervising, looks after

A contemporary drawing of a USLSS surfman, complete with oilskins, a cork life-vest and a heaving-stick.
USCG

several factors – not the least of which was thousands of miles of sparsely populated or uninhabited coastline. The first maritime safety measures established in the New World consisted of lighthouses and other aids to navigation. Many shipwrecks occurred at or near these lights, and the keepers, who were paid employees of the government, would also conduct rescues using their own boats.

Eventually surfboats and lifeboats were supplied by the government and many lightstations became humane establishments as well. At Sable Island, 200 miles off the coast of Nova Scotia, the first state-funded humane establishment in North America was set up in 1801 under the direction of a superintendent, or keeper, with a crew of salaried lifesavers. With no natural residents on the islands the concept of a volunteer-style crewing system was simply not possible.

In the United States the first paid employees of the early government lifesaving stations on the coast of New Jersey were, in addition to the Officers of the Revenue Marine assigned to manage them, the 'keepers'. The use of the term was probably connected to that used for the employees of the early lightstations. In fact, one of the first Bills tabled before the American Congress in 1847 requesting funding for lifeboats and lifesaving apparatus, actually called for the provision of that equipment to the existing lightstations, to be used by 'keepers and their charges'.[181] The first salaried keepers were hired in 1856 for the New Jersey lifesaving stations funded by the US government. Beginning in 1869 permanent pay for the crew, or surfmen, of these stations was provided on a seasonal basis, 'though only at alternate stations'. Although this measure was only partially effective, it was still considered to be 'a measure of signal benefit, chiefly because it opened the door to the subsequent employment of crews at all the stations'.[182] After 1871 and the reforms of the government lifesaving organisation that eventually led to the official establishment of the United States Life-Saving Service in 1878, the old system of having volunteer crews who were paid only for call-outs and training was gradually phased out in favour of salaried crews. A similar pattern of employment emerged in the Canadian Life-Saving Service towards the end of the century.

One of the chronic problems associated with salaried crew in the 19th Century, particularly where these positions were funded by public money, was that of the patronage appointment. The appointment to government jobs was deemed to be the privilege of local politicians and many selections were based on political contributions and one's political or family affiliation, rather than on individual merit and experience for the job. This remained a problem even after the establishment of the much more efficient USLSS. The

the lifesaving appliances and is responsible for their being kept in a proper state, while it is his duty to conduct the actual work of lifesaving whenever there is danger'.[180] The superintendents were not, however, expected to go to sea. This was the duty of a coxswain and crew who also received an annual salary. To compensate for such costs the Danes saved money by using small surfboats at most of the stations. In comparison to the large English style self-righting lifeboats and by virtue of being standardised throughout the fleet, the surfboats were relatively cheap. The Danish and Belgian services both remain in existence and still use paid crews, augmented in some cases by volunteers. In Belgium the lifeboats are still manned by pilot-boat crews.

In the United States and Canada, the concept of an annual salary for coastal lifesavers was the direct result of

General Superintendent of the service, Sumner Kimball, had this to say as late as 1890:

The crews are selected by the keepers from able-bodied and experienced surfmen residing in the vicinity of the respective stations. This privilege is granted the keepers in view of the obvious necessity for mutual confidence between a leader and his followers in hazardous enterprises involving their own lives and the lives of others, and in view of the strict responsibility to which each keeper is held for the good repute of his station and the conduct of its affairs.

In the absence of strong counteracting inducements these considerations would naturally lead to the choice of the very best men to be had. It was early found, however, that political, social, and family influences were often strong enough to so control the selection as to materially affect the efficiency of the crew. To oppose them certain regulations were established, the most important of which provided that the selection of keepers and crews should be made solely with reference to their fitness and without regard to their party affiliations. This, after being enforced for several years, received in 1882 the sanction of Congress, being at the same time extended to the appointment of district superintendents and inspectors. This enactment greatly aids against the most insidious and potent evil that has ever threatened the welfare of the service.[183]

The reasons for employing paid crews, rather than volunteers, were not always specific to geography or lack of available and experienced manpower. Some of the early European privately funded lifeboat organisations hired full-time crews, albeit mostly on a seasonal basis, to man 'cruising lifeboats' (see Chapters II-11 and II-15). The use of cruising lifeboats with live-aboard accommodations was pioneered by the Norwegians in the 1890s and was adopted by other early organisations in Sweden, Iceland, Germany, and, to a lesser extent, Finland. For obvious reasons, the nature of the operation was not conducive to having volunteer crews as the vessels could be away for extended periods, sometimes for weeks at a time. The interesting point in this development was that, for the first time, salaried crew were employed by independent private organisations, rather than by wholly state-funded bodies. This structure remains to this day in Germany and Norway, where fully-paid crews are used to man the patrolling vessels of non-governmental organisations.

The reality of many crewing structures today is that nothing is really as black and white as it was in the 19th Century. Like all large organisations emerging into the new millennium, many maritime rescue services have recognised that, in order to survive, they have to adapt. This includes the adoption of different staffing methods, one of the most common being a combination of paid, part-time and voluntary crew within the same organisation. Many of the most efficient organisations recognise the merits of integrating various crewing structures under a common umbrella, as manning and resource demands within the same country generally vary from place to place, and from season to season.

In Germany, for example, paid crews man the large 'Rescue Cruisers', while volunteers man some of the smaller coastal rescue boats. To a large extent, other than requiring personnel with nautical certificates on the larger vessels, both the paid crew and the volunteers receive exactly the same training. The system works well as they are all part of a single organisation with a common goal. There is no doubt that the joint-manning structure will be the wave of the future in the world's non-military maritime rescue organisations as state-funded entities continue to feel the pinch of balanced budgets and government cut-backs, and private societies that rely on private contributions also see their sources of revenue diminish in the increasingly competitive world of charitable organisations. There will always be a need for both the continuity and experience of the paid crewman and the vitality of the volunteer.

Sources of Funding & Styles of Management; Private verses Public

The system of supplementing the collected income of a voluntary association by a state grant would seem to be an excellent one. At any rate it has been adopted as a working proposition by many countries. In England, however, we are wedded to the theory that State aid must imply State control.[184]
Noel Methley, *The Life-Boat and Its Story*, 1912.

It is the only exclusively governmental establishment of the kind in the world, the lifesaving institutions abroad being all voluntary societies, supported by the donations of benevolent persons; and to this country belongs the eminent distinction of having organized an elaborate system of relief for seafarers wrecked upon its coasts, backed by the means and energies of the Government.[185]
W.D. O'Connor, Assistant General Superintendent, United States Life-Saving Service, 1878.

Methods of funding and management are inextricably connected. The non-governmental lifesaving organisations are, for the most part, privately funded, while the principal government-run organisations are, obviously, maintained by tax dollars. In the case of the RNLI, to which Mr Methley referred in 1912, independence from state control has always been at the core of operation. A similar approach has been taken by several of the other European lifesaving organisations, which continue to view freedom from state involvement as the key to maintaining the freedom and flexibility to develop their own procedures and resources. They prefer to be unhindered by slow-moving bureaucracy and to focus on the job in hand – saving the lives of seafarers in difficulty. In almost all cases where voluntary crews are the principal source of manning, the preferred funding source is also voluntary. It is perhaps this connection of independent philanthropy, whether serving directly as crew, or dropping money into the collection box, that allows all contributors to feel that their efforts are going directly to the aid of those in peril.

In the case of Mr O'Connor's statement of 1878, total state control was deemed to be the most favourable system. It provided the efficiency and, more importantly, the financial continuity, to establish a lifesaving system across the vast territories of a young America. The reality, however, was that an entirely state-funded lifesaving organisation was unique at the time.

Almost all lifesaving organisations have derived income from sources other than charitable donations. The use of levied funds, whether originating from shipping or port dues collected by private bodies, or direct tax monies provided by governments, have been used either continually or during specific periods to augment the income of societies, both state-run and private. The early Chinese lifesaving societies were funded by a combination of sources, including levies on shipping transiting through the gorges, and subsidies from local governments. The first local lifeboat service in Great Britain, that of the Liverpool Docks Trust, originating around 1776, was funded by port dues and groups of underwriters. In the case of the now fully independent DGzRS of Germany, a temporary state subsidy was provided to help the service restructure after the Second World War. In 1957 when the society, its resources and finances had sufficiently improved to allow it to become independent once again, the subsidy was stopped.

Even the RNLI accepted an annual grant of £2,000 from the Mercantile Marine Fund from 1854 to 1869. But, when the British Government placed a condition on the allocation, it was respectfully declined.

Like all highly visible public organisations, the RNLI was not without its detractors over the course of its development, many of whom felt that lifesaving should

be the responsibility of the state, and that the lifeboats should be entirely manned by paid crews. In 1897 a Parliamentary Board of Inquiry was established to review this very question, instigated by the continuous attacks on the RNLI by a few prominent individuals, some of whom were being motivated by issues of self-interest. After four months of extensive interviews and intensive research Sir Courtenay Boyle, Permanent Secretary of the Board, concluded that:

> *No Government Department could ever do the work as well as the National Life-Boat Institution; no Government Department would ever maintain the alertness and alacrity which the Governors of that Institution have always exhibited; and no Government Department could ever evoke that generous sympathy with the heroism that has characterized the work of the Institution...I trust the time will never come when the English public will abdicate their duty and their highest privilege of supporting such a noble institution.*[186]

The RNLI would suffer through several more inquests over the next century, most of which coincided with either the unfortunate loss of a vessel, or of a lifeboat itself. Thus, in 1970, the loss of the Longhope and Fraserburg lifeboats in Scotland brought another call for the review of the service and the possible 'nationalisation' of the institution, integrating it into a new government-run air-sea rescue service. Again, however, cooler heads prevailed, and the obvious benefits of a voluntarily funded and operated lifeboat service for the coasts of Britain and Ireland won out.

There are very few private organisations in the world today that can say they are entirely free of state support. But, whether subsidised or not, voluntary societies continue to pursue the independent donor, for the independent dollar. Private sources of revenue vary from country to country, but include individual and corporate donations, memberships and subscriptions, income accrued from invested revenue, lottery funds, the sale of technology such as lifeboats and equipment, and, increasingly, from estate legacies, a common practice in many countries where rescue craft are actually purchased with such funds and named after the benefactor. In one interesting and innovative example, the Chilean Lifeboat Society in Valparaíso actually supplements their income through the operation of a restaurant and nightclub, strategically located above their boathouse! In other cases, private lifeboats may be chartered for pilotage delivery services, or local towage, both of which provide revenue for the lifesaving societies.

Charity Made Public -
The Lifeboat Saturday Campaign

The tragedy that occurred at the wreck of the German barque *Mexico* on 9 December 1886, in which two RNLI lifeboats from Southport and St Anne's and 27 men were lost, fostered many debates within the institution, not least of which concerned the design of the standard self-righting lifeboats themselves (see Chapters I-13 and II-19). The tragedy also served to induce some soul searching within the Institution, which led to the development of the first populist charitable fund-raising campaign in Britain, as well as many other progressive social changes aimed at helping lifeboatmen and their families.

The loss of the St Anne's crew had closely touched a successful Manchester businessman named Sir Charles Macara. He maintained a summer residence at St Anne's and was the Chairman of the St Anne's branch of the Institution, where he was well known for warming and feeding the local crew after a call-out. After the disaster, Sir Charles started investigating the organisation's finances. To his dismay, he discovered that the RNLI was then spending twice as much as it was earning and that, incredibly, two thirds of its income came from the nation's 100 wealthiest people. Macara recognised the popular appeal of the lifeboat, and how the tragedy of the *Mexico* had caught the attention of ordinary people throughout the country.

On 1 October 1891 Macara organised the first 'Life-Boat Saturday' in the City of Manchester. Several lifeboats and carriages were drawn through the streets. An estimated 30,000 people attended and, in one of the earliest examples of organised street charity, £5,000 was raised by women carrying nets on the ends of long poles around the crowd. Life-Boat Saturdays became weekly events all over the country for years to come.

Sir Charles next set about reorganising the fund-raising structure of the RNLI into six districts around Britain and Ireland. Marion Macara was instrumental in establishing the successful ladies' fund-raising committees throughout the country. By making the lifeboat a common cause for all, Macara's vision increased and stabilised the finances of the RNLI.

Before the loss of the *Mexico*, widows and families of lost lifeboatmen could only expect a £100 lump-sum payment. The loss of the family's main wage-earner and the lack of any social assistance whatsoever would leave his family destitute. This too, was unacceptable to Charles Macara and, aside from raising thousands to assist directly the families of the *Mexico* disaster, he helped to introduce widows' pensions so that, in his own words, 'at least every lifeboatman ought to have the satisfaction of knowing that, if he never returned, those dependent on him should not suffer pecuniary loss through his self-sacrifice'.[187]

Charity goes public. The RNLI, through such measures as the establishment of the Lifeboat Saturday Fund in 1891, became one of the first humanitarian organisations to pursue fund-raising from the public at large. Parades and pageantry put the lifeboat cause centre stage and volunteers walked alongside the boats collecting money from the crowd.
RNLI

Above: Lifesaving then: a German lithograph of 1867 depicting a rescue by lifeboat and line-throwing gear.
Deutsches Museum
Below: Lifesaving now: a Valentijn RHI lifeboat of the Dutch KNRM assists a beam trawler aground in the surf zone, 2001.
KNRM

PART II

THE EVOLUTION OF COASTAL RESCUE CRAFT; ORIGINS TO THE PRESENT DAY

INTRODUCTION

The Unknown Lifeboat

It is quite certain that the first vessels used for lifesaving were not designed specifically for such purposes. Small boats were built for basic survival; primarily as a means of transportation and to acquire food from the sea. The characteristics of each particular craft were products of the environment in which it operated; it would be those vessels best adapted to face the hazards of local conditions that, in the end, would also prove to be the best rescue craft.

Thus, the first lifeboat would have been a conventional, unaltered vessel specifically stationed at a particular location for the explicit purpose of saving lives and property. Just where this occurred is a matter of pure conjecture. We know that lifesaving benevolent societies were established in ancient China and that boats were probably used for lifesaving as early as 1737. We can assume that these would have been traditional river sampans (see Chapter I-3). In The Netherlands, in 1769, the Government of West Friesland attempted to establish some early lifeboats. Contemporary images show these to be barge-like, unwieldy-looking vessels, not at all suitable for work in the surf. In fact, it is not even known whether these craft were ever built, let alone used (see Chapter I-5). In England, at the port of Liverpool, the lifeboat crews of the local docks trust also used conventional small boats, probably quite similar to those used as ships tenders in about 1776, such as the whaleboat. There is no evidence to suggest that they were modified in any way. The lifesaving station permanently established at Sable Island, Canada, in 1801 would have used surfboats while the first station in the United States, established at Cohassett, Massachussetts, in 1807, was said to have utilised a local whaleboat design (see Chapter I-6).

Indeed, it would not be until the revolutionary efforts of men such as de Bernières in France and Lionel Lukin in England, both of whom pioneered the alteration of conventional small boats into unsinkable vessels, that safer rescue craft would be created; it would be in 1789 that the world's first purpose-built lifeboat was constructed in England by Henry Greathead.

The story of the development of coastal rescue craft, and of the lifeboat in particular, is an interesting one. It is full of claims of discovery and invention and, of course, counter claims. As is commonly the case in technological development, particularly where many nations and interests are represented, opinions on the best approach varied widely and led to some very lively debates, both good-natured and otherwise. Similarly opinions would vary on the best overall boat for the job, whether it be for surf, inshore waters, or deep sea. The debate would rage for more than two centuries and, whether well-intentioned or not, had positive results. The public exchange of information, whether it be in the newspapers and gentlemen's magazines of the early 19th Century, or in the technical papers of today's conferences, has allowed designers and operators to review and accept different opinions, giving rise to safer and more effective rescue craft best suited for the particular environment in which they will operate.

The following pages deal with the evolution of coastal rescue craft from the earliest known origins to the present day. The term 'rescue craft' has been used in a broad sense as there are many categories of vessel whose principal, or secondary, function has been to save lives at sea. These include, but are not limited to: lifeboats, surfboats, cruising rescue craft, coastal patrol boats and offshore cutters.

CHAPTER 1

Lifeboat
Terminology &
Definitions

Before delving further into the development of rescue craft and the chronology of events surrounding their evolution, it is important to understand a few relevant terms and definitions regarding types of rescue craft and the design modifications that characterise a rescue craft in comparison to more conventional vessels (see Glossary of Terms).

LIFEBOATS

The term 'Lifeboat' (originally hyphenated as life-boat) refers to simply that: a boat built for the principal purpose of saving life. There are some variations within the term, however. For example, when many people think of lifeboats they conjure up images of small craft loaded with survivors from nautical calamity, such as those surrounding the ill-fated RMS *Titanic* as it glided vertically into the icy depths of the Atlantic. True, these craft were designed to save human life, but generally only until help could arrive. Coastal lifeboats are considerably different, they are designed to be launched from a base ashore, to face the harshest sea and weather conditions, to seek out those in distress and recover them, and to return all to safety. The lifeboat has specific safety and construction features incorporated into its design that make it different from conventional small craft and allow it to carry out rescues that would overwhelm ordinary boats. The origins of early shore-launched rescue craft go back to at least 1776. The term life-boat began to be associated with such vessels around 1802, whereas, in the case of survival lifeboats, their relative place in history

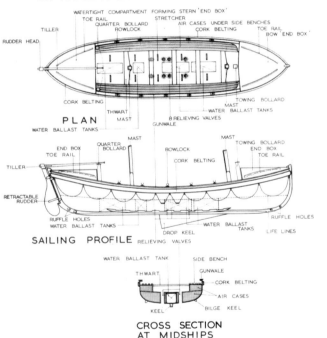

The RNLI's Standard Self-Righting (SR) Pulling and Sailing Lifeboat. One of the most widely adopted designs of rescue craft ever, derivations of the basic design were used by almost all principal lifesaving nations during the 19th Century and beyond. The drawing serves as an excellent example of the standard qualities of a lifeboat, namely ample reserve buoyancy (air cases), a low centre of gravity (drop keel), the ability to self-bail (relieving valves), ample stability (water ballast tanks) and the ability to self-right (a combination of the aforementioned factors).
Eric Fry, RNLI

can be illustrated by the fact that as late as 1863 the Lord Commissioners of the British Admiralty were still discussing whether survival lifeboats should even be installed on HM ships.[188] Beginning in the 1850s many coastal lifeboats became both self-bailing and self-righting, features which further separated them from conventional small craft. The term lifeboat then, in the context of this book, refers to the original coastal type, and it is on the development of these vessels that this chapter is chiefly focused.

DESIGN FEATURES

Just what, exactly, separates a lifeboat from more conventional small craft? Due to the extreme conditions in which these vessels are expected to operate, certain features have been introduced to make lifeboats and other rescue craft able to withstand the rigours of their service, and return the crew and survivors in one piece. Throughout history lifeboats have utilised some, or all, of these features and the following innovations, developed in the 18th and 19th Centuries, are used on most rescue craft to this day.

Extra Buoyancy

The original lifeboats were described as 'unsubmergible' or 'unimmergible'; essentially they contained within their design and construction additional features that provided more buoyancy than a conventional boat. Originally this came in the form of cork flotation, placed, like a long fender, along the exterior gunwale of the boat, where it also provided protection for the lifeboat when coming alongside a wreck. In many cases the cork was also placed internally beneath the thwarts or floors. There was also the incorporation of watertight air cases into the hull. The idea is said to have originated in China, this intrinsic feature of modern naval architecture having been witnessed by Marco Polo on one of his visits to that empire.[189] In some early boats such air cases may have been merely airtight barrels, strapped into a conventional boat. These evolved into hollow wooden boxes covered with calico, or gutta percha, and moulded to the shape of the hull. Later modifications involved large fixed air cases at either end of the lifeboat, as well as additional longitudinal and/or horizontal airtight compartments under the floors or decks. The original open lifeboats generally had enough extra buoyancy to remain afloat, even when totally awash. Retaining positive buoyancy, however, did not prevent the vessel from capsizing nor hold it afloat in that position. In 1872 the reserve buoyancy provided by water-tight air cases in RNLI standard self-righting lifeboats was described as follows: '…in a 33 foot Lifeboat the buoyancy obtained by the end air-cases above the line of flotation is $4\frac{1}{4}$ tons; in the side air-cases the buoyancy is equal to $1\frac{1}{2}$ tons; and the buoyant space under the deck is equal to $5\frac{1}{2}$ tons'.[190] This was considered sufficient reserve buoyancy to hold the lifeboat's sides above the water in an inverted position. By the mid 1850s most lifeboats incorporated both cork flotation and watertight air compartments. Today, most modern rescue craft have flush decks, enclosed wheelhouses and several watertight compartments, allowing the reserve buoyancy to be maintained within the vessel's hull and superstructure.

Increased Range of Stability

One of the earliest design considerations in coastal lifesaving boats was a lower than average centre of gravity. This was originally created by giving the vessel a heavy iron keel, in order to make it less prone to capsize. The downside of this was that the boat was very quick to recover from being heeled over and thus much more lively in rough seas. Some sailing lifeboats had an additional swing, or drop keel, to lower the centre of gravity still further when under sail.

The shape of the hull also affected stability. The earliest lifeboats, from the time of Henry Greathead in 1789, had been characterised by large sheer-to-length ratios. This resulted in high stems at either end, as the vessel was designed to operate in either direction. Stability was improved by these high bows; when underway in breaking seas the ample sheer, and subsequent increase in reserve buoyancy in the ends, would allow the vessel to rise over the waves. It also meant that less water came into the boat where it could have a profound effect on stability. Greathead's boats incorporated a curved, or rockered keel – a feature that has been attributed to William Wouldhave, another inventor from South Shields. This, too, lowered the centre of gravity beyond that of a conventional flat-keeled boat. Both Greathead's boats and the early non-self-righting beach yawls seen in Norfolk and Suffolk had very large beam-to-length ratios providing greater transverse stability. On the self-righting lifeboats that appeared towards the 1850s, this ratio was substantially decreased, as was the amount of reserve buoyancy on the sides of the vessels – a wide beam became detrimental to the re-righting ability of the lifeboat.

Another feature used quite extensively to provide stability when underway was the water-ballast system – no longer in common use. Tanks were placed in the lower part of the vessel, generally beneath the floors and, using seawater and manual pumps, could be filled up or discharged at will, thus altering the trim, draught and displacement of the lifeboat. In some early boats, particularly of the non-self-righting variety, a water-ballast system also provided the additional weight needed to stabilise the craft and allowed it to pound through a heavy sea.

In modern lifeboat and rescue craft design, a large range of stability is still of paramount concern. The introduction of mechanised propulsion has allowed naval architects to substitute the weight of the machinery for the weight of the iron keel. Hull dynamics such as the length-to-beam ratio, and the amount of hull sheer on modern boats vary considerably, depending on the conditions in which they are designed to operate.

Self-Bailing (SB)

In early open lifeboats the shipping of seawater was of major concern. The stability and performance of the boat would decline, as any water shipped into the bilges of a boat would slosh around, creating a free-surface effect on stability. The movement of this water through the lifeboat would alter the vessel's centre of gravity resulting in a change of trim or heel with, in many cases, deadly consequences. Furthermore, lifeboatmen who were needed to pull at the oars would instead be assigned to bailing, increasing the overall fatigue factor on the entire crew.

Certain design features were thus developed to allow any water shipped into a lifeboat to be freely expelled without manual effort on the part of the crew. In the early lifeboats this was generally done through the use of relieving tubes or scuppers. Relieving tubes were enclosed pipes that ran from the deck of the lifeboat through to the exterior of the hull, thus allowing the water to flow out. The additional reserve buoyancy in most lifeboats generally meant that the deck was above the load waterline and that the top of the relieving tube was also above the waterline. Thus, seawater would flow out but not in. In the earliest boats the relieving tubes had removable plugs on the top. Later self-righting designs had one-way valves, thus blocking any ingress of water through the tube, but allowing it to drain out freely. On some lifeboats, where the enclosed deck was placed a considerable distance above the load waterline, scuppers were introduced similar to those on larger ships. Scuppers are merely wooden or metal flaps on the outside of the vessel's hull that are hinged so that they can only open outward. Some scuppers have no flaps at all, but are just openings, or freeing ports, through which water can be expelled. Most modern rescue craft have flush decks and seawater is designed to flow freely off them. If a modern lifeboat has a cockpit or bulwark of any sort, relieving tubes are still commonly used. Inflatables and rigid hull inflatables (RHIs) – the only open rescue boats in common use today – will, depending on their size, have either open transoms for drainage, or hypalon relieving tubes, sometimes known as 'elephant trunks', which extend off the stern of the boat; both allow the water to drain out as it rushes aft due

to the forward momentum of the vessel. Some larger RHIs, such as those in use in The Netherlands, also have relieving tubes in their decks.

Self-Righting (SR)

If a vessel can fully recover, unaided by an external force, from a capsized position to an upright position through the inherent properties incorporated in its design and construction, it is said to be self-righting (see Chapter II-19).

The innovations outlined above: an increase in reserve buoyancy, design features which improved stability and the ability to automatically expel water; all combine to make a self-righting lifeboat. In comparison to the early unimmergible boats, which had a range of stability sufficient to make them not 'likely' to capsize, self-righting lifeboats had such a large range of transverse and longitudinal stability that if one did find itself 'red side up' it would return to its normal upright state.

The lower weight created by an iron keel, did not, unto itself, guarantee that an early lifeboat would re-right after a capsize. Further design features had to be added and enhanced to create the first true self-righting lifeboats after the Duke of Northumberland's competition in 1851. The air cases placed at either end of the lifeboat, were increased so that, 'the cubical contents…from the thwarts upwards, are sufficient to bear the whole weight of the boat when she is placed in the water in an inverted position, or keel upwards'.[191] It was also essential that the air cases were placed at a considerable distance above the vessel's centre of gravity, thus increasing the re-righting lever – still a common feature on modern rescue craft. The beam-to-length ratio was decreased, resulting in a lessening of reserve buoyancy along the sides of the vessel where it provided resistance to re-righting from a state of capsize. In some early self-righters, static water ballast provided additional weight low in the boat and, in an inverted state, assisted in the re-righting process. Certain more modern rescue craft, such as the early Dutch motor lifeboats, and the RNLI's Oakley type, had water-ballast transfer systems that automatically moved water between bilge and wing tanks in the event of a capsize, thus adjusting the vessel's centre of gravity as it rolled over and so creating a tendency for the vessel to re-right itself.

Modern self-righters utilise these same elements of hull and superstructure design: flush decks for self bailing, larger superstructures for greater positive buoyancy, and a relatively low centre of gravity to maintain the capability of 360° stability. In the case of many RHIs a large automatic or manually discharged air bag, mounted high on the vessel, is used for re-righting. These air bags have also been deployed on certain non-self-righting lifeboats over the years, as emergency equipment in the event of a capsize.

PROPULSION

Pulling Lifeboats

A pulling lifeboat is propelled by men and oars. The crew faced the stern of the vessel, and expended most of their effort pulling at the oars. The oars themselves were chosen for lightness, stiffness and strength and were generally built from pine or ash. The earliest lifeboats used grummets, small rings of rope used to secure the oar to the gunwale; as with those balanced on an iron pin, the rower could let go the oar without losing it overboard. Other early boats used thole pins where a small lashing would be used to secure the oar to the boat. Later boats had balanced swivel crutches, which also had a lanyard to hold the oar to the vessel. Prior to the introduction of tillers and rudders the coxswain would steer with an oar that could be quickly moved to either end of the boat, thus avoiding the potentially disastrous consequence of having to turn the boat in a heavy sea. Pulling lifeboats were either single or double banked, meaning that there was either one crewmen with one oar rowing per thwart or two crewmen per thwart, one on either side of the vessel. Pulling lifeboats, like surfboats, were generally used for rescue work within a mile or two of shore, the range being limited by the mode of propulsion.

Sailing Lifeboats

Sailing lifeboats were simply that: rescue vessels whose primary mode of propulsion was the wind and sails. They developed in countries where long distances needed to be traversed in the cause of lifesaving and were predominant in the Scandinavian countries at the beginning of the last century where winter patrols worked in conjunction with the offshore fisheries. The Colin Archer design of Norwegian sailing lifeboat is the most well known.

Pulling and Sailing Lifeboats

In many locations boats were developed to work well under sail in order to traverse long distances and also under oar for close-quarters manoeuvring at the wreck site or when being launched from shore.

Steam Lifeboats (SLB)

Steam was one of the earliest forms of mechanised propulsion in lifeboats. Steam lifeboats were generally much larger than contemporary conventional lifeboats as additional space was needed for the boilers and machinery. They also required new crew in the form of stokers and engineers but the overall complement was generally less than that of a conventional pulling and sailing lifeboat. Both the British and Dutch societies experimented widely with steam, the Dutch using it for over 30 years. It never became widespread, however. The internal-combustion engine that was developed in the late 1800s was far more lightweight and compact and could therefore be installed in existing non-mechanised lifeboats – a far cheaper alternative than building an entire boat.

Motor Lifeboats (MLB)

Lifeboats with one or more internal-combustion engines as their principal mode of power began to appear in the 1890s with the advent of smaller petrol engines. These were originally placed in conventional pulling and sailing lifeboats. The United States Life-Saving Service embraced this new technology very rapidly and had almost half its fleet, close to 100 lifeboats and surfboats, converted to motorised propulsion by the start of the First World War. The term Motor Lifeboat in a modern context generally refers to self-righting, self-bailing vessels specifically designed for coastal lifesaving and operations in extreme sea conditions. They may have propeller or water-jet propulsion. Most modern vessels are powered by twin high-performance diesels, and can cruise at speeds in excess of 25 knots. In the UK the fast afloat boats (FAB's) are excellent examples. However, not all MLBs have been, or are, self-righting.

MEANS OF LAUNCHING & STORAGE

Carriages

Owing to the fact that wrecks could occur several miles from where the surfboat or lifeboat was stationed, it was often necessary to transport the rescue craft overland for launching. It was not feasible for men to carry the boats down the beach as they could weigh anywhere from 1,000 to 15,000lb (450-6,800kg)! Nor could the crew be expected to row these boats great distances, generally in horrible conditions, and still have enough energy to conduct a rescue. Early rescue boats designed to be launched from the beach had special carriages built for them that could be hauled by either horse or manpower. In many cases it was prudent to launch upwind of the wreck, so that the natural forces would allow the lifeboat to bear down on the vessel. The carriages had large wheels that made them easier to pull and provided enough height above the ground that the lifeboat could be dragged into deeper water for a launch. Various other means of traction were used in other countries: in Denmark steel rollers were placed directly on the beach beneath the keel of the lifeboats and in Germany sand plates, tank-like tracks that surrounded the carriage's wheels, were used. Both methods were designed to prevent the carriage's wheels from digging into the soft

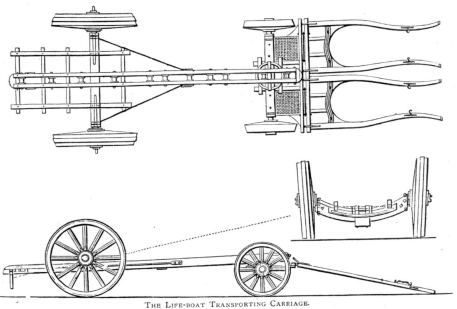

THE LIFE-BOAT TRANSPORTING CARRIAGE.

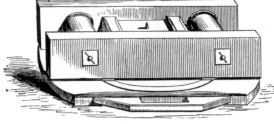

A transporting carriage for one of the RNLI's SR-type lifeboats. Due to the heavy weight of these large lifeboats, teams of horses were used for long-distance transport, but manpower was required for the final push into and pull out of the sea. The drawing also shows a portable turntable-style roller-skid used to move the lifeboat about the beach and shallows while off the carriage.
Author's Collection

sand. Generally, the carriages had a type of roller system on the keelway that allowed the boat to slip on and off with greater ease. Beach launches are still required today, but carriages are now made of materials such as aluminium, and are pulled by special tractors that can drag a heavy MLB or RHI in and out of the surf. Some modern carriages even have hydraulic lift capabilities that allow them to be raised or lowered according to the prevailing conditions as well as to clear themselves of the lifeboat when launching.

Lay Afloat

When lifeboats and other rescue craft began to increase in size, particularly after the introduction of steam and motor power, the ability to transport them on carriages became limited by their weight. As is the case with a great deal of contemporary rescue craft, many of the larger and heavier vessels were designed to lay afloat, either secured to a mooring, or tied to a wharf or dock. The increased range of these rescue craft meant that they could be strategically placed wherever there was a suitable safe haven and, in many cases, the older stationary carriage and slipway boats became redundant.

Slipways

At some locations the steep or rocky nature of the coast may not have allowed for a beach launch or there may have been no safe haven nearby in which to moor a rescue boat. Here slipways were developed to launch the lifeboat directly into the sea. Using the natural elevation of the boathouse as a starting point, the vessel was pulled

out of the house by its crew, and placed at the top of the slipway ready for launch. When all the crew had boarded and made ready for sea, the order was given, the cable was disconnected, and the lifeboat and its crew would slide down the channelled concrete path on the vessel's keel until it crashed headlong into the waiting sea, the forces of gravity providing more then adequate headway. Some of the slipways were constructed of wood or metal and utilised a roller system throughout most of their length, while others were more akin to a marine railway, with a trolley on tracks. With the advent of the internal-combustion engine, winches were used to lower and recover the boats. There are still slipway launched MLBs in service to this day.

Davit Launched

Some mention should be made regarding another, albeit relatively uncommon, method for launching coastal lifeboats. In some locations where a great pier jutted out into the ocean, large ship-style davits were used to suspend the lifeboat above the water, for the crew to board and to be lowered when ready. Such systems were used in the United States, Canada, Britain, Australia, The Netherlands, and Belgium, although they are no longer common.

A new RNLI lifeboat station at Skerries, Ireland. An Atlantic 75 inshore lifeboat is seen resting on its carriage ahead of the launch tractor.
Nicholas Leach

OTHER TYPES OF RESCUE CRAFT

Surfboats

Many conventional small boats through the ages were built and designed to be launched to and from a beach and to transit through the surf safely. When one considers this it is quite obvious that a surfboat would make an ideal rescue craft. These vessels were generally of lighter construction than lifeboats and were no more then 30ft (9.1m) in length. Easily transported by horse-drawn carriage and by hand, generally designed with high bows to pierce the surf, and light enough to be agile in a strong sea, the original lifesaving surfboats would not be a great deal different than the conventional craft. Most were self-bailing but not self-righting. In the modern context, some lifeboats used in surf, such as the American 44 and 47 Footers, are frequently referred to as surfboats but, by definition, are actually motor lifeboats.

Motor Surfboats

Some of the earliest experiments with motorised propulsion were in the United States on existing pulling surfboats. The adaptation of this traditional small boat created the non-self-righting motor surfboat. The closest vessel to a modern motor surfboat is the USCG's 30ft (9.1m) surf rescue boat (SRB), developed in the 1980s. Although self-righting, this vessel maintained the traditional surfboat elements of being relatively small and lightweight. With the introduction of the 47ft (14.3m) MLB

these vessels are being phased out by the USCG although one was still in service, at Depot Bay, Oregon, as of 2002.

Cutters

In the context of lifesaving the term cutter, or Coast Guard Cutter, refers to large offshore patrolling vessels, generally in excess of 82ft (25m). They are not self-righting and are not specifically designed for rescue at sea. The original vessels used for customs and revenue patrols along the coasts of both Britain and the United States during the latter part of the 18th Century and well into the 19th Century were known as cutters because of their rig. Eventually most cutters in the days of sail were topsail schooners and brigantines. They were chosen because of their speed and ease of handling under sail, issues of primary concern when chasing pirates and smugglers. Such features made the cutter rig suitable to various pilotage services around the British Isles, including the highly competitive Bristol Channel trade. To this day Trinity House, the principal pilotage authority in the UK, continues to call its pilot launches 'cutters'.

In 1915 one of the public bodies amalgamated to form the United States Coast Guard was known as the Revenue Cutter Service – hence today's reference to the large offshore patrol boats of various state-run organisations around the world, as cutters. Even after the introduction of steam and diesel propulsion for these vessels, the term cutter remained. In some countries craft of this type under 82ft (25m) are referred to as coastal patrol boats. They are principally used by navies and enforcement agencies but are also used as lifesaving resources.

Rescue Cruisers

The Rescue Cruiser, developed in Germany by the DGzRS in around 1957, is as large as many offshore cutters, extending up to 145ft (44m) in length, but has two distinct differences. It is designed specifically for rescue at sea and to be self-righting. They also carry the *tochterboot* (daughter-boat), a small diesel-powered SR-SB lifeboat that can be launched and recovered from a ramp on the cruiser's stern. Some large non-self-righting cruising lifeboats are also referred to as rescue cruisers.

Cruising Lifeboats

Cruising lifeboats are essentially just that, boats specifically designed and used for the sole purpose of lifesaving, with onboard accommodation so that crews may remain at sea for extended periods. In the context of this book this definition is used as a general term – many nations refer to these large patrolling lifeboats as rescue cruisers, although they are not self-righting and may not carry a daughter boat. Some large patrolling lifeboats may also be referred to as MLBs.

CHAPTER 2

The 'Canot Insubmersible'

Fance was the first nation to construct a purpose-built survival craft, although it would seem that the inventor's intention was not to build a lifeboat for saving the shipwrecked, but to design a general-purpose vessel that was inherently safer for those in it.

In 1765 one Monsieur de Bernières, Controller-General for all the Embankments and Bridges in the country and an obvious tinkerer of his own accord, developed what he termed a *canot insubmersible*, or 'unsubmergible' boat. This craft was designed, according to de Bernières's own description, as a vessel 'not like ordinary vessels liable to be overset or sunk by winds, waves, water-spouts, or too heavy a load...'.[192] One noteworthy feature was the introduction of air boxes at either end of the boat, a feature that would become almost universal in lifeboats of the future.

The craft was tested on the Seine and compared with a conventional craft of similar shape and description but not segmented by air compartments. Although the unsubmergible boat flooded, it did not sink like the conventional craft and remained upright with nine men onboard. It was also dragged over on its beam-ends and successfully recovered to a level position when the lines were let go. In spite of the vessel's innovative design, it seems that de Bernières's canot was never put to use for the purposes of lifesaving.[193]

As time went on other inventors, particularly in Great Britain, would espouse many of de Bernières's ideas for increasing the safety of small boats in general, including Lionel Lukin (see following chapter). Much later, in 1807, the Royal Society of Arts awarded a gold medal to a Mr Wilson of London for his invention of a 'neutral-built self-balanced boat' that apparently utilised the space between a double-hull as an air case. A silver medal was awarded to Captain Gabriel Bray for recommending the use of sealed air cases fastened under a boat's thwarts as well as being lashed to the exterior of the vessel in 1817. A Mr Bremner from the Orkney Islands also promoted the idea of lashing empty casks into conventional boats to make them less prone to sinking and was awarded a silver medal by the society in 1810. A similar idea was promoted by George Manby, one of the inventors of the wreck gun in 1821. Again, with the exception of Lukin, all these men sought primarily to invent a safer small boat for general use, or to rapidly adapt such boats in an emergency. The focus was principally on small boats carried onboard larger ships to convey the ships' crews safely to shore in the event of calamity. The true coastal lifeboat was yet to come.[194]

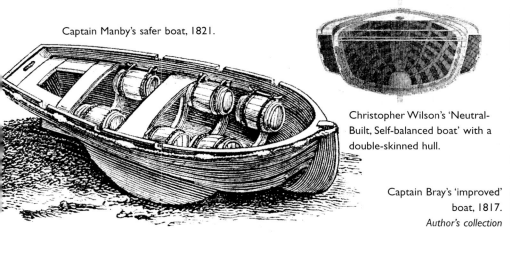

Captain Manby's safer boat, 1821.

Christopher Wilson's 'Neutral-Built, Self-balanced boat' with a double-skinned hull.

Captain Bray's 'improved' boat, 1817.
Author's collection

CHAPTER 3

Lionel Lukin and his 'Unimmergible' Boat

Later, in Britain, similar efforts were pursued to develop an inherently safer small boat. Here enters a name that would become very prominent in the history of lifeboat development, Lionel Lukin (1742-1834). A coachbuilder by trade Lukin had made significant inroads in society through the success of his business. During the 1780s he began experimenting with different types of vessels with the intention of creating what he would later term an 'unimmergible' boat. Like de Bernières before him, Lukin did not set out with the intention of designing a rescue craft. He was merely trying to produce a much safer version of a conventional boat. The craft Lukin chose to modify was a surfboat, known as a Norwegian yawl, then quite popular in the North of England. The type was ruggedly built and characterised by high ends and a rounded keel, in many respects much like a smaller version of a Viking longboat. It was ideal for piercing surf and operating in adverse conditions offshore. Lukin merely added a cork belt around the gunwales and cork flotation under the thwarts. In addition, like de Bernières he placed air cases on either end, as well as in the sides of the craft. He also added a heavy iron keel for stability. Although this vessel would never be used for lifesaving, it appears that its fine sea-keeping qualities may have been put to another more common use for the times. On 'the advise of the Deputy-Master of the Trinity House, Lukin entrusted this boat to a Ramsgate pilot to be tested in bad weather. He never heard from this man nor saw his boat again, but he learned that she had frequently crossed the channel when no other boat would venture out, and he surmised that she was employed in smuggling, and eventually captured and destroyed.'[195]

Lionel Lukin (1742-1834). During his long life Lukin would convert conventional craft for use as lifeboats, as well as constructing new lifeboats based on proven hulls, including the *Frances Ann,* the first sailing lifeboat known as the Norfolk and Suffolk type, launched in 1807.
RNLI

Lionel Lukin realised the lifesaving potential of his new unimmergible boat and, in 1785, he applied for, and successfully received, a patent on the design.[196] His efforts had not gone unnoticed, for in the following year Doctor John Sharpe of the Bishop Crewe Charitable Trust, curate of the Northumbrian village of Bamburgh and a man quite sensitive to the plight of the many who suffered the wrath of wind and weather on the nearby

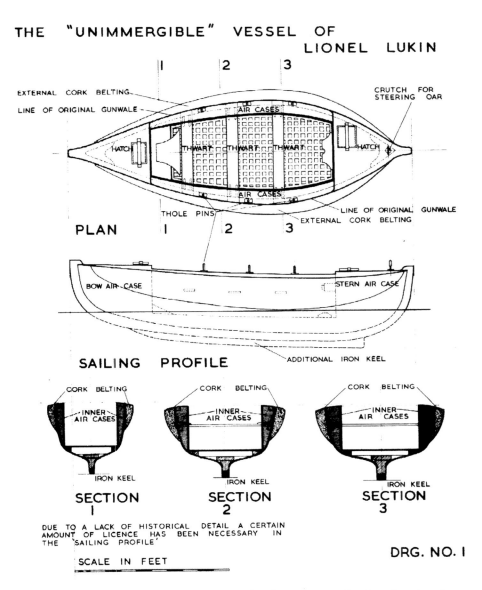

THE "UNIMMERGIBLE" VESSEL OF LIONEL LUKIN

PLAN

SAILING PROFILE

SECTION 1

SECTION 2

SECTION 3

DUE TO A LACK OF HISTORICAL DETAIL A CERTAIN AMOUNT OF LICENCE HAS BEEN NECESSARY IN THE 'SAILING PROFILE'

SCALE IN FEET

DRG. NO. 1

Lionel Lukin's 'Unimmergible' Boat. Lukin, like de Bernières, believed in modifying conventional craft with additional safety features such as inner air cases and external cork belting. Lukin, however, believed that these vessels could also be used as rescue craft to save lives on other vessels. In this diagram, the conventional boat which had been altered is a Northumberland coble.
Eric Fry, RNLI

coast, contacted Mr Lukin (see Chapter I-2). After seeing his work, Dr Sharpe commissioned Lukin to alter another conventional vessel of local preference, this time a Northumberland coble. Although this boat cannot be referred to as the world's first purpose-built rescue craft, there is no doubt that the alterations (similar to those rendered to the Norwegian yawl) would make it the world's first vessel re-designed for the express purpose of saving lives at sea. There is some debate as to whether Lukin's converted coble was ever put to use at Bamburgh. There is no record of its involvement in actual rescues and it may not even have been returned to Bamburgh from Mr Lukin's shop until after the construction of Mr Greathead's first purpose-built lifeboat in 1789 (see Chapter I-5).

Whether or not the converted coble was ever used at

Bamburgh, the fact remains that the seeds of the purpose-built lifeboat had been sown. Lukin tried extensively to promote the construction and use of boats with added safety features for the next several years. Even though the Prince of Wales himself had been Lukin's prime supporter, he was unable to convince such other notables as the First Lord of the Admiralty and the Deputy Master of Trinity House of the usefulness of his invention.[197]

Lionel Lukin had, however, proved that his design modifications, when combined with the heavy weight of an iron keel, provided a very stable and seaworthy craft. The concepts would not be forgotten by future designers and builders and Lukin himself would carry on for many more years altering local vessels into some of the world's first dedicated coastal rescue craft.

CHAPTER 4

The Gentlemen of the Lawe House

In the year 1789, not far from Bamburgh Castle and around the same time that Mr Lukin was working on the alterations to the coble, another group of men would hold the first competition for a boat designed as a purpose-built rescue craft (see Chapter I-5). This boat was to be 'calculated to brave the dangers of the sea, particularly of broken water' and to be able to rescue the shipwrecked and return them safely to shore. A prize of two guineas was offered for the best design. Several models were submitted, including one from Lionel Lukin, which, for reasons unknown, was rejected. In the end, only one entry caught the attention of the committee. It came from William Wouldhave (1748-1821) of North Shields, an amateur in the world of boat design. Wouldhave is attributed with several professions including painter, singing teacher, and Parish Clerk. He was also widely known for certain inventions, including an 'organ, a clock, and an electric machine'.

Wouldhave's boat, interestingly enough, was intended to be built of iron or copper, a recommendation considerably ahead of its time, and 'she was to have a straight keel, high peaked ends fitted with water-tight cases containing cork, cork along her sides within board and above the floor amidships, and great sheer of gunwale'.[198] The vessel had one other innovative feature. Due to its high ends and ample positive buoyancy, it was advertised as being inherently self-righting. It was said that, somewhere in his daily travels, Wouldhave came across a woman who requested his assistance in removing a heavy bucket of water from a well. In the course of his conversation with the lady, Wouldhave, like most continual tinkerers, began to fiddle with the water dipper, which was one half of a round wooden dish. He soon realised that regardless of which way he placed the dipper in the water, it would always re-right itself, with both high ends pointing upward. Wouldhave immediately recognised the principle that, if allowed to move freely in a body of water, a quarter-spheroid shape would always regain its stability with the convex side downward. In later years, when the debate about who could claim to be the inventor of the first true lifeboat began to rage, Wouldhave and his supporters would argue that his model, and his recognition of the principle of self-righting, made him the true inventor. Subsequent facts would seem to undermine this argument, although there is no doubt that, through his promotion of such innovative principles, William Wouldhave did make a considerable contribution towards future designs of rescue craft.

One of the rejected entries in the competition came from a local boatbuilder by the name of Henry Greathead (1757-1816). Greathead's entry was also unique. It was described as barge-like in appearance (although it was quite probably similar to one of the long, flat-bottomed troop-landing boats that Greathead had worked on while serving in the Royal Navy during the American War of Independence), and it was not self-righting.[199]

In the end there was no outright winner although the committee did offer Wouldhave half the prize money – according to all reports the offer was vehemently refused. Two of the committee members, Mr Nicholas Fairles and Mr Michael Rockwood, then took it upon themselves to come up with what they thought might be the best design of lifesaving vessel, incorporating some of the best ideas of several of the entries. Ironically enough, Mr Rockwood had been rescued some years previously by a Norwegian yawl off Memel in Lithuania. Both men felt that the new boat's basic hull shape should be '...something in the form between a coble and a yawl [Norway]...',[200] and that it should have the qualities of 'buoyancy, and the ability to divide the water with the least possible resistance – each end of the boat to be similar; that in leaving a wreck, there might be no occasion to turn the boat about; and thereby the danger of being laid athwart, or in the hollow of a sea would be avoided – that great elevation at the ends was necessary, to prevent agitated broken water from entering the boat when contending against a head sea and wind...'.[201] The two men then decided to mould a clay model based on their own design criteria. So pleased were they with the results that they commissioned the building of a full-sized craft. The person assigned the task of building the new design was none other than Henry Greathead.

CHAPTER 5

The Pulling Lifeboat; Greathead's 'Original'

The boat constructed by Henry Greathead to the design recommendations of the Lawe House Committee was launched from his yard in South Shields in September 1789. It would become the first purpose-built coastal rescue craft in the world. Some time later, after others of the type were constructed, this first boat would be aptly called the *Original* and, within a very few years, the term life-boat would come into common usage when referring to one of Greathead's boats – also referred to as the Shields or North Country Type. The *Original* is best described in a quote from Mr Nicholas Fairles himself, as extracted from Surtees's *History of Durham*;

The committee was unanimous that a boat somewhat resembling a Norwegian Yawl, with both ends alike, having great spring at the bow and stern, and with the bottom flatter, might answer the purpose... She was called the Original, *and was thus described:*

Length from stem to stem:-   *30 feet [9.1m]*
Breadth in midships:-   *10 feet [3.1m]*
Depth in midships from gunwale to keel
                         3 feet 3 inches [1m]
Height of each stem above the keel:-
                        5 feet 9 inches [1.75m]

Her sides from the floor-heads to the gunwale 'flaunched off', or extended outwards, in proportion to rather more than half the breadth of the floor, thus making her broad in the beam, compared with the fineness of her bottom. Her breadth was well continued towards her extremities, thus giving her good bearings at the bows; and her sheer was considerably increased towards each stem, in order that they might the better divide an overtopping wave, and thus prevent the boat shipping water when rowed against a head sea; a casing of cork, 16 in. [400mm] deep from the gunwale and 4 in.

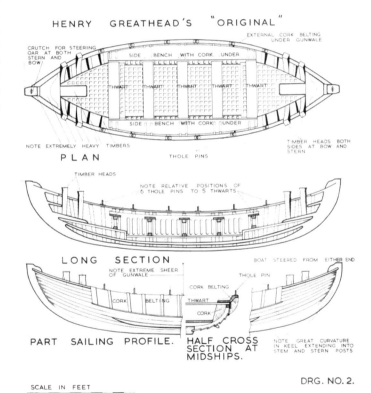

A drawing of Henry Greathead's 'Original' life-boat by Eric Fry. The unique curvature of the keel is evident in this side profile.
Eric Fry, RNLI

[100mm] thick extended for 21 ft. 6 in. [6.6m] along each topside, giving her at once additional buoyancy, and serving as a fender should her side come in contact with the side of a ship.

The inside of the boat, from the thwarts to the floor, was also lined with cork in a similar manner. She was built of oak, and was copper-fastened; the quantity of cork used in lining and casing her weighed 7cwt [356kg]. She had six thwarts for rowers, which, from her breadth, held two men each; and she thus rowed twelve oars, six on each side. The oars were not worked in 'rowlocks' or between 'thowls' as in most other boats, but a small ring of rope, called a grummet, being passed loosely over the loom of each oar, was afterwards slipped over an upright iron pin, which thus formed the fulcrum for the rower's stroke. The rower, by this means, could occasionally leave his oar without its being broken or unshipped.[202]

An early depiction of a Greathead type lifeboat heading out to a wreck. Note the helmsman operating the steering oar in the stern; this could be done from either end of the vessel.
National Maritime Museum, London

Published by William Miller, Albemarle Street Jan.1.1805

The *Original* cost a grand total of £76 to construct and, despite the committee's original request, sported a rounded, rather than a 'flat' keel. (Henry Greathead claimed this innovation as his own, having adapted it from his experience with round-bottomed surfboats in the Caribbean and the Americas.) She would start saving lives within months of her launch, beginning in January 1790 when she rescued the entire crew from a vessel stranded on the Herd Sand (see below). This stalwart craft would continue in service at the mouth of the Tyne for over 30 years, saving thousands in her lifetime, until finally wrecked on the Black Middens.

A contemporary portrait of Henry Greathead (1757-1816), boatbuilder of South Shields and co-designer and builder of the first purpose-built lifeboats. These vessels were commonly known as the Greathead type, but were sometimes referred to as North Country or Shields boats. Greathead's lifeboats were also used in Sweden, Prussia, Holland, Portugal and possibly even the United States.
Newcastle Central Library

At Shields, about the year 1820, Greathead's original life-boat, in taking the crew of the ship Grafton *stranded on Tynemouth Rock heads under the Spanish battery, struck upon a rock, bilged, and swamped, but she nevertheless remained upright and brought both crews safely to land.*[203]

From 1790 to 1810 Henry Greathead produced 44 more of his lifeboats based, more or less, on the *Original*. Many would be built for use in foreign countries and, in some cases, the plans would be provided for the boats to be built overseas. In some locations Greathead's boats remained so popular that they were still being built well after his death in 1816. For example, in 1833, another Shields type would be constructed to replace the *Original*. The lifeboat *Tyne* continued in operation at the mouth of her namesake until 1887 and, in her 54 years of service, is said to have saved over 1,024 lives.[204] The Shields type lifeboat *Zetland*, built by Greathead in 1800 and based at Redcar in 1802, was still in service there as late as 1880 when, incredibly, she was used to rescue the entire crew of the brig *Luna*. She is preserved there to this day, the last known example of one of Greathead's boats still in existence.

The Tyne Lifeboat Society, which was also created by the Gentlemen of the Lawe House back in 1789, continued to build these boats until 1886, with the construction of the *Bedford*. The only differences from Greathead's *Original* being the inclusion of some more modern features such as watertight compartments at the ends and in the floors, as well as relieving tubes.[205] Unfortunately, this exuberant acceptance of Greathead's lifeboat was not entirely widespread and beyond the northeast of England many of his boats fell into disrepair due to neglect and lack of use. In some locations, such as at Lowestoft, Suffolk, there was outright refusal on the part of the beachmen to even use the vessel, which they regarded as unseaworthy and not well suited to the local area (see Chapter II-7).

The First Rescue by a Lifeboat

Although details of the earliest rescues conducted by the first actual lifeboat remain rather scanty, it would appear that in the midst of a winter's storm in February 1790 the *Original* set out with a crew of more than 20 men to assist an unidentified sloop that had struck upon the Herd Sand at the mouth of the River Tyne. This was the same treacherous location where the brig *Adventure* had been lost less than a year before with all her crew, but the fate of the shipwrecked in 1790 would be considerably different: much to their surprise, through the blinding sleet and spray, a beamy surfboat with high pointed ends appeared and, easily surmounting the massive surf, came alongside their vessel to offer assistance. The *Newcastle Courant* of 6 February 1790 reported:

We hear from Shields, that the boat lately built by Mr. Greathead, for the purpose of preserving the crews of ships coming on the Herdsand, was tried out first on Saturday last, and far exceeded the expectations of those who had the most sanguine hopes of her utility, for, in going off three times to a vessel then onshore, through a very heavy sea, she scarce shipped any water, and rendered the crew infinite service — we have the satisfaction to add that the sailors present were extremely ready in offering themselves upon the occasion.[206]

CHAPTER 6

The Great Debate: Who Invented the 'Lifeboat'?

To claim that one individual invented the first purpose-built coastal rescue craft would be an injustice to historical fact. The truth is that several ingenious and creative contemporaries contributed to its development. Whether there was prior knowledge of one another's efforts will never be known. In the end, however, the first purpose-built lifeboat would be that built by Henry Greathead and stationed at South Shields, Northumberland, in 1789.

Lukin, Wouldhave and Greathead shared many traits. They were ingenious, creative, and industrious; they were all also completely lacking in humility, each claiming sole responsibility for this wonderful new invention.

In 1802, when Henry Greathead began his publicity campaign through the efforts of the likes of Rowland Burdon (see Chapter I-5) and petitioned the House of Commons for an award and credit for having invented the lifeboat, a rather vociferous and sometimes openly malicious public competition was initiated regarding the claim for the overall invention. Greathead's successful claim (he received an award of £1,200 from the British Parliament Committee reviewing his petition) and his very public promotion of the new lifeboat combined with the resultant acceptance of the type greatly annoyed William Wouldhave who had so staunchly refused the half-prize offered by the Lawe House Committee back in 1789. Wouldhave felt that he was the inventor by reason of his promotion of the concept of self-righting, and that some of the features in Greathead's boats were very similar to his own original model. Wouldhave's self-promotion was taken up by a local pamphleteer by the name of W.A. Hails, who wrote an attack on Greathead's claim entitled *An Enquiry Concerning the Invention of the Life Boat*, which was published in 1806. Hails would eventually publish some of the claims from his pamphlet in a popular British journal of the day called *The Gentleman's Magazine*. It was at this point that an anonymous third party would become involved in the controversy and would openly dispute Mr Hails's opinions regarding Wouldhave's originality of the idea in subsequent issues of the same magazine. The anonymous writer eventually revealed himself as none other than Lionel Lukin!

Mr Lukin might have been baited to respond publicly when Mr Hails stated his opinion of Lukin's altered lifesaving vessels, such as the converted coble that Lukin claimed was used at Bamburgh.

...Mr. Lukin had never turned his thoughts to such a vessel as the life-boat; the vessels he describes were by no means fit to go alongside a stranded ship, in a heavy and broken sea. There his gingerbread work of air-boxes, and projecting gunwales, would soon be torn away, and the vessels, stripped of their flimsy preservatives, be left to contend with the boisterous element, to which they would doubtless become a prey.[207]

Lukin responded to Hails's claim by stating that he had no wish to get involved in 'the local squabbles of a remote country town [South Shields], nor any ambition to take a part in the unimportant discussion, whether Mr. Wouldhave or Mr. Greathead is most entitled to the gratitude of the public'. In further public correspondence he challenged Mr Hails to justify his claim of the uselessness of the cork gunwales by stating, '…that if Mr. Hails should be so convinced by his own arguments, as to make in a stormy sea an experiment of dependence on the FORM of the life-boat, without the cork gunwales, either externally or internally applied, I believe the chances would be very much against his ever favouring the publick on any further lucubrations on the subject of the life-boat'.[208]

The reality was that William Wouldhave could lay little claim to having invented the first lifeboat. The vessel built by Henry Greathead to the Lawe Committee's recommendations incorporated none of his competition entry features: unlike the *Original*, his tin model was purported to be self-righting and had a straight keel; also, as was expressed so fervently by Mr Hails, his design had no projecting cork gunwales, a principal feature on the first Greathead boat.

Henry Greathead, too, could provide little evidence to support his claim. The rockered keel he professed to have invented was standard on certain coastal surfboat designs with which he was familiar. Indeed, from a lifesaving perspective, this feature seems to have first appeared on Lionel Lukin's well-publicised unimmergible boat.[209] Greathead even claimed Wouldhave's 'spheroidal' principle of hull design (the key to maintaining a boat in an upright position and to the principle of self-righting), in his 1802 submission to parliament.[210] It is also probably no coincidence, that Henry Greathead's petition was not initiated before 1802, at which time Lukin's patent was due to expire.

As for Lionel Lukin, his claim to be the sole inventor of the lifeboat was also somewhat limited. His boats were never purpose-built but were always altered versions of contemporary designs. This, according to Lukin, was much more successful than constructing a purpose-built lifeboat, as it was more readily accepted by local boatmen, and the modifications could be applied to all forms of small boats including 'Packet Boats, Pleasure Boats Etc'.[211] That said, it would appear that Lionel Lukin did have the best argument for having the greatest influence in the invention of the lifeboat. The *Original* did incorporate his well-advertised design features, namely the iron keel and the extensive use of cork inside and out. Furthermore, Mr Lukin would go on to convert other conventional craft into lifeboats for many years to come, while the other two gentlemen would disappear into the woodwork.

In reality, the most powerful forces in the development and introduction of the first purpose-built lifeboat were Mr Fairles and Mr Rockwood of the Lawe House Committee. It was their design recommendations that were incorporated in the original lifeboat, obviously in conjunction with the expert boatbuilding opinions of Henry Greathead. Interestingly, when Greathead was making his claim before Parliament, he would ask for the written support of the original five members of the Lawe Committee who had reviewed the models. In the event, two signatures were noticeably absent – those of Nicholas Fairles and Michael Rockwood, who, in all probability, had no desire to re-invent the facts.[212]

In the end the facts are these: William Wouldhave had put forward the idea of incorporating self-righting capabilities into a lifesaving boat; he had also promoted the concept of the metal hull for strength and durability. Both ideas were 60 years ahead of their time and, although they would have little or no effect on the creation of the first lifeboat, they would most certainly have a profound effect on the designs of rescue craft in generations to come. Lionel Lukin could undoubtedly claim credit for the concept of combining air cases, cork flotation and an iron keel to produce an unsinkable and stable vessel, unlikely to be upset by a sea – these ideas were incorporated into the *Original*. Henry Greathead contributed as the master boatbuilder whose skills as a craftsman, extensive knowledge of small-boat design and expertise in self-promotion, would result in the physical reality of the first purpose-built lifeboat and its eventual acceptance, both in form and in name, by the general public. Thus, the case is made that, in conjunction with the coordinating efforts of Mr Fairles and Mr Rockwood, all had a part in the creation of the first true lifeboat.

CHAPTER 7

Pulling & Sailing Lifeboats; The 'Norfolk & Suffolk' Type

One of the earliest local lifeboat societies to be established in England was at Lowestoft in Suffolk. In September 1800 a Mr Robert Sparrow, led a consolidated fund-raising effort to purchase one of Mr Greathead's boats. With further financial assistance from the local Trinity House a 30ft (9.1m) model, the largest of the type, costing £165, was delivered in 1801 from Mr Greathead's boatyard in South Shields. From the outset the Shields-type lifeboat was unpopular with the Suffolk beachmen and pilots. They viewed its strange, beamy mass and its high-peaked ends and rounded bottom as unsuitable for the local conditions. Due to the steepness of the beach, boats found themselves in breaking seas close inshore while many shipwrecks occurred on the treacherous sandbanks 1 to 3 miles (1.6 to 4.8km) offshore, well beyond the safe range of a pulling boat. Thus, for several years, the new lifeboat sat relatively unused, the beachmen preferring to use their local sailing yawls for rescues.

There were other mitigating factors in the apparent derision of the lifeboat. It was common practice that the entire salvage award for ship, cargo and life could be claimed by a beach crew using their own boat whereas, if the official lifeboat was used, the rewards must be shared with the humane society.[213] Furthermore, when a large crowd gathered on the beach at Lowestoft to witness the first trial of the Shields boat, the plug was 'inadvertently' left out. The boat had to return to shore

A Norfolk and Suffolk lifeboat belonging to the Suffolk Humane Society, under the command of Lt Carter, RN, departs to aid a ship in distress off Lowestoft beach, 22 October 1821.
National Maritime Museum, London

full of water, the exercise incomplete, her reputation permanently tarnished.

Thus Greathead's lifeboat saw little service at Lowestoft and, by 1804, a frustrated writer, thought to be Robert Sparrow himself, sent the following letter to a local paper, addressed to 'the pilots, sailors and seafaring men of the town of Lowestoft'. It unreservedly expressed his emotions on the subject of the boat's lack of use.

...whence comes it then that the lifeboat operating with so much success in all other places, is at Lowestoft an object of dislike, that so far from resorting to her when opportunities offer, few occasions are lost to lower her services in the opinion of the public?... To endeavour to rouse you from the languid state in which you are, or from the disgraceful prejudice you have adopted, I offer you, from the remainder of the subscription left in my hands, a reward of ten guineas for every exertion, fairly and fully made, with the lifeboat, and if the exertion be attended with the success of saving human life, the reward shall be extended to fifteen guineas – it rests with you to bring this fortunate system forward; should my present attempt fail, I shall first state the failure to the public, and then look for a situation where a more worthy race of men will gladly accept the advantages you have so blindly refused.[214]

The intensity of Mr Sparrow's discourse and his pleas to the local boatmen to make use of the new lifeboat would all be in vain; their minds were set. Eventually, he stood by his word and moved the boat to Gorleston where a small harbour made it easier to launch the vessel. But the boat's reputation had preceded her and again the local beachmen would have nothing of it. On 25 January 1806 Robert Sparrow would write one final letter to the *Ipswich Journal*, advising the public that attempts to use the boat had failed, and that the Greathead lifeboat would be sold at public auction.

I removed her to Gorleston, upon the haven, where she might be launched with great ease in a short time, but here also the same dislike attended her, and when, in a late terrible storm the scene of distress was so great as to induce some humane gentlemen to offer twenty guineas as a reward for the use of the lifeboat, the refusal at once convinced me that nothing was ever to be expected of her from this part of the coast.[215]

Unbeknownst to Mr Sparrow and other members of the local lifeboat committee Lionel Lukin was in town and had kept apace of the debate. No doubt he had added to the vessel's lack of acceptance through his discussions with some of the local beachmen and pilots. As an

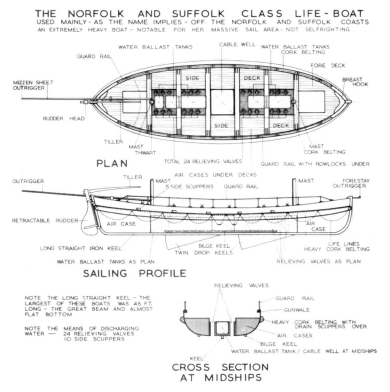

Norfolk and Suffolk pulling and sailing lifeboat, originally adapted by Lionel Lukin from a local of beach yawl.
Eric Fry, RNLI

alternative, he promoted his well-known method of making conventional craft more seaworthy. His opposition to the Shields type had been well publicised through his debates with Mr Hails a few years earlier. The pilots wrote a letter of reply to the dejected Robert Sparrow requesting that he consider modifying one of the local boats for the express purpose of lifesaving, and thus provided a glimmer of hope that a proper rescue craft could be established for Lowestoft.

In November 1805 the Suffolk Humane Society was formed out of the old local lifeboat society and, in 1807, the committee of management, including Robert Sparrow, commissioned Lionel Lukin to superintend the construction of a purpose-built boat, based on his own ideas. Lukin graciously offered to extend his stay at Lowestoft for some weeks in order to oversee the project. As ever his design considerations were based on a proven local craft, this time one of the large yawls popular with the local longshoremen. Well-suited to working around the offshore sandbanks, the Norfolk and Suffolk beach yawls were large open boats averaging around 40ft (12.2m) in length and ranging up to 70ft (21.3m), very beamy and shallow in draught – in short, very stable heavy-weather boats well suited to the shoals off East Anglia.

The first of this type – to become known as the Norfolk and Suffolk class – was built by Barcham of Lowestoft, under the supervision of Mr Lukin. Named the *Frances Anne* after the daughter of Lord Rous, one of the members of the Suffolk Humane Society committee, she was 40ft (12.2m) long, 10ft 4in (3.2m) beam, and had a shallow draught of just over 3ft (0.9m). The *Frances Anne* would be the first purpose-built lifeboat to use sails as a primary mode of propulsion, making her the first of many future generations of pulling and sailing lifeboats. She was a three-masted yawl, with a dipping fore-lug, a standing main and an outrigger which extended well beyond the stern. In winter months the masts were traditionally reduced by one (in time the two-masted rig became standard). She also had 14 oars, double-banked. There were external cork gunwales, which also contained integral air cases, a false iron keel and, as had been the case with some of Lukin's earlier unimmergible boats, a multitude of hollow casks were placed along the inside of the gunwale, under the thwarts, and at both ends. These were sheathed in copper and lashed to eyebolts in the hull. In one of the first experiments with water ballast as a means of stability, some of the casks were designed to be filled with water, in order to increase the displacement of the boat at will. As with all early lifeboats, she was not self-righting. The local boatmen favoured a larger, more stable craft that could ship plenty of water and keep going – considerable distances were traversed, so a comfortable ride was much preferred over the relative liveliness of the cork-like Greathead boat. The Norfolk and Suffolk boat was essentially an offshore sailing lifeboat while the Greathead boat was for inshore use; two roles, two boats.

The extra buoyancy was particularly important for the Norfolk and Suffolk boats as they were essentially underwater most of the time when operating in heavy weather. It was believed that the large amount of shipped water actually served to stabilise the vessel. These lifeboats rammed through the seas instead of going over them and the theory was that they should have such inherent stability as to render the rockered keel and the extreme height of the ends unnecessary. The water ballast was kept in an open space low down and amidships, between the air cases. The water would slosh around and could be expelled if plugs were pulled. After the competition and trials of all the RNLI's sailing lifeboats at Lowestoft in 1892, it was decided to enclose the water-

ballast tank on all Norfolk and Suffolk type lifeboats after one of the class flooded and some of the crew were injured while attempting to beach her.

Although based on a traditional design, the *Frances Anne* was purpose-built and cost approximately £200 to build. In Lukin's own words, 'It is particularly advisable that all lifeboats should be built of the form most approved by the pilots or seamen on the coast where they are to be used; as no one form will suit all shores, and these principles of safety are applicable to every form'.[216]

The Norfolk and Suffolk class would remain in service for over a century (well after the amalgamation of the local societies into the RNLI). Later models would even have internal-combustion engines. The last to be built for Lowestoft, was the *Agnes Cross*, launched in 1921 and remaining in service until replaced in 1939. The last Norfolk and Suffolk, the *Mary Scott* built for Southwold in 1925, was sold out of service in 1953.[217]

The First Launch of the Lifeboat *Frances Anne*

Frances Anne, built in 1807, served out of Lowestoft from 1807 to 1850. Her first two rescues were recorded thus:

The Frances Anne *made her first launch on the 24th of February, 1808, being launched to a boat aground on the sands off Lowestoft. The wind and tide being against the Lowestoft boats – yawls had also been launched – Gorleston yawls got to the vessel first. They [the beachmen] did not attempt to board her until the Lowestoft lifeboat was very near. Then afraid that they might loose their prize, they made the attempt. No further launch is recorded until the end of 1809, when on 14th December, she went out in a tremendous gale. The beach was strewn with wreck and many vessels were ashore between Lowestoft and Yarmouth. The* Catherine…*from Sunderland, with coals for Chatham, upset on the Holm Sands off the town. As soon as it was known that there was a survivor on the wreck, the lifeboat was launched, and with great difficulty managed to rescue him. He was the ship's carpenter, and in the rescue, unfortunately had several ribs broken. The Norwich* Mercury *about a month later reported that the crew who had carried out this rescue, had received the thanks of the Suffolk Humane Society, and rejoiced to add that the carpenter was recovered from the injury occasioned by the wreck, and now enabled to return to his friends.*[218]

CHAPTER 8

The Duke's Lifeboat Competition

The year 1824 saw Sir William Hillary succeed in his efforts to establish a national sea rescue organisation in Britain. One of the first tasks of the Royal National Institution for the Preservation of Life from Shipwreck was to seek out a suitable standard lifeboat. Alas, the Institution soon realised that no one boat was best suited to all parts of the coast – it was to be a truly national organisation, then local preferences were going to have to be considered, including those designs already in use by some of the local societies.

The Sailor Duke. Algernon, the Fourth Duke of Northumberland, had been First Lord of the British Admiralty and, as such, had a keen understanding of ships and seafaring. He was instrumental in revitalising the cause of the lifeboat and assisting the shipwrecked, principally through his sponsoring of a second competition for a better design of lifeboat in 1851.
RNLI

From 1825 to 1828 the Shipwreck Institution constructed some 29 lifeboats, three of which were the original Shields or North Country-style pulling lifeboats. Another was a 26ft (7.9m) pulling and sailing whaleboat adaptation designed by George Palmer. This vessel had a straight keel and an external cork fender, as well as 12 internal air cases that rose to the height of the gunwale; she was purported to be self-righting. Shallow in draught at 1ft 3in (0.4m), she was also relatively lightweight, resulting in a lifeboat that was easily rowed and could be launched from a beach. Although somewhat limited in self-bailing qualities (a concept which had yet to catch on), she became quite popular within the Institution and was later adapted as the standard design built until 1852.

Another design adopted by the RNLI in the early years was that of Mr Pellew Plenty. Even smaller than Palmer's craft, at around 24ft (7.3m) in length, this vessel was compared to a Norfolk wherry but according to Methley the comparison was probably 'used merely in its generic sense to mean a light, open boat used for both rowing and sailing' as a wherry is essentially a shallow-draught river or canal boat, not suitable for heavy weather.[219] Plenty's boat was exceptionally beamy at 8ft (2.4m) and, quite uniquely, had cork cemented externally along the entire length of the bottom for extra buoyancy and as a protective buffer for groundings, both intentional and unintentional. She was not self-righting, although she did incorporate some self-bailing features, having six scuppers. Although a step in the right direction, this limited self-bailing capacity was still not entirely adequate for the purpose. It seems that the design did not gain as much favour with the early lifeboatmen as that of Palmer. It should be noted that both the Palmer and the Plenty types also carried a small stormsail for stability purposes.

The fortunes of Sir William's Shipwreck Institution dwindled after 1828. For a variety of reasons, both economic and political, support for the organisation fell to such an extent that, by the fiscal year 1849-50, only £354 in donations were raised. Lifeboat development also came to a standstill, although there were notable exceptions in some of the local societies. The non-self-righting, pulling and sailing lifeboats constructed for the Liverpool Docks Trust would eventually be adapted by and constructed for the RNLI after the merger of the two organisations in 1894, and would be fitted out as one of the Institution's first MLBs (see Chapter II-12).

On 4 December 1849 the brig *Betsy* ran afoul of the Herd Sand, the same infamous shoal that had claimed the hapless crew of the *Adventure* more than 60 years earlier. This time, however, efforts were made to assist those onboard the stricken vessel. A crew of 24 local pilots set out in the Shields-type lifeboat. The consequences were disastrous. The lifeboat flipped end-over-end and her entire crew was tossed into the sea. Only four of the men returned to shore alive (see Chapter I-13). Once again nautical disaster became the catalyst for change and the fuel for rekindling public sympathy. Algernon, Fourth Duke of Northumberland, also known as 'The Sailor Duke' because of his Royal Navy background and appointment as First Lord of the Admiralty, became the second President of the Institution. He immediately began the process of rebuilding the organisation. First and foremost, from the perspective of lifeboat development, the Duke recognised that progression had to be made in the field of lifeboat design. A safer, more standardised craft was needed to avoid future lifeboat disasters. Even before he became President he initiated a competition for the most promising lifeboat design. The Duke of Northumberland Award offered 100 guineas and designer's models had to be forwarded to the Surveyor's Office of the British Admiralty by February 1851. An incredible 280 models were received from all over Britain as well as from the United States, France and The Netherlands – all of which were to be reviewed by a panel of experts. Unlike the earlier competition solicited by the Gentlemen of the Lawe House, the committee for the Duke of Northumberland Award had specific guidelines or, as we might call them today, a statement of requirements for the parameters of the ideal lifeboat. Points would be awarded based on the following prescribed design characteristics:

Qualities as a rowing boat in all weathers...
20 points.
Qualities as a sailing boat...   *18 points.*
Qualities as a sea-boat – as stability, safety, buoyancy forward for launching through a surf etc...   *10 points.*
Small internal capacity for water up to level of thwarts...   *9 points.*

Means of freeing boat of water readily... 8 points.
Extra buoyancy; its nature, amount, distribution, & mode of application...   *7 points.*
Power of self-righting...   *6 points.*
Suitableness for beaching...   *4 points.*
Room for and power of carrying passengers...
3 points.
Moderate rate of transport along shore...3 points.
Protection of injury to bottom...   *3 points.*
Ballast as iron (1), water (2), cork (3)...3 points.
Access to stem or stern...   *3 points.*
Timber heads for securing warps to...   *2 points.*
Fenders, life-lines etc....   *1 point.*
Total...   *100 points.*[220]

It is interesting to note how the design characteristics were prioritised. For instance, in previous designs the 'means of freeing [the] boat of water readily' was not a primary concern. Suddenly this design characteristic was rated fifth in terms of points, above even the 'power of self-righting'. The recognition and prioritisation of the need for better self-bailing qualities in lifeboats may have been a result of the *Betsy* incident. As described, the Shields type lifeboat had flipped end-over-end, or pitch-poled, suggesting that a considerable amount of water may have been shipped on launching. Without proper rapid bailing features, the water ran to one of the vessel's ends as she was lifted by a sea, thus sending her somersaulting into oblivion.

What the Duke of Northumberland competition truly signified was an almost universal recognition in the British lifesaving community for the need of a more standardised rescue craft incorporating design features of various disparate craft. The road was thus paved for the lifeboat of the future, one whose basic features remain in use to this day – the self-righting, self-bailing (SR-SB) lifeboat. An incredible variety of designs were submitted for review. Some of the more unorthodox included a 'momentary-motion' lifeboat from Aberdeen, a series of paddle-wheel boats entered by a parson from Stowmarket, a 30ft (9.1m) craft made of 'gutta-percha' designed to be rolled out on the beach and costing only £26 to produce and an 'infallible' craft of 'whimsical construction', which was open to the sea at the bottom.[221]

One of the more interesting entries was the Tubular lifeboat designed by Henry Richardson of North Wales. It was considered too radical by the committee but Mr Richardson and his son thought otherwise. Following the competition they built a boat on their own and apparently sold her to the Portuguese government. In 1852 following two lifeboat disasters at Rhyl and Lytham, the Richardsons were able to convince the RNLI of the redeeming features of their craft and thus constructed the

40ft (12.2m) iron-tubed lifeboat *Morgan* stationed at Rhyl in 1856. Other tubular lifeboats were constructed and performed heroic rescues, being particularly well suited to shallow sandbanks owing to their wide beam and extremely shallow draught of 1ft 4in (0.4m). The later craft were constructed of wooden tubes to make them lighter and more suitable for beach launchings. The tubular boats were inherently self-bailing, as the floors between the pontoons consisted of wooden slats that allowed for free drainage of any water shipped. They were not self-righting, however, and were best suited for operations in river estuaries such as the mouths of the Dee and the Mersey. The last tubular lifeboat in the RNLI, the *Caroline Richardson*, remained in service at Rhyl until 1939.[222]

The eventual winner of the competition was a much more conservative design, more in line with the guidelines as laid down by the committee. Although still 16 points short of the 100 total, the winning entry came

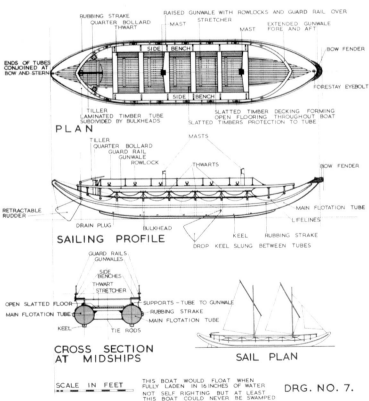

RICHARDSON'S TUBULAR LIFE-BOAT
THE DRAWING ILLUSTRATES **The Second CAROLINE RICHARDSON**
THE FIRST TUBULAR LIFE-BOAT WAS SUBMITTED FOR THE DUKE OF NORTHUMBERLAND AWARD

Richardson's Tubular Life-Boat. One of the more unique entries in the Duke's Lifeboat Competition.

Eric Fry, RNLI

from Yarmouth boatbuilder James Beeching, whose pulling and sailing design resembled a traditional whaleboat with straight stems and both ends alike. In many ways Beeching's boat looked remarkably like Greathead's original lifeboats, such as was lost at the shipwreck of the *Betsy*, but there were considerable differences. Beeching's boat had a straight, rather than rockered keel; she also had large air cases at either end and it was suggested that these be longitudinally divided to provide access to the stems; there were smaller side air-cases in the bilges; for stability, a heavy iron keel was added and 2.5 tons of water ballast could be admitted to a centreline water tank when the vessel was launched. Most important were the design's excellent self-bailing qualities, which consisted of 12 large relieving tubes that 'would rapidly free the boat of water, down to the level of her draught, which, with her crew on board, would not be less than a depth of some inches above the floor'.[223] At 36ft (11m) in length, and 9ft 6in (2.9m) beam, she was a large vessel designed to carry as many as 70 persons, with 12 oars double banked. She was rigged with a lugged foresail and mizzen, and had an innovative retractable rudder for steering. Cost of construction at the time was estimated at around £250. This was not Beeching's first attempt at designing and building lifeboats. In 1825 he had built a boat co-designed by Captain Manby, creator of the life-saving mortar, for the Norfolk Shipwreck Association. This vessel, modelled after local craft and quite similar to Lukin's Norfolk and Suffolk type, was also yawl rigged. In spite of the fact that she outsailed the *Frances Anne* in trials at Lowestoft in 1826 she never gained favour with local lifeboatmen.[224]

Although Beeching's lifeboat had won the prize, the committee felt a more comprehensive and suitable lifeboat design could be developed, incorporating the best features of Beeching's boat with some of the innovations of other entries – when it comes to lifeboat design it seems that further refinement is always a prerogative of the committee. To give evidence that further improvement could be obtained, two of Beeching's self-righting lifeboats and several crewmembers were lost in 1852 at Rhyl and Lytham. Many believed that these accidents had been caused by access doors being placed in the end cases so that they could be used for storage, resulting in the loss of the air-tight integrity and reserve buoyancy. This was further complicated by the water ballast system, which inadvertently drained through a pump hole every time the boat rolled, thus causing greater instability. However, another of Beeching's lifeboats built along the same lines as those that had been lost, for the trustees of Ramsgate harbour prior to the competition, 'was a complete success, continuing to give excellent service until

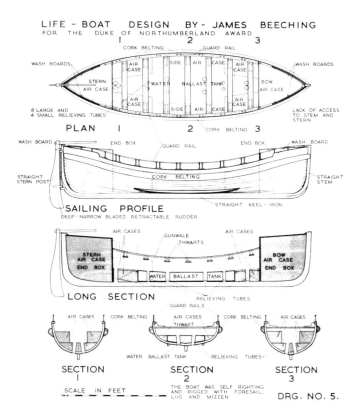

LIFE - BOAT DESIGN BY - JAMES BEECHING
FOR THE DUKE OF NORTHUMBERLAND AWARD

DRG. NO. 5.

The self-righting, self-bailing, pulling and sailing life-boat designed by James Beeching of Yarmouth, England. The winner of the Duke's 100-Guinea prize for the best design in 1851.
Eric Fry, RNLI

absolutely worn out, and saving hundreds of lives from the treachery of the Goodwins'. This suggests that local habits, such as the lack of cork life-jackets and the alteration of the original design, may have had more to do with the failure of the boats at Rhyl and Lytham than the design itself.[225]

The RNLI Committee of Management was particularly unhappy with the reliance on unsealed air chambers and the effectiveness of water ballast for inherent self-righting. Motivated by the 1852 losses, they commissioned master shipwright James Peake of HM Dockyard at Woolwich, also a committee member, to construct a lifeboat incorporating the best points of all the models. Peake's pulling and sailing SR-SB lifeboat, like Beeching's, was based on a whaleboat design, but used no water ballast. The earliest version was much smaller and lighter than Beeching's, at 30ft (9.1m) LOA and pulling only 10 oars. The new boat was more amenable to the entire coast as it could be more readily transported. The design had the same pronounced air cases at either

end but they were permanently sealed and purposely shaped to allow through access to within 2ft (0.6m) of stem and stern. Like Plenty's lifeboat, extensive cork flotation was placed along the bottom of the boat, only this time it was fixed internally, and the air cases below the floor were also filled with cork, all providing about 3 tons (3.06 tonnes) of additional buoyancy. The self-bailing capabilities were expanded through tubes 'fitted with self-acting valves, which open downwards only, so that they will allow any water shipped to pass downwards, whilst

The committee reviewing the various lifeboat designs entered in the Duke of Northumberland's competition were not entirely satisfied with the overall merit of the winning design. As a result they set about designing a new lifeboat that would combine the best features of all the competition entries. James Peake, one of the committee members and a master shipwright at HM Dockyard, Woolwich, penned the new design, later referred to as the Peake-type lifeboat. It was most notable for its sealed air-cases which allowed access to either end-post and the reverse-sheer evident at either end.
Eric Fry, RNLI

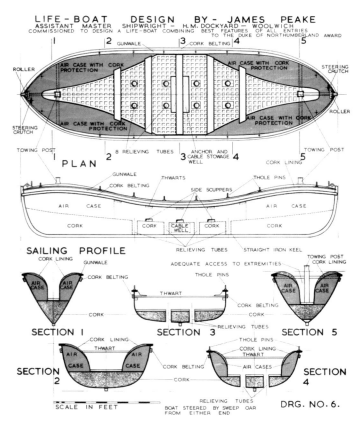

LIFE - BOAT DESIGN BY - JAMES PEAKE
ASSISTANT MASTER SHIPWRIGHT - H.M. DOCKYARD - WOOLWICH
COMMISSIONED TO DESIGN A LIFE-BOAT COMBINING BEST FEATURES OF ALL ENTRIES
TO THE DUKE OF NORTHUMBERLAND AWARD

DRG. NO. 6.

none beyond a trifling leakage can pass upwards through them'.[226] For the first time, self-righting and self-bailing tests were conducted on every new lifeboat prior to going into service. Peake's design re-righted itself from an inverted state in an astonishing five seconds and, when filled to the gunwales with water, could free itself in 55 seconds. Further refinements included making the SR-SB lifeboat even smaller at 27ft (8.2m), averaging around 2 tons (2.04 tonnes) in weight. Requiring smaller crews – averaging between six to eight oars, double-banked – and being suitable for more remote locations where large crews were not always available.

As a result of the competition – the best designs from which were exhibited at the Great Exhibition of 1851 in London – and the subsequent revival of the lifesaving institution in Britain, the new Peake-type lifeboats would not only become quite popular throughout the country but overseas as well, as the RNLI began to spread its positive influence around the globe. Lifeboats were purchased by the Prussian Government where they were called Peakeschen boats, and several more were built in the British Colony of Australia.[227] The first of the Peake lifeboats was given to the Duke of Northumberland who had a further three constructed, as well as one of Beeching's boats, to be placed at various locations throughout the British Isles.

The RNLI were pleased that the designs of both Beeching and Peake had included the necessary self-righting and self-bailing properties, but still felt that further refinements could be made. From these refinements would evolve the Standard Self-Righting lifeboat of the RNLI (see drawing in Chapter II-1 p.83). So successful was this design that, by 1899, of the RNLI's 290 boats, 237 were of this class.[228] Known as the Standard Self-Righter, this vessel had much finer lines than previous self-righting lifeboats, and varied in size according to the needs of the location in which they were placed. They ranged from 34 to 45ft (10.4 to 13.7m) in length. They were pulling and sailing boats with an iron drop keel to assist in the latter.

The standard had now been set for many years to come: large sealed air-cases at either end and along the sides, integral water ballast to assist in self-righting and ample relieving tubes for self-bailing, all placed in a heavier package than previous self-righters. Finally a compromise had been reached between the cork-like surfboat and the larger more stable offshore lifeboat. Refinements to the design would be made over the next few decades. It would seem that the proponents of the self-righter had won out, but within a few years the issue would again become a point for debate within the institution.

In 1886 one of the most infamous disasters in the history of coastal lifesaving occurred when 27 lifeboatmen were lost in one day while trying to rescue the crew of the German barque *Mexico*. Three Standard Self-Righters departed into the fury of the gale, and only one returned intact (see Chapter I-13). In the wake of this shocking calamity, the benefits of self-righting would be seriously questioned. One of the problems was that self-righting capabilities had been based on lightship calculations – that is, calculated based on the weight of the boat minus the lifesaving gear, oars, sails and people. From 1887

A 'Peakeschen' type lifeboat of the German Life-Saving Service, the DGzRS.
Author's Collection

onward, stability calculations were based on the vessel being fully loaded, with ballast tanks full and all sail set, the foresheet being free. Then adjustments were made to the standard design to even further enhance self-righting capabilities: the end air cases were made even larger, the drop keel was made heavier, and the beam was decreased.[229]

In spite of the modifications, the non-self-righting camp had re-established itself within the Institution. They advocated larger, more stable, unsinkable boats. As a result, in 1887, the Committee of the RNLI hired George Lennox Watson as a consultant naval architect to design a larger non-self-righting lifeboat. G.L. Watson was world renowned for his designs, which included the Royal Yacht *Britannia*. It was his strong belief that two types of lifeboats were needed in the RNLI fleet: the small inshore carriage-launched lifeboat, which by the very nature of working in the surf needed to be inherently self-righting; and the larger offshore boats, which needed to be beamier and more stable, and thus unsinkable, rather than 'uncapsizable'. It would be this train of thought that would rule the drawing boards of the RNLI for more than 50 years.

Early development of pulling and sailing rescue craft in continental Europe had also begun at this time. The Dutch lifeboat societies took a somewhat different approach based on the demands of their geography – long, low-lying beaches, and extensive offshore shallows and sand bars. The English lifeboats, although suitable for certain parts of The Netherlands where the water was deep enough for launching, were too heavy and deep for most areas. That said, lifeboats adapted from the English Standard Self-Righting type were used, and were similarly described as being approximately 34ft (10.4m) long with end and side air-cases, containing eight relieving tubes and also having a water-ballast system and a heavy iron keel, being double-diagonally planked and rigged with a mast and lugsail. For most of their coastline however, the Dutch preferred a lighter surfboat of common local design and usage, which they adapted and altered into a lifesaving craft. The boats became known as Strand lifeboats and were generally described as follows:

They are 27 feet, 8 inches long by 8 foot beam [8.4m x 2.4m], with a straight keel, high rounded stem and stern, and good sheer. They are provided with air-cases at either end and along the sides, and with eight relieving tubes to free the surplus of water. The planking is of teak, and stem and stern posts of oak. The boats are unsinkable and self-emptying, and have thwarts for six rowers. An unusual adjunct, and one which is seldom met with in any other country, is the reservoir of oil at either end, to be used for the purpose of smoothing the surf.[230]

It is important to mention the development of these first Dutch surfboats, as similar designs would be adopted by other emerging lifesaving societies in neighbouring countries with the same low-lying coastlines, such as Belgium, Denmark and Germany.

The Wreck of the Steamship *Admella*

As rescue organisations began to flourish after 1850, particularly in continental Europe and in the British colonies, the RNLI received increasing orders for the best available design of SR-SB lifeboat. As a result, many of James Peake's lifeboats were built in Britain for use overseas, while still more were constructed abroad. The following story describes a rescue conducted by one of the Australian Peake boats, based out of Portland, Victoria, in 1859, just a year after its launch (see Part IV).

The SS *Admella* was an iron cargo and passenger ship named after her principal trading ports of Adelaide, Melbourne and Launceston, Australia. In the early morning of 5 August 1859, in the midst of the southern winter, she had departed Port Adelaide for Melbourne with 113 passengers and crew on board as well as a cargo of copper, wheat and 'race horses'. The sea conditions were such that the captain became concerned for the welfare of the horses (one wonders about the passengers) and he altered course closer to shore. This fateful decision, combined with a stronger than average onshore current, resulted in the *Admella* violently striking a reef near Carpenter's Rocks about a mile off the South Australian shore. Almost immediately, the ship broke into three pieces, with the midships section falling into deeper water, taking more than 30 people along with it. As it turned out, these individuals may have been the more fortunate ones.

Most of the 70 or more remaining people stayed huddled together on the separated fore and aft sections, which were both constantly awash in the storm-driven seas. Others perished in valiant but ill-fated attempts to reach shore. At one point a line was connected between the two sections and many made the trip to the more stable after part of the ship; others were washed off the rope. Families were separated and, within a few hours, those who were left on the fore-section met their fate when it broke up and fell into the sea. Ships went by both at night and day, but the rockets failed and no one could hear their cries. Finally, on the second day, several men reached the shore on a make-shift raft and got word to the authorities. It would be only a matter of hours before news spread in the local area and people showed up on the shore, but the seas were too fierce to launch any small boats. For those unfortunates who remained on the God-forsaken reef with almost no food and water, help would not arrive until a week after their initial striking.

As any attempts at rescue with conventional small boats, including a lighthouse keeper's gig and one of the ship's own lifeboats that had washed ashore, failed, the authorities dispatched the steamer *Lady Bird* towing behind her the newly constructed Peake type lifeboat from Portland, over 200 miles (320km) from the disaster. It was hoped that the new lifeboat might succeed where others had failed. Upon arrival the following Friday, only 22 people remained on the *Admella*. The *Lady Bird* shot two lines towards the wreck but they failed to attach. On the lifeboat's first attempt, Coxswain Fawthrop and his crew were almost lost when an immense sea swamped the boat breaking six of the oars and smashing the rudder. But the boat remained upright and the men were able to return safely to the *Lady Bird*. A second attempt was made that day and, once again, the lifeboat was beaten back. They had to wait until the following day to make another approach and this time the crew was able to get a line onboard the stern section of the stricken *Admella* and haul 18 survivors onboard. Four others would be rescued by the lighthouse keeper in his gig and the ship's lifeboat – both vessels would either be swamped or capsized but with the loss of only one of the survivors.

CHAPTER 9

Early American Surfboats and Lifeboats

Of course, it was not only in Europe that people were becoming interested in developing better types of rescue craft. Lifesaving organisations began to appear all over the world. Across the Atlantic other unique developments in design and construction were taking place. As in Britain and The Netherlands, perspectives on the type and style of craft best suited for rescue work tended to sway towards local favourites. With the creation of the Massachussetts Humane Society in 1785 came the birth of organised coastal lifesaving in America. The first lifeboat station, established at Cohasset, Massachussetts, in 1807, used a whaleboat of local design and construction. For lack of any contradictory material, it would appear that until the 1830s any rescue craft built for this Society was like the Cohasset lifeboat, a conventional craft best suited to deal with the prevailing conditions.

The early lifesavers along the coasts of Massachussetts, New Jersey and Long Island faced problems similar to their counterparts in the lowland countries of Europe: long stretches of beach and extensive sandbanks that ran for miles along the coast, although generally not far offshore, and which formed almost impenetrable lines of breakers – natural death-traps for countless ships. Shipwrecks generally occurred within sight of the shore. Lightweight, highly manoeuvrable, well-built and shallow-draughted boats were needed. The wreckers, salvagers and local fishermen used what were locally referred to as surfboats. In part these owed their origins to Swedish immigrants to South Jersey and were characterised by 'lapstrake hulls with a generous sheer, a narrow flat bottom with no keel, a pointed bow, and a square "raked" stern'.[231]

In 1848, following an Act of Congress that provided the first funding for the creation of government-sponsored lifesaving facilities for New Jersey, a Committee was established to review the needs of the new stations and, in particular, the type of boat best suited for the area. Led by Captain Douglas Ottinger of the Revenue Marine, and Major Henry Wardell, a recognised expert on shipwrecks and surfboats associated with the New York Board of Underwriters, a group of 'intelligent and experienced surfmen' from the New Jersey shore were canvassed for their opinions. Not surprisingly they chose the boat known as the New Jersey Surfboat. The construction contract was awarded to Joseph Francis who owned the Novelty Iron Works in Brooklyn, New York. The boats were to be built as closely as possible to the prescribed design of surfboat but, according to Francis's recommendations, the hull was to be of corrugated iron with a wooden bottom. The reasoning behind the use of metal was that, being a voluntary service, there was no regimen in place for either maintaining or operating the boats on a consistent basis. It was felt that a wooden boat, which might be out of the water for considerable periods, would dry out in the seams and would leak considerably upon entering the water; there was also the problem associated with dry rot and decay in the rather primitive boathouses.

Joseph Francis was born in 1801 and spent almost his entire adult life developing and working on equipment for rescue at sea. Even as a child his inventive personality shone through when he constructed a small boat at his uncle's shipyard, to which he added cork for extra buoyancy.[232] Francis also recognised the need to keep a lifeboat's weight to a minimum, as was preferred by the surfmen of the local societies and government stations. He also realised that what the American surfboat sacrificed in weight, it also sacrificed in strength. He believed that lighter weight and strength of hull could be achieved by building a lifeboat out of moulded sheets of corrugated galvanised iron riveted together. Francis also placed air cases on either end of the craft providing a certain degree of self-righting capability, although the original vessels were not self-bailing.[233]

Francis's 'metallic lifeboat' (or surfboat), otherwise known as the Francis type, would gradually fall from favour at home, but was quite successful elsewhere in the world. The early state-run lifeboat service of Prussia purchased several of Francis's boats, which were highly suitable for the surf and shallows of the North Sea. They continued to make modifications to the type, eventually creating what become known as the 'German' lifeboat, a derivation of the original Francis craft, and also constructed of steel. A Francis lifeboat was also purchased by the Portuguese Government in 1852 for use at Oporto, and was named the *Valente*.[234] Canada, then known as British North America, also used the metallic lifeboat quite successfully. Four of the craft were donated through the concerted efforts of Boston philanthropist and humanitarian, Dorothea Dix (see Chapter I-14 and Part IV).[235]

An early American lifesaving crew hauling a traditional wooden surfboat.
USCG

The first metallic lifeboats built for the New Jersey stations and the Massachussetts Humane Society, had almost the same dimensions as the chosen surfboat, being approximately 26ft 6in (8m) in length, 6ft 6in (2m) in breadth, and having a draught of just 30in (0.8m). The main difference between the traditional wooden surfboat and the metallic version was, of course, its weight. Where the cedar-planked and oak-framed traditional surfboat

weighed in the range of 900lb (408kg), the Francis version came in at 1,500lb (680kg). This added weight became one of the chief complaints of early American lifesaving crews. The lifeboats had the characteristic square Jersey-style stern, 'India rubber fenders placed outboard of their gunwales...to protect the boats when alongside a wreck', and 10 watertight compartments built into the hull. These compartments, and the ease with which the thin metal hull could puncture, were also sources of complaint, as the spaces were prone to filling with water making the craft unwieldy and dangerous to operate. Furthermore, the wooden bottoms of the original versions were prone to cracking. The next generation of Francis boats had the entire hull made of corrugated iron, with an external wooden runner on the bottom; it was considered a vast improvement.[236] These smaller and lighter versions were provided to the next stations established on the southern coast of New Jersey and Long Island in 1849 to 1850.

In spite of the metallic lifeboat's relative ease of maintenance the type still had many detractors. One of the most notable was R.B. Forbes of the Massachussetts Humane Society, who wrote:

> It has long been the opinion of our surf men that the metallic lifeboats placed by the Government on the coast of New Jersey, and those given to the Massachussetts Humane Society by the same, are practically valueless as surf-boats. The Humane Society were very glad to receive and house these boats at the time, thinking there might be cases where ships with emigrants might find them useful.[237]

In 1858 the US Congress approved funds for more lifesaving vessels, with an expressed preference for vessels of the 'self-righting' type, recently perfected in Britain. The Treasury Department convened a three-man Board of Commissioners to experiment with various types of lifesaving vessels and to recommend to the department, 'for its consideration the life-boat which may be best adapted in all its conditions for the saving of human life from shipwreck on the coast of the United States'. The commission was to recommend a boat 'most suitable for the life-saving stations on the coasts of New Jersey and New York'.[238] The trials were conducted on two separate occasions in 1858. The first took place at Spermaceti Cove Life-Saving Station, New Jersey, on 9 October where seven different boats were tested. The second evaluations took place on the Long Island shore at Fire Island, New York, on 20 October, with nine different models being tested. Francis-type metallic lifeboats were on trial at both stations and the Commission felt that...

Her great weight, the liability of her air cells to puncture or fracture (sometimes by little force, in consequence of rust), her loss of buoyancy in this condition, and liability to sink end first under her crew, are the chief objections urged by the surf-men against her. When in perfect order she is capable of rendering great service.[239]

As the best for overall use around the country the committee chose Buckman & Camp's Empire City Life-Boat. It was described as a 'self-righting and self-freeing' wooden vessel, clinkerbuilt of cedar, with air chambers at each end and under the deck, as well as a manually controlled water-ballast tank. The lifeboat was further described as being 28ft (8.5m) overall, with a 6ft 3in (1.9m) beam, 30in (0.8m) draught and weighing only 900lb (408kg). The self-freeing, or bailing, feature of the boat was created by the inclusion of 'self-acting' delivery valves. Given the relative failure of the Francis-type boats, and the government's stated preference for a self-righting lifeboat, it is not surprising that this was the boat chosen. Whether any were actually purchased and put into service is not known, however, although any plans for procurement were probably severely disrupted by the tumultuous years of the American Civil War, that were soon to follow.

For the New Jersey and New York stations the Commission reverted to the tried and true wooden surfboats of old. It recommended the selection of a lighter vessel, with lifeboat-like features incorporated, known as Bunker's Model Surfboat, which had a striking resemblance to the standard Jersey surfboat being, '...made of cedar, 3/4 inch thick [19mm]; clinker built; copper fastened and riveted, with a square stern, 3 feet wide on top [0.9m]; rows four oars; has detached air chambers at stem and stern, and one on each side under the thwarts, extending fore and aft, 9 inches in diameter and 10 feet long [0.23 x 3.1m]; weighs about 700 pounds [318kg]'.[240]

The Commission's report then goes on to describe an added benefit of the smaller, lighter vessel in the context of the early American lifesaving stations, and the limited availability of manpower.

This boat possesses great buoyancy, lightness and strength; her model makes her peculiarly serviceable in the surf. In connexion with a boat of greater capacity, she is calculated to meet the existing wants of the life-saving stations. The small number of men required to man her will enable a communication to be established with a wreck at times when a sufficient force is not at hand to man a boat of greater weight and capacity.[241]

The types of early lifesaving vessels in the United States had a profound effect on the type of coastal lifesaving organisation which was established. Following the Committee's decision in 1858, the metallic boats fell out of favour, and were replaced by the preferred cedar surfboats. These vessels required more constant maintenance and use to keep them watertight and ready for service. This led to the introduction of paid surfmen at the government stations, beginning as early as 1869. In addition, the extra costs of a paid service meant that it was fiscally prudent to keep the rescue vessels somewhat smaller than conventional lifeboats, as smaller boats meant smaller crews (see Chapter I-16).

In 1871 the United States Life-Saving Service was established and Sumner Kimball, then head of the Revenue Marine, set up another commission, 'consisting of officers of the Treasury and Navy and experienced beachmen', to evaluate boats and equipment. Trials were conducted at Seabright, New Jersey, in May 1872. Once again the commission found that:

While firmly believing that metallic boats are best adapted for the service required, we are of the opinion that some advantage may arise from the use of wood, and would state that the self-bailing apparatus can be applied to such boats as readily as to those constructed of or from iron, and that when protected from swamping surf-men would be enabled to go to sea in weather when no ordinary boat could live for a moment.

While at Seabright, on the 27th, we conversed with nearly all of the surf-men present at the trial of the life-saving apparatus, and found that without exception they considered the self-bailing, or emptying principle of great importance, and that, if applied to their cedar boats, the greatest obstacle to a passage through the surf would be removed.[242]

The commission also felt that a surfboat should be placed at almost every station in the new service, as it was well suited and adaptable to almost all conditions.

From the limited examinations we were able to make, we were convinced of the superiority of the cedar boats over any other for general service on the coast of New Jersey. That these boats have been found by the long experience of practical surf-men to be the best adapted for any sort of work in the surf, is sufficient argument in their favour, without more then a passing allusion to the fact that these men could never be induced to use any of the boats of different shape supplied to the stations since their first establishment. Therefore we recommend that a boat of similar model be placed at every station.[243]

A USLSS Beebe-McLellan self-bailing, pulling surfboat. This boat was built in large numbers for the USLSS and was preferred by many surfmen over the much heavier, self-righting lifeboat. *USCG*

Several variations of standard surfboat types would be adopted for the service, including, but not limited to, the Jersey type, as well as the Excelsior, Monomoy and Beebe style of surfboats. By the 1880s alterations had been made to the traditional design. Almost all the rescue surfboats had a small keel and the flat-transom stern had been replaced by a double-ended one with equal sheer at either end. By 1890 the only surfboats being used by the USLSS were the Beebe and the Higgins & Gifford types, as well as a newer version of the former, known as the Beebe-McLellan type, which incorporated the self-bailing features requested by the members of the 1872 commission.

Like almost all surfboats the standard Beebe-McLellan was not self-righting. Instead, it was considered insubmergible, with a water-ballast system and side air cases. This stout little craft was an excellent self-bailer and was designed so that its deck would be above the waterline when loaded to full capacity with crew and survivors, thus allowing shipped water to depart via six square tubes on either side of its keel. There was even a self-righting version, of which very few were built, with high air cases at either end, much like a small lifeboat. Apparently these self-righting prototypes did not gain favour with the surfmen of the USLSS, who preferred the combination of a lighter, more stable, non-self-righting version, and opted to take their chances with the oft-practiced manual re-right. The manual re-righting of the surfboat could be an extremely arduous task given the environment in which the crews operated, and many a surfman was lost in the process. Nevertheless, the crews practiced the drill on a weekly basis in all conditions. At the Louisiana Purchase Exposition at St Louis in 1904, a USLSS surfboat crew was able to carry out a full capsize drill in less time than it took a larger SR lifeboat to re-right itself.[244]

The standard Beebe-McLellan surfboat was 25ft 4in (7.7m) in length and weighed about 1,300lb (590kg). According to one of its designers, Lieutenant C.H. McLellan, a man who would go on to make further significant inroads in lifeboat development in years to come, the double-ended, self-bailing design had significant advantages over the old square-transom surfboats. It shipped less water and, with the self-bailing feature, allowed the rowers to remain at one of the 12 pulling stations rather than having to bail by hand. According to McLellan, so successful was the design that by the turn of the century around 200 of the type were stationed throughout the country and, he added, the 'men

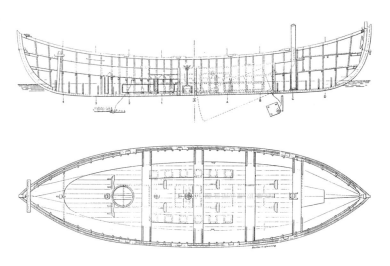

The USLSS Beebe-McLellan surfboat. *USCG*

of one crew on the New Jersey coast, who have made some of the most perilous rescues, declare, that if they had to go back to their old open boat, they would leave the service'.[245]

At many locations, however, it was felt that, in addition to the venerable surfboat, a larger, longer-range vessel was required. To this end the USLSS began to look at the proven design of the Standard Self-Righting lifeboat of the RNLI. Wisely recognising the decades of development that had gone into the type, they purchased one of the vessels in 1873. This new boat, which became known as the 'English lifeboat' or, simply, the lifeboat, gradually gained acceptance, particularly on the Great Lakes and at

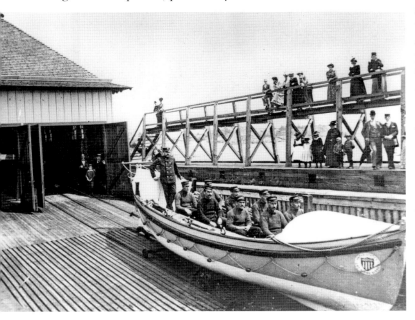

A USLSS crew at Marquette, Michigan, ready to launch in an 'English' type self-righting, self-bailing, pulling and sailing lifeboat similar to the one purchased from the RNLI in 1872. These boats were used extensively on the Great Lakes and at locations where greater distances needed to be traversed to attend a wreck. *USCG*

the Pacific stations. It became the design seed for a long line of American lifeboats and motor lifeboats (MLBs) well into the next century. The original vessel was 30ft (9.1m) long, but future US-built models were generally about 26ft (7.9m). In all some 77 American lifeboats would be built for the USLSS from 1876 to 1897, with 64 of them serving on the Great Lakes, seven on the Atlantic, and four on the Pacific.[246] The original 1873 English lifeboat has been preserved, and remains on display at the Mariner's Museum in Newport News, Virginia.

The Americans also sought to develop a compromise design between the popular lightweight surfboat and the heavier lifeboat. The solution was invented by David Porter Dobbins, a District Superintendent who designed a smaller, lighter version that could be manually launched through the surf. The Dobbins Pattern lifeboat, as it became known, was self-righting and self-bailing, weighed anywhere from 1,600lb (725kg) to 1 ton (1,016kg), and varied in length from 24 to 30ft (7.3 to 9.1m). It was very popular on the Great Lakes and on the Pacific Coast, where the combination of a heavier 'surfboat-like' lifeboat was well suited to face the harsh bar and beach conditions. Both the Beebe-McLellan surfboats, and the Dobbins lifeboats were also widely used by the Canadian Government's lifesaving stations, starting a tradition in that country of using primarily American-designed rescue craft. The Canadian version of the Dobbins type was described as 'a heavy self-righting lifeboat about 25 feet [7.6m] in length. Fitted with a full set of oars, airtanks at the ends, and outside rudder with yokes and lines...'.[247] The Dobbins boats were also self-bailing, using a series of hinged scuppers at deck level, rather than traditional relieving tubes. However, it appears that, because of their weight, draught and high freeboard, the Dobbins lifeboats were not very popular at the Atlantic stations in either the United States and Canada. By 1914 they were generally no longer in use in either country.[248] Eventually they were replaced by newer versions of the Beebe-McLellan surfboat. In Canada, some of the self-righting versions of the surfboat were introduced, which, in the earliest days of mechanisation, were fitted with small 8-hp internal-combustion engines.

USLSS Dobbins lifeboat on surf drill off the Coquille River life-saving station, Oregon, c.1900. These boats combined the lightweight characteristics of a surfboat with the tendencies of a larger lifeboat, and were most popular at Pacific coast stations. *USCG*

Rescue by Surfboat, Point Allerton, Massachussetts

The following tale is drawn from the first Annual Report of the USLSS, published in 1888. It serves as an excellent example of just how effective surfboats could be when in the hands of capable surfmen.

On 25 November 1888 a storm was rising to hurricane force and Keeper James realised that 'business' was coming his way. Many vessels were attempting to regain safe haven or trying to ride out the storm in the roadstead off Nantusket, southeast of Boston. James wasted no time in mustering his crew from the best of the local fishermen. By afternoon, the schooner *Cox and Green* had been driven ashore and her crew found themselves helpless in the mounting surf. The seas were of such ferocity that James felt it best to first attempt a rescue by line-throwing apparatus. A line was shot and, within a short time, all the crew were transferred ashore by breeches-buoy.

Similar scenarios were now occurring all around. The coal-schooner *Gertrude Abbott* was on the rocks and flying distress signals less than a mile to the east. The lifesavers immediately set off down the beach and discovered the wreck too far offshore for the line-throwing apparatus to be effective. Hurricane-driven seas were creating an impenetrable wall of surf and it was getting dark. James decided it was best to wait for a lower tide before launching the surfboat. A signal fire was lit to provide a small measure of reassurance for those unfortunates on the schooner. It was soon realised that the storm was only increasing and that the only chance was to make a rescue attempt sooner rather than later. According to the *Annual Report*, 'Captain James warned his crew that they would probably never return alive from this desperate rescue.... All the men stepped forward to volunteer.'

The surfboat crew somehow mounted the breakers, although two of the crew had to release their oars and bail to keep the boat from swamping. Upon arrival, the eight sailors on the *Gertrude Abbott* swung off ropes suspended from the wreck and were grabbed by those aboard the surfboat. But the trials of the rescuers had only just begun. The conditions were now so frenzied that the surfmen could not control the direction of their boat. All they could do was head somewhat towards the shore, and concentrate on keeping the vessel upright. Close to the beach they struck a rock. The surfboat was stove, but did not capsize; the passengers and crew shifted to the windward side and kept the damaged part of the hull above water. One man was lost overboard but was quickly recovered. Now totally out of control, the surfboat crashed along a series of rocks and reefs at the mercy of the elements. Keeper James advised all onboard to remain with the boat as long as possible. Fortunately, the vessel met its final demise much closer to shore, whence all were somehow able to scramble to the beach.

One of the most famous lifesavers in American history, Joshua James served with both the Massachusetts Humane Society and later the USLSS for 60 of his 74 years. He is shown here wearing both Congressional and MHS life-saving medals. *USCG*

In spite of their fatigue, James and his men continued patrolling through the night. At 3am the wreck of the schooner *Bertha F. Walker* was sighted further down the coast. There were seven men clinging to her rigging in driving rain and sleet. James ordered a second surfboat brought up, hauled by horse and carriage four miles overland to the wreck site. With several fresh crewmembers he again drove out into the fury of the storm and somehow retrieved the men from the *Bertha F. Walker*, returning them safely to shore.

Still the carnage was far from over. On the beach, a messenger was waiting to advise James of two further wrecks. One was the schooner *H.C. Higginson*, which was being assisted by both the crew of the USLSS Station at North Scituate and another from the MHS. Lines had been shot and one made fast to the wreck but it was soon fouled. Joshua James and his crew set off. Twice they struck a rock and were holed and, in spite of 45 minutes of almost super-human effort, they failed to make it; they were forced to return to shore. Exhausted but undaunted, James had the surfboat patched and went out yet again. This time they were successful and the schooner's crew of five were returned to shore.

Now there was another wreck, the *Mattie E. Eaton*; this time all James and his men had to do was help her crew ashore – she had been blown safely past the surf-line. The night was almost over, but not quite. While James and his crew were returning to the station, battered and bruised from their incredible exploits, they chanced upon the sixth and final wreck of the storm, the brigantine *Alice*, whose crew had already been saved. Onboard, however, were two would-be salvage men who had wasted no time in taking advantage of the tempest's spoils. They had stayed too long and were now trapped by the tide and the sea. With little or no idea of what James and his crew had been through in the previous 12 hours, they happily boarded the agile surfboat and were returned to the safety of the beach.

Joshua James won both a Congressional Gold Medal, and a Gold Medal from the MHS for his efforts in 1888 and would carry out many other daring rescues in his long career with both the MHS and the USLSS. On 19 March 1902, at the age of 74 and while still a keeper at the USLSS Station at Point Allerton, Massachussetts, Joshua James returned from surf drill and, commenting to his crew that 'the tide is ebbing', stepped from the bow of the surfboat and fell dead at his post of duty; a fitting end for a venerable surfman. [249]

CHAPTER 10

Steam-Powered Lifeboats

When the concept of steam-generated power was still in its infancy, people were advocating its use on lifesaving vessels. One of the original supporters of the idea was Sir William Hillary. In September 1824 he wrote and published a pamphlet entitled, *A Plan for the Construction of a Steam Life-Boat, Also for the Extinguishment of Fire at Sea*, in which he expressed ideas that were decades ahead of their time and some of which would eventually become reality. He predicted that the steam lifeboat would have to be somewhat larger than the conventional pulling and sailing boat in order to provide space for the machinery; that it would have to be self-bailing, and that a power windlass and capstan could be attached. All were features

Demonstrating the RNLB *Duke of Northumberland* to dignitaries at Harwich in the 1890s. She was the world's first steam-powered lifeboat as well as the first lifesaving vessel to use water-jets for propulsion.
RNLI

of the first steam lifeboat built 64 years later. Quite intuitively, Sir William hypothesised that 'The important point will consist in ascertaining the smallest size vessel calculated to receive an engine that, in proportion to her bulk, would have a commanding power over her'.[250] The reality was, however, that the primitive state of steam technology in the first half of the 19th Century rendered the earliest engines too large for practical use on small vessels such as lifeboats. In addition, the reliability and efficiency of such early engines and their boilers were very suspect. It would be some time before such issues were addressed and, even then, the concept of steam propulsion on lifeboats would have its detractors.

In 1851 Captain John Washington, RN, a member of the Committee that published the report for the Duke of Northumberland's design competition, had the following comments to make:

> *Remington of Warkworth, boldly proposes the use of steam, and Coryton of atmospheric air as a moving power. The time may come when steam may be so under control as to be made directly applicable to a lifeboat (and in the form of a steam tug it is already of great use, and might be much more used with advantage), but for the present the Committee do not feel that they should be warranted in recommending any other propeller than oars.*[251]

Both inventors mentioned by Washington had entered plans in the competition. Remington's design was a screw-propelled lifeboat, approximately 40ft (12.2m) long, propelled by a 10-hp steam engine. Given the low horsepower of this early engine compared to its relative size and weight and the complications of installing it, it is not surprising that the committee saw no merit in its application. The atmospheric boat was even stranger. Designed by an inventor named Erskine, it was propelled by 'New pinion wheels and a self-acting syphon pump', which was probably akin to the 'caloric-drive' engine promoted by Swedish-American inventor John Ericsson around the same time. Another lifeboat was purported to be mechanically propelled by a hand crank that turned a propeller. All such ideas were rejected.

By the 1870s steam engines had become much smaller, more efficient and more powerful. Steam pinnaces and launches were becoming quite common sights and, once again, people in Britain were advocating the use of steam in lifeboats. Still, the powers that be felt quite strongly that it had no practical application in coastal lifesaving. In 1871 an article was written in the 1 August edition of the RNLI's journal, *The Life-Boat*, entitled 'Steam Life-Boats'. It was probably written by then Secretary of the Institution,

Sir Richard Lewis, as it quite closely reflects comments that he makes in his very informative book, *History of the Life-Boat, and Its Work*, published three years later. The article responds to the contemporary advocates of steam propulsion by outlining a potential benefit. A steam lifeboat, the writer argues, would be safer in that there would no longer be a need to place upwards of 20 men in peril on a heavy-weather rescue, as was the case with the traditional pulling and sailing boats, for the boat would require a crew of only four. That said, however, the specialised crew would be a radical departure from the Institution's previous manning structure, as a full-time engineer and firemen would be required. In addition, the appropriate mechanical training required for such crew would be far beyond the previous prerequisites for the traditional lifeboat crew, which primarily consisted of excellent boat-handling and seamanship skills together with knowledge of the local marine environment. It could not be expected that the lifeblood of the fleet, the local fishermen and boatmen, could man and operate such a vessel. It was also deemed that such vessels would be far too large for carriage launching, that the violence of the seas in which such a boat would be expected to operate would extinguish the fires, and that this, combined with the shallow draught necessary for working alongside wrecks and in shoal waters, would render the propellers useless as they would be prone to 'racing' once they came out of the water. The problems associated with a steam-driven lifeboat were thus considered 'insurmountable' and the idea was put to rest for the next several years.[252]

The article did, however, share the opinion of the 1851 Committee, that the use of steam tugs to tow pulling and sailing lifeboats to the scene of the disaster, thus limiting the fatigue and saving the energies of the crew, was of paramount importance. This was particularly vital at some locations where wrecks occurred a considerable distance offshore and where steam tugs could lie afloat, and 'co-locate' with a traditional lifeboat. This method of mutual assistance in lifesaving had been utilised for decades and, in the future, the Institution would commission the construction of a steam tug of its own.

The loss of two lifeboats and 26 men in 1886 not only had a profound effect on the design of British rescue craft with the resurgence of the non-self-righting lifeboat, it also served to revive the question of whether mechanised propulsion would have made a difference in the outcome? In the year following the wreck of the *Mexico*, the committee of the Institution, spurred on by G.L. Watson, decided to hold a third competition for the best design of lifeboat, this time mechanically propelled, and '...resolved to offer a gold and silver medal for drawings or models of a mechanically propelled life-boat best adapted to meet the conditions under which life-boats are called upon to perform their work…'.[253] Although several designs and models were submitted and publicly demonstrated at the Liverpool Exhibition of 1887, a verdict was never made and an award never granted. Once again a lifeboat-design review committee exercised its prerogative. Almost all the Institution's coxswains felt that the best use of steam rested with the co-working of pulling and sailing lifeboats and steam-powered tugs and so rested the opinions of the panel.

The decision was short-lived, however, for that same year the boatbuilding firm of R & H Green of Blackwall presented an alteration to their original competition design. It appeared to address some of the 'insurmountable' concerns of the committee – principally the potential racing and the physical protection of the propellers. In 1888 the RNLI ordered the construction of the first steam-driven lifeboat (SLB) from Messrs. Green; it would incorporate what was described as a 'hydraulic' propulsion system. In truth, the hydraulic system was really an early version of the modern water-jet drive so common on many of today's rescue craft. The idea was that the steam engines would drive a turbine, which pumped sea water inducted through a scoop on the bottom of the craft and then transferred the water at a much higher velocity through a series of nozzles, or jets, at the ends and sides of the vessel, thus propelling it in any direction.

The first steam lifeboat ever constructed, the *Duke of Northumberland*, was launched in 1889 and, after extensive trials in 1890, was stationed at Harwich in May 1891. This prototype steam lifeboat was probably the largest purpose-built rescue craft yet built. She was 50ft (15.2m) long, 14ft 3in (4.3m) beam, and 3ft 6in (1.1m) draught. She weighed an astounding 30 tons (30.6 tonnes), and the flush-decked steel hull had 72,000 rivets, which held together 15 water-tight compartments. In addition to the jets she had a rudder and, just as Sir William Hillary had predicted, also had power on deck for a capstan and windlass. She was not self-righting, but could be heeled to an angle of 110° before losing her upright stability. In addition to the steam hydraulic propulsion system, which was driven by two Thornycroft compound steam engines mounted horizontally and putting out an estimated 170hp, she also carried two masts and sails stowed on deck. On her original trials the *Duke of Northumberland* obtained a maximum speed of 9.17kt, but her effective cruising speed was more in the vicinity of 7kt. The cost of the vessel was estimated at £5,000, and it was said that she could carry 60 to 70 passengers, 30 of whom could be seated below deck.

As proof of her seaworthiness, within weeks of entering service the *Duke of Northumberland* was

credited with saving 33 lives.[254] On 20 December 1900, while still stationed at Harwich, she was instrumental in saving lives from two vessels in the same day. The details of the rescue are quoted from Methley.

At 5.30 p.m., with a tremendous sea running and a heavy gale from the south-west, she was summoned to the assistance of the White Star liner Cufic, *which was in distress off the Skerries Rocks. She did her work magnificently, and succeeded in taking aboard forty-one persons, and bringing them safely ashore. Having returned to her moorings, she learned that the other life-boat, a self-righter, had put out to a vessel in distress, and having lost her anchor, had been obliged to return for another. At past midnight the* Duke of Northumberland *put out again, and rescued the crew of the schooner* Julia of Gloucester, *regaining her station at three o'clock in the morning after nearly ten hours' service. In his report the Hon. Secretary of the branch remarked that, since the steam life-boat had been there, she had never been out in such a sea, but in spite of it she behaved perfectly.*[255]

The SLB *Duke of Northumberland* would remain in service for 33 years, finally being decommissioned in 1923. In that period she would be launched 175 times and be responsible for saving 295 lives, a monumental record of longevity for a vessel that was the first of her kind.

Word of the success of the new steam lifeboat soon spread to other countries. In The Netherlands, the ZHRM recognised the merits of such a design for the shallow sandbanks off the southern part of the country. As a result, they ordered the next steam lifeboat from the yard of Messrs. Brown. The vessel was to be called the *President Van Heel* but, for reasons unknown, the ZHRM cancelled the contract and, ultimately, ordered a steamboat of slightly different design from the Thornycroft yard.[256] At about the same time as the first *President Van Heel* found herself without a buyer, a series of marine disasters off the coast of South Australia had the government there scrambling to reorganise its almost non-existent local lifeboat service. Robert Barr Smith, MP and local businessman in Adelaide, heard about the ownerless steam lifeboat and paid £3,500 for her out of his own pocket. He donated her to the people of the colony in 1895, under the condition that the government establish a structure to operate and maintain the vessel. Renamed the *City of Adelaide* she was stationed at Beachport, where she remained in service until 1930. Strangely there is no record of her ever being used for a

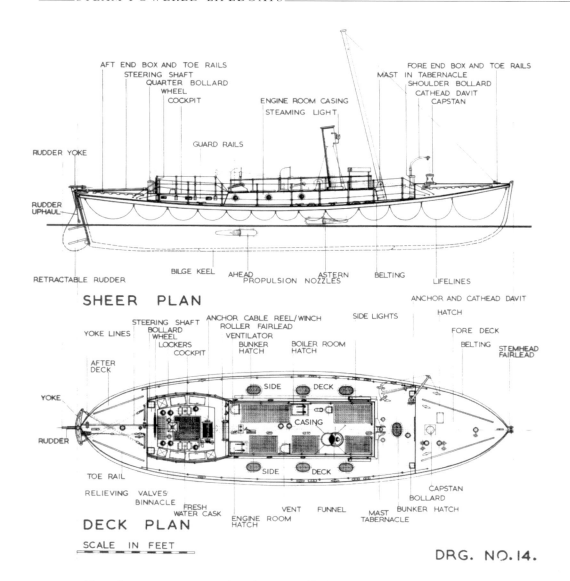

SHEER PLAN

DECK PLAN

SCALE IN FEET

DRG. NO. 14.

The RNLI's steam lifeboat *Queen*, the last SLB constructed for the RNLI and the last in service, retiring in 1924 having saved 196 lives. Note the water-jet propulsion nozzles on the lifeboat's sides. *Eric Fry, RNLI*

rescue, although one writer states that she was called out in 1911, on a service to the steamer *Time*.[257][258] The *City of Adelaide* is preserved to this day at the maritime museum in Port Lincoln, South Australia.

In 1893 the RNLI also ordered a second steam lifeboat from Messrs. Green. This vessel, christened in June 1894, was called the *City of Glasgow*, and had the same expanded dimensions and alterations as her Australian sistership. These two lifeboats, built at the same time, were 53ft (16.2m) long, with an extreme beam of 16ft (4.9m) and a draught of 3ft 1in (1m). They were also slightly heavier at 31 tons (31.62 tonnes). Their engines were of the Penn type with an increased capacity of 230hp and, instead of one horizontal turbine as in the *Duke of Northumberland,* they had two vertically-mounted turbines. It would appear that this alteration was not very successful in Britain. The *City of Glasgow*

was replaced by another steam lifeboat of the same name just seven years later having been called out 26 times and saving 26 lives.

The last water-jet-driven, steam-powered lifeboat to come out of the Green boatyard was the *Queen*, built for the RNLI and placed in service at New Brighton in 1897. The *Queen* had an experimental oil-fired boiler which does not appear to have been more efficient, as the vessel was later converted to coal, the principle fuel source of all previous steam lifeboats. G.L. Watson had a further say in the design of the lifeboat, and followed the lead taken by the Dutch in the construction of the Thornycroft version of the second *President Van Heel*, which had been launched in 1895. These vessels were even longer at 55ft (16.8m) overall, but had the same beam as the previous boats. Both boats switched back to the horizontally-mounted turbine, and the *Queen* had a quoted power range of 222hp.[259] Unlike previous steam lifeboats, both the *Queen* and the *President Van Heel* had self-bailing cockpits towards their sterns. Both vessels also maintained the hydraulic propulsion system.

Further foreign interest was shown by the fact that the '...Chief Inspectors of the French and German Life-Boat Institutions, both of whom have always shown a keen interest in the development of steam life-boats, were on board during the trials on the 25th of August'.[260] The *Queen* would remain in service at New Brighton for 27 years, finally being laid up in 1924, after having been called out on 81 rescues in which 196 lives were saved. The *President Van Heel* would be the last steam lifeboat to serve anywhere in the world, having remained operational for over 36 years, until being put out to pasture in 1931. During her long and illustrious life she was responsible for several famous rescues, including that of the *Berlin* in March 1907 (see p.118). The *President Van Heel* actually capsized in 1921, with the loss of six of her seven-man crew. But, regardless of the calamity, she was recovered and rebuilt, still favoured by her Dutch crews. By 1908, only a third of the way through her career, this fine vessel had been responsible for saving some 350 lives from shipwreck.[261] In 1909 the ZHRM would order the construction of another steam lifeboat from the Feyenoord yard in Rotterdam. Unfortunately this vessel was lost with all hands in 1929.[262]

Only three more steam-powered lifeboats were constructed for the RNLI after the launch of the *Queen* in 1897. The spread of the idea was limited because the vessels were relatively expensive to maintain, at around £800 per annum, and there were only a few locations on the coast where such a craft was actually needed. These factors, combined with the recognition that smaller and lighter internal-combustion engines were now beginning to appear as auxiliary power on small boats, meant that the costs of expensive steam lifeboats could probably no longer be justified.

In 1898 the first of the last three steam lifeboats, the *James Stevens No3* was launched. She came from a different shipyard, J. Samuel White and Co. of Cowes, on the Isle of Wight, a firm which had been associated with the Institution almost since its inception. The Samuel White yard had come up with a design modification that would replace the relatively inefficient hydraulic drive with a single large propeller recessed in a tunnel for protection from the ground. All the remaining boats were propeller driven. The length was slightly longer at 56ft 6in (17.2m) overall but, aside from the change in propulsion systems, these vessels were essentially newer versions of the second-generation boats such as the *Queen*. The engines were rated at 180hp, considerably less than the previous steam lifeboats, with the increase in efficiency of

the propeller making up for the loss in power. The *James Stevens No3* remained in service until 1928 and was the last operational steam lifeboat in Britain, having saved 54 lives in 83 call outs. The third boat constructed by the White yard, the *City of Glasgow No2*, which replaced her inefficient namesake after being launched in 1901, stayed in service at Harwich until 1917 and had an illustrious career of 99 launches, with 87 lives saved. She was the last steam lifeboat built for service in Britain. The second boat constructed at Cowes did not, unfortunately, share the longevity and success of the other two. The *James Stevens No4*, launched in 1899, was the only RNLI steam lifeboat lost at sea. In April 1900 she was rolled over by a large breaking sea near her base at Padstow, north Cornwall, with the loss of eight men.

In 1902 another steam-powered, propeller-driven lifeboat was constructed by J. Samuel White and Co., this time for use in Australia. The *Lady Forrest* arrived in Fremantle, Western Australia, in July 1903 for work as a combination pilot vessel and lifeboat. During her sea trials in the Solent, the *Lady Forrest* obtained an impressive speed of 10.126kt with her 226-hp 'inverted compound surface condensing steam' engine. This venerable steamer would lead a distinguished career. Forty-four years after her delivery, she was still in service in her original role, and, in 1946, the Fremantle Harbour Authority that operated her, said 'This vessel has given very satisfactory service ever since it was placed in commission...and at no time has there been a failure of this vessel to put to sea in the heaviest of weather'.[263]

The *Lady Forrest* had her steam power plant removed and replaced with a diesel engine in 1947, and incredibly, remained in service until hauled in 1967. In 1970 she was donated to the Western Australian Maritime Museum where she was fully restored to original condition and where she remains on public display.

The loss of the *James Stevens No4* in 1900 revived the debate in Great Britain about the effectiveness of large mechanised lifeboats as opposed to steam tugs pulling conventional lifeboats to the scene of a shipwreck. The tragedy may also have had some bearing on the Institution's decision not to construct any further steam lifeboats. Instead, the RNLI ordered the construction of their own steam-powered rescue tug, the *Helen Peele*, to be stationed at Padstow, to work in conjunction with the pulling and sailing Standard Self-Righter, the *Edmund Harvey*. The *Helen Peele* was designed by G.L. Watson and was a twin-screw vessel of 231 tons (235.62 tonnes) displacement and 95ft (29m) length. She would remain in service for 27 years, ending her days with the Institution in the Bristol Channel. Before she retired in May 1928 to carry on as a private tug on the Clyde she was the last serving British steam-driven rescue craft.[264]

The use of steam for maritime rescue craft was not limited to coastal lifeboats, of course. As was the case with the *Helen Peele*, they were widely used in ocean-going lifesaving vessels. In the United States, the cutters of the Revenue Marine were all steam-powered by the late 1800s and were used quite frequently for lifesaving work. In France, the Société Centrale de Sauvetage des Naufragés had a steam 'life-ship' stationed at Royan in 1902. This vessel, the *Amiral Lafont*, was said to be of 374 tons (381.5 tonnes) displacement and was strategically stationed so as 'to assist all distressed vessels in the wide area of the mouth of the Gironde'.[265]

The idea of a steam life-ship had been put forward in England as well. In 1886 Sir Edward Watkin, MP promoted the idea of placing such vessels at different stations around the coast. Acting on his submission, the South-Eastern Railway Co. ordered a 120ft (36.6m), 320-hp screw-driven steamship that could cruise at 12kt. Although designed to earn its keep in the coastal trade, 'She was fitted for towing, and carried two life-boats and mortar apparatus. Moreover, she was provided with a hot bath for assisting to restore the apparently drowned – a feature which bore witness to the foresight of her designer.'[266]

There is, however, no record of the vessel ever being used for such service. Considering the shallow waters in which ships such as the *Mexico* were lost, it is not surprising that the use of large-draught steam-driven rescue craft never gained widespread acceptance.

The Loss of the Passenger Steamer *Berlin*

The story of the loss of the Great Eastern Railway Company's Harwich to the Hook-of-Holland steamer *Berlin* is principally one of tragedy – 128 of the 143 passengers and crew being lost. But sometimes the weather and sea conditions, and the perilous position of the wreck itself, can create a situation where even the rescue of one life can be seen as a miracle of lifesaving. Such was the case in this disaster, and it was partially through the incredible efforts of the crew of the steam lifeboat *President Van Heel* in horrendous conditions, that 15 lives were saved over the course of two long and dreadful days. An excellent description of the events is provided by Noel Methley, in his book *The Story of the Lifeboat*.

The story of the wreck of the English passenger steamer Berlin bears magnificent witness to the devotion of the Dutch life-boat men. This vessel struck on a spit of sand at the extreme end of the North Pier of the Hook of The Netherlands at about five in the morning of Thursday, 21st February 1907. It was blowing a hurricane from the northwest; the seas made a clean breach over her, and she broke up speedily. The steam life-boat President van Heel went out at once in charge of Captain Jensen with a crew of nine men. It was only with the utmost difficulty that she could get out at all, so terrible was the force of the wind, but she succeeded at last in coming within three fathoms of the Berlin. The seas lifted her up and tossed her high above the wreck, and disaster seemed not imminent but certain. However, the captain succeeded in getting his anchor to hold for a space, and fired two rockets. The second established communication, but only for a few minutes; the line was fouled by wreckage and was severed.

Then the anchor chain parted, and the lifeboat was forced to back away clear. She returned to the harbour for a fresh anchor and more rockets, and, during that brief space, the Berlin went to pieces and the majority of those aboard were drowned. By ten the President van Heel *was out again and alongside the wreck, but she could not get a line aboard. Later in the day she tried again, and on the Friday she put out to the wreck three times, but still the sea was so tremendous that nothing could be done.*

On the Friday afternoon, at 1:30, she left the harbour in the teeth of a blinding snowstorm. Accompanying her was the pilot boat Hellevoetsluis, with Prince Henry of the Netherlands aboard. On approaching the wreck, Captain Jensen of the life-boat with four volunteers made a dash for it in a small boat. A rope was thrown, and to it he succeeded in making fast another line, thus securing communication. Then joining hands and wading up to their necks in water, these five brave men reached the lighthouse. The rope was made fast, and three women slid down to safety. They were taken aboard the pilot ship.

Seven men followed without accident, and there were now only two women and a child left aboard, who were too terrified to essay the perilous journey. The falling tide drove the vessels back into the harbour, but it was decided to make another attempt at two in the morning, and to rescue the survivors, if need be, by main force. On the previous day one man was picked up by the life-boat, who had abandoned the wreck of his own accord and endeavoured to reach the shore by swimming.

The story of the Berlin will go down to posterity as one of the most terrible in the annals of the sea. But though we may fail to remember the fearful total of more than one hundred and twenty drowned, we shall never forget how those five men led the forlorn hope and rescued the handful of survivors in the face of almost certain death. Even if the Netherlands life-boat men had not a thousand tales like it to their credit, they could point to that one service and hold up their heads with the best and bravest on the coasts of the seven seas.[267]

CHAPTER 11

The Twilight of Sail

Depiction of a competition amongst different designs of the RNLI's sailing lifeboats, similar to the contest held at Lowestoft in 1892. The lifeboat on the right is of a tubular design.
National Maritime Museum, London

Following the loss of the Southport and St. Anne's self-righters in 1886 and the RNLI's decision to switch to larger more stable non-self-righting boats, G.L. Watson designed two new lifeboats. The first was a self-bailing, pulling lifeboat which, at 38ft (11.6m) in length and 9ft (2.7m) beam, was meant to be carriage-launched. The other was a much larger, offshore capable, pulling and sailing lifeboat, much like an updated version of the Norfolk and Suffolk type. It became known as the Watson type and was 43ft (13.1m) long and 12ft 8in (3.9m) beam. More a sailing boat than a pulling boat.

She had low end boxes, not for righting purposes, but in order to decrease the space which could be filled by shipping a sea. Her cork wale was 15 inches by 8 inches [380 x 200mm], and she had no fewer than fourteen relieving tubes. Her ballasting arrangements were six water tanks and a lead keel 3 tons 2cwt. in weight. She was fitted with a drop keel, and rigged with fore and mizzen lugs and jib.[268]

In 1892 competitive sailing trials were held by the RNLI at Lowestoft between lifeboat types then being used by the Institution. They included a Norfolk and Suffolk type, a large Standard Self-Righting type, one of Richardson's larger Tubular boats and a new Watson type. It appears that the Watson was the reviewing committee's favourite. By 1896 a further 19 of these boats would be constructed.[269] [270] A similar lifeboat trial, this time to evaluate the pulling qualities of the various lifeboats, was held in March 1893 at Montrose, Scotland. The general conclusion was that many of the RNLI's lifeboats were far too heavy and cumbersome to be beach-launched from a carriage.

The original Watson would be the last pulling and sailing lifeboat designed for the RNLI. But the use of sail would not diminish overnight with the introduction of mechanisation. While motors did become more common, for decades they were considered auxiliary to sails, rather than vice-versa.

At around the same time that the RNLI was experimenting with steam and conducting competitive trials with its pulling and sailing boats, an entirely different approach was being taken in Norway, where a new coastal lifesaving organisation, the Norsk Selskab til Sibbrudnes Redning (NSSR) had recently been formed and was designing and building lifeboats powered by sail only. In essence these would be the first of what would become known as Cruising Lifeboats.[271] [272]

The reasons for such a rescue craft were simple. The NSSR required a vessel that could patrol from October to April with extended periods offshore. The only small vessels capable of doing this cheaply and efficiently would be those powered by sail. The design was based on the famous Norwegian pilot ketches, stout and seaworthy craft capable of operating in all forms of heavy weather. The designer was a Norwegian of Scottish descent by the name of Colin Archer, who was also a founding member of the Society and its Committee. His plan for the first Norwegian sailing lifeboat, RS1 the *Colin*

119

THE 'WATSON' PULLING AND SAILING LIFE-BOAT

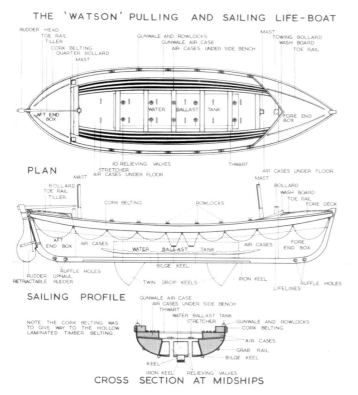

PLAN

SAILING PROFILE

CROSS SECTION AT MIDSHIPS

Although not self-righting, the Watson, and later the Barnett-type lifeboats were much heavier and beamier than their self-righting predecessors and were considered to have far greater initial stability, making them more comfortable in heavy seas and less likely to capsize in the first place.
Eric Fry, RNLI

Archer, was a phenomenal success – so much so that derivatives of the design (in many cases with very few alterations) can be seen sailing all over the world to this day. The boats, which in Norway earned the nickname 'storm petrels', were flush-decked, generally in the range of 46ft (14m) in length, with a large beam of 15ft (4.6m), and a draught of 7ft (2.1m). The prototype had a yawl rig, and weighed in at 26 tons (26.5 tonnes). The scantlings could only be described as massive. The outer planking was of oak and the lifeboat was triple-ribbed at every frame – two frames of yellow pine, grown to shape, sandwiching another of oak, which was in turn fastened to the outer planking. There was a watertight inner skin extending upwards from the cabin floor, which was also watertight, so that, even if stove in, the lifeboat would still float. Interestingly, although designated as RS1, the *Colin Archer* was actually the fourth sailing lifeboat to be built. The previous boats were RS2, *Langesund*, the RS3, *Tordenskjold*, and the RS4, *Feie*, all of which were entries

in a design competition initiated by the Society in September 1892, which had been won by a shipowner/boat designer named Lauritz Christian Stephansen. It would appear that Stephansen's entry, although not entirely accepted by the design committee, did meet with Archer's approval, as the hull was very similar to his own pilot vessels. In the end the *Colin Archer* was an amalgamation of both men's ideas. The two-masted rig, which eventually became standard, was attributed to Mr Stephansen.[273]

On one of *Colin Archer*'s early cruises in May 1894 she encountered a severe storm off the northern coast of Norway and, in resounding testimony to her sea-keeping qualities, saved more than 36 lives in one day. This one action, at a time when the NSSR was in its infancy, resulted in an incredible upsurge in public support, donations, and the founding of many new local NSSR branches.[274] The rescue further entrenched the design as the mainstay of the NSSR and 35 storm petrels were built between 1893 and 1924. There were three series of vessels, the first being the original, RS1 to 11 (1893-96). The second series, RS12 to 20 (1896-1907) had a somewhat different bow and were known as the Svolvær type. The last series, RS21 to 35 (1907-24), was the Solli type.[275]

In 1909 Colin Archer built the last of his boats for the

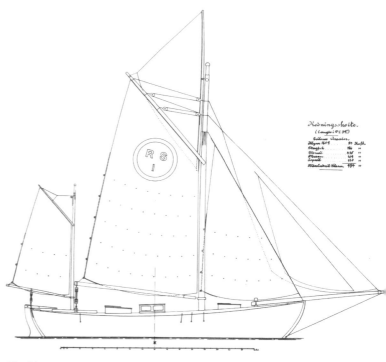

The Norwegian lifeboat RS #1 *Colin Archer* launched in 1893. This was the first lifeboat designed to cruise for extended periods offshore with onboard accommodation for the crew.
Bård Kolltveit, Norsk Sjøfartsmuseum, Oslo

NSSR, the *Vardø*, in which the veteran proponent of sail made provision for the installation of an engine – sail was almost sacrosanct in the NSSR at this time. The society had begun experimenting with internal-combustion engines in fishing vessels as early as 1897 but had encountered so many problems that vessel and engine had to be sold separately. It was probably these failed experiments, combined with a long-entrenched tradition of the use of sail that led to the Society's serious mistrust of anything even verging on the mechanical for decades to come. Even the motorised lifeboats built after 1930 varied little (except for an increase in length and breadth) from the original *Colin Archer* design. The larger vessels of the 1930s were the first NSSR lifeboats designed for motors, but only as 'secondary' propulsion. However, the engines did increase the operational range and efficiency of the vessels and allowed the NSSR to increase their patrol areas to the fishing grounds around Iceland and the Shetland Islands. Even as late as 1936 the hierarchy of the NSSR still espoused the virtues of sail, as an important mode of propulsion on lifeboats.

We maintain the principle that our craft shall have sails as the chief motive power, the motor coming in as secondary power, and used chiefly for assistance when undertaking heavy towage, and to enable the craft to get along faster, and more reliably in a light breeze. Regarded from the economical point of view it is also cheaper to drive the craft by sails, and the driving power, the wind, does not fail us, it being just when it has exerted all its power to destroy whatever is afloat on the sea, that our Life-Saving boats utilize this same power to save those, who are on the point of foundering.[276]

Other organisations and countries recognised the merit of sailing cruising lifeboats. In Norway itself, the Salvation Army had a sailing lifeboat of the Svolvær type built in 1897. This fine vessel, named the *Catherine Booth*, served off the coast of Finmark and the Lofoten Islands for more than 30 years, and was still working when transferred to the NSSR in 1931. In 1902 two of the Norwegian sailing lifeboats were built for use in the Kola Sea by the Imperial Russian Lifeboat Society.[277] Before 1911 the DGzRS in Germany had four 37ft (11.3m) wooden sailing lifeboats 'stationed in bays and river mouths on the North

Sea coast, from where they were able to undertake long trips, as they were provided with accommodation enabling their crews to sleep onboard'.[278] They were eventually fitted with auxiliary engines. In Sweden sailing and cruising lifeboats would be converted from the British Watson type equipped with auxiliary engines (see Part IV). In the 1930s Finland, too, would build a sailing MLB for cruising the outer coasts. In time, the sailing MLBs increased to around 64ft (19.5m), providing more space for both machinery and crew.[279]

Colin Archer, renowned Norwegian boatbuilder and designer. Archer also helped found the Norwegian Lifesaving Society, the NSSR, in 1892.
Wilse, Redningsselskapet

'Storm Petrels' at rest. A fleet of Norwegian sailing lifeboats at anchor in Bergen, circa 1900.
Redningsselskapet

The original Norwegian sailing lifeboat, the *Colin Archer*, remained in service for 38 years before being sold in 1933. In that period she rescued 67 boats, saved 237 lives and towed, or otherwise assisted, an additional 1,522 vessels. Eventually she was resold and crossed the Atlantic to become a floating template for the many future generations of cruising yachts.[280] Today RS1, *Colin Archer*, is maintained as a floating exhibit at the Maritime Museum in Oslo. In 1999 she sailed from Norway to attend the 175th Anniversary celebrations of the RNLI at Poole in Dorset, England – she was more than 100 years old.

A Storm at Havningberg, Northern Norway, 1894

On 20 May 1894 *Colin Archer*, RS1 of the NSSR, arrived at the port of Vardö, on the Barents Sea. This was her maiden cruise and hurricane-force winds heralded her arrival. In the well-protected harbour, the fishing fleet sheltered behind the breakwater but to the north, at the fishing port of Havningberg, the situation was much worse — several small fishing boats and a steamer had been caught on a lee shore and were dragging anchor in the mounting seas. Requests for assistance were dispatched and received by the harbourmaster at Vardö who, like most of the local populace, had little faith in the seagoing merits of the new rescue boat.

Although we had no strong hopes that the newly arrived Rescue-boat could be of any help in this juncture, we nevertheless went aboard her, and showed her skipper the telegram. Captain Anthonisen at once declared himself willing to sail to Havningberg and see if he could be of any help, and promptly hoisted sail and set off. Soon after, steam was made on the Heimdal, and we put forth in her from the harbour.... But we had not gone far before it became clear to both Captain Isaksen and to the rest of us that we could not possibly render help to the vessels in Havningberg or their crews. The storm was so violent and the waves so enormous that the Heimdal could barely hold her own in the open sea, and it would have been utterly impossible to manoeuvre her amongst the breaking seas in the harbour. We decided then, after consultation, to make our way back to Vardö.... On getting back, I telegraphed to Havningberg telling of our unsuccessful attempt...and asking if they had seen anything of the Rescue-boat. Very soon after I received this reply: 'The Rescue-boat has taken off from the vessels in danger about 20 persons, among them Capt. Monsaas' wife, and is now on her way back to Vardö. A steamer can do nothing here, but we beg that the Rescue-boat may be sent back, as a number of the vessels are still signaling for help.'

The *Colin Archer* would rescue 36 people that day, not only proving her own effectiveness but also establishing the Norwegian lifesavers' reputation for incredible seamanship. The following excerpt provides Captain Anthonisen's concise account of the Havningberg rescue and gives an idea of what the crew of the *Colin Archer* were up against.

We made sail on the Rescue-boat and set out as quickly as possible under a press of sail, steering for Havningberg. The snowstorm was so thick that we had great difficulty in keeping our course, the distance at which the land was

visible being never more than one eighth of a mile, and sometimes only a few ships' lengths. About half-past eight we sighted Havningberg. The sea was then extraordinarily heavy; we stood down towards the breakers, going as near as was possible. At the entrance to the inlet the whole sea was practically one great breaker. We then went about and put her on the port tack, with two reefs in the foresail. From here we could make out the boats and vessels lying in the harbour.

The conditions were peculiarly difficult, as there was very little sea-room, and the waves were breaking at depths of 10 to 12 fathoms. We sailed round the vessels, poured oil on the sea and manoeuvred in such a way as to get the boats into the stream of oil, which moderated the sea considerably.

We carried on in this way, backing, filling, tacking, gibing, as seemed best from time to time; and with good results, as in the course of three-quarters of an hour we took on board twenty-two souls, one of them a lady. The persons rescued were ordered below, and we thereupon sailed out past the worst of the breakers, and hove to, waiting for signals of distress from other vessels in the harbour. I may be allowed to remark here that I did not venture to lie further in among the ships and the breakers, as we had the vessel full of people, and there was a raging sea as already described. When we had lain there about a quarter of an hour looking out for signals without seeing any, we set our course back to Vardö. The snow drove thicker and the storm increased. We learnt after that the other vessels too had distress signals hoisted, but we could not see them.

At the mouth of Porsfjord a sea broke over us that would undoubtedly have buried us all if the vessel had not been as solid and seaworthy as she is. The whole of her after-part was completely under water, and the pram we carried was smashed; but otherwise there was no damage. We were, I may remark, under suitably reefed-down canvas. At midnight we reached Vardö and landed all our passengers safely.

On our arrival we found telegraphic orders from the scene of the disaster directing us to return as quickly as possible. We went out again at once. The storm was then abating, but the sea was still exceedingly heavy. We reached Havningberg again at 3:20a.m. and by manoeuvring in the same way as before, succeeded in picking up fourteen more people. We then once more laid our course for Vardö. About 10a.m. we arrived at Vardö, and put the people ashore. Thereafter we moored the vessel and turned in, as there were no more boats at sea.[281]

CHAPTER 12

Early Motor Lifeboats

The development of smaller and more powerful internal-combustion engines towards the end of the 19th Century would forever change the ways of rescue at sea. Until now lifeboat mechanisation had been limited by the inefficiencies of steam power. In some countries the development of the motorised lifeboat, or MLB, surged ahead at a rapid pace, while in other nations, especially in Europe, it would follow a more conservative route. Here the motor was considered 'auxiliary' back-up power for traditional pulling and sailing lifeboats well into the 20th Century. Not surprisingly, given the vast expanses of territory in which they were to provide rescue coverage, the USLSS became a frontrunner in the development of the MLB.

Lt. Charles H. McLellan, co-designer of the popular USLSS surfboat and an officer of the United States Revenue-Marine began experimenting with internal-combustion engines mounted in existing pulling and sailing surfboats and lifeboats. In 1899 he received

authorisation to fit a 'twelve horse power, two cylinder Superior gasoline engine' into a 34ft (10.4m) pulling and sailing lifeboat of the 'English' Type. The arrangement was evaluated at Marquette, Michigan, on Lake Superior, and appears to have become quite popular with both the station crew and McLellan himself, who reported:

The boat was tested under sail and power during a gale blowing at the rate of from 28 to 40 miles an hour, as registered at the Weather Bureau. She was taken five miles outside of the harbour...and tried under all directions of wind and sea, and behaved as well as could be desired. Under the same conditions of wind, and without the engine, a tugboat's assistance would have been necessary, or several hours consumed in beating the lifeboat out against the wind. It is the unanimous opinion of the officers of the Service who have witnessed the trials of this boat that the Service would have a very valuable auxiliary by its general adoption.[282]

The 34ft (10.4m) prototype boat had some very innovative features, which would become standard in almost all MLBs of the future. First it was twin screw, having two shafts and propellers geared off the same engine – an idea considerably ahead of its time. The engine itself was housed in the sealed, air-tight compartment in the stern of the lifeboat, with all controls externally mounted and recessed into the forward bulkhead of the compartment. This allowed for all the engine controls – starting, stopping, changing revolutions, propeller direction, and basic lubrication – to be handled from the open cockpit. The sealed engine room had a unique air-induction system that drew the engine air through vents located on the forward bulkhead of the after whaleback/engine room, just above deck-level and, if the vessel were inverted, would remain out of the water in the trapped air beneath the boat. The twin-cylinder, two-cycle engine could obtain 400rpm, turning two 18in (460mm) propellers with reversible blades, which could be adjusted with the use of a wheel

A USCG 36ft Self-Righting, Self-Bailing (SR-SB), Pulling and Sailing Motor Lifeboat (MLB) from the station at Barnegat, New Jersey, returns from sailing drill. This boat, with the basic hull-design of an English Self-Righting (SR) type, was the first purpose-built, production-line MLB in the world.
USCG

on the forward end of the whaleback. The propellers were not recessed into tunnels – as had been the case on the European and Australian steam lifeboats – but were placed in protective cages to guard against fouling or grounding. During its sea trials the prototype obtained a speed of 7.5kt at a fuel consumption rate of 2 gallons per hour and, despite the additional weight of the engine, the vessel righted itself in three seconds from an inverted position.

The primary design flaw was the 12-hp engine itself, which, with all the appropriate attachments, weighed a whopping 1,500lb (680kg)! By 1906 however, the USLSS had switched to a 25-hp 'Standard Automotor' that provided twice the horsepower at half the weight of its predecessor. Several more English-type pulling and sailing lifeboats were built in the US with the idea of incorporating auxiliary engines. However, they were made somewhat longer, at around 35ft (10.7m), and had further design modifications including the use of a single propeller, rather than two. The Electric Boat Company, otherwise known as Elco, of Bayonne, New Jersey, built almost all these early MLBs and worked closely with McLellan. The firm was instrumental in developing a safety mechanism for automatically shutting off the engine in the event of a capsize. This circuit breaker would become standard equipment on almost all future MLBs around the world.

These early American MLBs were still, however, merely altered versions of the traditional pulling and sailing lifeboat. By 1907 McLellan, now a Captain, had been paid out of the Revenue Service but he remained closely involved in the development of US lifeboats. During his travels he had spent some time in England and visited the RNLI to witness developments in motor installations. Unlike his British colleagues, however, he believed that motors should be the primary propulsion in a lifeboat, with oars and sails being the back-up power. He realised that, to create a true MLB, the boat would have to be purpose-designed and -constructed. McLellan and the USLSS also wished to retain the quality of self-righting in their lifeboats and this would have to be considered in the original design.

The result was one of the most successful lifeboat designs ever: the 36ft (11m) by 8ft 7 1/2in (2.6m), SR-SB MLB. (These sturdy craft would begin the 'Footer' terminology for American MLBs, which continues to this day.) So successful was the design that various versions of 36 Footers would be constructed for both the United States and Canadian lifesaving services right into the late 1950s. Two would continue in service as relief lifeboats on the Pacific coast of both countries through to the 1980s, being stationed at Depot Bay, Oregon, and Bamfield, British Columbia, respectively. The original 36 Footers were constructed at the Holmes Motor Co. of West Mystic, Connecticut, as well as at the Elco yard. As the procurement contract for the USLSS service expanded, full production would eventually switch to the much larger Elco facility, with Holmes still supplying the motors and working closely with McLellan on development. The motors were described as a '6-cylinder, 4 cycle, open base auto-marine motor of 40 horsepower'. The Bamfield Lifesaving Station on the west coast of Vancouver Island received the first Elco 36 Footer at the end of 1907, the first of three to be provided to the station over the years. The following year the first Holmes 36 Footer would go to the USLSS station at Waddah Island (Neah Bay), directly across the Strait of Juan de Fuca from Bamfield. In 1909 the Holmes yard would also build the first 36 Footer for the Atlantic seaboard at Sandy Hook, New Jersey. Although several versions evolved over the decades, the hull remained relatively unchanged; the whalebacks, location and type of power (gas to diesel), number of screws and size of engines were all modified. Despite it all, however, the original design still had a full set of 10 oars, double-banked, and was rigged with two hollow spruce masts carrying fore and main lug sails and a jib.[283][284]

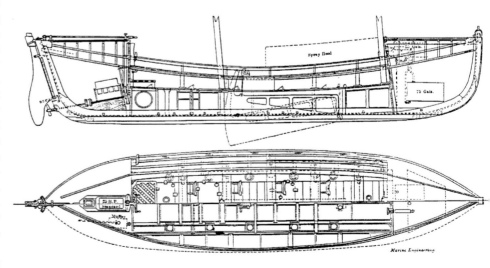

The USLSS 36ft MLB with the petrol engine beneath the after air case, and the retractable drop keel used if the MLB reverted to sail. *USCG*

The original 36 Footer of 1907 was designated as an E type – the E being a reference to its 'English' origins. Future generations included the H type, built between 1918 and 1928 and named after two USCG naval architects instrumental in the update of the design – Frederick A. Hunnewell and Alfred Hansen – who moved the engine from the after compartment to amidships, and shortened the end boxes. This was followed by the T type built between 1928 and 1931, TR (T Revised) built between 1932 and 1937, and TRS (T Revised and Simplified) built from 1937 to 1956. All of the Ts were characterised by a much longer bow compartment/air case and engine cover than seen on previous versions.[285] [286]

As an interesting footnote, in 1951 three TRS 36 Footers were built in Quebec for the Canadian Department of Marine and Fisheries. One was sent to Bamfield to replace the ageing E type (the second at the station) that had been in service since 1910. Upon the arrival of the new boat Coxswain John Logvinoff and Engineer Boris Hoskins were rather perturbed to find that there was still only an open cockpit where, in their opinion, a wheelhouse should be. Not pleased with the prospect of spending another 20 years facing the storms of the North Pacific head on, Logvanoff, Hoskins and the crew set about building a small wheelhouse over the cockpit. However, they never advised the bureaucrats in Ottawa of this 'minor' alteration. When the Department's marine agent next visited the remote station and discovered the wheelhouse, the coxswain was threatened with severe disciplinary action. In the end cooler heads prevailed and the rationale behind the Bamfield crew's addition was validated – Hoskin's hand-drawn sketches were used as a template on the service's other 36 Footers.

The 36ft MLB provided a link between past and future. Essentially, the hull and its components differed little from the first SR-SB pulling and sailing lifeboat built for the USLSS by the RNLI in 1873. In turn, that design was a direct descendent of the Duke of Northumberland's competition in 1851. Now, the successful integration of mechanical propulsion in the United States in 1906, utilising the same traditional design of lifeboat, resulted in the creation of the first true SR-SB MLB and provided a design basis for future generations. Thus, for well over a century, the principles of lifeboat design developed by men such as Beeching and Peake, remained relatively unchanged.

Encouraged by the early success of the MLB, Sumner Kimball, General Superintendent of the Service, and Captain McLellan, now Supervisor of Construction, started a major building programme to replace all the pulling and sailing boats in the fleet with MLBs. In 1908 Kimball reported:

With respect to the serviceability of these boats for the purposes of life-saving service, I am pleased to be able to state that the results thus far obtained have been very satisfactory. During the comparatively short period that they have been in service, we have had numerous instances of notable rescues of life and property, some of which would have been impossible, and others exceedingly difficult without the motorboats. These boats have greatly increased the effective radius of operation in a life-saving station, but the most important advantage, perhaps, lies in the fact that the crews reach a wreck quickly and in good physical condition for their crowning work.[287]

In that same year, a USLSS MLB from the Monomoy Point station, on Cape Cod, rescued the crew of a sinking schooner, in extremely perilous circumstances, and 'went over the same cross seas in which a crew of six men from the Monomoy station was lost five years ago, when the life-savers had to rely upon their own strength at the oars. The motorboat reached the wreck in less then an hour....' The writer of this contemporary account went on to say, 'The equipment of all important life-saving stations with suitable motorboats cannot be brought about too quickly'.[288]

Within four years there were 68 36 Footers in commission, and the Elco boatyard was building them at the rate of one per week; the average cost per boat was estimated at $6,975. By 1912 there were several of the original prototype 34ft MLBs still in service, and approximately 30 of the small, non-self-righting surfboats had also been provided with engines. The 'motor surfboats' had their engines housed amidships – European style – and many were twin-screw vessels with a unique shaft and strut system that allowed the exposed shafting and propellers to be folded 'up against the hull under each quarter'. This feature was necessary as the motor surfboats were still primarily launched from carriages and were designed to operate in extremely shallow water. By 1914 over half of the entire USLSS fleet of rescue craft had been motorised.

In Britain internal-combustion engines were being installed as 'auxiliary power' in existing pulling and sailing lifeboats. In 1904 G.L.Watson passed away at the rather young age of 53. Prior to his death however, he had advocated experimenting with internal-combustion engines as a back-up means of power. His work was taken on by J.R. Barnett, a partner in the Watson firm. Barnett, whose name would become synonymous with future generations of British lifeboats, immediately hired the specialised mechanical firm of Messrs. Thelluson to help supervise the RNLI's experiments with petrol engines.[289]

In August 1904 a 38ft (11.6m) pulling and sailing, Standard Self-Righting lifeboat, the *J. McConnell Hussy*, was fitted with a 10-hp, twin-cylinder, two-stroke 'Fay and Bowen' petrol engine beneath a water-tight cowling amidships, under the supervision of J.R. Barnett and a consulting engineer from Thelluson. After sea trials in the Solent, where she obtained a speed of 6kt, and a further period of testing at Newhaven, Sussex, she was sent to Tynemouth, Northumberland, as the permanent station boat. But the local lifeboatmen were leery of the new prototype and the rather cantankerous engine and, as had been the prerogative of lifeboatmen since the earliest days of organised lifesaving in Great Britain, they made their mistrust evident by refusing to use the boat. In reply Captain H.E. Burton, an army officer and member of the local lifeboat committee, mustered a new volunteer crew from his own men. Soon, these new recruits carried out a successful rescue with the motorised lifeboat and without any assistance whatsoever. The local crew, somewhat humiliated and now recognising the potential merits of the new form of propulsion, signed up once again. But they did so on one condition: Captain Burton and his men, who obviously had some mechanical expertise, were to remain in charge of the station and assume responsibility for maintaining the mysterious internal-combustion engine! (see p.132).

Local preferences differed around the UK. Before the *J. McConnell Hussy* was stationed at Tynemouth, she had

been tested by the Newhaven crew. There 'she had won such golden opinions from the coxswain and crew that when she was transferred to Tynemouth as the Station lifeboat, the Newhaven men promptly asked to have their own lifeboat (a 37 feet by 9 feet 3 inches [11.28 x 2.82m] self-righting boat) fitted with a motor'.[290] It was all a matter of opinion.

In July 1905 three more conventional lifeboats, all larger vessels designed to be launched from a slipway, or lay afloat, had more powerful four-stroke petrol engines installed. A 43ft (13.1m) by 12ft 6in (3.8m) non-self-righting Norfolk and Suffolk type had a 40-hp Blake engine added. The other two vessels were Standard Self-Righting boats: a 38ft (11.6m) version that had a four-cylinder, 24-hp Thornycroft engine, and a 42ft (12.8m) model from Ramsgate that had a 30-hp Taylor engine installed. All encountered design and mechanical problems throughout their trials, but the RNLI remained upbeat:

> ...*the ordinary irritating little troubles well known to owners of motor-boats and motor-cars have been experienced in a more or less degree in each of the life-boats. Until the boats have had some years' work at their stations it will be difficult to gauge the exact degree of success which has been attained; at any rate so hopeful does the outlook seem that the Committee of Management have felt justified in ordering four more motors for life-boats which have been specially built for them, instead of, as in the case of the three experimental boats, simply adapting existing boats.*[291]

The first of the four purpose-built motor lifeboats for the RNLI would be a 42ft (12.8m) Standard Self-Righter destined for the Stromness station in the Orkneys; she went into service in 1909. For the first time the British had designed a boat around an engine – a 30-hp Taylor driving a Villinger propeller. The British SR-SB MLB differed considerably from the American 36 Footer, as the engine was housed amidships with its air intake located in the forward air-case. Air would pass through a ball-valve at the intake, from which it ran the entire length of the vessel to the after air-box from where it went by pipe to the engine compartment itself, thus 'reaching the air intakes of the engine unladen with salt water spray'.[292] Another interesting innovation was the incorporation of a tunnel in the hull for protecting the propeller, an idea that stemmed from the development of the steam-powered, screw-driven lifeboats, and which had been already tried on an experimental MLB in The Netherlands. This feature would become a standard on all British MLBs of the future.

The RNLB *Anne Allen*, an early English MLB based on the Liverpool type of non-self-righting, pulling and sailing lifeboat, undergoing sea trials on the Thames.
RNLI

The arrangement resolved itself into a tunnel, which is constructed of mahogany, and is of a turtle-backed shape, rising from the top of the iron keel, commencing from a position about one third of the length of the boat from her sternpost. A hatch is provided in the deck of the boat to enable ready accessibility to the propeller boss and blades. In this tunnel the propeller does its work. The effect of racing has been materially reduced, any possible difficulties to be met with when dealing with a slipway have been overcome, and lastly, and not the least important, partial immunity from the fouling of the propeller arising from wreckage alongside a vessel, pier, ropes and the various other matters liable to cause this and put the motor out of action, has been provided.[293]

All four purpose-built MLBs incorporated tunnels and alterations had to be made to their keels in order to accommodate the feature. In some cases, as with the standard self-righters, a single heavy drop keel replaced two smaller ones. The next three MLBs included another Standard Self-Righter – somewhat smaller at 40ft (12.2m) long by 10ft 6in (3.2m) beam, powered by a 24-hp Taylor engine driving a Meisner propeller, and stationed at Fishguard, Wales – and two non-self-righting Watsons; one was 40ft (12.2m) long with an 11ft (3.4m) beam and a 40-hp Taylor engine (again driving a Villinger propeller) stationed at Thurso, Scotland; the other a somewhat larger 43ft (13.1m) by 12ft 6in (3.8m) boat with a 40-hp Blake engine driving a Gaines reversing propeller, stationed at Stronsay, Orkney.[294] The variety of power plants, propeller types, and even styles of lifeboat used in these early years indicates that the RNLI was serious about auxiliary engines, and recognised that the installation of motors would have to be considered for each type on an individual basis.

Probably the best evaluation of these new purpose-built MLBs occurred during their delivery voyages. In April 1909 the 43ft Watson MLB for Stronsay, and the 42ft Self-Righter for Stromness, left London along with a Watson pulling-and-sailing lifeboat destined for Thurso. The entire trip was fraught with trials and tribulations, particularly with the finicky petrol engines. For the first part of the trip to Tynemouth, the 40-hp Stronsay lifeboat towed the other two in tandem, making fairly good speed. From there to the Orkneys however, the weather changed for the worse and, nearing the northern tip of Scotland, all the boats separated. It became a veritable free-for-all, that tested the sailing capabilities of the fledgling MLBs and their crews. It is best described in a contemporary account by the Commander of the voyage:

A hard northerly wind was prevailing with a dirty sea, but the spirits of all the men were buoyant because they were nearing their destinations, and little thought was given to Pentland Firth. Rounding the head at 10:30, the full force of the ebb tide picked up and the wind drawing to the northeast the effects of the 'races' were soon felt. Passing southward to Stroma, the masts were raised and canvas put on, the tow being kept as before, with the result that, soon after, the flotilla headed into the last part of the 'race' known as the 'Merry Men of May'. Here the force of the sea was so strong that all three boats became free of their tow and were left to their own individual merits. The spectacle was simply magnificent. The sea was a veritable churn, but the boats made light of it and came through without a murmur. The Stronsay boat showed the Stromness boat a clean pair of heels, whilst the Thurso boat, at times showing three parts of her keel, proved that the 'Watson' boats can do with plenty of wind and when close hauled. Neither of the Watson boats took any heavy water on board.[295]

All three boats did eventually reach their destinations. The merits of sail over the early engines under certain circumstances and of the fine sea-keeping qualities of the Watson lifeboats themselves had been further enhanced.

In terms of testing the 'auxiliary engine' on a delivery voyage, the 40ft MLB that went to Fishguard had much better luck: 'no hitch of any kind was found, the motor proving itself thoroughly reliable, and giving all the satisfaction that could be desired'. In particular, the use of a governor to control engine revolutions in the inevitable event that the propeller came out of the water, was highly praised. One of the crew of the vessel advised that

…when passing through a heavy 'race' off St. Alban's Head, the propeller on two occasions was half out of the water, the speed of the engine in that instant being reduced to 250 R.P.M. and as the load came on again the governor gently opened the throttle, allowing the engine to run at its proper speed. Had it not been for the activity of the governor at the different loads, when the boat was thrashing her stern, there would appear to have been every possibility of her shedding her propeller.[296]

By 1914 and the outbreak of the First World War the need to install internal-combustion engines in the RNLI's lifeboats and to design future vessels for engine installation, had become widely accepted. However, the focus on the war effort would have a detrimental effect on the delivery of such boats to the service. Between 1912 and the cessation of hostilities in 1918 only two more MLBs would be built, bringing the grand total of motorised vessels in the RNLI to 19 – just 1/16 of the entire fleet.

Following the war and the well-publicised rescues that had been carried out by some of the MLBs, a massive lifeboat-building and -design campaign was begun in Britain – its aims, to create an all-MLB fleet. J.R. Barnett would focus on mechanising the large and expanding fleet of non-self-righters while F. Rubie, the Institution's surveyor, would work on the RNLI's fleet of self-righters. In addition, a special type of petrol engine was to be developed, specifically for lifeboats, that could be submerged up to the level of the air intakes. The standard MLBs included the 43ft (13.1m) and 45ft (13.7m) Watson and the Standard Self-Righter. All of these vessels had single screws housed in a tunnel and must be launched from a slipway or lay afloat.

In 1923 Barnett came up with a new design of MLB that, at 60ft (18.3m) long by 15ft (4.6m) beam, was a radical departure from previous British rescue craft. The large Barnett MLB had twin propellers, housed in tunnels, driven by two new D.E. six-cylinder, 80-hp 'submersible' petrol engines. Each engine was housed in its own engine room, with entirely separate fuel and cooling systems. The Barnett MLB could cruise at 9.5kt and had a range of 300 nautical miles. It was the first British MLB with flush decks, similar to the earlier steam lifeboats. It also had a deck shelter, or semi-enclosed cabin for the on-deck helm position and to keep the crew out of the weather. It had a below-decks cabin for 24 people and, if necessary, could carry a total of 130 survivors. The wooden hull was also divided into 15 watertight compartments. This was the first RNLI lifeboat to rely solely on its engines for motive power; there were no oars on board for, at slightly over 40 tons (40.8 tonnes), any manpowered efforts would have been fruitless. The only canvas carried was 'a small staysail and trysail for steadying purposes'.[297] Each of the submersible engines was 'itself watertight, and will continue to run when the engine room is flooded and the engine itself entirely submerged, the air-intakes being well above the water-line even when the boat is waterlogged'.[298]

The Barnett type also had a line-throwing gun, an electric searchlight and capstan, and a life-saving net placed amidships – an innovation borrowed from the Dutch lifesaving societies. The first of the type, the *William and Kate Johnston*, went on station at New Brighton on the Mersey in 1923, replacing the venerable steam-driven lifeboat *Queen*. Her cost was estimated at an unprecedented £20,000.

The 60ft Barnett was closely followed by a new version of the Watson MLB utilising one of the 80-hp submersible engines, and adding flush decks and a cabin. The after cockpit had a shelter built around it as per the Barnett type. The Watson (Cabin) MLB, as it became known, was around 45ft (13.7m) long, with a 12ft 6in (3.8m) beam. It was based on the larger pulling and sailing Watson lifeboat but, although it carried a full sailplan, the engines were now considered sufficiently reliable to be the primary motive power. By 1927 a twin-screw version of the Watson (Cabin) type was in service, with two four-cylinder, 40-hp submersible engines. Massively built with seven watertight compartments and 142 separate air-cases, as well as 10 relieving scuppers, this version had two cockpits, one at either end of the vessel, both with shelters for protection. Its cruising speed was 7.5kt, and it had a range of 116 miles. By 1933 there were 29 Watson (Cabin) MLBs in the RNLI fleet.[299] In 1933 a special 41ft (12.5m) Watson MLB was built, which, like earlier versions, had an open cockpit, rather than a covered deck; shelters were added forward and amidships, similar to those on the Liverpool and SR MLBs. Several of this type would be built before the Second World War.[300]

In 1928 a smaller version of the Barnett MLB was constructed; if necessary this could be launched from a slipway but the type generally remained afloat. Weighing 26.5 tons (compared to 40) the 51ft (15.5m) Barnett MLB, had a beam of 13ft 6in (4.1m) and a draught of 4ft 1in (1.2m). It also had a heavier keel producing a greater range of stability than that of its larger predecessor. It was twin screw and powered by two six-cylinder, 60-hp submersible engines. It had a top speed of 9kt and could cruise for 270 nautical miles at 7.5kt. By 1933 there were two of this type in service. They were the first British MLBs to be characterised by a small ship-like funnel, located approximately amidships, used to vent the engine exhaust.[301]

By 1929 however, there still remained the problem of mechanising the RNLI's fleet of carriage-launched boats, primarily smaller Standard Self-Righters. In 1921 the Institution had begun to experiment with internal-combustion engines in a series of lightweight Self-Righters, but had not arrived at the proper combination of weight and strength necessary for the rigours imposed on beach-launched boats. Through a series of tests and adjustments, a 35ft 6in by 9ft 6in (10.8m by 2.9m) SR lifeboat was settled on. This wooden lifeboat, which weighed slightly in excess of 6 tons (6.12 tonnes), was still very similar to the original Standard Self-Righter, having the prominent air-cases at either end and being divided into six watertight compartments fitted with 110 separate air-cases. It was powered by a comparatively lightweight, purpose-designed AE6 petrol engine, producing 35hp and a maximum speed of just over 7kt with a range of 106 miles (171km). The engine was mounted amidships under a watertight cowling. By 1933 there were 10 SR MLBs in the RNLI fleet, with more under construction – they replaced older carriage-launched pulling and sailing boats all over the country.[302]

As had been the case since the invention of the self-righting lifeboat, however, not all the carriage-launched stations wanted such craft, many preferring the more stable, non-self-righting boats. To this end, in 1930, the Institution began experiments with another traditional pulling and sailing lifeboat: the non-self-righting 35ft 6in by 10ft 3in (10.8 x 3.12m) Liverpool type. Weighing 7 tons (7.14 tonnes), somewhat more than the Standard Self-Righting MLB, the Liverpool MLB was nevertheless powered by the same 35-hp engine. The hull was divided into six watertight compartments with 129 separate air cases. Its self-bailing capabilities consisted of 18 relieving scuppers, which could 'free her of water entirely in 20 seconds'.[303] The engine was housed amidships beneath a large whaleback in the open cockpit of the vessel that served the dual purpose of housing the engine and providing protection and shelter for the crew.

Another type of British MLB developed for launch from a carriage was the Beach or Aldeburgh type. Certain stations such as Aldeburgh, Suffolk, located close to the notorious Goodwin Sands, required a larger and heavier boat then the SR and Liverpool MLBs. The flat nature of the foreshore precluded the use of a slipway and, with no suitable harbours, it was not possible to keep a heavy Watson or Barnett lying afloat. The Aldeburgh type was thus designed to fill the void. It was approximately 41ft by 12ft 3in (12.5m by 3.73m) and weighed just under 16 tons (16.32 tonnes). Its very wide beam made up for its shallow draught. It was twin-screw, with the propellers housed in tunnels and was powered by two 35-hp engines, producing a top speed of 7.5kt with a range of 122 miles. The first of the type, of which only a few were made, was launched in 1931.[304]

Other specialised MLBs were also constructed in Britain. Several of the reliable old Norfolk and Suffolk type boats were built as MLBs in the 1920s, to continue serving the needs of the East Anglian coast. Due to their shallow draught, shaft tunnels were not incorporated, and the more modern versions were twin screw, running two 80-hp submersible engines. The British developed their own version of a motor surfboat in the late 1930s, similar to the lightweight carriage-launched surfboats used in Denmark, Germany and The Netherlands. Called the Surf type MLB, they were 32ft by 9ft (9.75m by 2.74m) and had a reduced handling weight of 4.5 tons (4.6 tonnes). Initially two of the Surf type were built with two specially designed 12-hp petrol engines called F2s. The first boat

had the traditional three-bladed propellers housed in tunnels, while the second had two 'Hotchkiss Cone Propulsion' units – an early form of jet propulsion. In the end it was decided that the safety advantages of the jet-drives outweighed the slight speed advantage of the propellers, and seven more Hotchkiss-propelled surfboats were constructed.[305]

An early specialised MLB was the high-speed launch built by Thornycroft in 1929. The *Sir William Hillary* was a 64ft (19.5m) wooden craft driven by two 12-cylinder engines producing a top speed of just over 17kt. Designed to meet the immediate demand for rescue services caused by the birth of cross-Channel air traffic, she was stationed at Dover with a full-time crew (see Chapter II-21). By the outbreak of the Second World War, the RNLI's goal of creating an all-MLB fleet had been almost realised. By 1945 out of a fleet of 151, there remained only two pulling and sailing lifeboats in service, one Liverpool type, and one Standard Self-Righting type. The latter, at Whitby, Yorkshire, remained in service until 1957, when it went on display at the local museum.

In France the first motorised-lifeboat experiments began in 1908, when a 'Marchand petroleum engine was installed in an old boat for experimental purposes. It was ballasted to bring its displacement to 6 tons, and with an 11 H.P. engine could obtain a speed of 5.5 knots.'[306] It seems that this first boat was not very successful. Any use of the oars – still considered the primary method of motive power – was now hindered by the extreme weight of the engine, which gave the lifeboat an overall weight in excess of 10 tons (10.2 tonnes). The engine also interfered with the rowing positions and lowered the available freeboard.[307] Another pulling and sailing lifeboat was altered to an MLB in about 1910, this time a 32ft 9in by 8ft 3in (10m by 2.5m) model displacing just over 6 tons (6.12 tonnes). The 24-hp motor was said to have driven a turbine, instead of a screw, although this was probably an early form of water-jet. It obtained a speed of 7kt.[308] In 1914, further efforts to mechanise the fleet of the Société Centrale de Sauvetage des Naufragés were hindered by the outbreak of war.

In 1919 the French turned to purpose-built MLBs. The first was a fully decked, 43ft 6in (13.25m) by 11ft 6in (3.5m) non-self-righting lifeboat, powered by a 42-hp petrol engine driving a single screw recessed in a tunnel. It was designed to be launched from a slipway or to lay afloat. It had a cruising speed of 8kt. At almost 13 tons (13.26 tonnes) it was too large to be driven by oars and was considered a true MLB, although it did have sails as back up.

When it came to fitting engines into the lighter carriage-launched lifeboats, the French ran into the same problems of weight and strength that would plague other countries with similar boats. They attempted to strengthen their carriages instead of their boats although ultimately it was decided to scrap carriage-launching altogether and slipways were built instead.

In 1923 the first twin-screw version of the larger type of MLB was built with a covered engine room and a shelter for the crew. This vessel also had an interesting rudder arrangement – the entire device was located within the skeg of the vessel, and was thus protected from striking the bottom, or being damaged during launch. It was further described as 'a compensated rudder interposed in the deadwood, abaft the propeller and between the double tunnels, and completely protected by the keel and the sternpost'.[309] By 1928 the French Lifeboat Society had 10 twin-screw MLBs in service and another three on order. There were two models: a 36ft (11m) type driven by two 24-hp gas engines with a top speed of 7.5kt, and

a 41ft (12.5m) type with two 35-hp engines and a top speed of 8.5kt.

In Germany the first trial of a motor lifeboat took place at Laboe in Kiel Bay 1911. The vessel had a twin-cylinder Sleipner engine producing a grand total of 15hp and, unlike the earlier metal pulling and sail lifeboats of the German Lifeboat Society, was built of wood. In all, eight of these open wooden MLBs would be built; three for the North Sea and five for the Baltic. The hull type remained similar to the early German pulling and sailing lifeboats, which were a combination of the American Francis-type metallic boats and the Peake-type self-righters which had been purchased by the Prussian Government back in the 1850s and '60s. They had air tanks, double bottoms and self-bailing characteristics. The motor was the primary means of propulsion but the boats had oars and sails as back up. A ninth boat of the type was built of galvanised steel in 1918 and was stationed in Schleswig-Holstein. Eventually the engines in these boats would be upgraded to 28-hp versions constructed by the Daimler Motor Co. of Berlin.[310] Five of the DGzRS's sailing lifeboats, designed for cruising offshore, also had internal-combustion engines installed between 1911 and 1913. In 1926, as finances improved, the Germans were the first lifesaving nation to begin experimenting with diesel engines. Two of their sailing lifeboats had their petrol engines removed and replaced by 'two-cylinder 40 H.P. crude oil Diesel engines without compressors, constructed by the Deutz Engine Works'.[311]

The perils of petroleum engines, and the fuel itself, were well known, and the advantages of diesel power in lifeboats were aptly described by the German representative at the 2nd International Lifeboat Conference in 1928:

MOTOR-RETTUNGSBOOT

LÄNGE ÜBER DECK	17,10 M.
LÄNGE IN DER WASSERLINIE	15,60 „
BREITE ÜBER SPANTEN	4,20 „
SEITENHÖHE	2,125 „
TIEFGANG	1,25 „
SPRUNG	0,75 „

An early 56ft (17m) twin-screw German MLB of the 1930s. The DGzRS was the first lifesaving organisation to install and use diesel engines in their rescue craft and also led the way in the use of steel for lifeboats.
Deutsches Museum München

Experience has shown that the high-speed petrol engine possesses serious disadvantages for Life-Boat work. As it is necessary in the case of such engines to ignite the fuel by means of an electric spark, a complicated arrangement of magneto, wires and sparking plugs is required. The dampness which is unavoidable when engaged on rescue work in rough weather often occasions a breakdown and troubles are caused by short circuits, as a result of which the engine stops; thus there is no guarantee for certainty of operation in stormy weather. Similarly, as has actually been experienced, an outbreak of fire originating from the carburetor can have serious results on account of the explosive nature of the fuel employed. Consideration of these factors has led the Society (DGzRS) to direct their attention to the development of the slow-speed Diesel engine without a compressor and using crude-oil fuel, because the operation of such an engine appears to be considerably more simple.[312]

Three new purpose-built MLBs were ordered in 1926, all of them diesel-powered. Two of the boats, the *Bremen* and the *Hamburg*, were single-screw models, 38ft 6in by 11ft (11.7m by 3.35m). The third was a twin-screw model, the first of its kind in Germany, named the *Hindenburg*. She was somewhat larger at 45ft 6in (13.9m) long and 12ft 4in (3.8m) in beam. Uniquely, these were steel-hulled boats, built to class, and divided into approximately nine watertight compartments separated by longitudinal and transverse bulkheads. As on the British MLBs, the propellers were protected in tunnels. The early German MLBs were not self-righting and every compartment had a pump driven either off the engine(s) or manually. The single-screw versions were powered by a twin-cylinder, two-cycle 45-hp Deutz diesel producing a top speed of 8.5kt. The *Hindenburg* was powered by two four-cycle, 45-hp MAN diesels, which could push it along at 9.5kt. This latter boat also had 'a wireless telegraphy installation with a radius of fifty sea miles'.[313] From now on communications between lifeboats and the shore would play a crucial role in coastal lifesaving, directly and indirectly saving the lives of tens of thousands of distressed mariners, and even of lifeboat crews themselves.

During the Second World War, two cruising type MLBs were constructed by the DGzRS, the *Norderney* and a new *Hindenburg*. These 57ft (17.4m) boats were the first to have the high, conning-tower-like wheelhouses that would become so typical of many future DGzRS rescue craft. The Germans continued to build diesel-powered, full-displacement MLBs after the Second World War but would eventually begin experimenting with a high-speed self-righting offshore MLB, known as the 'Rescue Cruiser,' (see Chapter II-14). Other nations would soon follow the German model of utilising diesel rather than petrol engines, with the RNLI beginning the switch in 1936.

In Denmark, the state-run lifesaving service began converting some of its fleet to MLBs in 1914 when a lightweight beach-launched surfboat, 25ft 3in by 6ft 7in (7.7m by 2m), was fitted with a 12-hp 'Aristox' engine, resulting in a trial speed of 6kt. Like the American motor surfboats the external shafting and propellers could be raised and moved out of the way when launching. There were problems with both the engine and the lifting shaft and propeller system however and within the year the boat was 'eventually destroyed by fire'.[314] Undaunted, the Danes decided to skip any further alteration experiments and ordered the construction of a 41ft (12.5m) Watson MLB, similar to the 1909 British version with the original propeller tunnel. She had a 40-hp Taylor engine and was built at the naval arsenal at Copenhagen.

Several more carriage-launched motor surfboats were built, albeit somewhat larger at 33ft 6in by 9ft 2in (10.2m by 2.8m). Originally they were fitted with the 12-hp engine but by 1923 they were all being refitted with a 25-hp Fordson engine, which appears to have greatly improved their performance. By 1927 three more Watson 42ft (12.8m) MLBs had been built for Denmark the last of which was equipped with a 'Dixon and Hutchinson motor, developing 50 H.P. and giving a speed of seven and a half knots'.[315]

Internal-combustion engines were finding their place in diverse modes of transportation all over the world, and it is quite probable that other rescue craft were similarly converted. Belgium, for instance, had two MLBs in service as early as 1910, and in 1911 it was reported that Portugal had a metallic MLB based on the French Henry style pulling surfboat stationed at Duoro, near Oporto.[316]

The Loss of the Hospital Ship *Rohilla*

Owned by the British India Line, the 7,400-ton liner *Rohilla* had been converted to a hospital ship for the war effort and, in October 1914, was en route from Queensferry to Dunkerque with 229 passengers and crew on board. Very early in the morning of 30 October, storm-force southeasterly winds began to buffet the ship, driving her aground near Saltwick Nab, in the vicinity of Whitby, Yorkshire. At 4am the *Rohilla* sent up distress rockets – she was on the rocks about 400 yards from shore. Within an hour, she began to break up and dozens of men were thrown into the sea and perished.

The signals were seen by Thomas Langlands, coxswain of the Whitby Lifeboat who quickly realised that the seas were of such an enormous magnitude that trying to set out from the harbour would be tantamount to suicide. The only option would be to transport the Whitby No2 pulling and sailing lifeboat, the *John Fields*, overland from the east pier and then down the steep cliffs to the beach. By first light a large group of men had succeeded in doing just that, but the lifeboat had suffered in the process and was stove in in two places, partially as a result of being manhandled over an 8ft-high stone wall. Regardless, the Whitby crew launched into the boiling surf and made their way to what remained of the *Rohilla*. On the first run, they recovered 17 survivors from the main accommodations section, including the ship's five nurses. On the second attempt, 18 more men were taken off but, striking more rocks, the lifeboat was damaged beyond repair. A call went out to the pulling and sailing lifeboat from Upgang, many miles away.

The Upgang boat and her crew would also travel overland. Upon arriving at the wreck site, the lifeboat was gingerly lowered down the cliff by rope. It was now 2pm, both wind and seas had grown in ferocity. The Upgang crew would have to wait for better weather. At first light they made an attempt but were driven ashore by the powerful seas. Some of the men huddled on the *Rohilla* became so despondent upon witnessing the lifeboat's failed attempt that they jumped off the ship in a desperate attempt to make it ashore. Not one of them survived.

Two more pulling and sailing lifeboats, one from Scarborough and one from Teesmouth, were despatched as word spread of the prolonged agony of the *Rohilla*. The Scarborough lifeboat, which had been towed to the scene by a steam trawler, attempted to reach the wreck from offshore, but eventually gave up. The Teesmouth lifeboat, also under tow, was swamped by an immense sea and her crew was rescued by the tug that had been assisting her. Coxswain Langlands did manage to get the Whitby No1 lifeboat out of the harbour but she, too, was beaten back.

Extreme measures were needed and a call was made to the lifeboat station at Tynemouth, some 40 miles to the north, where an experimental motor lifeboat, with a 40-hp petrol engine was located. It would be a long offshore trek in terrible conditions, but Coxswain Robert Smith of the motor lifeboat *Henry Vernon* mustered his crew. Making the journey to Whitby alone, the *Henry Vernon* crossed the harbour bar at 1am of 1 November, to pick up Commander Basil Hall, who had come to help organise the rescue effort.

At first light the *Henry Vernon* approached the wreck from seaward and, in full view of an expanding throng of journalists and onlookers, appeared to hesitate outside the breakers, as if she, too, was no match for the situation. In fact Coxswain Smith was dropping oil to quell the seas. One chronicler wrote:

> …the lifeboat turned about, raced at full speed outside the line of breakers, past the stern of the wreck, and then turned directly towards shore. The most dangerous moment came when she was inside the surf and broad-side on to the waves; but, guided with splendid skill and courage, she moved forward steadily, and a cheer of relief went out from the shore when she reached the lee of the wreck, immediately beneath the crowded bridge. The feelings of those on board as they saw salvation at hand can only be imagined.[317]

Now alongside the *Rohilla*, with the lifeboat's petrol engine still purring away, and green water still pummelling over the top of the wreck, Coxswain Smith wasted no time in getting the survivors on board. Initially he decided to take a load of 30 ashore, but after being almost capsized by two immense waves that had combed over the *Rohilla*, he decided to take all 50 remaining survivors at once; the risk of attempting another trip was too great. The run back was far from uneventful. En route, the *Henry Vernon* was swept over on her side by the surf, but ever so slowly she came back up, with all her human cargo intact; she eventually made the beach to a hero's welcome. The motor lifeboat had proven its worth.

The rescue of 85 survivors of the *Rohilla*, was a monumental feat. Not only did the rescue earn the RNLI Gold Medal for Thomas Langlands, Robert Smith and Captain Burton (an army officer who had been with Smith on the *Henry Vernon*), it also proved that motor lifeboats had a place in coastal lifesaving and that with reliable engines and trained engineers they could do what conventional lifeboats could not.

CHAPTER 13

The Dutch Motor Lifeboats

Another country that featured prominently in the early development of the motor lifeboat was The Netherlands. In the north of the country the NZHRM had begun experiments with petrol engines as far back as 1907, when the *Jhr Mr J.W.H. Rutgers van Rozenburg* was constructed in Amsterdam – a purpose-built MLB powered by a 45-hp Brooke's engine. She was the first MLB in the world to have a proper engine room and to incorporate tunnel protection for the propeller.[318] In 1910 the NZHRM would order the construction of a much larger steel MLB, called the *Brandaris*, which, at 38 tons (38.76 tonnes) and 58ft (17.7m) LOA was a considerable advancement. This vessel would be the first of a new design of large Dutch MLBs and of a style of lifeboat associated with coastal rescue in The Netherlands for decades to come. The *Brandaris*, and others like her, would be the catalyst for the construction of a larger breed of motorised cruising lifeboat that would become quite popular in other European countries.

The *Brandaris* was the dream-child of Hendrik De Booy, a retired naval officer who had been Secretary of the NZHRM since 1906. He had a vast knowledge of the needs of the Dutch lifesaving service and of the type of motorised rescue craft that would best suit. De Booy believed that a larger MLB that could be used to patrol offshore in stormy conditions, would be much more useful than an entire fleet of smaller, harbour-based and carriage-launched MLBs. The high volume of local and international maritime traffic around the country generally meant that whenever a severe storm hit the area, one or more vessels would inevitably get into difficulty offshore. Thus it made more sense to reduce response time by having a large, massively-built lifeboat already at sea, patrolling for vessels in peril. The philosophy was, of course, adapted from the Norwegian Society, already using their sailing lifeboats in this manner for over a decade. For the Dutch the distances were not as great as those in Scandinavia, but the principle was the same. The sea and surf conditions off The Netherlands are among the most severe in the world. The tendrils of shifting sand extend miles offshore and the treacherous currents that flow over them combine with northwesterly storms to produce impenetrable walls of breaking surf. Most lifeboat launchings in severe weather would be from protected harbours or rivers, which invariably meant that a coastal bar of some shape or form would have to be crossed. In De Booy's opinion this was the most dangerous part of any mission – the large cruising MLB would also offset this danger – when such a boat did have to return to or depart from port the larger size of the hull, and the weight and power of the boat itself would be better suited to cope with the conditions at a bar entrance.

The 38-ton Dutch MLB *Brandaris* of the NZHRM, the first of a long line of large MLBs designed to withstand the horrendous bar and shoal conditions on the Dutch coast and to stay out for extended periods if required. *KNRM*

The *Brandaris* was launched in 1910. The *M.C. Blankenheym* of the ZHRM, an MLB of similar type and construction, followed in 1912. The *Brandaris* was powered by a single twin-cylinder 76-hp Kromhout paraffin (kerosene) 'heavy oil' engine driving a large three-bladed propeller producing a top speed of 8.25kt with an underway endurance of 40 hours.[319] Aside from the unique approach of the design itself, other innovative features included a hull of riveted steel, which the Dutch felt was stronger than wood and was less prone to structural failure in the rather inevitable event of striking bottom. The *Brandaris* also had flush decks and two below-deck cabins for survivors and crew. This was the first rescue craft to install a 'rescue net' forward – a veritable trapeze net, into which survivors could jump. First of a long line of similar Dutch rescue craft, the *Brandaris* also had a full ketch rig. In 1921 while en route from her home port of Terschelling, in the outer Frisian Islands, to a schooner reported in distress, the *Brandaris* disappeared with all hands (see Chapter I-13). Not a trace of vessel or crew was ever found, but her reputation survived: in her relatively short career *Brandaris* had saved some 231 lives. On the day of her tragic loss conditions were so severe that the Southern Society steam lifeboat *President Van Heel* capsized with the loss of six of her crew. These two tragedies would inspire a fundamental reconsideration of self-righting qualities in future large Dutch rescue craft.

Following 1921 a new construction programme was undertaken in the NZHRM, again under the stewardship of De Booy. The merits of larger lifeboats, whether steam or motor propelled, had already been proven. In 1923 the society constructed the *Brandaris II*, a twin-screw version of the earlier boat and somewhat larger at 60ft (18.3m). In many respects the *Brandaris II* was similar to the British Barnett type that appeared the same year; she was powered by two single-cylinder 45-hp Kromhout engines housed in separate fully enclosed engine rooms, and had tunnel-housed propellers as well as a shelter over the cockpit for the crew. In contrast to the Barnett type, her hull was of riveted steel, but she was still non self-righting.

Eventually, De Booy himself promoted the idea of a large, self-righting MLB of the same length but less beam than the previous Dutch lifeboats. It would incorporate a heavier keel and a re-righting ballast system known as a 'kiptank'. The idea for such a boat had been brought to De Booy's attention by Coxswain Mees Toxopeus, a name that would be synonymous with heroic lifeboat rescues in The Netherlands for many years to come. In his mind, the ideal large lifeboat would be self-righting and, being completely watertight, would behave in rough weather 'like a submarine on the surface'. It would also include another first: a completely enclosed conning

position, or wheelhouse, extra to the standard exposed helm station.[320] The necessity for such an enclosed wheelhouse is now so universally accepted that one wonders how lifesavers of the past fought the elements face-on without some form of protection. But the conventional attitude at the time was that seamen were best left 'in the weather', in order to gauge the conditions and safely control the craft. It is an opinion that continues to this day, as evidenced by the addition of secondary 'flying bridges' on many coastal rescue boat designs.

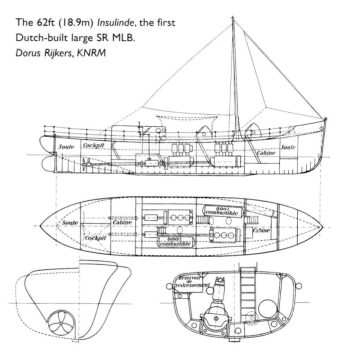

The 62ft (18.9m) *Insulinde*, the first Dutch-built large SR MLB.
Dorus Rijkers, KNRM

In the finest tradition of listening to the people that worked the vessels at sea, De Booy followed Toxopeus's suggestions to the letter. The result was the *Insulinde*, the first large self-righting MLB to be built in The Netherlands. Named after the Dutch colonies in the East Indies whence the funds for her construction came, she would become one of the most famous rescue boats in The Netherlands (see p.137).

The *Insulinde* was 62ft (18.9m) long and had a beam of just over 13ft (4m), giving her a length-to-breadth ratio of 3.86 – significantly less than the average 4.64 of earlier large non-self-righting MLBs in both The Netherlands and Britain. She was built of mild steel and the thickness of the bottom plating was significantly increased from previous Dutch MLBs, serving first to strengthen the bottom of the boat, and secondly, to increase the weight towards the keel. Along with the narrower beam the extra weight was essential for self-righting as was the new 'kiptank', designed to fill rapidly after capsizing and provide the additional momentum to re-right the boat from the inverted position. Displacing 42 tons (42.84 tonnes) *Insulinde*'s draught was a mere 4ft 3in (1.3m). She was powered by two 60-hp 'heavy oil motors' which, because of the narrow beam, were placed in isolated engine compartments positioned diagonally, one ahead of the other; she could cruise at 9.25kt. This was also the first MLB to have a 'boiler type' hull that helped create the lifeboat's submarine-like appearance. The semi-rounded decks, particularly pronounced along the sheerstrake, became a common feature on future large lifeboats in The Netherlands and Germany. They allowed water to flow off the deck in rapid fashion – an important feature for inshore rescue craft that often find themselves more beneath than above the water. She also had stanchions and hand-railings placed a considerable distance inboard from the sides of the vessel – another first that would be seen on many future lifeboats, particularly those commonly used in the surf. With her narrow, torpedo-like appearance, her crew nicknamed the *Insulinde* the 'ballasted bottle'. Although her narrow beam and self-righting features did not make her the most comfortable boat in a seaway, she always came back. All the large Dutch MLBs of the next 40 years would be basic derivations of the *Insulinde*.

The *Insulinde* was considered a radical departure from the traditional design of large MLBs at the time. At the 1924 and 1928 International Lifeboat Conferences, considerable debate was waged between Barnett, Consultant Naval Architect to the RNLI, and De Booy, regarding the merits of steel over wood, the potential dangers of an enclosed helm position and, more significantly, the advantages, if any, of having such a large boat designed as a self-righting vessel. These well-intentioned discussions continued for several years until, eventually, De Booy articulated the age-old truth of lifeboat design: a 'life-boat has to adapt herself to the circumstances she is going to meet; therefore where circumstances differ, life-boats will differ'.[321]

It was, indeed, as simple as that. From the time of the earliest proponents of different lifeboat designs, such as Henry Greathead, William Wouldhave and Lionel Lukin, this fundamental reality had not changed. Nevertheless, in the end, most countries would adopt self-righting designs, steel for hull construction, and enclosed wheelhouses.

The creation of a large all-weather self-righting MLB had also essentially eliminated the need for cruising offshore in heavy weather. Although the practice did continue with the new boats, the self-righters were designed to lay afloat and to safely cross the treacherous bars in all conditions. Patrols eventually became unnecessary. The *Insulinde* and her descendants would

remain in service through the Second World War right up until the 1990s. The *Neeltje Jacoba* built in 1930 would serve throughout her 38-year career at IJmuiden, for many years as a relief vessel, and would not be sold out of service until 1969.

In the 1930s the Dutch began experimenting with another design innovation. A large rubber fender, or rubbing strake, was permanently mounted on the exterior of the hull, running almost the entire length of the vessel. In 1936 Th. De Booy, who had taken over the reigns of the NZHRM from his father, presented a paper at the 4th International Lifeboat Conference in Sweden, in which he described the benefits of such a fender over the previous type of natural-fibre fenders that tended to break from their lanyards.[322] The system was similar to the external cork fendering of some of the early European pulling and sailing lifeboats. The cushioning effects and durability of hard rubber provided far greater protection to the more modern, and much heavier, MLBs when they came alongside a wreck. Permanent rubber fenders are now a standard feature on almost all lifeboats and large rescue craft.

The 1950s and '60s saw the construction of the next generation of large self-righting MLBs for The Netherlands' two lifeboat organisations. In 1951 the MLB *Prins Hendrik* was built by the H. Schouten Yard at Muiden for the NZHRM. Essentially a modernised version of the *Insulinde*, she was diesel powered (all Dutch lifeboats, including the *Insulinde*, had by then been converted to diesel), had more efficient five-bladed propellers, and the hull and stern tunnels had been re-designed to allow for a more efficient flow of water past the propellers at almost all angles of heel. Another new and important feature was the lightweight aluminium wheelhouse, similar to that already fitted on the veteran *Brandaris II*, which incorporated a secondary helm in a 'flying bridge'. The hull was of welded-steel construction and there were to be 'no more leaky rivets'![323] The newer hull form incorporated bilge keels providing greater transverse and longitudinal stability when underway, and also helping to stabilise any rollover tendencies should the boat strike the bottom. The *Prins Hendrik* was longer than the previous boats at 66ft 10in (20.4m) but still just as narrow at only 13ft 3½in (4m); she had a relatively shallow draught of 4ft 4in (1.3m). She was powered by two 120-hp Glennifer diesels, producing a maximum speed of 10kt, and remained in service at IJmuiden and Den Helder until 1997. The *Prins Hendrik* is now part of the Dutch Life-Saving Museum at Den Helder.

In 1960 the NZHRM developed the qualities of the *Prins Hendrik* with the Carlot class. The Society was receiving an increasing number of call-outs up to 50 miles offshore and there was a need for a more powerful and longer-range craft. The *Carlot*, therefore, was powered by

The KNRM (formerly KNZHRM) Carlot type lifeboat *Suzanna* underway with a rescue-net on her foredeck. Constructed in the 1960s this was one of the last designs of large displacement-hulled lifeboats in service, the type being characterised by the raised wheelhouse aft.

Kees Brinkman, KNRM

two 140-hp 8-TS-117 Kromhout diesel engines providing a top speed of 10.5kt and a range of 1,050 nautical miles. The earliest versions of the type had an enclosed flying bridge, or upper wheelhouse, which provided additional crew protection on long offshore calls. Later versions had an additional open flying bridge above this. Five Carlot MLBs were built during the 1960s, the other four being the *Gebroeders Luden*, *Bernard van Leer*, *Johanna Louisa* and the *Suzanna*.[324]

Around the same time that the northern society was developing the Carlot, officials in the south were working on a new design of MLB for the Hook of Holland station at the entrance to the Port of Rotterdam. The first of the Javazee class, was named the *Koningin Juliana*, and was launched in March 1963. The Javazee was the largest Dutch MLB class ever built. More than ever the design resembled the submarine-like qualities of the earliest boats. It was 70ft by 15ft 3in (21.3 by 4.6m), providing it with a somewhat larger length-to-breadth ratio then earlier vessels, although the engines were still diagonally mounted in separate engine rooms. One of the unique features of the type was that the self-righting ballast tank had been removed, but the design was still expected to re-right itself because ' a sea which can capsize a boat, will also right her again within a short time, provided the negative part of the curve of righting levers is small, as it is in this boat'.[325]

The inherent self-righting tendency of the boat would be assisted by the positive buoyancy of the large and prominent wheelhouse. The *Koningin Juliana* was powered by two 170-hp GM diesels providing a top speed of 10.7kt. She also had an integrated safety wire,

fitted from her wheelhouse to her bow and stern, to which the crew could attach safety lines when working on deck in heavy weather. Three of this type were eventually constructed, the other two being the MLBs *Javazee* and *De Zeemanspot*. All were still in service with the KNRM as relief lifeboats as of 2001.

In the 1970s both Dutch Societies realised that the changing demands of maritime search and rescue (SAR) required a faster speed of response in all weather conditions. The focus began to swing away from the large traditional steel MLBs towards other types of smaller inshore rescue boats and, in particular, to the development of larger rigid hull inflatables (RHIs). That said, the Dutch MLBs, some of the largest of their kind ever built, would continue to provide invaluable service right into the 21st Century. Some lifeboats continue in service to this day. In addition to being used as relief lifeboats in The Netherlands, several have been sold and now serve in Iceland where they are well suited to patrolling the harsh marine environment around that island nation.

The submarine-like KNRM (formerly KZHRM) lifeboat *Javazee*. This vessel was the namesake of her type and one of three built. The *Javazee* was still being used as a relief lifeboat by the KNRM as of 2001.

KNRM. Redding Museum Dorus Rijkers

The Dutch *Javazee* type MLB of the KNRM (formerly KZHRM).

KNRM

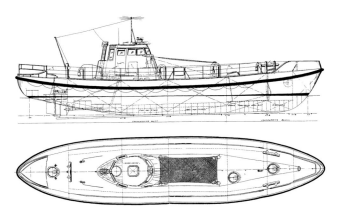

The Wreck of the *Bramov*

At 10.30pm on 16 September 1935, a strong WSW gale was blowing across the North Sea. A call was received by the lifeboat *Insulinde* of the NZHRM from the Ems River Pilot Boat, advising that an unidentified ship was aground on the treacherous Borkum Reef at the mouth of the Ems. Although this notorious obstacle to shipping was in German waters, the crew of the Dutch lifeboat disregarded the concept of national boundaries and carried on with the mission of saving lives.

While the *Insulinde* crossed the breaking surf of the Frisian Gap she was swept by a massive comber that 'rose above us in the dark, its white crest looming over the ship. With a terrific blow it thundered eight feet over us' and broke, leaving the clinging lifeboat crew soaked to the bone with more than three hours to go before they reached the stricken ship. In addition to the ravages of mother nature, the coxswain and crew were unsure what awaited them at Borkum Reef, for no radio messages had been received from the casualty and the dark and chaotic din of the evolving storm ruled out any chance of a visual signal. The Ems River Pilot Boat had also advised the *Insulinde* that a German lifeboat was already on its way; perhaps those onboard the ship had already been safely rescued.

In spite of the doubts, and with grim determination, the Dutch crew carried on into the increasing fury of the storm that had now reached Force 9. With daybreak came the loom of dawn and the dark shape of a stricken ship engulfed in the mist and foam of the breaking surf. Human figures were clearly visible scurrying about the boat deck; the bridge and charthouse had already been swept away by the giant waves. The name of the ship, *Bramov*, was clearly visible on her stern. The *Insulinde*'s coxswain, Mees Toxopeus, knew instantly that if they were to save the *Bramov*'s crew of 12, they would have to act quickly and decisively.

With a strong ebb tide confusing the breaking seas and providing even less water around the wreck, Mees Toxopeus brought the 62ft (18.9m), 42-ton *Insulinde* alongside the stricken *Bramov*, striking bottom on several occasions. The crew had set up the rescue net on the *Insulinde*'s long foredeck and in the first two passes seven of the *Bramov*'s crew successfully jumped on to the heaving *Insulinde*.

Six more attempts to come alongside the wreck were made under 'almost impossible circumstances', but to no avail. Either the *Insulinde* was too far away and heaving too much, or the remaining five crew on the ship, including the captain, had not enough courage to make the terrifying plunge at a pitching, heaving, safety net. One thing was certain, time was running out and the conditions were deteriorating – on the seventh attempt, near calamity struck when a monstrous breaker came crashing in over the Borkum Reef, picked up the *Insulinde* like so much flotsam and sent her careening towards the *Bramov* stern first. In the words of Klaas Toxopeus, a crewmember on the lifeboat, 'luckily the *Insulinde* came around at the last moment and we only scraped the wreck, but that "scrape" took our starboard pudding fender and stove in the whole stern'. On the eighth attempt, four more men jumped into the net, and only the captain of the *Bramov* remained. Three more attempts were made to recover the captain who seemed inseparable from his doomed vessel. The lifeboat crew knew that this could not go on and that, sooner or later, the odds would turn against them. On the 12th and final attempt the *Insulinde* was thrown aloft by a heavy sea and came level with the stricken ship's boat deck. Two lifeboatmen made a split second decision: one grabbed the captain by the leg, the other by his arm, and 'the Captain was ours. We got him aboard uninjured, and the first thing he said was: "Thank God"'.

Such was the chaos and confusion of this particular rescue that it was not until after the lifeboat was well away from the wreck that her engineer advised the coxswain that, during the recovery process, the starboard engine had been off-line for five minutes – apparently the *Insulinde* had struck bottom so hard that the throttle controls for that engine had severed; the coxswain, his undivided attention on handling his little ship (and keeping himself and his crew alive), had been totally unaware.

The *Insulinde*'s crew of five had saved all 12 men from the *Bramov* and carried them safely into Borkum Harbour.[326]

Unlike previous designs of large Dutch MLBs, the NZHRM's *Insulinde* was designed to be self-righting. This was done through the use of a water-ballast transfer system or 'kiptank', here being tested at her builder's trials.
KNRM, Redding Museum Dorus Rijkers

CHAPTER 14

The German Rescue Cruisers

The German Rescue Cruiser *Vormann Steffens* from the DGzRS Station at Hooksiel beating her way into heavy seas.
DGzRS

In 1959 a paper was presented at the 8th International Lifeboat Conference in Bremen, Germany, describing the DGzRS's newest style of rescue craft, of which three were then in service. The author of the paper was Captain John Schumacher, Inspector of the Society and a leading figure in the development of large lifeboats in post-war Germany. The conditions faced by the German rescue service were very similar to those of neighbouring countries, such as The Netherlands and Denmark, having 'shallow coasts, extended tidal sands, far advanced shelves and reefs, considerable distances of the shipping routes from the coast, and the (need for) safeguarding of the airways over a sea range of considerable extent…'.[327]

The DGzRS needed to design a large, fast, self-righting MLB capable of operating in shallow surf conditions close inshore. Rather than have two vessels respond to a shallow-water call, the simple solution was to combine two boats in one. The mother vessel would be large – 76ft (23.2m) – and considerably faster than previous German MLBs, attaining 21kt. It would carry, on a stern launch-and-recovery ramp, a *tochterboot*, or daughter-

boat, that could be launched in practically all sea conditions for shallow inshore work. The result was a new style of large self-righting MLB, aptly named by Captain Schumacher himself: 'The "rescue cruiser" for she has to cruise on position at sea and thus be ready for action in the shortest possible delay'.[328]

Another reason for the development of this type of fast offshore rescue boat was one of economy. The finances of the self-sufficient DGzRS were still reeling from the devastation of the Second World War, and it was felt that considerable operational savings could be gained by shutting down several of the old shore stations and replacing them with the new rescue cruisers.

The rescue cruiser was the first design to combine the benefits of self-righting, a steel hull, and high speed in a larger offshore-capable package. The development can be likened to the breaking of the sound barrier for aircraft – it led the way for the evolution of the self-righting MLB from the 10kt displacement hulls of the past to the 25kt plus wonders of the future.

The design evolution of the rescue cruiser began in 1950 with the old 52ft MLB *Bremen* launched in 1931 (see Chapter II-12). The *Bremen* was stripped down to a bare hull and completely re-engineered to test elements of the rescue cruiser concept. She was totally re-powered, had the typical conning-tower wheelhouse attached with a secondary steering station on top, and had a launching ramp and prototype daughter-boat placed on the stern. The *Bremen* was returned to service in 1953 at her homeport of Bremerhaven where the suitability of the alterations were monitored by DGzRS engineers.[329]

The improvements were well accepted but there still remained the question of speed – even with the new engines, the *Bremen* could still only reach 11kt. The next step was a purpose-built rescue cruiser. The DGzRS hired the engineering firm of Maierform to help design a hull that would provide the proper combination of stability, sea-keeping ability and speed. The result was the *Hermann Apelt*, launched in 1955 and powered by three Daimler-Benz diesels: one large 1,100-hp engine on the centre shaft, and two 150-hp engines on either side. The design followed the tradition of earlier German MLBs, such as the *Norderney* and *Hindenburg* of 1944, in terms of their conning-tower wheelhouses and rounded sheerstrakes. This prototype had no daughter-boat or stern ramp, however, as she was designed for use at the Heligoland Station where shallow-water was not an issue. Reaching the anticipated 20kt plus, the *Hermann Apelt* was a resounding success. The direction was now clear, the only thing remaining was to perfect the machine. In 1957 the *Theodore Heuss*, the first of a long line of modern rescue cruisers was launched. She was 76ft (23.2m) long, 17ft 5in (5.3m) beam, with a draught of 4ft 8in (1.4m). For the 'design of the new boat type it was an important demand to increase the speed and to combine the best qualities of "non-self-righting" and "self-righting" boats'.[330]

The Maierform hull design was entirely unique, and contributed greatly to the eventual success of the type in Germany and elsewhere. Captain Schumacher also advised that the 'bow lines of the boat have proven excellent under various sea conditions. In general the special form of the hull and the stern permit [the vessel] to keep continuous high speeds in heavy seas'.[331] The self-righting tendency of the boat was not dependant on any water-ballast arrangements but was a factor of the design itself. The combination of the vessel's low centre of gravity, the large amount of positive buoyancy within the hull and the prominent enclosed wheelhouse all served to assist in re-righting. The *Theodore Heuss* had seven watertight compartments, and her tank structure was designed to create a double bottom over the entire length for protection against puncture. Required to have good manoeuvring qualities in a ground swell and surf, the hull was also strengthened to withstand repeated groundings and the transverse impact stresses inherent when coming alongside vessels in adverse conditions. Lightweight, high-tensile steel was used and the framework was stiffened in a latticework of honeycomb-type frames for resistance.

The five rescue cruisers in service by 1960 were triple-screw with one 1,350-hp high-speed centreline diesel and two smaller 150-hp auxiliary diesels outboard. For economical cruising and slow speed manoeuvrability one or both auxiliaries could be used. The large engine could be used to bring the rescue cruiser up to its maximum speed of 21kt if required. The centreline fixed propeller could also be used in floating ice (not uncommon in German estuaries), as it was lower than the outboard variable-pitch propellers. The rescue cruisers had three separate rudders providing excellent handling characteristics – the boat was able to come around full circle, at full speed, in 20 seconds. On one of the smaller engines only, with a full load of fuel, the rescue cruiser's range was a phenomenal 6,500 nautical miles at 9kt.

DGzRS

Scale

Length over all	23.20 m
Breadth, moulded	5.30 m
Draught, max.	1.40 m
Speed	21 kn

Rescue Cruiser

The DGzRS Seenotkreuzer *Theodore Heuss*, launched in 1957, revolutionised maritime SAR as she was the first vessel to combine the advantages of high speed (in excess of 20kt) with a self-righting hull.
Deutsches Museum

The 21ft (6.5m) tochterboot was a stout little vessel sturdily built of light, salt-water resistant alloy and designed to be self-righting. It had a totally enclosed hull except for two self-bailing cockpits and there was a full-length rubber fender. The 34-hp diesel gave a speed of 8kt. The stern of the *Theodore Heuss* had a built-in launch ramp for the daughter boat, described as a 'recessed trough-shaped part of the after deck...fitted with seawater-resistant rollers running on ball bearings. The hinged stern is operated oil-hydraulically. This arrangement gives an incorporated slipway for launching or hauling up the daughterboat.'[332]

The concept of mother and daughter-boat has become a mainstay for MLB design in Germany and elsewhere in the world. In the 1960s it became apparent that the fleet of smaller beach-and-carriage launch boats was in need of replacement. After some consideration the DGzRS

decided upon a smaller, shallow-draught version of the rescue cruiser, this time with a high-speed, lightweight tochterboot powered by an outboard engine. The new vessel, the *Paul Denker* was launched in 1967; she had a length of 55ft (16.8m) and a relatively shallow draught of 4ft 6in (1.35m). The *Paul Denker* was the only version of this size to be built; subsequent designs of the inshore rescue cruiser known as the Otto Schülke class, launched from 1969 onwards, were 62ft (18.9m) long with a slightly deeper draught.[333]

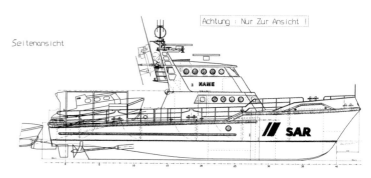

A contemporary drawing of one of the latest DGzRS rescue cruisers. The basic principles of the Maierform hull remain the same. An enclosed upper wheelhouse has been added for extra space and to allow for a sealed internal environment in the event of a SAR case involving a petroleum or chemical product tanker. *DGzRS*

The very large 144ft (44m) rescue cruiser *Wilhelm Kaisen*, one of two offshore control and command rescue ships launched for the DGzRS in the 1970s. Note the helicopter pad on the aftdeck. *DGzRS*

Later types of rescue cruiser included the 87ft (26.6m) *George Breusing*, launched in 1963 with a top speed of 24kt.[334] This class included the ill-fated *Adolph Bermpohl*, launched in 1965 (see Chapter I-13). The trend towards larger rescue cruisers continued through the 1970s when two very large examples were built for offshore work: the

John T. Essberger and the *Wilhelm Kaisen*, both an astounding 144ft (44m) long with a top speed of 26kt; they are still in operation, one on station in the North Sea, the other in the Baltic. More ship than lifeboat, these large SR vessels are equipped with a helicopter deck, a 29ft (8.8m) tochterboot and an inflatable rescue craft, as well as a hospital and massive fire-fighting capabilities. Their primary role is in offshore search-and-rescue (SAR). With such a large platform, they can act as a floating maritime rescue sub-centre (MRSC) in the event of a major offshore maritime incident involving either ships or aircraft.[335] As of 2001 work was underway to replace both vessels with slightly larger rescue cruisers in the 157ft (49m) range (see Chapter II-23).

In addition to these, several different variations of the rescue cruiser were designed and launched in Germany during the 1980s and 1990s. As of the year 2000 there were six of the 90ft (27.5m) Berlin type in service, seven of the Eiswette type, around 76ft (23.3m) in length, four of the larger inshore Otto Schülke type at around 62ft (18.9m) in length and, of course, the smaller inshore *Paul Denker*. In 1996 a rescue cruiser was delivered to the DGzRS that had an enclosed upper wheelhouse rather then a flying bridge. The *Hermann Rudolf Meyer* was the first of this type, based on the 76ft design. She was designed around the 'citadel principle', which provided full environmental protection for the crew in the event of a shipping casualty involving noxious chemicals or fumes – an increasingly common occurrence in German waters. As well as having an enclosed wheelhouse, the entire vessel becomes a sealed unit, allowing the crew to assess a situation without exposing themselves to the hazardous substances and thereby debilitating their own effectiveness to render aid.

The Loss of the Italian Steamer *Fides*

In the early morning of 20 January 1962 the Italian steamer *Fides* lost steerage and was blown on to the Vorgelsand at the mouth of the River Elbe. The area was well known as a graveyard of ships, and the *Fides* was grounded almost on top of the *Ondo* wreck, lost only the year before. The southwest winds were very strong and the ship was soon hard aground and overwhelmed by immense breaking seas. The DGzRS rescue cruiser *Ruhr-Stahl* was dispatched from the station at Cuxhaven with two large salvage tugs. When they arrived the tugs made a futile attempt to drag the *Fides* off the shoal. The tide was dropping however, and the coxswain of the *Ruhr-Stahl* knew the situation was only going to get worse; he immediately began to take soundings around the ship. By midday the storm was Force 7 from the SW with driving rain and the coxswain advised the master of the *Fides* of the impending predicament of his ship and crew; the captain ignored all advice of abandonment in favour of another salvage attempt. Two more tugs arrived and salvage men were placed aboard the stricken vessel. At about 1pm another attempt was made to drag the ship into deeper water, but it was too late. Green water was now making its way into the holds, and further soundings by the *Ruhr-Stahl* proved that the *Fides* was now one with the sands.

Within an hour the horrendous wrenching of tearing steel could be heard above the roar of the gale. The *Fides* was breaking up and rapidly. At 2.15pm the coxswain of the *Ruhr-Stahl* advised the ship's master that either the crew came off then, or probably they would not be coming off at all. Still they refused to give up the ship. Finally, at about 4pm, with the ship splitting in half, and both pieces being blown further into the breakers, the coxswain convinced the master to abandon his vessel. To come alongside was now much more hazardous: the current and wind had whipped the seas into an even more chaotic frenzy. But, somehow, over the next 45 minutes, all 32 of the Italian crew were recovered, plus the pilot and the salvage master. Two of the ship's crew were injured in the process, but all survived to tell the tale.[336]

One of the new generation DGzRS rescue cruisers, the 74ft (23.1m) *Herman Rudolph Meyer*, stationed at Bremerhaven.
DGzRS

CHAPTER 15

Other Cruising Rescue Craft

The NSSR's cruising lifeboat, the *J.M. Johansen*, was a radical departure from previous Scandinavian offshore boats. Launched in 1949, her houseworks were moved forward to amidships and the sails were no longer used for auxiliary propulsion but for steadying purposes only. *Redningsselskapet*

Starting in 1929 with the 51ft (6m) *Andreas Aaro*, the NSSR began the gradual switch towards mechanised propulsion as a primary source of power in Norwegian lifeboats. During the 1930s even larger sailing MLBs were constructed, with more powerful engines and far greater ranges of operation. In 1935 the society constructed its first cruising lifeboat to incorporate a full-size wheelhouse, the *Christian Bugge* (see p.145). Although equipped with large diesel engines, all these lifeboats still maintained a full set of sails and their hulls were essentially the same as that of the original Colin Archer design.

By the end of the Second World War, the NSSR recognised that its fleet was tired and that they required new vessels compatible with the change to year-round offshore patrols and to traverse the increasing distances travelled by the Norwegian fishing fleet. In 1949, in response to these changing demands, the cruising lifeboat *J.M. Johansen* was launched. At 75ft (22.8m) she symbolised a radical departure from previous NSSR designs and was to be the largest rescue craft in the fleet until 1958. Unlike her predecessors, this large displacement-hull vessel had limited sailing capabilities (staysails for steadying purposes only), and her superstructure was amidships, rather than aft, as had been the case on the motorised versions of the sailing lifeboats. On her maiden voyage, bound for Greenland, the *J.M. Johansen* saved the crew of 17 from a fishing vessel in a storm off the coast of Iceland.[337]

The trend towards larger offshore lifeboats in Norway would continue. Beginning in 1953 a new generation of steel rescue cruisers emerged, many of which are still in operation today. Six 55ft (16.8m) steel coastal lifeboats were built between 1958 and 1961; the last of the series, the *Tonnes Puntervold*, retired in 1990. Three 87ft (26.5m) offshore lifeboats, with steel hulls and aluminium superstructure were built between 1958 and 1960. Thirteen 75ft (22.9m) general-purpose cruising lifeboats were also built between 1963 and 1972 – some of the most beautiful 'small ships' ever constructed.

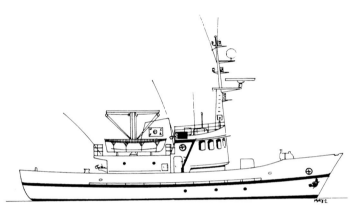

The 87ft (27m) Norwegian cruising lifeboat RS# 61, *Haakon VII*, originally launched in 1958, received a mid-life upgrading during the early 1980s. Her beautiful lines are typical of many of the NSSR's rescue craft constructed from 1946 until the mid 1970s; they were essentially small lifesaving ships.
Bård Kolltveit, Norsk Sjøfartsmuseum, Oslo

In 1973-74 the NSSR launched two 80ft (24.4m) derivatives of the popular 75ft (22.9m) design, the *R.S. Platou* and the *Ada Waage*, and built their largest offshore lifeboat ever, the 92ft (8.4m) *Sjofareren*. In style and design all these vessels maintained the superstructure amidships or slightly forward, as in the original *J.M. Johansen*, thus providing them with their 'ship-like' appearance.

A similar approach to lifeboat construction was taken in neighbouring Sweden after the Second World War. In order to cover more coastline with limited resources, a 62ft (18.9m) cruising MLB was constructed in 1948. The all-steel *A.E. Appelberg* was powered by a 'Super-Scandia crude-oil engine of 210 H.P.' and had a cruising speed of 9.5kt. She had an ice-strengthened hull and, like earlier Swedish cruising MLBs, was fully equipped with a ketch rig.[338] In 1954 a high-speed, steel-hulled, aluminium-superstructure rescue launch was built in Sweden for rapid response and coverage of the new air routes to and

from Europe. This vessel was not self-righting, and was very similar in design to wartime crash boats. The *Hjalparen* was 59ft (18m) long and, like contemporary German rescue cruisers, had a primary engine for high-speed use and a secondary engine for more economical, low-speed patrols. (Both the Norwegians and the Swedes referred to their large offshore lifeboats as 'rescue cruisers' for, although not as fast as their German counterparts, they, too, patrolled offshore for extended periods with crews being accommodated onboard.) The *Hjalparen* had a top speed of 20kt.[339]

Although the Swedish SSRS would continue to make advances in the development of faster rescue boats, they would also continue to build the North Sea-type cruising lifeboats for offshore patrols right up until the 1990s. By 1972 there were 10 rescue cruisers in the Swedish fleet, including a new type of ice-strengthened vessel designed in 1965 and launched in 1967. The rescue cruiser *Dan Bostrom* was 78ft (23.8m) long and was powered by four Volvo-Penta 210-hp diesels providing a top speed of 12kt. At 118 tons (120.36 tonnes) displacement, she was well suited for working in the harsh northern environment. A unique feature of the *Dan Bostrom* was her forward cabin and wheelhouse, which offered almost 360° visibility.[340] In 1981 another large offshore lifeboat design was initiated when the 70ft (21m) *Olof Wallenius* was launched. She was referred to as a 'medium heavy cruiser' and weighed in at 95 tons (96.9 tonnes) displacement. She, too, was

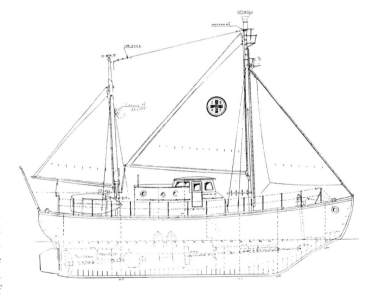

The transition from sail to power – a 64ft (20m) Swedish sailing MLB built in 1951. This boat had a steel hull with a reinforced ice-breaking bow. Although she sported a full ketch rig for auxiliary power the masts had been shortened.
RNLI

powered by twin Volvo diesels generating 656hp, providing a speed of 11kt over an operational range of 1,400 nautical miles. In 1995 the SSRS also launched the 146-ton (148.92-tonne), 13kt rescue cruiser *Astra*. With the recent switch to higher-speed, harder-chined rescue craft in Sweden and Norway, *Astra* was probably the last of her kind. Built to Ice class 1A, she is capable of holding 100 survivors, has an external de-icing system on the outer wheelhouse and railings, and a large fire pump and monitor system. Additionally, she has an aft control station in the wheelhouse to assist the master when setting up a tow, and a small stern ramp that can be extended off the after deck to allow a helicopter to land.[341]

Many of the large offshore displacement-type rescue craft built in Sweden since the 1960s were still in operation as of 1999, most in conjunction with smaller, high-speed craft. More recently however, the SSRS have been switching to the construction of high speed MLBs (see Chapter II-23 and Part IV).[342]

Norway and Sweden were not the only northern countries to establish patrolling rescue craft. In 1937 Iceland built a patrolling rescue ship to cover the offshore fishing grounds. The vessel, the *Sæbjörg*, was incredibly busy during the dark days of the Second World War and was responsible for rescuing an astounding 224 vessels and saving 1,257 lives. Following the war, it was recognised that a much bigger and more powerful rescue cruiser would be needed to keep up with the expansion in the fishery and the increasing size and range of the Icelandic fishing trawlers themselves. As a result, the original *Sæbjörg* was entirely re-built in 1947, much along the lines of the large Norwegian and Swedish rescue cruisers, but with her houseworks placed well aft, like most of the North Sea trawlers of the day. The 180-hp diesel was replaced with a 300-hp model, and her hull was made 15ft 8in (4.7m) longer. She was also updated with state-of-the-art electronics including radar.[343] In 1950 a new offshore rescue cruiser, the *María Júlía*, was added to the Icelandic service, being somewhat larger and more powerful than her predecessor at 137.4 tons (140,12 tonnes), 90ft (27.5m) long and with a 470-hp Petters diesel that could drive her along at 11.5kt.[344] Currently, the Icelandic Lifesaving Service maintains a large fleet of offshore lifeboats from around Europe, including a Clyde and several Aruns from the UK, two ex-German rescue cruisers, two of the old Dutch Carlot type lifeboats and an ex-Norwegian lifeboat. All these stout vessels are well suited to the harsh conditions and greater distances in which the Icelandic crews are expected to operate (see Part IV).

In Britain and Ireland, the role of the cruising lifeboat has always been limited. The vast number of stations meant that the bulk of rescue calls were almost within sight of one lifeboat station or another and there was no real need to provide lifesaving coverage offshore, or to cruise about. That said, there had been earlier proposals for large, mobile rescue vessels. These included the specially constructed rescue schooner *Peronelle*, designed and built in 1875 by Captain Hans Busk, and the 'lifesaving steamer' concept that had been proposed and built in 1886, in response to the urgings of Sir Edward Watkin, MP (see Chapter II-10).[345] In both cases, the concept of roaming rescue vessels around the British Isles, failed. Aside from the large 60ft Barnett type MLBs developed in the 1920s, the RNLI did not consider it necessary to build patrolling lifeboats. The all-volunteer nature of the service meant that permanent crew would need to be hired to man patrolling boats and, aside from the fast Dover lifeboat, *Sir William Hillary* of the 1920s and '30s for which a crew was hired to patrol the Dover Straits, the Institution has always prided itself on remaining an entirely voluntary service. The large Barnett type was designed for one or two specific locations where maritime traffic was heavy and a larger capacity lifeboat may have been needed to evacuate scores of survivors. Still, the Barnett was meant to lay afloat at a station and to respond to large casualties in high-traffic areas such as off the Thames and the Mersey.

In 1962 however, the Committee of Management of the RNLI decided to buck the trend and proposed the construction of a new type of large offshore lifeboat in the 70ft (23m) range. The previous year, on a visit to the Dutch and German lifeboat services, RNLI officials had been very impressed by the large station-and-patrol rescue craft.[346] The result was the Clyde class cruising lifeboats, only three of which were ever built.[347] The first two vessels, which had somewhat different hulls, were described as being 'high endurance, suitable for prolonged search and/or stand-by operations'. They had capacity for 120 survivors onboard, accommodation for a live-aboard crew of five, and were equipped with a 20kt, inflatable daughter-boat stowed on the large foredeck. The first large lifeboat, the *Charles H. Barrett*, Civil Service No5, was launched in 1964, and the second, the *Grace Patterson Ritchie*, in 1965. Both boats were built at the Yarrow and Co. yard in Glasgow, Scotland. They had a displacement of approximately 80 tons (81.6 tonnes), could cruise for 550 nautical miles and were powered by twin Gardner 8L3B engines developing 230hp each at 1,150rpm, giving a cruising speed of 10.4kt. It seems that the Clyde-type boats were never used as patrolling rescue craft, but rather as large station lifeboats for locations such as the Bristol Channel, where a lifeboat may have to travel a considerable distance offshore to assist a casualty. Two of the three Clydes served at Clovelly from 1968 to 1988. As of 2001, all had been sold out of service, one of them becoming the *Henry A. Hálfdansson* of the Icelandic Lifesaving Service in 1989.

In 1992 the RNLI began design work for two new GRP fast afloat boats (FABs). The result was the 46ft 9in (14m) Trent class and the 55ft 9in (17m) Severn class, which would eventually take over from the Aruns. In this photo, the Trent class *Esme Anderson*, stationed at Ramsgate, is seen on training.
Nicholas Leach

The submarine-like KNRM (formerly KZHRM) lifeboat *Javazee*. This vessel was the namesake of her type and one of three built.
The *Javazee* was still being used as a relief lifeboat by the KNRM as of 2001.
KNRM. Redding Museum Dorus Rijkers

The USCG cutter *Barracuda*, one of the new 87ft (26.5m) Protector class patrol boats capable of cruising at 25kt.
USCG

Right:
One of the new generation DGzRS rescue cruisers, the 74ft (23.1m) *Herman Rudolph Meyer*, stationed at Bremerhaven.
DGzRS

Above:
The KNRM (formerly KNZHRM) Carlot type lifeboat *Suzanna* underway with a rescue-net on her foredeck. Constructed in the 1960s, this was one of the last designs of large displacement-hulled lifeboats in service, the type being characterised by the raised wheelhouse aft.
Kees Brinkman, KNRM

An intermediate lifeboat of the SSRS.
The 40ft (12m) Victoria class is
powered by twin 450hp diesels and
water-jets resulting in an impressive
top speed of 38kt.
Note the extensive polyurethane
fender system.
SSRS

The JF class RHI lifeboat *Christien* crosses the surfzone outside her homeport of IJmuiden, headquarters of the KNRM.
Kees Brinkman, KNRM

An RNLI 24ft (7.3m) *Atlantic 75* type RHI, an updated version of the old *Atlantic 21* type with a re-designed hull and console system.
RNLI/Royal Bank of Scotland/Rick Tomlinson

New generation SAR helicopter. A Canadian Armed Forces CH-149 Cormorant SAR helicopter from Gander, Newfoundland, on training exercise with the CCG.
Deb Bowes-Lyon, CCG

Facing page top:
The 52ft (15.8m) *Arun* class (FAB2) RNLB *Kenneth Thedwell* underway in rough seas. Although the RNLI has been actively replacing this type in recent years, almost all these venerable lifeboats continue to operate in rescue services around the world.
RNLI/Royal Bank of Scotland/Rick Tomlinson

Facing page bottom:
A new French First Class lifeboat. Based on a popular pilot boat design, this will be the standard large lifeboat for the SNSM, replacing 26 other large lifeboats of various shapes and descriptions. She is 46ft (14m) long, carries a small inflatable in her stern and is characterised by a tapered bulbous bow for improved hydro-dynamics.
SNSM

Below:
Due to the success of RHIs in the Dutch lifesaving environment, the KNRM decided that they would develop an all-RHI lifeboat fleet.

In 1999, an even larger RHI lifeboat, the 62ft (18.8m) *Arie Visser* was launched, with several more following, known as the AV type. The increased length provides a larger after deck than the JF type and the twin 1,000hp diesels deliver a top speed of 35kt with a 16-hour endurance.
Peter Van der Laan, KNRM

The Norwegian cruising lifeboat, the *Sjoefarenen*, blasts through a North Atlantic swell. At 92ft (28.4m) she is the largest of the NSSR fleet and is designed to patrol for extended periods providing SAR coverage for both the fishing and offshore oil industries.
Hans Hvide Bang, Redningsselskapet

Below:
An 18ft (5.5m) Gemini type RHI gets some 'airtime' while training off Cape Town, South Africa.
NSRI

Above:
The Sumner Lifeboat Institution's 'jet surf rescue boat' *AID II*,
stationed at Christchurch, New Zealand, in 1970. The SLI, working in
close conjunction with the Hamilton Jet Company of New Zealand,
pioneered the use of modern water-jet technology in fast rescue craft,
a technological trend that continues around the world today.
SLI

Left:
Knock down. A USCG 47ft MLB heels over 100° while her crew
hang on for dear life. Incredibly stable, the self-righting MLB
recovered immediately after this photo was taken.
USCG

The new 66ft (20m) Swedish lifeboat *Gad Rausing*, the first of the SSRS's Rescue 2000 class. A personal water craft (seadoo) is used as a daughter-boat and is seen on the vessel's stern.
SSRS

The new 79ft (24m) SM Finland rescue cruiser *Jenny Wihiri*, launched in 2000 and based out of Helsinki. This rescue craft is equipped as a mobile training center for the society's lifesaving crews.
Jaakko Pitkäjärvi, SM Finland

A newer all-weather MLB of the SNSM, the *Jean Cam* was the
first of 21 of her type that began entering service in 1988.
She is stationed at l'Ile Molène, Finistère.
Philip Plisson

A new RNLI Severn class MLB based at Weymouth underway at high speed. The latest versions of the Severn have had a small hydraulic-crane added to assist in launching the daughter-boat.
Gilbert Hampton, RNLI

As the RNLI replaces its Arun class lifeboats with the Severn and Trent classes many of the Aruns are being sold to other lifesaving organisations around the world. ICESAR has purchased four as of 2002. This is the ICESAR lifeboat *Oddur V. Gislason* stationed at Grindavik, southwest Iceland.
ICESAR

An RNLI slipway launch station at St David's in Wales. The Tyne class lifeboat *Garside* is seen being recovered on the slipway. These 47ft (14.3m) vessels have been designed with a low superstructure so that they can be stored and launched from the smaller slipway boathouses, some of which date back to the 19th Century.
Nicholas Leach

Modern-day heroines. Boatswain's Mate Cassandra Peacock of the USCG manoeuvres New London's 47ft MLB into position as a HH-60 Jayhawk helicopter lowers a stretcher during a training exercise.
USCG

Facing page top:
Four new RNLI lifeboat stations became operational on the Thames in January 2002. In a break from the traditional manning structure of the institution, three of the four units will have full-time managers and paid crews. The photo shows three of the new lifeboats, all are water-jet propelled Tiger Marine FRCs, capable of 40kt. The new initiative is being operated in conjunction with the British Maritime and Coastguard Agency and the Port of London Authority.
Nicholas Leach

Facing page bottom:
A 54ft (16.25m) Odd Fellow class lifeboat of the Swedish Sea Rescue Society (SSRS). This vessel has a top speed of 32kts and a range of 375nm. The SSRS presently has plans in the works for 18 and 20m versions of the vessel.
SSRS

A Dutch Valentijn type RHI lifeboat of the KNRM underway at speed.
The Valentijns are used as intermediate rescue craft and are generally
beach-launched from a carriage.
Kees Brinkman, KNRM

The RNLI experimented with cruising lifeboats. Only three Clyde type lifeboats were ever constructed; these included ON 987, which served at Clovelly 1968-1975, ON 988 which served at Kirkwall 1967-1988, and ON 1030 which also served at Clovelly 1975-1988.
RNLI

This is by no means an exhaustive list of all cruising type, motorised rescue craft that have seen service, or continue in service. It is merely a sampling of the types and styles of rescue craft that have fulfilled the role. Many other countries, including Finland, Denmark and Poland also had patrolling rescue boats at one point or another and the concept of extending the arms of a lifesaving service beyond the bounds of the shore-based environment has been used the world over. In many countries, patrolling vessels used for search and rescue are also expected to fulfil many other tasks. Some of these are the subject of the next chapter.

The Loss of the Steamer, *Rokta*

One of the most famous rescues in the history of the NSSR, occurred on 3 April 1938, when the ship *Rokta* of Oystese ran aground in a blinding snow storm while carrying a load of slate from Alta to Leith in Scotland. The story is famous not only for the incredible human drama that unfolded over a few days, but also because it was the first NSSR rescue to be broadcast live over Norwegian Radio, thus captivating the entire country and drawing a great deal of attention to the workings of the service.

On the morning of 3 April 1938 the wife of the lighthouse keeper at Bjornsund, Norway, saw that a ship had gone aground at Gallerskjaerene in the night. The weather was foul with blizzard conditions and storm-force winds blowing from the north. The message was immediately sent to the nearest large cruising lifeboat of the NSSR, the 56ft (17.2m) *Christian Bugge*, then lying in Kristiansund. The *Christian Bugge* was one of the larger, second-generation sailing lifeboats, designed with an internal-combustion engine for 'auxiliary' purposes, and had been launched in 1935. At the time of notification, weather conditions were so poor that the identity of the stricken vessel was still unknown. One thing was certain, however, the location of the wreck was a day and a half away from Kristiansund, and if the *Christian Bugge* was to render any assistance at all, time was of the essence. The master of the *Christian Bugge*, Johan Bakken, realised that this would be a long and perilous rescue attempt and augmented his crew with three fellow lifeboatmen from the *Namsos* and the *Andreas Aaro*, both smaller Colin Archer-style lifeboats from the local area.

While preparations were being made in Kristiansund, another drama was unfolding near the wreck. True to the spirit of

mariners the world over, three local fishing vessels had set out in the teeth of the storm to attempt assistance. After arriving on scene, one of the vessels from Bjornsund with six men on board attempted to cross through the breakers to identify the wreck and see if there were any survivors. Bernhard Rindaroy, following on the fishing vessel *Korsk*, watched in horror as the vessel capsized and all six men found themselves in the cold, confused surf. By some miracle of seamanship, the *Korsk* was able to recover four of the six, but the other two were lost. In spite of the tragedy the local fishermen made several further attempts to reach the wreck but the mountainous seas repeatedly beat them back. It became clear that if there were any crew left on the stricken vessel their chances of survival were deteriorating with the weather and their only hope for rescue lay with the *Christian Bugge*.

In order to keep the public in touch with the proceedings of this dramatic event, Bergen Radio transmitted live radio communications from the *Christian Bugge* at regular intervals for the duration of the rescue. This would be the NSSR's first 'media rescue' and would provide an incredible public focus on the organisation and the men who served in it.

Upon arriving at the wreck the next day, Captain Bakken on the *Christian Bugge* made an attempt to cross through the surf of the Gallerskjaerene and look for survivors. The giant combers and surrounding rocks beat back the lifeboat, but she did get close enough to tell that there was little chance of anyone remaining onboard. After this first attempt Captain Bakken decided to proceed to the port of Rindaroy to pick up a pilot to guide them through the treacherous breakers. This was Bernhard Rindaroy's nephew, Peder, a local fisherman familiar with the rocks and shoals at the site of the calamity. On the next

The NSSR cruising lifeboat *Christian Bugge* and her crew carried out a daring rescue of 12 men from the wrecked steamer *Rokta* in 1938.
This rescue was the first to be covered live on Norwegian radio and drew considerable public attention to the cause of the lifeboat service.
Akliar Bardal, Redningsselskapet

CHRISTIAN BUGGE

A decision was made to attempt a rescue right then and there, and Captain Bakken swung the *Christian Bugge* around in the pounding breakers, taking the lifeboat right under the suspended stern of the stricken ship, ignoring the fact that at any moment the wreck could come crashing down on the comparatively minuscule *Christian Bugge*. With the aid of lifelines and one of the ship's lifeboats, one by one, the *Rokta*'s 12 crew emerged from the shelter of the hulk and clambered aboard the lifeboat. No one was more surprised at the continual flow of survivors than the lifeboat crew — it was a miracle that these men had survived after almost two days of freezing spray and exposure to the elements.

In the words of Peder Rindaroy,

It is with a lifeboat like the Christian Bugge and its capable crew that one can do truly wonderful work, even in the most demanding circumstances, such as it was in this case. Even I, who knew this area well, realized that the Christian Bugge was probably the largest vessel ever to make it through the narrow channel that was there and then through the mighty breakers of the shallows. What I was afraid of was that we could lose steering on the lifeboat in the surf, or foul the propellers in the incredible amount of wreckage surrounding the Rokta. The lifeboat proved itself however, and I found that its manoeuvring ability was entirely unique, and that she would rest fairly calmly even in the strong surf and undertow conditions at the wreck. The seamen understood the responsibility I felt as pilot for the area. If it had gone badly it would certainly be said by many that I should get most of the blame, but fortunately it went as well as it could go.
The impression I have from being onboard with Captain Bakken and his talented crew is that they will continue to make a name for themselves on many future rescues in the Lifeboat Service.

attempt, with Peder's help, the *Christian Bugge* was able to make it through the breakers and identify the wreck as the *Rokta*. Even more surprising, they saw a flag hanging over the stern of the vessel — it had not been there on their previous approach. Then, to their amazement, the lone figure of a man was spotted clinging to the wreck. By now only the stern of the ship was left hanging perilously over the rock that had impaled it, and the seas were pounding at the ship's remains. The crew of the *Christian Bugge* had little time before ship and man slipped away to a watery grave.

For this daring and successful rescue the entire crew of the *Christian Bugge* was awarded the King's Gold Medal of Merit. For the NSSR as a whole, the media coverage served to entrench the lifeboat service in the hearts and minds of many Norwegians. [348]

CHAPTER 16

Coast Guard Cutters and Patrol Boats

When she steams into the harbour
People don't flock 'round like bees;
For she ain't no grim destroyer;
No dark terror of the seas.
And there ain't a load a romance
To the guy that doesn't know,
In a ship that just saves vessels
When the icy northers blow.

When the old storm signal's flyin',
Every vessel takes a lee,
'Cept the cutter; which ups anchor
And goes ploughing out to sea,
When the hurricane's a'blowin'
From the banks to old Cape Cod
Oh, the Cutter; with her searchlight,
Seems the messenger of God.

The Coast Guard Cutter, by Arthur Summers Roche

In 1789 Alexander Hamilton, first Secretary of the Treasury of the United States of America was asked by President George Washington to establish a blockading force to control the increasing amount of illicit smuggling in and out of the fledgling nation. Hamilton proposed that 10 'Boats from 36 to 40 foot keel will answer the purpose, each having one captain, one lieutenant and six mariners and armed with swivels…'. The boats were constructed and placed in commission soon thereafter. Thus was born the United States Revenue Marine, an armed maritime branch of the US Government that preceded the establishment of the US Navy by some seven years. These first 10 vessels were actually two-masted topsail schooners, but were referred to as 'revenue cutters'. By 1797 there were 17 revenue cutters in service and they became renowned as the greyhounds of the seas, being primarily designed for speed and pursuit. The second-generation cutters were smaller forerunners of the famous Baltimore Clippers.[349]

Beginning in 1832 certain revenue cutters were requested by the Department of the Treasury to actively cruise off the Atlantic seaboard during the winter months for the express purpose of providing assistance at sea. In 1837 this lifesaving responsibility was further entrenched when the US Congress asked 'to cause any suitable number of public

The United States Revenue Cutter *Eagle*. Although termed a cutter, the rig was actually a hermaphrodite brig, similar to that of the famed Baltimore Clippers.
USCG

147

vessels adapted to the purpose, to cruise upon the coast, in the severe portion of the season, when the public service will allow of it, and to afford such aid to distressed navigators as their circumstances and necessities may require; and such public vessels shall go to sea prepared fully to render such assistance'.[350] The only vessels capable of maintaining such a service were the cutters of the Revenue Marine and so began the time-honoured tradition of cutters being used for coastal and offshore lifesaving that continues to this day (see Chapter I-6).

In 1844 the Revenue Cutter Service, as it had become known, began experimenting with steam propulsion, including two rather advanced screw-propelled cutters designed by the Swedish engineer John Ericsson, who would later design the gunship *Monitor* for the US Navy. The other four cutters were designed by a naval lieutenant named Hunt who had come up with the idea of vertically placing the paddle wheels in semi-submerged wells in the sides of the ships. All these vessels were, unfortunately, failures.[351] As a result, the service reverted to the tried and true, and built shapely brigs and topsail schooners. It was not until 1857 that a large wooden side-wheel steam cutter, the 180ft (55m), 164-ton *Harriet Lane* would be built.

By the end of the American Civil War, the number of steam cutters had increased, and the new Secretary of the Treasury, Hugh McCulloch described the perfect cutter as being of 'light draught, manned by a small crew, and able to navigate the shoal waters and penetrate the inland bays, rivers and creeks with which our sea, lake and gulf coasts abound, but of sufficient tonnage to perform efficiently and safely the duties of a coast guard at sea and to succor to vessels in distress'.[352]

Towards the turn of the century the standard revenue cutter began to increase in size to the 200ft (61m) range. In 1911 there were said to be 36 cutters of various shapes and descriptions in the service. All those cutters built between 1900 and 1921 bore Native American names such as *Tacoma*, *Seneca* and *Yamacraw*, and were quite easily recognisable by their gleaming white hulls and buff funnels. In 1915 the Revenue Cutter Service was amalgamated with the United States Life-Saving Service to form the United States Coast Guard, and the maritime safety role of these large vessels was expanded even further. Cutters would be responsible for saving thousands of lives as they patrolled their nation's coasts, carried out duties on far-away stations, and served their country faithfully in times of war.

Not long after the end of the First World War, the fledgling USCG found itself fighting another battle; the war was prohibition, the enemy was the rumrunner. A new vessel was needed that combined features of both the large offshore cutters and the small coastal picket boats, had onboard accommodations, could patrol the coasts for extended periods and, with superior speed and shallow draught, could pursue smugglers into the coastal inlets and harbours. The result was the small coast guard cutter, sometimes referred to as a coastal patrol boat, the first of which were wooden vessels of about 75ft (23m). The USCG today defines the term *cutter* as 'any CG vessel 65 feet [19.8m] in length or greater, having adequate accommodations for crew to live on board'.[353]

There have been several variations of the small coastal cutter since the 1920s including the 95ft (29m) Cape class, of which 35 were built between 1953 and 1959. Several of these were also built in Canada for the CCG in the early 1960s (see Part IV). The Canadian 95 Footers were powered by 4 V-16 Cummins diesels that produced a top speed of 20kt. These vessels were widely used for coastal lifesaving and many continued in service until the 1990s.[354] The 95 Footers were replaced by the 110ft (33.5m) Island class cutter/patrol boats that first came off the assembly line in August 1985. As of 2001 there were 49 of these high-speed vessels in service around the United States and its territories. Based on a British patrol boat design, the Island class can cruise for 1,580 miles at 15kt, and has a top speed in excess of 26kt.

The 110ft (33.5m) USCG Cutter *Washington* underway off the island of Oahu.
USCG

Another smaller American coast guard cutter is the 82ft (25m) Point class patrol boat, 79 of which were constructed between 1959 and 1970. Essentially a scaled-down version of the 95 Footer, 21 of these sturdy patrol and rescue craft were still in service as of 2001. They have a top speed of 22kt, and can cruise for 1,580 miles at

The USCG Cutter *Barracuda*, one of the new 87ft (26.5m) Protector class patrol boats capable of cruising at 25kt. *USCG*

2001, have two completely separate propulsion systems. The standard cruising power plant is a pair of 3,500-hp diesels that can provide the large cutter with a 14,000-mile cruising range at 11kt. However, if a more rapid response is required, the engineers can start up the two Pratt and Whitney gas turbines which, when combined, produce 36,000hp. This huge reserve of power can push the vessel at speeds in excess of 30kt, and she can cruise continually at 29kt for 2,400 nautical miles to attend a mid-ocean casualty if required.

The concept of the patrolling cutter used for lifesaving, and other duties, was eventually adopted by coastal states around the globe, particularly where the lifesaving organisation was a state-run body, a branch or ancillary duty of the military or the marine police, or in countries where both a state-run coast guard and an independent lifesaving organisation operated in conjunction with one another. In Canada, for example, the Canadian Coast Guard continues to operate a fleet of large patrolling vessels in the North Atlantic and the Pacific for fisheries enforcement and SAR work when required. State-run organisations which also use offshore cutters for lifesaving, include the Japanese, Indian and Argentinian Coast Guards.

10.7kt. Thirty-seven were refitted in the 1990s to extend their working careers to 30 years and beyond. The modern replacement for the 82 Footers is the new 87ft (26.5m) Marine Protector class patrol boats, with 21 in the fleet as of 2001. Compared to the old Point class vessels, the 87ft cutters have improved sea-keeping qualities, greater accommodation and wheelhouse space, as well as a small jet boat with a stern launch-and-recovery system; the maximum speed is 25kt.

In 1965 the USCG divided its large cutter fleet into two classes known as Medium Endurance (WMEC) and High Endurance Cutters (WHEC). Today's fleet of WMECs includes the 270ft (82.3m) Bear class, of which there were 13 in 2001, and the 210ft (64m) Reliance class cutters of which there were 16 in service in 2001. The 270ft cutters have a top speed of 19.5kt and can cruise for 10,250 nautical miles at 12kt. Like all the modern medium- and high-endurance cutters, they also have a helicopter pad. The 210ft cutters have a maximum speed of 18kt, or can cruise for 6,100 miles at 14kt.[355] The largest cutters in the fleet and, indeed, the world, are the 378ft Hamilton class vessels that are essentially akin to ocean-going naval frigates. The WHECs, of which there were 12 in service in

PL76 *King Shun*, a Divisional Patrol Launch of the Hong Kong Marine Police. There are 15 of this type in the HKMP fleet. Propelled by water-jets, the PL76 can cruise at 25kt. Although their primary role is law enforcement, the vessels of the HKMP also respond to hundreds of SAR cases every year. *HKMP*

CHAPTER 17

American Motor Lifeboats, the 52 and 44 Footers

In 1928 the USCG began experimenting with a prototype 52ft (15.85m) MLB, the largest American lifeboat yet, with a more powerful engine, limited onboard accommodation and a longer cruising radius than the standard 36ft MLB. Two prototypes would be constructed, referred to as Type F 52ft MLBs. One of these, the *Triumph* (CG-52301), would be stationed at Pt. Adams, Oregon, at the treacherous entrance to the Columbia River. The other, the *Invincible* (CG-52300), would be evaluated on the Atlantic coast, at Sandy Hook Coast Guard Station, just south of the busy port of New York.

The two lifeboats were designed and built by the Construction and Repair Section of the USCG at Curtis Bay, Maryland, and were launched in 1933. Like the 36ft MLBs, also built at Curtis Bay, the 52 Footers were of strong wooden construction with double-diagonal planking. The hull was divided by five watertight bulkheads and eight separate watertight compartments. There were flush decks and a small bronze-alloy enclosed wheelhouse positioned well forward, providing better visibility over the bow. The deck cabin had an external steering station placed on top, improving all-round visibility in fair-weather. Similar to contemporary large British MLBs such as the Barnett, the *Triumph* and the *Invincible* were not self-righting but instead 'an effort [had] been made to obtain the maximum of statical stability under all conditions'.[356] The boats had a beam of 14ft 3in (4.3m) and a draught of 6ft 8in (2m). The original 52 Footers were the first American rescue craft to have

diesel power, being single screw and driven by a 150-hp Buda diesel. There was no protective tunnel, instead a large skeg extended all the way aft guarding the rudder and the propeller in the event of grounding. The powerful diesel provided a continuous speed of 10kt and a range of 600 nautical miles. There was also an auxiliary diesel generator for electric power.

The Type F 52 Footer weighed in at 30 tons (30.6 tonnes) and had a survivor capacity of 60 persons below decks and 100 on deck, the latter only being of use in favourable weather conditions. In spite of the relative success of the two purpose-built prototypes, no further boats were built during the 1930s. Many USCG crews still preferred the smaller self-righting 36 Footers. Eventually the *Invincible* would find her way to the Pacific Northwest, home of the 13th District of the United States Coast Guard, where she would be stationed at Grays Harbour, Washington, adjacent to another treacherous bar crossing. Both original 52 Footers would survive until the 1960s. Even though the *Triumph* would be lost with all but one of her crew on the Columbia River Bar in January 1961 (see Chapter I-13), the large MLBs would remain a favourite of the crews in the 13th District where their size and power were of great benefit in the breaking-bar conditions. As a result the USCG decided to build a newer version of the type specifically for use in the Pacific Northwest.

In 1955 the USCG engineers at Curtis Bay began work on a new 52 Footer, with a steel hull and aluminum superstructure, twin diesel engines, expanded range and

The USCG 52ft MLB *Intrepid* takes a pounding while training on
the Coos Bay, Oregon, bar in 1987.
Fireman Phil Cross, USCG Ret'd

The USCG Type F 52ft MLB *Invincible* underway, showing her flush
decks and open helm station aft of the wheelhouse.
USCG

more extensive crew accommodations. The new design would be inherently self-righting. Once again the boats were built in-house. The first of the type, the *Victory* (CG-52312), went into service in the summer of 1956. Powered by two 6-71 GMC diesels producing 300hp in total, the new class cruised at 9.6kt and had a range of 1,071 nautical miles at full speed, 2,397 nautical miles at 60% power.[357] Eventually three more of the type would be built: the *Invincible* (CG-52315), the *Triumph II* (CG-52314), and the *Intrepid* (CG-52313). All would be strategically stationed to work the primary river bars of the 13th District – Grays Harbour and Cape Disappointment, Washington, in the north, and Yaquinna Bay (Newport) and Coos Bay, Oregon, in the south. Following the original evaluation phase of the MLB *Victory* at Yaquinna Bay, the Officer-in-Charge of the station had the following comments:

> *In the 17 months that the CG-5312 has been in service at this unit she has proven to be the finest example of lifeboat design in the World. Local opinion of the fishing fleet is the same. The CG-52312 has been involved in 89 actual assistances involving about $570,000.00, has traveled 1493 miles in 230 hours on those assistance cases, actually pulled from the water six persons who would have otherwise drowned as well as removing a great number (estimated at 75 to 100) of sports fishermen and others from positions of peril. These figures do not include countless hours of patrol and standby on rough bars. In these instances*

particularly every type of marine casualty has been encountered. In fact it is our firm opinion that some of the assistances, involving the actual saving of life could not have been performed with any other type of Coast Guard vessel. In one assistance case the CG-52312 was driven hard aground on the ocean beach in heavy seas to effect the rescue of four persons foundering in the surf. These persons not only were saved, but the CG-52312 was made to take herself off the beach under her own power with the only damage sustained after 45 minutes of heavy pounding on the sand beach being loss of steering.[358]

As of 2003 all four steel 52ft MLBs were still in service in the 13th District, although, with the introduction of the new aluminum high-speed 47ft (14.3m) MLB beginning in the 1990s and the overall trend in the USCG for standard national boat types, their future is now in question. These massive and powerful lifeboats have been responsible for saving thousands of lives off the coast of Oregon and Washington over the last 40 years and there remains many a qualified surfman in the USCG who will regret their passing.

In spite of the success of the large 52ft MLBs on the coastal bars of the Pacific Northwest, the 36ft SR SB MLB remained the primary, and preferred, workhorse of the lifeboat stations throughout the United States until the 1960s. In 1938 research began on the development of a replacement for the 36 Footer and a rather unique prototype was launched from the Curtis Bay facility in July 1940. This MLB, which became known as the CG-40300, was of welded, galvanised-steel construction. Steel had been chosen because of the realisation that wooden lifeboats were not only becoming more and more difficult to maintain, they were also becoming difficult to construct. The exacting standards of heavy-scantling lifeboat construction required straight-grain, high-grade lumber, which was becoming an increasingly rare commodity. The 40ft (12.2m) MLB had other design features that made it noticeably different from its double-ended, wooden predecessors. It had a small, slightly squared stern, and a single, self-bailing cockpit placed amidships where the helm also was located. This was a considerable departure from the traditional American style of having the helmsman located aft. The CG-40300 also had a unique enclosed survivor's cabin aft of the cockpit. Power was from a single 120-hp Sterling petrol engine that could push the boat along at approximately 9kt. The 40 Footer was tested at several Atlantic lifeboat stations in varying sea conditions until 1943 when she was permanently stationed at USCG Station Plum Island, Wisconsin, on Lake Michigan.

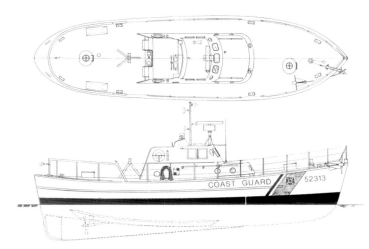

In 1955, the old wooden Type F 52 Footers were reaching the end of their service life and a decision was made to build several newer versions, this time out of steel, with twin-diesel propulsion in a self-righting design.
USCG

The innovative features of the 40ft MLB did not catch on however, and lifesaving crews remained enamoured of the handling characteristics of the familiar wooden 36 Footer. This, combined with the entry of the United States into the war only months after the 40 Footer's introduction, meant that any efforts at research and development for coastal lifesaving craft would now be refocused on military small craft. In the end CG-40300 would be the only one of her type ever built. Incredibly, she remained in service at Plum Island until 1979 and was still being used as a Harbour Authority workboat at Sault Ste. Marie, Michigan, as late as 1994.[359]

After the war the USCG would continue building the proven 36 Footers, constructing 36 more of the type between 1946 and 1956. In August 1956 the last of the 36 Footers, a Type TRS, rolled out of the Curtis Bay yard. A new MLB was now required and coxswains and surfmen from all over the country were petitioned to solicit their opinions for a replacement.[360] Criticisms of the old MLB included poor visibility from the helm position, poor towing capabilities with the tow post located too far aft, and a lack of power and speed. Up to this point, most SR lifeboats the world over rarely exceeded 10kt and the round bottoms and displacement hulls eliminated any possibility of higher speed. It would take some innovative thinking to come up with a self-righting lifeboat with an increased speed threshold, although the Germans were working on precisely that problem at that time, resulting in the development of the high-speed rescue cruiser. By 1960 a statement of requirements (SOR) for the new lifeboat was established. In addition to the increase in speed, the SOR included twin-diesel propulsion for handling and manoeuvrability, an incredibly strong corten-steel hull for greater strength when bottoming out and in ice operations, improved survivor spaces and accommodation, improved rescue-zone recovery and towing capabilities, and an increased full-speed range of operation. Most importantly, however, the new lifeboat would maintain the American tradition of being self-bailing and inherently self-righting through the combination of substantial reserve buoyancy and a low centre of gravity. This new MLB, 44ft (13.4m) in length, needed to operate and maintain crew and passenger survivability in some of the worst surf and coastal bar conditions in the world.

The design process for the new 44 Footer was a lesson in how to do things right and would set the precedent for lifeboat-design processes of the future. After exhaustive consultations and the establishment of design requirements, a preliminary hull plan was completed. A 1/12 scale model was then constructed and stringently tank-tested. Wooden mock-ups were made of the crew stations, accommodation, coxswain's flat and mastworks to discern the best arrangement and weight distribution.

The prototype USCG 44ft MLB shown during her initial sea trials off Curtis Bay, Maryland, in 1962. This vessel, USCG MLB *44-300* would remain in service for the next 35 years, ending her days as one of the training boats at the USCG's National MLB School at Cape Disappointment, Washington.
USCG

The prototype was launched from the Curtis Bay Yard in February 1962 and quickly earned a favourable reputation as she toured the eastern seaboard. She met all design requirements and with her semi-displacement hull had a top speed of 16kt, thus representing a revolutionary step forward in inshore self-righting-lifeboat design. Not surprisingly, the 44ft MLB prototype incorporated some of the design features from the old CG-40300. In addition to the steel hull, these included the single, 'midships cockpit, the relatively square stern and the aft survivor's cabin, which became affectionately known by many as the turtleback, or simply the 'turtle'. The 44 Footer took full advantage of technologies that had been developed in the intervening war years such as the use of much lighter aluminum for the houseworks, and the installation of lightweight, more powerful diesels.

The USCG had successfully combined the visibility, manoeuvrability and good handling characteristics of a utility-type workboat with the SR-SB features and excellent heavy-weather handling characteristics of the old full-displacement lifeboats. This was probably the most versatile near-shore rescue craft then designed and would become the mainstay of the United States Coast Guard's lifeboat fleet for the next three decades. Starting with the original prototype, *44-300* (which this writer trained on at the USCG's National Motor Lifeboat School at Cape Disappointment, Washington, in the 1980s), 110 of these vessels would be built and put in service. After the design's successful introduction at the 9th

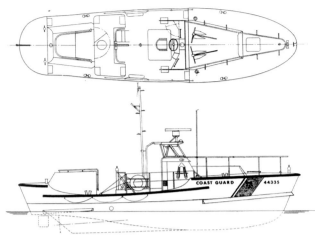

A USCG 44ft MLB training from the NMLBS works close to the beach in the shadow of Cape Disappointment, Washington, at the mouth of the Columbia River.
Lynda Wilcox

One of the most successful designs of lifeboat in the world. The USCG's 44ft MLB was adopted by rescue services in Britain, Canada, Iran, Italy, Norway, Portugal and Tunisia. Many remain in service around the globe.
USCG

International Lifeboat Conference held in Scotland in 1963, the Canadian and Italian Coast Guards, as well as the Norwegian and Portuguese Lifeboat Services and the RNLI would all begin constructing 44ft MLBs, with minor variations, for use in their own fleets. In 1975 Iran had 10 of these craft constructed for use by the Iranian Navy by Fairey Marine in the UK.[361] Many 44

Footers continue in service today in various parts of the world, (see Part IV). For the RNLI, the introduction of the 44 Footer would lead to an evolution in British lifeboat design with the Waveney-type 44ft MLB instigating a move towards the development of the Fast Afloat Boats (FABs) and the predominant designs in service today, (see Chapter II-21).[362]

The 44ft MLBs conducted countless rescue missions in their almost 40 years of lifesaving service. The following are brief accounts of two such rescues.

In December of last year [1963], the CG-44300 received her baptism in a serious assistance case. In a south-westerly gale a tug was towing two barges north along the coast. At a point about 33 miles north of our station (Yaquinna Bay, Oregon), while the tow was four miles offshore, the second barge came adrift and would have eventually gone on the beach. This barge was 150 feet in length and loaded with dredging pipe. The 44-footer arrived on the scene in two-and-a-half hours and soon had a towline on the drifting barge. She towed the barge for three hours until the crew were able to secure the towline to the first barge and the tug continued on its way. The CG-44300 towed the barge for approximately 8 miles in seas up to 15 feet.[363]

_____

Three crew members of the pleasure craft Koala were saved May 25, 1982 when two 44-footers from Humboldt Bay

responded at 11 p.m. to a request for an escort into Humboldt Bay. The skipper of the 56-foot Koala reported that his vessel had one engine down and a sick, fatigued crew.

With seven miles of visibility, 10-knot winds, and seas peaking at 18 feet, the two Coast Guard boats set out to aid and retrieve the distressed vessel. During the escort over the Humboldt bar, one rescue boat took the lead position while the other acted as a break. Although both Coast Guard boats' radars were inoperative, the rescue progressed smoothly until midnight when Koala was thrown in the air, spun around and reduced to splinters by a 20-foot breaker.

Immediately, both rescue boats maneuvred to rescue the three crew members. Flares were set off to illuminate the area. The men in the water were spotted and assisted on board. The crew mates were pulled to safety and treated by the Coast Guard teams for hypothermia, cuts and bruises. One of the victims appeared to have suffered a heart attack. At the station the crew of the ill-fated Koala was turned over to waiting medics.[364]

CHAPTER 18

American Utility Boats

Although not specifically designed for lifesaving, it is worth including the American 'Utility Boats' (UTBs) in the category of rescue craft, as they have been responsible for saving thousands lives in the United States, Canada and around the world since the 1950s. Their story begins after 1915, with the amalgamation of the United States Life-Saving Service and the Revenue Cutter Service into the United States Coast Guard.

The USCG was both a lifesaving and a law-enforcement agency and the 1920s era of Prohibition created the need for small, high-speed boats to patrol the coasts and intercept smugglers at sea. The first vessels were called 'Picket Boats', in reference to the blockade-type work for which they were used. Averaging around 38ft (11.6m) in length, they were constructed of wood, and had 225-hp to 250-hp petrol engines that could push them along at a substantial 18kt, fast enough to catch many of the early rumrunners infiltrating the coast from Canada and Mexico. Although designed primarily for law enforcement, many were co-located at lifeboat stations alongside 36ft MLBs. The lifesaving crews soon saw that the fast boats were very useful for rapid response in calm to moderate sea conditions.

By the end of the Second World War most of the wooden picket boats had seen hard use and were in dire need of replacement. The USCG naval architects set about developing a new 'multifunctional design' of fast workboat that would be even better suited to saving lives at sea while still having the ability to carry out the other missions of the Coast Guard. The multifunction nature of the new design 'was crystallized in the name "Utility Boat", which was given to the new class before even the first line was laid down on the drawing board'.[365]

The naval architects came up with a new 40ft (12.2m) design that was diesel powered, had increased deck space, a self-bailing cockpit, improved manoeuvrability and towing abilities, and increased cabin and survivor space. It was designed to lay afloat and be used either in conjunction with a slower, self-righting MLB, or on its own if the prevailing coastal conditions did not warrant the use of a heavy-weather boat. Prior to the construction of two 40ft UTB prototypes, one with a wooden hull, the other of galvanised steel, the Curtis Bay engineers modified one of the old wooden picket boats to resemble

the proposed design. Although the modified boat had a single 275-hp diesel engine, it was decided that two motors would be better and thus the two prototype UTBs had twin 190-hp 6-71 GM diesels. The wooden prototype reached a top speed of 20kt, while the metal boat obtained 22.15kt. In typical USCG fashion the boats were tested at various stations. The wooden UTB with its deeper hull received the most accolades from a sea-keeping perspective, while the steel UTB gained approval from the maintenance point of view. In the end it was decided to build 15 wooden UTBs and 100 galvanised-steel versions that would incorporate the modified hull form of the wooden boats. All would be built at the Curtis Bay facility, with the first being launched on 1 June 1951.

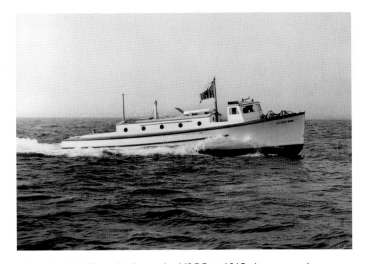

When the USLSS evolved into the USCG in 1915, the many roles of the new organisation, particularly that of law enforcement, required a faster, more versatile platform. The result was the high-speed, wooden picket boat, similar to those used by the US Navy. It also proved to be extremely versatile as a fast rescue platform. *USCG*

A CCG 40ft UTB, the *Mallard*, based out of Kitsilano Coast Guard Station in Vancouver, British Columbia. Several of these USCG UTBs were purchased by the Royal Canadian Air Force for use as rescue craft in the 1950s and became part of the CCG's fleet when it was established in 1962.
CCG

(The production of these boats would see the first use of assembly-line techniques by the USCG and, in short order, they were producing 40 Footers at the rate of one per day. [366] A rotary jig was used to spin the hulls around above ground while all the components were being welded, a practice now common in metal boat construction.) The only other prominent alteration from the prototype phase to the post-production version was the addition of an external steering station and windbreak on the after part of the cabin. The metal version was 40ft (12.2m) long, had a beam of 11ft 2in (3.4m) and a draught of only 3ft (0.9m). The cruising range was 270 miles.

Not all the 40ft UTBs were built of wood and steel however. For the first time in the history of rescue craft, the use of fibreglass reinforced plastics, or FRP, was tested as a hull material in the late 1950s and early 1960s. [367] Experimental use of FRP for small boats had begun in the US Navy during the Second World War with the construction of a series of small workboats, and even a version of the 26ft Monomoy surfboat. [368] The material brought potential benefits in terms of ease of construction and maintenance, as well as potential cost-savings. However, there were problems and structural defects occurred with the FRP boats. Although these were rectified as part of the research and development of the concept of 'plastic boats', in 1966 the USCG decided to drop the construction and development of FRP 'pending the re-evaluation of operating requirements, construction materials and methods', for any future UTBs. These

pioneering developments were not a failure, just somewhat ahead of their time. By the 1970s and '80s, fibreglass was being used in rescue-boat construction all over the world, from the early RHIs, to large MLBs, starting with the Arun class in Great Britain as well as the Skomvaer-type lifeboats in Norway, with many more to follow.

The 40ft UTB was a modern workhorse, and hundreds were built for the USCG as well as for the US Navy. The Royal Canadian Air Force (RCAF) had several 40 Footers constructed for use as crash boats near their bases and when the Canadian Coast Guard was formed in 1963, many of these became part of that fledgling organisation. The CCG was still operating two of the 40ft UTBs in its Pacific Region, at Ganges in the Gulf Islands, and at Kitsilano, in Vancouver, until the mid 1980s.

The introduction of the UTB in the early 1950s coincided with the phenomenal growth in demand for rescue services as people took to sea in the pursuit of pleasure. By the late 1960s therefore, the 40ft UTBs had already seen incredible service, and had been re-engined on several occasions. The reality was that the workload had increased immensely and the boats, as strong as they were, were getting tired. But the concept of the multi-purpose UTB was here to stay and, once again, the USCG put together a design team to survey the options for a newer, improved, version of the same boat. This time, external design proposals were accepted, along with an in-house proposal. The SOR issued in October 1969 differed considerably from the parameters of the old 40 Footer. It called for a vessel approximately 42ft (12.8m) long, 14ft (4.3m) beam, with a draught of 3ft 6in (1.1m). It was to be constructed of aluminium and have an increased range of approximately 300 miles.[369] Four different prototypes were delivered and, over the course of four months, they toured all over the United States, spending a week at every station visited. In the end, the in-house prototype received the highest praise and, in the finest American tradition of 'go big, or go home', the USCG subsequently ordered the construction of 180 new 41ft UTBs.

The first 24 were built at Curtis Bay with aluminium hulls and fibreglass and balsa wheelhouses. Eventually the boats would become all aluminium, and after the first was delivered on 2 August 1973 they were produced at the rate of 30 per year. Hundreds remain in service today in both the United States and Canada. The CCG replaced its old fleet of 40ft UTBs and several other non-standard lifeboats with the 41ft UTB during the mid 1980s. Both the more modern re-engined American 41 Footers and the Canadian versions built by Matsumoto Shipyard in Vancouver, British Columbia, have twin turbo-charged 325-hp diesel engines that provide a top speed of 27kt. The 41ft UTB was one of the first coastal rescue craft in North America to have a powerful, integrated fire pump, operated by a power take-off attached to one of the main engines, a versatile feature that provided an incredible fire-fighting capability for such a small boat.

The CCG 41ft UTB *Osprey* underway off the city of Vancouver. These stable, high-speed vessels have always been extremely useful for SAR and port security duties in and around major cities. *Brian Rempel, CCG*

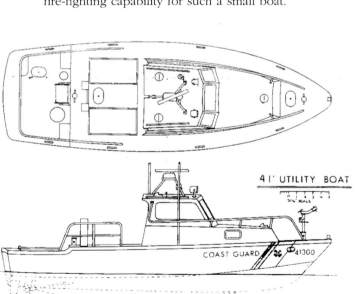

The USCG 41ft UTB; the first all-aluminium boat built for the service. Powered by twin 325-hp diesel engines the 41 Footer can cruise at 27kt. *USCG*

With the introduction to the US and Canadian rescue services of the high speed 47ft self-righting MLB in the mid 1990s the demand for stationing two types of boats, the MLB and the UTB, at one station was somewhat alleviated. That said, there are many locations on the extensive coasts and waterways of North America that still require both a purpose-built MLB and a versatile utility boat. As a result of these continuing demands, work is presently underway for the development of a new generation of UTB. There has been some mention of following the example of the KNRM in The Netherlands, with the introduction of a large, versatile, jet-propelled rigid hull inflatable in the 40ft (12.2m) range. In the aftermath of the attack on the World Trade Center, 2001, the USCG has purchased hundreds of smaller utility RHIs in the 30ft (9.1m) range, principally to provide increased port and coastal security. Regardless of what direction the USCG decides to take in the future, the key ingredients behind the success of the old UTBs must remain: seaworthiness, manoeuvrability, speed, adequate cruising radius, adequate deck space and economy of operation and maintenance.

CHAPTER 19

To Right or
Not to Right?

Gone in an instant. The RNLI's Fraserburgh lifeboat *Duchess of Kent*, a non self-righting *Watson* type is capsized by an immense rogue wave while attempting to assist a fishing vessel in difficulty in 1970. Four of her five man crew were lost. This tragic incident and several others involving non-SR lifeboats resulted in a decision to create an all self-righting fleet for the RNLI by 1980.
RNLI

The pros and cons of inherent self-righting qualities, a feature which most lifesaving crews around the world today take for granted, has been one of the most hotly debated topics in the history of rescue-craft development. There have been those who have argued in favour of its use only in inshore, surf-type boats, while others have argued that the principle is best adapted for offshore, deepwater boats; still others have argued that all rescue craft should have the capability, while some say none should have it.

From the earliest unsinkable boats of de Bernières and Lionel Lukin until the Duke of Northumberland's competition for a safer design of lifeboat in 1851, the belief had always been that it was better to design a boat with a more-than-adequate ability to remain upright in the first place, rather than to rely on the capability to re-right after a capsize. William Wouldhave felt quite differently (see Chapter II-6). But, while the idea of

designing a self-righting lifeboat may have originated with him, any design configurations he submitted with his model of 1789, were subsequently removed. After several tragic losses of non-self-righting lifeboats in Britain development turned to the Standard Self-Righting design (see Chapter II-8). SR lifeboats became the preferred resource in Britain and Ireland after 1851 and, within 30 years, there were no fewer than 249 self-righting lifeboats in service in those two countries.[370]

In the United States some of the earliest lifeboats constructed for the Massachussetts Humane Society and the early government lifesaving stations in New Jersey and Long Island, were said to be inherently self-righting (although in reality this was probably a rather dubious claim). But in time the self-righting principle was not deemed desirable for the predominant workhorse of the government lifesaving service in America, the surfboat. The review committee of the 1872 lifeboat and surfboat trials that took place at Seabright, New Jersey, concluded that:

From the light now had upon the subject, we are of the opinion that the self-righting principle, however advantageous in the open water, is of little or no use in the surf, and that therefore, it should be dispensed with in boats intended for the purpose above named, by which means the weight and cost of the boat could be reduced nearly or quite one-third, and the improved device rendered far more easy to handle than would otherwise be possible.[371]

The virtues of the non-self-righting surfboat for inshore use were still being extolled by Sumner Kimball, the General Superintendent of the United States Life-Saving Service, in 1890. Using the statistics available at the time, he compared the safety records and overall use of both the surfboats of his service, and the self-righting lifeboats of the RNLI, over an 18-year period, from 1871 to 1899. In comparison, Kimball stated that:

During the eighteen years they (non self-righting surfboats) have been in the hands of our crews they have been launched 6,730 times in actual service, and have landed 6,735 persons from wrecked vessels. In all this service they have capsized but 14 times. Six of these instances were attended with loss of life, the number of persons perishing being 41, of whom 27 belonged to the service and 14 were shipwrecked people...I learn from the annual reports of the institution (RNLI) that during the same period of eighteen years her boats have capsized 21 times attended by loss of life, the number perishing aggregating 75, of whom 68 were lifeboatmen and 7 shipwrecked people.[372]

In spite of the definite preference for non-self-righting boats for surf work in the United States, there was a recognition of the merits of a self-righting design for more extended offshore work, hence the 1873 purchase of one of the RNLI's Standard Self-Righting type pulling and sailing lifeboats, which became the first of a long generation of American self-righting lifeboats constructed well into the next century. In fact, by 1924 the trend towards non-self-righters had been almost completely reversed, with most of the old surfboats in the United States being converted to self-righting boats or being replaced by the 36ft SR-SB motor lifeboat, used for both surf and offshore work.[373]

Although after 1851 many of the early continental European coastal lifesaving organisations, purchased, adapted and built their own designs of self-righting lifeboat based on the standard RNLI designs, from the Peake type to the Standard Self-Righting type, the predominant rescue boat remained the small, portable and lightweight, non-self-righting surfboat that could be easily drawn by carriage. Some large self-righters remained, but they were primarily used to lay afloat in the relatively few safe harbours available in Germany and The Netherlands. In northern Europe the generally low opinion of self-righting type boats was expressed by the Danish delegate at the 1924 International Lifeboat Conference.

We built three, but the men did not go out in them. After we had them in service for two or three years they were put aside, and we have never taken on

the principle again. It is possible that the objection to these boats is that the manoeuvring of them close to wrecks is more difficult with the high forecastles.[374]

In Britain the move away from the predominant Standard Self-Righting design had begun back in the 1880s following a series of capsizes of self-righting lifeboats culminating in the loss of the St. Anne's and Southport lifeboats at the wreck of the barque *Mexico* in 1886 (see Chapters I-13 and II-8). As a result of the subsequent re-evaluation of lifeboat design, the non-self-righting Watson type (see Chapter II-11) was developed. This was followed by the various Barnett type motor lifeboats, as well as other motorised versions of conventional non-self-righting lifeboats such as the Liverpool and Norfolk & Suffolk types. The trend continued until, by the beginning of the Second World War, there were very few Standard Self-Righting lifeboats left in service. By 1957, out of 178 lifeboats in service around the country, only six were self-righters (see Chapter II-12).[375]

The concept of large, stable lifeboats designed with a high degree of initial stability and not likely to be upset, had been thoroughly entrenched in Britain. In the view of the proponents of non-self-righting lifeboats, chiefly the RNLI's Consultant Naval Architects G.L. Watson and J.R. Barnett (both of whom had a profound influence on the design of the Institution's lifeboats, their respective tenures lasting from 1887 to 1947), the need for inherent self-righting was only necessary in small inshore lifeboats working in shallow water and surf (this being the exact opposite of Sumner Kimball's opinion). At the First International Lifeboat Conference, held in London in 1924, J.R. Barnett presented a paper on the subject of self-righting in lifeboats, in which he stated that:

A Self-righting Life-boat is essentially a shallow-water boat, and the self-righting principle ought to be confined to comparatively small and light boats. In fact, the Self-righting Boat has been devised simply because deep-water boats were impossible in certain places, and as long as Life-boats are required on coasts where there is shallow water, the self-righting type may be expected to survive.[376]

Barnett felt there was no need to make deepwater lifeboats self-righting as the large, highly stable, non-self-righting Watson lifeboats had already proven themselves over and over since their inception in 1890. Furthermore, he had devised a new large 61ft (18.6m) non-self-righting motor lifeboat that had been launched the previous year.

An entirely different opinion was held by another delegate at the same conference, Mr Hendrick De Booy, of the Dutch NZHRM, who felt that the tendency to inherently self-right should most definitely be applied to lifeboats utilised offshore.

I cannot see why a Self-Righting Boat is essentially a shallow water boat. We are going to build a boat of 62 feet, and she will be self-righting. I remember going out in a motor-boat of 28 tons displacement in heavy weather, and when coming in I noticed that we did not use the drogue. It is, therefore, quite possible that such a boat might capsize, in which case it would be good for her to be a Self-righting Boat.[377]

The 62ft lifeboat to which De Booy referred was the *Insulinde*, a very innovative design of large, narrow motor lifeboat created for the Dutch coast and launched in 1927 (see Chapter II-13).

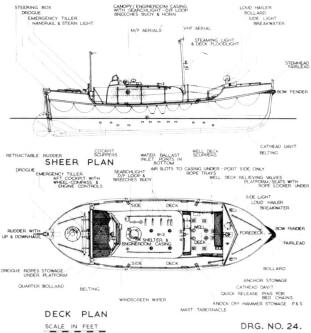

37 FT 'OAKLEY' TWIN SCREW SELF-RIGHTING TYPE MOTOR LIFE-BOAT

SHEER PLAN

DECK PLAN

SCALE IN FEET

DRG. NO. 24.

In 1958, Richard Oakley, the RNLI's resident naval architect re-introduced self-righting to the Institution's fleet. The new Mk I lifeboat was much beamier than traditional self-righters and utilised a water ballast transfer system that provided both a high degree of initial stability as well as the mechanism for re-righting in the event of a capsize. The best qualities of both the old self-righting and non self-righting lifeboats had now been combined.
Eric Fry, RNLI

The shift to predominantly self-righting lifeboats throughout Europe, a pattern which continues to this day, began in the 1950s. In 1950 the German DGzRS would begin experiments with alterations to one of its older motor lifeboats, the *Bremen*, launched in 1931, which would lead to the eventual development of the German rescue cruiser. In 1955 a prototype rescue cruiser, the *Hermann Apelt* was launched which, like the large Dutch motor lifeboats to the south, was inherently self-righting, although without the use of a water-ballast system. In 1957 the self-righting rescue cruiser *Theodore Heuss* was launched with the first daughter boat and stern ramp combination. The daughter boat, too, was self-righting (see Chapter II-14).

In Britain and Ireland, perspectives on the requirements for self-righting were changing as well. From the end of the Second World War to 1954 the RNLI lost five of its non-self-righting lifeboats, an unfavourable trend made worse by the fact that such disasters generally claimed the lives of the entire crew and any passengers onboard. The RNLI re-evaluated their policy regarding self-righting and asked its resident Naval Architect, Richard Oakley (who had replaced J.R. Barnett in 1947), to design a new carriage-and-slipway-launched self-righting lifeboat. The first Oakley type, self-righting motor lifeboat, the 37ft (11.3m) Mk I, was launched in 1958 and placed on station at Scarborough for evaluation. In many ways the new boat was a combination of the Institution's previous non-self-righting and self-righting boats. She had a double-diagonal wooden displacement hull, was twin-screw, with the propellers protected in tunnels. She had a low hull profile and a wider beam, more in line with the standard Watson and Barnett non-self-righting types. As far as the similarities to the self-righters of old were concerned, the large air cases were once more placed at either end, although they were not quite so predominant in size. The biggest difference from older self-righters was that the means of re-righting the vessel was not created by such features as a narrow beam, extremely low centre of gravity and high air cases, but by an ingenious transferable water-ballast system, a derivation of that used on the Dutch *Insulinde*. The system, which automatically transferred sea water from a ballast tank located below the lifeboat's engine room into higher wing tanks when the vessel heeled beyond a certain point, could rapidly adjust the lifeboat's centre of gravity and create a tendency to re-right. This 1.54 tons (1.57 tonnes) of ballast seawater flowed into the vessel when launched and drained away when hauled out. The system was designed so that any capsize to starboard would result in a roll of 360 degrees, but to port only 180 degrees before reversing direction.[378] The new self-righting lifeboat also had a greater range of stability than even the non-self-righting lifeboats of the institution, which also made the

Oakley a more comfortable sea-boat than the old Standard Self-Righting type lifeboats.

The other particulars of the 9.12-ton, 37ft Oakley Mk1 included the generous 11ft 6in (3.5m) beam, and a 3ft 4in (1m) draught; there were twin 43-hp Perkins diesels producing a top speed of 8kt with a range of 180 nautical miles. In 1972 the Mk II 37ft Oakley, which became known as the Rother class lifeboat, was built. Significant changes included the elimination of the two open cockpits and the addition of a large enclosed cabin and flush decks over the entire vessel, as well as a large semi-enclosed wheelhouse aft, which protected the more modern navigational equipment such as radar. This large cabin also provided enough internal buoyancy to allow the exclusion of the water-ballast self-righting system.

The original 37ft boat had been a resounding success and plans were made for a larger version designed to lay afloat. The 48ft 6in (14.8m) Oakley was the first lifeboat in the RNLI designed to have radar onboard and, like the Watson and Barnett boats, had a large superstructure and small wheelhouse, although the latter was located well aft. This larger version used the same water-ballast system for self-righting, although the relative size had increased with 2.75 tons (2.8 tonnes) of water being shipped. At the capsize trials she 'proved capable of righting herself from the bottom-up position in from five to seven seconds'.[379] The larger Oakley was 14ft (4.3m) in beam with a 4ft 8in (1.4m) draught, and weighed approximately 30 tons (30.6 tonnes) with ballast water. It was powered by twin 101-hp 6LX Gardner diesels producing a top speed of 9kt.

In 1966 a Mk II version of the 48ft 6in Oakley was built. This dispensed with the small after cockpit and moved the wheelhouse amidships making it similar in appearance to the later versions of the Barnett and Watson lifeboats. It was followed by a Mk III in 1969 known as the Solent class. The Solent resembled the previous version in appearance, the primary difference being the use of steel rather than the traditional wooden construction, with the houseworks being of aluminum. This method of construction had already been used by the RNLI in the new Waveney-type fast-afloat boats. In addition, as with the smaller Rother class self-righters, the water-ballast system was negated by the increased cabin volume. The Solent class was the last design of the traditional displacement-type lifeboat, self-righting or not, to come from the drawing boards of the RNLI. Although the Institution has replaced all these boats in recent years with more modern and faster SR MLBs, many still remain in operation around the world.

The re-emergence of SR lifeboats in Britain and Ireland had only been partial, however. By 1968 there were only 27 Oakley type MLBs, and six of

The Solent lifeboat was the last version of the RNLI's Oakley self-righters, the only one constructed of steel and the last RNLI lifeboat with a displacement hull. This photo is of the Uruguayan *Solent* type lifeboat *ADES 12* stationed at Punta del Este. *Author's collection*

the new Waveney type 44ft (13.4m) SR MLBs in service. There were plans to build more, but the enormous costs of replacing a large fleet of non-self-righting lifeboats combined with a still ingrained preference in some quarters for the non-self-righters meant that progress was slow, if sure. But subsequent tragic events would quicken the pace. In 1969 and 1970 two of the traditional non self-righting Watson type lifeboats were lost in Scottish waters. After the ensuing public inquiry, the RNLI decided to undertake one of the largest building programmes in its history, doubling the number of boats in its new-building schedule and setting 1980 as its target for an all self-righting fleet.[380] In the interim, all non-self-righting type motor lifeboats would have supplemental self-righting systems installed, in the form of large automatically deployed airbags similar to those on modern RHIs, which would remain in place until the vessels were retired. The stage was now set for the development of the next generation of fast British lifeboats and, in Britain at least, almost two centuries of debate on the question of self-righting had ended.

Following the loss of several non self-righting lifeboats, the RNLI installed automatically-deployed airbag systems. In November 1979 the Barnett lifeboat at Barra in the Outer Hebrides was capsized by an immense sea. With the airbag, she rapidly re-righted. *RNLI*

CHAPTER 20

Inflatable Rescue Boats

An RNLI 24ft (7.3m) *Atlantic 75* type RHI, an
updated version of the old Atlantic 21 with a
re-designed hull and console system.
RNLI/Royal Bank of Scotland

In the 1960s an increase in pleasure boating around
the world resulted in many coastal rescue services re-
evaluating their mandates and their rescue craft – a
speedier response was needed for the increasing number
of call-outs. When considering design criteria for faster
rescue craft the question was: did all call-outs require the
launching of a large lifeboat which, in most cases, still
only did 10kt? Many of the mishaps were now occurring
inshore within sight of piers and beaches; common
incidents now included swimmers and small sailboats
which, to the rescuers at least, seemed to spend more
time upside down than right side up.

In France, the 'inshore rescue' problem had become
particularly acute and, in the early 1960s the Société des
Hospitaliers Sauveteurs Bretons (HSB) established
inshore-rescue boat (IRB) units along popular beaches.
For this purpose the society chose 15ft (4.6m) Mk III soft-
bottom inflatables built by the Zodiac Company and
powered by a single Johnson outboard. They were
perfectly suited to the role: they were extremely stable,
light enough to be hauled on a trailer, required a small
crew (generally two) and minimal maintenance. They
were fast and highly manoeuvrable, essentially
unsinkable and, most significantly for any volunteer
rescue service, were relatively cheap to build.
Furthermore, being the equivalent of a floating fender,
the inflatable boat was well adapted to coming alongside
vessels in rough seas without damaging either boat or
persons, as well as recovering people from the water.

So successful was the use of inflatables as rescue boats
in France, that by 1963 the HSB had 90 such craft in

operation, including five in the French protectorate of La
Réunion.[381] In time, some stations began to operate year-
round and worked in conjunction with the larger lifeboat
stations, thereby establishing the concept of the co-
location of heavy-weather lifeboats and fast inflatables, or
fast rescue craft (FRC) – a highly efficient system that
continues in many of the world's lifesaving organisations.

From Britain, the RNLI had been keeping a curious eye
on French experiments. In 1962 a visit was paid to the
HSB and a recommendation made to purchase and
experiment with a similar 15ft 9in (4.8m) inflatable to be
built by RFD Company in England. The boat was tested

In 1962 a team from the RNLI visited the HSB in France to view
the new inflatable inshore rescue boat at work. In 1963
several 15ft 9in (4.9m) inflatables were purchased from RFD in
England and tested at stations around the country. The new
D type inflatables were a resounding success and by 1966 there
were 72 in service.
Nicholas Leach

during the winter of 1963 and proved highly popular, with nine more being purchased for further trials around the country. In their first summer these vessels were dispatched 39 times and were responsible for saving 10 lives. Eventually, three were maintained for year-round operations and by 1966 only four years after the original trials, there were 72 inflatables in operation in Britain and Ireland; between them they had been launched 1,449 times and could claim credit for saving 613 lives.[382]

At about the same time that inflatables were being pioneered in both France and Britain, the first United World College was being established at St. Donat's Castle on the coast of South Wales. Atlantic College (United World College of the Atlantic) nestled on the shores of the tempestuous Bristol Channel and, soon after its founding in 1962, became the site of one of the RNLI's new inshore rescue stations. But before long the strong local currents that created short steep seas had proved too much for the small, soft-bottom inflatables. The Headmaster of the College, Admiral Desmond John Hoare, was also a naval architect and engineer and became deeply interested in improving the hydrodynamics of these small rescue craft.

One of the problems of the 15ft 9in inflatables, which would become known as the Type D, was that their soft bottom and segmented-plywood flooring buckled in the short, steep seas and the boats folded in on themselves. Even the introduction of a single piece, solid floorboard did not remedy the fault to any great extent. Admiral Hoare designed a 'rigid' fibreglass and plywood hull that could be joined to the inflatable sponsons and would overcome the problem. In the small boat shop at Atlantic College the staff and students set about creating the first rigid-hull inflatable, or RHI. Becoming known as the Type C, the RHI was 16ft (5.8m) in length, and its inflatable sponsons were compartmentalised into five sections. The hull itself was of deep-V design and had five watertight compartments. The experiment was a grand success – the RHI had far superior handling characteristics in short, steep sea conditions; the longitudinal flexing of the sponsons was minimised; the boat had superior tracking and turning qualities, was more comfortable in a seaway and had greater speed for the given horsepower due to the lessening of hydrodynamic resistance of the Glasply hull. The first of these vessels, the X1 was launched by Queen Elizabeth II during a visit to the College in 1965.

The experimentation did not stop there: prototypes were developed between Atlantic College and the RNLI with subsequent increases in length. In 1969 a 21ft (6.4m) RHI was launched to become the first of the RNLI's Type B RHI, later to be known as the Atlantic 21. This new RHI had a smaller beam-to-length ratio than the Type C, as well as a hybrid hull divided into six longitudinal

watertight compartments and incorporating a deep-V forward, lessening to a relatively flat stern section. This new hull provided a relatively smooth entry as well as an ability to remain stable upon beaching, a very important feature in an inshore rescue boat. The Atlantic 21's increased size, more responsive handling characteristics, increased height of eye and improved hull speed all combined to give enormous improvements in vessel performance and crew comfort. The ability to self-bail was also addressed with the adoption of an open-transom design. The original Type Bs had twin 40-hp outboards but Admiral Hoare, on the RNLI's Committee of Management, continued to experiment with larger engines and the Atlantic 21s were soon cruising at an impressive 29kt.

The use of inflatables, both rigid-hull and conventional, was becoming so prolific in the RNLI that the Institution decided to set up their own depot for the construction and repair of such vessels at Cowes, Isle of Wight, which also later became the RHI training centre. Under the

THE 'ATLANTIC 21' INSHORE RESCUE BOAT

SADDLE SEATS WITH WATERTIGHT LOCKERS UNDER CONTAINING BATTERIES / PORTABLE VHF RADIO / FIRST AID KIT & PROVISIONS

TWIN 50 HP OUTBOARD ENGINES

A

FAIRLEAD

THROTTLES   WHEEL & COMPASS

FAIRLEAD

FAIRLEAD

SPRAY STRIPS

LIFELINES   HAND GRIPS   PLYWOOD HULL

SHEER PLAN

INFLATED NEOPRENE RUBBER TUBE SUBDIVIDED BY INTERNAL BULKHEADS

NON SLIP DECKING

COMPASS   WHEEL   A

FAIRLEAD

TUBE   TUBE

FLEXIBLE FUEL CONTAINERS P & S   WT WT WT WT   BOX GIRDER CONSTRUCTION OF PLYWOOD BASE HULL

SPRAY STRIPS

FAIRLEAD

SECTION A-A FUEL CONTAINERS   A   **BOW VIEW**

ANCHOR & ROPE STOWAGE CLEAT VALVES

OAR STOWED P & S

FAIRLEAD

WATERWAY

50 HP ENGINE

TIMBER TRANSOM

STRETCHER   POSITION

NON SLIP DECKING

50 HP ENGINE

WATERWAY

TUBE

TUBE

BULKHEAD

EMERGENCY PADDLE

BULKHEAD

HAND GRIPS   THROTTLES   LINE OF JUNCTION OF HULL & TUBE

PLAN   FUEL CONTAINERS   A   SADDLE SEATS & STEERING POSITION

SCALE IN FEET

DRG. NO. 33.

The RNLI's Atlantic 21 RHI. Note the water-tight compartments in the hull and the flat skeg for beaching. Later versions also incorporated a self-righting airbag.
Eric Fry, RNLI

Rigid hulls were first married to the inflatable sponsons at the RNLI's inshore lifeboat station at Atlantic College in Wales. Several developmental boats were constructed at the College under the direction of its Headmaster, Admiral Desmond Hoare, the end result being the Atlantic 21.
RNLI

leadership of Depot Superintendent Lt. David Stogden (RNVR), the Atlantic 21 continued to evolve and many features, such as the use of self-righting air bags and waterproof outboards, now inherent in the literally hundreds of RHI designs around the world, were pioneered and introduced by the design team at Cowes.

By 1970 the number of people rescued by the RNLI's inflatable inshore rescue boats actually exceeded that of the Institution's old displacement lifeboats by 702 to 555. In 1977 the RNLI decided that a fast lifeboat was required that would bridge the gap between the Atlantic 21 inshore rescue boat and the larger traditional MLBs. The proposal was that the new 'intermediate lifeboat' would be in the 35ft (10.7m) range, capable of speeds in the order of 25kt, and able to launch from a slipway or carriage or lay afloat. The design team at Cowes was asked to investigate the proposal and based their calculations around the concept of a large RHI that would meet the criteria. The result was, essentially, a much larger version of the Atlantic 21 driven by twin diesels.

The prototype of the RNLI's Medina class was the *Earl Mountbatten of Burma*, completed in 1979. She was approximately 40ft (12.2m) long, powered by two Sabre diesels producing 212hp per side, running on inboard/outboard-style stern drive units and could achieve 26kt. She was an open-console boat that relied on a large manually deployed air bag for self-righting, similar to that on the smaller RHIs. Her hull was of cold-

moulded wood and epoxy to allow for easier alteration as further tests were conducted, this being the 'test bed' for future models of large RHI.[383] The original hull was much like that of the Atlantic 21, with a fine deep-V entry leading to a flat beaching shoe, or 'ski sole', on the after third of the skeg, which allowed for greater transverse stability when aground, as well as when underway. Considerable sheer was added to the hull and tube form forward and the tubes themselves were tapered towards the bow, the narrower diameter providing less wind- and sea-resistance and better visibility forward.

In September 1980 Dutch officials from the KNZHRM, visited the Cowes Depot and were highly impressed with the speed, sea-keeping and manoeuvrability of the new large RHI. They, too, were in the process of re-evaluating and replacing their ageing fleet of slower lifeboats. The

The RHI. A bow-on view of one of the RNLI's experimental Medina type RHIs provides an excellent visual example of the marriage of rigid glasply hull and pneumatic tubes.
RNLI

KNZHRM had, in fact, been cooperating with the RNLI in RHI development since 1973, when they had ordered their first Atlantic 21. As a result of the 1980 meeting, a memorandum of understanding was established between the KNZHRM and the RNLI to co-develop the concept of a large RHI lifeboat under the directorship of the Cowes team and work continued on the Mk II Medina, the *Countess Mountbatten of Burma*.[384] This second boat was different from the Mk I in that it incorporated an enclosed wheelhouse rather than an open helm position. The positive buoyancy which was maintained within this superstructure provided the inherent self-righting ability of the vessel and an airbag was not necessary. Originally Volvo diesels and stern-drives were installed on the Mk II, but they proved too heavy and difficult to maintain. Eventually three 200-hp bracket-mounted outboard motors known as sea-drives were installed and pushed the RHI along at an impressive 34kt. However, the safety implications of large fixed onboard petrol tanks eventually outweighed the advantages of this propulsion concept.

In 1983 design problems still plagued the programme. The difficulties with the existing technology, such as the high-weight-to-low-power ratio of contemporary diesels, the excess weight and relative inefficiency of existing stern-drive legs, and the need to limit the weight of the entire package for reasons of hydrodynamics and methods of launch, all combined to make the RNLI reconsider and drop out of the project.

The KNZHRM maintained faith in the concept however and in 1984 they recruited David Stogden on to their design team. (The KZHRM to the south had worked with Stogden in the development of a large RHI lifeboat, launched in 1984.) The 42ft (12.8m) *Koningin Beatrix* incorporated a fully enclosed wheelhouse and was the first large RHI to use water-jet propulsion. Another interesting feature was the engine configuration that was staggered diagonally fore and aft – a detail inherited from some of the early Dutch steel MLBs. The use of water-jets was vital in the Dutch rescue environment, as the ability to operate in extremely shallow water was crucial. Utilising innovations proven in the Medina project and in the development of the *Koningin Beatrix*, the KNZHRM team continued to push the idea of a large self-righting RHI lifeboat, propelled by water-jets, with an enclosed wheelhouse for protection and an external steering station. They took advantage of improvements in diesel-engine technology with the introduction of lighter, smaller and more powerful diesel engines, as well as lighter more efficient water-jet propulsion units. In addition, lightweight composite materials, such as carbon-fibre, were used to reduce the overall tonnage. In

spite of the technological innovations, the design team still calculated that the RHI lifeboat would have to be about 47ft (14.5m) in length, and weigh about 13.5 tons (13.77 tonnes), making it far too heavy for the conventional Dutch beach-launching carriages; it would thus be designed to lay afloat.

The concept was given to the Marine Engineering firm of Bureau voor Scheepsbouw de Vries Lentsch for final design configuration and, after extensive tank tests, tenders for construction of the prototype were invited in 1986. The first of the new generation was launched in 1988 and named *Johannes Frederik*. She proved herself to

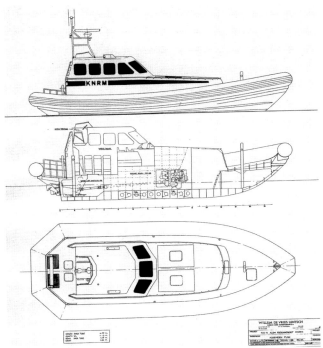

Designed to lie afloat, the KNRM's Johannes Frederik (JF) type RHI lifeboats first launched in 1988, boasted a top speed of 34kt. These vessels are self-righting, with the twin diesel engines housed forward of the wheelhouse for even weight distribution, and a small flying bridge located aft.
KNRM

The 42ft (12.8m) Dutch RHI lifeboat *Koningin Beatrix* was the first of a new generation of large RHIs to use water-jets for propulsion.
KNRM

be a fine heavy-weather rescue craft, more than capable of replacing the ageing fleet of large steel MLBs. The *Johannes Frederik* became the namesake for an entire class of large RHIs known as the JF Type of which eight had been launched by 1997. Although they do vary the boats average around 47ft (14.4m) in length with a 17ft 8in (5.4m) beam and an extremely shallow 2ft 6in (0.75m) draught. They are powered by twin 680-hp turbo-charged diesels running through stainless-steel

165

Due to the success of RHIs in the Dutch lifesaving environment, the KNRM decided in the 1990s that they would develop an all-RHI lifeboat fleet.

KNRM

seen. One of the waves actually pitch-poled the vessel, sending her tumbling end over end. In spite of some rather limited electronic damage and a somewhat shaken but still intact crew, the RHI suffered minimal damage, and righted herself rapidly both times with no loss of motive power (see Sidebar).

The two Dutch lifeboat societies amalgamated to form the KNRM in 1991 and continued to work on developing RHIs. There still remained the problem of replacing the carriage-launched beach lifeboats with a suitable RHI of smaller weight and overall dimensions than the JF class. In 1990 a 34ft 10in (10.6m) water-jet driven RHI was launched to become the namesake of a new class of Dutch RHI known as the Valentjin type. Propelled by two 430-hp diesel engines placed well forward, she could speed along at 34kt and had a semi-enclosed wheelhouse topped by an enclosed self-righting bag. An entirely new self-propelled beach-launch carriage was developed with a hydraulic launch-and-recovery system. There were 12 of the Valentjin class RHIs in service with the Dutch Lifeboat Institution as of 2001, and many more being built for service elsewhere in the world, including Italy and Turkey.

In keeping with the KNRM's goal of building an entirely RHI lifeboat fleet by 2002, further developments continue to this day (see Chapter II-23) including the standardisation of all the smaller inshore rescue boat RHIs. The RHI that has been chosen is the 28ft (8.6m) Harder type with twin diesel water-jet propulsion.[385] In 1999 the KNRM launched the first of its Arie Visser (AV) class 62ft (18.8m) RHIs, designed to deal with the increasing number of calls from further offshore. Essentially this is a stretched version of the JF class RHI lifeboat, and certainly one of the largest RHIs in the world. The AV type are powered by twin 1,000-hp MAN diesels producing a top speed of 35kt that can be maintained for 16 hours duration. It has improved accommodation, engine-room access and greater cockpit space in the stern. The longer hull offers a softer ride in heavy seas, which helps eliminate crew fatigue on extended offshore calls.[386]

Inflatables are probably the most popular rescue craft in use in the world today. The Medina type RHI has been utilised in both the Danish and the Norwegian lifeboat services and the Italian Coast Guard has also recently completed a large building programme of modified Valentjin type RHIs. Many countries and maritime rescue organisations around the globe have developed their own specialised versions of RHI, or have worked in close conjunction with manufacturers to develop boats best suited to local operating conditions. (For more on inflatable and RHI development within other countries see Part IV.)

KaMewa water-jets that provide an impressive top speed of 34kt. Unlike earlier large RHIs the diesel engines were placed forward of the wheelhouse, which moved the vessel's longitudinal centre of gravity (LCG) forward, a consideration of paramount importance for RHIs designed to operate in large head seas and surf.

The sea conditions faced by Dutch lifesaving crews are some of the worst the world has to offer and any doubts in the ability of the large RHIs were eliminated on 21 February 1993 when the *Jan van Engelenburg*, stationed at Terschelling, responded to a distress call from the German container vessel *Linda Buck*, going aground after having her wheelhouse windows blown out by 59ft (18m) seas. In the process of coming up to the wreck, the *Jan van Engelenburg* was capsized twice by incredibly powerful waves, the magnitude of which the coxswain, with more than 20 years local experience, had never

The Storm of 21 February 1993, Terschelling, The Netherlands.

On 21 February 1993 the wind had been blowing storm force from the northwest for two solid days. The seas, which were pounding the outer Frisian Islands off the north coast of The Netherlands, were an average of 26ft (8m) high, with the occasional 50 footer (15m). An unmanned platform in the vicinity of the island of Terschelling was found later to have had all its railings swept off; its height above sea level was 60ft (18m). According to the Dutch Meteorological Office, it was the worst weather to hit this notoriously storm-prone stretch of coast in 20 years. The following narrative describes the events of that night from the perspective of the crew of the KNRM's large JF class RHI, and is quoted from a paper presented at the 17th International Lifeboat Conference by Sip Wiebanga.

At 0410, 21 February 1993, the front windows of the German container vessel Linda Buck *were smashed in by huge waves. Because of the damage done by the seawater, the ship was not under control. The aids to navigation were destroyed. At 0645 the* Linda Buck *made a distress signal. Both Terschelling lifeboats put to sea on receiving the message: the old slow lifeboat* Carlot *and the new modern lifeboat* Jan van Engelenburg. *The water level at the port of Terschelling was so high, that access to the boats was flooded and the crew had to wade to board them.*

Jan van Engelenburg *passed the dangerous Stortemelk very well. On the bar conditions can be hazardous with confused seas coming from any seaward direction.* Carlot *was hit by a heavy ground sea which deformed a side window and damaged the video plotter, radar mast and chart table.*

Two merchant navy ships were in the vicinity of the Linda Buck. *One, the German* Humling, *got into difficulties because her engine stopped. Water came into her air inlets. A Russian ship was at anchor close to the beach. She was also in a dangerous position. However the* Humling *and the Russian ship avoided grounding.*

The Linda Buck *did not follow the advice of the lifeboat coxswain to drop the anchor quickly enough. So slowly she came into the groundsea area, two lifeboats accompanying her. The lifeboat crews felt safe. Seatbelts were not worn and sausages were cut to provide breakfast.*

Jan van Engelenburg's *coxswain decided to take the lifeboat outside the breakers area because nothing could prevent the* Linda Buck *from running aground. Before he could execute*

his decision, Jan van Engelenburg *was hit by a breaker on the beam. The maximum list was 160°. Footstraps and hand holds kept the crew in position. After that experience, the coxswain decided to order the seat belts to be fastened, he steered to seawards and saw a huge sea coming towards him. His first reaction was to give full speed ahead to try to break through the crest of the sea. The result...a bow over stern screw capsize. Within a few seconds (nobody could give an exact time bracket in which the capsize actually happened) the boat righted itself.*

The JF class RHI lifeboat *Christien* crosses the surfzone outside of its homeport of IJmuiden, headquarters for the KNRM.
Kees Brinkman, KNRM

None of the crew had realized the danger or had found the time to think. It went just as smooth and natural as in the capsize trial which they had experienced themselves. The boat itself was in good condition after the capsize. The navigator antenna was missing; the flying bridge windshield was gone, the antenna of the DF was bent and the radar performance was bad because of salt water damage to the inside of the scanner.

The real dangers were inside the wheelhouse. An axe, a knife, a shackle for the drogue had been flying around the wheelhouse during the capsize. 'The ashtray was emptied,' said the coxswain's report.

After restarting the engines and testing the equipment, the coxswain and the crew decided to stay outside to finish the job. Just before stranding, the crew of the Linda Buck *had been taken off by a helicopter of the Dutch Navy.*[387]

CHAPTER 21

The United Kingdom; The Fast Afloat Boats

The recognition of the 'need for speed' came quite early in the history of motorised rescue. In 1915 for example, the Canadian Lifesaving Service had two high-speed launches capable of speeds in excess of 20kt built for their Toronto Station. In 1929 the RNLI constructed a specialised lifeboat for another kind of emerging oceanic casualty: the aeroplane. As cross-Channel air-transport increased so did the number of at-sea ditchings. This type of predicament required a far more rapid response and a new hybrid lifeboat was constructed by the well-known Thornycroft yard. The boat was named the *Sir William Hillary* after the 1824 founder of the Institution and was stationed at Dover in 1930 for close access to the congested aircraft and cross-Channel ferry routes. She was 64ft (19.5m) long and was powered by two 375-hp engines, which provided a top speed of just over 17kt – something almost unheard of in large rescue craft at the time.

The *Sir William Hillary* was an anomaly in rescue craft design and was the only one of her type to be built. Unlike most motor lifeboats she was not self-righting, in fact, she was more rescue launch than lifeboat. In terms of rapid response she served her purpose and, in many respects, was a great deal ahead of her time. Although recognition of the need for faster rescue vessels would not truly take hold in Britain until well into the 1960s, the *Sir William Hillary* would establish a trend for the military crash boat and rescue launch that would follow. During the Second World War armed forces around the world and, in particular, the RAF in the English Channel saw the RNLI's prototype for what it was: the precursor of the fast rescue launch. She was followed by a variety of even faster craft for rescuing the crews of downed aircraft and sunken warships during the years of European conflict.

The *Sir William Hillary* was transferred to the Admiralty for wartime air-sea rescue duties in 1940.

As previously stated, the 1960s saw a revolution in the approach to lifeboat design in Britain. There was now a trend towards much faster designs, which would really come to fruition during the 1970s. At the 9th International Lifeboat Conference, in Edinburgh in 1963, the RNLI and other lifesaving organisations from around the world, were impressed by the new workhorse of the USCG, the 44ft MLB. Following the conference, representatives of the RNLI visited the USCG's production facility at Curtis Bay, Maryland, and acquired Hull #28. She arrived in the UK in May 1964 and, as 44-001, began sea trials around the coasts of Britain and Ireland and was even tested by

The RNLI's fast rescue launch, the *Sir William Hillary*, built at the Thornycroft yards, seen here on her builder's trials in 1929 cruising at an impressive 18kt. Recruited for military service during the Second World War, this vessel would become the predecessor of many generations of naval and air force fast rescue launches. *RNLI*

the Dutch in December 1964. On trials 44-001 covered approximately 5,000 miles[388] and, while not accepted by all traditionalists, her 14-kt speed and manoeuvrability impressed many and six more were built in Britain. They were known as the Waveney type and began a trend in the RNLI for naming new classes of lifeboats after rivers rather than designers.

All future Waveneys would be built in Britain; the principle differences from the American versions being aluminium rather than steel for the houseworks and main deck, and the addition of wave-subduing strakes along either side of the vessel aft. Many British lifeboats were still slipway or cradle launched and one of the potential drawbacks of the steel-hull was its weight, which forced the vessels to lay afloat in deepwater harbours. With speed came greater coverage and it was soon seen that such a fast afloat boat (FAB) could eventually eliminate the need for many of the slower lifeboats. In the end 22 Waveney lifeboats would serve in the RNLI, the last one being launched in 1982. They remained in British service until 1999, leaving in their wake an astounding legacy of over 7,000 call-outs and 2,800 lives saved.

As of 2001 most of the original RNLI Waveneys are still in service around the world, including several that have been sold for use by various local branches of the Royal New Zealand Volunteer Coast Guard Federation and the Royal Volunteer Coastal Patrol of Australia. One is in service in Walvis Bay with the Namibian Sea Rescue Institute, others have gone to Montevideo, Uruguay, and British Columbia. Still more have been sold into private service for use as pilot vessels and heavy weather excursion boats in both Britain and the Falkland Islands.[389]

Although the RNLI continued to focus on more traditional displacement-style lifeboats such as the Oakley, Solent and Rother, by 1970, following the loss of the Longhope and Fraserburgh lifeboats off Scotland, the push was on to develop an all self-righting fleet by the end of the following decade and other designs were sought. Those who favoured the FAB were ready to further develop the concept introduced with the Waveneys. A larger and somewhat faster FAB was needed, of about 50ft (15.2m) in length.[390] Design work was begun on two self-righting prototypes. The first, a 50-footer, would essentially be a larger version of the Waveney. With a corten-steel hull and an after 'turtle', like its smaller cousin, the Thames class was designed to have a top speed of 19kt and would be inherently self-righting (no ballast system required). Another FAB project took a considerably more radical approach: this was the 52ft (15.8m) Arun class MLBs, built in wood, with diagonal planking, laminated frames and cold-moulding techniques, a construction chosen for reasons of cost and the reduced strength-to-weight ratio.[391]

Of the two new designs the Arun would become the clear winner. This new vessel represented a fundamental departure and would lead the way from full-displacement lifeboats to faster, hard-chine craft in the RNLI and other rescue organisations. The first Arun, 52-01, was launched in 1971 and introduced radical design features such as reverse sheer forward for better visibility at high speeds, greater flaring to the bows for spray dispersal, more breadth for greater lateral stability in a beam sea, and self-righting capabilities dependant on the positive buoyancy of the superstructure. The new class combined the speed of a rescue launch with the survivability features of a traditional lifeboat. The 52-01 had a top speed of 18kt and a cruising range of 230 miles.

After over 12,000 miles of extensive sea trials 52-01 was stationed at St Peter Port, Guernsey. Within hours of her arrival, she was called out to rescue the crew of a French trawler. The speed and success of the operation solidified the future of the FAB concept within the RNLI.

Further Aruns were built with several design modifications, including one built of steel with aluminium houseworks, and several made out of glass-reinforced plastic (GRP). Although several 54ft (16.4m) versions were built, by the time of the eighth Arun a return to the 52ft hull was made with GRP as the material of choice. The refined lifeboat would have several new features including a larger wheelhouse, space for the carriage of a small inflatable boat, a flying bridge and the characteristic 'inverse' wheelhouse windows, a feature designed to minimise the penetration of sea water by reducing the surface area exposed to direct contact. Another distinctive

The Canadian Coast Guard Arun class MLB based out of Bickerton, Nova Scotia. This was the original vessel purchased by the CCG directly from Halmatic, UK, and constructed out of GRP. Subsequent CCG versions of the vessel have been constructed out of aluminium.
CCG

feature introduced on 52-02 was the lowering of the decks on either side of the wheelhouse towards the stern of the lifeboat. This innovative concept was intended to get the rescuer closer to the person in the water for ease of recovery and would be copied on many designs to come. The Arun would become one of the most successful MLB designs ever, paving the way for the development of high-speed self-righting MLBs in other rescue services around the world. In all, 46 would be built, the last, the *Duke of Atholl* being launched in 1990.[392]

The newer high-speed FABs would have a service life of about 20 years and it was early recognised that many would need replacing in the early 1990s. In addition, the venerable Waveneys were getting on and a smaller design of FAB was needed to replace them. In 1989 the RNLI established SORs for two new vessels, which included an upgraded operational speed of 25kt, better semi-tunnel

An ocean-going MLB. The RNLI's largest rescue craft, the Severn type MLB is powered by twin 1,050-hp diesels in a U-drive configuration to maximise internal space. First introduced in 1996, the 40-ton *Severn* has a top speed of 25kt and can cruise for 250 nautical miles. She also carries a small daughterboat on the upper deck.
RNLI

propeller protection, and the ability to take the ground.[393] It was decided that fibre-reinforced composite would be the hull material of choice and, in 1992, after extensive testing and trials all around the UK, the Institution announced the launching of FAB 3, the 55ft 9in (17m) Severn class to replace the Arun, and FAB 4, the 46ft 9in (14m) Trent class to replace the Waveney type.

Both vessels required a considerable increase in horsepower in order to maintain the 25kt operational speed. In order to test the handling characteristics of a FAB at these higher speeds, the RNLI successfully re-powered an Arun with the larger engines. The Severn would require two 1,050-hp diesels, and the Trent two 800-hp. Both vessels would maintain many of the design characteristics inherent in the Arun. One major modification was the installation of an aft engine-room utilising u-drive propulsion. This allowed for easier access to the engines, which could also be removed through hatches on the aftdeck, and provided more space forward. At the 1995 International Lifeboat Conference it was noted that the FAB 3 and 4 prototypes had experienced some cracking and stress fractures in frames and shell laminates after some months of heavy-weather testing. As a result the overall scantlings of the hull components were increased to produce an incredibly strong GRP hull, which has stood the test of time. It is anticipated, in the RNLI's present building programme, that approximately 60 of the Severns will be constructed, as well as some 30 of the Trent class. It is a long time since the days of Lionel Lukin and Henry Greathead, but like these great innovators, the British continue to recognise the merits of operational input and a good design, and the Severn and Trent are products of that resolve.

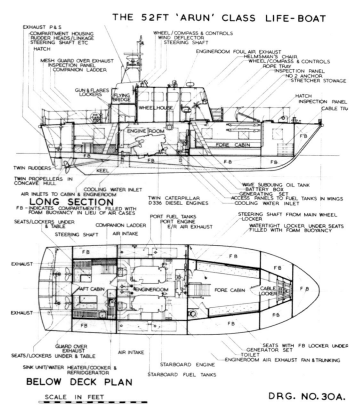

THE 52FT 'ARUN' CLASS LIFE-BOAT

LONG SECTION
FB – INDICATES COMPARTMENTS FILLED WITH FOAM BUOYANCY IN LIEU OF AIR CASES

BELOW DECK PLAN

SCALE IN FEET

DRG. NO. 30A.

The prototype RNLI Arun class self-righting MLB. The original had a double-diagonal wooden hull while subsequent versions were constructed of fibreglass. Future modifications included lowered side-decks for man-overboard recovery, a much larger wheelhouse with cantilevered windows forward, and the inclusion of a small inflatable daughterboat.
Eric Fry, RNLI

The Wreck of the Cargo Ship *Green Lily*

Many modern coastal rescues, particularly when lives are in grave danger and survival time is limited, are handled by rescue helicopter services. But what happens when the weather and sea conditions become so violent that they overwhelm the capabilities of airborne machines?

For three days a horrendous storm with consistent Force 11 winds had been battering the Shetlands. The seas could only be described as massive and were estimated to be in the range of 50ft (15.2m). On the morning of 19 November 1997 the 3,000-ton refrigerated cargo vessel *Green Lily*, about 15 miles (9.3km) southeast of the lifeboat station at Lerwick, reported to HM Coastguard that she was experiencing engine failure and was adrift. Almost immediately the RNLI's local honorary secretary was apprised of the situation and advised that a large tug, the *Tystie*, and the oil-rig supply vessel, the *Gargano*, were en route to assist. The *Gargano* was the first to arrive and quickly established a towline to the stricken ship. Within 90 minutes however, the *Gargano* reported that the towline had parted and that the *Green Lily* was now drifting rapidly towards the rocky shores of Bressay. The Coastguard immediately scrambled the Severn-type lifeboat *Michael and Jane Vernon* and their large helicopter, *Rescue Lima Charlie*, to the scene.

Once out of the relative protection of Bressay Sound, the *Michael and Jane Vernon* was confronted by 40ft (12m) waves, the tops of which were tumbling off in immense walls of white water. But, as she rounded Bard Head and swung to the northeast, the sea came on to the quarter, and she was able to maintain 20kt. Time was running out for the *Green Lily*. The ship had been drifting towards shore at a rate of 2kt and, with only 1.5 miles to go, something had to be done, and quickly. At 1.50pm the lifeboat, the helicopter, and the *Tystie* were all on scene. The rocky cliffs were in sight but the *Green Lily* was lying beam-on to the seas and her violent motions were preventing the helicopter from hoisting. By 2pm three brave souls on the bow of the heaving *Green Lily* helped to secure another tow-line from the tug, and, for a few brief minutes, the great bow was brought to seaward. Ten minutes later the tow-line parted, and the coxswain of the *Michael and Jane Vernon*, Hewitt Clark, advised the master of the ship that his only chance was to drop anchor and hope.

Almost 30 minutes later, and within half a mile of the shore, the port anchor was finally dropped on a short scope. It was not sufficient to stop the ship's drift but it did serve to slow it somewhat and bring her bow about 45° into the wind.

Realising that the ship's fate was now sealed and a helicopter evacuation was still not an option, Clark began to drive his lifeboat into the only recovery zone possible – the partial lee on the port side of the ship – placing the boat between the massive drifting hulk and the cliffs. He advised the master of the ship to muster his crew and, with his own crew standing by on life-lines he made his first approach. As if in a dazed state of denial, the ship's crew slowly made their way on deck one by one. With every second they were coming closer to destruction. At one moment the huge lifeboat would be suspended high above the deck of the ship, on the next, the coxswain, now at the flybridge helm position, was staring at the ship's water-line. One at a time, five of the ship's crew were hauled off the heaving, rolling ship. Each time Hewitt had to take a separate approach and run in. At one point the *Michael and Jane Vernon* became pinned beside the ship but with the brute force of the powerful diesel engines Hewitt was able to pivot away. In the process, some stanchions were ripped off the lifeboat and one of her crew was slightly injured but all carried on.

Unbeknownst to the lifeboat crew, another oil-rig supply vessel, the *Maersk Champion*, had now arrived on the scene and, through an incredible feat of seamanship, had grappled the *Green Lily*'s anchor line and was swinging her bow back to sea. Within 200yd (183m) of the cliffs, the lifeboat lost her lee and was forced to head offshore. But the *Maersk Champion*'s valiant efforts stabilised the stricken ship and the helicopter moved in. With the *Green Lily* now aground and being combed by the gargantuan seas, winchman Bill Deacon was lowered from *Rescue Lima Charlie* and, one at a time, recovered the remaining 10 crew, literally as the ship was torn apart beneath them. Tragically, towards the end of the operation, Deacon was washed overboard from the deck of the *Green Lily* by a huge breaking sea. The helicopter, with its winch line fouled, had no choice but to sever the connection. Both helicopter and lifeboat scoured the area for the lost winchman but with daylight fading and survivors onboard, they had to return to base. Bill Deacon was lost.

The RNLI awarded its Gold Lifesaving Medal, for the first time in 16 years, to Hewitt Clark, and the Bronze to each crewmember of the *Michael and Jane Vernon*. Both the crew and the new Severn-type FAB had proved their mettle in the toughest of conditions.

The Severn class RNLB *Michael and Jane Vernon*, based out of Lerwick in the Shetland Islands comes alongside the stricken freighter *Green Lily* about to go ashore in massive seas off the coast of Bressay on 19 November 1997. Coxswain Hewitt Clark and his crew made several attempts to come alongside in the lee of the ship and were able to rescue five of her crew one by one. This rescue earned Clark the RNLI's Gold Lifesaving Medal, the first to be awarded in 16 years. *RNLI*

CHAPTER 22

The New American MLB; The 47 Footer

The last 44ft MLB to be built in the United States came out of the USCG's Curtis Bay Boatyard in November 1972. In all, 110 of these sturdy boats had been built at Curtis Bay, 106 for service in the United States and four for foreign rescue organisations.[394] Incredibly, when one considers the environment in which these vessels operated and the thousands of heavy-weather SAR incidents that were answered by the boats and their crews, only two of the USCG's 44 Footers were ever damaged beyond repair. As of 2002 most of the 44 Footers have been replaced by the new thoroughbred of the surf, the latest generation of American MLB: the 47 Footer.

By the 1980s the 44ft MLB was outdated. They had been well built, but the incredible demands placed upon them by the ever-increasing caseloads around the US coasts meant that many were rapidly becoming tired. In 1984 Naval Engineers at USCG Headquarters dispatched a preliminary design outline to lifeboat crews and coxswains around the country asking for input into a better design of MLB. The primary objective was to 'design a boat that retained the durability and survivability of the 44ft MLB combined with 30 years of technological advances'.[395] After extensive research the basic operational requirements of a new MLB were to include the ability to operate safely in 20ft (6.2m) breaking seas, improved speed, stability and internal crew accommodation as compared to the old 44 Footer. By 1987 a preliminary design concept had been developed and a contract went out to tender for the finalisation of the schematics and the construction of a prototype vessel. The contract also provided for the construction of a further five 'pre-production' MLBs if the initial design and prototype was deemed successful.

The new MLB was built by Textron Industries of New Orleans, Louisiana, entirely of high-grade corrosion-resistant marine aluminium and its approximate dimensions were 47ft (14.3m) long with a beam of 14ft (4.3m) and a draught of 4ft 6in (1.4m). The hull was of relatively hard-chined deep-V form and the new boat was able to cruise in excess of 200 miles at over 25kt with twin 425-hp turbo-charged diesel engines. Unlike all previous American MLBs – other than the 52 Footers – the new boat had a fully-enclosed wheelhouse and a flying

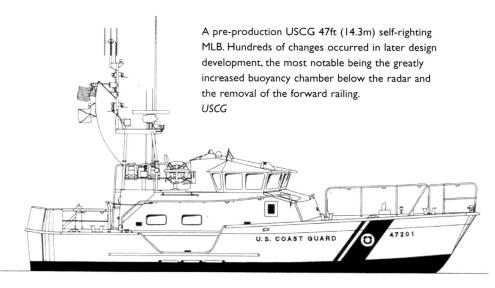

A pre-production USCG 47ft (14.3m) self-righting MLB. Hundreds of changes occurred in later design development, the most notable being the greatly increased buoyancy chamber below the radar and the removal of the forward railing.
USCG

bridge with two-topside steering stations, both of which were positioned so that the helmsman could control the boat and look directly down at the man overboard (MOB) recovery zones on either side of the vessel. The concept of the lowered recovery zones was similar to that on the British Arun and future FAB-type RNLI MLBs except that the American 47ft MLB prototype had a deck grating that could be raised for recovery, or lowered to allow regular level access around the deck.

Following a successful roll-over test in Louisiana, the prototype was sent across the United States in the fall of 1990 to Cape Disappointment, Washington, home of the USCG's National Motor Lifeboat School (NMLBS) where a test team was established to evaluate the new boat and put her through her paces on the dangerous waters of the Columbia River Bar. The evaluation included a trip north to the Canadian Coast Guard's Pacific Region where CCG lifeboat crews were also allowed to trial the boat in their home waters and where the design was also well received. After exhaustive evaluations the test team advised 'that the 47' MLB met, or in many cases exceeded, the operational requirements' as defined.[396]

Nevertheless, 100 recommendations for design changes were made. One of the most significant was the alteration of the rudder system from canted to vertical to provide greater stability when underway at high speeds and to allow the vessel to track better and turn more efficiently. The prototype was then turned over to the operational crew of USCG Station Cape Disappointment where further evaluations could be made during regular 'working' conditions. Approval was then given for the construction of the five pre-production boats and they were delivered by the Textron Yard in 1993 and early 1994. They were placed at Gloucester, Massachussetts, Cape May, New Jersey and Oregon Inlet, North Carolina on the Atlantic, and at Umpqua River and Tillamook, Oregon, on the Pacific. The idea for the operational testing and evaluation phase of these boats was that they would spend the next 18 months being used on 'normal cases and sorties by normal crews'.[397] Various evaluation criteria were developed to measure such human factors as crew fatigue and instrument ergonomics and, for the first time in the development of a new rescue craft, a Marine Data Recorder (MDR) – a seagoing version of a jetliner's black box – was placed on all the boats to continually monitor performance when underway. The MDR provided vessel motion and operations data on a long- and short-term basis. When a near rollover occurred, a more concise data burst was automatically or manually triggered so the effect on machinery and electronics could be analysed in greater detail.[398]

The operational evaluation and testing of the pre-production boats proved the new 47 Footer to be a considerable improvement on the old 44ft MLB. The obvious increase in speed was, of course, the most noteworthy change, but station crews also noticed a considerable improvement in towing capabilities with a bollard pull of 9,000lb (4,082kg) at 1,500rpm, and the ability to easily tow a vessel of about 150 tons (153 tonnes). Visibility from the open steering stations topside was also greatly improved, particularly when working in surf and when setting up a tow. Nor were the boat operators in any doubt that the handling characteristics of the 47ft MLB were considerably different: the new boat had far more windage due to the large superstructure; the large bow meant that she could be uncomfortable when underway at speed in a head sea and the small rudders meant that the boat required a greater distance in which to turn about than the old 44 Footer. However, all such characteristics were merely 'quirks' – the 36ft and 44ft MLBs also had their own bizarre 'behaviour patterns'. As with any new design, crews would be trained to recognise the tendencies and, in some cases, use them to their advantage.

In 1996 a contract for full production of the 47ft MLB was awarded to Textron Industries, with the first of the post-development boats, MLB *47206*, being delivered for duty at Cape Disappointment in May 1997. By March 1999 29 of the new boats had been placed in service. With the average on-site delivery of one every 18 days, the overall production run was scheduled to conclude in 2002 after the delivery of the 100th 47 Footer (there is a strong possibility that even more will be constructed for the USCG).[399]

In 1998 the Canadian Coast Guard took delivery of its first 47ft MLB, constructed by Metalcraft Industries in Kingston, Ontario. The Canadian boat differs from the US version in its propulsion and control package, ventilation and certain safety appliances pertinent to Canadian regulations. At the time of writing a contract for the construction of 24 more CCG 47ft MLBs has been awarded to Victoria Shipyards, with deliveries taking place from 2003 to 2006.

The Canadian Coast Guard 47ft (14.3m) MLB *Cape Calvert* stationed at Bamfield, British Columbia. By 2005, over 30 of this type will be in service with the CCG.
Mark Kelly, CCG

CHAPTER 23

Trends and Innovations

L ike the lifeboats of yesteryear, today's modern rescue craft must be able to operate safely and capably in the harshest of sea and weather conditions. They must also be able to respond rapidly to a call, carry out the rescue operation, and return crew and survivors safely to shore. Although the natural environment in which rescue craft and their crews must operate has changed little over the last two centuries, the operational environment has changed immensely. Increased traffic and larger coastal populations mean more frequent maritime casualties. At the same time, in today's cost-conscious world, greater efficiencies of service are required. It is not surprising, therefore, that recent trends in design and technology include the demand for increased speed, larger, more versatile designs, standardisation of design, simplification of onboard systems, and an increased emphasis on ergonomics and crew comfort.

The Need for Speed

The principal directive in coastal lifesaving in recent decades has been the demand for more rapid response to a casualty. Thus today's rescue craft are becoming faster with some designs approaching or exceeding 40kt. At one time this kind of on-water speed was only possible with air-cushion vehicles, high-speed RHIs and other inshore rescue boats, but no longer. Many conventional lifeboats can now cruise in the 30 to 35kt range.

The demand for increased operating speeds has come hand-in-hand with a demand for much larger and more versatile long-range rescue craft. In The Netherlands, for example, the KNRM continues to develop its fleet of RHIs, all of which have operational SAR speeds in the mid-30kt range. In Sweden, the latest designs of rescue craft continue with the high speed traditions established by the *Victoria* and *Odd Fellow* lifeboats with a new 66ft (20m) vessel that can top out at an amazing 37kt. The latest designs for the SNSM in France and for the RNLI in Britain and Ireland, all have operational speeds of 25kt or better. For the most part the days of the displacement lifeboat seem to be numbered even though many remain in service around the world.

Bigger Boats

Although most of the world's maritime rescue organisations began as 'coastal' lifesaving organisations, today many are asked to provide effective SAR coverage at greater distances offshore; far beyond the traditional 50-mile zone of influence for most coastal lifeboats. This has meant that rescue craft have had to increase in size to accommodate larger engines, greater fuel capacity and, in some cases, crew accommodation for extended offshore SAR operations. In many ways the result is a marriage between the design merits of the fast coastal lifeboat and the offshore cruising lifeboat. The trend towards larger, fast, offshore lifeboats originated in Germany with the DGzRS rescue cruisers (see Chapter II-14) and continues there today with a massive 160ft (49m) rescue cruiser planned to replace the 141ft (44m) *John T. Essberger* type, which are now approaching 30 years of service. Recently the NSSR of Norway has led the way in this category with the development of two classes of large, high-speed offshore rescue craft: the 65ft 6in (20m) Emmy Dyvi and the 82ft (25m) Ulabrand class vessels (see Part IV). As mentioned, the SSRS of Sweden, is developing the 65ft 6in (20m) SSRS Rescue 2000, a 14-ton, water-jet, offshore rescue cruiser with a service speed and range of 33kt for 10 hours.[400]

To accommodate the modern demands far out in the North Sea the KNRM has been experimenting with a project entitled the 'Enlarged Ship Concept', or ESC. Having decided many years ago to construct an all RHI fleet (see Chapter II-20) the Dutch service had been increasing the size of their RHI lifeboats over time, culminating in the launching of the 59ft (18m) Arie Visser class prototype in 1999. ESC has been developed for the production of high-speed monohulls in private industry. The objective is to achieve the optimum hull length and breadth for given demands and sea conditions. Its ultimate goal is the maximum limitation of vertical movement and acceleration for a given design – the principal limiting force of speed and response in adverse conditions. In simple terms, an existing design is taken and then lengthened by 25% to 50% with no increase in deadweight or initial hull speed. The result is a vessel with a much smaller length-to-beam ratio and a much lighter overall weight. As a result of the ESC calculations based on the traditional Dutch 47ft (14.4m) Johannes Frederick class, the optimum RHI size for offshore operations has been determined to be 63ft (19.2m). The new self-righting Ejape class RHI configured for this optimum length will be powered by two 500kw Man turbo-diesels driving Hamilton 362 water jets and will be capable of cruising at 30kt for 16 continuous hours. From a historical perspective, it is interesting to note how the increase in the length-to-beam ratio of these RHIs closely resembles the development of the early motor lifeboats by both Dutch societies (see Chapter II-13).[401]

Standardisation

Regardless of the funding mechanism, the most efficient use of limited financial resources is often the bottom line in the survival of that organisation. As a result of such economic reality, standardisation and rationalisation of rescue-craft design and systems has been an ongoing trend for many years. Since the earliest days of the industrial revolution the manufacturing sector has proven that interchangeable components amongst different production lines have immense economic benefits. For rescue craft such inter-changeable components might include main engines, propulsion units and pieces of navigational equipment. For instance, the Canadian Coast Guard's Pacific Region has recently decided to re-engine part of its fleet of USCG type 41ft UTBs with the same engine type fitted in its fleet of SR lifeboats. The spare inventory and

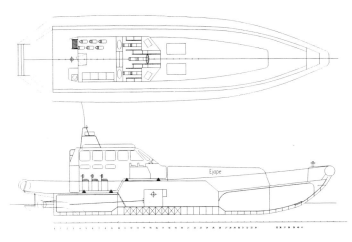

Inshore rescue boats no more. The KNRM's trend of developing even larger RHI lifeboats continues with the Ejape class proposal. The new RHI would be 63ft (19.2m) long and its two 500kw turbo-diesels with water-jets would provide a top speed of 30kt for 16 continuous hours and would allow this 'rubber' boat to operate at far greater distances offshore than its predecessors.
KNRM

technical repair advantages of such a move are obvious. Training crews for standardised vessel types also provides economic and safety benefits.

Recent standardisation has involved limiting the types of rescue craft within a particular fleet. Many large maritime rescue organisations have a multitude of craft 'types' at their disposal. This variation has resulted from localised operational requirements but today design developments are tending towards the rationalisation of types, so that a particular design may fulfil more than one traditional role. For example, currently in development for the RNLI is a lifeboat capable of being launched from a slipway or carriage or laying afloat.[402]

In 1997 the RNLI carried out a study of its boats and equipment with the aim of rationalising types and providing a template for lifeboat construction for the next 20 years. The outcome was the decision that the RNLI's 11 rescue craft types could be combined into four. From largest to smallest these included the GALB (General All Weather Lifeboat), the FRB1 (Fast All Weather Response Lifeboat), the FIB1 (Fast Inshore Lifeboat) and the IB1 (Inshore Lifeboat). The existing Severn and Trent classes of all-weather lifeboats fit the bill for the GALB and a new prototype was not required. The FRB1 project, renamed the FCB2 (Fast Carriage Boat 2) project, aims to provide a fast medium-endurance lifeboat to replace the Mersey (carriage-launched) and Brede (lay afloat) types as well as some of the inshore rescue boats where a somewhat larger resource is required. The FIB1 aims to replace and standardise the RNLI's fleet of RIBs, while the IB1 project aims to replace the fleet of ageing D class soft-bottom inflatables. As of 2003, the FSB2 (Fast Slipway Boat 2) project is well underway, aiming to replace the RNLI's Tyne (slipway-launced) MLBs and, potentially, certain of the RNLI's lay-afloat fleet of MLBs as well.

Similarly, as already mentioned, the KNRM plan to limit their rescue craft types to four, all of them RHIs. From largest to smallest these are the approximately 62ft 4in (19m) Arie Visser class, the 47ft 3in (14.4m) Johannes Frederik class, the 34ft 9in (10.6m) Valentjin class and the new 29ft 6in (9m) class of Harder type inshore rescue boats. The latter will replace no fewer then five separate models of smaller RHIs within the KNRM's present fleet.[403] In France, the SNSM is standardising its fleet of large all-weather lifeboats, the First class launches. The new 46ft (14m) design, which will replace some 26 older lifeboats of various dimensions, is based on a successful pilot-boat design built by the Bernard shipyard in Brittany. It will be self-righting, of fibreglass construction and will carry a small inflatable on a stern ramp. It has a rather prominent 'beak', resembling a narrow and tapering bulbous bow, familiar on many larger vessels. The advantages of this protrusion appear to be more efficient hull dynamics and speed due

A new French First class lifeboat. Based on a popular pilot boat design, this will be the standard large lifeboat for the SNSM, replacing 26 other large lifeboats of various shapes and descriptions. She is 46ft (14m) long, carries a small inflatable in her stern and is characterised by a tapered bulbous bow for improved hydro-dynamics.
SNSM

to the greater waterline length as well as reduced pitching due to the increased resistance to bow submergence and impact dampening with waves and spray head-on.[404]

Simplification of Onboard Systems

Part-in-parcel with the move towards greater standardisation has been a shift towards greater simplification of onboard systems. The wheelhouses of modern high-speed rescue craft bear more resemblance to the cockpit of a large aircraft than to the lifeboats of old. Rapid developments in navigational technologies in the last two decades, such as Global Positioning Systems (GPS), types, sizes and models of radar, and electronic-chart systems, have all lent to the clutter and ergonomic chaos within the small confines of rescue craft wheelhouses and on the consoles of open fast rescue craft. In many respects this has been unavoidable – technologies have developed and improved since the vessels were designed and many indispensable devices have to be added as afterthoughts. However, it seems that wheelhouse clutter might be a thing of the past: a simplified onboard electronics package may now exist that will also allow for a much more stream-lined integration of future technologies.

The RNLI has taken a page from the aviation industry with the implementation of a fully integrated Systems and Information Management System (SIMS) for their new lifeboats. SIMS is presently being tested on the new Fast Slipway Boat (FSB2) prototype being developed in Great Britain and involves a unification of the operation and monitoring of the lifeboat's primary navigational and operational systems from a single control and monitoring unit. Flat computer screens at the various helm locations monitor information from navigation, internal and external communications, mechanical, electrical, and hull systems as well as all alarm and data-recording functions. All systems can now be controlled and monitored from the station without the crewmember even having to leave his or her seat – a potentially hazardous activity in the modern, high-speed, heavy-weather environment. The system is mouse driven and track balls have been integrated at all helm positions for ease of access. The operator can easily switch between navigational information such as radar and engine system status with the flick of a finger. In the FSB2 prototype six screens have been placed throughout the vessel, allowing crew to access and control systems from any of these stations. Thus, more than one crewmember can monitor the vessel's navigation at any particular time by simultaneously bringing up radar and/or the electronic chart system at another station. All systems can still be operated manually and primary components have been placed in an easily accessed location for back-up operation and servicing. Locating devices away from the wheelhouse dash and deck-head has considerably decreased equipment clutter and eliminated many of the sharp edges associated with protruding devices. In addition, fibre-optic cables have been used to integrate all systems into the SIMS monitors thus eliminating the potential for RF interference within the rescue craft. Crew training will be simplified as well through the common commands of a Windows-driven screen, which also eliminates the button-and-nob nightmare of many electronic devices, particularly when operating in adverse conditions.

Ergonomics

Ergonomics is defined as 'the fit between people, the activities they wish to carry out, the tools, machines and systems they use to aid them and the environments in which they are performed'. In modern high-speed rescue craft the human-machine interface involves two principal elements: cognitive/information ergonomics, or the ability for the human mind to interact with the machine; muscular/stress ergonomics, or exactly how the vessel's layout and handling characteristics affects the body's performance.[405]

For the relationship between cognitive and information flow, the recent large increase in instrumentation has provided an audio-visual overload on board many rescue craft. The brain's ability to monitor and accept this plethora of information can vary according to circumstances. The fact that this information might have to be interpreted while driving a high-speed dynamic platform makes it even more complicated.

The modern approach appears to be moving towards the elimination of excess instrumentation in front of the boat operator. One concept, as seen in the case of the RNLI and the SIMS application, has been to integrate technology as much as possible. Another is to maintain separate control units but to place only those instruments crucial to the safe operation of the vessel at the helm station. The Swedish Lifeboat Society has done a considerable amount of work in this regard. Realising that excess instrumentation was not only causing sensory overload but, in some cases also beginning to block the crew's vision out of the wheelhouse, future designs of Swedish rescue craft such as the Rescue 200 will have non-primary systems and instrument panels placed behind the helm stations in order to eliminate clutter and confusion.

The Dutch have also been working on the ergonomics of team operating procedures (bridge management) in high-speed, heavy-weather operations and the KNRM's new large Arie Visser class RHIs have a simplified instrumentation system designed for extended offshore operations with a crew of six. Here there are three separate consoles, each seating two crew, fore and aft. The port console controls engine monitoring and communications, the starboard console, navigation, and the centreline console, steering, depth and electronic-chart information. The coxswain generally sits aft of the helmsman at the centreline station and can monitor all instruments from there. The crew in the forward seats can remain primarily focused on the instruments in front of them, which correlate with their onboard duties. In extreme weather or when coming alongside a casualty, the coxswain can still move to the forward seat and take the helm. For many, this teamwork approach to navigating and operating a high-speed rescue craft seems unnatural, but the concept of an integrated 'cockpit' team has been successfully implemented in the aircraft world for many years.

Another recent ergonomic trend has been the increasing use of onboard communication systems, or ICS, in high-speed rescue craft. Many rescue organisations, such as the RNLI and the KNRM, have used standard aircraft-style ICS units for many years. These have wired-in headsets that provide internal communications amongst all the crew, hearing protection in a noisy environment, and external communications through a range of shipboard radios and other communication devices. The operational and health-and-safety advantages of such systems are enormous. The crew can communicate with one another at all times and can also monitor all radio traffic while going to a casualty, thus eliminating crucial briefing time upon arrival. Various 'wireless' systems have been developed by companies

and agencies around the world and are used in many small high-speed RHIs that may need to monitor only one external device, but they do have some limitations in terms of monitoring capacity. Many lifesaving organisations are presently experimenting with different onboard communications systems and, as time goes on, the technology will undoubtedly become more cost-effective and versatile.

Finally, a great deal of ergonomic research and development has been conducted to make rescue craft more amenable to the human body, safer and more comfortable to operate for extended periods in adverse conditions. The Swedish Lifeboat Society has spent many years developing innovative ergonomic technologies, such as the well-known semi-sitting Ulmann seats and motorcycle-style helm stations on their 26ft 3in (8m) RHIs (see Part IV). Cockpit seats with hydraulic shock absorption have become quite common on many vessels. Vertical impact in large seas has always been one of the principal causes resulting in crew injury and overall fatigue. It is expected that, as populations and crews continue to age, research and development into human-stress reduction will become an increasing priority for all lifesaving organisations.

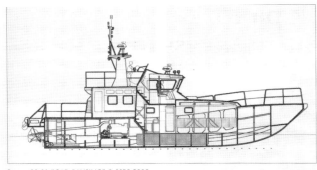

Rescue 20-01 "GAD RAUSING" © SSRS 2002

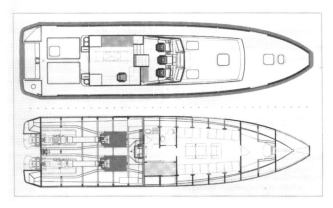

The new 66ft (20m) Rescue 2000 type lifeboat of the Swedish Lifeboat Service.
SSRS

PART III

THE OCEANIC SAFETY NET

CHAPTER 1

Saviours from Above

Perhaps no other element of the oceanic safety net maintains a stronger connection to those who crew and operate lifeboats and other rescue craft than the men and women who work the world's helicopter and fixed-wing rescue units. Whether acting together on an actual rescue mission, or simply on exercise, the aircraft and the boat on the surface combine to make an extremely versatile team. Although the focus of this book is on boats, it would be inappropriate to conclude a text on rescue at sea without describing the history and development of air-sea rescue. Many excellent books have been written on air-sea rescue and so this chapter has been kept intentionally brief and by no means does justice to the subject.

On 29 November 1945 two men found themselves trapped aboard a large fuel barge that had come adrift and been blown by strong winds on to Penfield Reef in Long Island Sound, New York. Large, wind-driven seas were breaking right over the barge; the winds had risen to 60kt with driving rain. In such conditions rescue from ashore would be extremely difficult. Suddenly, over the roar of wind and seas, a strange engine sound was heard. As if from nowhere, an aircraft appeared and, instead of flying past, just hovered above the barge, its pilot staring down at the astonished men. The strange machine was an experimental Sikorsky R-5 helicopter, flown by the company's chief test pilot Dmitry 'Jimmy' Viner. The lightweight R-5 was being buffeted by the high winds and Viner was doing everything he could to keep his machine stationary. Also onboard was Captain Jackson Beighle of the US Army Air Force, present to operate the new experimental power-driven winch, or 'hoist'. A line was dropped down to the barge and, as if scooped by the angels themselves, both men were lifted, one at a time, into the helicopter. Without even getting their feet wet, they were taken to the safety of shore.[406]

Thus ended the first successful rescue at sea by a helicopter with hoist. The relative simplicity of the exercise, especially in terms of manpower and speed of response and recovery (mind-boggling for 1945), was not lost on authorities in the United States and around the world in years to come. These men had pioneered a rescue technique that would become commonplace – it was the dawning of a new era in coastal lifesaving.

The story of flying machines and their relationship to rescue at sea also began in the United States, many years before the events at Penfield Reef. In fact, the connection between the two goes back as far as the birth of manned flight itself. On 13 December 1903 three surfmen from the USLSS Station at Kill Devil Hill, North Carolina, were summoned by signal flags to return to the scene of a strange experiment that had been unsuccessfully attempted the day before. Their assistance was required by two inventive brothers named Orville and Wilbur Wright who were once again hoping to fly for the first time in their experimental machine. The surfmen helped carry the fragile biplane to the launch site at Kitty Hawk, and one of them, J.T. Daniels, took the only photograph of the first flight, with the Wrights' own camera.

In 1915, the same year that the USLSS and the Revenue Cutter Service were combined to form the United States Coast Guard, two lieutenants of the new service, Elmer Stone and Norman Hall approached the Curtiss Aircraft and Motor Company at Newport News, Virginia, regarding the viability of using their flying boats for coastguard work, particularly as a search platform. As a result of these initial enquiries, Stone and five other USCG personnel were sent to the relatively new Naval Aviation School at Pensacola, Florida, the following year, while Hall was assigned to the Curtiss Factory to study aeronautical engineering. Following 1917 and America's entry into the First World War many more USCG pilots were trained, serving at home and overseas, on coastal patrol and amphibious aircraft. Hundreds of lives were saved off the coasts of the United States and Europe thanks to their eagle eyes. In May 1919 Lt. Elmer Stone, USCG, and his crew made history when he piloted a US Navy Curtiss NC-4 seaplane in the first successful transatlantic crossing. What Stone and Hall had helped to create was the first military air-sea rescue service in the world. A similar service was initiated during the First World War in Great Britain operated by men and aircraft of the Royal Naval Air Service, who carried out many daring rescues with primitive flying machines in the worst conditions.

Following the war, however, memories were short in both countries and the provision of dedicated aircraft for civilian lifesaving did not materialise. This, in spite of the fact that in 1916 the famous early aircraft designer, Glenn Curtiss, had designed what he termed the first 'life boat' plane.

It was not until the 1920s that aviation found a permanent role in the USCG. The introduction of prohibition resulted in the smuggling of alcohol all along the coast and the benefits of aerial surveillance as a counter-measure were obvious. This, combined with the improved reliability of aircraft, led Congress in 1925 to come up with sufficient funds to purchase the first dedicated coast guard aircraft and establish the first coast guard air stations at Gloucester, Massachusetts, and Cape May, New Jersey. In 1928 the man assigned to run the newly created aviation section at USCG headquarters was none other than then-Commander Norman Hall. Knowing full well the benefits of aircraft for lifesaving, Hall oversaw the establishment of additional air stations around the country and the development and purchase of the first 'flying lifeboats'. These amphibious aircraft were General Aviation PJ-15s with boat-like hulls and two large engines suspended high above the wings. All the PJ-15s came into service in the early 1930s and were named after prominent stars: *Acamar*, *Antarea*, *Altair*, *Acrux* and *Arcturus*. They were the first aircraft to be specifically constructed with a lifesaving role in mind. They were long-range, could land in relatively rough seas and were built to take a beating. They continued in service until 1941 and were responsible for saving hundreds of lives. An example of one such daring exploit in the early days of air-sea rescue is quoted as follows:

A USCG General Aviation PJ-15 'Flying Lifeboat'. These amphibious aircraft were purchased primarily for lifesaving and were responsible for saving hundreds of lives, principally on the Atlantic seaboard, from the early 1930s until they were decommissioned in 1941. *USCG*

A passenger onboard the Army transport Republic *en route from Panama to New York became critically ill. An emergency operation beyond the transport's facilities was necessary. Help was sought.* Arcturus *was lowered down the ramp at the Miami air station; she taxied into Biscayne Bay and flew three hours in darkness and storm. Using radio bearings, the ship's searchlight beams were located.* Arcturus *circled and landed off the ship's bow. The patient and his wife were transferred by ship's lifeboat.* Republic *indicated wind direction by searchlight and* Arcturus *rose out of the rough sea. This difficult mission took seven hours – and a life was saved.*[407]

The onset of the Second World War saw the next great resurgence in the use of aircraft for lifesaving at sea. Countries on both sides of the conflict established or re-established their air-sea rescue services. New designs of long-range flying boats were constructed, principally for anti-submarine patrols, but were also useful for search and rescue (SAR). The German Luftwaffe established an air-sea rescue service using flying boats and high-speed rescue launches as early as 1939. After the Norwegian campaign, the service was expanded with a fleet of Heinkel 59 floatplanes specifically equipped for rescue. In late 1940, during the height of the Battle of Britain, the Luftwaffe established a rather unique lifesaving measure. Approximately half way across the English Channel a large buoy-shaped float was positioned as a refuge for any fliers fortunate enough to reach it. The float was equipped with a large quantity of food and survival supplies – enough to sustain four men for a considerable period of time. It was painted bright yellow with a red cross on either side. Eventually it became the sanctuary of aircrew from both sides of the conflict and was considered neutral territory. The only problem was that an airman's future – free man or prisoner of war – depended entirely on whose rescue launch arrived first.

From 1939 to 1945 USCG aircraft were directly responsible for locating 1,000 survivors at sea and directing surface vessels to their rescue. In addition USCG flying boat crews recovered some 100 survivors of torpedo attacks and other losses by landing their aircraft at sea in what must have been extremely hazardous conditions. Many lives were also saved by air-dropped lifeboats invented by the British yachtsman and designer Uffa Fox. These lightweight detachable lifeboats were dropped by passing aircraft to parachute down to a casualty. They were entirely enclosed and contained survival rations and gear as well as navigation and sailing instructions. Similarly the USAF developed a glider-borne lifeboat that could glide down to shipwrecked victims and then, after disposing of its wings, power back to shore like a conventional rescue craft. From the time the British Air Sea Rescue Service was officially established in January 1941 to war's end the organisation saved 13,629 lives of which 8,000 were downed air crew.

Like many emerging technologies, experiments with autogyros and other vertical-lift aircraft had actually commenced much earlier than 1939 but were accelerated by war. In the United States an inter-agency board, co-chaired by a member of the USCG, had been established in 1938 to evaluate the helicopter for coastal patrols and lifesaving. After 1941 this team switched its focus to anti-submarine warfare but USCG personnel, in particular Cdr Frank Erickson, remained key players. The USCG Air Station at Brooklyn, New York, commanded by Erickson, received the first Sikorsky HNS-1 and HOS-1 helicopters, and training began in conjunction with Naval and Air Force personnel in 1941. The USCG took the lead role in training other agencies and nations in the operation of the new helicopter. In 1942 they began training several British Royal Air Force and Navy pilots at Brooklyn. The Royal Navy then purchased the largest number of Sikorsky R-4 helicopters ever ordered from the factory; they called them 'hoverflies' and established 705 Squadron, the first helicopter unit outside the United States. (In 1953 this unit, and other helicopter detachments in the UK, would be instrumental in evacuating hundreds of citizens from the disastrous flooding that struck The Netherlands.)

In January 1944 Cdr Erickson carried out the first humanitarian mission to be conducted at sea by a helicopter when he transported a load of blood plasma to the US Navy destroyer *Turner* after she had suffered a serious explosion off Sandy Hook.

As the war neared its end, the focus of the helicopter evaluations returned to search and rescue. In 1945 a USCG HNS-1 helicopter was disassembled at the Brooklyn Air Station and loaded onboard a C-54 transport aircraft for delivery to Goose Bay, Labrador. The machine was then reassembled and flown across 185 miles of frozen tundra to rescue the crew of a downed Royal Canadian Air Force bomber. In addition, ship-based trials were conducted by Sikorsky and the USCG during and after the war. Eventually helicopters would become the chief aerial search-and-rescue tool onboard both US Navy aircraft carriers and the Coast Guard's patrolling cutters.

After the War increasing use of aircraft by military organisations around the world meant that most air force bases close to the ocean had their own SAR capability. As pleasure boating increased exponentially, these SAR resources were used more and more for civilian and commercial casualties. In 1953 Flight Lieutenant Danny Kearns of 705 Squadron, Royal Navy, was tasked with

establishing the first dedicated peace-time helicopter SAR squadron in the UK – 275 Squadron at Linton-on-Ouse, Yorkshire. The squadron's aircraft were painted brilliant yellow with 'rescue' written on the side – the colour scheme is still used to this day. More helicopter SAR squadrons were established around the UK in the 1950s. Eventually the much larger three-crew Wessex Whirlwind Mk II helicopters were purchased to greatly increase the range and effectiveness of the units.

Coming on line in 1963, the Sikorsky HH-52 was the USCG's first amphibious helicopter. Designed in conjunction with the US Navy, this helicopter and its offspring became the USCG's primary SAR helicopter for several decades.
USCG

In many other countries as well, military units, particularly those that had had an air-sea rescue role during the war, were tooled up for peacetime SAR. In Canada the RCAF established SAR squadrons across the country, purchasing early versions of the two-bladed Boeing Vertol helicopters in the mid 1950s and using converted B-17 bombers and PBY flying boats for long-range SAR.

At the 1955 International Lifeboat Convention in Portugal Commander James Cornish of the USCG described the advances in helicopter technology and shared his dream of having a USCG Air Station equipped with helicopters located every 80 miles along the coast of the United States and its protectorates; this would provide 30-minute SAR coverage over all US waters. By 1963 his

A Spanish S-61 SAR Helicopter hovers over the Greek oil tanker *Aegean Sea* fully engulfed off the port of La Coruña in December 1992.
SASEMAR

dream was becoming a reality. Following a review of USCG aviation, 15 new air stations had been built around the United States and a new amphibious SAR helicopter had been developed in conjunction with the US Navy: the Sikorsky HH52A. This incredible machine, and future versions of it, would become the mainstay of the USCG helicopter fleet for decades to come. It was more powerful, had a longer range and, most importantly, it could float. The HH52A could land, and cruise, in a fairly heavy sea and was considered by many to be the first true 'flying life-boat'. The days of the amphibious fixed-wing aircraft being used for SAR were numbered and there was no looking back.

Air search and rescue squadrons had become a principal element in the maritime SAR structure of most coastal states by the 1970s. In many countries today they are merely an adjunct of the national armed forces. In some cases, such as in Spain, and to a certain extent in the UK, Ireland, and Canada, non-military government agencies operate helicopters and fixed-wing resources for SAR, but this is very rare. Long-range maritime patrol and SAR aircraft continue to be key components of the oceanic safety net. Aircraft such as C-130 Hercules and P-3 Orions are used by many nations for offshore patrol work and for reaching the scene of a distant distress rapidly. In the United States the Coast Guard augments these larger aircraft with a fleet of HU-25 Guardian medium-range jet aircraft. The maritime rescue role of the world's fixed-wing SAR aircraft includes on-scene commander duties (communication and control) for rescue missions, top-cover for helicopters en route, air-to-air refuelling, para-rescue deployment and the ability to drop SKAD kits (survival kit air droppable) and pumps to sinking vessels.

The Loss of the *Prinsendam*

On 4 October 1980 the Dutch cruise ship *Prinsendam* was underway in the Gulf of Alaska having departed Vancouver, British Columbia, three days previously for a one-month cruise to exotic destinations in the Far East. At 427ft (130m) she was the smallest of the company's cruise ships. Around midnight a fire broke out in the engine room. The captain immediately had everyone muster at their lifeboat stations on the promenade deck and sent out the following distress message to the USCG's rescue co-ordination centre (RCC) in Juneau, Alaska.

PASSENGER SHIP PRINSENDAM/RJTA POSITION 53-18 DEGREES NORTH AND 140-25 DEGREES WEST. FIRE! FIRE IN THE ENGINE ROOM FLOODING ENGINE ROOM WITH CARBON DIOXIDE. CONDITIONS UNKNOWN. PASSENGERS 320. CREW 190.

By 1:30am the largest helicopter sea rescue operation in peacetime history was underway. When Richard Schoel, the USCG Commander in charge, was advised that the liner was 120 miles out at sea, he began diverting merchant ships to the area, including the massive 1,000ft (305m) supertanker *Williamsburgh*, southbound from Valdez with a load of Alaska crude oil. Various large Coast Guard cutters and buoy tenders, including the 378ft (115.2m) USCGC *Boutwell*, were dispatched from positions at sea and from ports all over the Pacific Northwest. Still, the nearest surface rescue unit was at least a day away. If the fire was not brought under control the only hope for rapid rescue of the 524 (14 more than reported) persons on board the *Prinsendam* was by air. But such a massive helicopter rescue operation, so far offshore, had never before been conducted. The logistical problems of fuel availability, landing sites and casualty reception points alone were staggering.

The first rescue resource on scene was a USCG HC-130 out of Kodiak, Alaska. This giant aircraft would, until relieved by another HC-130, act as a communications platform, on-scene commander, and an air-to-air refuelling resource for the helicopters if required. Also en route to the *Prinsendam* were two HH-3, Jolly Green Giant helicopters from Kodiak, another two HH-3s from USCG Air Station Sitka and one USAF version from Elmendorf (all in Alaska). In addition, two Canadian Air Force CH-113 Labrador helicopters were en route from Comox Air Force Base in British Columbia, over 600 miles away.

By the time the Kodiak HC-130 had arrived the situation on the *Prinsendam* had deteriorated. Far from being extinguished the fire was now raging out of control. Smoke was filling all the

4 October 1980.
A Canadian Armed Forces
CH-113 Labrador helicopter
hoists a woman from one of
the *Prinsendam*'s lifeboats adrift
in the Gulf of Alaska, 120 miles
(193km) offshore. More than
500 passengers were airlifted
from the burning cruise liner,
making it the largest helicopter
sea rescue operation in
peacetime history. Incredibly,
given the conditions, not one
life was lost.
Canadian Armed Forces

ship's compartments, and the passengers and crew were being forced to stay on deck on the cold, windward side of the ship. Many of the passengers were elderly and in various states of attire, and exposure was becoming a problem. By 6:30am Captain Cornelius Wabeke of the *Prinsendam*, a 30-year veteran of the Holland America Line, decided enough was enough. Nothing could be done to save the ship. He gave the order to abandon ship, and the process of boarding the lifeboats and launches began. The ship had developed a list and, although the evacuation was described as a combination of order and chaos, almost all were lowered in the boats. A skeleton crew, including Captain Wabeke, remained on board. By now the first of the rescue helicopters had arrived, the crew on board one of the HH-3s from Sitka watched in awe as the tiny flotilla backed away from the massive burning hulk. A USCG fire-fighting expert and some equipment were dropped on the *Prinsendam* but it was too late.

At 7:45am the massive *Williamsburgh* arrived on scene. Fully laden, and with a draught of 65ft (19.8m), this monstrous floating island was incredibly stable in the large sea conditions. She also had two helicopter pads, and could house up to 500 survivors within her accommodations section alone. The casualty reception point had arrived. At first, scramble nets were placed over the side of the tanker but it soon became apparent that the predominantly aged passengers, many of whom had been violently seasick in the heaving lifeboats, were no match for the 40ft (12.2m) climb. The only way to get most of the people on to the tanker would be by helicopter hoist. Thus, seven large helicopters transferred the cold and exhausted survivors from the lifeboats in groups of 10 to 15 to the *Williamsburgh*. Eventually, when fuel became a priority, the helicopters departed for Yakutat, some 120 miles to the northeast, with a full load of survivors onboard, dropped them off, refuelled and returned. It was probably the first time in recorded history that a supertanker required an air-traffic controller in its wheelhouse.

There were some hiccoughs however. During the operation, a Canadian helicopter lost its navigational equipment and had to be escorted to Yakutat by a C-130. One of the USAF HH-3s had its hoist line snag on the tiller of Lifeboat No 6, and had to make an emergency landing on the SOHIO *Intrepid*, another tanker that had arrived to assist. In all the confusion the On-scene Commander lost track of Lifeboat No 6, which still had 18 survivors and two USCG parajumpers on board. Some 18 hours after their ordeal had begun, these remaining survivors were rescued by the USCG Cutter *Boutwell* that had returned to search for them after dropping off 80 other survivors at Sitka. Finally, those left aboard the doomed cruise ship were airlifted to the *Boutwell*, Captain Wabeke being the last to leave.

So ended one of the most incredible sea-rescue sagas of all time. The helicopters and their crews, with the aid of the fixed-wing aircraft and surface vessels, had pulled most of the 524 persons from small lifeboats tossing about in the North Pacific. Not one life had been lost from what could have been one of the worst maritime disasters in history.[408]

CHAPTER 2

The Offshore Patrol

Not all rescue at sea is performed by coastal lifesaving organisations. There are also the men and women who patrol the open oceans on board coast guard cutters, ice breakers, buoy tenders, scientific survey ships and designated naval vessels. In most cases, these large vessels are multi-tasked with search and rescue being but one of their missions. Generally, such vessels are state-owned and belong to either military or maritime-safety organisations. Unlike many coastal lifesaving organisations, the world's coast guards, maritime safety agencies and navies can provide dedicated full-time crews capable of working extended periods offshore or in remote areas of a nation's coastline.

The origins of organised lifesaving on the high seas go back to the creation of the earliest state-funded efforts to patrol offshore. In Great Britain and the United States, the early customs and revenue cutters were the first government vessels assigned such duties (see Chapters I-6 and II-16).

Following the *Titanic* disaster of 1912, an International Ice Patrol was established, whereby two United States Revenue Cutters were to patrol the offshore waters of the Grand Banks of Newfoundland to search for, and report, any icebergs or other hazards to navigation and to relay the information to shipping. The sinking of the *Titanic* also resulted in the 1st International Conference for the Safety of Life at Sea (SOLAS) held in London in 1913, at which 13 signatory nations agreed to subsidise the service. There was now a capable lifesaving platform at sea in the North Atlantic from September until April. Aside from the obvious benefits of iceberg and derelict avoidance, the patrols began directly saving lives within the first two years of their inception. On the second international ice patrol in 1914 the USCG Cutter *Seneca* rescued four British seamen from the Leyland steamer *Columbian*. The ship had exploded and sunk west of Sable Island two weeks previously, and two of her lifeboats and some of the crew had already been recovered by other ships. The third lifeboat had been given up for lost and those onboard, having little time left, would not have survived had it not been for the keen eyes on board the *Seneca*.

The onset of the Second World War heralded the next

The USCG 378ft Hamilton class high-endurance cutter *Gallatin* (WHEC 721) at sea. Fulfilling the many missions of the USCG, both civilian and military, these massive cutters are the largest vessels on the planet with a dedicated SAR role.
USCG

advancement in offshore rescue coverage, particularly after the entry of the United States in late 1941. During the war, more and more aircraft, men and materials were flown across the vast expanses of open ocean in the Atlantic and the Pacific. In the early days of the war many aircraft simply took off into no-man's land and disappeared forever. Once they departed from shore, say from Goose Bay, Labrador, bound for Iceland, there was no contact. In response to the growing losses, the Allied countries established a global network of 11 offshore weather and rescue stations within which large patrolling vessels would be permanently stationed. The 'ocean stations' were located at equidistant intervals along the principal great-circle air routes. They were named phonetically from east to west and each station consisted of a body of ocean bounded by 210 nautical miles on all sides. The chief duty of the cutters, weather ships or naval units within these zones was to provide meteorological information to passing aircraft and to weather offices ashore. Secondly, prior to the days of electronic navigational aids, the ships were able to provide a fixed position to ships and aircraft in mid ocean. Most of all, however, the ships were there to provide reassurance to those transiting the area: if something went wrong, they were there to help. Six of the ocean stations were manned by vessels of the USCG, four by European countries, and one by Canada.

Following the war, the ocean-station system remained in operation and was even expanded. The programme provided excellent offshore rescue coverage in the northern hemisphere for more than 30 years. In that time thousands of lives had been saved from downed aircraft and vessels in distress. Eventually, however, the invention of long-range, high-altitude jet aircraft signaled a decline in demand for the stations, while weather satellites and offshore data buoys could replace the meteorological reports. In the mid 1980s the ocean-station programme was scrapped and the network of offshore standby vessels was removed.

Today, many large rescue vessels still patrol offshore waters but they are no longer part of an international grid network. Generally, coast guard or naval vessels are at sea for fisheries patrol, law enforcement or scientific duties. Nevertheless, their positions are constantly monitored and, where opportunity permits, will be called upon for search and rescue by the appropriate authorities. Improvements in SAR alerting technology, the development of more effective long-range maritime patrol and SAR aircraft, and advances in global communications have allowed other resources, including merchant ships, to be tasked at very short notice to the scene of a disaster.

The Rescue of the Downed Aircraft, *Bermuda Sky Queen*

On the early morning of 14 October 1947, the USCG Cutter *Bibb* was on routine patrol in the North Atlantic within its designated standby area known as Ocean Station Charlie. The cutter's role was to transmit and relay weather and navigational information to trans-oceanic flights. At 1:55am the largest transatlantic aircraft NC612, the *Bermuda Sky Queen*, called the *Bibb*'s radio operator for a weather update. The huge flying boat had departed Ireland the previous afternoon, and was now en route for Newfoundland. There were 69 people on board, including 7 crew, 20 women and 12 children. Ocean Station Charlie was a standard check-in point for this flight; it was the point of no return. The *Bermuda Sky Queen* advised the radio operator that they were at 6,000ft and carrying on.

At about 5:00am the flying boat's navigator made the startling discovery that they were not going to make their destination; they had been battling a 60kt head wind for several hours, and they did not have enough fuel to reach Newfoundland. The pilot, Charles Martin, decided their best chance was to go back the 310 miles to Ocean Station Charlie and the *Bibb*. In the three hours it took for the plane to return, the crew of the *Bibb* wasted no time in making preparations. Scramble nets were deployed, surfboats made ready and rescue swimmers donned their wet suits.

By the time the *Bermuda Sky Queen* emerged from the clouds the sea was in a confused state. The large oceanic swells were now being criss-crossed by storm-driven seas from another developing system. Landing the big machine in such conditions would be next to impossible. Nevertheless Martin lowered the huge aircraft close to the wave-tops and, assessing the conditions, circled the *Bibb* several times. Suddenly he announced over the radio that he was going to land: the plane touched the top of a wave and, almost immediately, pulled up for another attempt. Martin had almost lost control but somehow he found a momentarily flat stretch of water and, nosing the flying boat down behind the crest of a massive rolling wave, touched the ocean. The *Bermuda Sky Queen* followed the back of the big sea and stopped dead in the water.

The passengers and crew had been saved from the perils of flight, but now they faced the perils of the sea. The flying boat had been designed to take off and land in relatively calm water. Now it was being buffeted by extreme oceanic conditions and was soon beam-on to the huge seas, which threatened to smash in a window or break the fragile machine apart. Martin now used the aircraft's rudders to keep it head to sea. He remained in the cockpit, steering the aircraft for the

14 October 1947. One of the surfboats from the USCGC *Bibb* is seen attempting a rescue in heavy seas from the rapidly drifting flying boat *Bermuda Sky Queen*.
USCG

next day and a half, over which time the relatively-light wind-driven aircraft would drift an astonishing 100 miles.

On the first attempt to transfer all to the *Bibb*, Martin tried to power the aircraft up to the cutter. But the windage was too severe: one of the aircraft's engines struck a ship's davit and was disabled; a wing was almost torn off. Next, Captain Paul Crook of the *Bibb* came to windward of the *Bermuda Sky Queen* and dumped oil to quell the seas. He then launched a 10-oared surfboat in an attempt to transfer a line, but the aircraft was being blown across the ocean's surface at too great a speed and the pulling boat could not catch up. The cutter's crew also realised that if they came alongside the thin-walled aircraft with a heavy surfboat, they could quite easily punch a hole in its side, sending all its passengers and crew to a watery grave. An updated weather forecast was received from Washington advising that another cold front was moving in to the area but that it might be preceded by a period of relative calm. Captain Crook decided to wait.

On the *Bermuda Sky Queen* the situation was horrendous. Almost everyone on board, including the captain, was in the throes of extreme seasickness as the stricken aircraft pitched and rolled. To add to their dismay, water was finding its way into the plane and Martin feared the tail was going to break off. They tried to deploy one of their small inflatable rafts, but it was quickly blown away by the strong winds. In the afternoon three

of the strongest passengers on board, seamen by profession, made it to the *Bibb* in another raft but they had taken such a beating in the process it was felt the women and children should not make an attempt.

Back on the *Bibb*, three 15-man inflatable life rafts were brought on deck. First, they tried to drift one down to the aircraft from the stern of the cutter, but the ropes were almost immediately sucked into the ship's propellers. Next, they launched the cutter's 26ft (7.93m) motor surfboat to tow one of the rafts to the aircraft. At first the massive raft was blown on top of the surfboat, but eventually the crew fastened it alongside and made their way to the *Bermuda Sky Queen*. Captain Crook then had Martin and his crew weight one of the plane's remaining small liferafts and have it drift down to the surfboat. The line from this raft was then secured to the big raft and the air crew hauled away. As soon as the raft was alongside the plane's escape hatch, Martin began loading it with passengers, entire families at a time. The motor surfboat then came alongside the raft and the first group were transferred aboard and taken to the scramble nets on the side of the cutter, where the rescue swimmers were waiting to help them over the rail. By 7pm 31 people had been rescued in three boatloads. On the fourth run, the large raft broke loose and, with 16 survivors on board, rapidly disappeared into the darkening gloom of the North Atlantic. Somehow the surfboat – itself now leaking after being pummelled alongside the cutter – located them. But there were too many people to be transferred and four of the USCG crew jumped into the raft to make room for survivors – three remained on the raft with the lifesavers. Now, however, the surfboat was no longer manoeuvrable but, by mere providence, the *Bibb* was soon drifting down on their position. Both surfboat and raft were dragged to the nets by the valiant efforts of the rescue swimmers. All on board were transferred over the railing of the *Bibb*. In the process, two of the survivors were blown off the net by a large sea; one was recovered by the collar, the other by the hair. In the now pitch-black darkness, both would surely have been lost.

With only one liferaft left and the motor surfboat disabled, the only hope for the still-stranded survivors now rested with the cutter's old pulling boat. With a new crew of volunteers the boat was launched into the darkness with the last raft in tow. When close enough to the aircraft, they fired a number of messenger lines with the shoulder gun, one of which reached its target. The raft was hauled to the plane but no one appeared. All the remaining survivors were either too tired or weak from seasickness to even move. A decision was made to wait until first light and the boat was recalled. The decision was fortuitous. By the following day the weather had calmed enough to launch the *Bibb*'s motorised gig. Quickly, the rest of the plane's passengers and crew, including Martin, were brought to the waiting arms of the rescue swimmers. Their ordeal was over.[409]

CHAPTER 3

The Global SAR & Communications Network

Bermuda Harbour Radio atop historic Fort George. Like many modern maritime communications facilities around the world, Bermuda Harbour Radio incorporates the services of a coast radio station, a rescue coordination centre and a vessel traffic management system under one roof.
Bermuda, Marine and Ports Services

INTERNATIONAL LAW OF MARITIME SEARCH AND RESCUE

The earliest laws and edicts promoting the saving of those in peril at sea (see Chapter I-2), as well as those shipwrecked upon the coasts, were national in scope. Throughout the latter part of the 19th Century many international maritime safety conferences would be held around the world, but the focus was on exchanging lifesaving technology, not creating international standards. This changed in 1910 when many of the world's principal maritime powers gathered in Brussels to sign a Convention on Assistance and Salvage at Sea. Article 11 stated that, 'every master is bound, so far as he can do without serious danger to his vessel, her crew and her passengers, to render assistance to everybody, even though an enemy, found at sea in danger of being lost'.

These first multi-lateral efforts at codifying the requirement to save lives at sea were soon followed by similar provisions

at the 1st International Conference for the Safety of Life at Sea (SOLAS) in 1913, following the loss of the *Titanic.*

In 1959 a new body of the United Nations was established in London, England, called the International Maritime Co-operative Organisation, or IMCO. The 'Cooperative' was removed from the title at a later date and the organisation is now simply referred to as the IMO. One of the first duties of the fledgling body, through the auspices of its Maritime Safety Committee (MSC) was to convene an updated SOLAS Conference, which was held in 1960. The 1960 SOLAS articles were extended beyond the mere provision of assistance at sea by vessels of a signatory nation to promoting the establishment of dedicated search-and-rescue facilities, such as vessels and aircraft (search-and-rescue units, or SRUs), Coast Radio Stations (CRS), Rescue Coordination Centres (RCC), and Maritime Rescue Sub-Centres (MRSC) within individual countries. In addition, the 1960 agreement promoted the ideas of a merchant ship position reporting system for offshore waters; the use of emergency position indicating radio beacons, EPIRBs (a carry-over from the aviation industry); and greater cooperation between other associated international bodies with an interest in maritime SAR. These included the International Civil Aviation Organisation (ICAO), the International Telecommunication Union (ITU) and the World Meteorological Organisation (WMO).

In 1970 the MSC of the IMO published the first Merchant Ship Search and Rescue Manual, or MERSAR, designed to provide a common set of guidelines for vessel masters who may be required to provide assistance to other ships at sea. At about the same time, a Search and Rescue Seminar was held in the United States at which many SAR experts from around the world recommended the implementation of a new international convention dealing specifically with maritime search and rescue. A committee was established by the MSC to work on the recommendations, the end result being the International Convention on Maritime Search and Rescue (ICMSAR) signed in Hamburg in 1979. The provisions of ICMSAR were similar to those of the 1960 SOLAS Convention, in that they focused on the establishment and maintenance of national SAR organisations within a common international framework. In addition a new reference manual, the IMO Search and Rescue Manual (IMOSAR) was developed as a guideline and international template for the structure and management of a national SAR organisation, as well as providing information on standard search and rescue procedures. Finally the ICMSAR called for the creation of 13 separate Maritime SAR Areas around the globe where memorandums of understanding and mutual assistance agreements would need to be drawn up between proximate coastal states.

Over the course of the next 14 years the IMO and its staff would work diligently with representatives from all over the world at a series of regional maritime SAR sub-conferences to establish these agreements and to ensure that all the oceans of the world were provided with some form of SAR coverage. One of the primary goals was to decide on the scope and extent of the individual Search and Rescue Regions (SRR) for a particular country within each of the 13 larger Maritime SAR Areas. Once these boundaries were agreed upon, the particular coastal state was then responsible for the establishment, maintenance and provision of SAR facilities adequate to cover the entire SRR within their jurisdiction. Signatories to the convention were also obligated to update the IMO, as the leading international maritime SAR agency, on a regular basis regarding any changes to the status of SAR resources and facilities within their country, so that this information could be absorbed into regional SAR plans.

In 1997 the IMO and ICAO decided that the provisions of their respective SAR manuals were so similar that a combined manual should be drawn up to unify both trains of thought. In most cases of maritime SAR both marine and air SRUs are involved and it was of utmost importance that all rescue resources working on a particular case be thinking and talking in the same technical language. The result of these joint efforts was the three-volume International Aeronautical and Maritime SAR Manual (IAMSAR) published in 1999. This comprehensive SAR tool provided uniform guidelines for organisation and management of the national SAR system, mission coordination for the responsible agency, and information of use to mobile facilities, ie the actual search and rescue units. As a result of this new combined approach to maritime SAR, many coastal states have now combined what were once separate marine rescue coordination centres (MRCC) and air rescue coordination centres (ARCC) into common joint rescue coordination centres (JRCC).

SAR COMMUNICATIONS

In the early days of sail, vessels in danger exhibited visual signs of distress, such as signal flags, the burning of oil in barrels on deck, and the firing of cannons or carronades. As time went on, better distress signals were developed, such as rockets and flares (see Chapter I-14, regarding Martha J. Coston). However, in many cases signals of distress were not required as the severity of the ship's predicament was obvious to those witnessing the calamity from ashore. If vessels were in distress beyond the sight of the human eye, their only hope was that a vessel of opportunity would pass and witness their plight. Early rescuers on shore utilised similar methods to both signal the shipwrecked that help was on the way and to notify the lifeboat crew to muster at the station.

In 1901, high atop the entrance to the harbour at St John's, Newfoundland, an event would occur that would forever change the way maritime affairs were conducted on the world's oceans and help lay the foundations for an electronic safety net that would eventually span the globe. On this day, the Italian-born inventor Guglielmo Marconi, seated in the tower at Signal Hill, received the morse code signal 'S', which had been transmitted from another experimental telegraph station at Poldhu in Cornwall, England. Eventually, with a subsidy provided by the Canadian Government, Marconi set up a permanent radio-telegraphy station at Glace Bay, Nova Scotia. By 1907 radio telegraphy had become commonplace. Now ships could communicate great distances across the seas, both to stations ashore and other vessels. Almost overnight a distress-monitoring network had been established that expanded rapidly as more and more ships and shore stations purchased the new wireless technology and began to monitor a common radio frequency. Around the world, wireless telegraph stations were set up to be the forerunners of today's coast radio stations (CRS). By 1908, for example, the Canadian Department of Marine and Fisheries, the predecessor of the Canadian Coast Guard, had 18 wireless telegraphy stations in operation on both coasts as well as on four of its ships.[410]

Following the Second World War, ships and shore-based stations began to utilise radio-telephony to a far greater extent as technologies improved, although telegraph messages were still the main method of communications for those far off shore. The coast radio station became the information source for vessel traffic, weather information, ship-to-shore communication and distress monitoring and assistance. In 1958 a new search-and-rescue system was developed for oceanic waters known as the Automated Mutual-assistance Vessel Rescue System, or AMVER. Using the network of coast radio stations that had developed around the world, merchant ships would relay essential passage information upon departure, such as intended tracks, speeds and destinations. These details were fed into a central computer managed by the USCG in the United States. If a CRS received a distress call, the coordinates would be transferred to AMVER HQ who could then provide a surface picture, or SURPIC, of the surrounding area to determine if any other ships were close by and able to assist. Originally this system only covered the busy shipping lanes of the North Atlantic but in 1971 it was expanded to cover the entire planet. Surprisingly, improvements in communications technology have not reduced the need for AMVER. In 1999 there were still some 12,000 ships from 143 separate nations participating in the system and on an average day approximately 2,700 ships were being maintained 'in the plot', with numbers increasing annually.

In more recent years another global distress communications network emerged that would be of great benefit to mariners the world over. In the early 1970s initial discussions began between the United States and Canada regarding the feasibility of a satellite-aided tracking system for downed aircraft. The military system at the time involved the use of emergency locating transmitters, or ELTs, which could be triggered manually or automatically and which generally broadcast on 121.5 or 243 MHZ. Search aircraft had to have a very good idea of where a crash occurred, as the transmissions could only be picked up on line of sight, basically within a few miles of the target. If the location of the crash site was vague – a common problem in the vast expanses of North America – then search aircraft had to practically fly right over the downed aircraft to pick up the signal on their direction finder, or DF. If ELT signals could be tracked from space automatically and around the clock, it would be a vast improvement.

After the initial reception tests with the AMSAT Oscar 7 Satellite proved favourable, a third nation became interested in the project, the Soviet Union. Further money and technical support arrived to begin full-scale implementation of the system. Considering that these developments were taking place at the height of the Cold War and that rather sensitive satellite technology information had to be transferred between the interested parties to ensure system compatibility, the successful completion of this undertaking was a stirring testament to both the tenacity of the individuals who worked on the project and the power of joint humanitarian endeavour. In June 1982 the first satellite in the system, the Russian COSPAS 1, was launched and by September the new COSPAS/SARSAT System had already helped to solve its first case, that of a downed aircraft in Canada.

In the end, six polar orbiting COSPAS/SARSAT satellites would be launched, all of which were capable of analysing the changes in Doppler shift of the ELT signals they received to determine a relative fix on the earth's surface. Soon other countries such as France, the United Kingdom, and Norway all furnished additional financial support for the project and established satellite mission control centres, or MCCs, of their own. The lifesaving implications for maritime traffic were obvious and eventually ELTs found their way on to both coastal and deep-sea vessels. In a marine context they were known as Emergency Position Indicating Radio Beacons, or EPIRBS. By the mid 1980s a newer, more efficient SARSAT network was in place for use by ships and aircraft, this time broadcasting on 406 MHZ. The new system was not only more accurate, it also allowed the transmitting party to be identified and could automatically be picked up by the earth's various Geo-stationary Orbiting Environmental Satellites (GOES). Although they could not pinpoint an EPIRB's position, they could pick up the signal right away – the previous system having to wait for a satellite to pass.

One of the ongoing problems faced by rescue agencies around the world has been how to provide distress communications coverage to those remote areas of the planet where no communications services are available. Even as late as the 1980s large merchant ships were still going to sea and disappearing without a trace. As a result of this gap in the global safety net, Resolution 6 of the 1979 ICMSAR requested that the IMO investigate the development of an integrated Global Maritime Distress and Safety System, or GMDSS. Technical research in and development of the system continued for more than a decade and, starting in 1992, all sea-going ships to which SOLAS applied had to begin installing GMDSS equipment, with full-implementation to be carried out by 1999. GMDSS is an integrated distress monitoring and alerting system which, through the use of satellite communications and EPIRBs, digital selective calling VHF and HF radios, and navtex, allows ships in distress to immediately notify other vessels within their vicinity or to respond in kind. The system is also linked to the global coast radio station and rescue coordination centre network where GMDSS land stations are maintained and monitored.

In spite of such major advances in maritime communications technology and in the oceanic safety net, the bulk of calls for assistance today are still received through the human operators of the world's coast radio stations. Radio operators around the world have been responsible for saving tens of thousands of lives over the last century, having the ability to solve problems before they occur, relay crucial medical information, rapidly pass on the distress message to the nearest RCC (many of which are co-located at the radio station), serve as a watchdog for rescue units at sea in perilous conditions and provide valuable information that can only be gained through local knowledge and years of experience. In the context of coastal communications, the human element will always remain the best tool in the lifesaving arsenal.

CHAPTER 4

Other Roles of Rescue Agencies

The vast majority of organisations profiled in this book have a single mandate, to save lives at sea. They are lifeboat and lifesaving services using rescue craft under 82ft (25m) in length as their main tool and principally operating in coastal waters. Many are private non-governmental organisations (NGOs). A few of these mostly-voluntary-crewed and -funded organisations also provide additional services for the public, such as boating safety education, and for commercial interests, such as survival systems training. In the Åland Islands, the private lifeboat society provides towage and pilot delivery services for local ports. In Germany, the DGzRS mans and operates the principal MRCC in Bremen on contract for the government. Some of the private maritime rescue organisations also work on contract for their respective governments, providing platforms for fishery patrols and pollution prevention. Primarily however, the lifesaving NGOs remain dedicated to their principal objective of saving lives at sea.

In the public realm, however, where tax dollars are at work, the focus changes somewhat and crews find themselves fulfilling a multitude of other important tasks both on land and at sea. A variety of specialised seagoing vessels are required for many of these duties with highly trained crews, skilled in their particular mission. At any given time, although they may not be specifically designated for SAR, these vessels can be called upon to respond to maritime distress. The Canadian Coast Guard is a good example of one of these multi-faceted agencies. The CCG is a civilian public organisation that acts as the federal government's operational arm on Canadian waters. It exists to fulfil the government's legislated mandate to provide a number of services, one of which is maritime search and rescue. To this particular end the CCG has over 40 lifeboat stations, dozens of seasonal inshore rescue boats, supports a large coast guard auxiliary to augment the system and maintains large sea-going vessels on constant SAR standby for calls offshore and in remote areas. Although maritime SAR is a key element in the CCG's mandate there are many other vessels and resources in the organisation designed to fulfil other important tasks. These include the buoy tenders that maintain aids to navigation and the many ice breakers that keep the eastern shipping lanes and ports open in the winter months and head north in the summer to provide support in the Canadian Arctic. There are also many scientific research vessels in the CCG fleet undertaking fishery and oceanographic exploration, both inshore and offshore; on the Grand Banks of Newfoundland these vessels are often called upon to assist foreign vessels in difficulty. The CCG also has a fleet of patrol boats and offshore cutters whose primary role is fisheries law enforcement. At times, these vessels are also used for other elements of maritime law enforcement including customs patrols and drug interdiction. Many are not only equipped and readily available to respond to SAR calls, they are also able to respond rapidly to environmental emergencies when required. Like many other coast guards around the world, the CCG also has an airborne division, with both rotary and fixed-wing aircraft on standby for SAR and other duties. On shore, the CCG also provides maritime communications and vessel traffic control services. This includes not only the provision of coast radio services, but also rescue coordination at the various JRCCs operated in conjunction with, and under the command and control of, the Canadian Armed Forces.

Many other maritime safety agencies and coast guards around the globe also perform a military function. These organisations provide coastal and port security and, in times of armed conflict, can form a principal part of their nations' armed forces. Other government rescue organisations fulfil a large regulatory role. They inspect vessels, both foreign and domestic, they draft legislation – a great deal of it safety related – and they may also supervise the granting of nautical certificates to seafarers. Many agencies are involved in safe-boating education, sometimes through the auspices of their respective auxiliary organisation.

The Loss of the FV *Kella-Lee*

CCGS *John P Tully* is primarily a science research vessel with search and rescue (SAR) duties. On 26 October 2001 *John P Tully*, under the command of Captain Paul Frost, was on primary SAR standby patrolling in Fitzhugh Sound on the central coast of British Columbia. A storm warning was up for the entire north coast. Second officer Daryl Mintenko had just come on duty and provides this account of the crew's call to duty that night and into the next day.

At watch change, close to midnight, a mayday call came in from the fishing vessel Kella-Lee. Tofino Coast Guard radio responded to the call and relayed that the boat was sinking and the crew had decided to abandon to a life raft. The crew donned survival suits and took their EPIRB with them. They radioed their position as 13 miles north of remote Cape Scott in Queen Charlotte Sound. There was one last transmission from Kella-Lee, then silence.

Captain Frost immediately ordered John P Tully to come about and we proceeded toward the vessel's last known position. As John P Tully entered Queen Charlotte Sound, winds were steady at 45-50kt and gusting as high as 80kt. Seas were seven meters and rough. A Canadian Forces Buffalo aircraft arrived on scene from the Comox Air Base and the crew spotted two lights in the water. They couldn't determine exactly what the lights were, but thought it was possibly a life raft. John P Tully was not due to arrive until 7:00am, as it was initially 70 miles away. The deep-sea vessel CSX Anchorage was also proceeding to assist. The Buffalo updated the light's position and relayed coordinates to John P Tully via Coast Guard radio. At 4:30am the aircraft dropped a data marker buoy in the water, then left the scene to re-fuel. Captain Frost ordered John P Tully to alter course to the last known position and at 6:15am one of our lookouts spotted a light in the water. The wind was still 45kt and gusting, with seven metre seas. By now the Buffalo had returned and dropped illumination flares to assist in sighting the object. Sea conditions made it difficult, but soon we determined that the light was being waved by a person in a survival suit – the person had been in the water in a storm for almost seven hours!

We had to determine the best way to recover the person as conditions were still extreme. We finally decided to launch the 733 (a rigid hull inflatable boat) with experienced seamen Mike Burdon, Ian Copping and Kirk Hesketh. They recovered the fisherman, who was still conscious, and returned to the ship. The crew were elated

when we found the first survivor and in such good shape. However, there were still three people missing and no life raft yet sighted. We continued to search through the morning, now with two Buffalo aircraft as well as the deep-sea CSX Anchorage. Each unit had a specific area to search, and debris from Kella-Lee was soon spotted. At 11:40am one of John P Tully's spotters saw a person in a survival suit floating face down in the water. Conditions had subsided a little by this time and the 733 was again launched to recover the body.

All units, including the fishing vessels Frosti and Hope Bay, continued searching. Frosti's crew had heard the initial mayday call but had been held back from proceeding right away because of severe conditions of 100kt winds at the entrance to Goletas Channel. By early afternoon a Canadian Forces Labrador helicopter joined the search. Another fishing vessel, the Pro Surveyor, was proceeding from Cape St. James to assist. More debris was found. Soon after, at 2:45pm, the Labrador's crew spotted another person in the water and John P Tully's 733 went out to recover the third person.

At 4:00pm one of the Buffalo crews spotted a life raft with a person waving. It had drifted approximately 15 miles further upwind. The Labrador recovered the person and John P Tully's 733 recovered the life raft. The fisherman in the life raft was in fairly good condition after drifting for 17 hours. The first survivor that we'd picked up told us a bit about his feelings when he first saw the lights of our ship. He said he was tired, sore and feeling hopeless with darkness surrounding him and the constant howl of the wind. He thought about drifting off to sleep when he saw lights come over his horizon. At first he felt elated but when the lights came closer, he thought it looked like a cruise ship and his spirits fell because he didn't see how they could get him out of the water. Then when it got closer yet, he saw CANADA on John P Tully's side and he knew then that he would be OK. He began to swim for all he was worth to make his way to the ship, shining his flashlight and sitting up so he was visible in the water.

It was a long night for Captain Frost and the crew of *John P Tully*. All of *Kella-Lee*'s crew were recovered; unfortunately however, only two had survived. A successful combination of teamwork, the experience of the crew aboard *John P Tully*, the skills in navigating, launching and manoeuvring a small boat in heavy seas, search techniques, and medical response resulted in excellent work for a crew not always called upon for search and rescue duties.[411]

PART IV

TODAY'S MARITIME
RESCUE SERVICES

ÅLAND ISLANDS

Coastal Conditions & Hazards
Located at the entrance to the Gulf of Bothnia, approximately halfway between the coasts of southern Finland and eastern Sweden are the Åland Islands, an autonomous, demilitarised and uni-lingually Swedish province of Finland. The archipelago consists of about 6,500 islands and skerries, of which 6,400 are larger than 1.16 square miles (3sq.km). Fast (Main) Åland is the principal island in the group, with more than 70% of the entire land mass and around 40% of the 25,000 residents. Mariehamn, the capital and main port is here, once famous as the home base of the Erikson Line, the last great fleet of commercial windjammers. For Åland's coastal and climactic conditions, see 'Finland' p.217 and 'Sweden' p.254.

History of Coastal Lifesaving
The Åland Islands hold a very significant place in the history of coastal lifesaving, as it was in the southeastern region of the group, around the Island of Kökar, that one of the western world's first organised measures for providing succour to the shipwrecked was initiated. Historical records indicate that the Catholic Monastery on Kökar, built around 1472, was instrumental in providing spiritual and physical relief to mariners in distress; most would probably have been members of the local population who relied on the Baltic herring and cod fisheries for their survival. The best seasonal fisheries were far removed from the main islands, and fishermen would spend many weeks on the fringes of the archipelago living in small huts, which were used to dry and store the catch as well as for shelter – in around the year 1549 there were estimated to be approximately 400 small fishing boats on Mörskären, near Kökar.

In the following centuries the sovereignty of the islands switched back and forth between warring Baltic nations such as Sweden, Finland and Russia. Little is known regarding coastal lifesaving measures until Åland became a semi-autonomous, demilitarised zone in about 1856. Due to the islands' close association with Finland and Sweden there has always been a strong link to the lifeboat services in those countries; in 1938 *Anna Gadd*, a 34ft (10.4m) single-screw MLB built specifically by the Turku Sea Rescue Women's Circle, was stationed in the Åland Islands. This lifeboat is preserved at the maritime museum in Turku, Finland.[412]

Ålands Sjoraddningssallskap (ASRS)
Operating Model: Non-Profit Voluntary Organisation
Source of Income: Private Contributions and State/Commercial Subsidy
Manning Structure: Volunteer/Employee Crew

The ASRS was created on 3 August 1965 initiated by members of the Åland Shipmasters' Society. Soon after the birth of the organisation as a voluntary, non-profit entity, two benefactors, Eva Hohentahl and Edgar Erikson, provided enough funds for the society to construct a 55ft 6in (16.9m) ice-strengthened cruising lifeboat, the *Gustaf Erikson*, which went into service out of Mariehamn in 1967. She was soon joined by a small inflatable. The ASRS continued to operate with these boats as well as members' vessels as auxiliary rescue craft until 1990, when they purchased the fast lifeboat

The Ålands MLB *PAF 2*. This 48ft (15m) rescue craft is water-jet propelled and can cruise at 25kt.
Åland Lifeboat Society

Vikaren secondhand from the Swedish Sea Rescue Service. In 1992 the Åland Islands government helped finance the ASRS to design and build a new high-speed MLB. The result was the 52ft (15.9m) SR lifeboat *PAF*, launched in 1995, a lightweight aluminium vessel powered by two 485kw MTU diesels and propelled by twin Hamilton Jet-Drive units with a top speed of 30kt.[413]

Today, the ASRS still has all these rescue boats in operation, as well as the displacement lifeboat *Hans Helenius* and the RHI *Mobben*. It also operates the oil-pollution landing craft vessel *Svärten*. The principal stations, aside from the society's headquarters at Mariehamn, are located at Vårdö, Lumparland, and Brändö. The society has a permanent staff of five, which includes one organising manager and four permanent crew who man the fast lifeboat *PAF* out of Mariehamn; they also operate the oil-pollution boat when requested by the government, and ASRS vessels are used for some commercial activities such as crew deliveries, docking assists and harbour ice breakouts. There are 40 volunteer lifeboat crew located at the outer island stations. Also, in addition to the single operating manager, there are 15 committee members who oversee the management of the society. Aside from state and commercial subsidies the ASRS also receives funding from private and corporate contributions and collects fees from the approximately 600 members. Other SAR resources for the Åland Islands area are drawn from the services of Finland and Sweden (see 'Finland' p.217 and 'Sweden' p.254).

ARGENTINA

Coastal Conditions & Hazards
The coast of Argentina is 3,100 miles (4,989km) in length and stretches down the Atlantic shores of South America from the mouth and estuary of the Rio de la Plata in the north to the

fjords of Tierra del Fuego in the south. The Argentine side of the Rio de la Plata consists of low-level bluffs with an extensive shallow sandbank paralleling the coast; this type of coast extends for some 420 miles (627km) to the west and offers few prominent features to assist in navigation. Tidal and freshwater currents intermingle and can create offshore tide rips and areas of confused seas, hazardous for small craft. South of the Rio de la Plata, from Cabo San Antonio to Punta Delgada, the coast consists of areas of long beaches with high sand dunes, followed by areas of steep cliffs and elevations that increase in size and stature as you approach the southern archipelago. There are very few sheltered havens here. Wind and weather off the coast of Tierra del Fuego can only be described as atrocious in the winter months. For more on the coastal conditions and hazards see 'Chile' p.212.[414]

Prefectura Naval Argentina (PNA)

Operating Model: Military Agency Managed by Government
Source of Income: State Funded
Manning Structure: Employee Crew

A Super Puma SAR helicopter of the PNA drops a rescue swimmer on training exercise.
Prefectura Naval Argentina

The origins of the PNA stem from the 'Compendium of Laws Governing the Indias' established by King Charles II of Spain in 1680. In essence this Royal Edict made the laws of Spain the laws of her possessions. Thus when, in 1793, King Charles IV passed a Royal Decree regulating such activities as port captains, pilots, inspections of vessels, rules concerning maritime law etc., it also became law in Argentina. The Prefectura was created in response to these new regulations and became the government's administrative arm for all maritime matters. Prior to 1940 records indicate that both pulling and motorised lifeboats were strategically placed along the Argentine coastline and were co-located at various light and signal stations including Martin Garcia, San Antonio, Recalada a Bahia Blanca and Isla Leones.[415]

Today the PNA, also known as the Argentine Coast Guard, is similar in model to other national maritime safety agencies around the world: it not only has responsibility for SAR and safety of life at sea, but also for such duties as maintaining a vessel registry, the certification and training of mariners, oil-pollution prevention and vessel salvage, marine casualty investigations, customs and immigration enforcement on the

water, maintenance of marine communications and vessel traffic centres as well as boating-safety education aimed at the recreational user. Due to the vast size and varying geography of Argentina these roles and duties vary from region to region. Along the river frontiers with Uruguay, Paraguay and Brazil, customs and immigration work is paramount, while in the Rio de la Plata, control of vessel traffic in the busy shipping lanes is a primary consideration. Off the Atlantic seaboard, sovereignty patrols within the exclusive economic zone (EEZ) are the key demand. The waters around Buenos Aires and in the Argentinian Lake District close to the Chilean border are very popular with pleasure craft, placing particular demands on the service when the boating season is in full swing during the summer months.[416]

In terms of search and rescue, there are four principal 'Services' within the PNA. First, the Cutter Service, which was established in 1955 and provides large patrolling vessels for rescue work strategically located along the Atlantic coast as well as smaller vessels on rivers and certain inland lakes. As of March 1994 the PNA had some 43 inshore and offshore patrol vessels varying in size from fast launches in the 65ft (20m) range right up to 1,500-ton cutters approximately 300ft (91m) in length.[417] Next comes the Aviation Service, which originated back in 1946 and now boasts a number of rotary- and fixed-wing aircraft strategically stationed at San Fernando Aerodrome near Buenos Aires, at Mar del Plata Air Station on the Atlantic coast, and at Comodoro Rivadavia Air Station in southern Patagonia. Helicopters in service include both the heavy capacity Super Puma and the medium endurance Daulphine. The Aviation Service provides continual SAR response within the Argentinian SAR region and is used for medical evacuations from ships and isolated communities. Large fixed-wing maritime surveillance aircraft are also available for SAR duties at short notice. The third service is the Salvage, Fire-Fighting and Pollution Control arm of the PNA which, although not specifically established to save life, can be called upon to assist in large-scale calamities and to prevent any potential deterioration of a situation. Last, but not least, is the PNA Communications Service, which operates a string of essential coast radio stations throughout Argentina, providing a necessary lifeline to vessels at sea as well as to many isolated communities, particularly in the south. The PNA is a branch of the Argentinian military and, as such, is responsible to the Minister of Defence. Rescue Coordination Centres (RCCs) are located at Buenos Aires, Puerto Belgrano and Ushuaia, with additional sub-centres co-located at most of the coast radio stations.

AUSTRALIA

Coastal Conditions & Hazards

Australia has a coastline of 12,210 miles (19,650km) – equivalent to half the circumference of the planet. There is a tremendous variety of sea and coastal conditions, not all of which are particularly friendly to the unwary mariner. The tropical north is subject to severe cyclones, while in the northeast the Queensland coast is bordered by the world's largest coral formation, the Great Barrier Reef, more than 1,243 miles (2,000km) long. There are many treacherous river bars around the country and, due to the relative scarcity of natural harbours – approximately 20 along the entire coast – these must be crossed regularly. There are areas of high cliffs and long stretches of uninhabited coastline. On the northwest coast of Western Australia the extreme tidal range causes dangerous races, while the shores can be lashed by storms developing across one of the largest unobstructed fetches in the world. The southern coasts of South Australia, Tasmania and Victoria are subject to severe storms developing in the Antarctic. The Tasman Sea can be as temperamental as any location on earth – a fact best exemplified by the weather system that overtook the famous Sydney-Hobart sailing race in December 1998 with catastrophic results. As on any coast there are also local anomalies and hazards. One such location is the approaches to the large city of Melbourne, at Port Phillip Heads, where a narrow passage, outlying reefs, and a strong rip current were the demise of many a ship in the early days of commercial sail.

History of Coastal Lifesaving

The history of sea rescue in Australia is full of tragic stories of disaster and shipwreck. By the mid 19th Century, isolated efforts to establish lifeboats and line-throwing apparatus began to appear adjacent to the major centres of population and trade such as Sydney and Newcastle in New South Wales and, with the frenzies of the Australian Gold Rush from 1850 to 1860 in the south, near the approaches to the cities of Melbourne and Adelaide as well. To a large extent these efforts were local in nature or at least administered at state level by government authorities such as the local ports and harbours boards. In fact, the individual state and local governments remain principally responsible for the provision of coastal lifesaving services in many parts of Australia to this day; the federal government provides assistance with coordination of services and operational support. As a result it is easiest to describe the early development of lifesaving services in the country on a state-by-state basis, beginning with the earliest known organised measures in New South Wales (NSW).

The port of Newcastle located about 62 miles (100km) up the NSW coast from Sydney, was an extremely busy haven in the mid 19th Century, being the principal point of export for the large deposits of coal. Many shipwrecks occurred around the entrance to Newcastle and records that began in 1837 state that local pilots used a surfboat or whaleboat manned by 'a crew of convicts' to rescue the crew of the cutter *Vulcan* wrecked on Stockton Beach.[418] As was the case at many of the earliest dedicated lifesaving facilities, it would appear that additional boats of conventional design would be provided to the local pilots for lifesaving work, these men having superior skills at handling small boats in heavy weather as well as an excellent knowledge of the local

perils. Mention is also made of two purpose-built lifeboats being constructed for use in NSW around 1847, but apparently both were soon found to be unseaworthy.[419]

The tragic loss of the clipper ship *Dunbar*, on 20 August 1857 off Port Jackson, near Sydney, resulted in calls for better lifesaving equipment.

Twelve hours passed before the news reached Sydney. The following day sightseers were horrified to see dozens of bodies amongst the wreckage on shore. James Johnson, the sole survivor, clung to a spar when the ship grounded and was thrown by a huge wave on to a rocky ledge from where he was able to climb to a higher position of safety. It was not until 36 hours later that a volunteer who had climbed down the rocky face saw him and he was hauled to the top.[420]

This event was unacceptable to the people of Sydney, many of whom were well aware of the recent growth of humanitarian efforts on behalf of the shipwrecked in other nations. So began the supplying of lifeboats and rocket apparatus by both national and local governments. This equipment was strategically stationed around the coast of NSW and even, rather uniquely, at one location far offshore on an uninhabited reef. Approximately 300 miles (480km) east of Cape Byron are the treacherous low-lying atolls known as Elizabeth and Middleton Reefs which, in the mid 19th Century claimed scores of unwary vessels. As a remedial measure a lifeboat was placed at a mooring inside the lagoon at Elizabeth Reef in 1870, the money having been raised by public subscription. If any shipwrecked souls made use of the lifeboat, they were to leave a message in a float attached to the mooring providing particulars such as the name of the ship that had been wrecked, the number and names of the survivors thereof and the direction in which they had departed. There is no mention of this isolated resource ever being used – although certainly well-intentioned, it must have been extremely difficult to maintain.

On 27 May 1897 a new RNLI Standard Self-Righting type lifeboat was officially launched and christened in the waters of Port Hunter, Newcastle, NSW. She was a 39ft (12.1m) version with a 9ft 3in (2.9m) beam, propelled by 12 oars; she had been built by Forrest and Sons of London for £800, named *Victoria* in honour of the reigning British Queen. By 1904 the *Victoria* had already been instrumental in saving scores of lives after attending 11 shipwrecks near the port and, in that same year, conducted one of her most famous rescues – 32 sailors from the French barque *Adolphe*, wrecked on 30 September.

The tugs, Hero *and* Victoria *had the four-masted barque in tow but the* Victoria's *tow line parted one kilometer off the Stockton Breakwater. Almost immediately the grey ship was swept sideways by the huge waves and driven broadside onto the wrecks of the* Lindus *and* Colonist. *The lifeboat passed between the wrecks on the Oyster Bank under the skilful control of Coxswain McKinnon in 'raging seas' and came up unto Adolphe's starboard side where the crew slipped down a line from her rigging. Not one life was lost and the lifeboat crew were well praised for their efforts.*[421]

This stalwart old Self-Righter continued in service for many decades. In 1909, while rescuing the captain and crew of the American schooner *Alpena*, the *Victoria* capsized in a large sea and threw 24 men into the water. Incredibly, the three men who remained onboard the lifeboat after she re-righted were able to regain control and recover every man from the tumultuous seas and take them to shore. Records indicate that the old lifeboat remained in service until 1940 and, having been continually manned and maintained by employees of the Navigation Department of NSW, was still in tip-top condition, so much so that following a further restoration in 1988, she remains on public display at the Newcastle Region Maritime Museum at Fort Scratchley, NSW.[422] As for other lifeboats and rescue apparatus in the early days in NSW, there is mention of an additional lifeboat being stationed at Sydney Heads as of 1911, and rocket and line-throwing apparatus still being in place at various locations along the coast.[423]

During the same period Victoria and South Australia were also developing dedicated coastal lifesaving facilities. By 1858 the outer shores of Victoria and King Island in the Bass Strait had witnessed approximately 95 recorded wrecks and the loss of 880 lives.[424] As previously stated the entrance to Port Phillip Bay, south of Melbourne, was particularly treacherous, the notorious tidal race and huge standing waves that could develop here claimed many lives as vessels foundered or were driven on to the adjacent reefs and rocks. As had been the case at Newcastle the earliest organised measures involved the use of the local pilots and their vessels – a pilot service having been established at Port Phillip Heads as early as 1838. In 1853 the Chief Harbour Master of the Port of Melbourne, Captain Ferguson, a man who would be the chief proponent of the provision of lifeboats and lifesaving facilities in the area for decades to come, requested that the cruising pilot cutter *Boomerang* carry boats to be used for lifesaving and that these be kept fully equipped, and be deployed and exercised once a month.[425] In 1856 this service was expanded to include the provision of a dedicated rescue boat, probably a whaleboat of conventional design, to be moored near the Customs House and maintained under the supervision of the Head Light Keeper at Shortland's Bluff (later known as Queenscliffe).[426]

In 1857 Captain Ferguson and others in the Department of Ports and Harbours for the State of Victoria had correspondence with the Committee of Management of the RNLI who had forwarded, at their request, 12 plans for the most up-to-date lifeboat being constructed in England – the relatively new SR-SB pulling and sailing vessel designed by James Peake (see Chapter II-8). In 1858 a contract was made

for the construction of five of these boats in Australia, to be built at the Naval Dockyard at Willianstown and stationed around the outer coasts of Victoria.[427] The first was provided to Queenscliffe the following year, stationed in a new overhanging boatshed at the end of a long pier, the boat being hauled up and down by block and tackle. The crew were all volunteers and included the station's superintendent, a coxswain, a bowman and 10 oarsmen, who were still drawn primarily from the local 'Health Officers, Customs and Pilot Crews'.[428] Other similarly managed stations were also established on the outer coasts of Victoria, adjacent to the entrance to Port Phillip, utilising the other new lifeboats. These were at Portland, Port Fairy and Warrnambool to the west, and Port Albert to the east. All became scenes of massive activity around this period as a huge influx of ships and men arrived to access the gold fields of the interior. The lifeboats of the Victorian Ports and Harbours Department were involved in several famous rescues in their day, including that of the American barque *Asa Packer* by the new Queenscliffe lifeboat in the autumn of 1861. The vessel had run afoul of the rocks below Point Nepean on the east side of the channel to Port Phillip, in a strong westerly gale and, with her entire crew remaining onboard, was being torn asunder by the massive breakers, when:

A line was eventually made fast ashore by the pilot tender Empire, *then the lifeboat, manned by a combined crew of Customs and Health Officers made several attempts to rescue the crew from the rigging but the boat, swept by three rolling seas, was quickly filled to the gunwale. Eventually, at slack tide the lifeboat crew rescued the thirteen seamen, but the boat's rudder had been broken on rocks, making her difficult to handle on the way back to Queenscliffe.*[429]

The Portland lifeboat, which arrived on 22 September 1858, was also instrumental in the rescue of 18 lives from the tragic wreck of the steamship *Admella* on 6 August 1859, one of only two recorded services; the lifeboat remained on station until 1915 (see Chapter 11-8).[430] The Warrnambool lifeboat arrived at her new home in April 1859, and appears to have made herself most useful many years later, in 1905, when she was used to rescue five crew from the wrecked ship *La Bella*.[431] In 1911 the old Warrnambool Peake-type lifeboat was replaced by a new 40ft (12.4m) lifeboat built at Willianstown to the latest design, said to be 'practically non-capsizeable' – leading the author to believe it was probably a derivation of a Watson-type pulling and sailing lifeboat. This boat remained in service until the 1960s and is preserved to this day at Warrnambool. The lifeboat at Port Fairy arrived on 27 September 1857 and was kept in a boathouse with a slipway; there is no information as to whether it was ever used. Sadly, both the Warrnambool and Port Fairy lifeboats spent the twilight of their years afloat lashed together as pontoons for a river dredge. In recent years however, both have been rescued and, along with the original Portland lifeboat, have been preserved in their hometowns, the Port Fairy lifeboat even returning to sea! These are thought to be the oldest European-designed Australian-built vessels still in existence and are probably the last surviving examples of the Peake-style SR lifeboats in the world today.

The Peake lifeboat at Queenscliffe was eventually replaced by a Standard Self-Righting type; originally built in 1888 for a new lifeboat station at Port Lonsdale, at the outer entrance to Port Phillip. The boat had proved too heavy for the falls on the overhanging shed at the new pier so the older and lighter Peake boat went to the new station, while Queenscliffe received the new and improved self-righter. The old lifeboat at Port Lonsdale would remain ready for action at the end of the pier for the next 40 years, but her services were never required. In 1926 the Queenscliffe self-righter, which had served until the First World War, was replaced by a modern 46ft (14.3m) Watson MLB, *Queenscliffe*, built at the A. MacFarlane and Sons boatyard in Adelaide with a double-diagonal-planked kauri hull. This would be the last lifeboat operated by the government of Victoria, with volunteer crews on a small retainer, and eventually she would be kept in a boathouse and slipway on shore. The new MLB responded to approximately 40 calls for assistance during her career, one of the more notable events occurring in 1967, when the *Queenscliffe* was instrumental in the search for Australian Prime Minister Harold Holt, who disappeared while swimming off Cheviot Beach. By the 1970s however, she was being used less and less and, with the government lacking the will to finance a replacement, the service was discontinued in 1976.[432] She, too, remains restored and on display, at the Queenscliffe Maritime Centre, south of Melbourne.

In South Australia the original lifeboat and lifesaving apparatus stations were established by the State Marine Board after a series of calamitous wrecks on the approaches to Adelaide, including that of the *Admella* in 1859 with the loss of 91 lives. In 1866 the President of the Board wrote to the RNLI to say that a lifeboat had been constructed of a type similar to the Institution's standard plans 'but with some additions', and that certain rocket stations had also been established along the coast.[433] This first lifeboat was probably the *Percy*, stationed at MacDonnell Bay in South Australia and, although specifics are not available, one can assume it was probably similar to the Peake boats in Victoria. The *Percy* led an illustrious career:

In 1873 she saved twelve men from the three-masted schooner Prince of Wales, *which was wrecked at Port MacDonnell, and in 1876 five from the barque* Agnes *lost two miles east of Cape Banks lighthouse, and thirteen from the French barque* St Marc. *(However) In 1877 the captain of a brig, his wife and two daughters, and the cook were drowned when the vessel struck near Cape Banks, and the remainder of the crew got ashore on a raft made with spars before the lifeboat, which gallantly put out from Mac Donnell Bay, could arrive at the scene.*[434]

By the 1890s the small number of lifesaving facilities, which included the *Percy* and a small 'surf-gig' stationed at Robe, as well as a few pieces of line-throwing apparatus, were no longer deemed sufficient for South Australia. The state was experiencing a boom in immigration and the harbour of Port Adelaide was becoming a major centre for the export of Australian grain. Around this time, the ship *Star of Greece* was wrecked on the South Australian coast and, with the nearest line-throwing apparatus some 20 miles away, there was very little that could be done for the hapless souls onboard. Local protests that followed the disaster resulted in the recognition of shortfalls. Measures for establishing and administering coastal lifesaving facilities in the state became the responsibility of the Royal Navy – an arrangement that remained in effect until 1909, when the responsibilities were transferred to the new Government of Australia and the responsibility for coastal lifesaving reverted to the State Marine Board. In the 18 or so years that the navy did manage the service, however, certain improvements were made. In 1895 Mr R. Barr Smith of Torrens Park financed the purchase of a steam-powered lifeboat, which had been built in Great Britain in 1893. She was stationed at Beachport and named the *City of Adelaide* (see Chapter II-10). The State Government, upon the insistence of the Naval Branch, agreed to fund the operation and manning of this new lifeboat, which, with a speed of 8kt and an operational range of 180 miles, '...commands an easy sphere of action of 50 miles on either side of her station at Beachport, whence, with steam ready at twenty minutes notice, she can easily cover the distance to any point along the "prominence"'.[435]

In addition, two large pulling and sailing lifeboats were also built, one being a self-righting lifeboat built at Larg in 1908, the *Undaunted*, to replace the *Percy* at Port MacDonnell, described as a self-righting lifeboat built at Larg in 1908. The other being the *Lady Daly*, stationed at Victor Harbor and which, in 1911, was said to be in the process of being motorised.[436] Little information is available about the activities of these vessels, however, the steam lifeboat *City of Adelaide* was brought back from near oblivion in 1984, and totally refurbished as the centrepiece of a maritime museum in Port Lincoln, South Australia.[437]

There is little or no available information on coastal lifesaving in other areas of Australia in the early years, although in Western Australia the harbour authorities at the Port of Fremantle purchased a steam lifeboat, the *Lady Forrest*, from Britain in 1902, she was to be used as a pilot boat and rescue vessel in the Indian Ocean (see Chapter II-10). This followed the loss of two of four sailing vessels approaching the port in June 1899, when six crew aboard the *City of York* and the entire crew of the *Carlisle Castle* were lost. This venerable steamboat, although later converted to diesel power, remained in service for an incredible 64 years.[438]

It would appear that, aside from a few of the old state-managed lifeboats only one of which was still in operation after the Second World War, there were few other efforts to establish dedicated coastal lifesaving facilities in Australia in the first half of the 20th Century, with the responsibility for such services reverting to local police forces, the Australian Navy, and anyone else available in the area to help. In March 1937 a movement called the Volunteer Coastal Patrol was formed in NSW with its principal duty being to help the navy patrol the extensive Australian coastline for security reasons, as the clouds of future conflict were already developing. After the war, the organisation became known as the Royal Volunteer Coastal Patrol (RVCP) and it expanded its role to include the provision of rescue boats in specific areas, as well as boating-safety education. In 1961 the Australian Volunteer Coast Guard (AVCG) was formed, modelled somewhat after the United States Coast Guard Auxiliary. Its chief purpose was to form flotillas in each state so that member-owned vessels could supply rescue services; eventually this progressed to the provision of dedicated rescue boats and radio stations in some locales. Local harbourmasters and police remained responsible for SAR operations in their zone of responsibility and, although in many areas local air-sea rescue associations were formed, a problem regarding overlapping jurisdictions remained. In order to provide a coordinating body for major incidents, which taxed the limited resources to the maximum or which covered vast expanses of coastline, the Australian Government established a National Marine Operations Centre in Canberra in 1972. Today this centre is administered by a new governmental organisation called the Australian Maritime Safety Authority (AMSA) whose primary function is to '...direct, coordinate and control search and rescue operations within the Australian Search and Rescue Region (SRR) and to provide the organizational basis for cooperation between different SAR authorities'.[439]

In 1981 the Marine Rescue Association of Australia was formed in an attempt to provide some cohesion to the myriad of local, state, and national coastal rescue organisations. Its members included the RVCP, the AVCG, the Volunteer Marine Rescue Associations of NSW, Queensland and Western Australia, and the Air Sea Rescue Association of South Australia. The aim was to homogenise the needs and demands of the services around the country and to provide a unified voice in support of the cause – the ultimate objective was the creation of a single nationwide voluntary coastal lifesaving organisation.

Today, in addition to the vast number of volunteer coastal lifesaving organisations around the country that are operated on a statewide and local basis, the Australian Government also provides additional resources in the form of the Australian Navy, with some local and state police forces also having their own marine divisions to provide coastal SAR services. In the air there are various volunteer and affiliated lifesaving resources, both rotary and fixed wing, used by local authorities. The Royal Australian Air Force maintains a fleet of fixed-wing aircraft for offshore patrol and rescue work as well as Blackhawk helicopters that can be used for hoist work. There are also 11 coast radio stations around the country providing a communications network that feeds into the national MRCC at Canberra.

Royal Volunteer Coastal Patrol (RVCP)
Operating Model: Non-Profit Voluntary Organisation
Sources of Income: Private Contributions & State Subsidy
Manning Structure: Volunteer Crew

First called the Volunteer Coastal Patrol, this organisation was formed on 27 March 1937 and modelled along the lines of a similar body in Britain created during the First World War. The general idea was that experienced merchant mariners and yachtsmen with expertise in the operation of small boats as well as extensive knowledge of particular areas of coastline, would be signed on as naval auxiliaries, whose services could be used to augment those of the navy for coastal patrol duties during periods of armed conflict. During the war which soon followed, the security role of the new organisation rapidly expanded and, by 1941, the Volunteer Coastal Patrol was operating in three states, had more than 2,000 members and 500 small ships. During the course of the Second World War these crews patrolled over 128,000 miles (206,000km), putting in some 393,600 voluntary man-hours.[440]

After the war, the Voluntary Coastal Patrol, although still a paramilitary organisation, took on more of a marine safety role and continued to provide lifesaving services with its members' vessels. In 1974 Queen Elizabeth II bestowed the privilege of using the 'Royal' prefix. Today the RVCP provides dedicated lifeboats, marine radio communications and boating-safety courses throughout Australia. In 1981 the organisation expanded even further when it established 12 new coastal radio stations to be manned 24 hours a day, and 10 dedicated patrol vessels.[441] The RVCP is now divided into three levels of administration – National, State and Divisional – and, due to its continued links with the military, utilises uniforms and ranks. Present regions include Queensland, Northern, Central and Southern NSW, Victoria, Tasmania, and South Australia. The RVCP is now a numbered Australian Company, is operated by voluntary members and crews and organisational financing is largely raised by private subscription with some state support.

For years the RVCP has operated an ex-RNLI Solent class lifeboat stationed at Wollongong, NSW, south of Sydney. Recently, the service has been expanded through the purchase of six RNLI Waveney-type 44ft (13.7m) MLBs and one Arun-type 52ft (16.2m) MLB. The Waveneys began arriving in 1999 and are now in service at Botany Bay, Narooma, Ulladala, Sydney, Broken Bay and Batemans Bay, Australia.[442] (see Chapters II-17 and II-21).

Australian Volunteer Coast Guard Federation
Operating Model: Non-Profit Voluntary Organisation
Sources of Income: Private Contributions
Manning Structure: Volunteer Crew

This organisation was originally formed in Melbourne in 1961 by a group of influential yachtsmen who were deeply impressed with the workings of the United States Coast Guard Auxiliary and who decided to form a similar association in Australia. The organisation was formally named the Australian Volunteer Coast Guard Association (AVCG) in the 1970s and rapidly gained wide support and a large membership. The main difference from the RVCP is that the AVCG, which is also a volunteer-operated body, is not a paramilitary entity, although it has the same objectives: to provide dedicated rescue boats, communications services and boating safety education to the public.

High-speed fibreglass surfcats are used extensively by lifesaving services in Australia. This one belongs to the Australian Volunteer Coast Guard and is stationed at Southport, south of Brisbane.
Queensland Emergency Services

The AVCG is a NGO with no fully paid staff. As of 2001 there were some 9,000 voluntary members, 2,600 of whom were considered active – members who either crew on lifesaving vessels or man the communications centres. It had expanded to 63 operational flotillas in Queensland, NSW, Victoria, South Australia, and Tasmania and had some 92 dedicated rescue craft most of which were between 20 and 30ft (6 and 10m), powered by twin outboards or turbo-charged diesels. In addition to the 147 coast radio stations at the individual bases the AVCG also maintained approximately 30 vehicles, including mobile communications vans. Certain members also use their own fixed-wing aircraft in support of search and rescue.[443 444]

Surf Lifesaving Australia (SLA)
Operating Model: Non-Profit Voluntary Organisation
Sources of Income: Private Contributions
Manning Structure: Volunteer Crew

Australia has a proud tradition of surf lifesaving. In fact, the idea of having specialised clubs established at individual beaches whose members volunteer to assist in lifeguard duties and lifesaving for swimmers and surfers originated 'down under' and has now spread all over the planet. Although these lifesavers focus principally on beach rescue – in the area between the breakers and the sand – they do use rescue craft, including lightweight pulling boats, jet skis and small inflatable inshore rescue boats.

The first surf lifesaving club in the world was formed at Bondi Beach, Sydney, NSW, on 6 February 1906 and was called the Bondi Surf Bathers Life Saving Club. It seems that, until 1902, swimmers in the Sydney area were only allowed to bathe in the ocean at sunrise and sunset, and even then men and women were to do so at different times! In September 1902 a free spirit by the name of William Gocher advised the authorities that he was going to defy the ban and go for a swim at Manly Beach at the preposterous hour of twelve o'clock, noon. At the appointed time Mr Gocher entered the ocean and was arrested for his reprehensible actions. No charges were laid, however, and the floodgates were open for the local population, who subsequently flocked to the beaches in droves to take advantage of the sun, sand and surf. One of the immediate results was a staggering rise in accidents, and the surf lifesaving clubs were formed by groups of experienced swimmers and surfers to assist relative newcomers. Soon, clubs were appearing all over Australia and, in October 1907, a NSW Surf Bathing Association was formed. This organisation later became the Surf Lifesaving Association of Australia which, in 1991, became simply Surf Lifesaving Australia (SLA).[445]

The value of these volunteer surf rescue clubs was proven on Sunday 6 February 1938, at Bondi Beach – a day that would become known as 'Black Sunday'– when a series of enormous freak waves crashed down on hundreds of swimmers, creating a powerful rip that dragged most of them out to sea. In the end the surf lifesavers were able to rescue 300 of the swimmers, many of whom were brought ashore unconscious. As of 2001 member organisations of the SLA, Australia's largest water-safety organisation, can claim to have rescued an incredible 420,000 people along the nation's beaches.

Volunteer Marine Rescue Association Queensland (VMRQ) and Queensland State Emergency Service
Originally a state branch of the Air Sea Rescue Association of Australia, and known as the Air Sea Rescue Association of Queensland, the present title was adopted in January of 1990.[446] The Association itself dates back to 1965 when individual units were located at Point Danger, Mackay and Southport proximate to treacherous bar entrances and the heavy vessel traffic around Morton Bay near Brisbane. In 1968 the State Government of Queensland began to provide some financial support to the Association and continues this subsidy to the present day. After a public review of volunteer SAR services the following year, the VMRQ was provided with official areas of responsibility in terms of developing state-wide regulations for training and operations of all local volunteer marine rescue organisations within Queensland.

As of 2001 the VMRQ had 24 affiliated squadrons, or local chapters ranging along the 1,680 miles (2,700km) from Cape Danger in the south to Thursday Island on the northern tip of Cape York. In addition to the coordinating role the Association provides for its satellite organisations in Queensland, the VMRQ also ensures that these affiliate squadrons provide dedicated rescue vessels, monitor local communications and provide boating-safety and weather information to the public.[447]

BAHAMAS

Coastal Conditions and Hazards

The Bahamian Archipelago extends some 746 miles (1,200km) from northeast of Cuba to the southern tip of Florida and its approximately 700 constituent islands form a natural breakwater against the open Atlantic. The islands themselves are merely the exposed portions of the Great Bahama Bank, which extends south from the coast of North America. The name, Bahamas, is said to derive from the Spanish word 'bajamar', meaning shallow water. True to the name, there are extensive shallow banks and coral outcroppings that provide numerous hazards for the unwary mariner. The islands are very low in elevation – the highest point in the country, on Cat Island, is only 206ft (63m) above sea level. The hurricane season extends from June until November and tropical revolving storms are not infrequent at other times.

History of Coastal Lifesaving

There is no known record of any dedicated coastal lifesaving facilities in the Bahamas during the early days of sail. It is quite likely that any rescues were conducted by vessels of opportunity and by ships of the Spanish and British Royal Navies, both countries claiming possession of the islands during different periods. The fact is that the locals were probably quite busy defending themselves from the other contemporary peril of the sea – the pirate. The first dedicated lifesavers were probably customs and pilotage crews, and, eventually, the vessels and crews of the harbour and national police. The country's close proximity to the United States has also resulted in a strong working relationship with the USCG and excellent coverage has been provided by that organisation.

In 1958 Bobby Symonette, Speaker of the Bahamian House of Assembly, petitioned the government to form the Air Sea Rescue Board in the Ministry of Transport. A Harbour Pilot, Sir Durward Knowles, was appointed to head the board, which immediately began to organise vessels of opportunity, principally charter fishing vessels out of Nassau, to assist in the ever-increasing number of distress calls received from pleasure craft. However, it was soon realised that there were serious gaps in this system and that there were times when no rescue resources were available to respond. In 1963 the Outboard Marine Corporation (OMC) sponsored a boating-safety seminar in the Bahamas for 200 local boaters. During the course of the seminar Mr Knowles and the senior instructor, Ben Astarita, discussed the idea of establishing a dedicated, volunteer-style marine rescue service for the islands. Not surprisingly, the idea was widely accepted and half the attendees signed on, with Knowles becoming the first Director and Astarita becoming the Executive and Control Officer. The new organisation, which received a small subsidy of $15,000 to $20,000 per annum from the Bahamian Government, called itself the Bahamas Air Sea Rescue Auxiliary (BASRA).[448] The 'Air' designation

reflected the fact that some of the new members had also offered the services of their privately-owned aircraft, a definite asset in a country whose islands are spread over thousands of square miles of ocean. The new organisation received much needed SAR training and organisational support from the USCG who sent personnel to assist in the setup. By 1965 BASRA already had three Duty Crews, as well as 30 vessels and 7 aircraft, all owned and operated by volunteers.

Bahamas Air Sea Rescue Association (BASRA)
Operating Model: Non-Profit Voluntary Organisation
Sources of Income: Private Contributions & State Subsidy
Manning Structure: Volunteer Crew

In 1970 funds were raised to build a proper headquarters and training centre for BASRA in Nassau; it was officially opened by the Bahamian Prime Minister and the organisation changed its final prefix from 'Auxiliary' to 'Association'. The original dedicated lifeboats of BASRA included an 18ft (5.5m) powerboat originally supplied by OMC; this was eventually replaced by a 17ft (5.0m) whaler donated by a local entrepreneur. In addition, a 30ft (9.2m) Bertram sportfisherman was donated by the local Rotary Club. Major fundraising drives helped the expansion of BASRA to some of the outer islands, including a new base at Freeport on Grand Bahama where a donated 17ft (5.0m) Avon RHI was put into service. A communications network of small radio stations and repeaters throughout the Bahamas was also created with donated funds.

In 1985 a 38ft (11.6m) SR MLB the *Lady Pearl*, described as a Lochin type, was ordered from an English yard. She was shipped to the Bahamas aboard a Royal Navy Supply Ship courtesy of the British High Commission and, within two years of her arrival, had already been entirely paid for by private contributions. *Lady Pearl* has a top speed of 17.5kt and an operational range of 28 hours. In 1989 BASRA also received a new 25ft (7.5m) Boston Whaler, affectionately named the *Uncle Ben*, after Mr Astarita; it is still in operation. BASRA remains an entirely voluntary operation, having only one paid administrator. In 1997 the organisation handled some 600 SAR cases – all with an annual operating budget of just $100,000 US.[449]

In conclusion, mention should be made of the financial support provided to BASRA over the years by the Miami, Florida, Search and Rescue Charitable Foundation, known as SEARCH. This organisation is a charitable foundation of the United States whose principal goal is to assist in 'the improvement of volunteer, non-government, search and rescue facilities throughout the S.W. North Atlantic and Caribbean Sea'. This is done through the use of voluntary contributions chiefly drawn from yachting interests in the United States. Monies have been provided to purchase both rescue craft and communications systems for use throughout the region, including the Bahamas, the Netherlands Antilles, Turks and Caicos and the British Virgin Islands.

BELGIUM

Coastal Conditions and Hazards

The coast of Belgium may only be about 40 miles (65 km) long but the local hazards to shipping are just the same as in The Netherlands. Also known as the Flanders Coast, this is an almost straight line of beaches and large sand dunes extending from France to The Netherlands, which protects the lowlands of Belgium from the full force of the North Sea. The beaches are generally flat and there are shallow sandbanks offshore that run parallel to the coast through which deep channels are created either by man or by nature. The effect of the strong surface- and under-currents running through these passages, especially when opposed by a northerly gale, can result in deadly breaking seas. There are several harbours and ports along the outer Belgian coast, the most significant of which, listing from north to south, are Zeebrugge, Blankenberge, Oostende and Nieuwpoort.

History of Coastal Lifesaving

Early coastal lifesavers in what is now Belgium were presumably the local Flemish fishermen and boatmen, some of whom were probably engaged in the rather lucrative business of salvage as well. Many lost their lives salvaging ships and cargo and quite early the government intervened and established a state-sponsored lifesaving service, the earliest of its kind in Europe, initially using volunteer crews but later switching to paid crews, most of whom were also engaged in pilotage duties. The Belgian Lifeboat Service still exists today and can claim to be the oldest state-run coastal lifesaving organisation in the world.

Belgisch Loodswezen Zereddingsdienst
(Waterways & Marine Administration of Belgium)
Operating Model: Civilian Agency Managed by
                          Government
Sources of Income: State Funded
Manning Structure: Employee/Volunteer Crew

In October 1838 the original Belgian Lifeboat Service was established by Royal Decree, becoming a branch of the Pilotage Administration in 1840. There were several attempts by various European aristocracies and governments to establish publicly funded rescue services during the early part of the 19th Century but only Belgium was successful. The first lifeboat stations were established at Oostende, Nieuwpoort, Blankenberge and Knokke and, by the turn of the century, there were four more at Adinkerke, Coq, Zeebrugge and Heyst. Eventually, when the port of Zeebrugge was completed, another station was established there.[450]

The crews at these stations were paid an annual salary to train and remain available for the lifeboat service, although most were able to work at another trade, many being local fishermen. There was also a large corps of non-retained volunteers around each station who could be called upon if the permanent men were not available. All crew were paid an additional stipend for call-outs, or for remaining at the

A Danish type 32ft (10m) pulling lifeboat belonging to the Belgian Lifeboat Service, the oldest state-operated lifesaving service in the world. This boat was stationed at Oostende until the Second World War.
Urbain Ureel

station during periods of stormy weather.[451] Eventually many of the lifeboat crews were drawn from employees of the pilotage service who also operated the launches. The only exception was at Oostende where enough qualified volunteers were available to man the station. All the original stations also had line-throwing guns and breeches-buoy gear, in the same fashion as the early French rescue services. Due to the sandy nature of the Belgian coast most early rescue craft were lightweight surfboats (around 2 tons) of the Dutch type, launched off iron carriages (see Chapter II-8). In most cases boats were drawn by hand although horses could be used if greater distances were involved. The lifeboats averaged about 30ft (9.1m) in length, were self-bailing and had air cases at each end, rendering them 'insubmersible' but not self-righting. As of 1911 the stations at Zeebruge and Blankenberge were equipped with motorised lifeboats.[452] The lifeboat at Oostende was reported to be of a more robust nature and, when tasked for a rescue, was generally taken in tow to the wreck by one of the state-owned tugs.

In 1926 the Belgian Lifeboat Service was re-organised and motor lifeboats were added at the ports of Oostende and Zeebrugge. These were the _Minister Anseele_ and _Minister Baels_ 46ft (14m) Watson cabin-type lifeboats, built in Germany by Henri Oltmans Bootwerft, near Bremerhaven (see Chapter II-12).[453] In 1931 a smaller motor lifeboat, the _Minister Lippens_, was built for use at Nieuwpoort. She was built in Denmark along the lines of that country's lighter weight, shallow-draught, open MLBs and was approximately 34ft (10.3m) long with a draught of only 3ft 10in (1.16m);[454] she was used as a carriage-launched lifeboat. The last of the horse-drawn carriages were replaced in 1936 by six-wheel petrol-driven 'Latil' tractors, which had power winches and could drive great distances along the sand.[455]

The onslaught of the Second World War resulted in the

almost total obliteration of the Belgian service. Almost all the boathouses and stations were destroyed and only a fraction of the lifeboats survived. Attempts were made to get the three MLBs across to Britain: the *Minister Anseele* was retrieved as a derelict in the English Channel off Weymouth by the Royal Navy and became a relief lifeboat for the RNLI for the remainder of the war, serving in the Isle of Man, Ireland, Wales and England, before being returned to the Belgian Government in 1946. On 11 February 1945 the *Minister Anseele* actually responded to a distress call from the Belgian ship, *S.S. Persier*, torpedoed off the Eddystone Lighthouse. Unfortunately there were no survivors. Neither the *Minister Baels* nor the *Minister Lippens* survived the conflict, the former being damaged beyond all repair after being bombed at Dieppe, while the latter, although successful in her quest for freedom, was also destroyed.[456]

Only three of the seven stations were rebuilt – at Oostende, Zeebrugge and Nieuwpoort. Three new RNLI Watson MLBs, *Reddingboots 1, 2* and *3*, were built in England by Samuel J. White of Cowes and placed in service at these stations in 1948. The range and speed of these newer MLBs eliminated the need for extra stations, which were then relegated to lookout duties only; they were closed altogether in 1957. The Watson boats remained in service for more than 20 years. In the mid 1970s efforts were made to develop replacement rescue craft and two types of lifeboat were purchased. The first, stationed at Oostende, was the *R4*, a 54ft (16.5m) SR, steel-hulled MLB with an aluminium superstructure, with a top speed of 16kt delivered in May 1980. The second, purchased for both Zeebrugge and Nieuwpoort was the large Pacific 36 (11.2m) RHI, similar to the Medina-type RHI then being developed in Britain. These large boats have a top speed of 25kt and were still in service in June 1999. In 1994 the last carriage truck was sold, thus ending a long history in Belgium of using beach-launched lifeboats.

In addition to the lifeboats of the Belgian Lifeboat Service, the Belgian coast is also covered by Sea King rescue helicopters of the Royal Belgian Airforce based out of Koksijde Air Station. Pilot cutters, belonging to the parent organisation of the lifeboat service, the Waterways and Marine Administration of Belgium, are used to assist in emergencies. The pilot-cutter crews also volunteer to man the lifeboats and, when wind conditions exceed Force 6-7, they remain on permanent standby at the lifeboat station. The administration also maintains a large salvage and rescue tug, the *Zeehond*, also on standby. Rescue coordination services are conducted by traffic controllers located at the Oostende and Zeebrugge Traffic Centres. In 1996 the Belgian Lifeboat Service handled some 106 calls, 50% of which involved pleasure craft in difficulty.[457]

Vrijwillige Blankenbergse Zee Reddingsdienst (VBZR)
Operating Model: Non-Profit Voluntary Organisation
Sources of Income: Private Contributions
Manning Structure: Volunteer Crew

Most nations with state-operated lifesaving services also have voluntary counterparts and Belgium is no exception. In 1982 a group of dedicated individuals established the VBZR to assist in coastal lifesaving along the Belgian coast east of Oostende. The VBZR operates several RHIs and has Land Rovers equipped with trailers to transport the vessels closer to the SAR incident.

The all-volunteer crews consist of coxswains, paramedics and responders (persons who will board a stricken vessel). The VBZR also has divers who will assist in both rescue and salvage operations. The exact complement of the crew depends on the nature of the rescue. Due to the VBZR's close proximity to the Dutch border they exercise regularly with the Dutch KNRM. In 1998 the VBZR was averaging approximately 150 call-outs per year.

BERMUDA

Coastal Conditions and Hazards
The islands of Bermuda lie far out in the Atlantic, 555 miles (890km) ESE of Cape Hatteras, North Carolina. They are but a speck on a vast ocean, the entire land mass being only about 25 square miles (65sq.km). The islands – combined into one single piece of 'land' by a network of causeways and bridges – are the peak of the Bermuda Rise, a seamount that originates some 3,000 fathoms deep. The top, which includes Bermuda itself, consists of approximately 250 square miles (650sq.km) of coral plateau that extends a great distance to the north and west of the islands while, to the south, it falls away steeply close inshore. The reefs provide a natural barrier from the full onslaught of the sea, but have also been renowned throughout history as the bane of unfortunate mariners. Huge seas, driven by Atlantic storms, pummel the outer edges, and myriad natural and dredged channels that wind through the treacherous clusters of coral

Lifeboats of the Belgian service. The self-righting lifeboat *R4* based out of Oostende leads the way followed by two 36ft (11m) Medina- class RHIs, *R1* and *R2*.
Urbain Ureel

heads are areas of strong currents that can rapidly pull a disabled vessel far out to sea. There are also offshore banks, located some 20 miles (32km) to the south of the island, that are popular with both professional and sport fishermen but which, especially in light of the unpredictable weather in the area, are a precarious distance from safe refuge.

History of Coastal Lifesaving

Wrecks in and around Bermuda came aplenty in the early days of sail. Some of the islands' earliest inhabitants were, in fact, survivors of shipwreck. In 1609 the *Sea Venture* was wrecked on the uncharted island and some of her personnel returned in 1612 to become the first settlers. Little is known of the early lifesaving measures but it is certain that once the island became permanently inhabited, the local boatmen would have done whatever was in their power to help in times of shipwreck. Above all, for the island population there would always have been the importance of salvage. Undoubtedly it would have been impossible to attend or provide assistance to many wrecks as they were often far offshore, at the edge of the reefline where massive seas brought about a rapid end to many ships. The earliest organised parties of lifesavers probably came from either the Royal Navy, whose men built a spectacular base and dockyard here in the early 19th Century, or from local pilots who, to this day, provide part of the sea rescue service for Bermuda.[458]

Through most of the 20th Century, search and rescue around Bermuda was conducted by a combination of pilot boats and crews, police launches and naval vessels; both the US and Canadian Navy establishing bases there during the Second World War. For offshore work, the USCG usually had a large cutter on patrol in the vicinity and could generally be called upon for assistance when required. However, by the 1960s the military presence in Bermuda began to wane – a diminishment of SAR resources that coincided with a proliferation of small pleasure craft. By 1975 it was said that there was approximately one boat for every ten Bermudians – more than 5,000 small craft.[459] The old pilot boat and the wooden police launches tried to take the strain but they were answering many more calls. To add to the problem, traffic in and out of the international airport was rapidly increasing with the boom in tourism and a dedicated waterborne lifesaving service was required. As a result, a group of concerned citizens banded together in 1974 to form a new, voluntary, non-profit coastal lifesaving organisation, called the Bermuda Search and Rescue Institute (BSARI). It was officially established in 1975, just in time for a representative to attend the 12th International Lifeboat Conference, in Helsinki, Finland, the same year. Contact was made with representatives from the Sumner Lifeboat Institute (SLI) in New Zealand who had been experimenting with a small water-jet-propelled inshore rescue boat specifically designed for fast response in shallow conditions such as over coral reefs. BSARI purchased one of these vessels, a 15ft (4.6m) inshore rescue boat (IRB) built by Hamilton Marine in New Zealand.[460] Paid for by a local donor, the boat was put into service in June 1976 and, within its first week on station, was responsible for saving two lives during a perilous night rescue; before year's end it had saved a further five people.

The new boat greatly enhanced the government services for inshore and local rescue operations, but shallow-water SAR coverage for the airport was still an issue – a larger vessel, capable of handling multiple casualties, was needed. Since the purchase of the IRB, Hamilton Marine and the New Zealand Department of Civil Aviation had developed a 30ft (9m) water-jet-driven rescue boat, specifically designed as an airport crash rescue vessel. In 1977 a representative from BSARI flew to both New Zealand and the Cook Islands to view these vessels in operation and a decision was made to purchase one for Bermuda. In 1978 the new 30ft (9m) lifeboat arrived. Powered by twin 200-hp turbo-charged diesels running through Hamilton jet-drives, the boat could cruise at an impressive 24kt.

Both new boats were constructed out of GRP and were kept on trailers so that they could be moved to the best launch site. Over the next several years the boats of the BSARI responded to hundreds of calls but the spirit of a purely volunteer lifesaving service could not be maintained. Some thoughts on the subject of fund-raising, voiced in 1977, were possibly a sign of things to come.

The Institute is fully operational with crews and supporters, boats, but little money. Like all new operations it needs, regretfully, a disaster. The fact that it has in its first year saved seven lives is apparently of insufficient significance – but all are optimistic that sooner or later its worth will be understood and the financial support which is so badly needed will be forthcoming.[461]

By the early 1980s the vision of a substantial voluntary-style marine rescue organisation had not materialised and in 1983 the Government of Bermuda initiated a joint study by both the RNLI and the USCG to develop a new marine rescue system for the country.[462]

SAR Committee, Department of Marine and Ports Services, Bermuda

Operating Model: Civilian Agency Managed by Government
Sources of Income: State Funded
Manning Structure: Employee Crew

Following the SAR-needs analysis of 1983, the Government of Bermuda took a more direct role in maritime SAR. An inter-departmental SAR committee was formed with the Department of Marine and Ports Services, which operates the large berthing tugs in Bermuda as well as the pilot boat based out of St George and the principal communications and traffic centre known as Bermuda Harbour Radio; and the Royal Bermuda Marine Police who had operated small coastal patrol and inshore rescue craft for many years and was a major component of the rescue system. Other departments with a vested interest included Bermudian Customs and the Department of Civil Aviation. The results of the study concluded that additional lifesaving resources were needed, particularly in light of the continued withdrawal of personnel and air and marine resources from the various military bases (as of 1997 these were completely abandoned). As a remedial measure, a new pilot/lifeboat was purchased to operate out of St David in the north of the island, which could be used for offshore work. The new lifeboat was a commercial version of the RNLI's 52ft (15.81m) Arun-type hull built by Halmatic in the UK, with a pilot-boat style wheelhouse. The *St David* was still in operation in conjunction with the old displacement-hull pilot boat as of 2001. In addition, the Royal Bermuda Marine Police received two new Arctic 24 RHIs, built by Osborne in the UK, to support their existing fleet of small Boston Whalers. In 1992 the Marine Police were also provided with a large 54ft (16.5m) Hatteras sportfisherman to use as a patrol launch. All these resources are coordinated through the rescue coordination centre (RCC) at Bermuda Harbour Radio, which also serves as the principal communications centre for the island and the surrounding area, and the vessel traffic management facility that has radar repeaters all across Bermuda (see Chapter III-3).

BRITISH VIRGIN ISLANDS

Coastal Conditions and Hazards

The British Virgin Islands are located between the Caribbean Sea and the North Atlantic Ocean towards the eastern tip of Puerto Rico. There are some 36 islands in the archipelago, only 16 of which are inhabited on a permanent basis, that have a total landmass of 59 square miles (150sq.km) and a coastline of approximately 50 miles (80km). The geography of the islands varies from the mountainous, volcanic islands of Tortola and Virgin Gorda, to the coral island of Anegada, some 20 miles (32km) to the north, which at its highest point is only 28ft (8.5m) above sea level. Anegada was a notorious hazard to shipping in the early days of sail and there are some 300 wrecks around its shores to prove it. Situated in the sub-tropical zone, the British Virgin Islands are swept by the prevailing trade winds, which are predominantly from the E, or between NNE and SSE and, from July to October, are also subject to the constant threat of the hurricane season. With a small resident population of only 19,000, the demands for a sea rescue service might seem less significant than in other countries but when one considers that, on average, approximately 130,000 yachtsmen will visit the country in one year, it becomes apparent that an organised and efficient coastal lifesaving network is of dire importance to both the local populace and the tourist trade alike.

Virgin Islands Search and Rescue (VISAR)
Operating Model: Non-Profit Voluntary Organisation
Sources of Income: Private Contributions & State Subsidy
Manning Structure: Volunteer Crew

For generations the principal resources for sea rescue in and around the British Virgin Islands (BVI) were, essentially, whatever was available at the time. This would have included the launches of the Royal BVI Marine Police and visiting vessels of the British Royal Navy (BVI being a semi-autonomous Crown Colony of Great Britain). Due to their close proximity to the United States and its protectorates of Puerto Rico and the US Virgin Islands, a strong working relationship with the air and marine units of the USCG has always existed. In the early 1980s, however, a group of concerned BVI citizens recognised that the islands, then witnessing a rapid increase in local tourism and the influx of foreign yachtsmen, needed to create their own lifeboat society to provide SAR coverage in territorial waters. A non-profit charitable organisation called VISAR was formed in 1982. The operating model they followed was, not surprisingly, that of the RNLI.

Both the Government of the BVI and the RNLI supported the establishment of the new organisation, the former with funding, the latter with training and advice. Originally a vessel of local design and construction was purchased for operation out of the main port of Road Town, Tortola, but, in about 1989, an RNLI-style Atlantic 21 RHI was purchased to replace the original boat; she was named the *Spirit of Tortola*. This dedicated lifeboat was operated in conjunction with the many conventional boats owned by members of VISAR. In 1994 VISAR purchased an Arctic 22 RHI hull and tubes from Halmatic, UK, and had the console and helm position transferred from the original Atlantic 21. The wiring and motor installation were all done locally. This RHI had twin 70-hp OMC outboards utilising the latest waterproof-cowling technology developed by the RNLI. Christened the *Spirit of Tortola II* on 9 October 1994, she was purchased through the financial support of the BVI Government, SEARCH, and several corporate and individual donors.

In about 1998 a second rescue unit was opened up on Virgin Gorda, one of the other large islands in the BVI. The first vessel for this station, named the *Gorda Peak*, was a Hurricane 22 RHI that had been 'borrowed' from BVI Customs, and which, like the Tortola boat, was manned by a volunteer crew. With donated funds a new VISAR headquarters was built in Road Town to house the Tortola RHI, as well as provide space for training, administration and a search coordination facility (the VISAR HQ and personnel became the principal MRCC for the BVI). In 2000 sufficient funds were raised to purchase a new RHI for Virgin Gorda, another Atlantic 21, also named the *Gorda Peak*; she went into service in April. In December of that year, the engines of both boats were replaced and standardised with 85-hp Yamahas.

VISAR continues to operate as a charitable organisation with the Governor of the BVI holding the position of patron. The crews are drawn from all professions and walks of life, many of them being connected with the large marine and tourism industries in the islands. When a coast radio station or other relaying agency picks up a distress call it is transferred to the BVI Fire and Rescue Service who, in turn, will page out the duty VISAR crew proximate to the incident. VISAR volunteers not only man the lifeboat, but also activate the rescue coordination centre at VISAR HQ and monitor all radio traffic until an incident is resolved. In 1998 VISAR lifeboats and crews responded to some 102 SAR incidents, 25 of which were medical calls – a type of incident that appears to be on the increase in BVI waters with growing charter boat and cruising activity.[463] The VISAR organisation is an excellent example of what can be done in a small country with limited resources when a group of skilled and determined individuals band together for a common cause.

BULGARIA

Coastal Conditions and Hazards
The coast of Bulgaria is approximately 150 miles (240 km) long and borders on the western part of the Black Sea between Romania to the north and Turkey to the south. The country also has myriad inland waterways, including the River Danube, which skirts most of its northern border, and hundreds of lakes. Waves in the range of 42ft (13m) have been recorded in the southwest part of the Black Sea and along its western shores. South or southeasterly gales can produce large confused seas when they are opposed to the main southerly current. There is little tidal effect – the average spring range is only 3in (80mm).[464]

Water Life Saving Service of the Bulgarian Red Cross (BRC)
Operating Model: Non-Profit Voluntary Organisation
Sources of Income: Private Contributions
Manning Structure: Volunteer Crew

The Bulgarian Red Cross (BRC) was originally established in 1878 and became a member of the International Committee in 1885, providing relief services for their own country, as well as other nations, during times of epidemic, disaster and armed conflict. In 1964 the BRC set up a Water Life Saving Service (WLSS) after being approached by the national government; this was in response to the loss of hundreds of lives in water-related accidents in the previous year. Ostensibly a beach lifesaving organisation, the BRC also trained coxswains and crews to run rescue boats at the popular Black Sea resorts and along the extensive inland waterways.

Today the WLSS is extensively involved in promoting water safety throughout Bulgaria and in the training of lifeguards and water rescuers, with the objective of reducing the country's water accidents. To this end, the organisation maintains a Water Safety Training School at Sozopol on the Black Sea, which is accredited to the International Lifesaving Federation (the international body related to beach and water rescue activities). The WLSS also holds a 'Water Life Saving Week' at the beginning of every summer.[465]

CANADA

A CCG 47ft (14.33m) MLB cruises the remote west coast of Vancouver Island, Canada.
Canadian Armed Forces

Coastal Conditions & Hazards
At 151,500 miles (243,791km), the coastline of Canada is the longest of any nation on earth. The country is bounded by three oceans and has almost every conceivable coastal hazard other than those common to more tropical climes. On the Atlantic coast of what are known as Canada's Maritime Provinces the full fury of the North Atlantic crashes upon a generally rocky shore which, in the north around Newfoundland and Labrador, can be uninhabited for hundreds of miles. The tides in the Bay of Fundy are some of the largest in the world and can produce a treacherous tidal bore that has claimed many a small boat. Two hundred miles off Nova Scotia lies Sable Island, an isolated bastion of shifting sand that was a curse to shipping in the days of sail and is again receiving attention due to the recent development of offshore oilfields in the area. In the Gulf of St Lawrence, mariners deal with dangerous shallows and currents that have been known to converge with large oceanic swells driven by North Atlantic storms to produce massive seas that, even in recent years, have claimed several large deep-sea ships. Then, of course, there is the ice. The Gulf and many of the ports along the Atlantic seaboard freeze up during the winter months and in spring and summer there is the additional hazard of great icebergs that drift down from Greenland and the Baffin Straits before melting in the warmer waters of the Gulf Stream. In the Arctic the season for shipping is short and only ice-strengthened vessels generally venture forth. Self-sufficiency is the key to maritime survival in this part of the world for the expanses are so great and the resources so limited that total reliance on a 'safety net' is not possible.

On the shores of British Columbia the waters of the North Pacific crash against a rugged terrain of outlying rocks, reefs and islets that help to protect the entrances of the many large sounds and inlets, some of which stretch inland for more than 60 miles (100km). Some of the largest ocean waves ever recorded – in the range of 100ft (30m) – have occurred in the waters south and west of the Queen Charlotte Islands. There are literally thousands of islands along what is known as the inside passage, from Vancouver to Alaska, which is also the scene of some of the strongest tidal currents in the world making the waters more akin to a large torrential river than to a sea. Some of the currents have been known to reach speeds in the range of 17kt – a disconcerting figure for the pilots and masters of the many large cruise-ships that now ply these confined waters every summer. In the Canadian Great Lakes, part of the largest body of fresh water in the world, storms are commonplace and wind-driven waves can be very hazardous to the unwary mariner – the lower density water allowing seas to build up very rapidly. In addition, the perils of currents and floating ice in the large rivers such as the St Lawrence, keep mariners on their toes.

History of Coastal Lifesaving

The earliest efforts at establishing coastal lifesaving services in Canada began on the Atlantic coast in the Crown Colony of Nova Scotia. In 1798 a temporary Humane Station was founded on Sable Island by the then Governor of Nova Scotia, Sir John Wentworth (see Chapter I-6). This station became a permanent facility in 1801 and, although the Sable Island Humane Establishment undoubtedly had its own small boats that would have been used for both supplying the base and for rescuing the shipwrecked, there is no record of any purpose-built rescue craft being provided there until the 1850s.

The Crown Colony of Nova Scotia had become the haven for tens of thousands of British Loyalists who fled New England during the turmoil of the American Revolution. These people, along with the French-speaking Acadians already residing there, would, in just a few short decades, turn a relative hinterland into one of the most prosperous trading and shipbuilding regions in the world. Thousands of British-flagged ships were launched from the Atlantic colonies of British North America and the amount of seagoing traffic increased phenomenally – so, too, did the number of shipwrecks and the resultant loss of life. The first safety measures involved aids to navigation and, during the first half of the 19th Century manned lighthouses around Nova Scotia and the adjacent colony of New Brunswick. One of the locations promoted as a site for a new lighthouse was Seal Island, off the southwestern tip of Nova Scotia. Uninhabited and harsh of climate, the island had witnessed many a tragic shipwreck. In 1823 Mary Hichens persuaded her husband and other family members to move to the island so that shipwrecked mariners would no longer lack assistance on its shores. Eventually, through Hichens's efforts, and her lobbying of the Colonial Government, a lighthouse was constructed on Seal Island. The family tradition would carry on for generations, and Mary's sons would construct a purpose-built rescue craft of their own

design, making the Seal Island Humane Station the home of the first dedicated lifeboat in Canada (see Chapter I-14; Coastal Heroines).[466]

As more lighthouses were built in and around Nova Scotia, they became the responsibility of the Colonial Superintendent of Public Works whose job it was to travel annually around the coast on a Government schooner to check on the status of the facilities. One of the early Superintendents during the 1830s was Samuel Cunard, a prominent Halifax businessman who would later establish one of the first transatlantic steamer services in the world. Cunard, and his successors in the job, recognised the need to expand the safety services beyond just lighthouses and, before long, humane stations were co-established with the lights at some of the more treacherous locations. These included the humane stations all around Nova Scotia and Cape Breton Island; the principal facilities being at St Paul's, Scatterie, and Mud Islands. By 1857 some of these stations also had lifeboats, mainly of the Francis type (see Chapter II-9); then Superintendent William Condon, referring to the station at St Paul's Island in the Cabot Strait between Cape Breton Island and Newfoundland, recommended 'that one of Francis's "life-boats" be sent to this island…the life-boat now in use there, being small, and of very little service'.[467] Following the establishment of the permanent humane facility on St Paul's in 1837, many decades later both Nova Scotia and New Brunswick would, unknown to one another, establish temporary humane stations on opposite sides of the island – incredibly the two groups stumbled upon each other in the act of rescuing the few hapless survivors of the ship *Great Britain* in the winter of 1882.[468] Such events were not uncommon in the vastness of early Canada, where means of communication were practically non-existent.

The boats at the humane stations were manned by the light keepers and their hired men; the great expanses of desolate and relatively unpopulated coastline meant that a voluntary lifesaving service was not an option – manpower was a valuable commodity.

The CLS crew on Sable Island, Nova Scotia, circa 1900. The first humane establishment on the island was established in 1797 and remained in service until 1947.
Maritime Museum of the Atlantic, Halifax

Nova Scotia's early humane stations received a major boost during the 1850s, this time from south of the border in New England. Dorothea Lynde Dix (1802-87), a prominent Bostonian and a woman of substance, dedicated her life to humanitarian causes such as the reform of prisons and asylums on both sides of the border (see Chapters I-11 and I-14), and would also champion the cause of assisting the shipwrecked for, during her travels into Canada, she had witnessed several horrendous wrecks. Her tenacious spirit even took her out to the inhospitable shores of Sable Island on the government schooner *Daring*, where she met with the keepers of the humane station and witnessed the rescue of the crew from a stranded schooner. She returned to Boston where, with a group of like-minded philanthropists connected to the Massachusetts Humane Society, she set about raising funds for the purchase of four metallic lifeboats. These were eventually shipped to the Nova Scotia Humane Stations, most particularly to the facility at Sable Island, which also received a line-throwing gun, and one of Francis's patented life-cars (see Chapter I-12). Within days of the equipment's arrival it was put to humane use when the crew rescued approximately 168 men, women and children from the American ship *Arcadia* on 27 November 1854.

Dorothea Dix was an incredible woman, revered by the men of the humane stations and feared by many a government official, for she had no hesitation in undermining any obstructionist bureaucrat who dared get in the way of her humanitarian quest. In a letter to Admiral Seymour, Commander-in-Chief of Her Majesty's North American Squadron at Halifax in November 1853, regarding the provision of further lifesaving measures at Sable Island, she offered the following advice regarding some of the officials within his jurisdiction;

The opinions of most members of the civil government differ; but as they suffer none of the exposures, and encounter none of the dangers of maritime life, I presume they will concede the decision to those who unite prudence with courage, and who, while they unshrinkingly meet perils, do not despise aids for averting destruction. [469]

Dorothea knew that when the cause was just, and the potential results of success so great, there could be no excuses.

Canadian Lifesaving Service – Department of Marine and Fisheries

In 1867 the Dominion of Canada was formed, uniting the Atlantic with the Pacific and creating a huge new country. The control of the humane stations became the responsibility of the new Federal Government; the maintenance of the Sable Island facility becoming a constitutional obligation of the new Dominion. A Department of Marine and Fisheries was formed to oversee the territorial waters of Canada and, although the original focus was on building more lighthouses and other aids to navigation as well as

constructing large steamers to patrol the coasts and perform other duties, eventually the small number of lifesaving stations also began to grow in number. In 1871 the first new lifeboat station in the Dominion was established at Salmon Point on Lake Ontario. Another was established the following year at Nottawasaga Island, also in Ontario. Many more were soon to follow all across Atlantic Canada, the St Lawrence River and the Great Lakes.[470] By 1886 there were 20 lifesaving stations in central and eastern Canada.[471] Starting in 1875 a uniquely Canadian lifesaving service was put in place along the shores of the Gulf of St Lawrence, where 10 'lifesaving canoe' stations were established. The severe ice conditions in the river meant that ships were constantly beset in the flows. The massive canoes, which had steel runners on their bottoms, were a combination of lifeboat and sled and could hold up to 30 survivors. The six-man crews were local, mostly descendants of voyageurs – the French Canadian paddlers and fur traders who had opened up the vast hinterland of the country. By the 1890s, with the advent of the powerful icebreaker and the reduction of the number of sailing ships entering the St Lawrence, the demand for the lifesaving canoes diminished and the stations were closed.[472]

A rare photograph of what may be a CLSS lifesaving canoe. These unique rescue craft operated on the St Lawrence River 1875-90, primarily during the winter and spring months, when the ice was at its worst. They had a crew of six, could carry up to 30 survivors and had steel runners to aid in sliding over the floes.
National Archives of Canada

The Canadian Lifesaving Service (CLSS), although an integral part of the Department of Marine and Fisheries, began to develop an identity of its own. Rules were established, to a large extent based on those of the RNLI in Britain. A document known as the 'Regulations for the Government of the Lifesaving Stations of Canada' was drawn up to include all rules and routines from the lifeboat and line-throwing gun drills to the forwarding of monthly reports, the status of the annual inspections, and the methodology required to keep the station clean. Unlike in Britain however, the crews were not all volunteers. The coxswain was to be the only permanently paid employee, appointed by the department and receiving approximately $75 per year. According to the regulations he was to be of:

> *...good moral character, and sober and correct habits. A coxswain must not be less than twenty-one, nor more than fifty years of age and be able to read and write a fair legible hand, must be able bodied, familiar with the line of coast embraced within his district, and must possess a thorough knowledge of the management of surf and lifeboats, and of the use of the various apparatus employed in the service.*[473]

It was up to the coxswain to pick his crew of volunteers from 'able bodied and experienced men residing near the station' and they were paid $1.50 for each drill, as well as for call-outs. By the turn of the century, due to the transient nature of the Canadian population, most, if not all, the stations in the Canadian Lifesaving Service had full-time paid crews during the periods in which they were scheduled to operate. Some of the stations, such as those on the Great Lakes, were seasonal, closing during the winter freeze-up.

It was not until 1907 that any efforts were made on behalf of the Dominion Government to establish lifesaving facilities on Canada's Pacific coast. This, in spite of the pleas of countless citizens on both sides of the border, to say nothing of the loss of hundreds of ships and thousands of lives in the last half of the 19th Century as two gold rushes came and went and the Canadian and American West opened up to the world. The southwest coast of Vancouver Island was a notorious lee shore lying on the northern side of the entrance to the Strait of Juan de Fuca, gateway to the Pacific Northwest. The area was a sailing master's worst nightmare as the prevailing storms and currents would inevitably combine to push a ship into the countless hazards of this area, also known as the northern part of the 'Graveyard of the Pacific'. The reasons for the delay in establishing facilities in British Columbia will never be known, but could be attributed to the immense size of the country and the vast separation of some of its regions from the centre of power in Ottawa. In 1906, however, an event would occur which brought the plight of the shipwrecked on these shores to the attention of the government and helped to establish the first dedicated lifesaving facilities there. In the early morning of 22 January the American passenger steamer *Valencia*, northbound from San Francisco to Seattle, Washington, and Victoria, British Columbia, ran aground in thick fog on the southwest coast of Vancouver Island. Over the next three days the 164 passengers and crew made several attempts to reach shore with a line-throwing gun and ship's boats while being constantly pounded by the North Pacific. Except for a few crewmen and passengers who were washed ashore, all the attempts would be in vain. Eventually the *Valencia* succumbed to the massive breakers and slipped into the icy

depths of the North Pacific, taking 126 men, women and children to their deaths. Aside from two lighthouses in the area and the rickety telegraph wire that connected them, there were no lifesaving facilities on the outer Pacific coast to assist the *Valencia*. Two Commissions of Inquiry were held on either side of the border – at last the Government of Canada had to act. A decision was made to establish four lifeboat stations on the West Coast of Vancouver Island, at Bamfield, Clayoquot, Clo-oose and Ucluelet. In addition, the Victoria Life-Saving Association, a private voluntary society that had already been created in the colonial capital of Victoria in response to the government's previous lack of action, would receive a lifeboat and some support from the Dominion Government.[474] The old telegraph trail connecting the lighthouses along the southwest coast of Vancouver Island was widened into what became known as the West Coast Life-Saving Trail, and extended to cover approximately 32 miles (52km) of inhospitable coastline. The trail, which today has become one of the most popular hiking trails in the world, was chopped through incredibly dense forests and had to traverse countless ravines and rushing torrents. It would be interspersed with houses of refuge and another lighthouse would be constructed at Pachena Point, adjacent to the scene of the *Valencia* tragedy. The trail would not be completed until 1912. Additional isolated houses of refuge stocked with stoves and provisions were established further north on the west coast of Vancouver Island, between Bamfield and Cape Scott. On the American side the USLSS would also establish a new lifeboat station at Neah Bay, Washington, thus providing coverage to the southern entrance of the Strait of Juan de Fuca as well.

The relationship between the Canadian and American lifesaving services has always been, by necessity and circumstance, a strong one. The creation of the USLSS in 1871 coincided with the establishment of the Canadian service. The bond is most evident in the similarity of lifeboats and rescue craft used; a pattern of development that continues to this day. Aside from the early Francis metallic lifeboats provided by Miss Dix and the Colonial authorities in Nova Scotia, all the early Canadian lifeboats were exact copies or derivations of USLSS models, although almost all were built at Canadian yards. Originally many of the early CLS stations on the Atlantic and the Great Lakes were equipped with the Dobbins type self-righting lifeboat, a sort of American hybrid that combined the safety and sea-going qualities of the large British Standard Self-Righting lifeboat with the lighter and more portable American surfboat (see Chapter II-9). The Canadian versions of this small lifeboat were all built at Dartmouth, Nova Scotia, and Goderich, Ontario. The Dobbins boats were well received in the Great Lakes and on the Pacific but were not liked by the crews in the Atlantic stations as their relatively high ends and freeboard meant that they were much more difficult to pull in to a strong head wind and sea. Many boats were replaced by 25ft (7.6m) Canadian versions of the Beebe-McLellan surfboats, some of which were known as Doherty's Improved Beebe-McLellans, probably in reference to the inclusion of self-righting air cases on the traditionally non-self-righting design. These boats had 10 men pulling double-banked oars, they, too, were built in Canada by Morrison of Shelburne, Nova Scotia, and by Vancouver Shipyards on the west coast, where the contract price was $575 per vessel.[475] The new Canadian Life-Saving Station at Bamfield on Vancouver Island, which had responsibility for maintaining and patrolling the new lifesaving trail, would receive the first American-designed and -built 36ft (11.2m), SR-SB MLB in 1907. It was built by the Electric Boat Company (Elco), in Bayonne, New Jersey. The Dominion Government had been jarred by the loss of the *Valencia* and, being pressured to permanently station a large 'lifesaving steamer' in the area, quickly recognised that the emerging technology of the MLB provided a cost-effective solution. Nevertheless, it was a large expenditure for the time – the price of $10,900 would have purchased almost 20 of the smaller surfboats. Bamfield thus became the first lifeboat station in Canada to have an MLB and the first in North America to have one of the new Elco 36 Footers. Coincidentally, the Waadah Island Station of the USLSS, across the Strait from Bamfield, would also receive a 36ft MLB when it opened up the following year (see Chapter II-12).[476] In 1911 another of the 36ft MLBs was purchased by the Canadian service for use at Bayview, Nova Scotia, and two of the twin-screw Beebe-McLellan motor surfboats were built for the Cheticamp and Little Wood Island lifesaving stations, also in Nova Scotia. In 1915 two high-speed motor launches, which could reach speeds in excess of 20kt were built for the Toronto Lifesaving Station on Ward's Island in response to the ever-growing number of calls from pleasure craft.[477]

The year 1915 would be the heyday of the Canadian Lifesaving Service, with 40 stations plus a number of other locations where the government supported voluntary lifesaving organisations such as at Victoria, British Columbia, Halifax, Nova Scotia, Cape Tormentine, New Brunswick, and Wellington, on Lake Ontario.

The ravages of the First World War on the Canadian workforce combined with the post-war economic slump to result in the demise of the stations. During the war the lifeboat service had been transferred to the control of the newly formed Royal Canadian Navy, under whose administration the CLS essentially fell between the cracks and, subsequently, through bureaucratic indifference, almost entirely disappeared. The Sable Island Humane Station was the last of the shore-based facilities to be closed in 1947, after 148 years of continuous operation. In the Great Lakes the last station still in operation was at Point Pelee, where only the watchtower remained as of 1938.[478] Some of the stations were taken over by provincial and municipal authorities, such as the facility at Toronto, which became part of the city's police department. By the Second World War the administration of coastal lifesaving and, indeed, all the federal government's marine concerns, had become the jurisdiction of the new Department of Transport, formed in 1936.

By 1951 only a remnant of a coastal lifesaving service remained with but two of the original stations still in service

and still operating the same first-generation 36ft MLBs built before the First World War. Both were on Vancouver Island, at Bamfield and Tofino (Clayoquot). However, around the country coastal lifesaving services had been enhanced somewhat by the stationing of Royal Canadian Air Force (RCAF) crash boats, primarily adjacent to air bases, during and after the Second World War. The fast rescue launches, originally large modified versions of the Fairmile MTBs, were replaced in the 1950s by new steel 30ft and 40ft utility boats (UTBs), designed by the USCG. (see Chapter II-18). In 1952 the RCAF and the Canadian Department of National Defense would assume overall responsibility for search and rescue on the coastal waters of Canada, and would establish Rescue Co-ordination Centres (RCCs) around the country, as well as dedicated fixed- and rotary-wing SAR squadrons in the various regions. The crash boats, too, would be principally dedicated to coastal lifesaving. The onus was on the federal government to put some money back into lifeboat stations. With the boom in the post-war economy and the resulting increase in the number of near-shore fishing vessels and pleasure craft, SAR incidents were rising. In 1951 three new TRS versions of the 36 Footer were ordered by the Department of Transport to replace the old boats at Bamfield and Tofino and to reinstate the service at Bayview. By the 1960s however, the workload on these few shore-based units was becoming heavier and heavier – the time had come for Canada to create a more efficient maritime safety organisation that could offer better coverage and improved services.

Canadian Coast Guard (CCG)
Operating Model: Civilian Agency managed by Government
Sources of Income: State Funded
Manning Structure: Employee Crew

This organisation was formed in 1962 and encompassed all the duties and responsibilities of the old Marine Branch of the Department of Transport. Officially named the Canadian Coast Guard (CCG) in 1975, the organisation was responsible for the provision of primary SAR on the coastal waters and Great Lakes of Canada, as well as the maintenance of lighthouses and aids to navigation, steamship inspection, boating safety, ice breaking, re-supply to the Canadian Arctic and, eventually, the control of maritime telecommunications and vessel traffic services, and the protection of the marine environment. In many ways the CCG was quite similar to the USCG but the CCG remained principally a civilian agency, operating on the same principles as the merchant marine, while the American counterpart was military in structure.

The creation of the CCG brought about a revitalisation of dedicated rescue services all around the country. Many of the RCAF crash boats became part of the new organisation, as did the three self-righting lifeboats built in 1951. By 1963 a fleet of five 95ft (29m) cutters based on the USCG's Cape patrol boat design was purchased for use as patrolling SAR platforms. Known as the 'R' class in Canada, the CCGC *Rally* was stationed in Nova Scotia, the CCGC *Relay* patrolled the

St Lawrence River and the Great Lakes, and the CCGCs *Ready*, *Racer* and *Rider* were stationed on the Pacific coast (see Chapter II-16). In the late 1960s more lifeboat stations were added around the country and supplied with about 20 of the new USCG-designed 44ft (13.7m) MLBs that had replaced the old 36 Footers. The construction programme continued until 1975 (see Chapter II-17).

In the mid 1960s experiments were begun with air-cushion vehicles (ACVs) for use in SAR and other applications. In 1965 and '66 a Bell SK5 hovercraft was tested on Lake Ontario with favourable results. In June 1968 a British Hovercraft Corporation SRN5 was purchased by the CCG for Vancouver airport where its amphibious capabilities could be put to good use on the extended tidal flats at the mouth of the Fraser River and on the relatively protected waters of the Gulf of Georgia. The SK5 had a top speed of 55kt and could cruise at 40kt, its speed being dependant on sea and wind conditions.[479] In time two more hovercraft would be purchased from Britain, both the larger 48ft (14.7m), 1,100hp, turbine-driven SRN6 MkI for work in and around the Gulf of Georgia. In 1987 the CCG purchased a 79ft (24.5m), 1,760-hp diesel-powered British Hovercraft Corporation AP1-88, the CCGH *Waban-aki*, for work on the St Lawrence River at Trois Rivières, Quebec, where, in addition to year-round SAR, it was used for icebreaking. In 1998 the CCG's Sea Island Hovercraft Units at Vancouver and Trois Rivières received the latest versions of the diesel-powered AP1-88, 91ft (28.5m) in length and powered by four Caterpillar 3416 diesel engines producing 2,800hp to give a cruising speed of about 30kt and a top speed said to be in the 45kt range. Both were built in Canada by Hike Metal Products in Ontario under license to British Hovercraft. The new CCGH *Siyay* was assigned to Sea Island and the CCGH *Sipu-muin* to Trois Rivières.

The CCG ACV *Waban-Aki* based on the St Lawrence River. Although used as primary SAR vessels on the Pacific coast, particularly around the low-lying mud flats off Vancouver International Airport, these vessels are also extremely versatile in eastern waters, particularly for ice-breaking.
CCG

Building during the 1980s included the development of smaller coastal SAR cutters in the 70ft (22m) range. Two of these, the *Pt. Race* and the *Pt. Henry*, were stationed in the Pacific Region at Campbell River and Prince Rupert respectively, where they remain in operation to this day. The other two were stationed in eastern Canada, the *Cape Hurd* on the Great Lakes at Goderich, Ontario, and *Isle Rouge*, on the St Lawrence at Tadoussac, Quebec. Previously known as the Type 400 SAR Cutters, these vessels are non-self-righting, have a cruising speed of 15kt, a top speed of approximately 22kt and carry a small 12ft (4m) RHI located on a stern-launching ramp. Their range of operation is 500 nautical miles.

The CCGC *Pt. Race*, based out of Campbell River, BC, approaches a burning pleasure craft in the Strait of Georgia.
CCG

In 1986 two coastal SAR and patrol cutters were specifically designed and built for the harsh winter conditions of Newfoundland. CCGC *Harp* and CCGC *Hood* had ice-strengthened hulls to operate as large shore-based lifeboats for use in severe ice conditions. They were 79ft (24.5m) long, had a cruising speed of 9.5kt and a range of 500 nautical miles. The late 1980s also saw a move towards the replacement of the old 40ft UTBs around the country, as well as some of the non-standard-type fast rescue launches that had been inherited from such organisations as the Royal Canadian Mounted Police. The USCG 41ft (12.5m) UTB was chosen as the best replacement design and nine, all Canadian-built, remain in service across the country, from the St Lawrence River to the Pacific (see Chapter II-18) and have provided excellent service in rescue operations throughout their tenure.

In 1986 the CCG started experimenting with a design for a large RHI, constructed by Hurricane Rescue Craft in Richmond, British Columbia. In many respects the CGR 100 was similar to the Medina class RHI developed in the UK during the early 1980s (see Chapter II-20). It was 45ft (14m) long, had a top speed of 34kt and was self-righting and self-bailing; it remains in service today at Port Weller, Ontario, although in 1997 it was re-powered with twin 560-hp 3176B turbo-charged Caterpillar diesels, running Hamilton 362 jet drives. The prototype was the only large RHI ever constructed for the CCG, despite the fact that it appears to have gained high praise from lifeboat crews around the country during its initial trials and, by all reports, remains in high regard with the crew at Port Weller.[480]

The CCG did, however, recognise the usefulness of smaller inflatables and RHIs at a very early stage in their development. Small, soft-bottom inflatables were used quite widely as daughter-boats on all the CCG's patrolling craft during the 1960s and, by the early 1970s, a seasonal Inshore Rescue Boat (IRB) programme had been established in each region similar to the system established in France during the 1960s, which used a combination of trained personnel and university students as crew. Also in the early 1970s Lester B Pearson College of the Pacific (sister institution to Atlantic College in Wales, where the RHI was invented) was established at Pedder Bay, near Victoria, and it wasn't long before College staff had set up a volunteer rescue unit for the Victoria area and the Strait of Juan de Fuca. The CCG's Pacific Region quickly recognised the merits of the Atlantic 21 particularly for the IRB programme, and ordered two in the mid 1970s. Gradually the fleet of RHIs in the Pacific Region began to expand from the original Atlantic 21s, to 18ft (5.5m) Avons, and then to various styles of Zodiac RHIs constructed in Canada.

The RHI fleet has now been standardised to the 24ft (7.33m) Zodiac-Hurricane RHI, which is now found across the country at most shore-based units and on almost all CCG primary vessels. The SAR version is driven by twin 150-hp counter-rotating outboards, has a three-seat, delta-console configuration, and can cruise for over 200 miles at more than 45kt, depending on sea conditions. In many ways these small, versatile RHIs have become the primary workhorses of the CCG for SAR and other duties. In the mid 1980s a training programme was established for the Zodiac-Hurricane; it became known as the Rigid Hull Inflatable Operations Training or RHIOT. The original RHIOT School was established at Bamfield in 1986, and there are now similar training schools in every CCG Region across the country, providing training for CCG and USCG crews, as well as for the Canadian Coast Guard Auxiliary and other government agencies.

By the 1990s the search was on for a suitable replacement for the CCG's fleet of venerable 44ft MLBs. In 1991 it was decided that 15 of the 44 Footers would be replaced by a combination of the British Arun lifeboats (see Chapter II-21) and the large CGR 100 RHIs. Eventually the large RHIs were replaced in the contract by the new 47ft MLB, then being developed by the USCG, the prototype of which had been brought up to the CCG's Pacific Region for evaluation in 1992.[481] One 52ft Arun SR GRP-hulled MLB had been purchased from Halmatic in the UK in 1989 and had been stationed at Bickerton, Nova Scotia. In time 10 of this type would be built for the CCG, with another nine being constructed entirely of aluminium, also in Canada. All the

CCG's Arun-type MLBs are presently stationed in the Atlantic Region. In 1998 the first Canadian version of the USCG 47ft MLB, the CCG MLB Cape Sutil, was delivered to Port Hardy, on the north end of Vancouver Island on the Pacific coast. The Canadian version was almost identical to its American counterpart, the main difference being in the power plant, which is two 3196B turbo-charged Caterpillar diesels. By 2001 seven of the 47ft MLBs had been delivered to the CCG and a contract for 24 more was tendered that same year, the goal being to standardise the lifeboat fleet across the country (see Chapter II-22).

The shore-based units of the CCG are not the only SAR resources within the organisation. There are many other vessels and units, which, while being principally designated for other duties, conduct rescue missions as part of their overall responsibility. These include some 30 small, medium and heavy icebreakers and Navaid tenders, as well as nine coastal and offshore scientific survey ships, and 10 'cutter'-type offshore patrol vessels, not including a myriad of smaller coastal fisheries enforcement and survey craft around the country. The CCG also has an airborne wing, whose primary mission is to assist in the maintenance of coastal navigational and communications aids on thousands of miles of relatively uninhabited coastline. The aircraft are frequently called upon to assist in such activities as searches and medical evacuations. Resources include a fleet of rotary-wing MB 105s, Bell 212s and 206s and a large Sikorsky S-61 at Prince Rupert as well as two fixed-wing aircraft. The principal responsibility for the provision of air SAR services in Canada remains with the Canadian Air Force, which has several SAR Squadrons strategically located across the country flying the CH 113 Labrador helicopter (Boeing Vertol), the CC 115 DH 6 De Havilland Buffalo, and C-130 Hercules fixed-wing aircraft. The fleet of ageing Labrador helicopters is presently being replaced by the triple-engine Cormorant helicopter built by the Eurocopter Consortium.

Finally, communications is the essence of effective SAR, and the CCG's many Marine Communications and Traffic Centres (MCTS) provide an invaluable service along with the joint CCG and military RCCs, through the monitoring of the distress frequencies, the relaying of information to and from the rescue units, and the co-ordination and control of the SAR case itself.

In 1997 the Canadian Coast Guard was transferred under the umbrella of the Department of Fisheries and Oceans, with the CCG taking over that department's large fleet of fisheries-patrol and scientific-research ships and launches. The result is a nationwide combined fleet of approximately 100 vessels of various shapes and descriptions, from the largest heavy icebreaker down to the smallest hydrographic survey launch, not including the 34 shore-based lifeboat stations and the four air-cushion vehicles. In 1995 there were approximately 6,500 SAR incidents nationwide, with the CCG and its all-volunteer auxiliary, handling the bulk of the calls for assistance on the water. As of 2001 the CCG was divided into five separate regional entities: Newfoundland, Maritimes, Laurentian, Central and Arctic, and Pacific.

Canadian Coast Guard Auxiliary (CCGA)
Operating Model: Non-Profit Voluntary Organisation
Sources of Income: Private Contributions & State Subsidy
Manning Structure: Volunteer Crew

Coinciding with the birth of the CCG in 1962, a system of Volunteer Rescue Agents for the Federal Government was established around the country in order to fill the inevitable gaps in the SAR system. These rescue agents, many of whom had their own boats and excellent local knowledge were chosen by the Coast Guard and appointed by the Minister of Transport. They were administered from the newly created Rescue Coordination Centres, then and still run by the Air Force and the Coast Guard. Rescue agents monitored vessel activity in their area, responded to incidents when called, were provided with basic training and, in many cases, with equipment such as radios and pumps. Some rescue agents were further trained as searchmasters and, owing to the remoteness of many locations, were expected to be the on-scene commander for SAR incidents. Thus began the first truly voluntary force for coastal lifesaving in Canada.[482]

The Volunteer Rescue Agents were particularly active in the CCG's Western Region (now known as Pacific) and in 1978 local authorities decided that their role should be expanded and the amount of members increased. The Western Branch of the Canadian Marine Rescue Auxiliary (CMRA) was formed in December of that year. Many existing rescue agents became part of the new organisation, which now provided insurance coverage for its members and basic fuel costs for those who owned and operated boats used on SAR incidents. Similar organisations soon followed in the other CCG regions. The principal role of the new organisation was to assist the CCG in the delivery of SAR operational and prevention services. This latter duty included the running of a nationwide voluntary pleasure-craft safety inspection programme that greatly increased boating safety awareness.

Eventually the organisation's name was changed to Canadian Coast Guard Auxiliary (CCGA) and a satellite organisation now exists in each CCG region. The CCGA has various types of volunteer lifesavers, from those who own and operate their own vessels, to those who operate community- or society-owned purpose-built rescue craft, many of which are large RHIs. In some cases Coast Guard RHIs have been provided to CCGA Units for use as SAR craft, while in other locations, the CCGA provides auxiliary crew members for existing CCG shore-based lifeboat stations, particularly where there is a need to operate an extra RHI. The CCGA has now become a non-profit charitable organisation and is seeking to expand its financial base beyond the realm of public funding in the support of volunteer coastal lifesaving in Canada. Vessels and members of the CCGA responded to 26% of the approximately 7,000 SAR cases in Canada recorded in 1999 and more than 200 lives were saved.

Canadian Lifeboat Institution (CLI)
Operating Model: Non-Profit Voluntary Organisation
Sources of Income: Private Contributions
Manning Structure: Volunteer Crew

The Canadian Lifeboat Institution was formed in November 1981 by Phillip Matty, a long-time proponent of improved SAR services for the 16,800 miles (27,000km) of coastline of British Columbia. Matty had become disillusioned with the lack of government coastal rescue resources on the West Coast during the 1970s. He believed that the newly created CMRA, of which he was a founding director, would not be able to fill many of the gaps in the system, as its primary vessels at the time were fishing boats and yachts owned by members. These were neither always available nor, for obvious reasons, always the best vessels for rescue work.

Matty had been impressed by the various operating structures of some of the all-volunteer European organisations and set about creating a new Canadian society modelled on the RNLI. His main argument against the Canadian system was that it had been modelled after that of the United States, a country with over 10 times the tax base and less then half the coastline. In his opinion, the minimal government resources being allocated to lifeboats and other rescue vessels was a direct result of a public purse that could not afford the system.[483] Sadly, the concept of the all-volunteer CLI never came to fruition during his lifetime. There were many responsible factors, not least of which was the expansion of CCG facilities around British Columbia during the 1980s, as well as the creation of certain CMRA units with their own community owned lifeboats, which, in essence, created a parallel volunteer rescue force with purpose-built lifeboats, albeit with government funding.

The CLI concept has been revitalised in recent years. During the 18th International Lifeboat Conference held at Bournemouth, England, in 1999, the first Canadian vessel ever to attend such a conference was a 44ft Waveney type MLB, the *Roberts Bank* lifeboat, having just been purchased for the CLI. Since then, the organisation has expanded to include five other units, including owner/operator vessels, all of which are situated in and around the Gulf of Georgia, in British Columbia. As an interesting footnote, as of 2003 the CLI's *Roberts Bank* had also become part of the CCGA (Pacific).

CHILE

Coastal Conditions & Hazards
The coastline of Chile is 4,000 miles (6,435km) long, extending from the Peruvian border in the north down to the archipelagos and fjords of the southern peninsula and finally culminating in that most notorious of promontories, Cape Horn. The weather varies: in the north severe northerly gales are common in the winter months; in the south, the thousands of islands and inlets, including the Magellan Strait, are subject to the extremes of any sub-arctic zone with bracing outflow winds, and sudden blinding squalls, known

locally as williwaws. Anyone familiar with the folklore of the sea can attest to the ravages of the southern oceans and, for an apt description of a small vessel passage in and around Cape Horn in the days of sail, a read of Joshua Slocum's *Sailing Alone Around the World* is a must. Weather depressions, which approach the mountainous Chilean coastline from the Pacific, can produce violent squalls and downdraughts that race down the slopes and into the narrow channels, blowing with ferocious intensity and from all directions. Offshore, the wind and sea conditions of the Southern Ocean in the vicinity of the Horn are historically renowned as possibly the worst the planet has to offer. The *South American Pilot, Volume II* states that the predominant westerly winds are in excess of Force 7 for 30% of the year, and that in this area, 'Seas can increase still further to very high, or even phenomenal, when occasionally the winds reach hurricane force'.[484]

The Chilean RHI lifeboat BS 06 *Guardian Brito* operated out of Valparaiso by the CVBS.
CVBS

Cuerpo de Voluntarios de los Botes Salvavidas de Valparaiso (CVBS)
Operating Model: Non-Profit Voluntary Organisation
Sources of Income: Private Contributions & State Subsidy
Manning Structure: Volunteer Crew

The CVBS was officially founded in the great seaport of Valparaiso on 15 April 1925 by a group of dedicated lifeboatmen led by a Danish sea captain, Oluf Christiansen Lund. In Noel Methley's book, *The Lifeboat and Its Story*, published in 1912, there is brief mention of a Sociedad de Salvavidas being based in Valparaiso and supported by voluntary contributions and a government grant.[485] It is quite probable therefore, that the official founding was the

culmination of many years of effort by the local marine community. The port of Valparaiso, located at 33°01' South 71°07' West, is subject to severe northerly gales in the winter months and one of the primary duties of the original lifeboatmen was to protect the lives of the crews of vessels anchored in the harbour as they ventured back and forth.

The 1925 service used two British lifeboats, one built for the RNLI in 1905 and a smaller vessel built by Thornycroft in 1920. The tradition of purchasing and operating ex-RNLI lifeboats continues in Chile to this day where two fine old vessels still operate and prove their metal. The CVBS presently operates an ex-RNLI Watson type MLB launched in 1925 and purchased by the Corps in 1955 (see Chapter II-12). This venerable craft, the L.B. 03 *Captain Christiansen* was one of the lifeboats used for the evacuation of the British Expeditionary Force from Dunkerque in May 1940. The second classic lifeboat, the L.B. 05 *Valparaiso III*, is an ex-RNLI Barnett MLB, constructed in the UK in 1950 and purchased by the Corps in 1981. Both vessels are beautifully maintained and have been upgraded with state-of-the-art electronics. As of 2002 the CVBS has updated its fleet of ex-RNLI lifeboats with the purchase of an Arun class 52ft (15.8m) MLB (see Chapter II-21).

In 1994 the CVBS followed the lead of The Netherlands and had the large 41ft (12.66m) RHI lifeboat, B.S. 06 *Guardian Brito* built by Asmar Marine of Valparaiso. The *Guardian Brito* is powered by twin Volvo Penta diesels with Hamilton jet propulsion and cruises at 16kt with a top speed of 22kt. It is augmented by a smaller inflatable, a Pumar 640, used for inshore work and beach rescue.

The Corps is referred to by the population of Valparaiso as, simply, 'the Lifeboat', and as exemplified by the recent expansion of its fleet, maintains widespread physical, financial and logistical support from the community. The volunteers are drawn from all walks of life; all must pass stringent entrance requirements and attend a substantial training programme prior to being accepted as crew. Financial support is garnered from several sources including membership dues from the Corps (a true test of a volunteer's spirit and dedication if there ever was one), as well as public donations. The Corps receives logistical support from the Chilean Navy in the form of a fuel subsidy and access to training courses and facilities. One further fund-raising mechanism, which might be called a Chilean innovation, is the operation of a restaurant and casino by the Corps above the lifeboat station in Valparaiso... all for a good cause!

Modern coordination of SAR in Chile is conducted under the authority of the National SAR Agency, which consists of six MRCCs, located at Valparaiso, Iquique, Antofagasta, Talcahuano, Puerto Montt and Punta Arenas. In addition there are several MRSCs located at Arica, Caldera, Coquimba, San Antonio, Pascua, Juan Fernandez, Valdivia, Castro, Aysen and Puerto Williams. All the coordination centres are co-located at, and/or connected by, an extensive network of coast radio stations. In more remote areas, as well as further offshore, marine and air resources of both the Chilean Navy and Air Force remain on constant standby for SAR.

CHINA

Coastal Conditions & Hazards

China has a very extensive oceanic coastline, approximately 14,500 miles (23,300km) long. The southern and eastern coasts, from the Gulf of Tongkin northeast to the Formosa, or Taiwan Strait, are sub-tropical in nature, with many bays and river estuaries as well as myriad offshore islands. Here the climate and winds are directly affected by the local monsoon, which brings strong NE winds in the winter (November to March) and less severe SW winds in the summer (July and August), although violent SW squalls are known to occur near the mouth of the Zhujiang River around this time. Local tropical revolving storms are referred to as typhoons and an average of five such systems strike the south and east coasts of China every year, sometimes with catastrophic consequences for coastal shipping and the local population.

From the Formosa Strait to the border with North Korea, the coast of China varies significantly. As far north as Shanghai and the mouths of the Yangtze River, the topography is relatively similar to that in the south, with many outlying islands and reefs. From this massive estuary north to the Shantung Peninsula, which separates the Yellow Sea from the Gulf of Pohai, the coast is relatively flat and featureless with extensive shoals extending as far as 50 miles (80km) offshore. The Chinese coastline in the Gulf of Pohai is dangerously shallow given the large number of river systems which drain into it and is fringed with a multitude of small islands. These more northern waters are also affected by the monsoon and typhoon seasons, but less dramatically. However, the Formosa Strait is known for extremely strong winds during the winter months and the period of the NE monsoon, when funnelling gales in the vicinity of Force 8 are frequent.[486][487]

Brief mention should also be made of the dangers and conditions of China's main inland waterway, the mighty Yangtze. The river is an astounding 3,000 miles (4,827km) long and at one time was navigable by small coasters and other shallow-draught commercial vessels as far as Chungking, 1,300 miles (2,091km) inland from Shanghai. It was said that in earlier times over half the goods shipped out of China came down this one river – one of the principal hazards could be the volume of traffic itself. The dangers on the Lower Yangtze, which extends some 600 miles (965km) inland from Shanghai to Hankow and the Middle Yangtze, which is another 383 miles (616km) to Ichang, are the shifting sandbars created by the annual freshet and the resultant floods. Smaller vessels can fall victim to 'Chow Chow Water', an area of extreme turbulence created by the meeting of two opposing currents. Such powerful currents and standing waves have also been known to force larger river craft off course, to strike either the river-bank or a submerged rock. The Upper Yangtze, from Ichang to the source is a region of steep valleys and the famous gorges. The river pours through the narrow gaps with tremendous force, the seasonal effects of the rise and fall creating even larger rapids, especially in the spring months when the snow pack is melting. Modern vessels that operate in this region are usually shallow-draught, twin-screw craft with ample power and the ability to easily manoeuvre in the turbulent water.[488]

Early History of Coastal Lifesaving

The earliest known lifeboat and lifesaving societies in the world were those established in the various provinces of China bordering on the Yangtze River. These benevolent associations assisted victims of river accidents and drowning and actually began established dedicated river lifeboats at some of the gorges as early as 1737 (see Chapter I-3).

Maritime Rescue and Salvage Bureau

Operating Model: Civilian Agency Managed by Government
Sources of Income: State Funded
Manning Structure: Employee/Volunteer Crew

In the world of maritime rescue it is never prudent to generalise about the way systems or services operate in different nations. No two countries are exactly alike and, in some states, operating systems are entirely unique and well adapted for the environment in which they work. In China, for example, today's coastal rescue service runs part-in-parcel with the commercial operations of that nation's largest salvage company. Some might question why a lifesaving service would be part of a private, albeit state-owned, company whose primary objective is salvage? In China, until fairly recently, the amount of non-commercial vessel traffic was fairly minimal. The majority of vessels requiring assistance were, and are, commercial. At a relatively early stage in the development of the People's Republic it was felt that services for salvaging ships and the rescuing of their crews essentially went hand in hand. The duties of coastal rescue were thus relegated to the crews of salvage and 'rescue' tugs strategically located at different salvage and rescue stations on the Chinese coast.

With the formation of the China Salvage Company in the early 1950s came the establishment of three primary salvage and rescue bases: at Yantai in the north, Shanghai at the mouth of the Yangtze, and Guangzhou in the south. The company, which started with five vessels and 300 men would, by 1988, have expanded to 143 vessels of all descriptions and a staff of over 9,000. Three separate, self-sufficient bureaus would be created and headquartered out of the same three original bases. Although salvage was originally the primary objective, rescue and salvage sub-stations began to appear up and down the Chinese coast with dedicated life-saving vessels being strategically located at some. Eventually the China Salvage Company came under the auspices of the National Ministry of Communications, which also operates the Chinese Maritime Rescue Centre.

The monumental growth of the Chinese economy over the last decade has resulted in a significant change in the type and quantity of maritime traffic along the coasts and waterways of the nation. As was experienced in Europe and North America in the 1950s and 1960s the Chinese have more recently discovered the pleasures of boating. The result has been an increase in the number of salvage bases in order to minimise the gaps between stations to no more than 74 miles (120km) and a three- to four-hour response time, as well as increasing the number of dedicated life-saving vessels on the Chinese coast. As an additional response to the extra calls from pleasure and excursion boats, the Chinese Government and the Chinese Salvage Company have begun promoting a European-style rescue service in some locations with the provision of lifeboats where there is a seasonal demand, the promotion of 'social contributions' to the cause, and the establishment of local committees to operate and crew the vessels. All in all it is an excellent example of how a country can adapt a lifesaving service to meet its ever-changing needs.[489]

In March 2001 an official announcement was made by the Chinese Government regarding the expansion of civilian maritime SAR services under the auspices of the Chinese Maritime Rescue and Salvage Bureau. These included the purchase of two, state-of-the-art American SAR helicopters and the creation of SAR air stations on the Chinese coast. These would be the first non-military SAR air resources in the nation's history and would be combined with additional military SAR resources, which were also being procured. All Chinese marine and air SAR units would continue to be administered by the State (China) Oceanic (Maritime) Rescue Coordination Centre in Beijing and by the various MRSCs around the country during SAR taskings. The new resources would also be available to assist in pollution prevention and salvage duties, although their primary mission would be lifesaving. The Maritime Rescue and Salvage Bureau also finalised the installation of all its coastal DSC facilities in the year 2000. From 1996 to 2001 the bureau conducted some 2,925 marine SAR operations in Chinese coastal waters and along the Yangtze River, saving some 25,146 persons from imminent danger.

DENMARK

Coastal Conditions & Hazards

Denmark has a varied coastline facing both the North Sea and the Baltic. The western and northern coasts of Jylland (Jutland) consist primarily of long sandy beaches and high sand dunes all the way to the northeastern tip of the country, the Skager which faces out on to the Skagerrak separating Denmark from southern Norway. The west and northwest shores of Jylland take the full brunt of North Sea storms, and it is not uncommon for segments of the coast to redefine themselves during such tempests, with sand bars moving or being created anew and harbour entrances becoming silted up.[490] The stormy season is typically from October to March, with strong winds generally coming from the NNW and SSW and creating high seas and 'winds of force 10 can occur on occasions when deep East-moving mobile depressions transit the region, and usually give rise to very high and confused

seas near the storm center'.[491] In the winter months sudden rapidly moving squalls are another common feature of the North Sea, and are generally associated with cold fronts.

Once a ship passes through the Skagerrak, to enter the Baltic Sea it must sail down the eastern shore of the Danish Peninsula through the Kattegat, a myriad of islands and narrow shipping channels that separate Denmark from Sweden. One of the biggest dangers to navigation in this area comes from the immense volume of vessel traffic in confined waters and the subsequent risk of collision. Here, the roughest seas generally occur when a secondary depression is created over the Skagerrak or strong NW winds blow over the Kattegat. South of Copenhagen the worst sea conditions are created by strong to gale-force winds from the E or SE. Ice conditions may become so severe as to hinder navigation through this area approximately one year in 10.[492]

History of Coastal Lifesaving

When writing the brief histories of the individual rescue organisations, one discovers a common bond in their origins – the bond of shipwreck and the long lasting effects suffered by witnesses. Perhaps no greater nautical tragedy could be imagined than that which unfolded before the childhood eyes of the founder of the Danish Lifesaving Service on Christmas Eve 1811. On that day two English warships, the *St George* and the *Defense* were wrecked near Sønder Nissum and an astounding 1,337 men perished with only 13 said to have survived.[493] The child who witnessed the horror was C.B. Claudi, who would eventually become the 'Commissioner for the Supervision of the Dunes' in Denmark.[494] Claudi's lifelong ambition was to create a coastal rescue service that would help eliminate the carnage, particularly off the west coast of Jylland.

In 1845 Claudi travelled to England at his own expense, with the express purpose of studying the organisation and workings of the relatively new Royal Institution for the Preservation of Life from Shipwreck. On his return he espoused the virtues of the English system and the need to establish a similar service in Jylland. Initial interest resulted in private contributions for the construction of two lifeboats. The first was paid for by the 'Society for the Propagation of Navigation' and placed on the Agger Canal, while the second, complete with air cases, was donated by the Freemasons and stationed at Flyvholm harbour in 1846.[495 496] By 1847 the government had decided to put forward a sum to establish preliminary stations in Denmark and send Claudi to England once again, this time to purchase rescue apparatus and to check on the workings of the fledgling RNLI. On his return a commission was appointed to study the issue on a national basis and to decide on the best placement for the new resources. By 1851 20 stations had been established throughout Denmark and in the following year the Danske Redningsvaesenet (Danish Life-Saving Service) was officially established with Claudi appointed as the first superintendent. He would remain in this position until his death in 1909; 58 years in the service of lifesaving.

Under Claudi's stewardship the organisation continued to

expand and included the brief provision of a patrolling service. By 1912 there were 69 stations nationwide including 'fifty-four stations equipped with boats, and fifty with rocket apparatus', and, in its first 60 years, the service saved 8,837 lives.[497] Unlike many rescue services that developed in neighbouring coastal states during the latter half of the 19th Century, the Danish service was non-volunteer. It was similar to the service in Belgium, with crewmembers receiving an annual salary as a retainer for attending drills, rescues and beach patrols. Most still maintained other employment and only worked for the service when called.

The early lifeboats were clinkerbuilt of oak and equipped with brass air-cases at either end. They were pulling boats described as 'insubmersible and self-emptying', but not self-righting. They were all essentially light-weight surf-boats of the Dutch type, averaging about 30ft (9.3m) in length, just over 8ft (2.5m) in beam, and drawing a mere 12in (0.3m) for ease of shore-launching. They were mounted on a carriage and manned by a crew of 12 comprised of, 'one coxswain who directs the boat, ten men at the oars and one "petty officer"', leaving one wondering just exactly what the petty officer did?[498] There is also mention of two larger vessels, possibly lifeboats, which had drop keels, as well as a 'light American surf-boat' based at Thyborøn.[499] The MLB was introduced to Denmark in 1914 and initially was not a resounding success (see Chapter II-12). The next MLB purchased was apparently modelled after the English Watson, which was also equipped with sails and a much larger 40-hp motor. Eventually a lighter 35ft 6in (11m) version powered with a 25-hp Fordson engine was developed for beach-launching and surf work. The increase in effectiveness and range provided by the MLBs meant that many rowing lifeboat stations were closed and by 1928 there were 13 MLBs in service. Most of the early Danish lifeboats were built in the shipyard of the Naval Arsenal in Copenhagen. Over the years considerable expertise must have developed in the construction of rescue craft as lifeboats would be built there for 'Sweden, Portugal and, in one case, Holland'.[500]

The emergence of the MLB in Denmark was gradual and many pulling surfboats were maintained until well after the end of the Second World War.[501] Most of the Danish lifeboats were eventually stationed at harbours or launched on slipways, but seven stations remained on the Jylland coast where lifeboats were launched from the beach. In these places the boathouses were essentially on the beach, within about 100yd of the sea, making long-distance conveyance unnecessary. Due to this close proximity to the surf, combined with a gradual slope to the water, a rather unique Danish method of beach launching developed using a number of iron rollers. For such stations Danish MLBs were built with three keels that allowed them to remain upright when aground, a series of iron rollers was placed under each keel and the lifeboat glided into the ocean. On the boat's return from service winches were used to haul it back up into the boathouse, which was invariably high up the beach to take full advantage of any natural incline. Once again, ingenuity proved a prerequisite for the success of the early lifeboat organisations.[502]

Danske Redningsvaesenet (Farvandsvaesenet)

Operating Model: Civilian Agency Managed by Government

Manning Structure: Employee/Volunteer Crew

Source of Income: State Funded

Today the sea rescue service in Denmark is still a state-run operation and is administered by the Pilotage and Coastal Rescue Branch of the Royal Danish Administration of Navigation and Hydrography. The service has approximately 220 full-time staff and volunteers at a variety of stations operating heavy-weather and medium-endurance lifeboats, fast rescue craft, and mobile beach- and cliff-rescue units. Lifeboat design in Denmark remained fairly traditional up to the 1970s when a new type of rescue vessel was developed. Sadly, during a rescue operation outside the harbour of Hirtshals on the northwest coast of Jylland in 1981 one of these new craft, the RF-2, capsized with the loss of six of its crew. Various commissions examined the tragedy and it was discovered that the inherent stability of the boat was insufficient for proper self-righting and a completely new approach was taken to lifeboat design which would re-incorporate some of the more traditional features of the original lifeboats. As a result, two new lifeboat designs were initiated, the MRB Type 20 or Nordsø class, and MRB Type

The 16.5m (53ft) Danish lifeboat *Morten Stage* at the 18th ILC, Bournemouth, 1999. A somewhat smaller version of the traditional Danish MLB, this vessel is self-righting and has a top speed of 20kt. *Author's Collection*

23 or Kattegat class. The 64ft 4in (20m) Nordsø class returned to fundamentals with a rounded stern, full displacement hull, and maximum speed of 11kt. The first of the type was delivered in 1989 and, at over 50 tons displacement, cannot be considered 'lightweight'. With a steel hull which is ice-strengthened, double-shelled and divided into 17 watertight compartments (14 of which are filled with foam), an aluminium superstructure and a 5-ton

towing winch, the type is well suited for the notorious west coast of Jylland. The Kattegat class are larger, at 74ft (23m), and a little less traditional in design with a semi-planing, round-bilged hull and a softly rounded transom stern. They cruise at 17kt and, at over 60 tons, are the largest self-righting lifeboats in the world except for the German rescue cruisers.[503][504] In addition to the Nordsø and Kattegat types, the Danske Redningsvaesenet also operates several large, 29ft 4in (9.1m), RHIs, providing a combined rescue fleet of 35 vessels. These operate out of 26 shore stations augmented by 12 mobile vehicles.

The agency mandated for SAR in Denmark is the Ministry of Defence. Through the MRCC located at Århus and the ARCC at Karup, a variety of resources can be tasked. On the marine side, beyond the inshore scope of the lifeboat service, the navy provides dedicated platforms based on standby at Esbjerg, Thyborøn and Skagen. While the airforce provides SAR dedicated H-3 helicopters based at Ålborg, Skrydstrup and at Værløse, which also has long-range C-130 Hercules transport aircraft with airdrop capability. The Danish SAR mandate includes coverage for the Faroe Islands as well as Greenland.

ESTONIA

Coastal Conditions & Hazards
The independent Baltic nation of Estonia has a 2,358-mile (3,794km) coastline bordering on the Gulf of Riga to the west and the Gulf of Finland to the north and includes the islands of Hiiumaa and Saaremaa, which extend from the western part of the country to form a natural breakwater for the Gulf of Riga. The sea is relatively shallow here, with a maximum depth of only 32ft (10m) and there are extensive shoals. As in many other inland seas, the effects of tide are almost non-existent, any changes in sea level generally being the result of storm surges. Storms in the Gulf of Riga can produce waves in the 19ft (6m) range in winter months and can result in extremely dangerous conditions. The Gulfs of Riga and Finland only completely freeze over during extreme winters, while the channels on the western shores and the inland waterways, including some 1,400 lakes and 420 rivers, typically freeze up from January to April.

Winter storms in the Baltic have always been renowned for their suddenness and ferocity and have, over the centuries, been the curse of large ships and small coastal vessels alike. On 28 September 1994 the large roll-on/roll-off passenger and car ferry MS *Estonia* was en route from the nation's capital of Tallinn, bound for Stockholm, when her bow door was blown off in large seas. In less than 30 minutes after her initial mayday call, the *Estonia* lay on the sea bottom, having taken her 931 passengers and crew down with her. Only 137 people were lucky or fit enough to survive in the frigid waters until helicopters arrived from Finland, Estonia, Denmark and Sweden. The loss of the *Estonia* was a wake-up call for the international marine community, reminding all that modern technology does not make mankind immune from the vagaries of mother nature.[505]

History of Coastal Lifesaving
After the First World War, Estonia became an independent state and in 1921 had already formed a voluntary non-governmental lifeboat organisation called 'Poseidon'.[506] Records indicate that an RNLI Liverpool-type MLB, the *Vilsand*, was in service in Estonia in the 1920s.[507] Because Estonia had both an extensive saltwater and a freshwater coastline a lifeguard service was also established under the auspices of the Estonian Red Cross in the 1930s, but it would appear that both organisations ceased to exist following the Soviet occupation of the country during the Second World War. In 1956, however, a new voluntary lifesaving service was established, 'and training of specialists started again' with several new stations being constructed.[508] In 1971 the Eesti Vetelpaasteuhingu, a voluntary organisation that received considerable state funding was founded with the objective of combining the responsibility of coastal lifesaving and beach water safety into one organisation.

Eesti Vetelpaasteuhingu (ELA)
Operating Model: Non-Profit Voluntary Organisation
Source of Income: Private contributions & State Subsidy
Manning Structure: Volunteer Crew/Seasonal Employee

The objective of the ELA was to provide 'for the search and rescue of people in distress on the coastal waters, guarding on the beaches and encouraging children and adults to learn to swim, and teaching competent swimmers the methods by which a drowning person might be saved'.[509] In 1992, the year after Estonia regained her independence, the ELA had a fleet of 50 motorised rescue craft and one large rescue cruiser. There were 15 dedicated lifesaving stations on the outer coasts and 23 seasonal ones inland. However, it seems that many of the vessels were in dire need of repair, and were insufficient for their assigned duties. In 1993 Estonia received a Rother-type lifeboat from the RNLI, which was later stationed at Haapsula. More ex-RNLI lifeboats have been procured in recent years and in 1995 the ELA received a fleet of three Nimbus 26 RHIs from Sweden. As of 1998 there were reported to be 10 active lifeboat stations in Estonia.

Maritime SAR in Estonia is co-ordinated out of the main MRCC at Tallinn and MRSCs at Kuressaare, Kärdla and Narva Jõesuu. There are also two rescue radio stations located at Ruhnu and Kunda, as well as coast radio stations at Pärnu and Tallinn.[510]

FINLAND

Coastal Conditions & Hazards
Finland has a vast coastline consisting of approximately 180,000 islands, as well as myriad narrow channels and waterways. In addition, there are over 60,000 inland lakes used extensively for pleasure boating. The rocky sea coast borders on the Gulf of Finland to the south, and the Gulf of Bothnia to the west. Over 100 large ships transit daily

through the Gulf of Finland during the peak shipping season. The shallow nature of these waters is aptly defined in the *Baltic Pilot, Volume III*:

Navigation in the Gulf of Bothnia and the Gulf of Finland requires constant vigilance as many of the channels are narrow, shallow, and filled with shoals; maximum use should be made of all available aids to navigation.[511]

Although the effects of tide and current in the open waters are minimal, some of the narrow channels have much stronger funnel currents, and severe gales can create storm surges that can flood low-lying areas. Owing to the comparatively limited fetch of the Baltic Sea, large oceanic swells are a rare occurrence; in their stead, the Baltic has been known to produce steep wind-driven seas, which are predominantly found at the entrances to both gulfs in late autumn and winter.[512] These vicious seas, with a relatively short period between crests have been known to overwhelm and drive ships under; it was such conditions that caused the loss of the passenger ferry *Estonia* on 28 September 1994 (see 'Estonia' p.217). With much of the country located above the Arctic Circle, most of the Finnish coast is frozen from December to May. But shipping continues with the use of powerful escort icebreakers and ice-strengthened ships. Prior to the introduction of the lifeboat society in Finland, all sea rescue was conducted by vessels of opportunity such as local fishing vessels or pilot craft. Numerous were the tales of calamity along Finland's western coast and in the Gulfs of Bothnia and Finland. Not only did mariners lose their lives in the frequent winter gales that rolled in over the Baltic Sea, so did landsmen who set out to fish from the ice floes, only to find themselves drifting out to sea as the ice broke up in the same storms.

History of Coastal Lifesaving
The earliest measures to provide relief to the shipwrecked in and around Finland probably began in the Middle Ages on the Åland Islands (see 'Åland Islands' p.193). In Finland itself lifeboat stations began to appear as early as 1821 when records indicate that a boat was provided for Suursaari Island. This station was originally established by the government and had a paid crew, although eventually the local populace took it over as a voluntary organisation.[513] In 1855 the government opened another lifesaving station on Puolimatkansaari Island, apparently manned by the Russian garrison there. (Russia itself did not have a lifeboat service until 1872.)

In the early 1870s a committee led by the Finnish Pilotage Administration was established to review the state of lifesaving facilities in Finland following a series of tragic and notable shipwrecks. Initially the committee recommended that a full government station be established at Hanko, at the southernmost tip of the country, and by 1874 there were plans for 12 more of the state-run stations. By 1878 three more lifeboats had been built, described as 'large, covered

maritime rescue boats', stationed at Haapasaari, Rönnskär and Harmaja, but the momentum faltered.

Around this time a local voluntary lifesaving society had been established on the west coast of Finland at Vaasa and before long similar localised organisations followed including one at Viipuri in 1886. An umbrella organisation, the Finnish Society for Rescuing Persons in Distress at Sea was established in the 1880s to help coordinate the local bodies. With the obvious success of similar private lifesaving organisations in other European states during this period, the Pilotage Administration, which had been running the government lifeboats, began to transfer its rescue facilities to the voluntary societies.[514] Two shipwrecks occurred in the 1890s that would solidify calls for a more unified national lifesaving service. In 1892 a collision occurred between the *Ajax* and the *Runeberg* with the loss of 38 lives, and the following year 137 men were lost from the Russian military transport *Rusalka*, which sank in the Gulf of Finland.

In 1896 many prominent members of society, most of whom had connections with Finland's marine affairs began to discuss the concept of a more efficient national voluntary society. They included Nikolai Sjöman, Director of the Pilotage Administration, a man who had served in the Russian Navy and was well aware of the recent successes and growth of the Imperial Russian Lifeboat Society. As a result of their efforts, on 27 March 1897 Suomen Meripelastusseura or SM Finland was officially formed. In 1897 Finland was still considered a semi-autonomous province of Imperial Russia and at the time the lifeboat society was founded many Finns were seeking full autonomy from the Tzar's control. The inevitable climate of suspicion resulted in many attempts to crush any sign of assembly or organisation within Finland. It is a testament to the universal sense of philanthropy that surrounded the need to establish rescue facilities at this time that the Russian aristocracy not only did not interfere with the establishment of the society, but Tzarina Maria Feodorowna became the protector of the new organisation.[515]

In the early years the society used both pilot cutters and their crews. Many other crews were drawn from the island dwellers surrounding the coast of Finland who used local boats. In 1898 SM Finland sent its first Director, master mariner G.H. Roos, on a fact-finding mission around Europe. He visited the lifesaving services of Russia, Sweden, Norway and Denmark and returned deeply impressed with the Scandinavian concept of cruising lifeboats. In the end, however, the society decided that shore-based boats were right for Finland and three English-style pulling and sailing lifeboats were launched in 1900 and stationed at Valassaari, Koivisto and Lavansaari. They had been built in Finland at the yard of A.J. Backman, and were probably of the Watson type, then in favour in Britain (see Chapter II-11).[516] As SM Finland expanded, the now-typical red boatsheds of the lifeboat service began to spring up throughout the islands. The boatsheds contained 'lifejackets, manila rope, line throwing apparatus and skis and sleds for rescue from the ice'.[517] A lifeboatman's duty did not always cease when the waters froze. In 1912 the society built its first MLB based on a German design; she was built at the Andrée & Rosenqvist Yard in Turku and stationed the following year at Hanko.

The First World War brought work on new lifeboats to a halt and although the aftermath saw a newly independent Finland, the society entered the developmental doldrums. The economic chaos of the 1920s and 1930s saw remaining equipment fall into disrepair. A series of shipping disasters in the early 1930s, including the loss of the ships *Draken*, *Kustavi* and *Kuru*, revitalised interest in upgrading facilities and in 1935 the first Finnish cruising lifeboat, the 60ft (18m) *Outdoori* was launched from the Turku boatyard. This new cruising lifeboat had five watertight compartments and, in addition to its ketch-rigged sails, was powered by twin 80-hp diesel engines with the propellers housed in protective tunnels.[518] At about the same time, seven new shore-based motor lifeboats in the 34ft (10.4m) range were ordered and built in Finland, based on the RNLI's Liverpool type and having a single 70-hp kerosene/petrol Wickström engine. In 1937 it was decided that the shore-based boats should be somewhat bigger and should have more cabin structure and enclosed spaces for protection from the extreme cold of winter. Thus, future versions of the shore-based units were in the range of 43ft (13m) and were powered by two 50-hp to 70-hp Wickström engines. These larger MLBs were also based on the Liverpool design. In addition, a specialised MLB, the *Anna Gadd*, had been purpose-built for working around Turku by the local chapter of the society.

SM Finland continued to save lives during the Second World War. In 1944 lifeboats and crews from the southern lifesaving stations of Hanko and Utö were responsible for saving 50 lives and 10 ships. After the war the society began a period of reconstruction. Stations and vessels began to cater to an ever-increasing pleasure-boat population as the Finnish economy continued to diversify and grow. In the 1950s SM Finland began a switch to the construction of steel lifeboats and the cruising MLB, *Isokari*, was built in Finland based on the design of the contemporary Swedish lifeboat, *A.E. Appelberg*. The society continued to strengthen and solidify its organisational structure in the post-war years and began to adapt more efficient administrative and operating procedures. During the 1960s three more large rescue cruisers, the *Niilo Saarinen*, the *Gustaf Erikson* and the *Wilhelm Wahlforss* were launched, followed by a small rescue-boat building programme which began in the 1970s, principally aimed at providing more rapid SAR coverage for the coast, as well as shallow-draught lifeboat coverage for the very popular inland lakes.[519]

Suomen Meripelastusseura, SM Finland
Operating Model: Non-Profit Voluntary Organisation
Source of Income: Private Contributions and State Subsidy
Manning Structure: Volunteer/Employee Crew

The Suomen Meripelastusseura also known as SM Finland, remains primarily a volunteer organisation with the entire operation being managed by only six permanent staff in the central office. In addition, there are four salaried coxswains on the larger rescue cruisers. Finances have always come from volunteer contributions but in the 1930s considerable funding was gained from the proceeds of slot machines – a revenue source that continues to this day. In addition, SM Finland receives an annual state subsidy raised through a form of lifeboat levy on commercial shipping. Both the Finnish Coast Guard and Marine Administrations maintain a seat on SM Finland's Board of Directors. In 1997 there were 11,000 members of the society.

Today, the society has approximately 82 rescue craft in service, including 10 large lifeboats in the 53ft to 79ft (16-24m) range. These larger boats include the original Finnish cruising lifeboat, the *Outdoori*, built in 1935, and still in service at Uusikaupunki; a large 75ft (23m) ex-German rescue cruiser, the *Ossi Barck*, and a new 79ft (24m) Finnish-built rescue cruiser based out of Helsinki called the *Jenny Wihuri*. This last was launched in 1999, is of aluminium construction, has a stern ramp for an 18ft (5.4m) RHI and is driven by water-jets producing a cruising speed of 20kt (see colour section).[520] There are approximately 72 other smaller rescue vessels, as well as some 42 auxiliary boats, primarily RHIs, on the inland lakes. In recent years the trend seems to be towards shallow-draught jet-powered vessels such as the 37ft (11.25m) EMPA 95 class, and the 53ft (16.25m) MPA 90 (Rajakari class), both constructed of aluminium. Larger RHIs have also found favour, such as the impressive C-4000 RIB. This 43ft (13m) vessel, built of GRP, is powered by twin 350-hp diesels and has a maximum speed of 34kt.

The Finnish lifeboat *Rankki*, a 39ft (12m) aluminium, water-jet rescue craft capable of speeds in excess of 30kt. *Eastpress/Seppo J. J. Sirkka*

From 1930, when official records for SM Finland began, until 1997, the organisation was directly responsible for saving 1,309 lives, rescued 28,780 persons from serious danger and assisted some 10,030 vessels. In 1996 alone society lifeboats and crews were called out 580 times and were responsible for saving 21 lives. Additional maritime SAR resources include the Finnish Frontier Guard, which encompasses the Coast Guard and is the government agency responsible for SAR in Finnish waters. The Coast Guard operates a number of vessels and maintains a regional MRCC at Turku and two sub-centres at Helsinki and Vaasa. Air resources are provided by the Finnish Air Force, which maintains a fleet of Super Puma helicopters and other maritime patrol aircraft. Nevertheless, SM Finland remains the only agency, public or private, whose sole responsibility is the provision of marine SAR.

FRANCE

The French MLB *Ville de Paris* went into service in 1980 stationed at l'Ile de Seine.

Philip Plisson

Coastal Conditions & Hazards

The coast of France can be broken into four principal areas each with extremely different environmental conditions and hazards. These include the eastern shores of the Dover Strait, the English Channel, the Bay of Biscay and the coast of southern France, bordering the Mediterranean. Natural hazards to shipping in the Dover Strait include the shallow waters, which rarely exceed depths of 130ft (40m), and the shifting sandbars and sandwaves created by wave action in the winter months. There are also strong tidal currents due to the narrow nature of the Strait which, in a fresh gale, can produce a large, steep sea with a very short period between crests. There is limited natural shelter and the incredibly large volume of vessel traffic, which proceeds along and across various traffic lanes, results in its own form of organised chaos. The coast of Normandy, along the southern shores of the English Channel is exposed to the vagaries of the North Atlantic and is consistently blasted by east-moving low-pressure systems in winter. Rough seas occur along this coast in the order of six to seven days per month in winter and a large W to WSW swell is also commonplace.[521][522]

The west coast of Brittany, along the Bay of Biscay, is very similar in geography to that of the north, with significant rocky headlands and many outlying reefs and islands. Eventually however, the topography levels out and low-lying beaches and sand dunes become more predominant towards the border with Spain. The Bay of Biscay is fully exposed to North Atlantic storms and through history has been associated with fearful winds and massive waves, which at times appear to arrive from all directions. In the days of sail, and well into the era of mechanised propulsion, many fine ships simply disappeared in these waters. The Bay of Biscay is also notorious for poor visibility and westerly gales that produce heavy swells. In fact, 20% of all weather observations in the winter months report a heavy or very

heavy sea with winds of Force 8 or higher averaging seven to nine days per month. A local wind phenomenon, the Galernas can wreak havoc on the unwary mariner in the summer months when sudden and violent NW squalls occur with the passage of a cold front, the winds being intensified by the adjacent high ground along the Northern coast of Spain.[523] Finally, along the French Mediterranean coast from the Golfe du Lion to the Côte d'Azur varying wind and sea conditions prevail. In the westernmost region, the effects of the Mistral are widely felt when, in winter, NW winds of Force 5 to 6 funnel down the Rhône Valley creating dangerous conditions for small craft offshore. Also in the winter months, persistent SE winds known as the Marin may occur to cause a considerable swell and rough sea along the outer coasts. Violent squalls and downdraughts along the steeper areas of this region caused by the wide temperature variation between land and sea at certain times of the year are not uncommon.[524]

History of Coastal Lifesaving

The French relationship with coastal lifesaving dates back to 1765 and the experiments of Monsieur de Bernières and his 'unsinkable and uncapsizable skiff' (see Chapter II-2).[525] However, despite early efforts, it would be many years before any vestige of organised lifesaving would grace the coast of France. In 1824-25, at approximately the same time as facilities were being established in adjacent countries, local humane societies began to appear on France's Atlantic seaboard. The earliest of these was the Société Humaine de Boulogne (see Chapter I-8). Other locally supported lifeboats were established at Dunkerque, Calais, Le Havre, Marseille, Grau du Roi and Honfleur,[526] but most eventually fell into disrepair as political turmoil and a lack of continuity ruled the day. Others, such as that at Boulogne, survived through the support of local benefactors and merchants.

In 1854 one Monsieur Th. Gudin, who had tragically lost his brother to shipwreck, attempted to gain support for an organised national lifesaving institution in France, probably inspired by the re-emergence of the national lifeboat service in Britain at that time. At first Gudin met with minimal support but in 1861 the French Government recognised the dire need for a national service and set about establishing an inter-departmental committee to look into the concept. Gudin and other enlightened supporters of the cause decided to follow the British model and the Société Centrale de Sauvetage des Naufragés (SCSN) was formed by the official decree of Emperor Napoleon III on 17 February 1865. This new central body immediately set about coordinating the remnants of the local societies and promoting the establishment of additional facilities where they were in need. The new society, partially administered by the state, met with resounding success and expanded at an incredibly rapid rate. Within five years there were 40 lifeboats stationed around the coast of France and by 1890 the number had doubled. Stations were even established outside France in the colonial possessions of Corsica, the West Indies and French North Africa. One of the Directors of the SCSN,

Emile Robin, became very instrumental in the development of lifesaving services in other countries and helped to purchase lifeboats and other rescue equipment all over the world (see Chapter I-11).

From its origins, the SCSN closely followed the RNLI in operating structure, although it did receive support from the French government in financing the establishment of new stations. Coxswains received an annual stipend, volunteer crews were paid for training and call-outs and operating funds were derived primarily from private contributions. The service also maintained lifesaving apparatus as part of its overall responsibility. By the turn of the century there were over 500 stations in France. Various styles of boat were constructed for the differing demands of specific areas and local lifeboatmen. The committee, which helped establish the organisation in 1865, adopted the Standard Self-Righting design of the RNLI and over 100 of these were built (see Chapter II-8). The SCSN also built several non-self-righters similar to the RNLI's Liverpool, which were 'uncapsizable' and self-bailing. Another early French lifeboat design was the Henry. Like the boats of American inventor, Joseph Francis, and some early German lifeboats, these were constructed of steel (see Chapter II-9). They had considerable breadth and, although not self-righting, were termed 'uncapsizable and insubmersible'.[527]

In 1873 another lifeboat service was established for the coast of Brittany. La Société des Hospitaliers Sauveteurs Bretons (HSB) was originally formed to provide assistance to the families of lifeboatmen lost or injured in the cause. This all-volunteer society soon expanded its humanitarian endeavours to assist the shipwrecked and establish rescue stations and lifeboats on the coast and rivers of this part of France. The HSB was an extremely progressive organisation and, in addition to the above causes, promoted such other safety ideals as the establishment of commercial fishing schools, insurance for seafarers, greater safety regulations, and the promotion of navigational and nautical safety inventions, to name but a few. The society was also one of the first European lifesaving organisations to actively promote the holding of international conferences 'with rescue services of other nations to discuss safety at sea and other rescue matters'.[528] It had been one of the fundamental tenants of Sir William Hillary, founder of the RNLI, to promote international cooperation in the cause of coastal lifesaving back in 1824, and the motives of this French Society, along with the continual support to fledgling foreign lifeboat services provided by Great Britain throughout the 19th Century, would eventually lead to the establishment of the International Lifeboat Conferences starting in 1924.

By the early 20th Century, both French societies were flourishing. The SCSN even operated a 374-ton rescue steamer with smaller lifeboats onboard at the entrance to the Gironde. In 1904 some of the first attempts at developing a MLB in Europe were conducted by the HSB, but with limited success. The first successful MLB in France would enter service in 1912 (see Chapter II-12). Further mechanisation of the two fleets was delayed by the First World War and sailing lifeboats were still being commissioned as late as 1923.[529] The devastation of the Second World War essentially wiped out most of the facilities of both services. After 1945 massive efforts at restoring the lifeboat service were undertaken by both the SCSN, which envisaged some 56 new MLB stations. Led on by its new President, Monsieur Lepeltier, the HSB rebuilt all its pre-war facilities.

The economic boom of the post-war era heralded an unprecedented upsurge in waterborne leisure activities, especially in France. In 1958 Paul Renault became head of the HSB and soon realised that the organisation, and indeed the MLBs themselves, could not keep up with the volume of call-outs and the increasing need for rapid response. Many of these calls were beach oriented and did not always warrant the launching of a large MLB. Renault devised two solutions. First, he realised that there was a need for secondary stations, mostly on a seasonal basis, at which smaller, faster rescue craft would be placed. The concept of the inshore rescue boat, or IRB was thus born. Secondly, he decided that the type of craft best suited to this purpose was the small inflatable boat, or Zodiac, then becoming popular in France. The vessel had good sea-keeping qualities, was relatively low cost, portable, easy to operate and required low-level maintenance (see Chapter II-20). After the 9th International Lifeboat Conference, in Edinburgh in 1963, many countries, including Great Britain and Canada, developed IRB programmes of their own. Inflatables are probably the most widespread rescue craft in existence today and their origins can be directly attributed to the pioneering work of the HSB.

Société Nationale de Sauvetage en Mer (SNSM)
Operating Model: Non-Profit Voluntary Organisation
Source of Income: Private Contributions and State Subsidy
Manning Structure: Volunteer Crew

In 1967 the French Government felt that the public would be better served if both primary societies were merged into one organisation and on 1 January 1968 formed the Société Nationale de Sauvetage en Mer (SNSM). This new state-run organisation would be funded by a combination of national and local governments, as well as voluntary contributions. The combined rescue fleet was quite substantial: by 1974 the SNSM boasted 274 lifeboat stations (including seven in the Caribbean), which had 286 inflatable inshore rescue boats between them.[530]

As of 1995 the SNSM consisted of approximately 160 lifeboats and 200 inflatable rescue boats located at 161 lifesaving stations in France and her overseas possessions. The SNSM has volunteer crews for its vessels: the 'Sea Lifesavers' are approximately 4,000 full-time volunteers who operate year round, in both the lifeboats and the inflatables, while the 'Seasonal Rescuers' are approximately 2,000 young men and women hired for the summer months to work at roughly 300 summer IRB stations, generally near busy beaches, from where they report to local officials. The SNSM carries out about 40% of all the rescues on the coast of France.[531]

Starting in 1986 the SNSM began a major modernisation and standardisation of its lifeboats into three classes. These were the 58ft (17.6m) 'all weather' MLBs of which 21 were to be built; these vessels are powered by two 380-hp diesels and have a top speed of 22.5kt. A new medium-endurance lifeboat came in at 48ft 6in (14.8m), is self-righting and unsinkable; it has the same engine and horsepower as the all-weather boats but, due to its semi-protected propellers, has a top speed of 18kt. As of 1995 there were plans to build 30 such vessels. The third class of smaller lifeboat was to be in the 23ft to 30ft (7-9m) range and have a top speed of 25 to 30kt. Plans were also in effect to build up to 40 of these high-speed vessels (see Chapter II-23).

The overall responsibility for the provision of maritime SAR in the waters of France rests with the Maritime Area Commander of the French Navy. Coordination of SAR is conducted by an inter-departmental maritime commission, which operates the various regional centres for surveillance and rescue, similar to those of HM Coastguard in the UK. There are principal MRCCs in France located at Criz Nez, Jobourg, Corsen and Etel. The lifeboats and IRBs of the SNSM work in close conjunction with other state-funded marine organisations such as the French Navy, Customs, Gendarmerie and Home Office, in addition to the fixed- and rotary-wing resources of the French Air Force.

GERMANY

Coastal Conditions & Hazards

Germany has two separate and distinct coasts. One is on the North Sea between The Netherlands and Denmark. It has low-lying beaches, shifting offshore sandbanks and numerous barrier islands including the German Frisian group and the Island of Sylt to the north. There are extremely strong tidal and estuarine currents in this region as several large rivers, including the Ems, Weser, Elbe and Eidar, flow out here. When confronted by a large east-moving North Atlantic depression and its associated winds these currents can whip the sea into a fury of massive surf and blinding spray as large seas break over the shallow bars. The region has been the graveyard of thousands of vessels over the centuries. The Baltic shores, where a generally steeper foreshore predominates with cliffs in many areas, also has extensive coastal shallows, particularly in the southwest. To the west there can be extensive seasonal build-up of ice, and strong outflow winds are quite common from the Danish islands and channels south of the Kattegat. While relatively infrequent, storm surges also cause concern here. In 1872 a storm surge driven by strong and persistent easterly winds raised the coastal sea level approximately 10ft (3m) and caused severe damage to parts of Germany and Denmark. In 1995 a northerly wind caused a similar surge in the range of 5ft (1.5m), but on this occasion the German Storm Flood Prediction Service provided considerable warning.[532] [533]

The DGzRS crew of a pulling lifeboat heave hard on their way to a shipwreck during a winter's storm.
DGzRS

History of Coastal Lifesaving

The earliest introduction of organised coastal lifesaving facilities in and around what would become Germany (the country was a unified entity from 1871) involved the provision of one or two Greathead lifeboats in about 1802 (see Chapters I-5 and II-5). It would seem that both the Prussian Government and local shipping interests may have had a vested interest in establishing these measures on both the North Sea and Baltic coasts, but, like so many others, both the idea and the lifeboats rapidly deteriorated. In 1854 it was reported that an English-style lifeboat, of the self-righting type recently designed by James Peake had been built; it was to be the first of several new boats and stationsmanned by volunteers but administered by the local pilotage authorities (see Chapter II-8).[534]

In spite of these well-intentioned but rather localised measures, dozens of shipwrecks and loss of life continued almost unabated along the greater part of the German coast. In November 1854 for example, the emigrant ship *Johanne* departed Bremerhaven, her many passengers bound for a new life across the great Atlantic. The ship had barely reached open sea when the weather turned foul. For days the ship and the nearly 200 men, women and children onboard were tossed about within sight of shore. Eventually the badly-leaking ship was stranded off the East Frisian island of Spiekeroog and 84 people were lost with many more suffering serious injury.[535] Yet, in spite of this tragedy, the carnage continued until local officials took on the responsibility of aiding the shipwrecked. In the vicinity of Emden, where one of the first local lifeboat institutions was established, one of the founders, Georg Breusing, stated that 'seventy-six ships ran aground on our coast from 1854 to 1861, and 118 people lost their lives. Most of them could have been saved'.[536] Further tragedies, such as that of the brig *Alliance* that went down with all hands northwest of

Borkum in 1860, served to reinforce the efforts of men such as Breusing. The lifeboat concept spread: local societies were formed in Hamburg, Bremerhaven and Bremen on the North Sea and, soon after, at Kiel, Lubeck, Rostock, Stettin and Danzig on the Baltic.

Eventually, there were increasing calls for a national organisation along the lines of the RNLI. In Bremen, a navigation instructor, Adolph Bermpohl, and a lawyer, Carl Julius Kuhlmay, joined George Breusing in his pursuit of a national lifesaving service. These three were instrumental in establishing the local societies that would be the forerunners of the national service. But it would not be until 29 May 1865 that a consolidated attempt would be made under the leadership of Dr Arwed Emminghaus of Bremen and a national organisation, the Deutsche Gessellschaft zur Rettung Schiffbruchiger (German Society for the Rescue of the Shipwrecked), or simply the DGzRS, was formed.[537]

This new institution would be based in Bremen and its first president would be the prominent businessman, H.H. Meier, founder and Chairman of the North German Lloyd Shipping Line. Within 10 years of its inception the society would boast 91 lifeboat stations on the North Sea and Baltic coasts and over 870 lives saved. Such rapid growth and success must have been well-received vindication. By 1885 the DGzRS had taken over all the local societies, including the state-operated stations in Prussia and, by the turn of the century, there were over 120 stations established 'and more than one thousand voluntary lifeboatmen were at the institution's disposal'.[538]

The original lifeboats were primarily pulling and sailing boats based either on the original design of James Peake (these boats being transferred from the Prussian Government), or the American Francis-type patented surfboat (see Chapter II-9). The DGzRS found the metal craft quite promising, particularly its shallow draught and flat skeg, both advantageous features for shallow-water launching. Over time several modifications were made to the design and steel became the material of choice. The Germans also conducted some of the earliest experiments in the development of MLBs, including the introduction of less volatile diesel engines (see Chapter II-12).

The First World War had a devastating effect on the DGzRS, membership fell off and the large financial reserves became a total loss through depreciation. From 1925 considerable effort was placed in motorising the existing smaller pulling boats, which were either slipway- or carriage-launched. Smaller, lighter diesels became the motors of choice, the Germans quickly realising the fallibility and dangers of early petrol engines. In 1926 two new steel single-screw MLBs, 38ft 6in (11.7m) in length were built, and another, the *Hindenburg*, the first twin-screw MLB for the DGzRS at 45.5ft (13.9m) in length. All three were destined for the North Sea. The *Hindenburg* was stationed at Borkum, while the *Bremen* and *Hamburg* were stationed at Nordenoy and at Friedrichskoog on the west coast of Holstein (see Chapters II-12 and II-14).[539] The modernisation effort between the wars combined with the installation of wireless communications in the lifeboats allowed the DGzRS to

reduce its rescue stations to 101, with 84 lifeboats and 68 rocket installations in service by 1939.[540]

By the end of the Second World War what had been one of the greatest lifeboat institutions in the world once again lay in ruins, and now that the German Democratic Republic had been formed in the east, the activities of the DGzRS were confined to West Germany, which had a mere 23 rescue stations. Undaunted and with temporary government support, the DGzRS began a process of financial and infrastructure reconstruction. Its fleet had diminished to a few of the original 28ft (8.5m) and 34ft 6in (10.5m) light beach MLBs, and a few 43ft (13m) and 56ft (17m) heavy MLBs all of which were in the 7 to 9kt speed range.[541]

After 1945 the DGzRS began a programme that would eventually culminate in the first designs of German 'rescue cruisers', large self-righting lifeboats capable of almost unheard of speeds in excess of 20kt. The new style also had the revolutionary feature of a daughter boat on a stern launch-and-recovery ramp. (For a complete overview of the development of this vessel type see Chapter II-14.)

Deutsche Gessellschaft zur Rettung Sciffbruchiger (DGzRS)
Operating Model: Non-Profit Voluntary Organisation
Source of Income: Private Contributions
Manning Structure: Employee/Volunteer Crew

Since its inception in 1865, the DGzRS has evolved into one of the most inspirational and efficient lifesaving organisations in the world. Operating large 'rescue cruisers' the society has promoted the 'daughter-boat' approach to lifeboat operations and is one of the few privately operated lifeboat organisations granted the mandate to control and operate an MRCC on behalf of its country's government.

The society has established an astounding record of lifesaving: as of the year 2000, more than 65,832 individuals owed their lives to the German lifeboats. Today the DGzRS consists of 54 vessels, including two of the large 144ft (44m) offshore rescue cruisers, 17 of the standard rescue cruisers and 36 inshore rescue craft. The organisation employs over 200 full-time personnel, primarily as crew on the larger vessels, with a small administrative and maintenance staff. There are also over 500 volunteers stationed across the country, primarily crewing the smaller inshore vessels, as well as thousands of volunteer fund-raisers and support personnel spread amongst the various local chapters of the organisation.

On 9 October 1990 only six days after German re-unification, the first rescue mission of a re-integrated DGzRS took place in what had been East German waters when the crew of two yachts were rescued in high seas in the Baltic. The cost of re-establishing the DGzRS in the unified territory has been high. Several new lifeboats have been required and resources were also needed for the establishment of the necessary infrastructure to re-initiate a privately funded lifesaving organisation throughout unified Germany.

The DGzRS also operates the Maritime Rescue Coordination Centre (MRCC) in Bremen, which tasks all the maritime SAR resources for the country. In addition, the DGzRS has 16 SAR control points along the German coast to support vessel operations and assist in communicating with the MRCC. The service maintains over 40 logistics storage depots at various locations with such items as spare engine parts; some of these depots also serve as bases of operation for the smaller inshore units.

The DGzRS is entirely supported by voluntary contributions and has only relied on government subsidy during the reconstruction periods following the two world wars. The fund-raising machine is very impressive. In 1994 the DGzRS raised DM 22.9-million in operating funds, over 76% of which was raised by member donations alone. The DGzRS works in close conjunction with other elements of the German maritime SAR system, which comes under the umbrella of the Federal Ministry of Transport. The German SRR includes a large section of the continental shelf in the North Sea, and the Bremen and Berlin Flight Information Regions (FIRs) in the Baltic Sea. The German Navy maintains an RCC at Glucksburg, which is utilised to assist in disaster scenarios, high seas SAR and aeronautical incidents, while the German Luftwaffe maintains an ARCC at Goch. In addition to the DGzRS's own internal radio-communications network, there are also two coast radio stations (CRS) located at Norddeich and Elbe-Weser. The German maritime SAR net can also rely on vessels of the Navy and Frontier Guard. The Luftwaffe maintains a fleet of SAR-capable Sea King helicopters based at Westerland on Sylt, Heligoland, and Borkum, as well as medium-range Bell UH-1D helicopters at Jever. Fixed-wing resources include long-range Atlantic-patrol aircraft based at Nordholz.[542]

The rescue cruiser remains the principal craft of the DGzRS; various derivations of this versatile lifeboat have been constructed. In addition to the two 144ft (44m) class vessels still in operation, the DGzRS maintains a fleet of six rescue cruisers of the 90ft (27.5m) Berlin class, seven of the 76ft 6in (23.3m) Eiswette class, four of the 62ft (18.9m) Otto

The DGzRS has a fleet of 18 27ft (8.5m) intermediate lifeboats that operate from bases ashore.
DGzRS

Schulke class, and the original pocket rescue cruiser, the 55ft (16.8m) *Paul Denker*. As of 2002 construction is also underway on a 160ft (49m) replacement for the John T. Essberger-class rescue cruisers (see Chapter II-23).

On the inshore side, the DGzRS maintains two shallow-draught 40ft (12.2m) lifeboats as well as five 29ft 6in (9m), eighteen 28ft (8.5m) and five 23ft (7m) lifeboats. There are also four 23ft (7m) mobile carriage-launched rescue boats towed behind special four-wheel-drive vehicles. The 28ft class lifeboats are the most recent arrivals combining the attributes of the other smaller vessels. Utilising the same incredibly strong 'rib-net' style of frame construction as the larger vessels as well as seawater-resistant light metal these vessels have a range of 150 miles at 17kt.

GREECE

Coastal Conditions & Hazards

The waters surrounding the mainland and islands of Greece conceal hundreds of shipwrecks, many of which are the working places of marine archaeologists from around the globe, while countless others rest undisturbed. Most of these vessels, some dating back to the ancient days of Homer, were victims of the thousands of rocks and reefs that are interspersed among the approximately 1,400 islands within Greek territory and which make up approximately 1/5 of the country's total land mass. Added to such physical hazards are the unpredictable weather and wind conditions that predominate at certain times of the year and can result in sudden, powerful squalls and storms.

Greece borders on the Ionian Sea to the west, the Mediterranean Sea to the south and the Aegean Sea to the east. Weather patterns in each of these areas are similar in many respects although strong regional winds can be found. In the Ionian the Bora and the Scirocco winds are the most infamous. The effects of the Bora, a strong NE wind that blows mostly in winter, are felt predominantly in the Adriatic. Cold winds funnel off the mountains of the Dalmatian coast and can produce hurricane-force winds offshore. The Bora is also renowned for its unpredictability and the potential speed of its onset. It has been known to catch the unwary seafarer offguard and too far from shore to reach shelter. In the Ionian the Bora is also called the Gregale. The Scirocco, on the other hand, is more predictable but just as dangerous. A southeast or southerly wind it blows from the Sahara desert at various times throughout the year and is associated with warm, humid conditions; it can produce a large SE swell along the Greek coast and visibility can be reduced due to the sand and dust carried across the Mediterranean from North Africa. In the Aegean, between Greece and Turkey, the effects of the Scirocco are somewhat broken by the natural barriers of Crete and the Cyclades archipelago, but the mountainous nature of the islands in this region can produce localised storms. The *British Admiralty Sailing Directions* offer the following caution for the Aegean region:

The area is occasionally affected by vigorous depressions and it is also subject to gales and squalls, which are often local phenomenon caused by topography. These storms can be violent and can develop with great rapidity so that little or no warning is possible.[543]

Today, the coastal waters of Greece are cruised by hundreds of thousands of yachtsmen from all over the world. Cruise and merchant traffic is heavy and there are many inter-island ferries. In 2001 two large passenger vessels foundered in Greek waters with significant loss of life.

A 60ft (18.6m) Arun class lifeboat of the Hellenic Coast Guard. Ten of these stretched versions of the RNLI lifeboat are stationed at strategic locations around Greece.
HCG

Hellenic Coast Guard (HCG)
Operating Model: Civilian Agency Managed by Government (Para-Military)
Source of Income: State Funded
Manning Structure: Employee Crew

There is no information available, to this writer's knowledge, of any organised measures to assist the shipwrecked in Greece before 1919 when the Mercantile Marine Administration was created. This government agency, which would evolve into today's Hellenic Coast Guard (HCG), had, as part of its official mandate, the responsibility for 'the protection of human life at sea', in Greek waters.[544] Like many similar state-operated coast guards around the world, the HCG also eventually took on the additional responsibilities of law and customs enforcement, ship inspections, public education, port activities, vessel traffic control and environmental protection. The organisation was made a ministry of the government in 1936 and by 1990

boasted a combined fleet of approximately 159 vessels, from small inshore rescue boats right up to large offshore cutters and four fixed-wing aircraft.[545] As an example of the magnitude of vessel traffic in the region, between 1985 and 1990 vessels and crews of the HCG responded to some 68,105 rescue missions, 6,555 of which were deemed to be life threatening.

As of 1999 a specific SAR focus has been initiated within the HCG following the purchase and construction of 10 new 60ft (17.9m) self-righting MLBs, based on the British Arun-type boats (see Chapter II-21). These new lifeboats, named HCG *511* through *520* have been strategically placed around the various coasts and outer islands of the country to ensure adequate all-weather SAR coverage and to provide resources in locations that have been historical hotspots for SAR. In addition to the new lifeboats, the service has also purchased four new Super-Puma rescue helicopters capable of carrying up to 15 survivors and operating over a range of 180 nautical miles.[546] All these new SAR resources are responsible to, and tasked by, either the primary joint marine and air RCC (JRCC), located at Piraeus, or one of the five rescue sub-centres located throughout the country. This method of administration was aimed at streamlining response and is a departure from previous operating procedures, which required approval from various levels, including, local harbour authorities and, in some cases, the military, before HCG resources could be utilised for lifesaving. The JRCC Piraeus is responsible for an SAR Region covering some 9,300 miles (15,000km) of coastline and 150,000 square miles (388,500sq.km) of ocean. In addition to its own vessels and aircraft, the HCG can call on ships and aircraft of the Hellenic Navy, as well as local police- and fire-department vessels and resources throughout Greece. Several strategically located large salvage tugs are on standby as well as a system of volunteer coastal lifeguards instituted after 1979.[547]

GUATEMALA

Coastal Conditions & Hazards
Guatemala borders on the Pacific Ocean to the west and the Caribbean Sea to the east; the entire coastline being only 250 miles (400km) in length. The eastern seaboard faces the Gulf of Honduras and is subjected to the occasional tropical revolving storm, or hurricane, in late summer or autumn. Such storms can produce 'mountainous and confused' seas, particularly ahead and in the path of the pressure centre of the system. The low-lying nature of the Guatemalan coast makes it particularly vulnerable to the deadly storm surges that can precede a hurricane.[548] The Pacific shores of Guatemala offer very few ports of refuge and heavy surf pounds the coast, particularly in a southerly wind. Hurricanes, although not as frequent on the west coast, do occur and are known locally as Cordonazos. Other prominent winds affecting maritime traffic are the winter northerlies, known as the Papagayos by the coastal fishermen of Guatemala and Costa Rica.[549]

Jefe del Estado Mayor de la Defensa Nacional
Operating Model: Military Agency Managed by
Government
Source of Income: State Funded
Manning Structure: Employee Crew

Responsibility for search and rescue in Guatemalan waters rests with the Ministry of National Defence and, in particular, the Guatemalan Coast Guard. The Coast Guard maintains dedicated rescue units at the principal naval bases on both coasts as well as on the major inland lakes and waterways. On the Atlantic side of the country there are seven stations at which multi-tasked SAR units are located, including the main naval base at Santo Tomás de Castilla, and on the Rio Dulce and Rio Motagua. Other units are stationed at Puerto Barrios, Puerto Livingston, Puerto de El Estor and Punta de Palma. The principal form of rescue craft are patrol boats including one 85ft (25.9m) vessel and three 65ft (19.8m) craft. There are also approximately 16 small patrol and rescue craft in the 16ft to 30ft (4.9m to 9.1m) range utilised in the Guatemalan Coast Guard's Atlantic region. On the Pacific side of the country, the main naval base is at Puerto Quetzal, and there are three separate sub-stations located at Lago Guija, Sipicate and Lago Amatitlán. Five Coast Guard patrol craft operate from these four bases.

The Guatemalan Coast Guard, like many other government maritime safety and enforcement agencies around the world, has a multitude of roles to fulfil. That said, one of its primary missions remains to protect and save lives at sea – a particularly onerous task during the holiday seasons when many Guatemalans take to the water for transport; approximately 75% of the country's SAR call-outs occur over the Christmas/New Year and Easter periods. Coordination of rescue services is conducted from the MRCC located at Guatemala City, which works in close conjunction with units of the Guatemalan Air Force and its SAR resources, namely two Bell helicopters and two Islander fixed-wing aircraft stationed at the Timehri Air Base.[550]

HONG KONG

Coastal Conditions & Hazards

The former British Colony of Hong Kong reverted to Chinese sovereignty in 1997 and remains one of the busiest commercial ports in the world. The territory of the now Special Administrative Region borders on the South China Sea and consists of approximately 240 islands with a combined total coastline in the range of 455 miles (733km). Weather and sea conditions in the archipelago are generally favourable although the climate is subject to the tropical monsoon. Maximum sea and swell conditions occur during the winter months and coincide with the strong winds of the NE monsoon. The steep and rocky nature of many of Hong Kong's islands give rise to local squalls and wind patterns, which funnel in various directions bringing havoc to small boats and motor sampans. Typhoons rolling in from the

South China Sea are not uncommon and average about one a month from July to September. Among the greatest hazards to shipping in the area are the ships and small boats themselves. The thousands of daily movements in and out of the area create innumerable close-quarter situations and collisions are frequent.[551]

Hong Kong Marine Police (HKMP)
Operating Model: Civilian (Para-Military) Agency
Managed by Government
Source of Income: State Funded
Manning Structure: Employee Crew

Established in 1842 as a means to provide some form of law enforcement within the waters of the British Crown Colony, this venerable organisation was initially referred to as the Hong Kong Water Police but was given its present name after a structural reorganisation in 1948. The principal duties of the original corps of two petty officers and 12 men were to curb illicit smuggling in and out of the port, as well as protect unwary mariners from coastal pirates. In 1848 one of the organisation's sailing gunboats and its crew of 17 were lost in a typhoon while on anti-piracy patrol. The first steam-powered gunboat came into service in 1870 and by 1894 most of the force's fleet had been mechanised; with pinnaces or launches for harbour work and larger offshore gunboats for coastal patrol work. By 1900 the number of staff had increased to nearly 200 officers and men and many great victories were won in battles with local pirates and gun-runners working between Hong Kong and the mainland during the early years of rebellion in China.

The battles with pirates continued well into the 20th Century and, although this aspect of saving life at sea might be somewhat removed from the general contents of this book, some of the events are no less noteworthy. For example, in September 1926, the steamer *Sai Kung* was seized by pirates off Tai Long Wan and its Indian piracy guard was murdered. The crew of the Hong Kong Water Police launch PL2 came upon the situation and started a pursuit, which continued ashore and ended in the capture of the rogues, two of whom were later hanged. In 1933 the Norwegian steamer *Prominent* was also captured by pirates, the entire crew being rescued by the police launch PL4. The scourge of the professional pirate seems to have ended in October 1947 when what was thought to be the last of the pirate strongholds within the territory of Hong Kong was raided by the Water Police, sending the pirate leader Lau Chun-ping fleeing into the hills never to be seen again.

The Marine Police have also always protected life from more common maritime perils, such as weather and shipwreck. In 1936 the officers and crew of three launches received awards from the Governor of Hong Kong for the successful rescue of the passengers and crew of the SS *Sunning*, wrecked and evacuated during the height of a typhoon. The following year the police launches were credited with saving hundreds of lives during the 'Great Typhoon' in which thousands were killed and three of their own vessels were destroyed. From 1936 to 1941 and the capitulation of Hong Kong to the Japanese, police launches were instrumental in saving many lives from Chinese and Hong Kong fishing vessels which were falling victim to Japanese gunboats. In June 1967 PL1, 2 and 3 rescued several survivors from a Thai International Airways jetliner that crashed in Hong Kong harbour. Five years later, in January 1972, one of the Hong Kong Marine Police's more famous rescues occurred when the massive *Seawise University* (Ex-RMS *Queen Elizabeth*) was destroyed by fire off Stonecutters Island. Launches rescued hundreds of passengers and crew; PL10, a harbour tug boat, took off 150 persons in one load.[552]

Today the Hong Kong Marine Police force is responsible for enforcing the laws of the Hong Kong Special Administrative Region on its territorial waters and outlying islands, which comprise some 714 square miles (1,850sq.km) of ocean. In addition to the responsibility for maritime SAR, the HKMP also has the duty of intercepting and stemming the flow of illegal immigrants from mainland China and other Southeast Asian nations.

As of 2001 the HKMP had a very diverse surface fleet of 145 vessels, including 69 inshore launches of various descriptions from small RHIs to fast jet-powered river patrol craft in the 52ft (16m) range. On the offshore and coastal patrol side there are also 76 larger vessels ranging from the 87ft (26.5m) Damen MkIII Divisional Patrol launches, right up to the large 130ft (40m) Divisional Command launches, PL3 and 4. New construction was in the works for six more inshore patrol launches and six more Divisional Patrol launches. In addition, the HKMP had also taken possession of five Dutch-built high-speed Damen Cougartek SS1500 Sea Stalker Interceptors for use in anti-smuggling patrols. Undoubtedly these extremely fast craft will also be useful for rapid response to SAR incidents.

By 2002 additional SAR resources had been purchased by Hong Kong's Government Flying Service (GFS) for use around the Special Administrative Region, including three new Super Puma AS332 L2 helicopters. The Hong Kong Fire Service has also constructed a new 'Command Boat', which has a top speed of 29kt and capacity for 600 survivors, its primary role being to respond to casualties involving large airliners. The fire service also maintains an airborne division, which can be used for maritime SAR and includes Sikorsky S-76 and S-70 helicopters and a Beech BE-20 aircraft. All these government resources now work in close conjunction with air and marine units of the People's Liberation Army (PLA) with annual joint SAR exercises becoming common practice (see 'China' p.214).

ICELAND

Coastal Conditions & Hazards

The island nation lies somewhat isolated in the North Atlantic, separated from the east coast of Greenland by the Denmark Strait to the west, and from Norway by 550 miles (887km) of open ocean to the east, with only the Faroe Islands between. The entire coast is approximately 1,100 miles (1,775km) long and is principally characterised by high, rocky shores indented by fjords, with many outlying islands and skerries. On the southeast coast, however, there is a low-lying stretch of coastline about 120 miles (193km) long, which has been formed over the centuries by the massive fluvial run-off from the interior glaciers. Over time the sediment has filled the fjords and extended into the sea. These gravel beaches have met their match in the heavy North Atlantic surf that pounds the region and which has gradually forced the large gravel deposits back towards the coast, creating a string of lagoons. Throughout the year, gale- and storm-force winds predominate but become most persistent in winter. In the Denmark Strait funnelling NE winds of extreme velocity are not uncommon. In 1931 the British Arctic Expedition, camped on the Greenland side of the Strait, recorded a consistent wind of 112kt before their anemometer was blown away. Like most areas with high mountainous coastlines and extensive fjords, incredibly strong and localised outflow and inflow winds occur along much of Iceland's coast and are an extreme hazard to small craft. The sandy shores of the southeast coast are treacherous because of the prevailing onshore wind and swell, which have driven many a fishing vessel aground. The high frequency of restricted visibility due to fog has also added to the area's reputation as the 'Cemetery of Iceland'. In the north and west, both pack ice and bergs can pose a threat to navigation, depending on the severity of the particular season.[553]

History of Coastal Lifesaving

Similar to other Nordic nations such as Sweden and Finland, some of the earliest laws of the land decreed that citizens of Iceland should provide whatever means were at their disposal to assist the shipwrecked.[554] The fishery was of supreme importance to the survival of the Icelandic people, with most coastal communities drawing their sustenance from the sea. In the early days it was not uncommon for fleets of small sail-driven fishing craft to be caught unawares offshore by a sudden gale. On 9 March 1685 just such a storm claimed 132 men of the coastal fishing fleet and on approximately the same date in 1700 136 more would be lost within sight of their loved ones onshore.[555] Lacking the population and resources of larger, more populous nations, the Icelandic people did what they could to rescue those in peril, but towards the beginning of the 20th Century a realisation had developed that to simply 'make do' was no longer acceptable. In 1888 Reverend Oddur V. Gíslason began promoting the cause of providing aid to the shipwrecked at the community of Stadur, in Grindavík. To further these goals he helped organise and fund lifesaving committees at various important fishing ports and also published a periodical on the cause called *Sea Rescue*.

Calamity along the rugged coast of Iceland had become an incredibly frequent occurrence with the rapid expansion of the offshore fishery and the arrival of thousands of steam and motorised fishing trawlers from many other nations. In

1903 the first of what would become a large network of coastal refuge huts was established, initially on the southern coast, with funding from the German Consul, after the loss of several German fishermen who had made it to shore only to succumb to exposure. In 1906 two ships ran aground off the western coast with the loss of 48 lives, while on the same day in Reykjavik harbour, another 20 people perished when the cutter *Ingvar* sank in sight of many of the inhabitants.[556]

In spite of such losses no further measures were introduced other than the refuge huts until 1925 when members of the Fisheries Association of Iceland established a committee of concerned citizens to propose a dedicated rescue service. This came after a disastrous year along the Icelandic coast when three steam trawlers and 80 men had been lost, most of them during what was called the 'Great Hali Banks Storm'. On 29 January 1928 a public meeting was held at which time the committee's recommendation to establish a national association with special responsibility 'to counter accidents at sea, drownings and other accidents and work towards the provision of help for people in peril at sea' was adopted. The result was the creation of the National Lifesaving Association of Iceland (NLAI). From this point on, Iceland's approach to maritime SAR, as well as survival training and accident prevention would change for the better.

The new organisation's primary motivation was to establish sea-rescue facilities and in 1929 they purchased their first lifeboat from the RNLI. It was a 35ft Standard Self-Righting type, the *George and Mary Berrey*, which had been stationed at Whitehills, Scotland, from 1901 to 1928 (see Chapter II-8).[557] The lifeboat was renamed *Thorsteinn* and was stationed in the southwest at Sangerdi. The second lifeboat, the *Herjolfur*, was stationed off the south coast in the Westmann Islands. The new organisation soon had local branches throughout the country and rescue teams were established to man the lifeboats, rocket-line and breeches-buoy stations, as well as to care for the houses of refuge strategically placed on the long stretches of uninhabited and inhospitable coastline. By 1937 there were six lifeboats in service plus a large rescue cruiser for offshore patrols (see Chapter II-15) and 26 rocket and line-throwing stations.

By 1947 the facilities had increased to 60 lifesaving stations around the country, and there were also 11 surfboats and a twin-screw MLB. In addition, there were now 18 coastal refuge stations, the first 11 having been established on the southern shores where they were primarily built on stilts above the sand and gravel, so that the drifts would blow beneath rather than against them. (Seven of these initial huts were funded by the emerging Women's Guilds of the local societies, a powerful organisational and funding source within the volunteer rescue movement in Iceland to this day.) Admirably, by 1947, one in six Icelanders had become a member of the NLAI. The rocket and line-throwing stations were highly successful and it was recently estimated that since 1928 more than 3,000 lives have been saved by this method alone. The NLAI has always fulfilled a second mandate of accident prevention and public education and from 1937 the association incorporated land-based accident prevention and assistance into its charter. In 1955 the NLAI

constructed their first fast rescue boat, the *Gísli J. Johnsen*, followed by the rescue cruiser *Albert* in 1957, which was partially funded by the government. This joint-funding regimen has continued in Iceland and has included financial support from both the state and the NLAI in 1965 for Iceland's first SAR helicopter, as well as two more in 1973. On 2 October 1999, the NLAI and Landsbjörg (Association of Icelandic Rescue Teams) amalgamated to form a unified land, air and sea SAR body known as the Icelandic Association for Search and Rescue (ICESAR).

Icelandic Association for Search and Rescue (ICESAR)
Operating Model: Non-Profit Voluntary Organisation
Sources of Income: Private Contributions and State Subsidy
Manning Structure: Volunteer/Employee Crew

The National Lifesaving Association of Iceland, NLAI, originally established as a sea-rescue organisation, has evolved into a national lifesaving and humanitarian entity on both land and sea and has gained incredible public support since its inception in the 1920s – out of a total national population of approximately 265,000, 30,000 are now members of the new combined SAR organisation known as ICESAR.

The association established by the lifeboat visionaries of 1928 has expanded into one of the more unique humanitarian organisations in the world today. ICESAR has over 214 branches throughout Iceland with about 100 rescue teams. To give the reader an idea of the community involvement, as well as the permeation of the humanitarian ideal into the Icelandic psyche, each branch is divided into separate teams for men and women, mixed teams and youth teams. In addition to the mandate of land, coastal and oceanic SAR and accident prevention and safety training, the association also runs the fully automated Icelandic Ship Reporting System (Duty) and the Icelandic MRCC, both managed from ICESAR headquarters in Reykjavik.

The organisation still maintains some 80 houses of refuge, which are fitted with emergency radio-telephones, food and first-aid kits. There is also a fleet of approximately 100 small inshore rescue craft (inflatables), and nine large heavy-weather lifeboats are maintained at six stations. Two ex-DGzRS rescue cruisers keep watch at Sangerdi and Siglufjorder, (see Chapter II-14). At Neskaupstadur and Raufarhofn, two ex-KNRM Carlot-class 66ft (20m) lifeboats are stationed (see Chapter II-13). There are also four ex-RNLI Arun MLBs stationed at Reykjavik, Grindavik, Isafjordur, and Rif (see Chapter II-21). One ex-NSSR lifeboat stationed in the Vestmannaeyjar Islands completes the heavy-weather fleet (see Chapter II-15).

ICESAR and the Icelandic Coast Guard maintain overall responsibility for the co-ordination of maritime SAR within Iceland's zone of responsibility and maintain an MRCC at Reykjavik. The Coast Guard also operates a network of five coast radio stations around the country. The Icelandic Air Force maintains an SAR flight at the Keflavik Air Station using Sikorsky HH-3E long-range helicopters and C-130 Hercules transport planes.

INDIA

Coastal Conditions & Hazards

The Indian sub-continent juts southward deep into the Indian Ocean creating, to the west, one side of the Arabian Sea and to the east, the western edge of the Bay of Bengal. On its southeast tip lies the Gulf of Manmar and the Palk Strait, separating India from Sri Lanka. There are approximately 4,350 miles (7,000km) of coastline, much of it low and estuarine. The climate is a product of the seasonal monsoons. Spring and summer, from June to October, is the time of the SW monsoon, while from December to March, the NE monsoon prevails. Off both coasts of India, the swell conditions generally follow the direction of the monsoon, with the SW monsoon producing the highest sustained winds. Off the west coast this is known as the 'fine weather season' even though gales of Force 7 and greater are not uncommon.

Along the shores of the Bay of Bengal, strong NW squalls can also occur close inshore, generally around the month of May. Also, during the SW monsoon, the 'Monsoon Burst' occurs and sustained SW winds of Force 4 to 5 prevail approximately 80% of the time over offshore waters. When large spring tides occur during this same period, many of the large rivers draining along the north and east shores of the Bay of Bengal, such as the Hugli, Meghna, Pegu and Sittang, are subject to dangerous tidal bores. These large standing waves creep their way upriver, consuming small and unwary vessels in their path.

One of the more notable marine hazards along the Indian coast – more prevalent along her eastern shores – is the tropical revolving storm, known locally as the cyclone. These concentrated weather systems can produce 'mountainous and confused seas' and 'in extreme cases an exceptionally huge wave (or storm surge) may precede the cyclone centre with catastrophic consequences'. Many of the floods that have claimed thousands of lives along the mouth of the Ganges and in Bangladesh have been a result of these surges.[558][559]

Indian Coast Guard (ICG)
Operating Model: Military Agency Managed by Government
Source of Income: State Funded
Manning Structure: Employee Crew

The Indian Coast Guard was officially established by an Act of Parliament on 18 August 1978 with the new organisation's official motto being 'Vayam Rakshamah', 'We Protect'. The creation of this new agency was a direct result of India's expanded claims to new offshore maritime zones and the need to exercise sovereignty over these areas. In addition, it was felt that a maritime law-enforcement agency was required to help deal with the increasing problem of seaborne smuggling off India's coasts. The ICG was modelled after similar state-run maritime safety agencies around the world, such as the United States Coast Guard and the Japanese Coast Guard and, as such, operates in parallel with the Indian Navy. It is considered one of the nation's military organisations.

Today the structure of the ICG is divided into three principal regions located in the west and the east of the country and in the Andaman and Nicobar Islands. Within these regions are several district bases and individual coast guard stations. Each region also has one or more coast guard air station. As the ICG is the principal maritime SAR co-ordinating authority for the Indian SRR, there are also rescue coordination centres in each of the regional HQs, located at Mumbai, Chennai and Port Blair respectively. Each region has divisional marine rescue sub-centres, which are generally co-located with coast radio stations. As of 2001, the ICG had some 23 small high-speed craft identified as 'interceptors', 15 inshore patrol vessels of the Thornycroft 110ft (34m) type, eight fast patrol vessels, and 12 large offshore patrol vessels with helicopter capability. The ICG also has one hovercraft in service, for use along shallow coastal waters and river estuaries. For airborne SAR the ICG maintains a fleet of 17 Dornier 228 fix-wing patrol aircraft and 17 Chetak single-rotor helicopters.

'The rescue of 11 persons from the ship *Alarm* of Belfast in Ballycotton Bay,' as published in the *Illustrated London News*, 14 April 1886.
National Maritime Museum, London

IRELAND

Coastal Conditions & Hazards

The shores of Ireland have been feared for centuries as the graveyard of thousands of ships and seafarers. Many of the hapless galleons belonging to the ill-fated Spanish Armada were lost on the craggy rocks and inlets of Ireland's west and northwest coasts as they tried in vain to return to their homeland. The western shores face the full fury of North Atlantic storms that can produce immense swells known to break in up to 100ft (30m) of water. Approximately one third of all the gales off the northwest coast of Ireland result in winds of up to storm Force 10; hurricane Force 12 is not uncommon and can result in 'confused seas of hazardous proportions', when sea and swell combine and begin to refract and reflect off a steep and irregular coastline.[560] On the east coast, the Irish Sea has claimed many a ship in its chaotic storm-driven waves, that can be very steep in form with a short period between crests – products of shallow waters and strong tidal currents. Both entrances to the Irish Sea, St George's Channel, and North Channel, are renowned for extremely rough seas produced by the funnelling effects of the wind. In January 1953 the Stranraer-to-Larne ferry *Princess Victoria* went down in the North Channel with the tragic loss of 133 passengers and crew. Along the Irish shores of St George's Channel from County Cork as far north as Dublin Bay there are numerous outlying rocks and islands. A greater hazard, however, particularly in the days of sail and early steam, were the offshore sand banks of the Leinster Coast, especially around the approaches to Dublin Bay. The southern shores of the island and the adjacent waters of the Celtic Sea have seen more then their fair share of tragedy including, in more contemporary times, the horrific storm that swept through the Fastnet yacht race in 1979. The heavily indented nature of the Irish coast also results in many local wind anomalies, such as unpredictable squalls and outflow winds in some of the inlets, all of which are perilous for small craft and deep-draught vessels alike.

History of Coastal Lifesaving

Prior to the introduction of dedicated safety measures in Ireland, such as lighthouses and lifeboats, the law regarding shipwreck was somewhat akin to the survival of the fittest. In fact, the Brehon Laws of ancient Ireland specifically stated that a man who survived a shipwreck was to be ensured hospitable treatment by any local coastal community proximate to the wreck, but that his surviving property was to be divided as spoil, whether he wished it or not, amongst the rescuers.[561]

Although the early Irish may have had a somewhat unorthodox approach to the rights of the shipwrecked, in later centuries this country would initiate some of the earliest and most progressive efforts at establishing an organised coastal lifeboat service in the world. The move towards such humanitarianism began as early as 1786 when the first independent Irish Parliament, recognising the need for safety measures around the approaches to Dublin Bay, set up the Dublin Harbour Authority. This organisation would establish the first dedicated lifeboat stations in the country starting in 1800. No doubt the strong trade links between Dublin and Liverpool, England, played a hand in these developments as the renowned William Hutchinson, who had helped establish the first recorded coastal lifeboat service in the world in Liverpool also played a part in the establishment of the fledgling Irish harbour authority (see Chapter I-5).

In 1800 the Corporation for Preserving and Improving the Port of Dublin – as the Port Authority was then called – received from the Irish Government the plans for Greathead's lifeboat (see Chapters II-4 and II-5). The Port Authority immediately set about ordering and constructing

three of these vessels for use around Dublin Bay. The first was built by John Clements of Dublin for £115 18s 9d and was stationed the following year at Clontarf. The second and third boats were also built by Clements and launched in 1803 and 1805, being stationed at Sandycove and Sutton respectively. Interestingly enough, the Irish stations were to be maintained by paid employees connected with the Port Authority. Unlike the early experiments with local lifeboats in England and Scotland around the same time, where a single boat was operated by a single community, the Irish experiment, like that of Liverpool and, to a certain extent the mouth of the Tyne, Northumberland, involved several vessels all belonging to a single administrative entity creating one of the first true lifeboat 'services'.

By 1820 there were some seven lifeboats in and around Dublin Bay, including additional stations at Howth, Dun Laoghaire and Pigeon House Dock. The proximity to the busy shipping lanes in and out of English ports as well as a massive increase in the amount of emigrant ships meant that the early Irish lifeboats were busy. Lives were saved and lives were lost, both shipwrecked and lifeboatmen alike. A good example of an early Irish lifeboat service occurred on 28 December 1821 when William Hutchinson, Haven Master for the Dublin Port Authority at Bullock and later at Dun Laoghaire, a man whose name would become synonymous with the early Irish lifeboats (and who would go on to win two gold and one silver lifesaving medals), responded to the wreck of the brig *Ellen* cast ashore in appalling conditions near Sandycove. In his own words:

> *It blew a most violent gale from the south-east...and on my arrival numbers of men were ready to launch the lifeboat. With a volunteer crew of 14 men, I embarked and with much difficulty reached the stern of the vessel, where we received a hawser to hold by. At this time the vessel was lying nearly head to the sea which broke completely over her, and while the crew (of the brig) were in the act of getting into the lifeboat she filled...while we were bailing out water with our hats a sea of which I shall never forget the aspect, overwhelmed the boat and washed six of us out of her. Two, fortunately, caught hold of the rope they had been holding by and three then unfortunately perished. I, with difficulty, regained the lifeboat and with the remainder of the crew were drove among the breakers without oars.[562]*

The account then went on to add that somehow, miraculously, the lifeboat made it to shore, although one more lifeboatman was lost, and the survivors then scrambled on to the beach whereupon they began to assist more survivors off the *Ellen*, which by this point had also been driven ashore through the breakers.

In 1824 Sir William Hillary's Shipwreck Institution was established in Britain and the effects of the universal approach to coastal lifeboats and lifesaving were being felt in Ireland with the implementation of the new society's system of awards and medals on both sides of the Irish Sea. In 1825 the first lifeboat medal, a silver, was awarded in Ireland to Coastguard Richard Ross of Rosslare for rescuing the crew of the ship *Mary and Eliza*. In 1826 the Shipwreck Institution established its first station in Ireland, at Arklow (it is still in existence today). As was the case in the British Isles, members of the Coastguard were instrumental in many of the earliest Irish lifesaving stations. The Irish Lifeboats and the Shipwreck Institution continued to work hand in hand for several decades allowing the Dublin Port Authority access to the latest in technological developments. Some of the original Greathead boats were replaced by Plenty-type lifeboats in the 1820s and later, after the Duke of Northumberland's Competition in 1851, with improved Standard Self-Righting lifeboats (see Chapter II-8).

From 1830 to 1860 Ireland was wracked by political turmoil and strife, and humanitarian efforts suffered. That said, the Irish lifeboats did remain in service, although manning and maintenance became a problem. Throughout this entire period William Hutchison, now Master of Pilots for Ireland, was in charge of the service, indeed he remained in the position until 1862 when the responsibility for the lifeboats of the Dublin Port Authority would be transferred to the RNLI. In 1852 there were but eight lifeboat stations in Ireland operated by both organisations. During the next 10 years this number would prove increasingly inadequate given the rising rate of shipwreck on the Irish Coast. In fact, between March 1850 and April 1858, no fewer then 142 large merchant vessels were lost between the Kish Bank off Dublin Bay and Carlingford Lough, where the counties of Leinster and Ulster meet.[563] One of the worst disasters in the area occurred on 19 January 1854, when the large clipper ship *Tayleur*, outbound from Liverpool to Melbourne, Australia, with 528 people onboard drifted in massive seas on to the shores of Lambay Island. Only three of the 250 women and children aboard survived. The following year the RNLI opened up a new lifeboat station at Skerries proximate to the wrecksite of the *Tayleur*. It was probably that disaster, and many others like it, that spurred the Dublin Port Authority into initiating negotiations with the RNLI in 1861 to transfer control of the port's lifeboats to the Institution. The means of the local port authority were insufficient to promote the expansion of a national service and the authority was having financial troubles of its own. In the end the RNLI agreed to upgrade all existing stations and provide the latest design of lifeboats for some, while the Authority would continue to provide an annual stipend of £50 towards their support. The end of an era had come.

Royal National Lifeboat Institution (RNLI)
Operating Model:　Non-Profit Voluntary Organisation
Source of Income:　Private Contributions
Manning Structure: Volunteer Crew

The RNLI is the principal coastal lifeboat organisation of both the United Kingdom and Ireland – in spite of the fact that the Republic of Ireland was formed in 1922 and with its formation came the severance of practically all ties to British influence. Although there were the inevitable detractors, those Irishmen who manned the boats knew that politics had no place in the world of the common seafarer, let alone in the realm of the lifesaver and so the Institution remained in Ireland. It was strong, efficient and provided excellent equipment, training, and support to its crews; there was no need to start afresh. Even during the Second World War when Ireland remained neutral, the Irish lifeboats of the RNLI sought no exception and saved hundreds of lives from casualties of conflict, wind and weather.

The RNLI remains a strong Irish institution to this day. Between 1985 and 1995 more new lifeboat stations were opened in Ireland than in any other district of the Institution. An Irish woman, Frances Gody, established a significant first in the history of coastal lifesaving when she became the first female crewmember of an all-weather lifeboat in the RNLI at the Dunmore East lifeboat station in 1981.[564] As of 2001 there were approximately 38 RNLI lifeboat stations around the coasts of both the Republic and Northern Ireland, including some 23 all-weather boats. The Irish lifeboats work closely with other SAR elements of the Irish Government as well as local community SAR groups and police forces. A particularly strong relationship exists with the resources of the Irish Coastguard (formerly known as the Irish Marine Emergency Service or IMES), which operates a network of coast radio stations and maritime rescue sub-centres (MRSCs) around the country and are jointly controlled through the principal RCC in Dublin. The Irish Coastguard operates in a similar fashion to its British counterpart having responsibility for the maintenance and provision of some 50 cliff- and shore-rescue units around the coast as well as operating a SAR helicopter service at strategic points in conjunction with the helicopter and fixed-wing resources of the Irish Air Corps. Three S-61 SAR helicopters and crews on long-term contract from CHC Helicopters of St John's, Newfoundland, are stationed at both Shannon and Dublin. On 6 March 2001 the Irish Coastguard helicopter from Shannon, along with a UK Coastguard helicopter and a Canadian maritime patrol aircraft, was instrumental in rescuing 10 crewmembers from the German-registered fishing trawler *Hansa*, which sank in the North Atlantic approximately 204 nautical miles northwest of Malin Head off the northern tip of Ireland.

ITALY

Coastal Conditions & Hazards
Italy has approximately 4,700 miles (7,600km)) of coast. The Italian Peninsula juts in a southeasterly direction into the Mediterranean Sea, with the Adriatic Sea to the north and east. Its coastline includes the larger islands of Sicily and Sardinia, and 70 smaller islands around the country. The west coast, facing the Tyrrhenian Sea, is one of the most seismically active regions on earth and there are strong indications of large seismic sea waves having occurred here throughout history. Various local winds wreak havoc on the

exposed west coasts, the more prominent of which include the Libeccio, a strong southwest wind that originates as far west as the Islas Baleares, the Tramontana from the north, and the familiar Scirocco which brings southerly winds and hot, dry Saharan air across the Tyrrhenian Sea. All these winds, when blowing over an extended period, can cause heavy swells, particularly in the case of the Scirocco at the most northern reaches of its fetch in the Gulf of Genoa. Strong katabatic winds are also common on both the Tyrrhenian and Adriatic coasts, particularly adjacent to the mountainous regions of the country where unstable air masses race down valleys and out to sea through river estuaries.[565]

On the Adriatic coast somewhat similar wind and sea conditions prevail. For the most part this coast is uniformly low, with sandy beaches and an almost constant string of tourist destinations. The northeast coast is backed by a low, marshy plain, through which flow myriad canals, rivers and channels. The entire Adriatic seaboard is subjected to the predictable effects of the Libeccio and the Scirocco, although it is also at the mercy of the much less predictable Bora. This phenomenon is a strong N or NE wind that can occur at any time of year but more commonly in winter. A cold, dry wind that can reach hurricane force as it blasts down from the Gulf of Trieste it can create extremely hazardous sea conditions along the Italian coast between Venice and Ancona.[566]

The number of marine SAR incidents in Italian waters is extremely high, principally because of the great number of yachts and pleasure craft cruising the coast. There are some 100,000 registered, and 600,000 non-registered pleasure craft in the country, not including foreign yachts. In addition, as of 1995, there were approximately 300,000 merchant ship movements in and out of Italian ports annually.[567]

History of Coastal Lifesaving
The recorded history of coastal lifesaving in Italy begins in 1871, when the Societa Italiana di Soccorso di Naufraghi (Italian Society for the Rescue of the Shipwrecked) was established. It would appear that the society was very active during the days of sail and that the main efforts at lifesaving were in the provision of lifeboats, rockets and line-throwing apparatus as well as awards and medals for private rescuers. By the turn of the century, however, and the switch to mechanised propulsion, the number of shipwrecks around the Italian coastline had begun to diminish significantly and so, too, had the demand for lifesaving services. By 1911 the Society decided to transfer its lifesaving resources to the 'Autorita Maritime', the Italian Ministry of the Merchant Marine. The Society then decided to focus its efforts on rewarding private individuals who rescued mariners in distress. In 1932, however, the Society did fund the construction of a motor lifeboat and the installation of wireless sets on fishing packers – vessels in constant transit around the coast as well as going to and from the offshore grounds. This latter measure was seen as an effective means of establishing a coastal radio monitoring system.[568]

Commando Generale del Corpo delle Capitanerie di Porto
Operating Model: Civilian Agency Managed by Government
Source of Income: State Funded
Manning Structure: Employee Crew

After the Societa Italiana di Soccorso di Naufraghi began to focus its efforts away from the provision of coastal lifesaving facilities it fell upon the state to fill the void. The Corpo delle Captanerie di Porto was established in 1865 to provide a co-ordinated administrative body for all the ports in a unified Italy. The individual port captains were responsible for all maritime matters within their respective jurisdictions, including law enforcement, customs and excise, registration of ships and, of course, the safety of mariners. Following the Second World War, the Corpo began to take on more specific lifesaving duties when they purchased the first all-weather Italian MLBs in the form of five 52ft (15.8m) Barnett-class vessels, all of which were constructed in Great Britain (see Chapters II-12 and II-19). Following the unveiling of the type at the 9th International Lifeboat Conference in Edinburgh, Scotland, 1963, the Corpo also purchased two USCG 44ft (13.7m) MLBs of the British Waveney type, which were powered by twin 200-hp Gardner diesels (see Chapters II-17 and II-21). Both were placed on the Adriatic coast at Ancona and Pescara. In addition to the 44 Footers, the Corpo also built two large rescue cruisers based on the German 'Maierform' design (see Chapter II-14)[569]. The first of these, CP 307, the *Michele Fiorillo*, was an 84ft (26m) design modelled after the DGzRS's rescue cruiser *George Breusing*, with a maximum speed of 24kt and a cruising range of 1,300 nautical miles. A second rescue cruiser, CP 312, the *Bruno Gregoretti*, was also constructed for the service in 1975, and was based on the Theodore Heuss-type of the DGzRS. She was slightly smaller at 75ft (23.3m), with a top speed of 19kt and a cruising range of 1,000 nautical miles. Both were considered high-endurance rescue craft to be used for offshore work. As of 1975 all the vessels operated by the Corpo, including the approximately 180 coastal patrol craft of various shapes and descriptions, were considered the property of the Italian Navy although operated by the Corpo.

Another interesting development was the introduction of the Inshore Rescue Boat or IRB. Also introduced at the 1963 Conference by the Breton Lifesaving Society of France, the idea of stationing seasonal rescue stations at strategic locations along the coast was especially adaptable to Italy with its extensive holiday beaches and tourist grounds (see Chapter II-20). By 1975 the Corpo had approximately 108 of these units in service used in combination with motorised caravans for accommodations;[570] this service has proven extremely versatile, affordable and effective, saving an estimated 1,500 lives in 1975 alone.[571] During the 1980s three stretched patrol versions of the RNLI's Arun-type lifeboat, CPs 313 to 315, were also constructed for lifesaving work (see Chapter II-21).

In 1989 the technical and operational components of the Corps were united to form a new arm of the service called the Italian Coast Guard, ICG. Soon after, a major vessel-building programme was initiated to replace the large fleet of coastal patrol craft and the various SAR vessels. By 1995 due to the increasing demands of international SAR conventions to which Italy had become a signatory, it was felt that specifically designed rescue craft should become dedicated for that purpose and no longer be multi-tasked for duties such as customs patrols and law enforcement. They were to be manned and available for call-out around the clock. It was also decided that the inshore SAR capability for the country needed to be significantly upgraded, and that a new, short-endurance lifeboat with excellent heavy-weather abilities would be required. The ICG had begun experiments with an Italian version of the 35ft (10.6m) Dutch Valentjin-class RHI as early as 1991 and by 1995 12 of these were in service with 14 more on order. They included several versions with totally enclosed wheelhouses to eliminate the need for a manually-operated self-righting apparatus. The Italian RHIs can cruise for 180 nautical miles at a top speed of 33kt; known as Type 800s, they now form the SAR core of the ICG, providing a two-hour SAR response time to the entire coast.[572]

Societa Nazionale di Salvamento (SNS)
Operating Model: Non-Profit Voluntary Organisation
Source of Income: Private Contributions
Manning Structure: Volunteer Crew

The Societa Nazionale di Salvamento (SNS) has roots that go back to 1871 when the organisation was founded in Genoa by such notable humanitarians as Professor Maragnano, who had worked on the development of the tuberculosis vaccine. The society must have had strong links with the Societa Italiana di Soccorso di Naufraghi, which was established the same year and the objectives of the two institutions were very similar, the SNS pursuing the fundamental goals of assisting the shipwrecked along the outer coasts, rivers and lakes and assisting the widows and families of mariners lost at sea, as well as educating the public in the resuscitation of the apparently drowned.

Today the SNS has evolved into the organisation that provides more of a public education and beach lifesaving role, although still keenly involved in all matters concerning safety at sea. In 1996 the SNS held an international conference at which some 50 separate nations attended. In 1998 the SNS became affiliated with the newly formed Italian Coast Guard Auxiliary with the two organisations working together in the pursuit of common goals of maritime safety and providing assistance to the ICG. The SNS is a primary civil protection agency for Italy, taking a major role in times of natural disaster or national emergencies. Aside from its primary water safety role, the SNS can also call upon its massive contingent of 5,000 volunteers to provide basic medical and first-aid services during such incidents. The SNS has also worked internationally, providing water safety and first-aid assistance in war-torn Kosovo during the most recent chapter in the collapse of the former Yugoslavia.

JAPAN

Coastal Conditions & Hazards
The Japanese archipelago consists of more than 3,200 islands and islets, as well as those surrounding the southern group of Okinawa. The principal islands in the north are Hokkaido, Honshu, Shikoku and Kyushu, which have a total national coastline in excess of 18,500 miles (29,751km). Weather follows the pattern of the monsoon, with the winter providing the most powerful wind and sea conditions, generally from the north and northwest. The summer monsoon brings warm and relatively weak southerly winds, although such conditions coincide with the typhoon season. These tropical revolving storms which generally form east of the Philippines and, on many occasions, slowly make their way north to bring destruction to coastal Japan. As is the case with any location that has high mountains, changing temperatures, and a massively indented coastline, many local weather patterns occur, generally in the form of strong katabatic winds that rush offshore after funnelling down the mountain slopes into narrow oceanic passages and channels. One of the most common perils to the unwary mariner however, and one which is duly noted under the 'Navigational Hazards' section of the three volumes of the Japanese sailing directions, involves the incredibly dense maritime traffic in Japanese coastal waters and the subsequent risk of collision. Such traffic conditions have brought the demise of many a fine ship and small craft.

History of Coastal Lifesaving
In 1888 Prime Minister Kuroda of Japan conducted a tour of European nations, including Russia, where he was deeply impressed with the workings of the Imperial Russian Lifeboat Society.[573] On his return to Japan, Kuroda visited a famous shrine devoted to the safety and protection of mariners located at Koto-hira in the Prefecture of Shikoku. The Chief Priest of the deity, known as the Konpira Shrine, was Hirotsune Koto-oka, who, after listening to the Prime Minister's description of the far-away service, felt that it was his civic duty to establish a similar organisation in Japan. Thus, in November 1889, using his own limited funds, Hirotsune established the Dainippon Teikoku Suiman Kiusai Kwai (DTSKK) – the 'Imperial Japanese Society for Saving and Succouring the Shipwrecked'. The new organisation received the support of certain members of the Japanese aristocracy including, most prominently, the Marquis Nabeshima. Although the new organisation was able to establish a few isolated stations, the passing of Hirotsune Koto-oka in 1892 meant that the society fell into a state of relative limbo for a number of years.

In the late 1800s and the early 1900s Japan's principal food source, other than rice, came from the sea and tens of thousands of inshore fishermen departed daily from coastal villages and harbours to eke out a living. As the population continued to increase in line with the industrialisation of the country so, too, did the size of the fishing fleet. By 1925 there were an estimated 42,000 Japanese-registered inshore fishing vessels. An organised coastal lifesaving force was more necessary than ever. In 1896 the Japanese Parliament requested that the government assume responsibility for organising a lifesaving service. Instead of creating a state-funded entity, the Japanese Crown Prince assumed the position of Patron of the DTSKK, and an annual public subsidy for the Society was established.[574] It was also at about this time that Count Kozo Yoshii became President of the organisation, a position he would maintain for almost 30 years. The Count was an ardent supporter of the cause of lifesaving in Japan and around the world. He stewarded the rapid expansion of the revitalised service in his home country and brought forward the idea of creating an international lifeboat body at the first international conference in London in 1924 (see Chapter I-11).[575] The new Japanese Society, which modelled itself upon the operating structure of the Spanish Lifesaving Institution, by 1899 had established '17 stations on the coasts of Japan fully provided with life-boats and life-saving apparatus, the boats being manned by volunteer crews'.[576] In that same year the Imperial Japanese Society was responsible for saving 1,211 lives and 269 vessels.[577]

By 1923 the Society had expanded immensely and boasted 83 lifesaving stations, including 176 rescue craft, most, if not all, of which were fishing vessels and coastal pulling boats with 9,700 volunteers to man them. By 1925 eight of the rescue craft were also motorised.[578] But it would not be until 1935 that the Society would begin to design and construct purpose-built MLBs based on European designs. These included three 40ft (12m), seventeen 50ft (15m), two 60ft (18m) and three 66ft (20m) lifeboats, the latter being based on the plans of the RNLI's fast rescue launch, the *Sir William Hillary*, built in 1929.[579] The first of these new purpose-built MLBs, the 48ft (15m) No.1 *Ryoha*, was launched in 1932 and must have been put to good use post-haste as the lifesaving statistics for the Society were rather astounding that year: there were an estimated 12,053 rescues and 64,173 lives being saved, most of which would have been related to the inshore fishery.[580] By 1935 there were 36 MLBs in service, it was also around this time that the Society decided to simplify its name to the Teikoku Suinan Kyusai Kai (TSKK) – the Imperial Japanese Lifesaving Institution.

Japan's infrastructure was all but destroyed by the ravages of the Second World War. The stations and lifeboats of the TSKK were spared none of the destruction and hardship. By war's end the once grand fleet of 214 lifeboats had been reduced to only 16 vessels and the Society had all but ceased to exist.[581] In 1948 the country was governed by the Allied Occupation Forces Command of General Douglas MacArthur and a decision was made to establish a maritime safety organisation, similar to that of the USCG, to be responsible for a multitude of tasks on the coast and oceans around Japan, including rebuilding the navigational aids and harbour entrances, hydrography, law enforcement and, of course, search and rescue. On 1 May 1948 the Japanese Maritime Safety Board was created to fulfil this overall

responsibility, with one of the satellite organisations being the 'Patrol and Rescue Group'.[582] As part of the national reconstruction programme, approximately 94 lifeboat patrol and rescue stations were established, strategically located at treacherous points on the coast and near high-traffic areas. The vessels provided were USCG 36ft SR-SB MLBs, two of which were generally co-located at any one station. In 1954 alone these new lifeboats were responsible for saving 593 lives and 110 vessels.[583] By 1955 the Board's fleet of resources had expanded to 303 patrol and rescue vessels, as well as six rescue helicopters. The political effects of the Korean War and Japan's lack of naval force (under the provisions of the post-world-war peace agreement) were undoubtedly two major factors behind this rapid expansion. The organisation is known today as the Japan Coast Guard and remains the primary maritime safety agency for the nation.

The concept of a non-governmental volunteer rescue service in Japan had not completely died, however. In 1948 the old Imperial Japanese Lifesaving Society was renamed the Nippon Suinan Kyusai Kai (NSKK) – the Japan Lifeboat Institution. By 1955 the NSKK had recovered somewhat from the years of conflict, with nearly 18,000 volunteers on its roster and a head office in Tokyo, as well as some 425 life-saving stations around the country using primarily owner-operated fishing vessels for rescue boats. The Institution was no longer subsidised by the government but instead received support in the form of equipment and training from the Maritime Safety Board. By 1963 the NSKK had 459 local lifesaving groups and 30 MLBs in service. Taking a page out of European operating models, the Society began to seek funds from large corporate donors and, in particular, those connected with the rapidly expanding Japanese shipping industry. By 1974 both the NSKK and the Japanese Maritime Safety Agency, or JMSA (the forerunner of today's Japan Coast Guard) were working closely together to save lives along the Japanese coastline. A prime example of this cooperation between the state-operated service and the volunteer society was the establishment of the Joint At-Sea First Aid Centre in October 1985. The Centre is operated around the clock with the objective of providing medical advice to ships and to establish a liaison between the ship, the nearest hospital and the Japan Coast Guard for patient transport.

Nippon Suinan Kyusai Kai (NSKK)
Operating Model: Non-Profit Voluntary Organisation
Source of Income: Private Contributions and State
                                            Subsidy
Manning Structure: Volunteer Crew

The primary objectives of the Nippon Suinon Kyusai Kai (NSKK) remains to save lives at sea and to assist in the preservation of property. With the establishment of the At-Sea First Aid Service this now includes the provision of medical services. Since its inception in 1888 the crews and rescue craft of the NSKK have been responsible for saving an awe-inspiring 187,018 lives from 35,899 vessels and other coastal mishaps.

A lifeboat belonging to Maritime Rescue Japan, formerly the Japanese Lifeboat Society. The rescue craft *Kyokuryu*, stationed at Inasa.
MRJ

As of 2002 the NSKK still maintained a large and efficient volunteer workforce of over 50,000 members, of whom more than 19,000 were directly involved in saving lives at sea.

The organisation is headquartered in Tokyo and is split nationally into 24 separate regions. The NSKK still maintains approximately 1,000 rescue stations around the country's extensive coastline with a wide variety of rescue craft at its disposal. Most of these are private fishing craft owned and operated by NSKk members. There are also 20 purpose-built rescue craft in the fleet, ranging from personal water craft right up to 66ft (20m) lifeboats, including such modern high-speed rescue craft as the 43ft (13m) Kyokuryu-class MLB, powered by twin 360-hp diesels with a top speed of 30kt. Funding comes from the Japanese Shipowners' Association and the Japanese Maritime Foundation as well as individual donations and contributions. All members receive basic compensation for call-outs as well as

PC 72, a 30m (97ft) patrol boat of the Japan Coast Guard carries out port inspection duties on deep sea shipping. Note the squared off bow and fender system to aid in boardings at sea.
JCG

insurance coverage for themselves and their vessels. Crews regularly exercise in rescue techniques as well as conducting research and development with new SAR and survival equipment. The NSKK conducts a very visible and popular fund-raising and public awareness drive every summer focusing on boating safety and saving lives at sea. This is known as the Blue Feather Campaign and, aside from attracting great public interest in the cause, serves to provide a considerable portion of the annually donated funds.[584] In 2001 the crews and vessels of the NSKK were responsible for saving approximately 500 lives.

Japan Coast Guard (JCG)
Operating Model: Military Agency Managed by Government
Source of Income: State Funded
Manning Structure: Employee Crew

The Japan Coast Guard (JCG) remains the chief maritime safety and coastal enforcement agency for Japan's maritime jurisdictions. In addition to the organisation's ever expanding role in SAR, other national obligations include peace and security, maritime traffic safety, marine environmental protection and, of course, international cooperation. The JCG is a very large organisation with a force of 12,249 personnel and, as of 2000, an annual budget of approximately 170-million yen. The JCG is headquartered in Tokyo and has a further 11 regional headquarters throughout the country. Each JCG Region has primary and secondary maritime communications and rescue coordination centres operated by the service. The JCG has a fleet of 517 surface craft, ranging from very large offshore patrol vessels right down to small coastal surveillance and rescue craft, as well as many specialised vessels for such tasks as buoy tending, hydrographic surveying and training. The JCG also has a large fleet of aircraft, including 29 fixed-wing units and 45 helicopters strategically stationed around the archipelago. Many of the JCG's aircraft have a primary SAR role, in particular the rotary-wing detachments with four Super Puma and seven Bell 412 machines, all of which work closely with the Special Rescue Section.

The JCG maintains a stand-alone SAR response unit known as the Haneda Special Rescue Section at the Haneda CG Station near Tokyo. First established in 1975 it is on standby 24 hours a day for rapid response anywhere in the country. There are five special rescue teams at the station, each comprised of six personnel, all of whom are trained in specialised rescue techniques such as underwater rescue and boarding vessels on fire. In 1999 the Haneda Special Rescue Section responded to 151 rescues and was directly responsible for saving 122 lives.

In 1999 the JCG responded to some 1,920 vessels in difficulty, assisted some 7,140 people in distress and conducted 178 medevacs. As of 2000 the organisation was implementing further initiatives to enhance its SAR role, principally through the re-positioning of some of its primary resources to provide better lifesaving coverage around the coast of Japan.[585]

MALTA

Coastal Conditions & Hazards

The Maltese archipelago consists of three main islands: Malta, Gozo and Comino. They lie in the Mediterranean approximately 58 miles (93km) south of Sicily and 143 miles (230km) from the North African coast. The history of Malta is inextricably linked to its strategic position in the world. Like a stationary ship at the crossroads of inter-continental trading routes, the islands were fought over for centuries yet the Maltese have also looked to the sea for their sustenance and survival.

The coastline spreads for some 87 miles (140km) with the ports being Grand Harbour, near the capital of Valletta, on Malta and Mgarr on Gozo. The Maltese coastline is indented by numerous small bays, creeks, sandy beaches and rocky coves. Climactic conditions are typical of the central Mediterranean region. Strong storm systems can strike in winter months and, on occasion, winds may exceed 60kt and waves can rise over 23ft (7m), breaching breakwaters and flooding coastal roads. Such storms are generally associated with the Gregale, a strong northeasterly wind that can occur when a high-pressure system exists over continental Europe and a low settles over North Africa. The most common wind comes from the northwest and blows about 40% of the time. In winter the Mistral can also bring weather problems to the islands' shores.

Armed Forces of Malta (AFM)
Operating Model: Military Agency Managed by Government
Source of Income: State Funded
Manning Structure: Employee Crew

A Super Vittoria SAR launch and an Alouette helicopter of the (AFM) practising hoisting operations.
AFM

Search and rescue in Maltese waters is the responsibility of the country's armed forces. The Maritime Squadron consists of three offshore patrol boats, four coastal patrol boats and two Super Vittoria class SAR launches. There are approximately 200 crew dedicated to the maritime arm of this service which is augmented by some 100 air crew belonging to the AFM Air Squadron. The squadron operates a fleet of two BN2B Islander fixed-wing aircraft for long-range patrols as well as five Alouette helicopters on 24-hour standby. These forces are directed by the 23 personnel at the Maltese Rescue Coordination Centre in Valletta, which was moved to a new facility in 2002. Recent upgrades to the provision of SAR in Maltese waters were to include the

commissioning of a new USCG-type Protector-class patrol boat in December 2002. From 1998 to 2001, the air and marine assets of the AFM responded to 1,562 SAR cases, assisting approximately 733 individuals in peril and saving an estimated 23 lives.

MOROCCO

Coastal Conditions & Hazards

The North African nation of Morocco has a total coastline of 2,175 miles (3,500km) extending from the Mediterranean and the Strait of Gibraltar in the north, down the Atlantic seaboard to the border with Western Sahara. There are approximately 26 harbours along its length, many of which have treacherous bars at their entrances. There are also long stretches that afford little safe haven for vessels and many fishermen still operate surfboats from these exposed beaches. Its profile from offshore is low and dangerous, with desert sand dunes extending outwards to meet the sea. The prevailing winds blow onshore and a large westerly swell produces a massive and practically impenetrable wall of surf. It was these conditions that made Morocco a natural trap for sailing ships and, if the local hazards did not claim those who ventured too close, there was also the terror of the Barbary Corsairs to consider. Northeasterly tradewinds prevail along the coast in the summer months and, occasionally, a hot, dry, south or southeasterly wind, known as the Simoun, brings clouds of dust from the deserts of Mauritania. A similar wind, called the Irifi, blows along the coast in spring and autumn bringing hazy air from the south and east and temperatures in the range of 38°C.[586] More than 100,000 Moroccans earn their living from the sea; most working on the approximately 20,000 fishing vessels of Moroccan registry, which range in size from small beach-launched surfboats to factory fishing trawlers.

History of Coastal Lifesaving

The coastal fishermen and boatmen of Morocco have braved the surf for hundreds of years and have undoubtedly saved thousands of lives in the process. Their early surfboats were large double-ended pulling boats, some with sails. A few of the larger surfboats, particularly those used in the vicinity of Rabat and Saffi, bore a striking resemblance to Greathead's original lifeboat and, according to Noel Methley in *The Lifeboat and Its Story*, both craft share a similar design genealogy (the *Original*'s design also owing much to Scandinavian and American influences; see Chapter II-5).[587]

In 1923 the Société des Hospitaliers Sauveteurs Bretons (HSB) began concerted efforts to establish a lifesaving service along those parts of the Moroccan coast under French colonial control. Initially it proposed three primary stations to be located at Casablanca, Rabat and Mazagan. These were to be equipped with line-throwing apparatus and the French Henry-type pulling lifeboat.[588] Funding was to come from a combination of voluntary contributions and port duties. There were also plans for the construction of seven more stations and lifeboats for other Moroccan ports. The HSB's efforts must have been effective as, by 1940, the International Hydrographic Bureau's *List of Lifesaving Stations of the World* included 13 lifesaving stations in Morocco, three having pulling lifeboats and one, at Casablanca, having an MLB.[589]

La Marine Marchande
Ministère des Pêches Maritimes
Operating Model: Civilian Agency Managed by
                                Government
Source of Income: State Funded
Manning Structure: Employee Crew

Following a Royal Decree announced on 9 September 1997 the principal responsibility in the Kingdom of Morocco for coordinating SAR operations was conferred to the Ministère des Pêches Maritimes (MPM). In order to achieve this objective the ministry maintains a fleet of twelve 60-66ft (18-20m) and eight 20ft (6m) rescue boats strategically located around the nation's coast and specifically designated for lifesaving. These surface resources are augmented by patrol vessels and aircraft of the Royal Moroccan Navy and Air Force. There are approximately 100 dedicated SAR personnel within the Ministry, 77 of whom crew the various rescue craft. The rest administer and coordinate SAR from the MPM headquarters and the national centre (CNRS) for SAR in Rabat and from the Moroccan MRCC in Casablanca, operated by the Merchant Marine. The CNRS coordinates and feeds information to four sub-centres around the country as well as to various coast radio stations and vessel traffic centres.

In recent years the MPM has focused on updating its SAR coordination and communication facilities to GMDSS requirements. Other initiatives include developing medical facilities available for seafarers at each large port and a national boating-safety campaign that has resulted in an annual decline in the average number of fatalities at sea. In 2001 personnel and rescue craft of the MPM assisted approximately 300 vessels in difficulty and saved 2,071 people.[590]

NAMIBIA

Coastal Conditions & Hazards
Namibia, formerly known as South West Africa, extends down the southwestern shores of the Horn of Africa a full 977 miles (1,572km) from Angola to the mouth of the Orange River and the border with South Africa. Its coastline is one of the most inhospitable on earth with the massive shifting sand dunes of the Namib Desert, some of which reach as high as 590ft (180m), forming the only backdrop. These shores have claimed many a vessel, both large and small, many of which are caught by the onshore set of the local currents. So numerous are the wrecks here that the area is sometimes referred to as the 'Skeleton Coast'. Today, many large wrecks that have been driven far ashore, sometimes

miles inland, are used as conspicuous radar targets for navigation, including the hulk of the SS *Eduard Bohlen*, wrecked in 1910 south of Walvis Bay, which remains in an upright position as if steaming through the desert. Phenomenal ocean swells, known locally as 'rollers', are not uncommon during the winter and are considered a serious hazard to coastal navigation. Created by ocean storms far offshore, these waves appear without warning and with no associated wind.

Throughout the year the coast of Namibia is subjected to a local anomaly known as the Berg wind, a hot and dusty gale from the east or northeast that can blow up to Force 7, acting like a natural blast furnace as associated air temperatures can be in the range of 40°C. At Walvis Bay, where Namibia's principal lifesaving station is located, local hazards include the relatively low nature of the coast which provides limited visual and radar references, particularly in restricted visibility, as well as strong easterly winds in winter, which can create a considerable sea in the bay itself.[591]

History of Coastal Lifesaving
Namibia gained independence from South Africa in 1990. Prior to this, lifesaving facilities in the country were maintained and operated by South African authorities. As of 1940 there were two South African government lifesaving stations located at Walvis Bay and Luderitz, both of which were equipped with tugs and line-throwing apparatus but had no dedicated lifeboats.[592] When the National Sea Rescue Institute (NSRI) of South Africa was officially registered on 15 October 1982, the South African government asked the non-profit organisation to arrange volunteer offshore rescue services for South West Africa and Mozambique as well. As a result, the first NSRI station in SW Africa was established at the port of Walvis Bay.

Sea Rescue Institute of Namibia
Operating Model: Non-Profit Voluntary Organisation
Source of Income: Private Contributions and State
                                  Subsidy
Manning Structure: Volunteer Crew

Following the country's independence, a new national coastal and offshore lifesaving organisation was established known as the Sea Rescue Institute of Namibia (SRIN). In 1994 when Walvis Bay was also incorporated into Namibia, the NSRI station became part of the SRIN. The objectives of the SRIN at the time of its establishment were described as 'to establish efficient lifesaving craft at specific points on Namibian waters, and undertake to organize and train crews capable of manning such lifesaving craft and boats at all times in cases of rescue or disaster'.[593] In recent years, as a result of the ever-increasing number of eco-tourists visiting Namibia, this mandate has been expanded to include the provision of surf (beach) lifesaving services and land SAR utilising all-terrain vehicles along the hundreds of miles of exposed beaches and sand dunes. SRIN Station #1 at Walvis

Bay remains the primary lifeboat station having an ex-RNLI Waveney lifeboat, the *Spirit of Standard Bank*, available for offshore service and to assist the Namibian Ministry of Fisheries and Marine Resources. Station #2, further north at Swakopmund, has taken on more of a beach lifesaving role to cope with the increases in beach tourism and inshore ski boat use. For this the station uses a small, portable RHI and an all-terrain vehicle. As of 2002, a third SRIN station is in the works, further south at Luderitz, where a new deep-sea port is being built.[594]

The SRIN is an all-volunteer-crewed organisation that relies primarily on voluntary contributions for its funding. The Institute does receive a small subsidy from the Namibian Ministry of Works, Transport and Communications as well as from local authorities, but the increasing costs of operations due to larger call volumes and rising maintenance requirements has meant that sources of additional funding need to be sought out. To this end, the SRIN Board of Directors appointed a designated fund-raiser in August 2000 with the aim of establishing more secure funding.

THE NETHERLANDS

Coastal Conditions & Hazards

The Netherlands rests on an alluvial plain most of which is below mean sea level, and the outer coast is essentially formed by an earthen dam that keeps the North Sea from pouring in. This natural and man-made barrier consists of large sand dunes fronted by extensive beaches as well as a string of offshore islands known as the Waddeneilanden, or West Frisian Islands, little more than large sand dunes themselves. The rest of the barrier is man made and, since the 12th Century, the Dutch have been reclaiming land from the sea through the construction of a massive network of dykes – over 3,100 square miles (8,000sq.km) of territory have so far been reclaimed.

The low profile of the coast and outer islands offers few natural features for navigating by and man-made structures must be used as reference points. There are many days of poor visibility and the combination of reduced visibility, shallow water and confined channels can be a challenging one. Rough seas are common from November to April. Winds from the NNW and SSW in the range of Force 10 are not uncommon and large seas pound the outer coast and break with great ferocity on the offshore banks. Waves can reach immense proportions and can be particularly aggravated by the conflicting currents sometimes found at the channel entrances.[595]

History of Coastal Lifesaving

The Netherlands has a strong history of coastal lifesaving. The Koninklijke Nederlandse Redding Maatschappi (KNRM), Royal Dutch Lifeboat Institution, is the product of over 175 years of organised lifeboat operations and the amalgamation of two separate Lifeboat Institutions in the northern and southern halves of the country.

Both the North and South Holland Lifeboat Institution (NZHRM), and the South Holland Institution for Saving the Shipwrecked (ZHRM) were founded in November 1824, just a few months after the Britain's Shipwreck Institution. Their formation was in large part due to the increasing public concern over the expanding number of shipwrecks and the enormous loss of life on the treacherous Dutch coast. In October 1824 the Dutch frigate *De Vreede* struck ground off the village of Den Helder, near the Frisian Gap, with heavy losses among both the shipwrecked and the fishermen who attempted to rescue them. This catastrophe solidified the calls for a more organised and reliable lifeboat service on the Dutch coast.[596] It should be noted that the lifeboats of these two organisations were not the first in The Netherlands. There is evidence to suggest that the government of West Friesland attempted to establish what would have been the first dedicated coastal lifeboat stations in the world as early as 1769 (see Chapter I-5). This was followed by a similarly ill-fated attempt to establish lifesaving stations initiated by the Dutch aristocracy and commercial interests around 1800 using lifeboats of Henry Greathead's design (see Chapters II-4 and II-5).

The reason for two separate institutions, the NZHRM being based in Amsterdam, the ZHRM in Rotterdam, was related to contemporary politics and the influence of The Netherlands Pilotage Authority, whose administration was split on the same geographic lines and who took 'an active interest in the formation of the rescue organisations'. Both institutions were governed by wealthy merchants who, if annual donations did not cover expenses, would provide their own funds to make ends meet. Although many of the local beachmen and salvagers were initially somewhat reticent to pursue the concept of saving lives, as well as property, the idea soon caught on. Within seven months of the institutions' inception there were 17 lifeboat stations in both the north and the south and hundreds of lives had been saved. Over the next 167 years the organisations would work closely together on thousands of rescues on the treacherous banks off the Dutch coast and the notorious lee shore created in the estuaries of the Rhine, Scheldt and Maas Rivers (see Chapters I-13 and I-15).

The NZHRM and the ZHRM also worked closely together in the development of lifeboats and rescue craft particularly suited to the perils of the Dutch coast. Strong links with the RNLI meant that many of the early Dutch lifeboats were derivations of British designs. It was soon found, however, that these were generally too heavy to be hauled great distances or to be launched with ease across the low-lying beaches. Many of the early Dutch pulling boats were thus considerably smaller and lighter and more along the line of a traditional surfboat (see Chapter II-8). Innovation in lifeboat design continued in The Netherlands towards the turn of the last century, first with experiments dealing with steam propulsion (see Chapter II-10), and later with the development of the first large MLBs, which could be used further offshore than any previous Dutch rescue craft (see Chapter II-13). Starting in 1980 the Dutch lifeboat institutions began working with the RNLI on the development of a new large RHI to be used as a high-speed medium-endurance rescue craft combining the capabilities of an inshore rescue boat and an offshore lifeboat. The concept of a rigid-hull inflatable lifeboat was eventually abandoned by the RNLI in favour of more conventional designs, but in The Netherlands development of the type continued, and today the Dutch lifeboat fleet consists entirely of RHIs ranging from 16ft (5m) to an astounding 62ft (18.8m) (see Chapter II-20).

In 1949, in honour of the 125th anniversary of both organisations, Queen Wilhelmina of The Netherlands granted the title Koninklijke, 'Royal', to both the NZHRM and the ZHRM. Although for many decades the possibility of combining the two organisations under one banner was considered and even promoted, the close working relationship, and the somewhat different means of financial support rendered any such move unnecessary. In 1991, however, they did amalgamate to form the unified Koninklijke Nederlandse Redding Maatschappij (KNRM).

A modern KNRM lifesaving station. Both rescue craft are beach-launched on carriages, the large RHI is a 34ft 10in (10.6m) Valentijn class.
KNRM, Kees Brinkman

Koninklijke Nederlandse Redding Maatschappij (KNRM)
Operating Model: Non-profit Voluntary Organisation
Source of Income: Private Contributions
Manning Structure: Volunteer Crew

In 2001, the KNRM consisted of 36 lifeboat stations spread along the coast from Cadzand in the southwest to Eemshaven in the northeast. Like the RNLI, the KNRM uses paid employees at stations where vessels require on-going maintenance and has approximately 11 full-time coxswains as well as five part-time physicians on-call for the radio medical service. The institution also has approximately 525 volunteer coxswains and crewmembers ready to man the vessels 24 hours a day, in all weather.[597] Administrative efficiency is the key and overhead costs are strictly

controlled. The entire shore staff consists of only 19 office and technical personnel. The KNRM prides itself on being non-governmental in terms of operating structure and raises the approximately 4.5-million euros needed for annual operating costs through voluntary contributions, annual donations, legacies, bequests and gifts.

Annie Jacoba Visser, a Valentijn RHI, was launched in 1993 and is stationed out of Lauwersoog.
KNRM, Kees Brinkman

In addition to its wide variety of rigid-hull rescue craft, the KNRM also has beach-launch and -recovery vehicles to cope with shallow coastline and relative lack of safe havens in which lifeboats can be stationed afloat. The Dutch have become masters at the art of launching in and through the surf. Until as recently as the 1950s the KNZHRM were still using a horse team at the Isle of Ameland. Today, purpose-built beach-launch and -recovery vehicles and lifeboat

This photograph provides an excellent representation of the increased size of the KNRM's new 62ft (18.8m) Arie Visser (AV) type when compared to its predecessor, the 47ft (14.4m) Johannes Frederik (JF) type.
KNRM

cradles are used such as the launch-cradle system for the 35ft (10.6m), 34kt Valentijn RIB that has a built-in hydraulic lift to raise the vessel until it is clear of the breaking surf and in a better position for launching.

The KNRM works closely with other European lifeboat institutions, the two original institutions having been founding members of the International Lifeboat Conference (Federation) in 1924. In addition, SAR activities in The Netherlands' maritime SAR region are conducted under the auspices of the Dutch National SAR Agency which helps coordinate the activities of the KNRM with the marine resources of other multi-tasked organisations such as the Royal Dutch Navy, and the Dutch Coast Guard, which maintains an MRCC at IJmuiden, and a coast radio station at Scheveningen. The Royal Dutch Air Force has rotary-wing SAR resources at both De Kooy AFB (Lynx helicopters), and Leeuwarden AFB (Bell 412 helicopters), as well as fixed-wing resources at Valkenburg and Schiphol AFBs.[598]

NETHERLANDS ANTILLES

Coastal Conditions & Hazards

The Netherlands Antilles consists of two separate island groups bordering on the Caribbean Sea. The largest group includes the islands of Curaçao, Aruba and Bonaire, all of which lay just north of the western coast of Venezuela. Far to the north, in the Leeward Islands, lies the Island of St Maarten, jointly administered by France (St Martin) and The Netherlands (for similar coastal conditions and hazards see 'British Virgin Islands' p.204). The total coastline of both groups is 226 miles (364km). The three main islands in the southern group are hilly in nature, with Bonaire having the most vegetation. Prevailing winds through the group are generally moderate, being in the path of the NE Trades, and can vary from ENE to SE, although local breezes are common off the slopes with changes in sea and land temperatures. The Guyana Current sweeps through the area in a westerly direction with currents in excess of 3kt. The northeast coast of the island of Aruba is exposed to heavy breakers and is generally unapproachable, while the southwest coast is fronted by barrier reefs that provide a further obstacle for those who wish to enter the tidal lagoons.[599]

St Maarten Sea Rescue Foundation (SSRF)
Operating Model: Non-Profit Voluntary Organisation
Source of Income: Private Contributions and State Subsidy
Manning Structure: Volunteer Crew

The SSRF was established on 1 November 1982 to provide a coastal lifesaving service for the Dutch dependency in the Leeward Islands. It has always been a voluntarily-funded and -manned organisation and during its initial years used members' private vessels for rescues. With the island's connection to The Netherlands, the SSRF has always maintained strong ties with the KNRM and its predecessor societies. Many

of the lifeboats and rescue craft presently run by the society have been purchased or donated from the KNRM.

The SSRF fleet today includes *Rescue 1*, a 30ft (9.3m) Pacific-class RHI built by Halmatic, UK, which has a top speed of 50kt with its twin 200-hp outboards. *Rescue 2* is a 42ft (13.0m) Neuville aluminium crewboat capable of 22kt, and *Rescue 3* is the large 65ft (20.4m) ex-KNRM Carlot-type MLB, the ex-*Johanna Louisa*, built in 1968 and is capable of extended heavy-weather cruising at 11kt (see Chapter II-13). This large lifeboat was transported across the Atlantic to Newport News, Virginia, courtesy of the Royal Dutch Navy, and delivered south to St Maarten by a KNRM crew. The two other rescue craft in the fleet are also ex-KNRM lifeboats; the *Rescue 4*, a 16ft (5.0m) RHI capable of 25kt, and *Rescue 5*, a 30ft (9.3m) aluminium rescue boat capable of 8kt. This latter vessel is the most recent arrival and is stationed at a new SSRF station at Simpsonbay Lagoon adjacent to Princess Juliana International Airport.

The SSRF operates with between 15 and 20 affiliated members and a small board of management of between five and seven of these members. On 14 December 1998 the small rescue society survived one of the greatest challenges in its history when it was instrumental in evacuating hundreds of passengers and crew from the sinking cruise ship, *Monarch of the Seas*, that had struck ground off Philipsburg Harbour. One of the founding members of the society, Robert 'Bobby' Velasquez, became On Scene Commander (OSC) for the incident and helped guide the rapidly foundering ship on to a sandbar so that its lower embarkation doors would not be submerged. All the local authorities were rapidly mustered by the OSC to provide tenders to recover those onboard and to provide humanitarian relief services for all once on land. Not a single life was lost.

The SSRF is not the only maritime rescue organisation in the Netherlands Antilles. Other entities include the Citizens Rescue Organisation (CITRO), which was originally established in Curaçao in 1966. CITRO went on to establish chapters in Bonaire and Aruba. CITRO operates ex-KNRM rescue craft, having two on Curaçao and two on Bonaire. The Aruba branch evolved into a separate organisation now known as the Search and Rescue Foundation of Aruba (SARFA). SARFA has a fleet of two ex-KNRM rescue craft and also has an air-borne resource at its disposal. There are two smaller lifesaving societies, the Sea Rescue Statia Foundation, located on St Eustatius, which operates two lifeboats, one of which was acquired from the DGzRS, and the Sea Rescue Saba Foundation which also has two lifeboats.

Starting in 1995 a movement was afoot to establish a Dutch Caribbean Rescue Foundation, a national maritime rescue umbrella organisation, similar to those already in place in New Zealand and Australia, to provide a more unified representation for all the local societies at international forums as well as to express their common interests through a single voice. As of 1999 both the SSRF and CITRO had joined the new foundation, which was also receiving support from the KNRM and SEARCH.[600]

NEW ZEALAND

Coastal Conditions & Hazards

The islands of New Zealand rest in their oceanic solitude between the notorious Tasman Sea and the vast expanses of the South Pacific. With its 9,400-mile (15,134-km) length, the coast of New Zealand is one of great diversity. The North Island boasts rugged headlands, long coastal beaches with treacherous offshore sandbars, as well as many protected harbours and archipelagos such as the Bay of Islands. The northern tip of the North Island, Cape Maria van Dieman, extends far out to sea where massive tide rips and over-falls meet large oceanic swells resulting in immense standing waves and, at times, an almost impenetrable wall of water extending out from the peninsula. The South Island has fewer natural harbours, treacherous bar conditions at certain ports like Greymouth and Christchurch, numerous fjords on the southwest coast, and sounds and islands in the north. The east coast of the South Island offers beautiful vistas from shore but very few ports of refuge and is subject to the full exposure of thousands of miles of unfettered Pacific.

The islands are separated by Cook Strait, an exposed body of water where tidal currents combine with the full onslaught of oceanic swells and funnelling winds from the NW or SE to produce some of the worst operating conditions in the world. On 10 April 1968 the New Zealand ferry *Wahine*, en route from Littleton to Wellington, had her steering gear disabled by an enormous wave and was eventually blown on to Barretts Reef, where she and 53 of her passengers and crew were lost. At the southernmost tip of New Zealand lies the Foveaux Strait with severe conditions similar to those in the Cook Strait and full exposure to the large westerly swells of the Southern Ocean, said to blow Force 8 for 15% of the year. Given this extreme operating environment, the need for a coastal lifesaving service is, and always has been, obvious.[601]

History of Coastal Lifesaving

The first record of any dedicated marine rescue facility in New Zealand comes from the port of Timaru on the east coast of the South Island. The original lifeboat here was purchased from Sydney, Australia, in 1860 and does not appear to have been used a great deal, although in October 1861 the local newspaper reported that 'the lifeboat stationed at le Crens could not be launched except by taking it a mile away'.[602] The need for lifeboats on the South Island came with the increase in immigrant ships and small sailing craft traffic to the new farming lands in South Canterbury and to the gold fields accessible from the west coast. On 18 June 1862 a 33ft (10.2m) lifeboat was ordered from Britain by the local Colonial Government for service at Timaru. This vessel, which cost a grand total of £300, arrived complete with launching carriage in 1864. Named *Alexandra*, she remained in service for decades to follow and in 1882 saved 43 lives from the sailing ships *City of Perth* and *Bienvenue* both wrecked on the Canterbury coast; in one of these rescues the *Alexandra* rolled four times with the loss of 10

The self-righting lifeboat *Alexandra*, stationed at Timaru on the South Island of New Zealand. In 1882 this lifeboat and her crew were instrumental in saving 43 lives from the ships *City of Perth* and *Benvenue*, wrecked on the Canterbury coast.
South Canterbury Museum

lives, including seven of her crew.[603] The *Alexandra* spent the rest of her days as a lawn ornament in a city park.[604] Other lifesaving measures were instituted in the vicinity of Timaru, however, including the establishment of one of the first rocket brigades in New Zealand in 1867.[605]

Down the coast, at Oamaru, harbourmaster Captain William Sewell established a local rocket brigade as early as 1860. From all accounts the rocket brigade had much more success than the lifeboat that was stationed here in May 1867. Only six days after her arrival, the lifeboat was needed to assist at the wreck of the schooner *Mary Ann Christina*. Unfortunately there was no proper launching carriage and, when the local lifeboatmen attempted to launch the lifeboat her bottom was stove in. Disgusted by the futility of the situation, the men left the boat to drift around the lagoon and rot into oblivion.[606] Other lifeboats soon followed including, on the west coast, at Okarito lagoon in 1865 where a 31ft 6in (9.8m) eight-man pulling boat was provided, and at Hokitika the following year.[607] On the North Island, mention is also made of a pilot/lifeboat being stationed at the approaches to the Manukau, west of Auckland, in the 1860s.[608]

In 1898 the first of the local coastguard organisations that make up the present federation was established. The Sumner Lifeboat Institution (SLI) was founded on the Pacific coast of the South Island northeast of Lyttelton. According to Methley, the original lifeboat was of the 'whale-boat type' and was supplied by the local authority, the Lyttelton Harbour Board. It was a four-oared lifeboat built in the Isle of Wight and was placed in commission at Sumner in August 1898.[609]

The new institution was modelled after the RNLI and, with resources in the country at a bare minimum, developed as a purely voluntary service similar to that in Britain. The rowing lifeboat, named *Rescue*, remained in service until 1930 at which time she was replaced by an ex-RNLI Standard Self-Righting type MLB with a petrol engine, the *Rescue II*, described as a 30ft (9.0m) 'J. Samuel White type' also built in the Isle of Wight (see Chapter II-12)[610]. This venerable lifeboat carried out many daring rescues over her fine career, including a famous service in 1942 when she steamed some 50 miles to Mortuna to rescue 45 crewmen from the wrecked steamship *Kaiwarra*.[611]

By 1970 other volunteer lifeboat and coastal rescue units were springing up in various parts of New Zealand where necessity and public empathy prevailed. The SLI recognised a need for a faster form of SAR response and began experimenting with high-speed jet boats. New Zealand has been a front-runner in the development of jet-powered rescue craft and the expertise of local firm Hamilton Marine, manufacturers of one of the first marine jet-propulsion systems, was used in designing the new craft. The 'Jet Surf Rescue Boat' was well suited for surf rescue work in New Zealand and Australia as it was relatively small – 16ft (4.9m) – providing the necessary manoeuvrability for close work in surf, had a speed in excess of 40kt. The jet-propulsion system was also useful for beach launch and landings as there were no rudders and props beneath the keel, and the boat could 'plane in as little as 5 inches of water'.[612] Many of today's rescue craft, designed to work in extremely shallow conditions, use water-jet propulsion units as their principal power.

Sumner Lifeboat Institute Inc (SLI)
Operating Model: Non-Profit Voluntary Organisation
Source of Income: Private Contributions
Manning Structure: Volunteer Crew

The SLI was one of the founding members of the New Zealand Volunteer Coast Guard Federation in 1976 and remains a key component of the federation today. Its headquarters are at the Scarborough lifeboat station, while the Institute's large MLB lies afloat in the harbour of Lyttelton, being constantly on standby for SAR call-out as well as to assist the harbour authority with other duties such as pilotage and tows. There were three principal rescue craft in service as of 2001, including a large 50ft (15.5m) Thames SR MLB of the RNLI, now named the *P&O Nedlloyd Rescue* (see Chapter II-21), a 19ft (5.8m) BFB jet-powered RHI, the *Caroline Nicholson*, and the *Lady Frances*, a 12ft (3.8m) conventional RHI.

Royal New Zealand Coast Guard Federation (RNZCGF)
Operating Model: Non-Profit Voluntary Organisation
Source of Income: Private Contributions and State Subsidy
Manning Structure: Volunteer Crew

The Royal New Zealand Coast Guard Federation (RNZCGF) has a similar background to other maritime rescue organisations in the Southern Hemisphere having been given the role of creating national sea rescue standards and providing unified representation for various local rescue organisations.

The use of the name Coast Guard started in Auckland in 1937 with the formation of a local organisation called the New Zealand Coast Guard. By 1964 interest in the Auckland-based service had waned and there were only 22 active members. Sea rescue in New Zealand has always been voluntary and this philosophy was entrenched when the word Volunteer was added to the title of this service. In 1976 eight of the country's separate local rescue organisations met at Taupo, North Island, to establish an umbrella body 'to develop a common approach to search and rescue'. On 31 July of that year the NZCGF was formed,with the original service gracefully renaming itself the Auckland Volunteer Coast Guard Service. In September 1990, following a visit to the Sumner branch of the federation by the Prince of Wales, the name 'Royal' was added to the NZCGF.

The Federation expanded rapidly and today boasts 67 subsidiary units around the country. Aside from the SLI, two of the Coast Guard units within the RNZCGF are also members of the ILF – Wellington and Manukau Volunteer Coast Guard. The latter currently operates a 30ft (9.0m) RHI from its base at French Bay on North Island, providing lifesaving coverage for the treacherous Manukau Bar. From 1986 to 1996 RNZCGF lifeboats and personnel responded to more than 20,000 calls and assisted 40,000 people. The RNZCGF uses a variety of rescue vessels. A new Brede-class MLB is stationed to cover Nelson Bay and the western approaches to the Cook Strait and two ex-RNLI Rother class MLBs operate over the dangerous bars of the South Island at Sumner and Greymouth. RHIs, both large and small, are used extensively throughout New Zealand. Trailered RHIs are stationed at many units and larger 41ft (12.6m) RHIs are at strategic locations, in particular at Picton to serve the Marlborough Sounds and southern Cook Strait, and at Wellington to serve the local harbour and the northern Cook Strait. Member organisations within the federation further enhanced New Zealand's offshore SAR capability with the purchase of six Waveney-class 44ft (13.4m) MLBs from the RNLI starting in 1999 (see Chapters II-17 and II-21). All these vessels are now on station at New Plymouth, Mana, Waiheke Island, Raglan, Napier and Kaikoura.[613]

Another very successful resource utilised by the RNZCGF is its Air Patrols. This service is quite unique, given the fact that the RNZCGF is a volunteer service and it has been highly successful in saving lives. It utilises a number of sponsored light aircraft to perform regular patrols and to assist in designated searches. These are equipped with GPS and electronic-chart systems that help to guide RNZCGF vessels to the scene of distress. In August 1994 the ASB Coast Guard Air Patrol out of Auckland was on a routine flight when the pilot spotted an object in the water in the Tamaki Strait – an overturned aluminium boat with four teenagers clinging to it. A distress signal was immediately forwarded and a smoke flare dropped to advise local marine traffic of the situation. All four were successfully rescued and undoubtedly owe their lives to the volunteer eye in the sky.[614] The RNZCGF provides valuable VHF radio coverage around the New Zealand coast and on the major lakes, and, along with the air patrols and the further upgrading and standardisation of the rescue fleet, this will further assist the organisation's expanding role as the premier marine rescue service in New Zealand. In addition the federation holds a primary role in public boating-safety education.

Overall responsibility for marine safety and SAR coordination in New Zealand is the responsibility of the Ministry of Transport and the New Zealand Maritime Safety Authority. The National Rescue coordination Centre is located in Wellington and there are three subsidiary coast radio stations at Auckland, Wellington and Awarua. The RNZCGF works in close conjunction with the New Zealand Police who are responsible for initiating many of the local call-outs. The New Zealand Police also have a large patrol-and-rescue vessel based in Auckland. Air SAR services are provided by the RNZAF which, in conjunction with surface vessels of the RNZN, provide surface SAR resources for vast offshore areas of the South Pacific ocean. These came to good use in June 1994 when a typhoon ripped through a fleet of offshore sailing vessels bound for New Zealand. Several yachts were dismasted and remained in the horrendous conditions, which were described as 'pretty rugged with 80 knots of wind and seas of up to 15 metres'. Through the efficiency of the MRCC in Wellington and the concerted efforts of local surface vessels including those of the RNZN, as well as continual over-flights by P3 Orions of the RNZAF, six complete yacht crews were rescued. Unfortunately, one yacht and three people were lost.[615]

NORWAY

Coastal Conditions & Hazards

Norway has an extensive seacoast with a relatively low, rocky shore facing the waters of the Skagerrak to the south (see 'Denmark' p.215), which evolves northward into an indented, mountainous coastline of many large fjords as well as thousands of islands. These islands and skerries form a natural breakwater for most of the seaward approaches to the coastal passages and inlets – and has been given the name Skœgården, rock rampart. In the Lofoten Islands, off the northwest coast of Norway, strong tidal currents flow through narrow channels creating great whirlpools and treacherous rips known locally as the Maelstrom. Along this outer coast, particularly between the latitudes of 62° and 68°N, there are several designated 'danger zones' for coastal shipping. Large freak waves are known to occur in these areas – a product of refraction and reflection of large oceanic swells off some of the steep outer headlands and islands, and a rapid rise and shelving of the ocean floor close to the coast. The winds vary, but localised squalls known as Sno or Elvegust frequent the fjords and inlets of south and southeast Norway in the winter months bringing strong katabatic-type outflow winds with corresponding sudden drops of temperature, sometimes as much as 15°C. Similar winds,

called Solgangsvind, occur in more northern fjords, particularly at night when the air cools. In terms of swell and sea conditions in the near coastal waters of the Norwegian Sea, the sailing directions have the following advice to offer:

High seas and heavy swell are relatively common in this area which is often affected by active Atlantic depressions and storms. On occasions when these Atlantic lows are deepest, with winds reaching hurricane force, then the seas can become confused and mountainous.[616]

History of Coastal Lifesaving

The first Norwegian lifesaving service was a child of tragedy and the product of a great philanthropic spirit. In the mid 19th Century it was estimated that approximately 800 people lost their lives each year along this coast, primarily in the herring and northern cod fisheries.[617] The Norwegian fishery was such an important mainstay of the national economy that by 1936 Commander Hans Holter, Secretary of the Norwegian Society for Sea Rescue (NSSR), estimated there were about 100,000 Norwegian fishermen at sea 'all the year round'.[618] The loss of life was enormous: a single winter's storm could wipe out an entire generation of seafarers and breadwinners.

The Norwegian Government was not blind to the sufferings of the shipwrecked and in 1854 established an organised lifesaving service under the auspices of the Norwegian Lighthouse Authority (then a branch of the Navy). Stations were established at Jaeran and Lista and were modelled after the Danish system with pulling boats, cannons, rockets and lifelines. These stations were instrumental in saving hundreds of lives over their years of operation. However, interest in the importance of the service gradually began to wane towards the end of the 1800s as did the annual allotments to the service. That said, these state-funded lifesaving stations did remain in operation until 1932, at which time they were handed over to the independent lifesaving service.

Norway's guiding philanthropic spirit was Dr Oscar Tybring who, almost single-handedly, brought about the creation of the NSSR. Tybring had witnessed death and destruction on the shores in front of his home in the outer islands when the entire crew of a vessel drowned before his very eyes.[619] The sight of the calamity induced him to devote the remaining part of his very busy life to the cause of organising a lifeboat service for the Norwegian Coast. Tybring was constantly inundated with apathetic and negative attitudes towards the idea of a Norwegian lifesaving service. Many felt that the vastness of the Norwegian coastline, coupled with its relatively small population, meant that the type of lifeboat society now in vogue in southern Europe was simply not possible in their country. His reply was, 'What we must do is to develop a service which is adapted to the (Norwegian) coast as it is!' In collaboration with the Khristiania (Oslo) Merchants' Association, who were also pursuing the idea, and after much research on foreign lifeboat institutions, lecturing, and touring of the country, Tybring was able to convince prominent Norwegians and the public in general of the need for an organised rescue service. Other prominent citizens involved in the movement included Heinrich Scheller, Ellert Sunot, Commodore Koren and, later, the famous designer of the first Norwegian lifeboat, Colin Archer. The result was that on 9 July 1891 Norsk Selskab til Skibbrudnes Redning was formed, with the rather large capital investment of about £7,500.[620]

In its infancy, the approach of the NSSR would be unique among European lifeboat societies. Due to cost considerations and the fact that a great deal of the demand for lifesaving services came from the mobile offshore fishing fleet, the Norwegians decided to design and build sailing lifeboats for range and efficiency. Indeed, the NSSR did not motorise any of its vessels until 1930, and even then the development came with much internal strife and soul-searching (see Chapter II-12). The reasons for sailing lifeboats were simple: the NSSR required a vessel that could patrol from October to April with extended periods offshore. The only small vessels capable of doing this cheaply and efficiently were powered by sail. The design was based on the famous Norwegian pilot ketches, known to be stout and seaworthy craft and capable of operating in heavy weather. The designer was Colin Archer and his first Norwegian lifeboat, RS#1 *Colin Archer*, was a phenomenal success (see Chapter II-11).

Twenty-eight of these sturdy craft were built and even the late sailing lifeboats departed little (except in increased dimensions) from the original. These larger vessels, built during the 1930s, were the first NSSR lifeboats designed with motors, but only as 'secondary' propulsion. The engines did increase the operational range and efficiency of the vessels however, and from a lifesaving perspective allowed the NSSR to increase its patrol areas to the fishing grounds around Iceland and the Shetlands.

The *Kaptein Skaugen* a 69ft (21m) Skomvær type has a GRP houseworks mounted on an aluminium hull, a top speed of 25kt and a range of 400nm.
Redningsselskapet

In 1932, when the NSSR assumed responsibility for the old government lifesaving stations, the society also accepted a small state subsidy, which continued until the onset of the Second World War. During the war, the NSSR continued its lifesaving duties in spite of the German occupation (see Chapter I-15). It was during this period that a decision was made to construct offshore patrolling lifeboats with motors as the principal mode of propulsion, although a set of sails would be maintained as back-up power. The result was a long line of offshore, cruising-type lifeboats, some of which remain in operation to this day (see Chapter II-15).

The Norwegian cruising lifeboat *Skomvær II* served with the NSSR for 25 years before being sold to the Swedish Society for Sea Rescue in 1986.
Fotoi Erlings Foto, Redningsselskapet

In the 1950s a state subsidy was reinstated for the society to provide for the costs of administration and the salaried crews. In turn, the NSSR was to provide a continuous SAR capability for the Norwegian authorities. This efficient and mutually beneficial financial arrangement remains in effect to this day.

Beginning in the 1960s a gradual move towards the introduction of station-mode lifeboats began. As a result, following the 1963 Edinburgh lifeboat conference, the NSSR decided to build two 44ft MLBs based on the popular USCG design (see Chapter II-17).

Norsk Selskab til Skibbrudnes Redning (NSSR)
Operating Model: Non-Profit Voluntary Organisation
Source of Income: Private Contributions and State Subsidy
Manning Structure: Volunteer/Employee

The brainchild of Dr Tybring has continued to flourish. In 1993 it was estimated that the NSSR had, since 1891, saved 5,407 lives and 1,882 vessels from certain death and destruction, and assisted more than 343,000 people and

97,594 vessels.[621] It utilises a combined staff of professionals and volunteers, having approximately 240 full-time staff (175 of whom work at sea) and 100 part-time staff for seasonal duties. The Society is also involved in public safety education and awareness, oil-pollution protection services, medical-transport duties, and even some towing and salvage assignments.

Although the NSSR has relied on a combination of government subsidy and voluntary contributions since the Second World War, its spirit is essentially non-governmental. Approximately 33% of the annual operating budget is provided by the Norwegian government to cover the costs of salaries and administration. The rest is solicited from private sources such as legacies, companies, associations and individuals. At present the NSSR is in the final stages of a massive vessel replacement programme to standardise and modernise its fleet. Raising the capital for this and the Society's running costs, rests with the employees of the Society, as well as with thousands of volunteer fund-raisers all over the country who belong to over 500 local rescue associations. Additional funding comes from membership dues, as well as the rather lucrative NSSR National Lottery and slot machines.

Following the construction of the two Norwegian versions of the American 44ft MLB, the next experiment with faster lifeboats came in the 1970s with the construction of a large Medina-type RHI, the *G.J. Kastor* (see Chapter II-20). In the 1980s the NSSR began experimenting with high-speed GRP and aluminium lifeboats. In the end they concentrated on the construction of three classes of vessels, all of which represent a departure from the traditional NSSR rescue craft in that operational speeds range from 25 to 30kt. The Skomvaer-class MLB, first delivered in 1986, is a medium-endurance vessel at 69ft (21m) LOA with a top speed of 25kt and a range of 400 nautical miles. The original vessel, the *Skomvaer III*, and three successive craft were constructed entirely of GRP. Within two years of operation, however, stress fractures were discovered in the hulls and subsequent craft have been built in aluminium.

The second class MLB was the 53ft (16m) Adeler, designed for inshore work. With an operational speed of 30kt and a range of approximately 300 nautical miles, the original Norboat version of this class was also constructed entirely out of GRP but was switched to the aluminium hull/GRP wheelhouse combination, with an increase of length of just over 3ft (1m). The third new type was a rescue cruiser designed to combine the traditional sea-keeping elements of the older Norwegian patrolling boats with the speed of the smaller inshore vessels. The first of the Reidar von Koss class built in aluminium with a GRP superstructure was delivered in January 1996. At 75ft 6in (23m) LOA with a speed of 25kt, this vessel was designed for offshore SAR and had a range of 800 nautical miles.

As of 2001 it seems that only one of the Reidar von Koss class had been built but that two more versions of large offshore rescue craft had been designed and built by the NSSR. The first of these, the 67ft (20.4m) Emmy Dyvi class,

One of two new classes of Norwegian offshore lifeboats, the 67ft (20.4m) *Emmy Dyvi* has replaced the traditional displacement lifeboats. In this photo the namesake of the class is seen cruising at an impressive 25kt.
NSSR

was launched in 1997 with a much more pronounced wheelhouse than its predecessor, providing better all-round visibility in heavy sea conditions. Top speed was once again rated at 25kt and power came from twin 1,200-hp Mitsubishis with an operational range of 600 nautical miles. In addition, a unique daughter-boat launch-and-recovery system was developed utilising a Norsafe midget RHI. Instead of losing valuable aft deck space with a conventional ramp system, the Norwegians store their small RHIs below the after deck, launching through the transom, which lifts vertically, like a conventional garage door. In 1998, a larger 83ft (25.25m) version, the Von Koss class, was launched,

The Norwegian rescue cruiser *Ulabrand*, 83ft (25.25m) long, has a top speed of 25kt and an operational range of 1,000nm. Like her smaller sister, the Emmy Dyvi class, this vessel has a unique daughter-boat launch-and-recovery system with an opening transom and a below-deck ramp in the stern.
NSSR

being powered by four 960-hp Cummins diesels producing a top speed of 25kt and a maximum range of 1,000 nautical miles. Both of these fine vessels are designed for extended patrols offshore in aid of the fishery and offshore-oil industries, as well as for rapid response in extreme weather conditions.

The provision of coastal lifesaving services in Norway 'is not assigned to any specific agency as its sole function'.[622] The sea rescue service is a cooperative venture between several governmental and non-governmental organisations, which ensures the efficient utilisation of whatever resources are available in the particular circumstances. These organisations include the NSSR, the Royal Norwegian Navy and Air Force, the Norwegian Coast Guard, Pilotage and Lighthouse Authorities, Port Authorities and Hospital Administrations.

The overall authority for the coordination of SAR in Norway rests with the Ministry of Justice and Police in Oslo. There are two Rescue Coordination Centres (RCCs), one in the north at Bodoe, and one in the south at Stavanger. In addition, there are five coast radio stations located at Oerlandet, Bodoe, Vardoe, Bjoernoeya and Isfjord. Airborne rescue units include four squadrons of Sea King helicopters at Bodoe and Banak in the north, and Sola and Oerland in the south; these are specially equipped and designated for SAR. In addition to Sea Lynx helicopters carried on vessels of the Norwegian Coast Guard, there is also a squadron of P3 Orion offshore patrol aircraft of the Royal Norwegian Air Force based at Andoeya and available as a secondary SAR resource.

POLAND

Coastal Conditions & Hazards
The Polish coast extends 300 miles (491km) along the shores of the southern Baltic Sea from Germany in the west to the Russian Federation in the east. The topography is generally low and there are many large lagoons. The southwest Baltic has many underwater hazards and shallow banks and shoals predominate. Ice is a severe problem in winter, appearing in mid December and reaching its peak around February. The annual freeze is most disruptive when strong onshore winds pile up the ice at the entrances to harbours and roadsteads. Strong winds are generally from the west and south and, although swell conditions are fairly rare, large storm-driven seas are not.[623]

Morska Sluzba Poszukiwania Ratownictwa (MSPiR)
Operating Model: Civilian Agency Managed by Government
Source of Income: State Funded
Manning Structure: Employee Crew

Starting in 1951, sea rescue in Poland was the responsibility of a state-run enterprise known as the Polskie Ratownictwo Okretowe (PRO). The company was responsible for the rescue of human life, as well as preventing oil pollution, salvage of property at sea, and wreck removal. Established

in January 1951, the PRO's primary duty, in addition to maritime rescue, was to remove the literally thousands of submerged wrecks sunk in Polish waters during the Second World War. One of the more significant wrecks raised by the company was that of the German battle-cruiser *Gneisenau*, intentionally sunk by the retreating German Navy.

The concept of marrying a salvage company with a rescue organisation assumed that in most marine accidents 'human life as well as property are involved and...both should be

A new lifeboat for the Polish Rescue Service (MSPiR). The *SAR-1500* class are based on a JF type RHI lifeboat designed in Holland and constructed at the Damen Shipyard in Gdynia, Poland. *MSPiR*

salved from disaster, if possible at the same time, because as often happens, the only way of saving life is to get the disabled floating object in tow'.[624] Another beneficial result is that in many cases the vessels can act under the auspices of the Lloyd's Open Form (No Cure - No Pay) of salvage agreement allowing some degree of compensation for the rescue organisation.

Poland has always maintained a variety of SAR resources including shore-based and patrolling lifeboats as well as large offshore salvage vessels capable of heavy-weather rescue of deep-sea shipping in the waters of the Baltic. The degree of local peril for larger shipping is somewhat limited but for smaller craft and fishing vessels the opposite is true. The coastal waters are so shallow that it can be impossible to get larger rescue craft close enough to the distressed vessels or to launch shore-based craft through the surf. As a result several mobile beach rescue units have also been established with four-wheel-drive lorries and line-throwing apparatus that can be taken to the site of a wreck.

One of the first lifeboats developed by the fledgling salvage company in the 1950s was the 82ft (25m) R1 class. These were very practical craft constructed along the lines of local fishing vessels, heavily built of pine with steel frames and were advertised as 'suitable for all conditions in the

Baltic Sea'.[625] With a cruising range of 1,500 miles the R1 lifeboats were also equipped with fire and salvage pumps, as well as a full set of diver's equipment and a hand air pump. In 1971 the company had six MLBs, six rescue cruisers (patrolling lifeboats), and two rescue and salvage tugs. About this time design work began on two newer classes of rescue and salvage craft, the R17 rescue cruiser, and the much larger R27 rescue and salvage vessel.

The first R17 was launched in 1972 and, although called an MLB by its builders, at 69ft (21m) it was more of a rescue cruiser in design and purpose. Six were built for use at all the shore-based rescue stations on the Polish coast and were still in service as of 1996. The R27 lifeboats resembled more of a deep-sea salvage tug. Four vessels were constructed for offshore service. At 100ft (30.4m) in length these vessels have a range of 2,100 nautical miles and a cruising speed of 13kt. The R27s were also ice-strengthened for winter operations. One of these large lifeboats, the *Sztorm 2*, remains in service as of 2003. In 1996 the PRO also commissioned a much larger offshore rescue platform, the 175ft (53.5m) *Kapitan Poinc*. This large OSV-type vessel continues the tradition of combining salvage and environmental services with maritime rescue.

The staffing of all Polish rescue vessels has always been and remains non-volunteer. As of 1983 the company was given sole responsibility for the provision of maritime SAR services within the Polish area of responsibility, with its personnel manning the RCC located at Gdynia and the MRSC at Swinoujscie. These services also included the stationing of a heavy MI-8 helicopter at Gdansk to cover the entire Baltic SAR region.[626]

In November 2000 a new Polish Safety at Sea Act was issued which would forever change the way maritime rescue was handled in Polish waters. A new state-operated maritime safety organisation was established with separate branches for SAR and oil pollution. The commercial salvage elements of the old PRO were also separated. Effective 1 January 2002 the new Polish Search and Rescue Service (MSPiR) began operations assuming responsibility for all the lifeboats and lifesaving facilities of the previous organisation. In addition to the *Sztorm 2* and the *Kapitan Poinc*, these include three of the original R17-type lifeboats, the *Powiew*, *Zefir* and *Mistral* and eight all-terrain vehicles equipped with RHIs on trailers. These latter mobile rescue teams are known as Coastal Rescue Units and are manned by crews of four professionals and eight to ten volunteers. The new SAR organisation has also continued the lifeboat construction programme started by the PRO in 1997 and has placed seven 49ft (15.2m) Dutch Johannes Frederik-type RHI lifeboats in service. These Polish-built lifeboats are known as the SAR-1500 type, have a top speed of 30kt and a range of 180 nautical miles; they are powered by a combination of twin 500-kw MAN turbo-diesels and Hamilton 362 water-jets.

Other dedicated SAR resources coordinated by the Polish Search and Rescue Service include several rotary- and fixed-wing SAR aircraft stationed at Gdansk, Gdynia and Darlowo. These include three long-range Mi-14p helicopters and four W-3 Rm Anaconda medium-range helicopters operated by the Polish Navy. The service operates the primary Polish MRCC at Gdynia along with a sub-centre in the western part of the country at Swinoujscie and three coast radio stations located at Gdynia, Witowo and Szczecin. In addition to the navy, the SAR service also works in close conjunction with units of the Polish Coast Guard, Fire Brigade, Health Authority and other national land SAR units.

PORTUGAL

Coastal Conditions & Hazards

Portugal lies on the western side of the Iberian Peninsula, its outer coast being fully exposed to the vagaries of the North Atlantic. The coastline (including the Azores) is approximately 1,114 miles (1,793km) in length and, although it is low and sandy on the extreme northern and southern shores, it has somewhat steeper features including many cliffs along the central coast. There are several large rivers, most notably the Douro and the Tagus, which have treacherous bar and shoal conditions at their entrances. With no natural breakwater, the coast is constantly pounded by oceanic swells and the fishermen and boatmen developed small craft that could safely transit the surf zone and could also be dragged up and stored on the beach. The north is hit by heavy swells for approximately 30% of the year. Prevailing winds in the area consist of the Portuguese Trades, a NW sea breeze that occurs in summer, while in winter strong SW gales known as Vendavales bring heavy rain and low, dark cloud that can obscure the coast for many days.[627] One of the main maritime hazards is shipping itself. Hundreds of vessels transit daily off Portuguese shores en route from the busy ports of western Europe to the Mediterranean and the Suez Canal, as well as deeper-draught vessels heading south for the coast of West Africa. Close-quarters situations are fairly common and the volume of traffic keeps the Portuguese vessel management systems extremely busy.

History of Coastal Lifesaving

In 1691, King D. Pedro II issued the following order for those residing on the coast of Portugal:

Because it has been shown that the maritime forts on this kingdom's coastline have no real means to assist and rescue the people and goods of the ships that are wrecked upon them by reason of bad weather or conflict, and it being necessary to take steps so that, as far as possible, the lives and property on the shipwrecks shall be salvaged, the War Council decrees that when at any time a maritime fort sees a shipwrecked vessel on its coast, the Life Guard should immediately send out any vessels in port to go to the shipwreck and save the people....[628]

However, it would appear that no further efforts were undertaken to assist the shipwrecked until 1776, when the Marquez de Pombal attempted to establish a lifeboat station at the mouth of the Tagus. Unfortunately, the Marquis suffered a political downfall and his dreams of a lifeboat station disappeared with him.

The first recorded efforts at establishing dedicated lifesaving facilities were in 1800, when the English Duke of Northumberland donated the third of Henry Greathead's lifeboats to the town of Oporto for use on their treacherous bar at the mouth of the River Douro.[629] The record also states that in 1828 King Miguel of Portugal recognised the merit of the Oporto lifeboat and ordered the construction of a newer station on the beach at St John. A new lifeboat was also purchased, as well as a line-throwing mortar (possibly a Manby type) and a house of refuge was built, complete with an infirmary and a stock of dry clothing.[630] Unfortunately, the Asilo dos Naufragos at Oporto eventually ran into disrepair through sheer neglect.

In spite of the earlier failure the Portuguese Government continued to show an interest in maintaining some vestige of a lifesaving service and following the Great Exhibition in London and the publishing of the Duke of Northumberland Report on the best design of lifeboat in 1851, they purchased the prototype Richardson 'Tubular Lifeboat' (see Chapter II-8).[631] In July 1852 the government also purchased one of the metallic lifeboats built by the American Joseph Francis (see Chapter II-9). She was named the *Valente* and was stationed at Oporto, to replace the older lifeboat that had suffered an accident the previous year.[632] The government's provision of lifeboats continued for some time. In 1862 six '32 foot single-banked life boat(s)' were ordered from Messrs. Forrest in England. Other local lifeboat societies were organised on the Portuguese coast in these early years operating entirely independently of one another. Many a valiant rescue and a heroic deed was carried out by these early crews. The Torre e Espada, the highest award for bravery in Portugal, was awarded by King D. Luis to the coxswains of the Paco d' Arcos and the Povoa de Varzim lifeboats. Nevertheless, by 1890 there remained only four stations on the entire coastline of the country, these being Povoa de Varzim, Vianna do Castello, Paco d' Arcos and, of course, Oporto.[633] In that same year, the Marquez de Sabugosa, the Minister of Marine, advocated the expansion of a proper national lifeboat service throughout Portugal, the Azores and Madeira.

In 1892 a severe storm claimed the lives of 105 Portuguese fishermen and Queen Amelia herself founded the Instituto de Socorros a Naufragos (ISN) – she would remain its President until 1910 and the creation of the Portuguese Republic. Initial development was rather slow. An Official Act was passed to establish an annual stipend of £1,230 and with this financial basis, good leadership and an ever-increasing amount of voluntary contributions the ISN began to grow. By 1902 there were 21 stations and by 1912 there were 36 with a wide variety of life-saving apparatus, including several of the RNLI's Standard Self-Righting lifeboats and two of the relatively new MLBs at Oporto and Cascaes. Records indicate that by 1909 the ISN had already saved over 4,000 lives and established an additional 120 lifeguard, or beach, stations.

After the revolution in 1910 the ISN was reduced somewhat but began to recover following a reorganisation in 1928 that saw its Naval subsidy significantly increased. During the 1950s six MLBs were purchased, including three Alphonso Sanches types and three D. Carlos types based on the RNLI's Oakley lifeboat (see Chapter II-19). By 1957, however, both the levels of funding and the number of volunteers had once again diminished and the ISN was absorbed into the Portuguese Navy. In the late 1970s two Waveney 44ft (13.7m) MLBs were purchased (see Chapters II-17 and II-21) as well as two 28ft (8.8m), DGzRS self-righting daughter-boats of the Wilhelm Hubotter type (see Chapter II-14). In the 1990s a significant number of Atlantic 21 RHIs was also purchased (see Chapter II-20). As of 1991 the ISN had been responsible for saving an estimated 36,000 lives in its 100 years of existence.

The new ISN lifeboat UAM 691, *N Sra Da Conceição*.
ISN

Instituto de Socorros a Naufragos (ISN)
Operating Model: Non-Profit Voluntary Organisation
Source of Income: State Funded with some Private Contributions
Manning Structure: Employee/Volunteer

The ISN remains a semi-independent branch of the Portuguese Navy. There are presently 31 lifeboat stations along the Portuguese coast as well as in the Azores. Each is the responsibility of the local Port Captain who ensures that a crew is available and trained at all times. The ISN is also deeply involved with public safety education and in the training of beach lifeguards. In April 1997 the first of eight new Queen Amelia class lifeboats was placed in service. In 1998 the lifeboats and crews of the ISN successfully carried out some 1,600 rescue missions. The principal maritime SAR coordinator is the Navy. There are maritime rescue coordination centres (MRCC) at Lisbon and Punta Delgada in the Azores. There is also a maritime rescue sub-centre (MRSC) at Funchal in the Madeira Islands. There are six coast radio stations at Apúlia, Leixõs, Cascais, Monsanto, Sagres, and Faro. Designated SAR helicopter flights are also maintained by the Portuguese Air Force at Lisbon and in the Azores.

RUSSIA

Coastal Conditions & Hazards

Russia has an extensive coastline extending approximately 23,400 miles (37,653km). It borders on three oceans and a multitude of seas, including the land-locked Black and Caspian Seas (see 'Bulgaria' p.205). Starting in the east, the Russian Federation has a geographically isolated stretch of coastline on the Baltic Sea between Poland and Lithuania. Here there are many shallows and few ports of refuge, the principal harbour being at Kaliningrad; in the winter months this port is kept open by large icebreakers. Thunderstorms are common and winds of Force 5 or greater are reported over 40% of the time in autumn and winter months.[634] Further north in the Baltic, on the eastern reaches of the Gulf of Finland, lies the next stretch of Russian coastline around the port of St Petersburg. This area is subject to extremes of weather and icing. There are many narrow, shallow channels and areas of strong current. Oceanic swell conditions are rare but storm-driven waves are not, with rough to very rough seas being experienced on approximately 12 to 14% of the time in autumn and winter. St Petersburg is icebound for most of the winter, although again, icebreakers assist commercial traffic in and out.[635]

The longest stretch of coastline lies north of the Arctic Circle extending from the Barents Sea to the Bering Strait and, although a description of most of this area is not worth noting in the context of maritime rescue, the ice-free period being so short and the amount of maritime traffic so minimal, there are one or two exceptions. The area around Murmansk and the Barents Sea is one, as many commercial vessels still ply these waters en route to the more southern ports of the Beloye More or White Sea. The coastline here is characterised by steep, snow-covered cliffs and many fjords and inlets. Weather in the Barents Sea is described as 'extreme'; the Vikings referred to this area as the Murmean Sea, the Lap word murman meaning 'the edge of the earth'. Rough seas predominate in the area until June and in coastal areas a ferocious katabatic wind, known locally as the Bora, can arrive suddenly and unannounced bringing with it blinding snow and winds in excess of 100kt.[636]

On the Pacific, the Russian coast borders on the Bering Sea and the Sea of Okhotsk, separated by the massive peninsula of Kamchatka. In the Bering Sea a large westerly swell predominates, created by powerful low-pressure systems transiting south of the area. Although sea conditions are not as extreme as in the Strait itself, strong, squally winds (similar to the Bora) blast out of coastal valleys and inlets, day or night, and wreak havoc on the fleets of small fishing vessels.[637] The west shore of the Sea of Okhotsk is mountainous, while to the north, many large river estuaries meet the sea, creating a lower more uniform coastline.

The coast along the shores of Sakhalin Island and the Sea of Japan as far south as Vladivostok is generally steep and mountainous. On Sakhalin itself there are many rivers, navigable by small craft as far inland as 10 miles. Most, however, have treacherous bars at their mouths. At the north end of the Tatarskiy Proliv, the body of water separating Sakhalin from the mainland, the Amur River, the 12th longest in the world, drains into the ocean creating many dangerous offshore bars.[638]

History of Coastal Lifesaving

In *The Lifeboat and Its Story*, written in 1911, Noel Methley stated that the 'Russian Society for the Preservation of Life from Shipwreck', which later became known as the Imperial Russian Lifeboat Society, was founded in 1872. This date is verified by mention in the RNLI's journal, *The Lifeboat*, in August 1872, that the merchants of the Russian port of Riga were establishing a lifeboat institution.[639] Soon after the founding of the new society, the British community in St Petersburg, in celebration of the marriage of the Duke of Edinburgh to the Russian Grand Duchess Marie, had two 33ft Standard Self-Righting lifeboats of the RNLI's design constructed in England as a gift for the Royal couple.[640] The two lifeboats, aptly named *Alfred* and *Marie*, were subsequently presented to the fledgling lifesaving organisation. They were to be stationed at Oesel, on the Baltic, and in the Black Sea at the port of Nicolaiev in 1874.

By 1891 the Imperial Russian Lifeboat Society had expanded quite significantly, having established 125 lifeboat stations around the country. Of these, 65 were said to be located on the coast, while the other 60 were along Russia's vast river system. Although the model upon which the Russian Society was based was that of the RNLI and most revenues were accrued through voluntary contributions, a small state subsidy was maintained. Lifesaving stations were broken into two categories described as First and Second class. First class Stations were equipped with lifeboats and line-throwing gear, while Second class units were provided with the latter equipment only. Prior to the outbreak of the First World War and the tumultuous years which were to follow, the society grew to monumental proportions. As of 1 January 1914 there were an incredible 1,890 lifesaving stations located throughout the Russian Empire, at which there were '800 Life-boats, two cruising boats for life-saving, and 1,000 line-throwing apparatus'.[641] The Imperial Russian Lifeboat Society also had over 8,000 members and, during the 44 years of its existence, had saved nearly 2,000 vessels and 25,000 souls.

Union of Soviet Socialist Republics

A small article in *The Lifeboat*, November 1921 entitled, 'Lifeboats in Bolshevist Russia' provided a brief glimpse of post-revolution coastal lifesaving in what became the Soviet

Union. The article stated that the Soviet 'Department of Salvage, Diving and Life-Saving Work' had been established and was seeking advice and help from the RNLI in matters of coastal lifesaving. Apparently the old institution was now defunct, most of its lifeboats and associated gear having not survived the period of revolution and turmoil. After a low in 1919, in which only an estimated 60 lives were saved by what lifeboats remained, services began to be re-established and by 1924 there were some 960 rescued lives recorded. A 'Central Committee for Saving the Shipwrecked' was formed in 1925 to helped coordinate the function as the fractionalisation of the old society had resulted in some 35 government bodies and 102 separate voluntary agencies being created. Interestingly enough, for many years the socialist bureaucracy of the Central Committee and the private volunteer lifesaving organisations worked together quite efficiently. Funds where raised from both state and private sources, which provided for the reconstruction of many of the destroyed stations, as well as the creation of a Norwegian-style cruising lifeboat service on both the Murmansk coast and the Caspian Sea.[642] In May 1928 all the societies were amalgamated into one central organisation and little information is available on coastal lifesaving in the Soviet Union from this period until after the Second World War, except that eventually all responsibility for coastal lifesaving would be assumed by the state.

The Soviet Rescue Service, like most of the Eastern Bloc services, was amalgamated into the marine salvage operations of the state. It was felt that, in most cases, salvage of the ship also meant the salvation of the people onboard. Thus it was only natural that powerful salvage tugs, which were strategically placed around the Soviet coastline and around the world, would also be used for rescue. The organisation was divided into different branches on the Barents, Baltic and Black Seas, as well as on the Pacific Ocean.[643] As outlined in a paper presented by the USSR delegation at the 8th International Lifeboat Conference in Bremen, Germany in 1959, it appears that many of the original lifesaving stations established by the old imperial society were still being used. The paper goes on to state that over 400 'lifesaving stations and posts on rivers, lakes and seas have been organised in all the 16 Republics of the Soviet Union'.[644]

State Marine Pollution Control, Salvage and Rescue Administration of the Russian Federation (MPESA)
Operating Model: Civilian Agency Managed by Government
Source of Income: State Funded
Manning Structure: Employee Crew

Following Russia's ratification of the 1979 International Convention on Maritime SAR (ICMSAR) in 1988, the government ensured that an organisation was established to coordinate all lifesaving measures within the nation's SRR and to ensure that all other public resources at the government's disposal could be combined and coordinated

to fulfil this objective. This organisation was the State Marine Pollution Control, Salvage and Rescue Administration of the Russian Federation (MPESA).

MPESA is an operative division of the Russian Ministry of Transport, which maintains several rescue coordination facilities around the country. The principal State Maritime Rescue Coordination Centre (SMRCC) is at Moscow, while six MRCCs have been established at Murmansk, St Petersburg, Kaliningrad, Novorossiysk, Astrakhan and Vladivostok. The administration also operates three maritime rescue sub-centres (MRSCs) located at Arkhangelsk, Yuzhno-Sakhalinsk and Petropavlosvsk-Kamchaytskiy. In addition to the many air and marine resources of the Russian military, the MPESA coordination facilities regularly task dedicated rescue tugs, icebreakers, commercial vessels and pilot boats to assist in rescue operations. MPESA operates approximately 12 coast radio stations around the nation, many of which are co-located with the RCCs. In 2001 MPESA was responsible for coordinating 149 SAR operations, which resulted in the rescue of more than 700 persons from perilous situations.

SOUTH AFRICA

Coastal Conditions & Hazards
Given South Africa's geographic station at the horn of a continent and the crossroads of two oceans, it would seem inevitable that some form of sea rescue service would be required. The country has vast stretches of exposed coastline with very few protected harbours, which, combined with a large and active boating population, provides for plenty of marine rescue activity. The entire coastline of South Africa is approximately 1,740 miles (2,798km) in length, running south along the Atlantic from the Namibian border around the Cape of Good Hope and then north to Swaziland and Mozambique. The topography varies from wide sandy beaches to rocky headlands and high bluffs with a backdrop of mountains and escarpments. There are several strong ocean currents but perhaps the most notorious is the Agulhas Current, which runs along the southeast coast from the Mozambique Channel, sometimes as fast as 5kt. Abnormally large seas are known to occur here, created when swells generated by storms in the Southern Ocean move northeast and pile upon one another as they are slowed by the conflicting southwest Agulhas Current. The result can be a giant sea wave in the order of 64ft (20m) which, unlike normal oceanic swells, does not have an even period between waves, but rather a very deep preceding trough followed by an almost-vertical face or, quite literally, a six-storey wall of water. Such waves have been known to swallow entire ships or break them in half – as occurred in 1968 to the SS *World Glory*.

Due to the mountainous nature of much of South Africa and the constant variations in temperature between sea and land, localised wind anomalies are commonplace. Between Cape Agulhas and Port Elizabeth on the southern coast, gale-force winds may last for several days. In the winter months, July in particular, a rough sea and heavy swell with squall-like conditions may persist and create 'considerable hazards' off exposed approaches. In the SE region hot and dry Fohn winds occur in the summer months as over-heated air masses funnel offshore from the central plateau.[645]

History of Coastal Lifesaving

The first mention of dedicated lifesaving facilities in what would become South Africa is recorded in a passage in _The Life-Boat_ 1 October 1861:

> _Read letter from the Agents-General of the Crown Colonies of the 16th April reporting that they were in communication with Messrs. Forrest respecting the building of a 33-feet lifeboat, thoroughly equipped, and a transporting carriage, for the Cape of Good Hope, and requested the cooperation of the Institution in the construction of the same._[646]

The lifeboat was of James Peake's design (see Chapter II-8) and was operated, along with two smaller lifeboats, Manby's line-throwing apparatus and various rockets, under the authority of the Port Captain for Table Bay. On 17 May 1865, a strong westerly gale wreaked havoc on the many vessels anchored off Cape Town. Several ships were wrecked and many lives lost. A considerable amount of public discontent was expressed towards the Port Captain, a man named Wilson, about the limited use of the lifeboats and lifesaving equipment during the disaster and the local newspapers called for an investigation. The report found that most of the accusations against Captain Wilson, in particular that he had refused to launch a lifeboat, were unfounded. In fact, one of the smaller lifeboats had almost immediately been manned by his own port authority boat crew and had headed out to render assistance. There were deficiencies in the system, however, the most outstanding of which was the lack of crews for the other two lifeboats and the need to station the large Peake lifeboat where it could be launched in all tides and weathers. In the end, the lifesaving service was maintained under the authority of the Port Captain, a new station was built at the end of the breakwater, and new equipment was purchased. Most importantly, the Port Captain was to hire dedicated coxswains for two of the lifeboats. These men would, in turn, assemble crews of volunteers who would be remunerated for exercises and rescues. The third boat was to be manned by the paid authority crew. Eventually, new lifeboats were ordered as more stations appeared around the coast.

As of 1912 these government facilities were still in place for, as Methley states:

> _At Table Bay life-boats are stationed under the control of the Port Advisory Board, and that they are up to date and efficient is proved by the fact that those in authority are contemplating the adoption of the newest form of motor life-boats. There are fifteen rocket stations altogether in South Africa, and six life-boats._[647]

By 1940 there were 17 lifesaving stations around the coasts of South and South West Africa.[648] Over the following decades, however, the need for a national marine rescue service became readily apparent. The concept was also promoted by the South African Society of Master Mariners during the late 1960s. In 1966 the entire 17-man crew of a fishing trawler was lost off Still Bay with no rescue resources to save them. Concerted efforts were then initiated to establish a volunteer organisation, particularly through the letter-writing campaign of Pattie Price. Miss Price had once been rescued by lifeboat from her sinking ship in the English Channel and understood the merits of such a service. The new organisation was originally called the South African Inshore Sea Rescue Service and boasted one two-man, 15ft (4.7m) inflatable based at Three Anchor Bay in Cape Town. In 1967 the title National Sea Rescue Institute (NSRI) was adopted and the organisation was registered as a non-profit society. The NSRI grew rapidly, filling the existing void in services and by 1971 there were 14 operational stations, two 30ft (9.0m) rescue boats were under construction, and a 46ft (14.0m), ex-DGzRS lifeboat was based in Cape Town.[649]

By 1975 20 stations were in operation and the NSRI set about designing and constructing larger rescue craft including 32ft (10m) vessels with a range of 300 miles, thus extending the organisation's range further offshore.[650] During the 1980s further rescue craft development was pursued with the search for a compromise between the larger 32-footers and the smaller 19ft 6in and 23ft inshore rescue boats (IRBs) that could operate in the surf. The solution was a 26ft (8m) lifesaving vessel known as the R8. Introduced in August 1980 it was considerably lighter than the 32ft boats and much faster – cruising speed of 25kt and a top speed of 40kt – while still being more economical to run. These vessels have successfully operated off the 'Cape of Storms in winds of up to 50 knots'.[651]

National Sea Rescue Institute (NSRI)
Operating Model: Non-Profit Voluntary Organisation
Source of Income: Private Contributions
Manning Structure: Volunteer Crew

Today the NSRI has 28 lifeboat stations, all on the coast except one inland on the Vaal Dam at Deneysville. There are 50 inshore and offshore lifeboats located at these stations. Each station is run by a Station Commander and a Station Deputy. Either of these two individuals, or the Duty Coxswain, has sole responsibility for authorising the launch of the rescue craft when required. Requests for services generally come from the local port authorities, or the South African Police, who receive the emergency call. If a rescue is offshore, or involves external organisations such as the South African Air Force or Navy, then rescues are coordinated by the South African Search and Rescue Organisation (SASAR) from their MRCC at Silvermine outside Cape Town. Additional South African SAR resources include short- and medium-range helicopters of the South African Air Force and C-130 offshore patrol aircraft. In addition, offshore SAR capabilities are covered by vessels of the South

African Navy as well as large private salvage tugs which generally remain on station adjacent to the main shipping routes from the Gulf around the Cape of Good Hope.

The stations themselves are similar to the English model and have communications facilities as well as training and operations rooms. Many have a four-wheel-drive vehicle fitted out as a mobile communications and ambulatory unit designed to operate on beaches as well as the less-accessible parts of the coastline in conjunction with the rescue craft at sea. Some of the shore vehicles are also equipped with search radar and are able to locate targets at sea and vector the lifeboats to them. Rescue vessels range in size from 10ft to 23ft (3-8m) inflatables to 43ft (13m) all-weather lifeboats.

The smaller rescue craft operate in a fast-response role, relatively close to shore. Operating inshore and in surf conditions, they deal primarily with call-outs to assist small boats, windsurfers, paddleskiers, swimmers, divers and rock fishermen. In recent years the NSRI has been standardising its inshore rescue craft to the Gemini 18ft (5.5m) RHI – now at the Mark 4 stage. As of 1995 the NSRI was operating 17 of these versatile craft, which have some special design characteristics for the South African environment. An interesting feature is the length of the sponsons, on either side, which have been extended well aft of the transom. This feature assists in surf by keeping the outboards from being swamped via the exhausts. The Institute states that these craft are capable of operating up to 20 miles offshore with a crew of three, and have been proven in conditions up to Force 8 or 9 for limited periods. As an interesting footnote, these same vessels have been used by the South African Antarctic Survey for eight years, an organisation whose favourite method of beaching on the icepack is 'to run the boat at full speed of around 30kt at the ice pack with the crew as far aft as possible to give the easiest angle of approach, with the motor tilt leavers in the released position'.[652] The larger lifeboats can operate up to 50 miles offshore, can remain on station for up to 24 hours, and deal

The *Spirit of Rotary,* a South African R8, underway in a training exercise. These fibreglass rescue craft cruise at 25kt and have a top speed closer to 40kt.
NSRI

primarily with cases involving ski-boats, dinghies, fishing trawlers and other commercial vessels.

The NSRI is an all-volunteer organisation and crewmembers come from all walks of life. All are trained in SAR techniques, seamanship, navigation, lifesaving, communications and first aid. Firefighting qualifications are also considered, as is advanced paramedic training. The NSRI has a small paid staff of 15 employees primarily involved in fund-raising activities to support the volunteer force of over 700.

The annual operating budget for the NSRI comes almost entirely from voluntary donations, with the corporate business sector donating the lion's share at about 40%. Another 16.5% comes from annual fund-raising drives, pledge weeks and collection boxes while the rest is contributed by public bodies, charities and other non-governmental organisations.

Since 1967, it is estimated that the NSRI, its crews and its vessels have saved over 1,800 lives and assisted over 17,453 people in distress. The 19th International Lifeboat Conference will be hosted by the NSRI in Cape Town in March 2003.

SPAIN

Coastal Conditions & Hazards

The Spanish coast borders France and the Bay of Biscay in the northwest, Portugal and the open Atlantic to the southwest and its southernmost tip forms the northern side of the narrow Strait of Gibraltar, one of the busiest shipping lanes in the world. The longest stretch extends along the Mediterranean shore from the Strait northeast to the coast of France. The total length of coastline, including the Spanish possessions of the Balearic and Canary Islands and places of sovereignty on the coast of Morocco is 3,100 miles (4,964km). The north and northwest coasts are high and rocky, with bold headlands protruding out to sea. In the southwest, the coastal terrain is predominantly low and sandy as far as Cape Trafalgar, then becomes much bolder towards the entrance to the Strait. Several large rivers meet the ocean along this stretch, one of the more significant being the Ria Guadalquiver, which is navigable by medium-draught vessels as far inland as Sevilla, approximately 54 miles (87km) from the mouth. The Mediterranean coast is generally much lower in profile, although interspersed with bold headlands. There are many long, sandy beaches that have made this area one of the more popular tourist destinations in Europe. One of the principal hazards in the southern zones is the sheer volume of maritime traffic that transits through the Strait of Gibraltar – estimated, in 1999, to be in the order of 70,000 vessels per year. The Strait is also affected by various local weather anomalies, in addition to being fully exposed to large oceanic swells from the south round to the northwest, there are strong easterly winds, known as the Levanter, that cause difficult sea conditions during spring and autumn. Further to the northeast a similar wind, the Lieventade, causes havoc along the Mediterranean coast. Other winds include the Ponientes, a strong westerly in the same area, the Vendevales, a strong southwesterly generally associated with cloudy weather and rain squalls and occurring near the northwest coast, and the Leveche, a hot, dry Saharan wind rising from the Moroccan shore, which sometimes appears as a brown cloud on the horizon. Off the northwest coast of Spain there are frequent strong gales, known as Nord-est pardo, or cloudy northeasterly, which frequently occur in the winter months.[653 654]

History of Coastal Lifesaving

The origins of organised lifesaving in Spain go back to 1773, when a Guild of Lifesavers was established in the interior of the Province of Seville, in the south of the country. The organisation may have been similar to the early benevolent societies in China as it, too, was based on a river, the 'Guadalquiver,' and was also concerned with the methods of resuscitating the apparently drowned.[655] It is not known what type of rescue craft were used by this early group. In 1798 the Spanish Navy issued a Decree stating that groups of local boatmen and fishermen would be provided with rescue apparatus at certain ports, Cadiz in particular, to be called upon when needed.

A pulling and sailing SR-type lifeboat of the Spanish Society for Saving the Shipwrecked (SESN), stationed at Torrevieja, Alicante, circa 1890s.

Museu Maritim Barcelona, Danblade

In 1861 the Spanish Government ordered 'two twelve-oared and five ten-oared boats', of the Standard Self-Righting type developed for the RNLI by Beeching and Peake (see Chapter II-8).[656 657] By 1872 it was becoming evident that the present system of a few, sporadically-funded lifeboat and line-throwing stations was inadequate. A committee was established led by Captain Ferdinand Guerra of the Spanish Navy to investigate the workings of the now very successful RNLI in Britain and the potential application of that model to the port of Cadiz.[658] It appears that this committee failed to

make any significant inroads into promoting the cause for, by 1879, little had changed.

In 1880, however, Martin Ferreiro, an employee of the Spanish Hydrographic Office, began to champion the cause. In his research on shipwrecks and the loss of life on the coasts of Spain, he discovered that no less than 1,800 lives had been lost in the previous 15 years, with very little effort being expended to prevent the carnage. Ferreiro started a publicity campaign, which captured the attention of the Spanish royal family, in particular, Queen Maria Christina. Funds were donated to establish a national lifesaving society similar to the RNLI, called the Sociedad Española de Salvamento de Náufragos (SESN). On 12 January 1887 the SESN was given official charter as a charitable organisation and, in consideration of the fact that it had assumed the operation of the old state-run lifeboats and rescue apparatus, the new society was granted a small government subsidy of £1,500. In addition to the seven government boats still in operation, the SESN immediately purchased seven more 'insubmersible' lifeboats from Britain.

The new organisation expanded rapidly, filling the void and fulfilling the civic duty of a well-organised national lifeboat service. By June 1892 the SESN already had 30 lifeboat stations around the country and

57 stations provided with rocket apparatus and other accessories for assisting shipwrecked mariners. About 1,000 men have been enlisted and trained to act as crews of life-boats, and to manage all the apparatus for saving life. The society has spent £19,000 on its material, and the boats and rocket apparatus have saved 712 lives. The society has also rewarded persons who contributed to save 1,590 shipwrecked persons.[659]

By 1912 there were approximately 50 lifesaving stations in operation, 13 of which had line-throwing apparatus only, the rest having lifeboats only or a combination of both. There were still several of the original English-built Standard Self-Righting boats, but eventually all lifeboats were constructed in Spain along similar lines. Like the RNLI, the Spanish Society had a central office that dealt with the provision and standardisation of boats and gear as well as a national fund-raising programme, while the actual operation and maintenance of the boats was left to the local chapters. A relatively small annual state subsidy of £2,200 continued to supplement privately contributed funds. There were also several lifesaving stations located in Spain's overseas territories and possessions, including the Canary Islands, Puerto Rico and North Africa. By 1932 the SESN had introduced MLBs and had 15 in service, averaging around 40ft (12.5m) in length, powered by 48-hp motors of the Hispano or Yeregui type. Three were actually stationed in Morocco, close to the entrance to the Strait of Gibraltar, at Larache, Ceuta and Melilla.[660]

The Spanish Civil War, from 1936 to 1939, was catastrophic for the SESN. Most of the society's lifeboats were commandeered for one reason or another and were damaged beyond repair. Although the organisation did eventually re-emerge, it was but a shadow of its former self. By the 1960s the only lifeboats in operation were those that had survived the conflict and had been maintained through the valiant efforts of the local chapters and their crews. In about 1970 several nautical disasters rekindled the cause and it was realised that the limited SAR coverage provided by the few remaining stations was now grossly inadequate.

To fill the void, the government approached the Spanish Red Cross to establish a voluntary maritime lifesaving service. The offer was accepted on the condition that the government provide financial support and, on 22 February 1971, the Cruz Roja del Mar was established. Three classes of rescue vessel were purchased including 25 A Type all-weather MLBs of French design, capable of operating up to 25 miles offshore; several B Type RHIs, including some British Atlantic 21s; and hundreds of C Type soft-bottom inflatables. Before the end of the decade there were some 570 of the small inflatables in service around the country, primarily used seasonally by students and volunteers on the popular beaches and coastal resorts, much along the lines of the French inshore rescue boat model. In 1972 the remaining organisational structure of the once prominent SESN was amalgamated into the Cruz Roja del Mar.

Sociedad Estatal de Salvamento y Seguridad Marítima (SASEMAR)

Operating Model: Civilian Agency Managed by Government
Source of Income: State Funded
Manning Structure: Employee Crew

The Cruz Roja del Mar remains in operation as of 2002, but with a much smaller fleet and a somewhat reduced role. Citing inefficiencies and administrative problems within the organisation, as well as the need to integrate several public and voluntary organisations involved with lifesaving around

the country, the Spanish Government decided to create a unified state-run rescue organisation in 1992, known as the Sociedad Estatal de Salvamento y Seguridad Marítima (SASEMAR). Established under the provisions of the State Ports and Merchant Marine Act the new organisation was designated with overall responsibility for '...safeguarding human life at sea and of promoting any actions that are directed toward increasing safety at sea'.[661] It has a large fleet of 11 offshore patrol vessels, most of which are converted oil-supply, anchor-handling and salvage vessels that help to fulfil SASEMAR's other responsibilities: pollution prevention and rescue-towing of large vessels. In addition, as of 1995 17 shore-based lifeboats were acquired and placed on station, with a further 16 new boats planned for purchase. The standard lifeboats are the Alusafe 1.500 and 2.000 semi-RHI, designed and built in Norway. These vessels are constructed entirely of aluminium with a small semi-rigid collar placed around the gunwale for sea-keeping and coming alongside other vessels. Both types are powered by twin diesels running water-jets, the 1.500 being 47ft (14.6m) in length and capable of obtaining 30kt with a 300-mile range, while the larger vessel, at 65ft (20.2m), can cruise for approximately 400 miles with a top speed of 34kt. The 2.000 type also carries a small soft-bottom inflatable on the after deck. In addition, SASEMAR has a fleet of five dedicated Sikorsky S-61 rescue helicopters, four of which are based around the coasts of Spain and one in the Canary Islands. As of 1995 the society also had 13 Rescue Coordination Centres (RCCs) and Sub-Centres, with another 10 planned. These also conduct general maritime communications and vessel traffic functions.[662]

SWEDEN

Coastal Conditions & Hazards

Swedish lifesaving services have to provide coverage over a massive coastline extending from the Skagerrak and the Kattegat in the southwest, around the southern tip of the country into the Baltic Sea and then northwards 600 miles (965km) up the eastern shores to the furthest reaches of the Gulf of Bothnia, at a latitude of about 68° North. Except for a few stretches in the south, the coastline is almost consistently shielded by a natural barrier of outer islands and skerries known as the Skärgård. Conditions and hazards in the southwest are similar to those of Denmark (see 'Denmark' p.215). As one enters the Baltic Sea there are navigational problems associated with bank and shoal areas with depths as shallow as 19ft (6m), as well as rocks and reefs that can extend offshore as far as 12 miles; all form part of the extensive Stockholm Skärgård. In winter fog, ice and storms, sometimes with heavy driving snow, are not uncommon. Ice is a very severe problem along Sweden's Baltic coast from January, and a strong persistent blow down the Gulf of Bothnia can create extremely heavy flows in the vicinity of Stockholm. Traffic is generally unhindered, however, due to the large number of ice-strengthened vessels and escort icebreakers. Winds are predominantly from the west and south in the winter months, with gales of

Two Spanish lifeboats rafted up: on the inside, an A type of the voluntary Cruz Roja del Mar and on the outside a 48ft (14.6m) Alusafe lifeboat of Norwegian design, the state-operated *Salvamar Alonso Sánchez*.
SASEMAR

Force 7 or above occurring about 14% of the time. The Baltic Sea between Sweden and Finland and south of the Åland Islands is infamous for its potentially extreme wind and wave conditions. A severe weather warning has been placed in the British Admiralty Pilot for this region (see 'Åland Islands' p.193 and 'Finland' p.217).[663]

Further north, in the Gulf of Bothnia, the offshore islands are interspersed with narrow, shallow channels. Floating debris, such as remnants of trees and logs, pose a threat to small craft as they funnel out into the ocean from the river mouths. The nature of the coastline becomes much more mountainous and localised outflow and longshore winds are more frequent. The most powerful winds along the Swedish side of the Gulf can be created by these local patterns, which can funnel together and flow quite strongly along the coast.[664]

History of Coastal Lifesaving

In the 13th Century, a Swedish Regent by the name of Earl Birger issued a proclamation against pillaging and the ill treatment of the shipwrecked; this being one of the earliest known laws to this effect. In 1692 the Sodra Dyerikompaniet (Southern Diving Company) was established with the primary objective of saving vessels and goods on the occasion of shipwreck. The Swedish King, Charles XI, issued an edict to this company, with instructions for the rescue and treatment of the survivors of such wrecks.[665] There is no evidence at this writer's disposal to indicate whether the 'Diving Company' used any dedicated lifesaving boats but there is no doubt that this was one of the first known examples of organised humanitarian effort towards assisting the shipwrecked anywhere in the world.

By 1831 the Diving Company had ceased to exist. From 1810 to 1820 concerted efforts were made by private individuals to convince the Swedish Parliament to purchase lifeboats of the 'English Type' to be placed at some of the more notorious locations on the coast. But the government decided against such measures, citing 'that it would be a difficult thing to get the necessary crew for the boats on the coasts of our country with their thin population'.[666] No further attempts to establish lifesaving facilities were made until the Royal Naval Society of Sweden took up the cause in 1852 and published a description of the facilities and vessels that had been established in neighbouring Denmark and, the following year, put forward a proposition to the government to establish a similar service and facilities, which was accepted. In 1854 a Naval Officer by the name of Carl Kleman was sent to Denmark to study the recently established lifesaving service. On his return he went to the southeast coast of Sweden to investigate locations for facilities. Kleman decided that two stations would be necessary in this area; one at Sandhammaren, where a Danish-style lifeboat and rocket apparatus would be located, and one at Brantevik, which would have rocket apparatus only. By March 1855 the stations were in place. Commander Kleman was made Inspector of the new state-run lifesaving stations with the service being designated to run under the auspices of the Swedish Royal Naval Administration. From

1857 to 1865 11 more stations were added to the Swedish Lifesaving Service, primarily on the west and southwest coasts, as well as on the islands of Gotland and Oland. In 1872 management was transferred from the Navy to the Pilotage Administration, similar to the services in Belgium and Denmark. By 1888 there were 18 state-funded lifesaving stations around the country.

A severe storm on 9-10 September 1903 battered the Swedish coast and resulted in considerable loss of life. The state-operated lifesaving service, now down to 15 stations, was inadequate and many concerned citizens believed that private efforts should be initiated to expand the facilities. Through the efforts of individuals and organisations, such as the Swedish Shipping Society, considerable funds were raised for the cause and in June 1907 the Svenska Sallskapet for Raddning of Skeppsbrutne (SSRS), Swedish Society for the Rescue of the Shipwrecked, was formed as a private, voluntary lifesaving organisation. It would seem that the biggest encumbrance to the proliferation and success of the government-run organisation had been the government itself with its rather parsimonious approach to the cause of lifesaving. The SSRS established itself quite quickly.

The Society's first lifeboat was a Danish pulling and sailing surfboat, built at the Royal Naval Shipyard in Copenhagen;[667] to be stationed at the small outport of Stafsinge, on the west coast of Sweden. It was just over 30ft (9m) in length, had cork belting around the gunwales, was self-bailing but not self-righting, and was powered by either five pairs of oars or by sail. Four more such boats were later constructed in Sweden.

The SSRS had the freedom to evolve with technology and, recognising the success of internal-combustion engines in the fishing industry around 1904, began experimenting with different kinds of mechanical propulsion including a rather unique, but unsuccessful, attempt at installing a '5-hp Archimedes outboard motor' on the surfboat stationed on the north end of Gotland.[668] By 1911 the Society was intent on constructing the first MLBs in Sweden and wrote to the RNLI for design recommendations. Subsequently a decision was made to construct three new MLBs similar to the RNLI's Watson type, with 30-hp crude-oil engines for propulsion (see Chapters II-11 and II-12). The RNLI was not the only lifesaving society from which the SSRS took advice. The Swedes also looked to Norway and recognised the merits of the cruising lifeboats. The SSRS followed the Norwegian suit, modifying their Watson boats and actually created ketch-rigged patrolling lifeboats out of the British design. Some limitations were noted with the modified Watson design, the lack of substantial freeboard being a particular problem. In 1917 a purpose-built offshore sailing MLB was constructed with a large 90-hp engine and accommodations for several crew. Two of these were built, one of which attended the 1st International Lifeboat Conference in London in 1924. The patrolling concept was a success in Swedish waters, particularly considering the vessels were only used seasonally from the beginning of October to the end of April. In 1927, for example, these two boats were directly responsible for saving more than 130 lives.[669]

The state-run lifeboat service also continued through this period and, in spite of limited financial support from the public purse, continued to carry out meritorious service. From its inception in 1855 until 1933 the Swedish Lifesaving Service was responsible for saving an estimated 2,289 persons using lifeboats, rocket apparatus and any other means at their disposal. The government service had itself lost 10 of their lifeboatmen in the call of duty.[670] The service carried on for several more years but eventually was surpassed by the success of the voluntary organisation. It is assumed that this branch of the Pilotage Administration eventually evolved into part of the modern Swedish Coast Guard, with the SSRS taking over the predominant role in the provision of lifeboats.

Following the Second World War, the SSRS continued to develop new lifeboats and soon recognised that different types of vessels would be needed for different conditions and demands (see Chapter II-15). Large rescue cruisers would still be needed to patrol the shipping lanes and several modern steel-hulled and ice-strengthened vessels, essentially miniature ships, were built to carry on where the sailing MLBs had left off. Several of these fine vessels are still in service today. Sweden was also one of the first nations to recognise the 'need for speed' as a basic tenet of SAR operations. The grand old man of the SSRS, Hans Hansson, while presenting a paper at the 6th International Lifeboat Conference, held in Oostende, Belgium, in 1951, asked the question:

Is it not possible, with the aid of modern technological resources, to revolutionize the sea rescue service by building lifeboats which make 20 or 30 knots but which are fully seaworthy in all weathers, and on board of which it will be possible to remain in all weathers without reducing speed?

Prophetic words – the fast German rescue cruiser and the USCG's 44ft MLB were a few years away, but Hanson certainly had the right idea.[671]

The Swedes began experimenting with high-speed-lifeboat design during the 1950s and by 1963 had the 34ft (10.3m) *Gustaf V*, with a top speed of 26kt, stationed in the Kattegat. She was followed by the rescue cruiser *Jarl Malmros*, built of light alloy and somewhat larger at 46ft (14.0m), a vessel that had the look and characteristics of many of the fast Swedish lifeboats of the future.[672]

Svenska Sjoraddningssallskapet (SSRS)
Operating Model: Non-Profit Voluntary Society
Source of Income: Private Contributions and State Subsidy
Manning Structure: Volunteer/Employee Crew

The Svenska Sjoraddningssallskapet (SSRS), as it is known today, consists of 45 lifesaving stations operating some 85 rescue craft. There are 11 paid crewmembers, as well as over 400 volunteer lifesavers. The entire operation is managed by

a staff of six at the SSRS headquarters in Götheborg. In 2000 the society responded to 657 SAR missions on the coast and inland waterways of Sweden, this being approximately 60% of all maritime SAR calls for the country.

Today the fleet of SSRS rescue craft consists of everything from large rescue cruisers to small RIBs. As of 1999 considerable efforts were being made to standardise the fleet. Changing demands, with the decline of the offshore fishing fleet, the rise in response to pleasure craft (85% of overall calls in 1995) and an increasing number of large-scale SAR incidents involving large passenger vessels, all became reasons for developing a fast-response capability. Three classes of high-speed rescue craft were then decided upon. The largest, at the time, was the 54ft (16.25m) *Odd Fellow* with a top speed of 32kt and a range of 350 to 400 miles. These vessels are designed for offshore work and as a fast-response tug for the fishing fleet. The new medium-endurance lifeboat is the Victoria class, a 40ft (12m) high-performance epoxy-composite rescue craft equipped with a polyurethane-foam fender system. This impressive vessel has a top speed of 38kt and has two 450-hp diesels powering the vessel through water jets. The new Swedish inshore lifeboat is a 27ft 6in (8.4m) RIB, which uses semi-rigid-foam-filled Polerutan fenders and is powered by a 300-hp diesel running through a single water jet. The SSRS has been experimenting with a semi-sitting seat arrangement called an 'Ullman Chair' on this class and seem to have overcome the problems of back fatigue and injury. Another unique feature is the motorcycle-style steering arrangement with an integrated handle bar and throttle system that allows the driver to adjust speed and steer without releasing the helm.[673] Recognising the merits of this design, several of the 27ft 6in RIBs have been purchased by the Swedish Coast Guard.

In addition to the above, a new 66ft (20m) rescue cruiser, complete with a small jet-powered daughter-boat was placed on station in July 2002. The Rescue 200 type *Gad Rausing* is stationed at Skillinge in the South Baltic.

An SSRS *Rescue 800* fast rescue craft. This water-jet propelled vessel has a top speed of 41kt and utilises a foam-filled polerutan fender system rather than a pneumatic collar. Another unique feature is the ergonomically efficient helm station which uses motorcycle style steering rather than the conventional wheel and throttle as well as semi-sitting shock absorbent 'Ullman' chairs. *SSRS*

Overall responsibility for the provision of maritime SAR within Sweden's designated jurisdiction is vested in the Swedish National Maritime Administration (SNMA). The SNMA operates an MRCC at Götheborg and an MRSC at Stockholm. Another branch of the administration, the Swedish Coast Guard, is responsible for law enforcement at sea and environmental protection and has several patrol boats and large cutters that can be tasked for SAR. The Swedish Air Force has two helicopter bases with designated SAR flights based out of Sola, Oerland and Rygge. For offshore maritime patrol and SAR, the Air Force also has a squadron of P3 Orion aircraft based out of Andoaya.

An intermediate lifeboat of the SSRS. The 40ft (12m) Victoria class is powered by twin 450-hp diesels and water-jets and has a top speed of 38kt. Note the polyurethane fender system.
SSRS

SWITZERLAND

Coastal Conditions & Hazards
Nestled along Switzerland's southwestern border with France lies Lac Léman, one of Europe's largest bodies of fresh water. It covers 225 square miles (586sq.km), 135 of which are in Swiss jurisdiction, the other 90 belonging to France; it is approximately 45 miles (73 km) long and some 9 miles (14 km) across at its widest point. It is a very busy body of water, not only with a considerable amount of commercial traffic but also with a large abundance of pleasure boats. Due to the strong prevailing winds, sailing is a favourite past time on the lake and there are several yacht clubs along the 104 miles (167 km) of coastline. Local winds include a southwesterly that generally occurs when a low-pressure system is passing over central Europe. This wind can blow Force 5 to 6 and can involve intense localised squalls with much stronger winds and wind-driven seas, particularly on the central and western part of the lake. A southeasterly wind, known locally as the Gaudier, is very unpredictable and can be strong and short in duration particularly around the port of Values. In addition to a fairly strong northerly wind known as the Base, which coincides with high-pressure systems in the area, other localised winds of note include the Forget, a northerly offshore afternoon breeze around Morges and the Bornan, a very strong southerly wind that comes from the French mountains over Thonon. All in all, this variety of localised wind and weather patterns can combine to push the fresh water of the lake into a frenzy of whitecaps and spray within minutes, making a boater's day on the water much less pleasurable in very short order.

History of Coastal Lifesaving
The story of organised waterborne lifesaving on Lac Léman begins around 1863. Commercial traffic on the lake was increasing and calamities were becoming more commonplace. In response concerned citizens in some of the small villages on the lakeside took measures to establish some form of lifesaving and salvage facilities. In the region of Vevy-la-Tour-Montreaux a Salvage Corps was established and funds were raised to purchase a rescue and salvage boat. Additional funds were raised over the next several years and, in 1883, the various villages consolidated their resources into an umbrella organisation known as the Société de Sauvetage du Lac le Doyen. Following several successful and well-publicised rescues, the new society continued to attract a considerable amount of interest from both business and government, which translated into further financial support. Around this same period, a prominent group of Swiss officials led by a Colonel William Hubert travelled to Paris to investigate the workings of the French lifesaving society, the Société Centrale de Sauvetage des Naufragés, incorporated in 1865 (see Chapters I-8, I-11; and 'France' p.220). They were greatly impressed with the international nature of the French society as well as its use of volunteer rescuers. As a result, on 6 September 1885, a new international lifesaving organisation was established for the lake with the name Société Internationale de Sauvetage du Léman (SISL).

Soon the new organisation had several pulling lifeboats strategically stationed around the lake in both Switzerland and France and many daring rescues were conducted. Many of these original pulling lifeboats remained in service for decades with the last being used on call-out as late as 1957. Motor lifeboats began to appear in about 1933, with the first being stationed at the village of Ouchy. Also, beginning in 1959, the SISL began to incorporate teams of trained divers into its stations, a service that it continues to provide to this day.

Société Internationale de Sauvetage du Léman (SISL)
Operating Model: Non-Profit Voluntary Organisation
Source of Income: Private Contributions and State Subsidy
Manning Structure: Volunteer Crew

The SISL operates today as an international humanitarian organisation dedicated to saving lives on Lac Léman. There are 34 stations strategically located around the lake, 26 in Switzerland and eight in France. The SISL's fleet of 45 vessels includes 19 patrol boats and 26 rescue craft including some RHIs. The stations are operated year round by approximately 2,200 dedicated volunteers. In 2001 vessels and crews of the SISL carried out 556 rescues, principally from pleasure craft and 38 lives were saved from imminent danger.

TUNISIA

Coastal Conditions & Hazards
Tunisia has approximately 715 miles (1,150km) of coastline facing the Mediterranean north and east towards Sicily and Malta. There are three large bights in the coastline, from north to south: the Gulf of Tunis, Gulf of Hammamet and Gulf of Gábes. Although a heavy swell is rare in this part of the Mediterranean, strong winds from the N and E can cause large seas along the eastern coast of Tunisia, especially near the port of Kelibia on Cape Bon. Large waterspouts are common here and some have been known to come ashore and wreak havoc.

The North African wind known as the Scirocco in other parts of the Mediterranean, is known in Tunisia as the Chihli wind. More violent versions of the same wind are referred to as the Simoon. This is a hot dry wind having just come from the adjacent desert, although it becomes moist and humid as it travels across the sea towards European shores. The Chihli is a south or southwesterly wind most common during the spring months. On the north coast of Tunisia, strong northwesterly gales are experienced in both winter and summer and topographical effects make the area 'especially liable to sudden shifts in the wind'. In this same area, off Bizerte, frequent thunder squalls cause local turbulent conditions and heavy seas from west through north can occur throughout the year.[674]

Service National de Surveillance Cotiere (SNSC)
Operating Model: Para-Military Agency Managed by Government
Source of Income: State Funded
Manning Structure: Employee Crew

In 1940 there were five principal lifesaving stations listed along the coast of Tunisia, two of which, Sousse and Bizerte, were equipped with pulling lifeboats. These stations were established during the period of French colonial rule.[675] In 1970 the Service National de Surveillance Cotiere (SNSC) was established to fulfil the following mandates in addition to coastal security: SAR, pollution prevention, vessel traffic control and fisheries enforcement. The organisation's headquarters are located at the main naval base at Tunis and there are two regional headquarters at Bizerte in the Northern District and Sfax in the South. The SNSC operates three primary maritime communications centres at Zarzis, Sousse and Tabarka at which VTS facilities are co-located.

There are 18 lifeboats and rescue craft at the disposal of the SNSC, these include 18 vessels over 33ft (10m) and seven smaller boats under 33ft (10m). The largest include nine high-speed patrol boats and nine 44ft (13.7m) MLBs located at eight lifeboat stations along the coast. These resources are frequently augmented by air and marine units of the Tunisian military, which are on SAR standby 24 hours per day.

TURKEY

Coastal Conditions & Hazards
Linking Asia and Europe, Turkey's coastline runs along the southern shores of the Black Sea to the north, the Aegean Sea to the west and the eastern reaches of the Mediterranean to the south. The Black Sea coast has very few ports and is primarily sandy in nature. In some locations there are strong anabatic and katabatic winds and heavy seas are created along the southern part of the Black Sea by strong northerly winds, enhanced locally by high ground rising steeply from the coast. These winds can switch directions to southeast at night as the cool air drains from the mountain valleys. On the northwest coast of Turkey lies the Sea of Marmara, a land-locked body of water that separates the Black Sea from the Aegean Sea. Access for shipping into the Black Sea is via the Bosphorous, and from the Aegean Sea through the Dardanelles. The Sea of Marmara has its own local weather anomaly, referred to as the Meltemi, similar to the Greek Etesian wind, which blows from the northeast, predominantly in the summer months. The west coast of Turkey is archipelagic in nature (see 'Greece' p.224) and has many rocky headlands and inlets. Along the southern Mediterranean coast, where the topography tends to be somewhat lower and less defined, Sciroccos, relatively moist southerly winds carrying dust and haze from North Africa are fairly frequent, although storms with winds in excess of storm Force 10 are a somewhat rare occurrence.[676] [677]

History of Coastal Lifesaving
Turkey's strategic position in the world, being situated between two important seas at the crossroads of two continents, has always meant that maritime commerce and traffic has abounded in its coastal waters. In 1866, after several maritime disasters in and around the Port of Constantinople (now Istanbul), discussions were initiated between representatives from several foreign embassies (principally those with considerable shipping interests such as Britain, Italy and France) and local officials regarding the necessity to develop some form of lifesaving service for that part of the Turkish coast. The result was the establishment of the first Turkish Lifeboat Service in 1869. This new entity was to be governed by an international board of delegates from the embassies concerned as well as a representative from the Ottoman Government. Its headquarters were to be at Constantinople and it was to be funded by a small levy on outbound shipping from the Black Sea. By 1880, however, the system had fallen into utter disarray.[678]

In 1886 the service was revamped through the concerted efforts of two Englishman, Matthew Summers and Captain Samuel Palmer. Summers was instrumental in establishing several lifeboat and rocket apparatus stations as well as a lightship for the Bosphorous. Captain Palmer became an employee of the service and would remain so for approximately 27 years during which time he is said to have helped save some 1,400 lives. He retired just prior to the outbreak of the First World War having received several lifesaving medals, including those of Turkey, Greece and Imperial Russia. By 1911 the service had become even more permanently entrenched with two separate districts being established, one in Europe and one in Asia. Captain Palmer trained and supervised the all-Turkish crews at the 15 lifesaving stations and numerous intermediate posts at which some 11 'insubmersible' lifeboats and 18 smaller rescue craft were placed.[679]

It seems that the Turkish Lifeboat Service survived the ravages of the 1914-18 war relatively unscathed and by 1923 had become a government-run General Directorate under the auspices of the Ministry of the Economy. The service did not stagnate; in fact it flourished after the Turkish Government employed the services of Hendrik De Booy, long-time director of the North and South Lifeboat Society in Holland, as an advisor (see Chapter II-13 and 'The Netherlands' p.238). Six new stations were established in the European zone, two with new lifeboats and all with rocket apparatus. Ten more were placed on the Anatolian coast with six new lifeboats. All were connected by telephone and each zone had caterpillar tractors where required for launching. At its peak the service employed some 250 men. By 1940 it boasted 18 lifesaving stations, five of which had pulling lifeboats.[680]

In 1950 a 35ft 6in (10.8m) MLB was purchased from the RNLI. The Lifeboat and Lighthouse Services were amalgamated into a single branch of the Turkish Maritime Association in 1952. By 1974 the organisation had been renamed the Turkish Sea Rescue Service and had come under the control of the Turkish Maritime Bank, a state-run company that also administered the levy on shipping. The new service had been split into three zones, Rumeli on the European side of the Black Sea and Anadolu and Kefken on the Anatolian side. The total number of stations had decreased to five lifeboat and 12 rocket apparatus units.[681] In 1984 the organisation was renamed the Turkish Coastal Safety and Lighthouse Department and in 1997 the present structure, Kiyi Emniyeti ve Gemi Kurtarma Isletmeleri Genel Müdürlügü (Coastal Safety and Salvage Administration) was established.

Kiyi Emniyeti ve Gemi Kurtarma Isletmeleri Genel Müdürlügü
Operating Model: Civilian Agency Managed by Government
Source of Income: State Funded
Manning Structure: Employee Crew

The Turkish Coastal Safety and Salvage Administration is today responsible for not only SAR in Turkish waters, but also the maintenance of lighthouses and other aids to

An Atlantic 21 RHI working for the Turkish DDD, a voluntary lifesaving service.
DDD

navigation as well as marine salvage and disaster management with a fleet of powerful ocean-going tugs on standby. The administration still maintains eight Tahlisiye (lifesaving stations) around the country, all of which have line-throwing apparatus and three of which, Harem and Kefken at either end of the Bosphorous, and Rumeli, have powerful 60ft (18m) MLBs. There are also three smaller fast rescue craft in service, approximately 10 Land Rovers and four large Unimog all-terrain vehicles. The stations are manned 24 hours per day, by approximately 200 specially-trained personnel.

The Administration is presently in the midst of a large-scale modernisation and lifeboat station expansion programme with approximately 30 new large high-speed RHIs being constructed by a Turkish-Norwegian consortium. These will be utilised at the existing lifesaving stations as well as at new units, which will be strategically located to fill any gaps in coastal SAR coverage. There are also plans for the purchase of 20 smaller RHI inshore rescue boats to augment the enhanced service as well as new all-terrain vehicles and ambulances. The plans also include the purchase of a dedicated SAR helicopter and upgrades to the facilities of the Administration's Coast Radio Stations at Samsun, Izmir, Fethiye, Antalya and Mersin to the latest GMDSS standards.

In addition to the dedicated SAR and salvage/towage resources of the Turkish Coastal Safety and Salvage Administration, a multitude of other waterborne resources are available for use in rescue at sea including craft belonging to the Turkish Navy as well as various port, pilot and customs authorities. On the air side, there are over a dozen bases at which both fixed- and rotary-wing resources are available, some of which are specifically assigned to SAR being co-located with para-rescue teams. The principal coordinator of all SAR within the Turkish SRR is the Ministry of Transport. To this end, a JRCC is located at Ankara with a sub-centre being located at Samsun.[682]

Denizciler Dayanisma Dernegi (DDD)
Operating Model: Non-Profit Voluntary Organisation
Source of Income: Private Contributions and
Commercial Activity
Manning Structure: Volunteer Crew

The DDD was established in the late 1990s as the first non-governmental organisation in Turkey since 1869 whose objective is saving lives at sea. As of 2002 the fledgling organisation could boast some 1,600 members, approximately 200 of whom crew on private vessels and motor yachts. The DDD also has at its disposal its first dedicated rescue craft: two Atlantic 21 RHIs on loan from the International Lifeboat Federation (RNLI) as well as an ex-naval landing craft. The main area of operation is at the southern entrance of the Istanbul Strait (Bosphoros) where the organisation has set up its first dedicated rescue station.

The DDD raises funds through various initiatives including voluntary contributions and members' fees. There is a commercial division of the DDD, which specialises in the sale of chandlery, the chartering of the organisation's landing craft and souvenir and gift sales. The main aim of the DDD is to introduce and spread the idea of volunteerism in SAR throughout Turkish waters as well as to promote issues related to boating safety and public education. From the obvious success of recent efforts it would appear that the DDD is well on its way to fulfilling its objective.

UNITED KINGDOM

Coastal Conditions & Hazards

Considering Britain's prominent role in the development of organised coastal lifesaving and the lifeboat, it is vital to understand the vagaries of her coastal geography and weather conditions. Beginning in the south and the southwest, along the English Channel the coast is generally high and rocky, particularly in Cornwall and Devon where there are relatively few large ports. Off Land's End, the southwesternmost tip of England, lie the Isles of Scilly, fully exposed to the North Atlantic. The many shoals and reefs surrounding these islands further complicate navigation in the area. The Atlantic shores of the West Country also have no natural breakwater and from the Bristol Channel to Land's End, monster waves come crashing ashore in winter.

In the English Channel, rough seas may be expected six to seven days a month in the winter and large oceanic swells may add to the chaos, particularly if it is from the west-southwest. In western sections of the Channel winds of Force 8 and above are reported for about 15% of winter. The coastal topography changes to the east, with a greater predominance of sandstone cliffs and an abundance of rivers and estuaries. There is a great deal of maritime traffic in the area, with hundreds of shipping movements every day and cross-channel ferries steaming to and from such major ports as Plymouth, Southampton and Portsmouth.

At its eastern end, the Channel narrows to form the Dover Strait, an area of incredibly dense vessel traffic and strong tidal currents – just 18 miles (29km) wide at its narrowest point and interspersed with a series of narrow, shifting sandbanks and countless submerged wrecks (the most recent being the car-carrier _Tricoleur_, sunk off Dunkerque in December 2002). Extreme sea and swell conditions can occur here in winter. To the west of the Strait, the coast is battered by predominantly southwest and westerly gales; within the Strait itself strong winds from the southwest or northeast can funnel, creating potentially hazardous sea conditions on this busy ferry route.

Around the corner to the north and east lies the estuary of the Thames. From here north along the outer coast of Essex to the port of Harwich there are many treacherous sandbanks, such as the notorious Goodwin Sands, which extend several miles offshore and upon which the sea can break with tremendous force. The low, sandy shoreline continues along the coasts of Suffolk, Norfolk, and as far north as the Humber estuary, where many large rivers flow into the southern reaches of the North Sea, and where again the English coast is characterised by outlying sandbanks complicated by treacherous tidal currents that can flow as fast as 4kt. Some of these banks extend 45 miles (72km) offshore and are marked in winter by the surging line of white breakers during onshore gales. The low, almost indistinguishable nature of the coast is affected by a high incidence of fog; again, there are relatively few safe ports of refuge.

From Humberside to Rattray Head, the northeast tip of Scotland, the coast becomes increasingly rocky in nature, with more pronounced steep bluffs and offshore rocks and islands such as the Farne group off Northumberland. This entire coast, from East Anglia in the south to the east coast of Scotland is at the mercy of the North Sea and, from October to April, gales from the NE and SE can blow with extraordinary violence. These winds and resultant seas have a particularly disastrous effect at certain locations such as in the Firth of Forth and further south off Great Yarmouth, where harbours are fully exposed to easterly gales. The notorious bars at the mouths of the Tees and the Tyne in Northumberland are susceptible to storms from the northeast, while at the Humber estuary it is southeasterly storms that bring problems. Off Scotland, between the Firth of Forth and Rattray Head, winds have generated waves of 'phenomenal' magnitude on rare occasions; wind gusts in this region have been recorded in the range of 95kt.

The north coast of Scotland becomes even more bold, craggy and indented as one rounds the top of Britain into the Pentland Firth separating Scotland from the Shetland Islands. The effects of this steeper topography are strong coastal winds that funnel down the valleys. In the Pentland Firth, the funnelling of the wind can work against strong tidal streams to create a large 'race', or tidal rip, a barrier of confused, breaking seas that behave as if standing still and pouring in on themselves, only to be revived and rise again. The Shetlands, and the Orkneys further to the north, have their own natural coastal hazards, not least of which are thousands of reefs and skerries. Localised winds and unpredictable, violent squalls are frequent occurrences and strong tidal currents pass through the narrow channels separating the islands. The *British Admiralty Sailing Directions* for the area state that the 'combination of high seas and a heavy swell is liable to create confused seas of hazardous proportions'.

The sailing directions for Scotland's west coast describe it as 'an almost uninterrupted succession of deep indentations fronted by bold rocky cliffs and headlands which are inhospitable and to be avoided'. Not exactly the stuff of tourist brochures, but this is one of the most ruggedly beautiful locations on earth. Here are the island chains known as the Outer and Inner Hebrides separated by a body of water known as the Little and North Minch and forming a natural breakwater for most of western Scotland. Coastal banks and rock pinnacles extend as far as 12 miles (19km) offshore from the Outer Hebrides. Winds in this region are Force 5 or higher 70% of the time. Continuous gale-force winds for more than 48 hours have been recorded on the Butt of Lewis. Sea and swell conditions can only be described as severe in the winter months and, although the outer islands do provide some protection from the open ocean, local wind anomalies and squalls regularly produce large wind-driven seas within the coastal channels and inlets. Similar conditions prevail over the remainder of the west coast of Scotland southward to the Mull of Kintyre.

The west coasts of England and Wales are characterised by bold headlands and rocky cliffs, although stretches of low coastal plain with extensive beaches and sandbars do occur in the vicinity of some river estuaries such as the Ribble in Lancashire, the Mersey, off Liverpool, and the Severn at the head of the Bristol Channel. The shores of England and Wales, from the Scottish border to the Bristol Channel, including the Isle of Man, are somewhat protected from the North Atlantic by the natural barrier of Ireland. One would think that this would make the waters of the Irish Sea less tempestuous than more exposed areas but, unfortunately, it is not the case. Some of the roughest seas in the Irish Sea are caused by strong winds from S to NW, although the north coast of Wales and the Isle of Man are particularly susceptible to easterly gales in winter. Violent squalls, although relatively rare, do occur in this region, again particularly in winter and adjacent to the steeper parts of the coast. Gusts in the range of 100kt have been recorded on the exposed outer coasts. The effects of tide and current are very pronounced here. In the Menai Strait, separating the Isle of Anglesey from North Wales, currents can reach as much as 8kt with similar rates being found in the Bristol Channel. Mean tidal ranges in certain ports in South Wales are as much as 40ft (12.3m). Tidal races occur throughout the channel and the effects of the outflow from the Severn Estuary and the Bristol Channel can be felt far out into the Irish Sea.[683]

History of Coastal Lifesaving

In terms of lifeboats and coastal lifesaving, Britain's historical record is full of firsts; it is for this reason that the nation is known as the 'cradle of the lifeboat'. Prior to the advent of the purpose-built lifeboat in Great Britain, most efforts to assist victims of shipwreck were conducted by private citizens who either worked on, or resided near, the coast. In 1751 one of the world's first charitable organisations in aid of the shipwrecked was established by the Trustees of the Bishop Crewe Estate at Bamburgh Castle in Northumberland and for the next 75 years the status of lifesaving around the British coast waxed and waned but, for the most part, remained local in its organisational structure. (For early history in Britain's lifesaving see Chapters I 4-9 and II 3-8.)

In 1824 the Royal National Institution for the Preservation of Life from Shipwreck was established to be reorganised as the RNLI in 1854. From then on the organisation would flourish into one of the most successful the world has ever known. The RNLI would help lead the way internationally with advice and assistance on both operating structures for lifeboat organisations in other countries as well as lifeboat designs and technology (see Chapter I-11).

From a technological perspective Great Britain and the RNLI pioneered in the development of steam lifeboats (see Chapter II-10) starting in the late 1880s, as well as MLBs (see Chapter II-11 and II-12) towards the turn of the century. In more recent years, the institution has switched from the old displacement-type lifeboats (see Chapter II-19) to high-speed self-righting lifeboats (see Chapter II-21). Another British innovation has been the invention and early development of the rigid-hull inflatable rescue craft, possibly the most widely used type of lifesaving vessel in the world today (see Chapter II-20).

Royal National Lifeboat Institution (RNLI)
Operating Model: Non-Profit Voluntary Organisation
Source of Income: Private Contributions
Manning Structure: Volunteer Crew

A tractor and carriage launch the 39ft (12m) Mersey class RNLB *Leonard Kent* at Margate. Note the tunnel-drive protection for the propellers and rudders that allows the boat to strike bottom without incurring damage.
Nicholas Leach

Today, the RNLI remains one of the largest and most successful private, volunteer maritime lifesaving agencies in the world. What originated as Sir William Hillary's dream back in 1824, now comprises some 224 lifeboat stations in the United Kingdom and Ireland (see 'Ireland' p.229). In 1999 lifeboats and crews of the RNLI responded to 6,574 SAR incidents and saved an incredible 1,030 lives. There are approximately 4,500 volunteer crewmembers within the organisation, including 240 women. Each all-weather lifeboat employs a full-time mechanic and every crewmember receives basic compensation to cover their expenses each time they are called out. The RNLI remains entirely dependant on voluntary contributions for income with a considerable amount of revenue now coming from private legacies. The Institution is also the permanent secretariat for the International Lifeboat Federation (ILF), whose headquarters are co-located at Poole, Dorset.

As of 2001 the RNLI had an active fleet of 309 rescue craft ranging from the smallest 16ft (4.9m) D class inflatable, right up to the large and powerful 55ft 9in (17m) Severn class self-righting MLB. There are another 110 additional lifeboats in the reserve fleet. Recent developments within the Institution include the introduction of a new standard RHI, the Atlantic 75, a replacement for the old Atlantic 21 type, as well as construction of a new slipway-launched prototype to replace the Tyne class (see Chapter II-23).

Of course the RNLI is not the only organisation in Great Britain concerned with coastal and maritime SAR. There are still a multitude of local and county organisations, both volunteer and state-funded, that provide vessels for lifesaving within specific jurisdictions. The Maritime and Coastguard Agency (formerly known as HM Coastguard) still oversees the volunteer coastal rescue units that operate the breeches-buoy apparatus, a responsibility they have steadfastly maintained since the 1850s, saving approximately 10,000 lives since that time (see Chapter 1-12). The Coastguard maintains the principal SAR coordination role for all UK waters through a network of integrated coast radio stations and rescue coordination centres. This service also charters a fleet of dedicated SAR helicopters strategically positioned around the country. Large S-61 helicopters are stationed at Sumburgh Airport in the Shetland Islands and at Stornoway in the Outer Hebrides. Additional machines have been located at Lee-on-Solent and Portland in the south of England. The Royal Air Force and Royal Navy also maintain several helicopter and fixed-wing SAR flights around England, Scotland and Wales. The principal SAR aircraft is the Sea King helicopter, and a flight of long-range RAF Nimrod maritime patrol aircraft is also on constant standby for rapid response offshore.

UNITED STATES OF AMERICA

Coastal Conditions & Hazards

The continental United States (including Alaska) has 12,400 miles (19,924km) of coastline bordering on the Atlantic and Pacific Oceans, the Gulf of Mexico and the Great Lakes. Starting in the northeast from the Canadian border, the coast

The 47ft (14m) slipway-launched Tyne class *Anne Blaker* stationed at Wicklow, Ireland. She is being escorted by a D-type inshore lifeboat.
Nicholas Leach

of New England as far south as Cape Cod abounds with rugged headlands, inlets, rocks, reefs and intricate channels. There are many offshore islands, particularly off the coasts of Maine and New Hampshire, that help form a natural breakwater from Atlantic storms. Fortunately for the coastal mariner and fisherman, there are many well-protected ports of refuge in this region. The shores around Cape Cod are sandy and low, the Cape itself consisting of a narrow strip of sand that juts out into the Atlantic some 40 miles (64km) before suddenly veering due north approximately the same distance. Like an arm reaching out to grab ships, the shoal waters, onshore gales and bad visibility in the area of the Cape have spelt disaster for many a ship trying to reach Boston in the early days of sail and steam. From Monomoy on the elbow of the Cape, to Montauk Point on the northeastern tip of Long Island, the coast is very similar to that in the north. From here, however, the character of the coast changes drastically. The outer coasts of Long Island and New Jersey, as far south as Cape May on the edge of Delaware Bay, consist of long, narrow beaches averaging from about 400yd to five miles (366m to 8km) in width, separated, in many locations, by narrow channels or bays. Some of these beaches are separated from the mainland by inlets, becoming barrier islands – essentially large sand dunes that poke out of the sea. Running parallel all along this coast is a treacherous sandbar from 100 to 400yd (90 to 365m) off the beach, and upon which tremendous walls of surf break during violent storms. In the days of sail the shifting bars of sand formed a natural deathtrap for many, particularly those driven on to a leeshore by the prevailing easterly storms in winter.

From Delaware Bay south to the vicinity of Cape Hatteras, the coast is very similar, although it is indented by more significant bays and sounds, including Chesapeake Bay. From North Carolina down to the Florida Keys it continues low and sandy, although the barrier beaches become less frequent. There are various coastal bars where rivers meet the sea, as well as low-lying islands and outflow currents from inshore waters that cause particular concern to small vessels returning from sea. This area is known as the hurricane coast, for it is often along these shores that tropical revolving storms come ashore after ripping a destructive path across the Caribbean. The US coast along the Gulf of Mexico is extremely low in profile and there are shoals a considerable distance offshore that necessitate the dredging of hundreds of miles of shipping channels throughout the region, such as at the entrance to the Mississippi River and the approaches to the Port of Galveston, Texas. There are various areas of swamps, river deltas and everglades all along the Gulf Coast, and storm surges are a problem for residents and mariners alike.

The Pacific coast of the United States is generally steep along its entire length, from Mexico to Canada, with bold headlands becoming progressively more frequent from Northern California to the northwestern tip of the continental United States at Cape Flattery, Washington. There are very few harbours along the coast of Southern California. Off San Pedro (Los Angeles) the famed Santa Ana winds act like a giant blow-dryer drawing warm, desert air offshore in the autumn and winter months, with velocities of up to 50kt. This wind can cause considerable grief amongst the incredibly large number of pleasure boats that frequent local cruising grounds off Los Angeles, San Diego and out in the Channel Islands. On the outer coasts of Oregon and Washington, almost all the principal ports are accessible only by crossing a treacherous river bar fully exposed to the North Pacific swells. On many occasions throughout the year dangerous conditions cause the local Coast Guard stations to close these bars to all traffic. Massive seas have been recorded along this stretch of coast. On 18 October 1912 the Tillamook Rock light station on the Oregon coast was struck by just such a sea. The next day the lighthouse lantern, about 132ft (40m) above sea level, was discovered to have had its lens broken, and the fog signal, 92ft (28m) above sea level, had been rendered inoperable, having been filled with small rocks tossed up from the ocean bottom. The northern regions of the United States Pacific coast are also characterised by large rock pillars that jut out of the sea hundreds of feet along the coastal beaches, and sometimes far offshore. The Strait of Juan de Fuca, that separates Washington State from British Columbia, is an area of heavy shipping as vessels make their way to and from the busy ports of Seattle and Vancouver. The relatively narrow entrance is further complicated by strong westerly winds at its western approaches in the spring and summer months as well as powerful tidal currents. Strong southerly winds in the winter months can also produce treacherous conditions off Cape Flattery, Washington, for vessels heading in and out of the strait.

The Alaska panhandle and the state's southern coastline as far as Kodiak Island has conditions very similar to that of the Pacific shores of Canada (see 'Canada' p.205). In the Aleutian Islands, however, things begin to change. Winds at Dutch Harbour, the principal haven in the group, frequently blow at hurricane force and at the Island of Adak, further to the west, winds of 104kt have been recorded. Although most harbours are ice-free in this area, severe icing of vessels can be a major problem and has claimed many vessels engaged in the lucrative crab fishery. The Bering Sea has some of the most atrocious weather on earth, the pilot stating that 'The weather over the Bering Sea is generally bad and very changeable. Good weather is the exception, and it does not last long when it does occur.'

Last but not least are the thousands of miles of navigable shoreline where the United States borders the Great Lakes. These bodies of water are navigable for approximately eight months of the year, with ice closing most of the ports in winter. Violent storms and squalls are known to occur throughout the region, particularly either side of the ice season, and can whip the lakes into a frenzy of breaking seas and spray, the prevailing shallow depths and the lower density of fresh water further expediting the rapid build up.[684]

History of Coastal Lifesaving

Like the United Kingdom the United States has a long history of lifesaving. The first organisation was a private and voluntary entity: the Massachusetts Humane Society (MHS), founded in Boston in 1785 (see Chapter I-4). In 1790 the United States Revenue Cutter Service, otherwise known as the Revenue Marine, was established as a branch of the US Treasury Department. The principal duties of the revenue 'cutters' were to patrol the coasts and intercept smugglers but soon they were being used for lifesaving as well (see Chapters 1-6 and II-16). In 1832 the US Congress passed an act decreeing that one or more of the revenue cutters would patrol off certain sections of the Atlantic seaboard in winter months on lifesaving duty and the offshore cutter remains one of the main components of the USCG's SAR response capability to this day.

By the 1840s lifesaving services began to spread south from New England. Ships loaded with hopeful immigrants were being lost by the score on the approaches to the ports of New York and Philadelphia and along the New Jersey shore. Spurred on by concerned New Jersey Congressman, Dr William Newell, Congress allocated $10,000 in 1848 to procure 'surfboats, rockets and carronades', and to establish volunteer lifeboat and line-throwing stations along the New Jersey coastline. More money would follow to establish similar stations in New York and Long Island, and to assist the MHS. Although manned by volunteer crewmen, the stations in New Jersey and New York were to be administered by an officer of the Revenue Marine. These early government-funded stations, although far from perfect, would help considerably in stemming the heavy losses in ships and lives along American shores. Eventually, the US Government would supply lifeboats and line-throwing apparatus for locations all over the country but the turmoil of the American Civil War would result in the deterioration and abandonment of most of these stations and their equipment (see Chapter I-10).

In 1871, the United States Life-Saving Service (USLSS) was established with Sumner Kimball as its General

Secretary. Massive reforms were undertaken, including guidelines for maintenance and training, and the hiring of both station keepers and surfmen, eventually on a permanent basis. Experiments with different types of rescue craft were conducted in order to standardise the boats within the service, the preference being for lightweight surfboats, although larger self-righting lifeboats would also be adopted from overseas (see Chapter II-8). The USLSS would also develop their own specialised line-throwing apparatus, principally through the efforts of Lt. David Lyle (see also Chapter I-12). By 1900 the USLSS would have established an incredible 269 lifeboat and lifesaving stations around the coasts of the United States and Alaska.

The USLSS would continue in operation up until the First World War and would lead the way internationally in the development of such lifesaving technologies as integrated communications between lifesaving stations and the development and acceptance of the MLB through the concerted efforts of Lt. C.H. McLellan and others (see Chapters I-10 and II-12).

In 1915 the service was amalgamated with the Revenue Marine to form the United States Coast Guard (USCG).

Although still managed by the Treasury Department, the USCG was now considered to be one of the nation's armed services and would become an integral part of the US Navy during times of war (see Chapter I-15). Following the amalgamation, cutters, and later aircraft, of the USCG continued to provide the service (see Chapter III-2). Starting in 1916 a number of officers in the USCG received training at the US Navy Flight School at Pensacola, Florida, and the USCG's air arm was born (see Chapter III-1).

Following the introduction of Prohibition in the 1920s, the resources of the USCG were expanded to help curb the illicit trade in alcohol. The first dedicated USCG Air Stations were created utilising flying boats and other designated fixed-wing aircraft. These were also used for search and rescue, and by the 1930s the first 'flying lifeboats' had been procured specifically for that purpose. The USCG would become a leading world expert in the use of aircraft for rescue at sea and, after 1941, in the initial development of one of the principal maritime search and rescue tools of the future, the helicopter.

Two other government agencies would be amalgamated into the USCG by 1942: the Lighthouse Service and the Steamship Inspection Service. In 1958 the USCG became a lead agency in the development and implementation of the Automated Mutual-Assistance Vessel Rescue System, or AMVER. This system, which remains in operation to this day, keeps track of ship's positions worldwide, allowing rescue coordinators to rapidly summon assistance to distress situations (see Chapter III-3). In 1967 the USCG left the Treasury Department, moving to the US Department of Transportation and additional roles of providing maritime law enforcement and environmental protection in US waters were added to its mandate. The USCG continued to be keenly involved in the development of coastal rescue craft, however. At the International Lifeboat Conference held in Scotland in 1963 the USCG introduced a revolutionary new

type of self-righting MLB, known as the 44 Footer. Several lifesaving nations attending the conference were deeply impressed with its qualities, not least of which was speed, and either ordered vessels from the US or built similar vessels of their own (see Chapters II-17 and II-21). Further developments in coastal rescue craft followed, including the use of multi-purpose utility boats, or UTBs and, more recently, the new 47ft (14.33m) self-righting MLB (see Chapters II-18 and II-22).

United States Coast Guard (USCG)
Operating Model: Military Agency Managed by Government
Source of Income: State Funded
Manning Structure: Employee Crew

Search and rescue remains one of the principal responsibilities of the USCG today. In 2000 the service responded to approximately 19,230 marine distress calls and saved an astounding 3,383 lives. Approximately two thirds of all SAR

Powering up the backside of a breaking wave, a USCG 47ft (14.3m) MLB crew watch attentively for more of the same.
Larry Kellis, USCG

incidents responded to by the USCG are handled by the service's small-boat stations. To accomplish this the USCG maintains a large fleet of approximately 1,400 small craft, including RHIs, UTBs and MLBs whose primary purpose is SAR, as well as approximately 200 larger patrol boats and offshore patrol cutters. There are presently some 130 lifeboat stations located in the nine separate districts that comprise the USCG.

There are also more than 200 USCG helicopters and fixed-wing aircraft at USCG Air Stations around the United States and its territories. These include everything from the medium-range HH-65 Dolphin helicopter to the larger, longer-range, HH-60 Jayhawk. On the fixed-wing side, USCG aircraft include the HU-

25 Falcon jet, which can be used for rapid response to a distress scene, and the large C-130 transport plane, used for International Ice Patrol, as well as long-range SAR duties.

The USCG is the lead agency in the coordination and resolution of maritime SAR incidents within the search and rescue regions (SRRs) falling under US responsibility. To this end it maintains a large network of coast radio stations and rescue coordination centres (RCCs) in the US (including Alaska and Hawaii) as well as a sub-centre in San Juan, Puerto Rico. On an international level the USCG remains deeply involved in providing assistance to other nations. In addition to the AMVER programme, the USCG also operates a National SAR School and UTB training centre at Yorktown, Virginia, and the National Motor Lifeboat School at Cape Disappointment, Washington. Both have been used to train crews and rescue personnel from other nations. The USCG has worked diligently with maritime rescue organisations from other countries in recent years to integrate international air and marine SAR procedures in the form of the new IMO IAMSAR Manual (see Chapter III-3).

United States Coast Guard Auxiliary (USCGA)
Operating Model: Non-Profit Voluntary Organisation
Source of Income: State Funded
Manning Structure: Volunteer Crew

The USCGA was established as the United States Coast Guard Reserve in June 1939. The idea was the brainchild of a Los Angeles yachtsman, Malcolm Stuart Boylan, and a USCG Lieutenant (later Commandant), F.C. Pollard. The idea was to utilise the burgeoning number of pleasure craft and yachts as a reserve fleet to aid the Coast Guard and to assist in the provision of public education in boating safety. The new reserve was to be a civilian organisation but, if members' vessels were used for Coast Guard duties, a CG Petty Officer was to be onboard. The core unit of the new reserve fleet was to be a flotilla of approximately 10 vessels, with five or more flotillas composing a division. Each division would coincide with a USCG district and an officer of the USCG would be assigned as liaison. The programme was quite successful: by June 1940 there were some 2,600 members and approximately 2,300 boats enrolled and a large-scale training programme was implemented.

During the Second World War the USCG Reserve provided enormous assistance in the near-coastal waters of the United States and was responsible for saving hundreds of victims of torpedo attack. The reservists also provided vessels and manpower for valuable picket (security) duty in and around US ports. One reservist who used his yacht on several picket patrols around Los Angeles was the actor, Humphrey Bogart. By war's end the USCG Reserve boasted a membership of 67,533 men and women. After 1945 with the Reserve's military role diminished, the term USCG Auxiliary was used to describe a more streamlined organisation. The USCGA reverted to its previous roles of assisting the USCG in search and rescue and providing courses for members and yachtsmen. In the 1950s the USCGA established air flotillas utilising members' private aircraft. Members with skills in HAM and other radio communications were utilised to set up local communications stations that could be used as back-up in the event of a large-scale disaster.

In the 1960s and '70s, the USCGA's role in educating the public about boating safety expanded greatly. Their ability to get out into the marinas and talk to boaters was put to full advantage. In the mid 1980s a boat crew qualification project was developed by the USCG to train members of the USCGA to assist the regular service at their small-boat stations. USCGA members have saved many lives with their own vessels over the years by being close to the scene of an emergency when disaster strikes. In the event of large-scale natural disasters, such as hurricane Andrew in Florida in 1993, the USCGA has been used to evacuate hundreds of people prior to, and in the wake of, a storm.

Today the USCGA remains the civilian, non-military component of the USCG. Its approximately 34,000 active members are responsible for saving an estimated 500 lives each year. In addition, on an annual basis the USCGA assists 11,000 other boaters in distress, flies 1,600 air patrols, operates 2,300 auxiliary radio stations, and conducts 29,000 safety patrols with its vessels. The public education role remains paramount, however, and it is estimated that the USCGA annually reaches some 500,000 students nationwide with its courses on safe boating, navigation and seamanship.[685][686]

Association for Rescue at Sea (AFRAS)
Operating Model: Non-Profit Voluntary Organisation
Source of Income: Private Contributions
Manning Structure: Volunteer

AFRAS is a non-profit charitable organisation whose aim is to promote assistance to those in peril on the sea. AFRAS was founded in 1975 by a group of American professional seamen and businessmen to address the needs of rescue organisations around the world, to raise funds, exchange information and provide international cooperation. Directors of AFRAS include working and retired members of the USCG and other marine-related organisations.

The focus is to raise funds to provide lifeboats and other rescue gear to voluntary lifesaving organisations around the world. To this end, members of AFRAS maintain a strong working relationship with the RNLI and the ILF, the KNRM in The Netherlands, and the USCGA. Over the years AFRAS has funded new rescue craft for Great Britain, The Netherlands and Estonia, as well as other countries. Recently AFRAS signed mutual fund-raising agreements with the KNRM, ICE-SAR of Iceland and VISAR in the British Virgin Islands.

AFRAS holds an annual banquet at which several awards are presented to lifesavers from around the world. These include the annual Gold Medal for an enlisted Coast Guard person who performed an act of extraordinary bravery during a rescue at sea, and the AMVER plaque for the most notable rescue by a ship and its crew participating in the system. AFRAS also maintains a close working relationship with Maritime Rescue International, an organisation that provides hands-on SAR training and technical expertise based in Stonehaven, Scotland.

URUGUAY

Coastal Conditions & Hazards

The coastline of Uruguay faces the northern reaches of the Rio de la Plata, from the estuary of the Rio Uruguay beyond Punta del Este where it borders the South Atlantic Ocean and begins to swing northward until it meets the Brazilian coastline in the vicinity of 33°45' South. The topography features rocky bluffs and cliffs interspersed with long sandy beaches. To the west of Punta del Este, the waters begin to shallow rather quickly and dredged channels are needed for access to the principal ports. Aside from the extensive shoals created by the silt brought down by the Rivers Uruguay and Paraná from the Amazon Basin, another substantial hazard is the innumerable wrecks. Tidal rates and directions vary in the Rio de la Plata being particularly influenced by the volume of fresh water outflow from the main rivers. The fresh water on the surface is easily turned into a breaking sea, particularly when the currents are confronted by an opposing wind. Local winds in the Rio de la Plata include the Pampero, which arises off the Argentinian pampas to the southwest and brings with it severe and sudden squalls, as well as the Sudestada, which can create extremely heavy seas.[687]

History of Coastal Lifesaving

A proud tradition of lifesaving exists in Uruguay. The Asociacion Honoraria de Salvamentos Maritimos y Fluviales (ADES), provides a valuable service for mariners in this busy part of the world where the waters of the Ria Plata meet the broad Atlantic. The river is, and always has been, one of the primary access points in and out of the South American hinterland, as well as to and from the Argentine ports to the south. In Noel Methley's 1912 book, *The Lifeboat and Its Story*, there is mention of a 'good salvage service with powerful steam tugs, which are sufficient to render any assistance which may be required either on the River Platte or on the coast'.[688] By 1940, however, the Uruguayan government had established 14 lifesaving stations along the coast, all of them equipped with lifeboats. The stations at Paysandu, Soriano, Colonia, Santiago Vasquez, Montevideo, Isla de Flores, Punta del Este and La Paloma all had MLBs at their disposal.[689] Unfortunately, by the mid 1950s, the service had waned somewhat and gaps had developed in the Uruguayan lifesaving system.

Asociacion Honoraria de Salvamentos Maritimos y Fluviales (ADES)

Operating Model: Non-Profit Voluntary Organisation
Source of Income: Private Contributions
Manning Structure: Volunteer Crew

After two nautical disasters resulting in the loss of 30 lives in 1954 and 1955 respectively, public opinion favoured the re-establishment of a coastal lifesaving service for Uruguay. The organisation known as ADES, a private, voluntary society

based on the model of the RNLI was founded in 1956. In the following year a 48ft (14.8m) Ramsgate-type lifeboat was purchased from the RNLI to be stationed at Montevideo. She was named the ADES 1 *Captain Francisco Alvarez*. Although she had been built in 1928 and had served in the evacuation at Dunkirk during the Second World War, this venerable lifeboat continued in service on the Plata until the mid 1980s and participated in over 800 rescues, saving many lives. Over the years, further stations were established. As of 1999 Station #1 at Puerto del Buceo (Montevideo) had an ex-RNLI Waveney MLB, and Station #2 at Puerto del Colonia and #3 at Punta del Este both had ex-RNLI Solent MLBs. Station #4 at Puerto de Carmelo on the Rio Uruguay had an 18ft (5.4m) Avon searider RHI as well as an ex-RNLI Rother MLB and an ex-DGzRS 21ft (6.5m) daughter-boat. At ADES Station #5, Puerto del Sauce, there is an ex-RNLI Watson type non-self-righting MLB. In 1999 there were also plans to establish a new, sixth station for Puerto Santiago Váquez.[690] The Association also has several small RHIs, used to augment the lifeboat stations and kept on trailers to be transported to other locations around the country if required.

The Uruguayan MLB, ADES 16, an ex-RNLI Waveney type now stationed out of Puerto del Buceo in Montevideo.
ADES

Since its inception, ADES lifeboats have set out on thousands of sorties and assisted more than 1,500 people. The Association is, and always has been, voluntary, being modelled after the RNLI. Members come from all walks of life with each station being manned by approximately 20 people in rotation. Funding is covered through donations and contributions from the Uruguayan government, private companies and public subscriptions. ADES works in close conjunction with the Uruguayan Navy and, on occasion, with the Prefectura Naval Argentina. To give an idea of the financial efficiency of this organisation, the average annual operating budget for all vessels and crew between 1989 and 1994 was approximately $35,175 US[691] – a far cry from the average annual costs of many other MROs around the world, whether professional or volunteer. In 1995 ADES was the host organisation for the 17th International Lifeboat Conference that took place in Montevideo. This was the first time the conference had been held south of the equator and the workload was handled admirably by this small but efficient organisation.

Other maritime SAR resources in Uruguay include the navy, which has a flight of Wessex helicopters with hoist-capability based out of the air station at Laguna del Sauce (Maldonado), and the air force, which has dedicated fixed-wing patrol aircraft. As of 1995 there were nine coast radio stations, the primary MRCC is co-located at the Montevideo coast radio station.

APPENDICES

Acronyms & Abbreviations

AC	Aircraft
ACV	Air Cushion Vehicle
ADES	Asociacion Honoraria de Salvamentos Maritimos y Fluviales (Uruguay)
AFB	Air Force Base
AFM	Armed Forces of Malta
AFRAS	Association for Rescue at Sea (USA)
AMSA	Australian Maritime Safety Authority
AMVER	Automated Mutual-Assistance Vessel Rescue System
ARCC	Air Rescue Coordination Centre
ASRS	Åland Sea Rescue Society
AVCGF	Australian Volunteer Coast Guard Federation
B	Centre of Buoyancy
BASRA	Bahamas Air Sea Rescue Association
BRC	Bulgarian Red Cross
BSARI	Bermuda Search and Rescue Institute
CG	Coast Guard
CCG	Canadian Coast Guard
CCGA	Canadian Coast Guard Auxiliary
CITRO	Citizens Rescue Organisation (Curaçao)
CLI	Canadian Lifeboat Institution
CLSS	Canadian Life-Saving Service
CMRA	Canadian Marine Rescue Auxiliary
COSPAS	Search and Rescue Satellite System (SARSAT)
CRM	Cruz Roja del Mar (Spain)
CRS	Coast Radio Station
CVBS	Cuerpo de Voluntarios de los Botes Salvavidas de Valparaiso
DDD	Denizciler Dayanisma Dernegi (Turkey)
DF	Direction Finder
DGzRS	Deutsche Gessellschaft zur Rettung Schiffbruchiger (Germany)
DR	Dead Reckoning
DSC	Digital Selective Calling
DTSKK	Dainippon Teikoku Suiman Kiusai Kwai (Japan)
ELA	Estonian Lifesaving Association
ELT	Emergency Locating Transmitter
EPIRB	Emergency Positioning Indicating Radio Beacon
ESC	Enlarged Ship Concept
FAB	Fast Afloat Boat
FLS	Finnish Lifeboat Society
FRC	Fast Rescue Craft
frp	Fibreglass Reinforced Plastic
ft	Foot/Feet
G	Centre of Gravity
GM	Metacentric Height
GMDSS	Global Marine Distress and Safety System
GMT	Greenwich Mean Time
GOES	Geo-stationary Orbiting Environmental Satellites
GPS	Global Positioning System
GRP	Glass Reinforced Plastic
GZ	The Righting Lever
HCG	Hellenic Coast Guard (Greece)
HKMP	Hong Kong Marine Police

HMCG	Her Majesty's Coastguard (UK)
hp	Horsepower
HSB	La Société des Hospitaliers Sauveteurs Bretons (France)
IAMSAR	International Aeronautical and Maritime Search and Rescue (Manual)
ICAO	International Civil Aviation Organisation
ICESAR	Icelandic Association for Search and Rescue (Formerly NLAI)
ICG	Indian Coast Guard
ICG	Irish Coastguard (Formerly IMES)
ICG	Italian Coast Guard
ICMSAR	International Convention on Maritime Search and Rescue
ILC	International Lifeboat Conference
ILF	International Lifeboat Federation
IMCO	International Maritime Consultative Organisation (IMO)
IMES	Irish Marine Emergency Services
IMO	International Maritime Organisation
IRB	Inshore Rescue Boat
ISN	Instituto de Socorros a Naufragos (Portugal)
ITU	International Telecommunications Union
JCG	Japan Coast Guard
JLI	Japan Lifeboat Institution
JMSA	Japanese Maritime Safety Agency
JRCC	Joint Rescue Coordination Centre (Air and Marine)
kg	Kilogram(s)
	Kiyi Emniyeti Turkish Coast Guard
km	Kilometre(s)
KNRM	Koninklijke Nederlandse Redding Maatschappij (Netherlands)
kt	Knot(s)
kw	Kilowatt(s)
lb	pound(s)
LCG	Longitudinal Centre of Gravity
loa	Length Overall
lwl	Length on the Waterline
m	Metre
M	Metacentre
MCC	Mission Control Centre
MCA	Maritime & Coastguard Agency (HMCG)
MCTS	Maritime Communications and Traffic Centre
MDR	Marine Data Recorder
MRI	Maritime Rescue International (UK)
MRJ	Maritime Rescue Japan (JLI)
MLB	Motor Lifeboat
MHS	Massachusetts Humane Society
MMFO	Moroccan Ministry of Fisheries & Oceans
MPESA	State Marine Pollution Control, Salvage & Rescue Admin (Russia)
MRCC	Marine Rescue Coordination Centre
MRO	Maritime Rescue Organisation
MRSC	Marine Rescue Sub-Centre

MSPiR	Morska Sluzba Poszukiwania Ratownictwa (Poland)
MV	Motor Vessel
NGO	Non-Governmental Organisation
NLAI	National Lifesaving Association of Iceland
nm	Nautical Mile
NMLBS	National Motor Lifeboat School (USCG)
NSKK	Nippon Suinan Kyusai Kai (Japan)
NSRI	National Sea Rescue Institute (South Africa)
NSSR	Norsk Selskab til Skibbrudnes (Norway)
NZHRM	North and South Holland Lifeboat Institution (later KNZHRM)
oa	Overall
OSV	Offshore Supply Vessel
PB	Patrol Boat
PL	Patrol Launch
PNA	Prefectura Naval Argentina
PRO	Polskie Ratownictwo Okretowe
RADAR	Radio Detecting and Ranging
RAF	Royal Air Force (UK)
RCAF	Royal Canadian Air Force
RCC	Rescue Coordination Centre
RHI	Rigid Hull Inflatable
RHIOT	Rigid Hull Inflatable Operations Training
RHS	Royal Humane Society (UK)
RIB	Rigid Inflatable Boat
RN	Royal Navy (UK)
RNLI	Royal National Lifeboat Institution (UK & Ireland)
RNZAF	Royal New Zealand Air Force
RNZCGF	Royal New Zealand Coast Guard Federation
RNZN	Royal New Zealand Navy
rpm	Revolutions Per Minute
RS	Rescue Ship
RVCP	Royal Volunteer Coastal Patrol (Australia)
SAR	Search and Rescue
SARFA	Search and Rescue Foundation of Aruba
SARSAT	Search and Rescue Satellite System (also COSPAS)
SASAR	South African Search and Rescue Organisation
SASEMAR	Sociedad Estatal de Salvamento y Seguridad Marìtima (Spain)
SB	Self-Bailing
SCSN	Société Centrale de Sauvetage des Naufrages (France)
SCTW	Standards of Training, Certification and Watchkeeping Convention
SEARCH	Search and Rescue Charitable Foundation (Caribbean)
SESN	Sociedad Española de Salvamento de Naufragos (Spain)
shp	Shaft Horsepower
SIMS	Systems and Information Management System
SISL	Société Internationale de Sauvetage du Leman (Switzerland)

SISN	Societa Italiana di Soccorso di Naufraghi (Italy)	SOS	Radiotelegraphy - Morse Code Signal of Distress	USLSS	United States Life-Saving Service
SKAD	Survival Kit Air Droppable	SR	Self-Righting	USN	United States Navy
SLA	Surf Life-Saving Association of Australia	SRB	Surf Rescue Boat	VBZR	Voluntary Sea Rescue Organisation Blankenberge (Belgium)
SLB	Steam Lifeboat	SRIN	Sea Rescue Institute of Namibia		
SLI	Sumner Lifeboat Institute (New Zealand)	SRR	Search and Rescue Region	VISAR	Virgin Islands Search and Rescue
		SR-SB	Self-Righting & Self-Bailing		
SM (Finland)	Suomen Meripelastusseura (also FLS)	SRU	Search and Rescue Unit	VMRQ	Volunteer Marine Rescue Association of Queensland
		SS	Steamship		
SNS	Società Nazionale di Salvamento (Italy)	SSRF	St Maarten Sea Rescue Foundation	VTS	Vessel Traffic System
				wl	Waterline
SNSC	Service National de Surveillance Cotiere (Tunisia)	SSRS	Svenska Sjoraddningssallskapet (Sweden)	WMO	World Meteorological Organisation
SNSM	Société Nationale de Sauvetage En Mer (France)	SURPIC	AMVER Surface Picture	WT	Watertight
		USAF	United States Air Force	yd	Yard(s)
SOLAS	Safety of Life at Sea Convention	USCG	United States Coast Guard	ZHRM	South Holland Institution for Saving the Shipwrecked (later KZHRM)
SOR	Statement of Requirements	USCGA	United States Coast Guard Auxiliary		

Chronology of Coastal Lifesaving

1300s
China. Chinese develop methods of resuscitation for drowning victims and establish first benevolent or 'humane' societies.

1357
Åland Islands. Kökar Catholic monastery provides shelter and aid to shipwrecked fishermen and distressed mariners.

1691
Portugal. King D. Pedro II issues edict – coastal forts must send out vessels to aid the shipwrecked.

1692
Sweden. Swedish Diving Company established, principally for salvage, with edict from King Charles XI to rescue the shipwrecked.

1708
China. Chinkiang Association for Saving Life established.

1722
Great Britain. Bishop Crewe establishes Charitable Trust at Bamburgh Castle, Northumberland.

1737
China. First river lifeboats introduced.

1751
Great Britain. Archdeacon Sharpe establishes permanent measures for assisting the shipwrecked at Bamburgh.

1757
The Netherlands. Methods of resuscitating the apparently drowned taught at Leidon University.

1765
France. de Bernières experiments with his 'canot insubmersible'.

1767
The Netherlands. The Maatschappij tot Redding van Drenkelingen established – first humane society in Europe.

1769
The Netherlands. First attempt to establish dedicated lifeboats in West Frisian Islands.

1774
Great Britain. Royal Humane Society (RHS) established.

1776
Great Britain. Liverpool Docks Trust establishes first known successful lifeboat service in the world at Formby, Merseyside.

1777
Spain. Guild of Lifesavers established in Seville.

1785
USA. Massachusetts Humane Society (MHS) established.

1786
Great Britain. Lukin invents 'unimmergible' boat, first vessel altered for lifesaving.

1787
USA. MHS establishes first 'houses of refuge' around approaches to Boston.

1789
Great Britain. Brig *Adventure* lost with all hands at Tynemouth; Gentlemen of the Lawe House hold a competition for a design of 'life-boat'.

1790
Great Britain. Henry Greathead builds the *Original*, and the Tyne Humane Society established, the world's first local private voluntary lifesaving organisation.

USA. Revenue Cutter Service established by George Washington.

1791
Great Britain. Artillery Sgt Bell conducts first experiments with line-throwing mortar and projectile at Woolwich Arsenal.

1797
Canada. Permanent houses of refuge and surfboats placed on Sable Island.

1798
Great Britain. Duke of Northumberland purchases Greathead lifeboat for North Shields.

1800
Portugal. Duke of Northumberland purchases Greathead lifeboat for Oporto. Ireland. Dublin Docks Trust establishes first lifeboats in Ireland using Greathead's type.

1802
Isle of Man. Lifeboat society established at Douglas.

Great Britain. Greathead petitions parliament for award and to fund more lifeboats. Lloyd's of London establishes 'Life-boat Fund' to assist local societies.

1803
Germany. Greathead lifeboats purchased for Prussia.

1806
The Netherlands. Dutch monarchy build several Greathead lifeboats.

1807
Great Britain. Henry Trengrouse conducts earliest experiments with line-throwing rockets in Cornwall.

USA. MHS establishes first lifeboat station in the USA at Cohasset, Massachusetts.

Great Britain. Norfolk and Suffolk Humane Societies established. Lionel Lukin develops Norfolk and Suffolk type pulling and sailing lifeboat.

1808
Great Britain. Captain George Manby conducts first rescue using line-throwing mortar.

1809
Great Britain. Preventive Waterguard established.

1821
Finland. First lifesaving station established in Finland at Suursaari Island.

1822
Great Britain. Preventive Waterguard and Coast Blockade combined to form HM Coastguard.

1823
Great Britain. Sir William Hillary's *Appeal to the British Nation*.

1824
Great Britain. First 'national' coastal lifesaving organisation in the world, the 'Shipwreck Institution' established.

The Netherlands. The ZHRM and the ZNHRM societies established (forerunners of today's KNRM).

France. First local lifeboat societies established at French ports such as Boulogne.

1828
Portugal. Portuguese monarchy establishes six lifeboat stations (replaced 1862).

1832
Great Britain. Lt Kisbee invents the breeches-buoy, or 'kisbee' ring.
USA. Congress requests that cutters of the Revenue Marine conduct winter patrols off Atlantic seaboard for the express purpose of saving lives at sea.

1835
Canada. Mary Hichens and family establish Seal Island lifeboat.

France. Société Generale des Naufragés et de l'Union des Nations established in Paris.

1838
Great Britain. Grace Darling and father conduct famous rescue of the *Forfarshire*.

Belgium. First state-funded lifeboat service established.

1842
China. Hong Kong Water Police established.

1847
USA. Joseph Francis and Douglas Ottinger co-invent the 'life-car'.

1849
Great Britain. Loss of the Tyne lifeboat and its crew.

USA. US Congress provides government funding for lifesaving measures in New England.

1850
Great Britain. In response to the loss of the Tyne lifeboat, 4th Duke of Northumberland initiates design competition for a 'self-righting' boat.

1851
Great Britain. James Beeching wins competition with self-righting, self-bailing (SR-SB) lifeboat, later perfected by James Peake and the forerunner of the Standard Self-Righting type lifeboat.
Sir Richard Lewis becomes secretary of Shipwreck Institution and initiates revitalising reforms.

Germany. More state-funded lifeboats for the Prussian coast.

Denmark. Government establishes first lifesaving service in Denmark under direction of C.B. Claudi.

1853
Canada. American philanthropist Dorothea Dix provides Francis-type lifeboats and a life-car for Sable Island humane station.

1854
Great Britain. Shipwreck Institution renamed the Royal National Lifeboat Institution.

Norway. First state-funded lifesaving stations established.

Sweden. First state-funded lifesaving stations established.

1858
Australia. Five Peake self-righters built in Australia for use in Victoria.
1859
Australia. Rescue of survivors from SS *Admella* by Portland lifeboat.

1860
New Zealand. First lifeboat station established at Timaru.

1861
Spain. Government purchases seven Peake self-righters from RNLI.

South Africa. First lifeboats established by Cape Town Port Authority.

1865
Germany. Deutsche Gessellschaft zur Rettung Schiffbruchiger (DGzRS) established.

France. Société Centrale de Sauvetage des Naufragés (SCSN) formed in France.

1867
Canada. Canadian Lifesaving Service (CLSS) established.

1869
Turkey. Turkish Lifeboat Society established for Bosphorus.

1871
USA. The United States Life-Saving Service (USLSS) established under the leadership of Sumner Kimball.

Italy. Societa Italiana di Soccorso di Naufraghi (SISN) established.

1872
Russia. Local lifeboat service established in Riga.

Finland. First government-funded lifesaving stations established.

USA. USLSS develops Beebe-McLellan surfboat.

1873
USA. USLSS Purchases 'English' type SR-SB lifeboat from RNLI.

France. La Société des Hospitaliers Sauveteurs Bretons (HSB) established.

1875
Russia. Imperial Russian Lifesaving Society formed.

1878
USA. Lt David Lyle invents Lyle Gun for the USLSS.

1880
Spain. Sociedad Española de Salvamento de Náufragos (SESN) established.

1885
Switzerland. Société Internationale de Sauvetage du Léman (SISL) established.

1886
Belgium. International Congress for Safety at Sea held in Brussels.

Great Britain. Loss of two RNLI Standard Self-Righting type lifeboats and 27 crew leads to development of Watson type lifeboats.

1889
Japan. Imperial Japanese Lifeboat Institution formed (DTSKK, later NSKK).

Great Britain. First steam lifeboat (SLB), the *Duke of Northumberland*, constructed by RNLI.

1891
Great Britain. The Macaras help to establish the Lifeboat Saturday Fund, one of the first 'public' charitable fund-raising efforts in the world, to raise money for the RNLI.

1892
Norway. Norsk Selskab til Skibbrudnes Redning (NSSR) established.

1893
Portugal. Instituto de Socorros a Naufragos (ISN) established.

1894
Norway. Norwegian sailing lifeboat *Colin Archer* launched.

1897
Finland. Suomen Meripelastusseura Unioninkatu (SM Finland) established.

1898
New Zealand. Sumner Lifeboat Institute (SLI) established.

1899
USA. USLSS and Lt McLellan begin earliest experiments with motorised lifeboats (MLBs).

1900
Canada/Great Britain. Marconi transmits first radio-telegraphy signal across the Atlantic.

1903
USA. USLSS surfmen assist Wright Bros with first flight of manned aircraft.

1904
France. HSB conducts experiments with MLBs.

1906
Australia. First surf lifesaving club in the world established at Bondi Beach, NSW.

1907
USA. First USLSS 36ft SR/SB MLB constructed. Purchased by CLSS for service at Bamfield, BC.

Sweden. Svenska Sjoraddningssallskapet (SSRS) established.

1908
France. International Congress on Maritime Lifesaving held at St Nazaire.

1910
Holland. First large Dutch MLB, the *Brandaris*, launched by the NZHRM.

1912
Great Britain. Loss of RMS *Titanic* results in the establishment of the first Safety of Life at Sea (SOLAS) Conference and Convention.

1913
USA. 1st International Ice Patrol conducted by US Revenue Cutter Service with funding from several nations.

1915
USA. USLSS and Revenue Cutter Service amalgamated to form the United States Coast Guard (USCG).

Canada. CLSS experiments with use of small, high-speed launches for lifesaving on Lake Ontario.

1918
Great Britain. First World War ends; RNLI have saved 5,332 lives in four years.

1919
USA. USCG Lt Elmer Stone pilots US Navy aircraft in first successful transatlantic flight.

1924
Great Britain. 1st International Lifeboat Conference (ILC) held in London to coincide with 100th Anniversary of RNLI. International Lifeboat Federation (ILF) established.

1925
Chile. Cuerpo de Voluntarios de los Botes Salvavidas de Valparaiso (CVBS) established.

1926
Germany. DGzRS begins to use diesel engines in its MLBs.

1928
France. 2nd ILC held in Paris.

1929
Great Britain. RNLI launches its first high-speed rescue launch, the *Sir William Hillary*.

1932
The Netherlands. 3rd ILC held in Amsterdam.

1936
Greece. Forerunner of Hellenic Coast Guard (HCG) established.

Sweden. 4th ILC held in Götheborg.

1937
Australia. Royal Volunteer Coastal Patrol (RVCP) established.

1938
USA. United States Coast Guard Auxiliary (USCGA) established.

1940
Great Britain. RNLI lifeboats help in evacuation of troops from Dunkerque.

The Netherlands. Dutch MLB *Zeemanshoop* evacuates 40 Jewish refugees to England.

1944
USA. First humanitarian missions conducted using a helicopter.

1945
USA. First rescue at sea using a helicopter and hoist, Penfield Reef, New York.
1947
Norway. 5th ILC held in Oslo.

1948
Japan. Japanese Maritime Safety Board, forerunner of the Japan Coast Guard (JCG) established.

1949
Norway. NSSR launches first non-sailing cruising lifeboat, the *J M Johansen*.

Switzerland. The Geneva Convention provides for the neutrality of all lifeboats during times of war and allows such vessels to exhibit the Red Cross.

1950
Poland. Polish Ship Salvage Company established.

1951
Belgium. 6th ILC held in Oostende.

1953
Great Britain. First peacetime SAR helicopter squadron established.

1955
Portugal. 7th ILC held in Estoril.

1956
Uruguay. Asociacion Honoraria de Salvamentos Maritimos y Fluviales (ADES) established.

1957
Germany. DGzRS launches first 'rescue cruiser', the *Theodore Heuss*.

1958
Great Britain. RNLI launches first Oakley self-righting MLB.

USA. Automated Mutual-Assistance Vessel Rescue System (AMVER) established.

1959
Germany. 8th ILC held in Bremen.

1961
Australia. Australian Volunteer Coastguard Association (AVCG) established.

1962
Canada. Canadian Coast Guard (CCG) established.

1963
Great Britain. 9th ILC held in Edinburgh. USCG 44ft MLB and inflatable IRBs introduced by the Breton Lifesaving Society.

Bahamas. Bahamas Air-Sea Rescue (BASRA) established.

1965
Åland Islands. Åland Sea Rescue Society (ASRS) established.

Great Britain. First experiments with rigid hull inflatables (RHIs) conducted at Atlantic College in Wales.

1967
France. 10th ILC held in Dinard.
South Africa. National Sea Rescue Institute (NSRI) established.

1968
France. The Société Nationale de Sauvetage En Mer (SNSM) established.

1969
Great Britain. RNLI launches first Atlantic 21 RHI.

1970
New Zealand. SLI begins experiments with high-speed water-jet-propelled IRBs.

1971
USA. 11th ILC held in New York.

Estonia. Estonian Lifesaving Service established.

Great Britain. First Arun Class FAB, *52-01*, launched by RNLI.

1975
Finland. 12th ILC held in Helsinki.

USA. Association for Rescue at Sea (AFRAS) established.

1976
New Zealand. New Zealand Coast Guard Federation (now Royal NZCGF) established.

1978
Canada. Canadian Marine Rescue Auxiliary, forerunner of the Canadian Coast Guard Auxiliary (CCGA), established.

1979
The Netherlands. 13th ILC held in Amsterdam/ Rotterdam.

Great Britain. First large Medina type RHI launched by the RNLI.

1982
Canada. First SAR 'case' handled by COSPAS-SARSAT system.

1983
British Virgin Islands. Virgin Islands Search and Rescue (VISAR) established.

1984
Sweden. 14th ILC held in Götheborg.

1985
The Netherlands. KZHRM launches RHI *Koningen Beatrix*, predecessor of today's large Dutch RHIs.

1987
Spain. 15th ILC held in La Coruña.

1990
USA. USCG launches first 47ft MLB prototype, MLB 47-200.

1991
Namibia. Sea Rescue Institute of Namibia (SRIN) established.

The Netherlands. KZHRM and the KNZHRM amalgamate to form the KNRM.

1992
Norway. 16th ILC held in Oslo/Bærum.

1995
Uruguay. 17th ILC held in Montevideo.

1999
Iceland. ICESAR, a new combined (land and sea) lifesaving organisation, formed. Great Britain. 18th ILC held in Bournemouth/ Poole. 175th anniversary of RNLI and the Dutch lifeboat societies.

2003
South Africa. 19th ILC held in Cape Town.

International Lifeboat Federation
West Quay Road, Poole, Dorset BH15 1HZ, UK

Åland Islands
Ålands Sjoraddningssallskap
Hamngatan 4, FIN 22100 Mariehamn, Åland Finland

International Lifeboat Federation Members Profiled in *Rescue at Sea*

Argentina
Prefectura Naval Argentina
Av Eduardo Madero 235,PB-Of.040,
1106-Buenos Aires, Republica Argentina

Australia
Royal Volunteer Coastal Patrol
P.O. Box 1494, 239 Spit Road, Mosman,
NSW 2088, Australia

Australian Volunteer Coast Guard Federation
National Commodore, 27 Southern Cross Way, Allambie Heights, NSW 2100, Australia

Volunteer Marine Rescue Association of Queensland
GPO Box 1425, Brisbane, Queensland 4001, Australia

Queensland State Emergency Service
(Associate Member)
GPO Box 1425, Brisbane, Queensland 4001, Australia

The Surf Life-Saving Association of Australia (SLA)
Surf House, 128 The Grand Parade,
Brighton le Sands, NSW 2216, Australia

Bahamas
Bahamas Air Sea Rescue Association (BASRA)
PO Box SS-6247, Nassau, Bahamas

Belgium
Belgisch Loodswezen Zeereddingsdienst
Sir Winston Churchillkaai 2, 8400 Oostende, Belgium

Bermuda
Department of Marine & Ports Services
PO Box 180, Hamilton HMAX, Bermuda

British Virgin Islands
Virgin Islands Search and Rescue (VISAR)
PO Box 3042, Road Town, Tortola,
British Virgin Islands

Bulgaria
Bulgarian Red Cross
61 Dondoukov Blvd., 1527 Sofia, Bulgaria

Canada
Canadian Coast Guard
5th Floor, 200 Kent Street, Ottawa,
Ontario, Canada, K1A 0E6

Canadian Coast Guard Auxiliary
200 Kent St., 5th Floor, Ottawa,
Ontario, Canada, K1A 0E6

Canadian Lifeboat Institute
401 East Waterfront Road, Vancouver, British Columbia, Canada, V6A 4G9

Chile
Cuerpo de Voluntarios de los Botes
Salvavidas De Valparaiso
Muelle Prat s/n 1'piso, PO Box 594,
Valparaiso, Chile

China
Maritime Rescue and Salvage Bureau Ministry of Communications PRC, 11 Jianguomennei Avenue, Beijing, 100736, China

Denmark
Royal Danish Administration of Navigation & Hydrography (Farvandsvaesnet)
Overgaden o Vandet 62B, Postbox 1919,
1023 Copenhagen K, Denmark

Estonia
Eesti Vetelpaasteuhingu
1 Tondi Street, 11313 Tallinn, Estonia

Finland
Suomen Meripelastusseura Unioninkatu,
SM Finland
Kalliolinnantie 4, 00140 Helsinki 14, Finland

France
Société Nationale de Sauvetage En Mer
31 Cité d'Antin, 75009 Paris, France

Germany
Deutsche Gessellschaft Zur Rettung
Schiffbruchiger
Werderstrasse 2, 28199 Bremen, Germany

Greece
Hellenic Coast Guard
150 Grigorius Labraki Street, 185 35 Piraeus, Greece

Guatemala
Jefe del Estado Mayor de la Defensa
Nacional
Palacio Nacional, Republica de Guatemala,
Central America

Hong Kong
Hong Kong Marine Police
Marine Police Regional Headquarters,
Tai Hong Street, Sai Wan Ho, Hong Kong

Iceland
Icelandic Association for Search and Rescue
Slysavarnafelagio Landsbjorg, Stangarhyl 1,
110 Reykjavik, Iceland

India
Indian Coast Guard
Tat Rakshak Mukhyalay, National Stadium Complex, New Delhi-110 001, India

Ireland
Royal National Lifeboat Institution
West Quay Road, Poole, Dorset BH15 1HZ,
UK

Italy
Commando Generale del Corpo delle
Capitanerie di Porto
Italian Coast Guard, Viale dell'Arte 16,
00144 Roma, Italy

Societa Nazionale di Salvamento
Via Luccoli 24/4, 16123 Genova, Italy

Japan
Japan Lifeboat Institution
(Marine Rescue Japan)

Nippon Suinan Kyusai Kai, Marine Building,
1-23-17 Shinkawa Cho-Ku, Tokyo 104-0033,
Japan

Japan Coast Guard
2-1-3 Kasumigaseki, Chiyoda-Ku, Tokyo,
Japan

Malta
Armed Forces of Malta
Headquarters, Armed Forces of Malta, Luqa
Barracks, Luqa CMR 02, Malta

Morocco
La Marine Marchande
Ministère des Pêches Maritimes, BD Felix
Houphouet Boigny, Casablanca, Morocco

Namibia
Sea Rescue Institute of Namibia
PO Box 1534, Walvis Bay, Namibia

Netherlands
Koninklijke Nederlandse Redding
Maatschappij, Haringkade 2, 1970 AK
Ijmuiden, Netherlands

Netherlands Antilles
St Maarten Sea Rescue Foundation
PO Box 383, Philipsburg, St Maarten,
Netherlands Antilles

New Zealand
Sumner Lifeboat Institute
Scarborough Boat Harbour, PO Box 17-515,
Sumner, Christchurch 8, New Zealand

Royal New Zealand Coast Guard Federation
Inc.
PO Box 91, 322 Victoria Road, Auckland,
New Zealand

Norway
Norsk Selskab til Skibbrudnes,
Postboks 500, N-1322 Hovik, Norway

Poland
Morska Sluzba Poszukiwania Ratownictwa,
10 Hryniewickiego Str, 81-340 Gdynia,
PO Box 375, Poland

Portugal
Instituto de Socorros a Naufragos,
Rua Direita de Caxias 31, 2780-438 Paco
D'Arco, Portugal

Russian Federation
State Marine Pollution Control, Salvage &
Rescue Administration (MPESA)
Ministry of Transport, 1-4 Rozhdestvenka
St., Moscow 103759, Republic of the
Russian Federation

South Africa
National Sea Rescue Institute of South
Africa
PO Box 154, Green Point 8051, Cape
Town, South Africa

Spain
Sociedad Estatal de Salvamento y Seguridad
Maritima

Maritime Safety and Rescue Agency, Avda
De Portugal 81, 28011 Madrid, Spain

Sweden
Svenska Sjoraddningssallskapet
Talattagatan 18, S-426 76 Vastra Frolunda
Sweden

Switzerland
Société Internationale de Sauvetage du
Léman
Case Postale 35, CH 1898 St Gingolph,
Switzerland

Tunisia
Service National de Surveillance Cotiere
Base Naval De La Goulette, 2060 La
Goulette Tunis, Tunisia

Turkey
Kiyi Emniyeti ve Gemi Kurtarma Isletmeleri
Genel Müdürlügü
Coastal Safety Department, Meclis-i
Mebusan Cad No: 18 Kat 4, 80040
Salipazari Istanbul, Turkey

Denizciler Dayanisma Dernegi (DDD)
Bahrige Caddesi Turabibaba, Sokagi No.13,
Kasimpasa, Istanbul, Turkey

United Kingdom
Royal National Lifeboat Institution
West Quay Road, Poole, Dorset BH15 1HZ,
UK

United States of America
United States Coast Guard
2100 Second Street SW, Washington DC
20593, USA

United States Coast Guard Auxiliary
c/o Auxiliary Center, 9449 Watson Industrial
Park, St Louis, MO 63126, USA

Association for Rescue at Sea
PO Box 5604, Arlington, VA 22205, USA

Uruguay
Asociacion Honoraria de Salvamentos
Maritimos Y Fluviales (ADES)
Rbla Rep Fed de Alemania 3571, Puerto Del
Buceo, 11300 Montevideo 12080, Uruguay

International Lifeboat Federation
West Quay Road, Poole, Dorset
BH15 1HZ, UK

Glossary of Terms

ENVIRONMENTAL TERMS [692] [693]

Backing
An anticlockwise change in wind direction.

Bank
An elevation of the sea floor, a submerged
plateau (sandbank)

Bar
An offshore ridge or mound, submerged (at
least at high tide). Commonly found at the
mouth of a river or estuary. Often a very
treacherous area of large *breaking* and
standing waves.

Beam Seas
Seas moving towards the side of the vessel.

Beaufort Scale
A numbered scale of wind speed and
relative sea conditions developed by Sir
Francis Beaufort (1774-1857). The word
Force is sometimes used to describe each of
the following Beaufort numbers. Today there
are 17 categories, each denoting a doubling
of the pressure (not velocity) of the wind.

Beaufort Number	Knots
0	<1

Dead calm: sea like a mirror.

1	1-3

Light airs: small ripples on the sea.

2	4-6

Light breeze: wind felt on face, small
wavelets on the sea.

3	7-10

Gentle breeze: wave crests begin to break.

4	11-16

Moderate breeze: frequent white horses
at sea.

5	17-21

Fresh breeze: small waves inshore,
moderate waves offshore.

273

6	22-27

Strong breeze: foaming wave crests and some spray at sea.

7	28-33

Near gale: foam from wave crests blown into streaks.

8	34-40

Gale: wave crests break into spindrift.

9	41-47

Strong gale: high waves with rolling crests and dense spray.

10	48-55

Storm: sea appears white, with high over-hanging waves and streaks of dense foam.

11	56-63

Violent storm: sea covered in streaks of foam, waves high enough to hide vessels, crests blown into froth; visibility restricted.

12	>64

Hurricane: sea completely white with driven spray; air filled with foam; visibility seriously impaired.

Breaking Wave (Breaker)
A wave which has become unstable because of steepness or because the crest has overtaken the trough in shallow water. Four principal categories:

Collapsing Breaker
Breaking wave that breaks in the middle or near the bottom of the wave, rather than on top.

Plunging Breaker
Breaking wave that tends to curl over and break with a crash.

Spilling Breaker
Breaking wave that spills gradually over a considerable distance.

Surging Breaker
Breaking wave that tends to peak up and surge up the beach face without spilling or plunging.

Chop
Short, steep waves.

Confused Sea
An area where many divergent *wave groups* and/or *wave trains* moving in different directions converge. See wave *reflection* and *refraction*.

Ebb Current
The movement of a tidal current away from shore or down a tidal stream.

Fetch
The distance that wind blows across the water from a constant direction and with constant speed.

Flood Current
The tidal current generally associated with the increase in the height of the tide. Generally setting towards the shore or in the direction of the tide progression.

Following Seas
Seas moving in the same direction as the vessel.

Gale Force Winds
A sustained wind speed of 34 to 47 knots.

Ground Swell
Waves that have travelled from a different weather system, where they were created. Characteristically long crested, low and regular waves, which tend to rise as they approach shore and interact with the sea floor. Also known as a hollow sea or roller.

Head Seas
Seas coming from the direction toward which a vessel is heading.

Heavy Weather
Stormy, windy weather, usually with rough or high seas and an element of danger or discomfort.

Hurricane Force Winds
Winds of 64kt or more.

Inflow Winds
Winds that blow up fjords and inlets from the sea to the land. Sometimes known as Anabatic winds

Lee Shore
The coast lying in the direction towards which the wind is blowing.

Longshore Current
A current located in the *surf zone* moving generally parallel to the shoreline; usually generated by waves breaking at an angle with the shoreline.

Knot
A unit of speed equal to one nautical mile per hour.

Outflow Winds
Winds that blow down fjords and inlets from the land to the sea. Sometimes known as Katabatic or drainage winds.

Overfalls
Areas of turbulent water caused by strong currents moving over submerged ridges or shoals. Sometimes known as a rip tide, tiderip, rip current or, in some areas of Scandinavia, maelstrom. Often associated with whirlpools.

Quartering Sea
Seas moving on to the vessel's quarter at an approximate angle of 45° to its heading.

Roller
See *ground swell*.

Seas
Combined wind waves and *swell*.

Spindrift
A spray blown up from the surface of the sea.

Spume
Foam or froth on the sea surface.

Squall
An increase of wind, generally lasting several minutes, usually associated with showers from a cumulo-nimbus cloud.

Standing Wave
Produced when strong currents (tidal, oceanic or river) move in the opposite direction of a wave, sea or *swell*. The result is a slowing down of the wave and a dispersion of the wave's energy upward.

Storm Force Winds
Sustained winds from 48kt to 63kt.

Storm Surge
A rise or piling-up of water against the shore, produced by wind stress and atmospheric pressure differences in a storm.

Surf
A collective term for *breakers*; also the wave activity in the area between the shoreline and the outermost limit of the breakers.

Surf Zone
The area between the outermost *breaker* and the limit of wave up-rush on the shore.

Swell
Long waves formed by a distant storm, more regular in appearance than wind waves and no longer growing in height.

Tsunami
Seismic sea wave.

Veering
A clockwise change in wind direction.

Wave Crest
The extreme top of a wave.

Wave Height
The vertical distance between the crest and the preceding trough.

Wave Length
The horizontal distance between two *wave crests* (or *troughs*).

Wave Period
The time, in seconds, it takes for successive *wave crests* (or *troughs*) to pass a fixed point.

Wave Refraction
The change in direction and size of sea waves when encountering shallow water. Waves tend to refract towards the shallower water.

Wave Reflection
The opposite change in direction and size of sea waves (generally to seaward) when encountering a parallel obstruction such as a headland or breakwater.

Wave Group
A series of waves in which the wave direction, length, and height vary only slightly. Also known as a wave series.

Wave Train
A series of waves from the same direction.

Wave Trough
The lowest depression between two waves.

Whitecap
The white froth on *crests* of waves in a wind, caused by wind blowing the crest forward and over.

NAUTICAL & LIFESAVING TERMS [694 695 696 697]

(See also Chapter II-1)

Beach Apparatus
The name given to the line-throwing mechanism (gun, rocket or mortar) in its entirety, including such items as the transport carriage, the lines, *breeches-buoy*, blocks and tackle etc.

Beach Company
In Britain of the 18th and 19th Centuries, small groups of 'beachmen' who resided on a specific part of coast and, with small boats, helped out with rescue, salvage and beachcombing for profit. Also known as 'hovellers' or 'jutters' in The Netherlands.

Beam
The maximum width of a vessel measured at right angles to the fore-and-aft centreline.

Bilged
When a vessel's bottom is stove (crushed) in.

Breeches-Buoy
A circular cork float, or life-ring, with canvas breeches (pants), sewn on the bottom. Used for transferring survivors from a wreck via rope and tackle. An adaptation of the 'Kisbee ring'.

Broach
A sudden, uncontrolled turning of the vessel so that the hull is broadside to the seas or wind.

Camber
The athwartships curvature of the decks, which rise from the sides towards the centreline.

Capsize
To turn bottom side up.

Carry Away
To break loose; said of gear that is stressed beyond the strength of its fastenings.

Centre of Buoyancy (B)
The geometrical centre of the underwater part of the ship.

Centre of Gravity (G)
The centre of all weight in a body. The point about which the body will balance.

Chine
The intersection between a boat's topsides and its bottom.

Clinkerbuilt
A type of hull construction in which each plank overlies the one below, also known as lapstrake construction.

Coastguard
First established in Great Britain, primarily as a means to curb illicit smuggling, when two earlier services, the Preventive Waterguard and the Coast Blockade joined forces in 1822. Became HM Coastguard, with additional lifesaving responsibilities for maintaining the 'beach apparatus'. Term is used widely by other maritime safety organisations. Internationally referred to as Coast Guard.

Cockpit
A space for the crew, lower than the deck and often watertight or self-bailing.

Coxswain
The helmsman or person in charge of a lifeboat.

Crash Boat
High-speed launches used by military air-sea rescue services to recover downed flyers.

Derelict
A vessel abandoned at sea.

Displacement
The weight of water displaced by a floating hull.

Displacement Hull
A vessel supported by its own buoyancy while in motion.

Double-Banked
On a pulling boat, to have two oars and oarsmen per thwart, one on either side of the vessel.

Double-Ended
A vessel having a sharp stern, resembling the bow in configuration.

Draught
The vertical distance from the waterline to the lowest point of the hull or attachments such as propellers and rudders.

Drogue
An open-ended cone, or sea anchor, used to slow the drift of a vessel in heavy weather. May also be used on a vessel underway to avoid broaching, as well as behind a vessel under tow.

Dynamical Stability
The amount of work done in inclining a vessel to any given angle of heel.

Flare
The flaring out of the bows of a vessel.

Fake/Flake
To coil a rope. Faking boxes were generally carried with the 'beach apparatus'.

Flotsam
Wreckage and debris floating in the water.

Flush Deck
The deck has no raised or sunken parts.

Freeboard
In the context of small boats, the distance from the line of the deck to the waterline.

Gunwale
The upper edge of the side of a vessel, usually a small projection above the deck.

Hard-Chined
Hull shaped with relatively flat panels joined at an angle.

Heaving Line
A light line, coiled and thrown from a vessel or from a vessel to shore. Generally used as a messenger line to pass over a larger line such as a towline.

Heaving Stick
A short stick with an oval weight at one end, generally attached to a *heaving line* for throwing.

Initial Stability
The statical stability of a vessel at a small angle of heel. Indicated by 'GM'.

Jetsam
Equipment or cargo deliberately thrown overboard to lighten a vessel.

Kedge
Name of a small anchor, also used to kedge a vessel off the beach by laying the anchor cable offshore in deeper water.

Keeper
In the USLSS, the person in charge of a lifesaving station.

Knock Down
When a vessel is forced over on its side by an overwhelming external force such as a large breaking sea.

Lagan
Goods or wreckage on the seabed.

Length Overall (LOA)
The total length of a vessel from the tip of the bow to the end of the stern.

Length on the Waterline (LWL)
The length of a vessel, including the rudder post, when measured at the line of flotation.

Lifecar
A small waterproof capsule resembling a small submarine, used to haul several survivors from a shipwreck through the surf after transfer lines have been established – no longer in use.

Lyle Gun
Principal line-throwing gun of the USLSS after 1872. Invented by Lt David Lyle, US Army.

Maroon
An exploding charge used as a warning signal or, by the RNLI, to summon lifeboat crews to the station.

Mayday
A radio-telephone distress call, from the French m'aidez (help me); indicates imminent danger to human life.

Metacentre (M)
The point at which the vertical line through the centre of buoyancy, at a small angle of heel, cuts the vessel's centreline. Only considered to exist for angles of heel up to 15°.

Metacentric Height (GM)
The height of the transverse metacentre (M) above the *centre of gravity* (G). The length of GM has a profound effect on how *tender* or *stiff* a given vessel will be.

Mizzen Mast
The aftermost mast on a vessel.

Nautical Mile (nm)
6,076.12ft (1,852m), an international standard; for practical purposes equals one minute of latitude.

Pitch Pole
To have a vessel *capsize*, or roll over, end over end.

Planing Hull
A hull designed so that forward speed creates water lift, reducing friction and increasing speed.

Pooped
A vessel is pooped when a heavy sea comes inboard over the stern.

Pulling
Rowing, to pull the oars.

Range
The maximum distance that a vessel can travel before refuelling.

Range of Stability
The angular range over which a ship will have positive statical stability (will return to upright). Also, the angle to which a vessel can heel before it will tend to capsize.

Relieving Tubes
Tubes in the deck that allow water to flow out of a self-bailing vessel, but not back in.

Reserve Buoyancy
The volume of hull between the waterline and the freeboard deck.

Righting Lever (GZ)
The perpendicular distance between the *centre of gravity (G)* and the vertical line through the *centre of buoyancy (B)*. The lever on the ends of which the weight of the vessel acts to return it to the upright when it is heeled.

Roll Over
To have a vessel *capsize* and re-right itself. A complete rollover would be a 360° revolution.

Scantlings
The dimensions of the various parts of the vessel.

Scudding
Running before the wind in a gale.

Scuppers
Drain holes on deck, in the bulwarks or drain pipes in the deck itself (self-bailing).

Sheer
The upward sweep of the deck or bulwarks of a vessel.

Stiff Vessel
A vessel with a large moment of statical stability. One with a large *metacentric height*, or *righting lever*.

Surfman
A designation in the USLSS for crew at the small boat stations. Today, specific qualification and rating at the USCG's small boat stations.

Swamped
To fill with water, not from a leak but from water coming over the deck and gunwales. Also referred to as being *pooped*.

Tender Vessel
A vessel which has a small moment of statical stability. One having a small *metacentric height*, or *righting lever*.

Thwart
A crossways seat upon which oarsmen sit; usually contributing to structural strength on small boats.

Tumblehome
The inward curve of the topsides above the waterline.

Tunnel Hull
A hull with tunnels shaped for the propeller in order to reduce *draught* and/or protect the rudder(s) and propellers.

V-Drive
A particular style of engine installation where the aft part of the engine faces forward and the engine is generally installed much further aft than on more conventional vessels.

Windage
A vessel's resistance to the wind working on its hull and superstructure.

Wreck Gun
Used initially to describe Manby's Mortar, also used to describe line-throwing guns used for lifesaving in general.

Wreck Master
Man designated to represent underwriter's interests and coordinate salvage efforts on New England coasts prior to the introduction of government lifesaving stations.

Wrecker
A person who lures vessels to destruction in order to plunder the wreckage. Sometimes used to describe a legitimate salvageman as well.

Endnotes

[1] K.J.R Langmaid, *The Sea, Thine Enemy: A Survey of Coastal Lights and Lifeboat Services* (London: Jarrold's, 1966), Chapter 1.

[2] Peter James & Nick Thorpe, *Ancient Inventions* (New York: Ballantine Books, 1994), 98-101.

[3] Langmaid, *The Sea, Thine Enemy*, 10.

[4] Noel Methley, *The Lifeboat and its Story* (London: Sidgwick & Jackson, 1912), 35.

[5] Erik Hagg, 'The Development of the Establishments Belonging to the Swedish State for the Saving of Shipwrecked', *Report of the 4th International Lifeboat Conference*, Göteborg (1936) 24-28.

[6] Methley, *The Lifeboat and its Story*, 26.

[7] Ibid.

[8] Ibid., 30.

[9] Great Britain, Admiralty, Duke of Northumberland Competition; *Report of the Committee Appointed to Examine the Lifeboat Models Submitted to Compete for the Premium Offered by His Grace the Duke of Northumberland: To Which is added a List of the Existing Lifeboat, Rocket, and Mortar Stations, and an Abstract of the Wrecks which Occurred on the Shores of the British Isles in 1850 with Appendix, Maps, Plans* (London: W.Clowes & Sons, 1851), 20.

[10] Dennis L. Noble, *A Legacy; The United States Life-Saving Service* (Bicentennial Publication, USCG, 1986), 2.

[11] Francis Metallic Lifeboat Company, *The Francis Metallic Lifeboat Corporation* (New York: W.C. Bryant & Co., 1853), 84-85.

[12] Patrick Howarth, 'The Origins of the Lifeboat Service in Britain', *Report of the 8th International Lifeboat Conference*, Bremen (1959), 25-27.

[13] Luisa Costa Gomes, & Gabriel Lobo Fialho, *Lifeboats; 100 Years of the Instituto de Socorros a Naufragos* (Lisbon: Quetzal Editores, 1992), (The Portuguese Lifeboat Society in English), 10.

[14] Erik Hagg, 'The Development of the Establishments belonging to the Swedish State for the Saving of Shipwrecked', 24-28.

[15] Methley, *The Lifeboat and its Story*, 22-24.

[16] Sima Qian, *Records of the Grand Historian Vol. I 209 to 141 BCE.*, translated by Burton Watson, Columbia University Press, New York 1961, 499-508

[17] Adrian Lee, 'Longboats of Asia Pacific', Chapter 6 in *Canoes in Canadian Culture*, ed. John Jennings (Trent University & Canadian Canoe Museum), Natural Heritage Press, Toronto, 1999.

[18] G.R.G. Worcester, *The Junks and Sampans of the Yangtze, Vol.II: The Craft of the Lower and Middle Yangtze and Tributaries* (Shanghai: The Maritime Customs III. Misc. Series: No. 54, 1948), 386-87.

[19] Ibid., *Vol.II*, 305.

[20] Ibid.

[21] China, Imperial Maritime Customs, Chinese Lifeboats Etc. (Shanghai: Statistical Department of the Inspectorate General of Customs, 1893).

[22] Worcester, *The Junks and Sampans of the Upper Yangtze Vol.I*, 28.

[23] Ibid.

[24] Untranslated works on the subject include the following; Ch'en Hu, *Hsing Ch'uan Pi Yao Hsia Chiang Chiu Sheng Ch'uan Chih* (A story of the Lifeboat Service in China, 1969), and *Ssu-ching Tu* (1235-1520), *Chi sheng pa ts'ui* (Collection on best works on lifesaving) (Shanghai: Han fen lou, 1938).

[25] Worcester, *The Junks and Sampans of the Upper Yangtze*, 29.

[26] Massachusetts Humane Society, *The Institution of the Humane Society of the Commonwealth of Massachusetts: With the Rules for Regulating Said Society* (Boston, 1788), 7.

[27] Worcester, *The Junks and Sampans of the Yangtze, Vol.I*, 184.

28 H. Th. De Booy, *Nederlandse Kustreddingboten* (Alkmar: De Alk,1970), 2.

29 Nicholas Leach, *The Origins of the Lifeboat Service; A History of the Development and Progress of Coastal Life-Saving Provision to 1810* (Birmingham: Published by Author, 1992).

30 IJsbrand't Hoen, *Memorie weegens eenige redressen op het Stuk van de Espargnes, by den Ondergeschreeven aan den Hove van Holland overgegeven* (Holland: Resolutions of the Staten van Holland, inv.no.222, 12 January 1769), 28-29. (Government memorandum regarding recommendations from IJsbrand't Hoen, Chairman of the Committee). Reference passed on from Leach, *Origins of the Lifeboat Service*.

31 Leach, *Origins of the Lifeboat Service*, 14-15.

32 William Hutchinson, *A Treatise on Practical Seamanship* (1777); reprinted 1979 by Scholar Press, London, with an introduction by Morin Scott; Introduction to 1979 reprint by Morin Scott. Reference passed on from Leach, *Origins of the Lifeboat Service*.

33 Leach, *Origins of the Lifeboat Service*, 22.

34 H.A.Gilligan, 'Captain William Hutchinson and the Early Dublin Bay Lifeboats', *Proceedings of the Old Dublin Society* (January 1979).

35 Adrian Osler, *Mr. Greathead's Lifeboat* (Newcastle upon Tyne: Tyne and Wear Museums Service, 1990), 4.

36 Rowland Burdon, *Report on Mr. Greathead's Petition* (London: 31 March 1802), 179.

37 Methley, *The lifeboat and its Story*, 50-51.

38 For an excellent analysis of the commercial implications in the early development of the lifeboat see Nicholas Leach, *Origins of the Lifeboat Service*.

39 Osler, *Mr. Greathead's Lifeboat*, 8-13.

40 Ibid., 86-87.

41 Richard Lewis, *History of the Lifeboat and its Work* (London: Macmillan & Co. 1874), 9.

42 Leach, *Origins of the Lifeboat Service*, 44-46.

43 Osler, *Mr. Greathead's Lifeboat*, 86-87.

44 Great Britain, Admiralty, *Duke of Northumberland Competition...*, 62-73.

45 *Newcastle Courant*, 20 March 1792. Reference passed on from Boswell Whitaker, 'How it all Began – 1789', in *Preservation of Life by Shipwreck; A Trilogy (The Story of the Tynemouth Lifeboat Society)* (South Tyneside Borough Council, 1979), 1-23.

46 Ralph Shanks, Wick York and Woo Shanks *The US Life-Saving Service, Heroes, Rescues and Architecture of the Early Coast Guard* (Petaluma: Costano Books, 1996), 2.

47 Massachusetts Humane Society, *The Institution of the Humane Society...* (Boston, 1788), 21.

48 Shanks, *The US Life-Saving Service...*, 3.

49 R.E. Johnson, *Guardians of the Sea, History of the USCG, 1915 to the Present* (Annapolis: Naval Institute Press, 1987), 1.

50 Ibid., 4.

51 Shanks et al, *The US Life-Saving Service...*, 3.

52 Robert F. Bennett, *Surfboats, Rockets and Carronades* (Washington, D.C.: US Government Printing Office, 1976), 6.

53 Ibid., 6

54 Ibid., 5.

55 Lyall Campbell, 'Sir John Wentworth and the Sable Island Humane Establishment', *Nova Scotia Historical Quarterly* (September 1976), 292-309.

56 Thomas Appleton, *Usque Ad Mare. A History of the Canadian Coast Guard and Marine Services.* (Ottawa: Department of Transportation, 1968), 130.

57 Campbell, 'Sir John Wentworth and the Sable Island Humane Establishment', 301.

58 Massachusetts Humane Society, *Rules for Regulating Said Society*, 21.

59 'A Manx Tale', *The Lifeboat* (Winter 1998-99), 22-23.

60 Osler, *Mr. Greathead's Lifeboat*, 69.

61 Methley, *The Lifeboat and its Story*, 58-59.

62 Hillary, *An Appeal to the British Nation...*(London: Whittaker, 1824).

63 Ibid.,

64 Sir John Cameron Lamb, *The Lifeboat and its Work, The Activities of the Royal National Lifeboat Institution since 1824* (London: Clowes, 1911), 33-34.

65 E.W. Middleton, *Lifeboats of the World: A Pocket Encyclopedia of Sea Rescue* (New York: Arco Publishing Co., 1978), 144.

66 Roger Swanston, 'French Lifeboat History', *Stations of the French Lifeboat Societies* (1996), 1.

67 Capt. Jaime H. Couceiro, 'A Few Abridged Notes on Life-Saving at Sea in Portuguese Waters', *Report of the 7th International Lifeboat Conference*, Estoril (1955), 70.

68 'Information on the Belgium Lifeboat Service', *Lifeboat International* (1990), 9.

69 France, 'Sauveteurs en Mer', *Historical Magazine* #1 (1992), 8-9.

70 Richard Lewis, *History of the Lifeboat and its Work* (London: Macmillan & Co. 1874), 20.

71 Ibid., 21.

72 Ibid., 23-27.

73 Great Britain, Admiralty, Duke of Northumberland Competition, *Report of the Committee...*, 23-24.

74 C. Walter Hodges, *The Overland Launch; The Heroic Story of the Lifeboat Louisa* (Lynmouth Lifeboat) (New York: Coward-McCann, 1970).

75 Bennett, *Surfboats, Rockets and Carronades*, 11.

76 Excerpt from Dr. Newell's Ammendment, in Bennett, *Surfboats, Rockets and Carronades*, 2.

77 Bennett, *Surfboats, Rockets and Carronades*, 12.

78 Ibid., 23.

79 Letter from Captain D. Ottinger of the Revenue Marine to the Hon. W.A. Newell, New York, January 16th, 1849 in Bennett, *Surfboats, Rockets and Carronades*, 21.

80 'The New York Life-Saving Benevolent Association', *The Lifeboat* (January 1856) 111-113.

81 W.D. O'Connor, 'Sketch of the United States Life-Saving Service', Appleton's Annual Encyclopedia of 1878, 750.

82 Bennett, *Surfboats, Rockets and Carronades*, 29.

83 O'Connor, 'Sketch of the United States Life-Saving Service', 751.

84 Ibid.

85 'The New York Life-Saving Benevolent Association', 111-113.

86 US Coast Guard, 'Physical Equipment of the United States Service; its Development and Adaptability', *Report of the 2nd International Lifeboat Conference*, Paris (1928), 79.

87 Dennis L. Noble, *A Legacy, The United States Life-Saving Service*, 5. (Available on USCG Historical Website http://www.uscg.mil/hq/g-cp/history/colect.html).

88 US Coast Guard, 'Physical Equipment', 80.

89 O'Connor, 'Sketch of the United States Life-Saving Service', 752.

90 Ibid., 755.

91 Ibid., 754.

92 Ibid., 767.

93 For an excellent in-depth photo-survey of the USLSS stations see Shanks's and York's book, *The US Life-Saving Service, Heroes, Rescues and Architecture of the Early Coast Guard* (Petaluma: Costano Books, 1996).

94 Shanks et al, *The US Life-Saving Service...*, 16.

95 Sumner I. Kimball, *Organization & Methods of the United States Lifesaving Service* (Washington: Government Printing Office,1890), 26.

96 Dennis Noble, *US Coast Guard: A Historical Overview*, 7. (Available on USCG Website http://www.mil/uscg.shtm)

97 Kimball, *Organization & Methods of the USLSS*.

98 'Lifeboat for Cape of Good Hope', *The Lifeboat* (January 1st, 1866), 19.

99 George Manby, *An Essay on the Preservation of Shipwrecked Persons: With a Descriptive Account of the Apparatus & the Manner of Applying It* (London: Longman, Hurst, Rees, Orme, & Brown, 1812), 85.

100 Luisa Costa Gomes, & Gabriel Lobo Fialho, *Lifeboats; 100 Years of the Instituto de Socorros a Naufragos*, 14-15.

[101] Edward J. Quigley, 'A Lifetime of Inventing Marine Lifesaving Apparatus', (n.p., n.d.), 18.

[102] Christian Ostersehlte, *Die Deutsche Gesellschaft zur Rettung Schiffbrüchiger* (Hamburg: Ernst Kabel Verlag, 1990), 97 & 136.

[103] *Memoria Referente a La Exposicion De Higiene Y Salvamento Verificada en Brussels en 1876* (Lifesaving Exposition, Brussels, 1876, very good graphics of early German lifeboats and coast rescue apparatus). (London, 1876).

[104] Count Yoshii, Imperial Japanese Lifeboat Society in *Report of the 1st International Lifeboat Conference*, London (1924).

[105] Lyall Campbell, *Sable Island Shipwrecks; Disaster and Survival at the North Atlantic Graveyard* (Halifax: Nimbus, 1994),108-13.

[106] *Repertory of the Arts for 1808, vol.xiii, 318* in Lt. D.A. Lyle, *Report on Lifesaving Apparatus: Guns, Projectiles etc.* (Ordnance Department, US Army, 1879), 292.

[107] Ibid., 318

[108] George Manby, *An Essay on the Preservation of Shipwrecked Persons*, vi.

[109] Lyle, *Report on Lifesaving Apparatus: Guns, Projectiles etc.* (Ordnance Department, US Army, 1879), 293.

[110] Methley, *The Lifeboat and its Story*, 282.

[111] Lyle, *Report on Lifesaving Apparatus: Guns, Projectiles etc.*, 303.

[112] 'Hunt's Gun and Projectile for Effecting Communication With Wrecked Vessels', *The Lifeboat* (1 November 1879) 593-94.

[113] Shanks et al, *The US Lifesaving Service...*, 69.

[114] Robert Bennet Forbes, *Lifeboats, Projectiles, & Other Means of Saving Life* (Boston: Wm. Parsons Lunt, 1872) 49-51.

[115] Ibid., 50-53.

[116] Methley, *The Lifeboat and its Story*, 289.

[117] There was a rival claim to this invention made by Captain Douglas Ottinger of the Revenue Marine. It is quite probable that Captain Ottinger had some early influence in the idea as he worked closely with the New York Lifesaving Benevolent Society, and the creation of the earliest lifesaving stations in New Jersey and Long Island, where he is said to have come up with the idea of a 'surfcar'. As was the case with many early lifesaving appliances including the lifeboat and the line-throwing gun, there were many rival claims as to their invention. Like Henry Greathead (lifeboat) and G.W. Manby (line-throwing gun), Joseph Francis probably deserves much of the credit for the invention of the life-car as he perfected the idea and put it into service. See Shanks, York & Woo-Shanks, *The US Lifesaving Service, Heroes, Rescues and Architecture*, and James L. Pond, *History of Lifesaving Appliances, and Military & Naval Constructions Invented & Manufactured by*

Joseph Francis, with Sketches & Incidents of His Business Life in the United States & Europe (New York: E.D. Slater, 1885).

[118] Gomes and Fialho, *Lifeboats; 100 Years of the Instituto de Socorros a Naufragos*, 88.

[119] Shanks et al, *The US Lifesaving Service...*, 69.

[120] Quigley, 'A Lifetime of Inventing Marine Lifesaving Apparatus', (n.p, n.d.), 15.

[121] Bernard Scarlett, Shipminder; *The Story of Her Majesty's Coastguard* (London: Pelham Book, 1971), 19.

[122] Great Britain, Admiralty, Duke of Northumberland Competition; *Report of the Committee*, 22.

[123] Ibid.

[124] Robert Malster, *Saved from the Sea* (Suffolk: Rerrance Dalton Ltd, 1974), 21-22.

[125] Gomes and Fialho, *Lifeboats; 100 Years of the Instituto de Socorros a Naufragos*, 80-82.

[126] James L. Pond, *History of Lifesaving Appliances, and Military & Naval Constructions Invented & Manufactured by Joseph Francis, with Sketches & Incidents of His Business Life in the United States & Europe* (New York: E.D. Slater, 1885), 52.

[127] Joseph Francis, *The Lifesaving Appliances of Joseph Francis: Action of the Congress of the United States in Recognition of His Services* (Congressional Record, March 1887), 43.

[128] Great Britain, Admiralty, Duke of Northumberland Competition; *Report of the Committee*, 16-19.

[129] Ibid.

[130] Ibid.

[131] USLSS Annual Report, 1886, 72-74 in Shanks et al, *The US Life-Saving Service...*, 89.

[132] 'The Lifeboat Disasters at Southport & St. Annes', *The Lifeboat* (1 February 1887), 213-16.

[133] Ray Kipling, *Strong to Save; Dramatic First-Hand Accounts of RNLI Lifeboat Rescues Around the British Isles* (Sparkford: P. Stephens, 1995), 13.

[134] 'The Lifeboat Disasters at Southport & St. Annes', 213-16.

[135] Ibid.

[136] Ray Kipling, *Strong to Save*, 13.

[137] Bjorn Foss, *HUNDRE ÅR MED REDNINGSSKØYTA* (Oslo: Grøndahl og Dreyers Forlag), 242-44. (Translated by Gail Evans)

[138] Middleton, *Lifeboats of the World*, 147.

[139] Ibid., 222.

[140] 'Day of Dread', *On Scene – Special MLB Issue* (2/92), 17-19.

[141] Germany, Maritime Court of Bremerhaven, 'The Judicial Enquiry into the

Accident at Sea of the Sea-Rescue Cruiser *Adolph Bermpohl* on the 23rd of February 1967', *Report of the 10th International Lifeboat Conference, Dinard (1967)*, 249-64.

[142] Ch. Van der Zweep, 'Lessons From a Tragedy, the Loss of the Lifeboat *Christiaen Huygens*, 26 March 1975', *Lifeboat International* (1976), 29-33.

[143] Kipling, *Strong to Save*, 117.

[144] Dennis Noble, *Lifeboat Sailors; Disasters, Rescues, and the Perilous Future of the Coast Guard's Small Boat Stations* (Washington, D.C†: Brassey's, 2000), 1-12.

[145] J. de Courcy Ireland, *Wreck and Rescue on the East Coast of Ireland* (Dublin: Glendale Press, 1983), 27-28.

[146] Tony Cranston, 'The Seal Island Lifeboat', *Disasters at Sea, Anthology of Nova Scotia Shipwreck Stories* (Sentinal, Yarmouth: 1986), 41

[147] *The Lifeboat* (January 1865), in R.M. Ballantyne, *Battles with the Sea or Heroes of the Lifeboat and Rocket: Being Descriptive of Our Coast-Life-Saving Apparatus with Some Account of the Glorious War and Our Grand Victories* (London: James Nesbet & Co., 1883), 121-23.

[148] *USLSS Annual Report, 1880*, 39-40. in Shanks et al, *The US Life-Saving Service...*, 127-28.

[149] Ibid.

[150] Oliver Warner, *The Lifeboat Service, A History of the Royal National Lifeboat Institution 1824-1974* (London: Cassell & Co, 1974), 106-107.

[151] Shanks et al, *The US Life-Saving Service...*, 125.

[152] Appleton, *Usque Ad Mare. A History of the Canadian Coast Guard and Marine Services*, 136.

[153] Shanks et al, *The US Life-Saving Service...*, 124-25.

[154] Oliver Warner, *The Lifeboat Service, A History of the Royal National Lifeboat Institution 1824-1974* (London: Cassell & Co., 1974), 102.

[155] Warner, *The Lifeboat Service*, 101-02.

[156] George Shee, 'The German Lifeboat Society During the War', *The Lifeboat* (November 1922), 328-32.

[157] Warner, *The Lifeboat Service*, 101.

[158] Dr. Robert L. Scheina, 'Coast Guard at War', *Commandant's Bulletin* 4-87 (13 February 1987).

[159] Warner, *The Lifeboat Service*, 89.

[160] Lt Col C.R. Satterthwaite, 'The British Lifeboat Service and the War of 1939-1945', *Report of the 5th International Lifeboat Conference, Oslo* (1947), 76.

[161] Capt. Ottar Vogt, 'The Question of the Desirability of an International Distinguishing Mark for Lifeboats', *Report of the 1st International Lifeboat Conference*, London (1924).

162 H. De Booy, 'Experiences of the Dutch Lifeboat Institution during the Years 1940-1945', *Report of the 5th International Lifeboat Conference, Oslo* (1947), 22-30.

163 Ibid., Holland, Protection of Coastal Lifeboats in War-Time', *Report of the 7th International Lifeboat Conference, Ostend* (1951).

164 Ibid., 'Experiences of the Dutch Lifeboat Institution during the Years 1940-1945', *Report of the 5th International Lifeboat Conference, Oslo* (1947) 22-30.

165 Ibid., 30.

166 Ibid., 29.

167 Ibid., 25.

168 NSSR, 'Relations with the German Occupation Authorities During the Years 1940-1945', *Report of the 5th International Lifeboat Conference, Oslo* (1947), 101-04.

169 Lt Col C.R. Satterthwaite, 'The British Lifeboat Service and the War of 1939-1945', 74-81.

170 Kipling, *Strong to Save*, 58-59.

171 Ibid., 59-60.

172 The coxswain of the Hythe Lifeboat refused to go, stating that his 15-ton vessel was not suitable for beach recovery, and that once touching ground, it would stay aground. Apparently, he convinced the coxswains of the Walmer and Dungeness lifeboats of the same, and they also refused to depart. The Hythe coxswain was dismissed from the RNLI after a Board of Inquiry. In reality, he was probably quite right, given the extensive damage and losses of the commandeered lifeboats operated by the navy, including that of the Hythe lifeboat. The independent nature of a lifeboat coxswain was not always the most conducive to taking orders from naval officers. The coxswain from Hythe, undaunted by his dismissal, 'swore that he would carry out rescues in his own fishing boat. Two months later he fulfilled his pledge by rescuing two British Airmen from a crashed bomber.' Kipling, *Strong to Save*, 61.

173 Lt Col C.R. Satterthwaite, 'The British Lifeboat Service and the War of 1939-1945', 76.

174 Angus MacVicar, *Rescue Call* (London: Kaye & Ward, 1967), 124.

175 Methley, *The Lifeboat and its Story*, 300.

176 Warner, *The Lifeboat Service*, 91

177 Lewis, *History of the Lifeboat and its Work* (London: Macmillan & Co. 1874), 136.

178 Ibid.

179 Middleton, 'Volunteer Crew in the 70s', *Report of the XI International Lifeboat Conference, New York* (1971), 173-78.

180 Capt. Jorgen F. Saxild, 'Some Aspects (Relating to Wages, Pensions and the Distribution of Money) of the Lifeboat Service in Denmark', *Report of the 2nd International Lifeboat Conference, London* (1924), 41-50.

181 Bennett, *Surfboats, Rockets and Carronades*, 62-63.

182 W.D. O'Connor, 'Sketch of the United States Life Saving Service', *Appleton's Annual Encyclopedia of 1878*, 751.

183 Kimball, *Organization & Methods of the United States Lifesaving Service* (Washington: Government Printing Office,1890), 12-13.

184 Methley, *The Lifeboat and its Story*, 303.

185 O'Connor, 'Sketch of the United States Life Saving Service', 749.

186 Quote borrowed from; Warner, *The Lifeboat Service*, 67.

187 Warner, *The Lifeboat Service*, 13-14.

188 Grant Uden, *Lifeboats* (Oxford: Basil Blackwell, 1962), 7.

189 Worcester, *Sail and Sweep in China* (London: Science Museum, 1966), 8.

190 Richard Lewis, *History of the Lifeboat and its Work* (London: Macmillan & Co. 1874), 48.

191 Ibid., 58.

192 Methley, *The Lifeboat and its Story* (London: Sidgwick & Jackson Ltd., 1912), 40.

193 G. De La landelle, *Le Tableau de la Mer: Naufrages et Sauvetages* (Paris: Hachette, 1867), 282 in Sir John Cameron Lamb, *The Lifeboat and its Work, The Activities of the Royal National Lifeboat Institution since 1824* (London: Clowes, 1911), 1-2.

194 Lamb, *The Lifeboat and its Work*, 23-24.

195 'Obituary of Lionel Lukin', *Gentleman's Magazine* (1834) in Lamb, *The Lifeboat and its Work*, 3.

196 Eric Fry, *Lifeboat Design and Development* (Devon: David & Charles Ltd, 1975), 38.

197 Lewis, *History of the Lifeboat and its Work* (London: Macmillan & Co. 1874), 4.

198 Ibid., 9.

199 Osler, *Mr. Greathead's Lifeboats*, 43.

200 Ibid., 44.

201 Ibid., 45.

202 Methley, *The Lifeboat and its Story*, 53-55.

203 Great Britain, Admiralty, Duke of Northumberland Competition; *Report of the Committee...*, 16.

204 Fry, *Lifeboat Design and Development*, 40.

205 Lamb, *The Lifeboat and its Work*, 17-18.

206 *Newcastle Courant* 6 February 1790 in Boswell Whitaker, Chapter 1, 'How it all Began-1789', *Preservation of Life by Shipwreck; A Trilogy* (South Tyneside Borough Council, 1979). 10.

207 'Letters from Lionel Lukin & His Refuters', *The Gentleman's Magazine and Historical Chronicle* (Volume LXXVI, 1806), 714.

208 'Letters from Lionel Lukin & His Refuters December 1806', 1112.

209 'Letters from Lionel Lukin & His Refuters September 1806', 819.

210 Rowland Burdon, *Report from the Committee on Mr. Greathead's Petition, Respecting His New Invention of a Lifeboat* (Reported by Rowland Burdon, Esq., 31 March 1802).

211 'Letters from Lionel Lukin & His Refuters September 1806', 820.

212 Burdon, *Report from the Committee on Mr. Greathead's Petition.*

213 Robert Malster, *Saved From the Sea* (Suffolk: Terrance Dalton Ltd, 1974), 77.

214 Jack Mitchley, *The Story of the Lowestoft Lifeboats, Part 1; 1801-1876* (Lowestoft: Port of Lowestoft Historical Society, 1974), 4-5.

215 Ibid., 5.

216 Malster, *Saved From the Sea*, 162.

217 Mitchley, *The Story of the Lowestoft Lifeboats, Part 1; 1801-1876*, 10.

218 Ibid.

219 Methley, *The Lifeboat and its Story*, 61.

220 Ibid.,66

221 Frances Collingwood, 'The Self-Righting Lifeboat and Beeching's Model', *The Nautical Magazine* (December 1958), 344-46.

222 Fry, *Lifeboat Design and Development*, 50.

223 Methley, *The Lifeboat and its Story*, 72.

224 Malster, *Saved From the Sea*, 166.

225 Collingwood, 'The Self-Righting Lifeboat and Beeching's Model', 344-46.

226 'Lifeboats of the National Lifeboat Institution', *The Lifeboat* (1 October 1856), 185.

227 Middleton, *Lifeboats of the World*, 166 & 195.

228 Fry, *Lifeboat Design and Development*, 52

229 Methley, *The Lifeboat and its Story*, 79.

230 Ibid., 217.

231 Bennett, *Surfboats, Rockets and Carronades*, 38.

232 Pond, *History of Life-Saving Appliances & Military & Naval Constructions Invented & Manufactured by Joseph Francis*, 5.

233 Ibid., 167.

234 Gomes and Lobo, *Lifeboats; 100 Years of the Instituto de Socorros a Naufragos*, 88.

235 Campbell, *Sable Island Shipwrecks; Disaster & Survival in a North Atlantic Graveyard*, 109-13.

236 Bennett, *Surfboats, Rockets and Carronades*, 40.

237 Forbes, *Lifeboats, Projectiles, & Other Means of Saving Life*, 13.

238 United States of America, 'Report of Commissioners Examining Lifeboats & Surfboats', *Report #44 from the Annual Report of the Secretary of the Treasury for the Fiscal Year Ending June 30, 1858* (Washington: William A. Harris, Printer, 1858), 367.

239 USA, 'Report of Commissioners Examining Lifeboats & Surfboats', 369.

240 Ibid., 368.

241 Ibid.

242 Letter from Life-saving Apparatus Review Committee to Chief Clerk, Treasury Department, Washington, DC, 3 June 1872

in Forbes, *Lifeboats, Projectiles, & Other Means of Saving Life*, 103.

243 Forbes, *Lifeboats, Projectiles, & Other Means of Saving Life*, 103.

244 Ibid., 108.

245 McLellan, 'The US Life Saving Service Self-Bailing Water Ballast Surfboat', *Marine Engineering* (March 1901), 94-99.

246 William D. Wilkinson, 'The 26-Foot, 8-Inch Self-Bailing Self Righting Sailing, Pulling Lifeboat of the US Life-Saving Service', *Wreck & Rescue; The Journal of the USLSS Heritage Association #6* (Fall 1997), 11-12.

247 Appleton, *Usque Ad Mare. A History of the Canadian Coast Guard and Marine Services*, 141-42.

248 William D. Wilkinson, Personal Correspondence Received 11 January 1997.

249 Shanks et al, *The US Life-Saving Service...*, 47-49.

250 'A Little Known Work by Sir William Hillary; Plan for a Steam Lifeboat', *The Lifeboat* (June 1931), 281-83.

251 Great Britain, Admiralty, Duke of Northumberland Competition, *Report of the Committee...*, 7.

252 'Steam Lifeboats', *The Lifeboat* (1 August 1871), 141-43.

253 Warner, *The Lifeboat Service*, 70.

254 Ibid., 71.

255 Methley, *The Lifeboat and its Story*, 98.

256 Gil J. Robertson, 'Steam Lifeboat to be Exhibition Centre-Piece', *Australian Sea Heritage* (Winter 1986), 18-19.

257 Robertson, 'Steam Lifeboat to be Exhibition Centre-Piece', 18-19.

258 'What South Australia is Doing', *The Lifeboat* (1 February 1897), 665-67.

259 'The Steam Lifeboat Queen', *The Lifeboat* (1 February 1898), 1-6.

260 Ibid., 4.

261 'Veteran Jet-Propelled Steam Lifeboat', *The Rudder* (July 1908), 49.

262 Vandermissen, Zeeman, Brinkman. 'Summaries in English', in *Lifesavers, 175 Years of the Royal Dutch Lifesaving Institution, 1824-1999* (Wormer, Inmerc, 1999).

263 Western Australian Maritime Museum, 'Description of Early Coastal Lifesaving off of Fremantle, W.A.', and 'Description of the Steam Lifeboat, *Lady Forrest*, 1902'.

264 'The End of Steam', *The Lifeboat* (September 1929), 310-11.

265 Noel Methley, *The Lifeboat and its Story*, 103.

266 Ibid., 102.

267 Ibid., 220-22.

268 Methley, *The Lifeboat and its Story*, 81.

269 'Competitive Trials with Sailing Lifeboats', *The Lifeboat* (1 August 1892), 219-31.

270 Fry, *Lifeboat Design and Development*, 59.

271 Hans Holter, 'Will Our Sailing Lifeboats Have a Renaissance?' *Report of the 4th International Lifeboat Conference, Götheborg, Sweden* (1936), 204-217.

272 An earlier attempt to fit an engine in a Norwegian lifeboat had failed in 1895. See Bjorn Foss, *One Hundred Years with the Norwegian Lifeboats* (Oslo: Grondahl Dreyer, 1994).

273 Norwegian Lifeboat Association, *For Those in Peril*, A History in English, (Alesund: Northwest Publishing, 1991), 33-37.

274 M. Jacobsen, 'The Development of the NSSR Fleet, In Relation to the Development of the Norwegian Fisheries', *Report of the 9th International Lifeboat Conference, Edinburgh* (1963) 202-203.

275 Norwegian Lifeboat Association, *For Those in Peril*, 42-43.

276 Hans Holter, 'Will Our Sailing Lifeboats Have a Renaissance?', 211.

277 Norwegian Lifeboat Association, *For Those in Peril*, 42.

278 J. Rosing Esq., 'Motor Lifeboats Stationed on the German Coast, with Special Reference to the Latest Boats fitted with Crude Oil Diesel Engines', *Report of the 2nd International Lifeboat Conference, Paris* (1928), 29.

279 Grahame Farr, 'Cruising Lifeboats', *Sea Breezes* (January 1964), 7-16.

280 James Archer, *Colin Archer, A Memoir*, '...Sailing Boats Favoured...', Chapter 6 (Gloucester: John Bellows), 93.

281 Ibid., 86-89.

282 McLellan, 'Twin Screw Lifeboat for the US Life Saving Service', *Marine Engineering* (January 1900), 25-26.

283 McLellan, 'The Evolution of the Lifeboat', *Marine Engineering* (January 1906), 7-11.

284 Wm. Washburn Nutting, 'The Sturdy Motor Lifeboat; Some Impressions of the Life Saving Service & its Splendid New Self-Righting Motor Boats', *Motor Boat* (January 1912), 14-15 & 47.

285 William D. Wilkinson, 'The US Coast Guard 44-Foot Motor Lifeboat', *The Quarterdeck*, Vol.24, No.1 (Winter 1998), 7.

286 Shanks et al, *The US Life-Saving Service...*, 113.

287 'Motor Lifeboats', *Motor Boat* (30 April 1908), 38.

288 'The Motorboat As a Life-Saver', *Motor Boat* (25 January 1908), 28.

289 Warner, *The Lifeboat Service*, 78.

290 R.W. Crowley, 'Motor Lifeboats in Great Britain', *Motor Boat* (10 July 1911), 3-11.

291 'The Experimental MLBs', *The Lifeboat* (1 August 1907), 243-47.

292 Lt Cmdr. W.L.B. Dutton, 'A Review of the RNLI's Lifeboats in the Twentieth Century', *Report of the 12th International Lifeboat Conference, Helsinki* (1975) 63-79.

293 Crowley, 'Motor Lifeboats in Great Britain', Motor Boat, 3-11.

294 Ibid., 9.

295 Ibid., 10.

296 Ibid., 11.

297 Motor Lifeboats of the Institution #1; 'The 60 Foot Barnett Type', *The Lifeboat* (February 1932), 434-37.

298 Ibid., 437.

299 Ibid. #3; 'The 45'6" Watson (Cabin) Type', *The Lifeboat* (March 1933), 27-30.

300 Ibid. #7; 'The 41 Foot Watson Type', *The Lifeboat* (June 1934), 274-77.

301 Ibid. #2; 'The 51 Foot Barnett (Stromness) Type', *The Lifeboat* (November 1932), 590-93.

302 Ibid. #4; 'The 35 Feet 6 Inches Self-Righting Type', *The Lifeboat* (June 1933), 76-78.

303 Ibid. #5; 'The 35 Feet 6 Inches Liverpool Type', *The Lifeboat* (September 1933), 122-24.

304 Ibid. #6; 'The 41 Foot Beach (Aldeburgh) Type', *The Lifeboat* (November 1933), 173-76.

305 Dutton, 'A Review of the RNLI's Lifeboats in the Twentieth Century', 63-79.

306 Methley, *The Lifeboat and its Story*, 244.

307 France, 'The Development of the MLB Stations. The Station of Goury-la Hague', *Report of the 2nd International Lifeboat Conference, Paris* (1928), 15.

308 Methley, *The Lifeboat and its Story*, 244.

309 France, 'The Development of the MLB Stations', 17.

310 J. Rosing, 'MLBs Stationed on the German Coast, with Special Reference to the Latest Boats fitted with Crude Oil Diesel Engines', *Report of the 2nd International Lifeboat Conference, Paris* (1928), 29.

311 Ibid., 29.

312 Ibid., 30.

313 Ibid., 31.

314 Capt. Topsoe-Jensen, 'The Sea-Coast Life-Saving Service in Denmark', *Report of the 2nd International Lifeboat Conference, Paris* (1928), 67-73.

315 Topsoe-Jensen, 'The Sea-Coast Life-Saving Service in Denmark', 70.

316 Methley, *The Lifeboat and its Story*, 251.

317 Warner, *The Lifeboat Service*, 94.

318 Vandermissen et al, 'Summaries in English', in *Lifesavers, 175 Years of the Royal Dutch Lifesaving Institution, 1824-1999* (Wormer, Inmerc, 1999).

319 'The Frontispiece', Story of the Dutch Lifeboat *Brandaris*, *Motor Boat* (February 1912).

320 Vandermissen et al, 'Summaries in English', in *Lifesavers, 175 Years of the Royal Dutch Lifesaving Institution*.

[321] H. De Booy, 'Description of the Twin-Screw Self-Righting MLB Insulinde ', *Report of the 1st International Lifeboat Conference, Paris* (1924), 53-61.

[322] H. Th. De Booy, 'Rubber Fenders for MLBs', *Report of the 4th International Lifeboat Conference, Göteborg* (1936), 189-92.

[323] Prof. Ir H. E. Jaeger, 'The New Dutch MLB *Prins Hendrik*', *Report of the 6th International Lifeboat Conference, Ostend* (1951), 108-20.

[324] Lt. Comdr. Ch. Van der Zweep, 'Some Notes on the New Dutch MLB Carlot', *Report of the 9th International Lifeboat Conference, Edinburgh* (1963), 35-37.

[325] The Netherlands, 'Twin Screw MLB of the Royal South Holland Lifeboat Society', *Report of the 9th International Lifeboat Conference, Edinburgh* (1963), 19-33.

[326] Klaas Toxopeus, *Wild Water* (London: Victor Gollancz Limited, 1954), 9-20.

[327] Capt. John Schumacher, 'The New Rescue Cruiser', *Report of the 8th International Lifeboat Conference, Bremen* (1959), 93.

[328] Ibid., 94.

[329] Grahame Farr, 'Cruising Lifeboats', *Sea Breezes* (January 1964), 7-16.

[330] Schumacher, 'The New Rescue Cruiser', 94.

[331] Ibid., 97.

[332] Ibid., 95.

[333] Schumacher, 'Lifeboats for Supplementary and Auxiliary Stations on the Coast of the Federal Republic of Germany', *Report of the 10th International Lifeboat Conference, Dinard* (1967), 33-40.

[334] The rescue cruiser *George Breusing* was sold to private interests in the United States, and became the pilot vessel *Peacock* based out of Astoria, Washington, for operations on the Columbia River Bar. Several rescue cruisers have been sold to foreign rescue services including those of Finland, Morocco, Portugal, Iceland, and Italy.

[335] Germany, 'The Development of Rescue Cruisers', *Report of the 12th International Lifeboat Conference, Helsinki* (1975), 121-25.

[336] Hans Wirz, *Seenot – Opfer, Siege 100 Jahre DGzRS* (Bremen: DGzRS, 1975), 258.

[337] M. Jacobsen, 'The Development of the NSSR Fleet, In Relation to the Development of the Norwegian Fisheries', *Report of the 9th International Lifeboat Conference, Edinburgh* (1963), 202-03.

[338] Capt. Hans Hansson, 'A New Swedish Rescue Cruiser & Radar on Lifeboats', *Report of the 6th International Lifeboat Conference, Ostend* (1951), 113-16.

[339] Hansson, 'Can the MLB be Made Faster', *Report of the 6th International Lifeboat Conference, Ostend* (1951), 139-40.

[340] Capt. Gunnar Alverman, 'R/K Dan Brostrom, A New Type of Rescue Cruiser for the West-Coast of Sweden', *Report of the 10th International Lifeboat Conference, Dinard* (1967), 41-48.

[341] Sweden, 'New Heavy Duty Rescue Vessel for Swedish Sea Rescue Institution', *Lifeboat International* (1993/94), 52.

[342] Swedish Society for Sea Rescue, 'Year Book, 1999', (Sölvesborg: SSRS, 1999).

[343] Henry A. Halfdansson, 'Icelandic Life Saving Ashore and at Sea', *Report of the 5th International Lifeboat Conference, Oslo* (1947), 43-47.

[344] Halfdansson, 'The Icelandic Patrolling Rescue Vessels', *Report of the 6th International Lifeboat Conference, Ostend* (1951), 168-71.

[345] Farr, 'Cruising Lifeboats', *Sea Breezes* (January 1964), 7-16.

[346] Commander F.R.H. Swan, 'Lifeboat Development', *Yachting World* (January 1973).

[347] Ibid.

[348] *One Hundred Years with the Norwegian Lifeboats*, trans. Gail Evans (Oslo: Grondahl Dreyer, 1994),150-54.

[349] Frank Donovan, *The Cutter* (New York: A.S. Barnes & Co., 1961), 17-18 & 25.

[350] Robert Johnson, *Guardians of the Sea: History of the USCG from 1915 to the Present* (Anapolis: Naval Institute Press, 1987).

[351] Donovan, *The Cutter*, 39.

[352] Johnson, *Guardians of the Sea*, 11.

[353] USCG, 'Cutter, Aircraft, and Boat Datasheets', http://www.uscg.mil/datasheet/dataindx.htm (30/01/01).

[354] Robert L. Scheina, *USCG Cutters and Craft, 1946-1990* (Annapolis: Naval Institute Press, 1990), 62-81.

[355] Scheina, *USCG Cutters and Craft, 1946-1990*, 37-43.

[356] C.L. Jennison, 'A Review of Hull and Machinery Design and Equipment of US Coastguard Lifeboats', *Report of the 4th International Lifeboat Conference, Göteborg* (1936), 218-35.

[357] H. Decatur Rice, Sr. 'Steel 52ft Diesel Lifeboat', *Report of the 8th International Lifeboat Conference, Bremen* (1959), 82-91.

[358] Rice, 'Steel 52ft Diesel Lifeboat', 86.

[359] William D. Wilkinson, 'One of a Kind', *On Scene*, (Summer 1996), 14-16.

[360] Ibid., 'The US Coast Guard 44-Foot Motor Lifeboat', *The Quarterdeck*, Vol.24, No.1 (Winter, 1998), 6-11.

[361] Leach, *The Waveney Lifeboats; An Illustrated History of the RNLI 44ft Waveney Lifeboats 1967-1999* (Bristol: Bernard McCall, 2001), 19.

[362] Lt. Cmdr. Robert W. Witter, 'Design and Construction of the United States Coast Guard 44-Foot MLB', *Report of the 9th International Lifeboat Conference, Edinburgh* (1963), 51-65.

[363] Capt. Richard Smith, 'Operational Characteristics of the United States Coast Guard 44-Foot MLB', *Report of the 9th International Lifeboat Conference, Edinburgh* (1963), 66-70.

[364] 'The 44 Footer', On Scene – Special MLB Issue (2/92), 28.

[365] Stephen H. Evans, 'The US Coast Guard's New 40' Utility Boat', *Report of the 6th International Lifeboat Conference, Ostend* (1951), 146-60.

[366] Ibid., 159.

[367] Cmdr. John F. Dunn, 'The Forty-One Foot Utility Boat: A New Work Horse for the US Coast Guard', *Report of the 12th International Lifeboat Conference, Helsinki* (1975), 82.

[368] R.T. Alexander, 'Plastic Lifeboats', *Report of the 6th International Lifeboat Conference; Ostend* (1951), 117-36 & 220-22.

[369] Dunn, 'The Forty-One Foot Utility boat: A New Work Horse for the US Coast Guard', 81-87.

[370] 'Our Lifeboat Work', *The Lifeboat* (1 February 1881), 211.

[371] Forbes, *Lifeboats, Projectiles, & Other Means of Saving Life*, 104.

[372] Kimball, *Organization & Methods of the United States Lifesaving Service* (Washington: Government Printing Office,1890), 18-19.

[373] Statement by Commander Harold D. Hinckley, USCG at 1st International Lifeboat Conference, London, 1924. in J.R. Barnett, 'Self-Righting & Non-Self-Righting Lifeboats', in *Report of the 1st International Lifeboat Conference, London* (1924), 7.

[374] Ibid. Statement by Captain Jorgen Frederick Saxild, Danish Lifesaving Service, 7.

[375] Patrick Howarth, *Lifeboat: In Danger's Hour* (London: Hamlyn, 1981), 60.

[376] J.R. Barnett, 'Self-Righting & Non-Self-Righting Lifeboats', *Report of the 1st International Lifeboat Conference, London* (1924), 6.

[377] Barnett, 'Self-Righting & Non-Self-Righting Lifeboats', 6.

[378] Fry, *Lifeboat Design and Development* (Devon: David and Charles Ltd., 1975), 98.

[379] Ibid., 99.

[380] Stuart Welford, 'Is it Right to Right; the Development of the Self-Righting Lifeboat', *The Naval Architect* (July 1974), 96.

[381] Breton Lifeboat Society, 'France, The Use of Inflatable Boats as Lifeboats', *Report of the 9th International Lifeboat Conference, Edinburgh* (1963), 113.

[382] Capt. D.G. Wicksteed, 'Inflatable Boats, Development & Rescue Potential', *Report of the 10th International Lifeboat Conference; Dinard* (1967), 95.

[383] Lt. Cmdr. H.E. Over, 'Development of a Twin Screw Diesel Rigid Inflatable Lifeboat', *Lifeboat International* (1983), 27-43.

[384] Van der Zweep and E.D. Stogdon, 'A Large RIB for Dutch Lifeboat Institution', *Ship and Boat International* (June 1987), 13 -16.

385 Sip Wiebenga, 'Harder-Type Lifeboat With Carriage and Truck', *Report of the 18th International Lifeboat Conference, Bournemouth* (1999), 43-45.

386 Ibid., 'The Development of the Arie Visser Type RIB', *Report of the 18th International Lifeboat Conference, Bournemouth* (1999), 9-11.

387 Ibid., 'Experiences and Development of Fast Rescue Boats Johannes Frederik (JK)-Class and Valentijn-Class of the Koninklijke Nederlandse Redding Maatschappij (KNRM) since Oslo ILF-Conference 1991', *Report of the 17th International Lifeboat Conference, Montevideo* (1995), 61-66.

388 Leach, *The Waveney Lifeboats...*, 15.

389 For an excellent overview of the history of 44ft MLBs in the RNLI, see Leach, *The Waveney Lifeboats.*

390 Lcdr. W.L.G. Dutton, '52ft. Fast Afloat Boat (FAB) Concept', *Report of the 11th International Lifeboat Conference, New York* (1971), 69-71.

391 'Arun Development; A Break With Tradition to Maintain Tradition', *The Lifeboat* (Spring 1975).

392 Keith Thatcher, 'Looking at Lifeboats; the Arun Class', *The Lifeboat* (Winter 1990/1991).

393 'Fast Work for the RNLI', Safety at Sea (n.d.)

394 Robert L. Scheina, *USCG Cutters and Craft, 1946-1990* (Annapolis: Naval Institute Press, 1990), 193.

395 'The Road to the New MLB; Overview of the MLB Replacement Project', *On Scene – Special MLB Issue* (2/92), 44.

396 David M. Shepard, 'New 47ft MLBs', *Coast Guard Engineer's Digest* (Spring 1994), 6-13.

397 Lcdr Michael A. Monteith, '47-foot UPDATE!!!!', *On Scene – Special MLB Issue* (2/92), 46-49.

398 Cdr M.J. Lewandowski & LTJG Jerome A. Popiel, '47ft MLB Operational Test & Evaluation Results', *On Scene* (Summer 1995), 23-29.

399 Mark H. Dobney, '47 Foot MLB-Carrying USCG Securely Into the 21st Century', *Report of the 18th International Lifeboat Conference, Bournemouth* (1999), 27-28.

400 P.E. Person, 'The New Fast Rescue Cruiser for the Swedish Sea Rescue Society', *Report of the ILF Intermediate Operational Conference, IJmuiden* (2001).

401 J.A. Keunig, 'The Enlarged Ship Concept Applied to a Rigid Inflatable Lifeboat', *Report of the ILF Intermediate Operational Conference, IJmuiden* (2001).

402 Michael Vlasto, 'RNLI-New Lifeboat Development', *Report of the ILF Intermediate Operational Conference, IJmuiden* (2001).

403 S.E. Wiebenga, 'KNRM-Lifeboat Choice', *Report of the ILF Intermediate Operational Conference, IJmuiden* (2001)

404 F. Besson, 'A New Generation of First Class Lifeboats for the SNSM', *Report of the ILF Intermediate Operational Conference, IJmuiden* (2001).

405 Capt. Rolf Westerström, 'Ergonomics', *Report of the ILF Intermediate Operational Conference, IJmuiden* (2001).

406 John Charles, *Helicopter Rescue* (Ian Allan Ltd., London: 1980), 15-16.

407 USCG, Public Affairs Division, *Air Search and Rescue: 63 Years of Lifesaving* (Washington, DC: GPO, 1978), 11.

408 Josh Eppinger, 'Fire at Sea, The Story of the Prinsendam', *Pacific Northwest Magazine* (June 1981), 18-23.

409 Frank Donovan, 'To the Rescue', *The Cutter* (New York: A.S. Barnes & Co., 1961), 125.

410 Appleton, *Usque Ad Mare...*, 86.

411 Daryl Mintenko, 'Kella-Lee Rescue', *CCG Pacific Shorelines* (Vol.6, Issue 1, Spring 2002), 1&6.

412 Jouni Arjava, 'Wooden Lifeboat Rescued for the Museum; The Lifeboat *Haapasaari* and Purchases by the Finnish Lifeboat Association in the 1930s', *The Maritime Museum of Finland Annual Report,* 1994 (Helsinki: Finnish Association for Maritime History, 1995), 16-21.

413 Jan Gronstrand, 'The Difficult Design Process', *Report of the 17th International Lifeboat Conference, Montevideo* (1995), 75-88.

414 British Admiralty Hydrographic Office, *South America Pilot, Vol.1* (NP#5, 13th Edition, 1999).

415 International Hydrographic Organisation, *List of Lifesaving Stations of the World with their Equipment and Geographical Positions* (Monte Carlo: Quai de Plaisance, 1940), 76.

416 'The Argentine Coast Guard (Naval Prefectura)', *Report of the 16th International Lifeboat Conference, Oslo* (1991), 275-277.

417 International Maritime Organisation, *Information on National Search and Rescue Facilities* (London: IMO, March 1, 1994).

418 Middleton, *Lifeboats of the World: A Pocket Encyclopedia of Sea Rescue* (New York: Arco Publishing Co., 1978), 197.

419 Middleton, *Lifeboats of the World,* 197.

420 Max Colwell, 'Australian Lifeboats', *Ships and Seafarers in Australian Waters* (n.d., n.p), 110.

421 Richard Morgan, 'Victoria Lifeboat Rescued', *Australian Sea Heritage* #15 (1988), 31-32.

422 'Newcastle's Lifeboat Restoration is Completed', *Australian Sea Heritage* (Spring 1997), 1.

423 Methley, *The Lifeboat and its Story,* 261.

424 'A Lifeboat Rescue', (Australian Peake Boat, Port Fairy) (n.d.,n.p), 69.

425 Jack Loney, *The Queenscliffe Lifeboat; Wreck & Rescue at Port Phillip Heads* (Queenscliffe: Queenscliffe Lifeboat Preservation Society, 1989), 2.

426 Ibid., 3.

427 'Mention of Admella Rescue, Victoria, Australia', *The Lifeboat* (2 January1860), 234.

428 Loney, *The Queenscliffe Lifeboat,* 4.

429 Ibid.

430 'Portland Rescues Australia's Oldest Vessel', *Australian Sea Heritage* #27 (Summer 1990), 7.

431 'The Warnampool Lifeboats. Lifeboat 1859-1911', *Australian Sea Heritage* #26 (Spring 1990), 33.

432 Loney, *The Queenscliffe Lifeboat,* 29.

433 'Mention of Port Adelaide & Bombay Lifeboats', *The Lifeboat* (2 July 1866), 205.

434 Article in Adelaide Observer in Max Colwell, 'Australian Lifeboats', *Ships and Seafarers in Australian Waters* (n.d., n.p), 110.

435 'What South Australia is Doing', *The Lifeboat* (1 February 1897), 665-67.

436 Methley, *The Lifeboat and its Story,* 260.

437 Gil J. Robertson, 'Steam Lifeboat to be Exhibition Centre-Piece', *Australian Sea Heritage* (Winter, 1986), 18-19.

438 Western Australian Maritime Museum, 'Description of Early Coastal Lifesaving off of Fremantle, W.A., & a Description of the Steam Lifeboat, *Lady Forrest,* 1902'.

439 Australia, 'Search and Rescue Arrangements in Australia', http:///www.amsa.gov.au (26 February 2001), 1.

440 Royal Volunteer Coastal Patrol, 'History of the Royal Volunteer Coastal Patrol', http://www.shoal.net.au (26 February 2001), 3.

441 A.S. Onarato, 'Royal Volunteer Coastal Patrol, An Introduction', *Report of the 14th International Lifeboat Conference, Göteborg* (1983), 72-74.

442 Leach, *The Waveney Lifeboats.*

443 Graham Clarke, 'A Brief Summary of the Development of the Volunteer Sea Rescue Scene in Australia', *Report of the 17th International Lifeboat Conference, Montevideo* (1995), 169-72.

444 Australian Volunteer Coast Guard, 'Official Website', http://www.coastguard.com.au (26 February 2001), 1-2.

445 Surf Lifesaving Society of Australia, 'History of SLSA', http://www.slsa.asn.au (26 February 2002), 1.

446 P.J. Quirk, 'The Air Sea Rescue Association of Queensland, Australia', *Lifeboat International* (1984), 12-15.

447 Volunteer Marine Rescue Association of Queensland, 'History', http://www.vmraq.org.au (26 February 2002), 1-2.

448 Bahamas Air Sea Rescue Association, 'The Story of Basra', http://www.basra.org, 1-2.

449 BASRA, 'The Story of Basra', 1-2.

450 'Information on the Belgium Lifeboat Service', *Lifeboat International* (1990), 9.

451 Methley, *The Lifeboat and its Story,* 224.

452 Ibid.

453 Urbain Ureel, 'A Lifeboat History', http://www.ping.be/urbiehome/Lifeboat.html (24 February 2001).

454 Ibid., 4.

455 Ibid., 2.

456 Ibid., 5.

457 Ibid., 10.

458 N. Lishman, 'Bermuda-The Sea, Reefs and SAR', *Report of the 12th International Lifeboat Conference, Helsinki* (1975), 241-44.

459 'Bermuda-Rescue Problems and Solutions', *Lifeboat International* (1977), 30.

460 Ibid., 32.

461 Ibid., 35.

462 'Bermuda's Department of Marine & Ports Services', *Lifeboat International* (1989), 27.

463 Virgin Islands Search and Rescue, 'Virgin Islands SAR Statistics', www.ultimatebvi.com /visar (3 March 2001), 1.

464 British Admiralty Hydrographic Office, *Black Sea Pilot* (NP#24, 12th Edition, 1990), 16 & 20.

465 Bulgarian Red Cross, 'Official Website', http://www.usd.edu/dmhi/brc/brc/brcindex. html (5 March 2001).

466 Walter W. Hichens, *Island Trek; An Historical and Geographical Tour of Seal Island, Nova Scotia* (Nova Scotia: Lancelot Press, 1982), 15-16.

467 Nova Scotia, 'Superintendant's Report on Lighthouses', *Journal and Proceedings of the House of Assembly* (1858).

468 Roland H. Sherwood, 'St. Paul's Island', *Legends, Oddities and Facts from the Maritime Provinces* (Nova Scotia: Lancelot Press, 1995), 26-33.

469 'A Noble Example', *The Lifeboat* (6 October 1860), 334. (Letter from Dorothea Dix regarding establishment of lifesaving facilities at Sable Island).

470 Appleton, 'Lifeboats: How Search and Rescue Began in Canada', Canadian Shipping and Marine Engineering, Vol. 45, No. 11 (August 1974), 16-18.

471 Appleton, *Usque Ad Mare...*, 141.

472 Ibid.

473 Ibid., 143.

474 Appleton, 'Canada's First Motor Lifeboat', *The Bulletin of the Maritime Museum of BC* (Spring 1976), 1-4.

475 Ibid., 2.

476 Shanks et al, *The US Life-Saving Service...*, 111.

477 Appleton, 'Canada's First Motor Lifeboat', 144.

478 Ken McLeod, 'The Canadian Great Lakes Lifesaving Service', *Fresh Water, A Journal of Great Lakes Marine History, Vol.3, No.1* (Summer 1988), 16-17.

479 Rear Admiral Stors, 'Canadian Coast Guard Hovercraft in SAR', *Report of the 11th International Lifeboat Conference, New York* (1971), 135-38.

480 'High Speed SAR Vessel for CCG (Type 100 14m RHI)', *Lifeboat International* (1986), 11.

481 Allen Bilodeau, 'Introduction of the USCG 47 MLB into the CCG Fleet', *Report of the 18th International Lifeboat Conference, Bournemouth* (1999), 29-34.

482 Phil Matty, 'The Birth of a Lifeboat Institution', *Report of the 14th International Lifeboat Conference, Göteborg* (1983), 7-11.

483 Ibid.

484 British Admiralty Hydrographic Office, *South America Pilot, Volume II* (NP#6, 16th Edition, 1993).

485 Methley, *The Lifeboat and its Story*, 262.

486 British Admiralty Hydrographic Office, *China Sea Pilot*, Vol.I (NP#30, 4th Edition, 1987).

487 Ibid., Vol.III (NP#32, 4th Edition, 1982).

488 John Q. Stewart, *Coasts, Waves and Weather* (Boston: Ginn & Company, 1945), 100-06.

489 Lu Shengxuan, 'Based on the Chinese situation – To do our best in life-saving at sea', *Report of the 17th International Lifeboat Conference, Montevideo* (1995) 187-90.

490 British Admiralty Hydrographic Office, *North Sea (East) Pilot* (NP#55, 3rd Edition, 2000).

491 Ibid.

492 Ibid. *Baltic Pilot Vol.1* (NP#18, 8th Edition, 1998).

493 Captain Topsoe-Jensen, 'The Sea-Coast Lifesaving Service in Denmark', *Reports of the 2nd International Lifeboat Conference, Paris* (1928), 67-73.

494 Topsoe-Jensen, 'The Sea-coast Lifesaving Service in Denmark', 67-73.

495 Methley, *The Lifeboat and its Story*, 229.

496 This may not have been the first lifeboat in Denmark. E.W. Middleton states in *Lifeboats of the World* that previously 'a man named Hansen of Svanke...provided a lifeboat for the Island of Bornholm', although he provides no specifics as to dates.

497 Methley, *The Lifeboat and its Story*, 230.

498 Ibid., 69.

499 Ibid., 230.

500 Topsoe-Jensen, 'The Sea-coast Lifesaving Service in Denmark', 71.

501 Captain Niels Hansen, 'The Importance of Shore-Stations and/or Patrolling Lifeboats', *Reports of the 4th International Lifeboat Conference, Oslo* (1947), 105-06.

502 Hansen, 'Launching of Motor Lifeboats From the Open Shore', *Reports of the 5th International Lifeboat Conference, Ostend* (1951), 98-99.

503 Royal Danish Administration of Navigation & Hydrography, 'Nordsoe Class Lifeboat – Type 20', *Reports of the 16th International Lifeboat Conference, Oslo* (1991), 76-78.

504 Royal Danish Administration of Navigation & Hydrography, 'Development of the Kattegat Class Lifeboat', *Reports of the 16th International Lifeboat Conference, Oslo* (1991), 57-75.

505 R. Admiral Heimo Iivonen, 'Car Ferry Capsized – 137 were rescued, 94 were found dead and 837 are missing', *Report of the 17th International Lifeboat Conference, Montevideo* (1995), 149-52.

506 'A Brief Survey of the Estonian Life-Saving Association', *Lifeboat International* (1992), 21.

507 Jouni Arjava, 'Wooden Lifeboat Rescued for the Museum; The Lifeboat *Haapasaari* and Purchases by the Finnish Lifeboat Association in the 1930s', *The Maritime Museum of Finland Annual Report, 1994* (Helsinki: Finnish Association for Maritime History, 1995), 16-21.

508 Ibid.

509 Ibid.

510 British Admiralty Hydrographic Office, *Baltic Pilot, Volume II* (NP#19, 11th Edition, 1998), 27.

511 Ibid., Volume III (NP#20, 11th Edition, 1998), 1.

512 Ibid.

513 Juhani Merilahti, *Sadan Vuoden Meripelastustyo* (The Story of the Finnish Lifeboat Service, An English Summary), 293.

514 Ibid.

515 Lammi, J, *The Finnish Lifeboat Society, Safety at Sea International* (n.d.).

516 Arjava, 'Wooden Lifeboat Rescued for the Museum...' *The Maritime Museum of Finland Annual Report, 1994* (Helsinki: Finnish Association for Maritime History, 1995), 16-21.

517 Ibid.

518 Ibid.

519 Merilahti, *Sadan Vuoden Meripelastustyo*, 297.

520 Lauri Helaniemi, 'A 20th Century Rescue Cruiser for the Baltic', *Report of the 18th International Lifeboat Conference, Bournemouth* (1999), 13.

521 British Admiralty Hydrographic Office, *Dover Strait Pilot* (NP#28, 4th Edition, 1997).

522 Ibid. *Channel Pilot* (NP#27, 4th Edition, 1999).

523 Ibid., *Bay of Biscay Pilot* (NP#22, 7th Edition, 1998).

524 Ibid., *Mediterranean Pilot* (NP#46, 10th Edition, 1978).

525 See Chapter 2, 'The Canot Insubmersible'.

526 Roger Swanston, 'French Lifeboat History', *Stations of the French Lifeboat Societies* (1996), 1.

527 Methley, *The Lifeboat and its Story*, 243.

528 Swanston, 'French Lifeboat History', ii.

529 Swanston, 'French Lifeboat History', i.

530 Middleton, *Lifeboats of the World...* (1978), 178.

531 Admiral Michel Merveilleux de Vignaux, 'Lifesaving in France', *Report of the 17th International Lifeboat Conference, Montevideo* (1995), 183-86.

532 British Admiralty Hydrographic Office, *Baltic Pilot*, Vol.I (NP#18, 8th Edition, 1998).

533 Ibid., Vol. II, (NP#19, 11th Edition, 1998).

534 'Prussia', *The Lifeboat* (January 1854), 76.

535 'SOS - We're Coming', *State of Bremen Magazine* (Vol.4 89/90), 4.

536 Ibid., 6.

537 Bernd Anders and others, *See Not Rettung, 125 Jahre Deutsche Gesellschaft zur Rettung Schiffbruchiger* (Hamburg: Verlaghaus Die Barque, 1990), 60-64.

538 Captain Uwe Klein, 'Maritime Search and Rescue in the Federal Republic of Germany', *Report of the 14th International Lifeboat Conference, Göteborg* (1983), 182.

539 J. Rosing, 'MLBs Stationed on the German Coast...', 30.

540 Middleton, *Lifeboats of the World*, 167.

541 Capt. John Schumacher, 'Germany, The New Rescue Cruiser', *Report of the 8th International Lifeboat Conference, Bremen* (1959), 93-94.

542 IMO, *Area Search and Rescue Plans*, SAR 2/Circ.4, Annex 2 (London: IMO, 1 March 1994), 3-5.

543 British Admiralty Hydrographic Office, Mediterranean Pilot, Volume IV (NP#48, 11th Edition, 2000), 19.

544 'The Hellenic Coast Guard-Information on its Activities', Lifeboat International ((1992), 47-48.

545 Ibid., 47.

546 Greece, 'Ministry of Mercantile Marine Safety of Navigation Division Joint Rescue Co-Ordination Centre', *Report of the 18th International Lifeboat Conference, Bournemouth* (1999), 49-54.

547 Ibid., 53.

548 British Admiralty Hydrographic Office, *East Coast of Central America & Gulf of Mexico Pilot* (NP#69, 2nd Edition, 1993).

549 Ibid., *Pacific Coasts of Central America & United States Pilot* (NP#8, 9th Edition, 1995).

550 IMO. *Area Search and Rescue Plans*

551 British Admiralty Hydrographic Office, *China Sea Pilot, Vol.I* (NP#30, 4th Edition, 1987).

552 Royal Hong Kong Marine Police, 'A Report on History and Vessels of the Department' (Hong Kong: June 1993).

553 British Admiralty Hydrographic Office, *Arctic Pilot, Vol.II*, (NP#11, 8th Edition, 1986).

554 Sigurjon A Olafsson, 'Refuge Stations for Shipwrecked in Iceland', *Report of the 5th International Lifeboat Conference, Oslo*, (1947), 41-42.

555 Gunnar Fridriksson, 'A Brief History of the Activities of NLSA', *Report of the 12th International Lifeboat Conference, Helsinki* (1975), 179-82.

556 NLAI, 'About the National Lifesaving Association of Iceland', http://www.svfi.is /Deildr/enskar/einfo.html (13 March 1998).

557 Middleton, *Lifeboats of the World*, 164-65.

558 British Admiralty Hydrographic Office, *Bay of Bengal Pilot* (NP#21, 10th Edition, 1978).

559 Ibid., *West Coast of India Pilot* (NP#38, 11th Edition, 1986)

560 Ibid., *Irish Coast Pilot* (NP#40, 14th Edition, 1997).

561 J. de Courcy Ireland, 'The Leinster Coast and its Seamen', *Wreck and Rescue on the East Coast of Ireland* (Dublin: Glendale Press, 1983), 11-72.

562 Ibid., 39.

563 Ibid., 62.

564 Ray Kipling, *Strong to Save; Dramatic First-Hand Accounts of RNLI Lifeboat Rescues Around the British Isles* (Sparkford: P. Stephens, 1995), 211.

565 British Admiralty Hydrographic Office, *Mediterranean Pilot, Vol.II*, (NP#46, 10th Edition, 1978).

566 Ibid., *Vol.III*, (NP#47, 10th Edition, 1988).

567 Captain Romano Grandi, 'A New Italian Search and Rescue Organisation and Operational Criteria', *Report of the 17th International Lifeboat Conference, Montevideo* (1995), 177.

568 'Societa Italiana Di Soccorso Ai Naufraghi, its Past, Present and Future', *Report of the 3rd International Lifeboat Conference, Amsterdam/Rotterdam* (1932), 72-73.

569 'Coastwise Rescue in Italy (Port Authority)', *Report of the 11th International Lifeboat Conference, New York* (1971), 205-12.

570 'SAR on the Italian Coast', *Report of the 12th International Lifeboat Conference, Helsinki* (1975), 183-90.

571 Captain Romano Grandi, 'Safe Beaches Project', *Report of the 17th International Lifeboat Conference, Montevideo* (1995), 177-82.

572 Grandi, 'A New Italian Search and Rescue Organisation and Operational Criteria', 177-82.

573 In the 1 November 1882 edition of *The Lifeboat* (673) mention is made of a diplomatic attaché for the Japanese Government, a Mr N. Takayania, visiting the RNLI to obtain information with the prospect of starting a similar organisation in Japan. There is, however, no record of such an effort ever occurring.

574 Count Kozo Yoshii, 'The Lifeboat Services of the World: Japan', *The Lifeboat* (May 1925), 77-80.

575 Ibid., Imperial Japanese Lifeboat Society, *Report of the 1st International Lifeboat Conference, London* (1924).

576 'The Lifeboat Service in Japan', *The Lifeboat* (1 August 1900), 779.

577 Ibid.

578 Yoshii, 'The Lifeboat Services of the World: Japan.'

579 Viscount Takesada Togukawa, 'Standardisation of Japanese MLBs and Probable Application of Ordinary Japanese Fishing Craft', *Report of the 4th International Lifeboat Conference, Göteborg* (1936), 52-67.

580 Togukawa, 'Standardisation of Japanese MLBs', 52.

581 'Outline of Maritime Casualties and Rescue Operations in Japan', *Report of the 7th International Lifeboat Conference, Estoril* (1955), 174-81.

582 Ibid.

583 'Life-Saving Equipment in Japan, How are Maritime Safety Board's Lifeboats Used?' *Report of the 7th International Lifeboat Conference, Estoril* (1955), 186-91.

584 Japan Lifeboat Institution, *Japan Lifeboat Institution, Nippon Suinan Kyusai Kai, Voluntary Organisation for Saving Life at Sea* (Information Pamphlet, 1989).

585 Japan Coast Guard, Japan Coast Guard (Information Pamphlet, 2002).

586 British Admiralty Hydrographic Office, *Africa Pilot* (NP#1, 13th Edition, 1982).

587 Methley, *The Lifeboat and its Story*, 15-17.

588 'A Lifeboat Service in Morocco', *The Lifeboat* (March 1923), 8.

589 International Hydrographic Organisation, *List of Lifesaving Stations of the World with their Equipment and Geographical Positions* (Monte Carlo: Quai de Plaisance, 1940), 53.

590 'Search and Rescue in the Kingdom of Morocco', fax to author, including statistics (June 2002).

591 British Admiralty Hydrographic Office, *Africa Pilot, Vol.II* (NP#1, 13th Edition, 1982).

592 International Hydrographic Organization, *List of Lifesaving Stations of the World with their Equipment and Geographical Positions* (Monte Carlo: Quai de Plaisance, 1940), 53-54.

593 SRIN, 'History', http://www.srin.org.na, (15 July 2002), 1.

594 British Admiralty Hydrographic Office, *North Sea (East) Pilot* (NP#55, 3rd Edition, 2000).

595 Middleton, *Lifeboats of the World* (New York: Arco, 1978), 144-45.

596 Ibid., 144.

597 KNRM, *Lifeboats at Sea* (IJmuiden: Pamphlet, 1994).

598 IMO, *Area Search and Rescue Plans, SAR.2/Circ.4, Annex 2* (London: IMO, 1 March 1994), 6-8.

599 British Admiralty Hydrographic Office, *South America Pilot, Vol.IV* (NP#7A, 2nd Edition, 1982)

600 John M. Kooijman, 'Dutch Caribbean Rescue Federation Under Development', *Report of the 18th International Lifeboat Conference, Bournemouth* (1999), 7-8.

601 British Admiralty Hydrographic Office, *New Zealand Pilot* (NP#51, 14th Edition, 1987).

602 RNZCGF, 'Coastguard History', http://www.nzcoastguard.org.nz/information .htm (8 June 2001).

603 Ibid.

604 Charles E. Hassall, 'Life-Saving', *A Short History of the Port of Timaru; 1852-1955* (Timaru Harbour Board, 1955), 53, 60 & 113.

605 Hassall, 'Life-Saving', 53, 60 & 113.

606 Steven L. Bloxham, 'Wrecks', *A Brief History of the Oamaru Harbour Board; 1874-1978* (Oamaru Harbour Board, 1978), 42-44.

607 Max Dowell, 'Okarito and Hokatika Lifeboats (1860s West Coast of South Island)', (New Zealand National Maritime Museum).

608 T.B. Byrne, 'The Manukau Lifeboat', *Wing of the Manukau; Captain Thomas Wing: His Life and Harbour 1810-1888* (Auckland: 1991), 272-77.

609 New Zealand, 'Development of BFB Fast Rescue Craft', *Report of the 17th International Lifeboat Conference, Helsinki* (1995), 67.

610 New Zealand, 'Development of BFB Fast Rescue Craft', 67.

611 Angus MacVicar, 'The Brotherhood of the Sea', *Nautical Magazine* (Vol.197, No.4, April 1967), 198-202.

612 Sumner Lifeboat Institute, 'General Data on Capabilities and Performance of Jet Surf Rescue Boat', *Report of the 11th International Lifeboat Conference, New York* (1971).

613 Leach, *The Waveney Lifeboats…*, 86.

614 RNZCGF, *Coastguard New Zealand* (July/August 1994), 17.

615 Ibid., 1&13.

616 British Admiralty Hydrographic Office, Norway Pilot, Vol. IIIA (NP#58A, 6th Edition, 1982).

617 M. Jacobsen, ' The Development of the NSSR. Fleet, In Relation to the Development of the Norwegian Fisheries', *Report of the 9th International Lifeboat Conference, Edinburgh* (1963), 202.

618 Hans Holter, ' Will Our Sailing Lifeboats Have a Renaissance?' *Report of the 4th International Lifeboat Conference, Göteborg* (1936), 216.

619 Mr. Dagfinn Paust, 'Short History and Some Problems of the Norwegian Lifeboat Institution', *Report of the 5th International Lifeboat Conference, Oslo*, 95.

620 Paust, 'Short History and Some Problems of the Norwegian Lifeboat Institution', 96.

621 Foss, Bjorn, *HUNDRE ÅR MED REDNINGSSKØYTA* (Oslo: Grøndahl og Dreyers Forlag, 1994), 134.

622 O. Skjelbred-Knudsen, 'Summary Survey of the Sea and Air Rescue Service in Norway', *Report of the 12th International Lifeboat Conference, Helsinki* (1975), 143-45.

623 British Admiralty Hydrographic Office, *Baltic Pilot, Vol.II*, (NP#19, 11th Edition, 1998).

624 Zbigniew Kowalski, 'Poland, Experience Gained on the Polish Coast', *Report of the 8th International Lifeboat Conference, Bremen* (1959), 203-04.

625 Zbigniew Kowalski, 'The Polish 25 Metre Towing & Rescue Boat', *Report of the 8th International Lifeboat Conference, Bremen* (1959), 80-81.

626 Bogdan Prusinkiewicz, 'Development & Organisation of the Polish Maritime Rescue Service', *Report of the 14th International Lifeboat Conference*, Göteborg (1983), 291-92.

627 British Admiralty Hydrographic Office, *West Coasts of Spain & Portugal Pilot* (NP#67, 7th Edition, 1999).

628 Gomes and Fialho, *Lifeboats; 100 Years of the Instituto de Socorros a Naufragos*, 10-11.

629 Methley, *Lifeboat and its Story*, 55.

630 Capt. Jaime H. Couceiro, 'A Few Abridged Notes on Life-Saving at Sea in Portuguese Waters', *Report of the 7th International Lifeboat Conference, Estoril* (1955), 70.

631 Methley, *Lifeboat and its Story*, 118 & 250.

632 Gomes & Fialho, *Lifeboats; 100 Years of the Instituto de Socorros a Naufragos*, 88.

633 Vice-Admiral Hypacio De Brion, 'The Lifeboat Services of the World: Portugal', *The Lifeboat* (March 1926), 193.

634 British Admiralty Hydrographic Office, *Baltic Pilot, Vol.II* (NP#19, 11th Edition, 1998).

635 Ibid., Vol. III (NP#20, 11th Edition, 1998).

636 Ibid., *Southern Barents Sea and Beloye More Pilot* (NP#72, 3rd Edition, 1973).

637 Ibid., *Bering Sea and Strait Pilot* (NP#23, 5th Edition, 1980).

638 Ibid., *South and East Coasts of Korea, East Coast of Siberia and Sea of Okhotsk Pilot*, (NP#43, 6th Edition, 1983).

639 'Russia', brief mention in *The Lifeboat* (1 August 1872), 352.

640 'Russia & New Lifeboats', *The Lifeboat* (1 February 1875), 225.

641 Mr. Lachkevitch, 'Survey of the Present State of the Life-Saving of the Shipwrecked in the USSR in Russia', *Report of the 2nd International Lifeboat Conference, Paris* (1928) 91

642 Lachkevitch, 'Lifesaving of the Shipwrecked in the USSR', 92.

643 'Co-operation of Soviet Rescue Service with Other Life-Saving Services', *Report of the 12th International Lifeboat Conference, Bremen* (1959), 227-32.

644 'Organisation of Life Protection on the Rivers, Lakes and Coastal Waters of the Soviet Union', *Report of the 12th International Lifeboat Conference, Bremen* (1959), 233.

645 British Admiralty Hydrographic Office, *Africa Pilot, Vol.III* (NP#3, 13th Edition, 1980).

646 'Lifeboat for Cape of Good Hope', *The Lifeboat* (1 October 1861), 50.

647 Methley, *The Lifeboat and its Story*, 261-62.

648 International Hydrographic Organization, *List of Lifesaving Stations of the World with their Equipment and Geographical Positions* (Monte Carlo: Quai de Plaisance, 1940), 53-54.

649 South Africa, 'Search and Rescue in South Africa', *Report of the 11th International Lifeboat Conference, New York* (1971), 16.

650 Ibid., 'South Africa; Rescue Boat Development', *Report of the 12th International Lifeboat Conference, Helsinki* (1975), 133.

651 Ibid., 'A New 8 Metre Class Rescue Boat', *Report of the 14th International Lifeboat Conference, Göteborg* (1983), 116.

652 Ibid., 'Five Metre Rigid Hull Inflatable', *Report of the 17th International Lifeboat Conference, Montevideo* (1995), 55.

653 British Admiralty Hydrographic Office, *West Coasts of Spain & Portugal Pilot* (NP#67, 7th Edition, 1999).

654 Ibid., *Mediterranean Pilot* (NP#45, 10th Edition, 1978).

655 Enric Garcia Domingo, *El Salvamento Maritimo en Espana: La Sociedad Espanola de Salvamento de Naufragos (SESN)'*, (n.p.,n.d.), 1.

656 'Spain', brief mention in *The Lifeboat* (1 October 1861), 502.

657 Domingo, *El Salvamento Maritimo en Espana*, 1.

658 'Spain', brief mention in *The Lifeboat* (1 November 1872), 373.

659 'The Spanish Lifeboat Society', *The Lifeboat* (1 August 1892), 218.

660 'Organisation and Methods of the Spanish Lifeboat Society', *Report of the 3rd International Lifeboat Conference, Amsterdam/Rotterdam* (1932), 260.

661 SASEMAR, 'Spanish Plan for Maritime SAR and Pollution Control (Information Booklet)', (Sociedad Estatal de Salvamento y Seguridad Maritima, 1994), 17.

662 Ibid., 'Spanish Plan for Maritime SAR and Pollution Control', 17.

663 British Admiralty Hydrographic Office, *Baltic Pilot, Volume II* (NP#19, 11th Edition, 1998).

664 Ibid., *Volume III* (NP#20, 11th Edition, 1998).

665 Erik Hagg, 'The Development of the Establishments belonging to the Swedish State for the Saving of Shipwrecked', *Report of the 4th International Lifeboat Conference, Göteborg* (1936), 24-28.

666 Hagg, 'The Development of the Establishments belonging to the Swedish State for the Saving of Shipwrecked', 24.

667 D. Stenberg, 'The Peculiar Features of the Swedish Coast and Their Influence on the Choice of Lifeboats', *Report of the 4th International Lifeboat Conference, Göteborg* (1936), 107-17.

[668] Ibid., 108.

[669] Sweden, 'The Patrol Service for the West Coast of Sweden in Bad Weather', *Report of the 2nd International Lifeboat Conference, Paris* (1928), 34-35.

[670] Hagg, 'The Development of the Establishments belonging to the Swedish State for the Saving of Shipwrecked', 26.

[671] Capt. Hans Hansson, 'Can the MLB be Made Faster', *Report of the 6th International Lifeboat Conference, Ostend* (1951), 139.

[672] Capt. Gunnar Alverman, 'A New Fast 46-Foot Rescue Boat', *Report of the 11th International Lifeboat Conference, New York* (1971), 45-49.

[673] Rolf Westerstrom, 'Development of Three Types of Fast Rescue Boats', *Report of the 18th International Lifeboat Conference, Bournemouth* (1999), 1-8.

[674] British Admiralty Hydrographic Office, *Mediterranean Pilot* (NP#45, 10th Edition, 1978)

[675] International Hydrographic Organisation, *List of Lifesaving Stations of the World with their Equipment and Geographical Positions* (Monte Carlo: Quai de Plaisance, 1940).

[676] British Admiralty Hydrographic Office, *Black Sea Pilot* (NP#24, 12th Edition, 1990).

[677] Ibid., Mediterranean Pilot, Vol.IV (NP#48, 11th Edition, 2000).

[678] Djevdet Bey, 'Turkey-Organisation of the Rescue of the Shipwrecked', *Report of the 2nd International Lifeboat Conference, London* (1928), 93-94.

[679] Methley, *The Lifeboat and its Story*, 253.

[680] International Hydrographic Organisation, *List of Lifesaving Stations of the World with their Equipment and Geographical Positions*, 49.

[681] Middleton, *Lifeboats of the World*, 186.

[682] IMO, *Information on National Search and Rescue Facilities* (London: IMO, 1 March 1994).

[683] British Admiralty Hydrographic Office, *Channel Pilot* (NP#27, 3rd Edition, 1996).

Ibid., *Dover Strait Pilot* (NP#28, 4th Edition, 1997).

Ibid., *West Coasts of England & Wales Pilot* (NP#37, 13th Edition, 1996).

Ibid., *North Coast of Scotland Pilot* (NP#52, 3rd Edition, 1997).

Ibid., *North Sea (West) Pilot* (NP#54, 7th Edition, 1999).

Ibid., *West Coasts of Scotland Pilot* (NP#67, 11th Edition, 1974).

[684] US Coast Guard, 'Nature and Peculiarities of the Coastlines of the United States with Respect to Life-saving Operations', *Report of the 2nd International Lifeboat Conference, Paris* (1928), 76-78.

[685] John Tilley, 'History of the US Coast Guard Auxiliary', (Department of History, East Carolina University).

[686] Mark S. Kern, 'United States Coast Guard Auxiliary, Conducting Preventative SAR', *Report of the 18th International Lifeboat Conference, Bournemouth* (1999), 9-13.

[687] British Admiralty Hydrographic Office, *South American Pilot, Vol.I* (NP#5, 12th Edition, 1996).

[688] Methley, *The Lifeboat and its Story*, 263.

[689] International Hydrographic Organisation, *List of Lifesaving Stations of the World with their Equipment and Geographical Positions*, 76.

[690] ADES, 'Mayday' (Uruguay: 1999 Yearbook for ADES in Spanish).

[691] Ibid., 'Results of the Evaluation of the Voluntary System in the Tasks of Search and Rescue in Uruguay 1956-1994', *Report of the 17th International Lifeboat Conference, Montevideo* (1995), 9.

[692] Canada, Ministry of Supply and Services, *West Coast Marine Weather Hazards Manual* (Ottawa: 1990).

[693] Grant Gross, *Oceanography, A View of the Earth* (New Jersey: Prentice-Hall, 1977).

[694] Elbert Maloney, *Chapman Piloting, Seamanship & Small Boat Handling, 62nd Ed.* (New York: Hearst Marine Books, 1996).

[695] Great Britain, *Admiralty Manual of Seamanship, Volume One* (London: HSO, 1937).

[696] H.J. Pursey, *Merchant Ship Construction* (Glasgow, Brown, Son & Ferguson, 1978).

[697] Ibid., *Merchant Ship Stability* (Glasgow, Brown, Son & Ferguson, 1983).

Notes on Sources

There are very few books that provide an overview of rescue organisations and rescue craft from an international perspective. There are two exceptions, however. The first is *The Lifeboat and Its Story*, written by Noel Methley in 1912. I have referred to this book extensively throughout *Rescue at Sea* and in many ways it has formed a template for this modern-day update. Unfortunately, Mr Methley, who was associated with the RNLI as part of the Lifeboat Saturday Fund, passed away soon after his book was published and never personally received the accolades he deserved for such a worthy endeavour. For anyone interested in the early history of the lifeboat and lifesaving services around the world this book is invaluable. The second is E.W. Middleton's, *Lifeboats of the World*, published in 1978. This, too, is an excellent resource and many copies are still available on the internet. Other books, which have specific chapters on foreign rescue services, include Ray Kipling's, *A Source Book of Lifeboats*, Patrick Howarth's *Lifeboat, In Danger's Hour*, and Angus MacVicar's, *Rescue Call*.

Much of the research material for this book, particularly concerning the development of rescue craft, comes from unpublished sources, principally papers presented at the 18 international lifeboat conferences that have been held at various locations around the world since 1924. There is a wealth of material within these conference papers, all of which are available for viewing at the RNLI library at Poole, UK. Other unpublished sources include a multitude of pamphlets, brochures, and newsletters as well as organisational profiles, journals and magazines forwarded to me from around the world. Although rather specific in scope, these tidbits of information were instrumental in allowing me to keep track of the contemporary lifesaving scene.

Reference to these individual papers, articles and other academic works can be found in the endnotes for each particular chapter.

Another excellent reference work, a donated copy of which I was able to view at the RNLI library, was *Water Safety & Rescue*, a series of notes by Denis J. Horgan of the Lifeboat Enthusiasts Society. Mr Horgan has spent a great deal of time and effort accumulating information on rescue services around the world and his notes were very helpful in verifying some of my research, I thank him for providing a copy of this work to the library.

For the earliest history of lifeboats and lifesaving, particularly in the UK, I relied a great deal on the approach taken in two excellent works of research, namely *Mr. Greathead's Lifeboats*, by Adrian G. Osler and an essay entitled *The Origins of the Lifeboat Service*, by Nicholas Leach. Both provide excellent insight and persuasive counter-arguments to many of the historical conventions that have surrounded this period and have been repeated time and again in other books on the subject.

Other fine works dealing with lifesaving in particular countries include, from a UK perspective, Robert Malster's, *Saved from the Sea*, an excellent survey of the development of the early societies, lifeboats and wreck guns in Norfolk and Suffolk. Also Ray Kipling's, *Strong to Save; Dramatic First-Hand Accounts of RNLI Lifeboat Rescues Around the British Isles*, for accounts of some of the historic rescues and lifeboat tragedies in the UK, and Jack Mitchley's, *The Story of the Lowestoft Lifeboats, Part 1; 1801-1876*, which provided an in-depth overview into the development of the original Norfolk and Suffolk type pulling and sailing lifeboats.

From Ireland, extensive use was made of Dr J. de Courcy Ireland's, *Wreck and Rescue on the East Coast of Ireland*, which covers in great detail the history of the earliest Irish lifeboats. *Lifeboats; 100 Years of the Instituto de Socorros a Naufragos* by Gabriel Lobo and Luisa Costa was a very useful source regarding lifesaving history in Portugal as well as for the story on the evacuation of the passengers and crew from the *Veronese*.

From the USA, special mention should be made of Dennis Noble's wonderful book, *Lifeboat Sailors; Disasters, Rescues, and the Perilous Future of the Coast Guard's Small Boat Stations*, which provided most of the detail regarding the lifeboat tragedy at Quillayute River. Also from the USA, Ralph & Lisa Woo Shanks's and Wick York's, *The USLSS; Heroes, Rescues and Architecture of the Early Coast Guard*, was constantly at hand as the bible of early American lifesaving history.

For the early history of lifesaving in Canada, one key resource was Lyall Campbell's, *Sable Island Shipwrecks; Disaster and Survival at the North Atlantic Graveyard*, which provided much of the detail regarding the efforts of Dorothea Dix and the rescue of the *Arcadia*. From The Netherlands, the story of the RHI lifeboat *Jan van Engelenburg* and the horrific storm of February 1993 has been used with the kind permission of its author, Sip Wiebenga of the KNRM.

Finally, from Norway, special mention should be made of two works, James Archer's *Colin Archer, A Memoir*, which provided great detail regarding the development of the famous sailing lifeboats and the first rescue by RS#1, *Colin Archer*, and Bjorn Foss's, *HUNDRE ÅR MED REDNINGSSKØYTA*, which includes an excellent chronology of lifeboat design in Norway as well as the famous rescue conducted by the RS *Christian Bugge*.

Selected Bibliography

Extensive use was made of articles published in the RNLI's journal *The Lifeboat* (which began publication in 1852), the ILF's journal *Lifeboat International* and from the many papers presented at the 18 International Lifeboat Conferences held since 1924. For the sake of brevity, these individual papers and articles have been cited in the endnotes. A list of the various International Lifeboat Conference dates and composite reports is provided below.

Alexandre, Georges, 'Valparaiso: The Maritime Paradise', *The Auxiliarist* (CCGA: January 2001), 10-11.

Anders, B, Lubkowitz and A. Wende, *See Not Rettung, 125 Jahre Deutsche Gessellschaft zur Rettung Schiffbruchiger*, Hamburg: Verlaghaus Die Barque, 1990.

Anonymous, 'The Frontispiece, Story of the Dutch Lifeboat Brandaris', *Motor Boat* (February 1912).

Ibid., 'Lifeboats for Danish Board of Navigation', *Small Ships* (Nov/Dec 1989), 20.

Ibid., 'A Canadian Life Boat', *Motor Boat* (25 September 1912), 50.

Ibid., 'Coast Guard Now Has New Type High-Powered Lifeboats', *The Rudder*, (September 1932), 26-7.

Ibid.,'Motor Lifeboats', *Motor Boat* (30 April 1908), 38.

Ibid., 'The Motorboat As a Life-Saver', *Motor Boat* (25 January 1908), 28.

Ibid., 'Veteran Jet-Propelled Steam Lifeboat', *The Rudder* (July 1908), 49.

Appleton, Thomas E., 'Canada's First Motor Lifeboat', *The Bulletin of the Maritime Museum of BC* (Spring 1976), 1-4.

Ibid., 'Lifeboats: How Search and Rescue Began in Canada', *Canadian Shipping and Marine Engineering*, Vol.45, No.11 (August 1974).

Ibid., *Usque Ad Mare. A History of the Canadian Coast Guard and Marine Services*, Ottawa: Department of Transportation, 1968.

Arbex, Juan Carlos, *Guarding the Ocean*, Madrid: SASEMAR, 1995.

Archer, James, *Colin Archer, A Memoir*, Gloucester. John Bellows, nd.

Australia, 'New Maritime Museum at Queencliffe', *Australian Sea Heritage* (Spring 1986), 9.

Ibid., 'Newcastle's Lifeboat Restoration is Completed', *Australian Sea Heritage* (Spring 1997).

Ibid., 'Rescues Australia's Oldest Vessel', *Australian Sea Heritage #27*, (Summer 1990), 7.

Ibid., 'The Warnampool Lifeboats. Lifeboat 1859-1911', *Australian Sea Heritage #26* (Spring 1990), 33.

Ballantyne, R.M., *Battles with the Sea or Heroes of the Lifeboat and Rocket: Being Descriptive of Our Coast-Life-Saving Apparatus with Some Account of the Glorious War and Our Grand Victories*, London: James Nesbet & Co, 1883.

Barnett, J.P., *The Lifesaving Guns of David Lyle*, Plymouth, Ind: Town 7 Press, 1974.

Bennett, Robert F., *Surfboats, Rockets and Carronades*, Washington, DC: US Government Printing Office, 1976.

Bloxham, Steven L., 'Wrecks', *A Brief History of the Oamaru Harbour Board; 1874-1978*, New Zealand: Oamaru Harbour Board, 1978, 42-44.

Burdon, Rowland, *Report from the Committee on Mr. Greathead's Petition, Respecting His New Invention of a Life-Boat*, 31 March 1802.

Byrne, T.B., 'The Manukau Lifeboat', *Wing of the Manukau; Captain Thomas Wing: his Life and Harbour 1810-1888* (Auckland, 1991), 272-77.

Cameron, Ian, *Riders of the Storm: The Story of the RNLI*, London: Weidenfeld & Nicholson, 2002.

Campbell, Lyall, *Sable Island Shipwrecks; Disaster and Survival at the North Atlantic Graveyard*, Halifax: Nimbus, 1994.

Ibid., 'Sir John Wentworth and the Sable Island Humane Establishment', *Nova Scotia Historical Quarterly* (September 1976), 292-309.

Canada, Ministry of Supply and Services, *West Coast Marine Weather Hazards Manual*, Ottawa: 1990.

Casson, Lionel, *Ships and Seamanship in the Ancient World*, Baltimore/London: John Hopkins University Press, 1971/1994.

Charles, John, *Helicopter Rescue*, London: Ian Allan Ltd, 1980.

China, Imperial Maritime Customs, *Chinese Life-Boats Etc*, Shanghai: Statistical Department of the Inspectorate General of Customs, 1893.

Cockcroft, Barry, *Fatal Call of the Running Tide: Lifeboat Rescues & Sea Dramas*, London: Hodder & Stoughton, 1995.

Collingwood, Frances, 'The Self-Righting Lifeboat and Beeching's Model', *The Nautical Magazine* (December,1958), 344-46.

Colwell, Max, 'Australian Lifeboats', *Ships and Seafarers in Australian Waters*, publisher and date n.a., 110.

Cox, Barry, *Lifeboat Gallantry*, Spink & Son, 1998.

Cranston, Tony, 'The Seal Island Lifeboat', *Disasters at Sea, Anthology of Nova Scotia Shipwreck Stories*, Yarmouth: Sentinal, 1986.

Crowley, R.W., 'Motor Lifeboats in Great Britain', *Motor Boat* (10 July 1911), 3-11.

Daunt, Achilles, *Our Sea-Coast Heroes, or, Stories of Wreck and of Rescue by the Lifeboat and Rocket*, London: T. Nelson & Sons, 1887.

Dawson, A.J. *Britain's Life-Boats: The Story of Heroic Service*, London: Hodder & Stoughton Ltd, 1923.

De Booy, H.T., *Grepen uit twee eeuwen geschiedenis der Maatschappij tot Redding van Drenkelingen, 1767-1967*, Asd., 1967.

Ibid., *Nederlandse Kustreddingboten*, Alkmaar: De Alk, 1970.

Domingo, Enric Garcia, *L'Estacio de Salvament de Naufragos de Fornells I el Salvament Maritim a l'illa de Menorca*, Menorca: Institut Menorqui' d'Estudis, 1996.

Ibid., *Viure O Morir Al Mar: El Salvament Maritim Al Maresme*, Montserrat, Spain: Oikos-Tau, 1998.

Donovan, Frank, *The Cutter*, New York: A.S. Barnes & Co, 1961.

Dowell, Max, 'Okarito and Hokatika Lifeboats' (1860s West Coast of South Island, New Zealand), NZ National Maritime Museum.

Du Buc Marentille, Abraham, *All People Wrecked at Sea Saved. Description of the Machines Invented for that Purpose and for Which Patents have been Obtained*, Elizabeth-Town: Printed by Shepard Kollock for the Author, 1803.

Du Manchi, 'China's System of Marine Rescue & Salvage', *Safety at Sea* (March 1988), 38-39.

Eisenreich, C.P., *Det Norrejydske Redningsvaesen. Dets tilblivelse, Organisation og Histoire*, Copenhagen:

E. Jespersens Forlag, 1927.

Elder, Michael, *For Those in Peril, The Story of the Lifeboat Service*, London: John Murray, 1963.

Eppinger, Josh, 'Fire at Sea, The Story of the Prinsendam', *Pacific Northwest Magazine* (June 1981), 18-23.

Evans, S.H., *The United States Coast Guard, 1790-1915: A Definitive History*, Annapolis: US Naval Institute, 1949.

Farr, Grahame, *British Lifeboat Stations; A Historical and Geographical List*, Portishead: the author, 1979.

Ibid., 'Cruising Life-Boats', *Sea Breezes* (January 1964), 7-16.

Ibid., 'William Plenty's Life Boats, 1817-29 & James and Edward Plenty's Life Boat Model,

1851', *Papers on Life-boat History, No.1*, Bristol: the author, 1975.

Floherty, John J, *Guardsmen of the Coast*, Providence, RI: Providence Lithograph Company, 1935.

Forbes, Robert Bennet, *Life-Boats, Projectiles, & Other Means of Saving Life*. Boston: Wm. Parsons Lunt, 1872.

Foss, Bjorn, *HUNDRE ÅR MED REDNINGSSKØYTA*, Oslo: Grøndahl og Dreyers Forlag, 1994.

Francis, Joseph, *The Life-Saving Appliances of Joseph Francis: Action of the Congress of the United States in Recognition of His Services*, Congressional Record, March 1887.

Francis Metallic Life-Boat Company, *The Francis Metallic Life-Boat Corporation*, New York: W.C. Bryant & Co, 1853.

Fry, Eric C., *Life-Boat Design and Development*, Devon: David and Charles Ltd, 1975.

Gomes, Luisa Costa & Fialho, and Gabriel Lobo, *Lifeboats; 100 Years of the Instituto de Socorros a Naufragos*, Lisbon: Quetzal Editores, 1992.

Great Britain, *Admiralty Manual of Seamanship*, Vol.1 London: HSO, 1937.

Ibid., The Admiralty, *Duke of Northumberland Competition; Report of the Committee Appointed to Examine the Life-Boat Models Submitted to Compete for the Premium Offerred by His Grace the Duke of Northumberland: To Which is Added a List of the Existing Life-Boat, Rocket, and Mortar Stations, and an Abstract of the Wrecks which Occurred on the Shores of the British Isles in 1850 with Appendix, Maps, Plans*, London: W.Clowes & Sons, 1851.

Ibid., Parliament, House of Commons, *Committee on Captain Manby's Petition*, London: 1810.

Greathead, Henry, *The Report of the Evidence, and Other Proceedings in Parliament, Respecting the Invention of the Lifeboat. Also, Several Other Authentic Documents...*, London: Luke Hansard, 1804.

Gross, Grant, *Oceanography, A View of the Earth*, New Jersey: Prentice-Hall, 1977.

Haanstra, *Redders Aan De Riemen: De Laatste Roeiredders Vertellen Over Hun Leven*, Amsterdam: Uitgeversmaatschappij Born BV, date n.a.

Hanson, Hans, *Srorraddningens Historia Rundqvists Boktryckeri*, Göteborg: Sweden, 1988.

Hassall, Charles E., 'Life-Saving', *A Short History of the Port of Timaru; 1852-1955*, New Zealand: Timaru Harbour Board, 1955, 53, 60 and 113.

Hichens, Walter W., *Island Trek; An Historical and Geographical Tour of Seal Island, Nova Scotia...*, Nova Scotia: Lancelot Press, 1982.

Hillary, Sir William, *An Appeal to the British Nation, on the Humanity and Policy of Forming a National Institution for the Preservation of Lives and Property from Shipwreck*, London: Whittaker, 1824.

Hodges, C. Walter, *The Overland Launch; The Heroic Story of the Lifeboat Louisa (Lynmouth Lifeboat)*, New York: Coward-McCann, 1970.

Hong Kong, *A Report on History and Vessels of the Department*, Royal Hong Kong Marine Police, Departmental Publication (June, 1993).

Hope, Eva, *Grace Darling; Heroine of The Farne Islands, Her Life and Its Lessons*, London: Walter Scott Ltd, 1892.

Horgan, Denis, *Water Safety & Rescue*, published by the author, RNLI Library.

Household, Capt. S.T.S., 'Severn & Trent: New Classes for the RNLI', *Seaways* (February 1993), 7.

Howarth, Patrick, *Lifeboat: In Danger's Hour*, London: Hamlyn, 1981.

Humane Society of the Commonwealth of Massachusetts, *The Institution of the Humane Society of the Commonwealth of Massachusetts: With the Rules for Regulating Said Society...*, Boston: 1788.

International Lifeboat Federation, *Report of the 1st International Lifeboat Conference*, London, 1924, RNLI Library.

Ibid., *Report of the 2nd International Lifeboat Conference*, Paris, 1928, RNLI Library.

Ibid., *Report of the 3rd International Lifeboat Conference*, Amsterdam/Rotterdam, 1932, RNLI Library.

Ibid., *Report of the 4th International Lifeboat Conference*, Göteborg, 1936, RNLI Library.

Ibid., *Report of the 5th International Lifeboat Conference*, Oslo, 1947, RNLI Library.

Ibid., *Report of the 6th International Lifeboat Conference*, Ostend, 1951, RNLI Library.

Ibid., *Report of the 7th International Lifeboat Conference*, Estoril, 1955, RNLI Library.

Ibid., *Report of the 8th International Lifeboat Conference*, Bremen, 1959, RNLI Library.

Ibid., *Report of the 9th International Lifeboat Conference*, Edinburgh, 1963, RNLI Library.

Ibid., *Report of the 10th International Lifeboat Conference*, Dinard, 1967, RNLI Library.

Ibid., *Report of the 11th International Lifeboat Conference*, New York, 1971, RNLI Library.

Ibid., *Report of the 12th International Lifeboat Conference*, Helsinki, 1975, RNLI Library.

Ibid., *Report of the 13th International Lifeboat Conference*, IJmuiden, 1979, RNLI Library.

Ibid., *Report of the 14th International Lifeboat Conference*, Göteborg, 1983, RNLI Library.

Ibid., *Report of the 15th International Lifeboat Conference*, La Coruña, 1987, RNLI Library.

Ibid., *Report of the 16th International Lifeboat Conference*, Oslo/Bærum, 1991, RNLI Library.

Ibid., *Report of the 17th International Lifeboat Conference*, Montevideo, 1995, RNLI Library.

Ibid., *Report of the 18th International Lifeboat Conference*, Bourenmouth/Poole, 1999, RNLI Library.

International Hydrographic Organization, *List of Lifesaving Stations of the World with their Equipment and Geographical Positions*, Monte Carlo: Quai de Plaisance, 1940.

International Maritime Organization, *Area Search and Rescue Plans*, London: IMO, 1 March 1994.

Ibid., *Information on National Search and Rescue Facilities*, London: IMO, 1 March 1994.

Ireland, J. de Courcy, *Wreck and Rescue on the East Coast of Ireland*, Dublin: Glendale Press, 1983.

James, Peter & Nick Thorpe, *Ancient Inventions*, New York: Ballantine Books, 1994.

Johnson, Robert, *Guardians of the Sea: History of the USCG from 1915 to the Present*, Annapolis: Naval Institute Press, 1987.

Jolly, Cyril, *S.O.S., The Story of the Lifeboat Service*, London: Cassell & Co, 1961.

Kelly, Robert, *For Those in Peril: The Life & Times of Sir William Hillary, the Founder of the RNLI*, Douglas, Isle of Man: Shearwater Press, 1979.

Kelly, Robert and Gordon Kniveton, *Sir William Hillary and the Isle of Man Lifeboat Stations*, Douglas, Isle of Man: The Manx Experience, 1995.

Kimball, Sumner I., *Organisation & Methods of the United States Lifesaving Service*, Washington DC: Government Printing Office, 1890.

Kipling, Ray, *Lifeboats, A Sourcebook*, London: Ward Lock, 1982.

Ibid., *Strong to Save; Dramatic First-Hand Accounts of RNLI Lifeboat Rescues Around the British Isles*, Sparkford: P. Stephens, 1995.

Lamb, Sir John Cameron, *The Lifeboat and Its Work, The Activities of the Royal National Lifeboat Institution Since 1824*, London: Clowes, 1911.

Langmaid, K.J.R., *The Sea, Thine Enemy: A Survey of Coastal Lights and Life-Boat Services*, London: Jarrold's, 1966.

Leach, Nicholas, *Lifeboat Celebrations. A*

Commemoration of the RNLI 175th Anniversary Celebrations in Poole, 1999, Birmingham: published by the author, 1999.

Ibid, *The Origins of the Life-Boat Service; A History of the Development and Progress of Coastal Life-Saving Provision to 1910*, Birmingham: Published by Author, 1992.

Ibid, *The Waveney Lifeboats; An Illustrated History of the RNLI 44' Waveney Lifeboats 1967-1999*, Bristol: Bernard McCall, 2001.

Lewis, Sir Richard, *History of the Lifeboat and its Work*, London: Macmillan & Co. 1874.

Loney, Jack, *The Queenscliffe Lifeboat; Wreck & Rescue at Port Phillip Heads*, Queenscliffe: Queenscliffe Lifeboat Preservation Society, 1989.

Ludviksson, Steinar, J., *Thautgodir a Raunastund: Bjorgunar-og Sjoslysasaga Islands*. Keflavik: Bokautgafan Hraundrangi, 1969.

Lukin, Lionel, *The Invention, Principles of Construction, and uses of Unimmergible Boats, Stated in a Letter to H.R.H. the Prince of Wales, by Lionel Lukin*, London: printed for the author by J. Nichols & Son, 1806.

Lukin & Others, 'Letters from Lionel Lukin & His Refuters', *The Gentleman's Magazine and Historical Chronicle* (Vol.LXXVI, 1806), 713-15, 818-20, 926-8, 1110-13.

Lyle, David Alexander, *Report on Foreign Lifesaving Apparatus*, Washington, DC: US Government Printing Office, 1880.

McLellan, C.H., *Beach Apparatus Drill*, Washington, DC: USLSS, 1883.

Ibid., 'The Evolution of the Lifeboat', *Marine Engineering* (January 1906), 7-11.

Ibid., 'Twin Screw Lifeboat for the US Life Saving Service', *Marine Engineering* (January 1900), 25-26.

Ibid., 'The US Life Saving Service Self-Bailing Water Ballast Surfboat', *Marine Engineering* (March 1901), 94-99.

McLeod, Ken, 'The Canadian Great Lakes Lifesaving Service', *Fresh Water, A Journal of Great Lakes Marine History*, Vol.3, No.1 (Summer 1988).

MacVicar, Angus, *Rescue Call*, London: Kaye & Ward, 1967.

Massachusets Humane Society, *The Institution of the Humane Society of the Commonwealth of Massachusetts: With the Rules for Regulating Said Society*, Boston, 1788.

Maloney, Elbert, *Chapman Piloting, Seamanship & Small Boat Handling, 62nd Ed.*, New York: Hearst Marine Books, 1996.

Malster, Robert, *Saved from the Sea*, Suffolk: Rerrance Dalton Ltd, 1974.

Manby, George, *An Essay on the Preservation of Shipwrecked Persons: With a Descriptive Account of the Apparatus & the Manner of Applying It*, London: Longman, Hurst, Rees, Orme, & Brown, 1812.

Ibid., *Illustrative Essay, Containing an Exemplification and Concise Description of Instructions for Affording Relief to Persons in the Hour of Shipwreck*, W. Meggy, 1824.

Marsh, George, 'Rescue 2000, RNLI's 21st Century Fleet', *Work Boat World* (April 1993), 11-12.

Merilahti, Juhani, *Sadan Vuoden Meripelastustyö* (English Summary of Book on Finish Lifeboat Society, SM Finland).

Methley, N.T., *The Life-Boat and its Story*, London: Sidgwick & Jackson, 1912.

Middleton, E.W., *Lifeboats of the World: A Pocket Encyclopedia of Sea Rescue*, New York: Arco Publishing Co., 1978.

Mitchley, Jack, *The Story of the Lowestoft Lifeboats, Part 1; 1801-76*, Lowestoft: Port of Lowestoft Historical Society, 1974.

Moll, F.G.E., 'The Berlin Disaster', *Sea Breezes* (February 1962), 112-32.

Morgan, Richard, 'Victoria lifeboat Rescued', *Australian Sea Heritage* #15 (1988), 31-32.

Morris, Jeff, *The History of the Port Erin Lifeboats (Isle of Man)*, Coventry: Lifeboat Enthusiasts Society, 1997.

Mouret, André. *Le sauvetage en Mer, un Siecle au Large de Sete*. Sete: A. Mouret, 1981.

Nathan, A.J., 'South African National Sea Rescue Institute Saves Seamen's Lives Off Rugged Coast', National Fisherman (September 1973), 16C & 31C.

Noble, Dennis, *Lifeboat Sailors; Disasters, Rescues, and the Perilous Future of the Coast Guard's Small Boat Stations*, Washington, DC: Brassey's, 2000.

Ibid., *A Legacy, The United States Life-Saving Service* (available on USCG Historical Website at http://www.uscg.mil

/hq/gcp/history/colect.html).

Noble, Dennis and Michael T. O'Brien, 'The Saga of the U.S. Coast Guard', *American History Illustrated* (June 1977), 4-7 & 37-43.

Nova Scotia, 'Superintendant's Report on Lighthouses', *Journal and Proceedings of the House of Assembly* (1858).

Nutting, Wm. Washburn, 'The Sturdy Motor Lifeboat; Some Impressions of the Life Saving Service & Its Splendid New Self-Righting Motor Boats', *Motor Boat* (January 1912), 14-15 & 47.

Oddvar, Nilsen ed., *For Those in Peril* (History of the NSSR in English), Alesund, Norway: Northwest Publishing, 1991.

O'Connor, W.D., 'Sketch of the United States Life Saving Service', *Appleton's Annual Encyclopedia of 1878*, 749-67.

Oosterwijk, Bram, *De Zee Was Onstuimig...* (History of the Royal South Holland Lifeboat Service, 1824-1991), Amsterdam: De Bataafsche Leeuw, 1994.

Osler, Adrian, *Mr. Greathead's Lifeboats*, Newcastle upon Tyne: Tyne and Wear Museums Service, 1990.

Ostersehlte, Christian, *Die Deutsche Gesellschaft zur Rettung Schiffbrüchiger*, Hamburg: Ernst Kabel Verlag, 1990.

Pearcy, Arthur, *A History of US Coast Guard Aviation*, Annapolis: Naval Institute Press, 1989.

Pursey, H.J., *Merchant Ship Construction*, Glasgow, Brown, Son & Ferguson, 1978.

Ibid., *Merchant Ship Stability*, Glasgow, Brown, Son & Ferguson, 1983.

Philipson, David, *All Her Glories Past; The Story of the Zetland Lifeboat*, Otley: Smith Settle, 1994.

Ibid., *Come Along Brave Boys, Come Along! A History of Redcar's Lifeboats*, Redcar: Sotheran, 1980.

Pillet, Jean, *Le Sauvetage au Temps des Avirons et de la Voile*, France: Douarnenez: Le Chasse-Marée, 1986. (France).

Pond, James L, *History of Lifesaving Appliances, and Military & Naval Constructions Invented & Manufactured by Joseph Francis, with Sketches & Incidents of his Business Life in the United States & Europe*, New York: E.D. Slater, 1885.

Poole, Francis, 'The Birth of the Lifeboat', *Sail* (July 1975), 72-74.

Portugal, *Exposicao do Estado Actual da Real Casa d'Asylo dos Naufragados*, Porto: Na Typ.de viuva Alvares Ribeiro & Filho, 1832.

Robertson, Gil J., 'Steam Lifeboat to be Exhibition Centre-Piece', *Australian Sea Heritage* (Winter 1986), 18-19.

Scarlett, Bernard, *Shipminder; The Story of Her Majesty's Coastguard*, London: Pelham Books, 1971.

Scheina, Dr. Robert, 'Coast Guard History', *Commandant's Bulletin 16-85* (4 August 1985).

Ibid., 'Coast Guard at War', *Commandant's Bulletin 4-87* (13 February 1987).

Ibid., *USCG Cutters and Craft, 1946-1990*, Annapolis: Naval Institute Press, 1990.

Schumacher, Capt. John, *Maritime Craft for Search and Rescue Suitable Also as Multi-Purpose Craft for Other Special Services*, Report for German Government (September 1977).

Scott, R. Bruce, *Breakers Ahead!*, Sidney, BC: Review Publishing House, 1970.

Shanks, Ralph & Lisa Woo and Wick York, *The US Life-Saving Service, Heroes, Rescues and Architecture of the Early Coast Guard*, Petaluma: Costano Books, 1996.

Sharpe, Mitchell, *The Development of the Lifesaving Rocket; A Study in 19th Century Technological Fallout*. Marshall Space Flight Centre: the author, 1969.

SNSM, 'Sauveteurs en Mer', *Historical Magazine* #1 (1992).

South Africa, *Cape of Good Hope, Report of the Commission Appointed by His Excellency the Governor to inquire into the Proceedings of the Port-Captain during the late Gale and the Organization of the Lifeboat Department*, South Africa: House of Assembly, 3 July 1865.

Spaans, Drs M., *De 'Nord'* (The History of the Royal North and South Holland Lifeboat Service, 1924-90), Amsterdam: De Bataafsche Leeuw, 1993.

Steinar, J. Ludviksson, *Thautgodir a Raunastund: Bjorgunar-og Sjoslysasaga Islands*, Keflavik: Bokautgafan Hraundrangi, 1969.

Stewart, John Q., *Coasts, Waves and Weather*, Boston: Ginn & Company, 1945.

Swanston, Roger, 'French Lifeboat History', *Stations of the French Lifeboat Societies* (1996).

Syme, Marten, 'A Lifeboat Rescue', Australian Peake Boat, Port Fairy. (date/source n.a.).

Tilley, John, *History of the US Coast Guard Auxiliary*, Department of History, East Carolina University.

Toxopeus, Klaas, *Flying Storm, The Adventures of the Skipper of a Rescue Boat off the Stormy Coast of Holland*, New York: Dodd, Mead and Company, 1954.

Uden, Grant, *Life-Boats, A Survey of Their History and Present State of Development*, Oxford: Basil Blackwell and Mott Ltd., 1962.

Ulvsgaard, Jorgen, 'Flying in the Teeth of the Storm', *Lighthouse Edition* #6 (1995), 16-18. (Norway).

USA, 'Report of Commissioners Examining Lifeboats & Surfboats', *Report # 44 from the Annual Report of the Secretary of the Treasury for the Fiscal Year Ending June 30, 1858*, Washington, DC: William A. Harris, printer, 1858.

United States Coast Guard, *Air Search & Rescue; 63 Years of Aerial Lifesaving; A Pictorial History*, 1915-1978, Washington DC: DOT, 1978.

Ibid., *On Scene - Special MLB Issue* (2/92).

Van der Zweep and Stogdon, E.D., 'A Large RIB for Dutch Lifeboat Institution', *Ship and Boat International* (June1987), 13-16.

VRIL, 'Lifeboats I; Manual Labour & Sail Propulsion', *Yachting & Boating Monthly* (May 1908), 43-46.

Ibid., 'Lifeboats II; Steam Power', *Yachting & Boating Monthly* (June 1908), 103-5.

Warner, Oliver, *The Lifeboat Service, A History of the Royal National Lifeboat Institution 1824-1974*, London: Cassell & Co., 1974.

Wake-Walker, Edward, 'The XVth International Lifeboat Conference, La Coruña, Spain, 1987', Safety at Sea (July 1987) 19-20.

Ibid., 'In Conference, 16th ILC, Oslo, 1991', *Safety at Sea* (n.d.)

Ibid., 'The 17th International Lifeboat Conference', *Safety at Sea* (June 1995), 16-17.

Ibid., 'Lifeboat Services Around the World', *Safety at Sea* (n.d.)

Waters, J.M., Rescue at Sea (2nd Edition), Annapolis: Naval Institute Press, 1989.

Welford, Stuart, 'Is it Right to Right; the Development of the Self-Righting Lifeboat', *The Naval Architect*, (July 1974), 93-97.

Whitaker, Boswell, *Preservation of Life From Shipwreck, A Trilogy, Volume 1, Skuetender Lifeboat*, Todmorden: South Tyneside Borough Service, 1979.

Whitnall, F.G., 'Lionel Lukin: Inventor of the Lifeboat', *Sea Breezes* (December 1967), 843-45.

Wigby, Frederick C., 'Invention of the Lifeboat', *The Mariner's Mirror* (August 1972), in *The Naval Chronicle* (Vol.VII, 1802), 485.

Wilkinson, William D., ' In the beginning...The English Origins of the Early American Coastal SR/SB Lileboat', *On Scene – Special MLB Issue* (2/92), 3-5.

Ibid., 'One of a Kind', *On Scene* (Summer 1996), 14-16.

Ibid., 'The 26ft 8in Self-Bailing Self Righting Sailing, Pulling Lifeboat of the US Life-Saving Service', *Wreck & Rescue; The Journal of the USLSS Heritage Association* #6, (Fall 1997), 11-12.

Ibid., 'The U.S. Coast Guard 44ft Motor Lifeboat', *The Quarterdeck*, Vol.24, No.1 (Winter 1998), 6-11.

Williams, M.S., 'A Hydraulic Propelled Steam Lifeboat', *International Marine Engineering* (December 1907), 516-17.

Wilson, Dorothy Clark, *Stranger and Traveller; The Story of Dorothea Dix, American Reformer*, Boston: Little, Brown and Co, 1975.

Wirz, Hans, *Seenot – Opfer, Siege 100 Jahre DGzRS*, Bremen: Carl Schüman Verlag, 1975.

Worcester, G.R.G., *The Junks and Sampans of the Upper Yangtze*, Shanghai: The Maritime Customs III. Misc. Series: No. 51, 1940.

Ibid., *The Junks and Sampans of the Yangtze, Vol.I: Introduction; and Craft of the Estuary and Shanghai Area*, Shanghai: The Maritime Customs III. Misc. Series: No.53, 1947.

Ibid., *The Junks and Sampans of the Yangtze, Vol.II: The Craft of the Lower and Middle Yangtze and Tributaries*, Shanghai: The Maritime Customs III. Misc. Series: No.54, 1948.

Yorke, Barbara, *Britain's First Lifeboat Station at Formby, Merseyside 1776-1918*, Liverpool: Alt Press, 1982.

Index

292